MOON HANDBOOKS®

IDAHO

D0778484

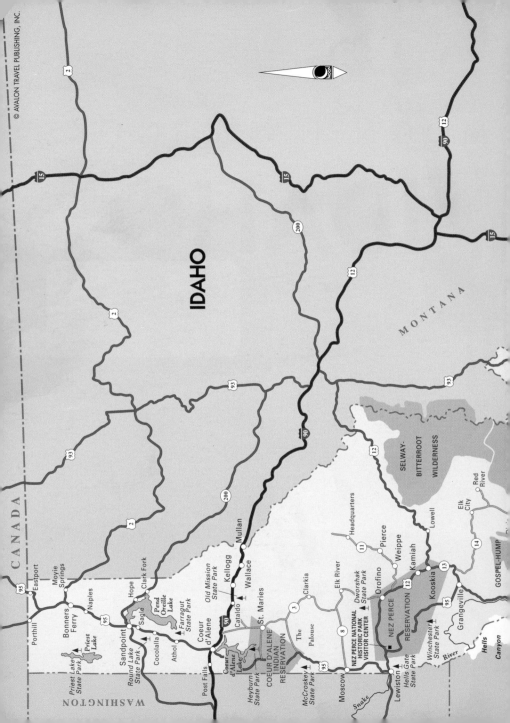

MOON HANDBOOKS®
IDAHO

FIFTH EDITION

DON ROOT

AVALON
TRAVEL

MAPS

CANADA
WASHINGTON
MONTANA
Sandpoint
Coeur d'Alene
Moscow
Lewiston
MOON
0
40 mi
0
40 km
MAP SYMBOLS
Divided Highway
Primary Road
Secondary Road
Unpaved Road
Railroad
Trail
U.S. Interstate
U.S. Highway
State Highway
County Road
State Capital
City/Town
Point of Interest
Accommodation
Restaurant/Bar
Golf Course
Ski Resort
Airfield/Airstrip
State Park
Campground
Mountain
Mountain Pass
Dam
Trailhead
Other Location

Introduction/On the Road

The Panhandle

North-Central Idaho

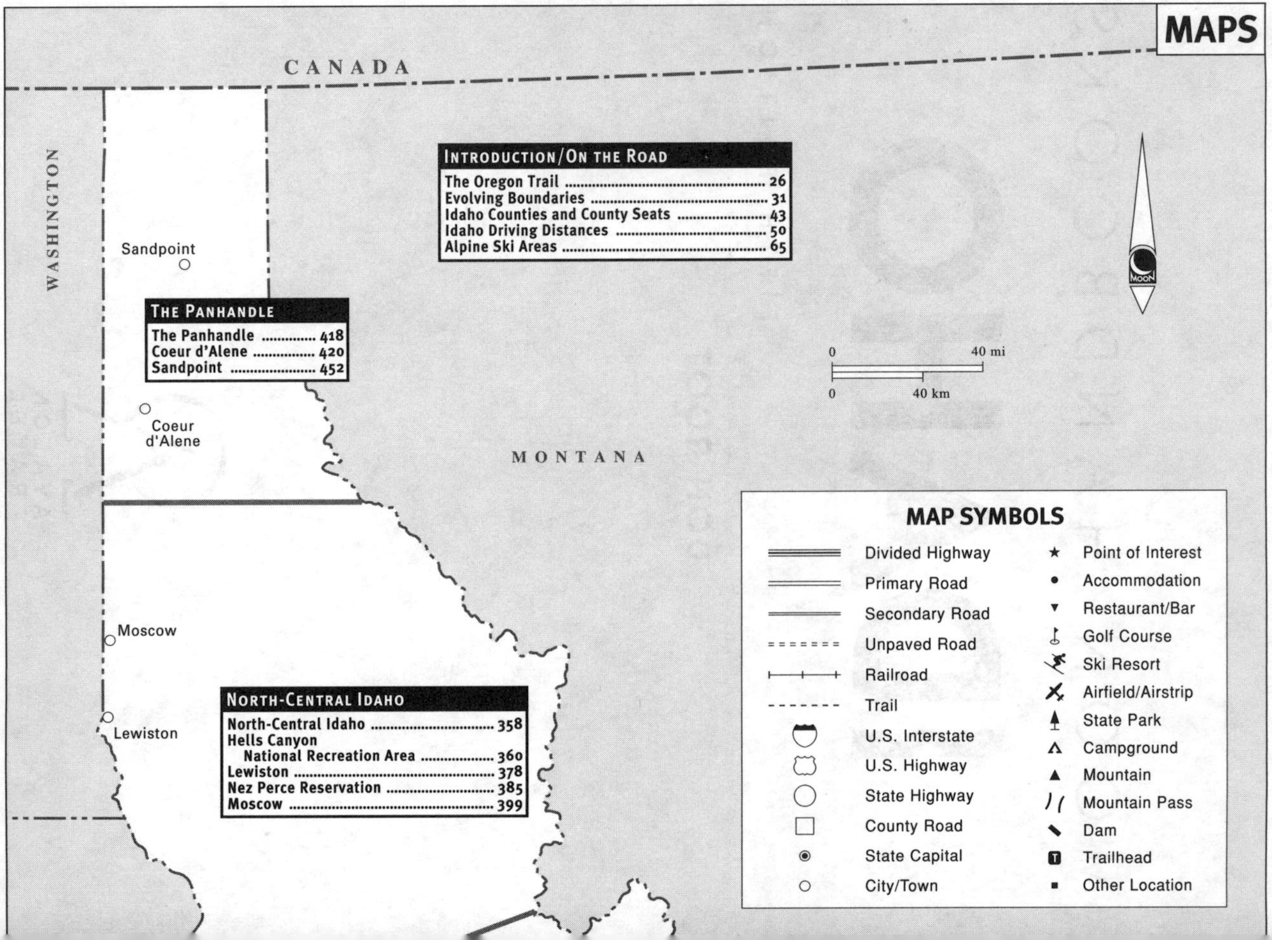

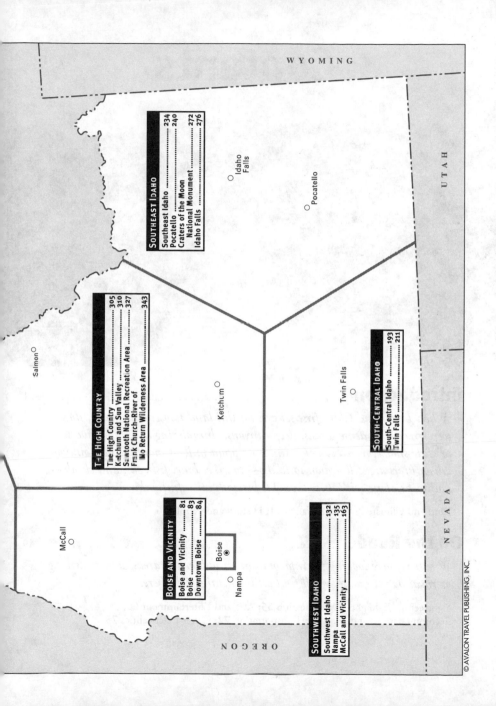

WYOMING

UTAH

NEVADA

OREGON

○ Idaho
Falls

○ Pocatello

Salmon ○

Ketchum ○

Twin Falls ○

McCall ○

Boise ◉

Nampa ○

© AVALON TRAVEL PUBLISHING, INC.

Contents

COURTESY OF THE IDAHO TRAVEL COUNCIL

Introduction 1

When Lewis and Clark first set eyes on this land two centuries ago, they were greeted by dense forests, deep canyons, shimmering lakes and rivers, pristine snow-covered slopes—and mile upon mile of space. Today's outdoor adventurers are still drawn to Idaho—to hike, bike, fish, ski, and climb—and to be alone with their thoughts beneath an infinite sky.

On the Road 49

Whether you're looking for information on wilderness areas, winter driving, or rural bar etiquette, you'll find all the details right here.

Boise and Vicinity

Early fur trappers lingered in this woodsy spot during their travels in the southern Idaho desert. Today, Boiseans still live as much outdoors as in—on the river, on the slopes, on the trails—and they enjoy the arts, from Shakespeare to the Oinkari Basque Dancers. Boise remains an oasis—for its culture as well as its geography.

Southwest Idaho

The state's most densely populated region offers sweeping rural vistas and abundant wilderness ready for exploration. White-water thrills await on the Boise, Payette, and Snake Rivers. You can also wet your whistle at the wineries of Sunny Slope, or dip into some fun in McCall, home to Idaho's biggest winter carnival.

South-Central Idaho 192

Take a detour off the interstate to see the best this region has to offer. In Hagerman Valley you'll find a miles-long stretch of cascading springs pouring out of basalt cliffs. Silver Creek's trout-filled waters lure fly-fishers, while rock climbers rise to the challenge at City of Rocks National Preserve.

Southeast Idaho 233

You'll find plenty of the big wide open here, punctuated by dramatic sights like the otherworldly Craters of the Moon National Monument and the surreal turquoise waters of Bear Lake. Along the Idaho-Wyoming border, the towering Tetons provide superb skiing— fans of fresh powder flock to Grand Targhee.

The High Country 304

Get closer to heaven in the High Country. Hit the slopes in glamorous Sun Valley, the West's oldest, grandest ski resort. Climb the granite walls and spires of the jaggedly beautiful Sawtooths. Bike in the lofty White Cloud Peaks. Or embrace solitude in the vast Frank Church–River of No Return Wilderness.

North-Central Idaho

This is the land of the Nez Perce and Coeur d'Alene, of Lewis and Clark's expedition, of gold miners drawn by dreams of wealth. Today's visitors are drawn by dreams of whitewater rivers: the Lochsa, the Selway, the Salmon, and the Snake, which powers through legendary Hells Canyon.

The Panhandle

Idaho's largest and most beautiful lakes bejewel its forested northern reaches. Coeur d'Alene Lake provides the backdrop and name for a buzzing summer resort town. Art colony Sandpoint perches on brilliant blue Pend Oreille Lake, with many bays and islands to explore. And remote, rustic Priest Lake is best known for huckleberries—and the bears who love them.

ABOUT THE AUTHOR
Don Root

Don Root grew up in San Diego and developed a taste for wild places early on. In his high school days, he spent every spare moment rock climbing at Joshua Tree and Tahquitz, backpacking the Sierra Nevada, and exploring the deserts of both Alta and Baja California. College brought a photojournalism degree and more travels, including a semester stint at the Université d'Aix-en-Provence in southern France.

After traveling hither and yon through almost every other state in the United States, he finally made his way to Idaho. It was love at first sight. "When I first went to Idaho," says Don, "I had planned to be in Boise six days. I ended up staying six weeks. It was just too wonderful to leave."

He soon found himself taking over the reins of *Moon Handbooks Idaho* and traveling through every nook and cranny of the state. In his tenure as author, Don has rafted the Middle Fork of the Salmon River, conquered Borah Peak (the state's highest), rock climbed outside Coeur d'Alene, and skied every possible part of Idaho. He's soaked in innumerable hot springs, crawled through caverns, caroused with cowboys, gotten stuck in the mud on the Snake River Plain, and spent a magical night in a fire tower high in the mountains, drinking Bigfoot Ale with the lookout operator while watching lightning illuminate the Owyhees for hours on end. Idaho has already given Don a lifetime worth of memories, as well as many lifelong friends.

For the moment, Don lives in San Rafael, California, working as a freelance writer, editor, and photographer. But who knows what tomorrow may bring? As for retirement? "Idaho, most definitely," he says.

Introduction

Of all the states in the tourist meccas of the Pacific Northwest and Rocky Mountains, Idaho comes across like the runt of the litter, the neglected stepchild. The state's high-powered marketing slogan, featured prominently on Idaho license plates, is "Famous Potatoes." Many people do associate Idaho with its justly famous potatoes, but honeymooners, vacationers, and conventioneers seldom plan trips around the availability of good spuds. So what *does* draw visitors to Idaho today?

Give me a minute to ponder that question while I strap on my skinny skis and glide off the back porch of a Sun Valley cabin—through the woods, past the frozen lake, and down to the hot springs. I'll mull it over from a rocky perch 300 feet above the desert floor near Almo, as I belay my partner up a towering wall of granite and watch the valley turn to gold in the late-afternoon light. Maybe the answer will come to me when I return from a two-week backpacking trip across Idaho's Frank Church–River of No Return Wilderness—a roadless area larger than Rhode Island and Delaware combined. Or maybe I'll head up to Silver Creek or the Big Wood River and see if Papa Hemingway's ghost will enlighten me, channeling his wisdom through that fighting five-pound rainbow trout on the end of my line.

Most residents and visitors alike would agree that the state's prize characteristic is the land itself. Nowhere in Idaho will you be out of sight of mountains. And at every turn, from one end of the state to the other, the landscape inspires awe—whether it be the dense forests, barren deserts, shimmering blue lakes and rivers, or pristine snow-covered slopes. More than two-thirds of the state is public land, mostly mountainous terrain unsuitable for factories, condos, or shopping malls. Generally speaking, you can't live or work on this terrain, but you sure can play on it. The rugged land that nearly foiled Lewis and Clark now provides a superlative setting, year-round, for almost every form of outdoor recreation imaginable. Best of all, you'll feel as if you have this paradise all to yourself. With only about 1.3 million residents spread out over more than 82,000 square miles, Idaho has one of the lowest population densities in the United States. A 10-minute drive outside any city in the state can put you in deep solitude. And in this day of cell phones, fax machines, and the Internet, imagine this: all of Idaho still has but a single telephone area code.

Idahoans are a varied lot—among the state's residents you'll find dedicated environmentalists, redneck ranchers, conservative business executives, liberal academics, and faded flower children—but most have one thing in common: they share a love of this great outdoors at their back door. They love to get out into the wilds—out with the wolves, coyotes, hawks, and eagles; with the bears, bighorn sheep, salmon, and steelhead; with the pines, firs, aspens, and cottonwoods—and see what they can see.

The state began attracting outdoor adventurers soon after Lewis and Clark first set eyes on Idaho's land in 1805. In that respect, not much has changed here in the ensuing two centuries. Today's visitors—whether on foot, on horseback, or behind the wheel of a large automobile—will soon find out that Idaho is still a magnificent place to explore.

Land and Climate

Idaho holds more than 82,000 square miles of land within its borders, making it the 11th largest state in the nation in land area. Most of the state's population is concentrated along the Snake River Plain in the south and along the state's western fringe, leaving vast amounts of land either sparsely settled or uninhabited.

MOUNTAINS

Virtually the entire state is covered with mountains. Even on the wide grin of the Snake River Plain, which arcs across the width of southern Idaho, mountains rim the horizon in most directions.

Southern Ranges

The mountains rising up right behind Idaho's capital city of Boise are, appropriately enough, the **Boise Mountains.** Their lower slopes mirror the brown desert that spreads out along the Snake River Plain, while the upper slopes are home to Boise's backyard ski resort, Bogus Basin. Across

the Snake River, in the state's southwest corner, are the **Owyhee Mountains.** Silver City, high in the Owyhees, was once one of the West's richest little towns, thanks to the vast seams of silver and gold found nearby.

East of the Owyhees, still on the south side of the Snake River, a string of north-south-trending ranges leads, one after the next, all the way to the Wyoming border. This incredible procession of peaks is a prime example of basin-and-range topography, caused by the slow stretching apart of the earth's crust. Just across the Wyoming border rise the impressive granite spires of the Teton Range.

Central Ranges

The Wood River Valley is the most common gateway to the lofty ranges of central Idaho: the **Smoky Mountains** (home of Sun Valley's famous ski hill), **Pioneer Mountains,** the **Sawtooth Range,** and the **White Cloud Peaks.**

All of these ranges are high and wild, but the state's highest point, the 12,662-foot summit of

INTRODUCTION

The magnificent Sawtooth Mountains are the crown jewels of Idaho's mountain ranges.

Borah Peak, is farther east in the **Lost River Range.** Experienced mountaineers who make it to the top of Borah will also have a great view to the east of the lofty **Lemhi Range.**

In the very center of the state, the **Salmon River Mountains** comprise most of the Frank Church–River of No Return Wilderness, south of the Salmon River. Farther west, the **Seven Devils Mountains** tower over Hells Canyon, providing spectacular views to hikers and horsebackers.

On the other side of the state, running north-south along most of Idaho's eastern border, is the **Bitterroot Range,** the towering rugged peaks that helped make Idaho the last of the Lower 48 states to be explored by whites. The **Beaverhead** and **Centennial Ranges** are subranges of the Bitterroots on the Idaho-Montana border.

Northern Ranges

North of the Salmon River, the **Clearwater Mountains** extend north all the way to the St. Joe River. Across the St. Joe are the **St. Joe Mountains.** North of I-90, the **Coeur d'Alene Range** extends north to Pend Oreille Lake. Finally, way up in the Panhandle are the **Selkirk, Cabinet,** and **Purcell Ranges.** The Selkirks are home to small numbers of rare woodland caribou, and both the Selkirks and Cabinets remain grizzly bear country.

RIVERS AND LAKES
Along the Snake and Salmon

From its abundance of famous whitewater rivers to its more than 2,000 lakes, Idaho is rich in water resources. Start with the mighty **Snake River,** which begins in Wyoming, then traverses the entire southern width of Idaho. The Snake enters Idaho at **Palisades Reservoir,** a popular lake with boating anglers; below Palisades Dam, it's commonly called the **South Fork of the Snake,** to differentiate it from the Snake's **Henry's Fork** tributary, which begins in a massive spring near Island Park. Both rivers are revered for fly-fishing.

As the Snake makes its way west across southern Idaho, it is dammed in many places—major turn-of-the-20th-century irrigation projects made Idaho the breadbasket it is today—forming reservoirs used for both water storage and recreation. Evel Knievel once tried to leap a rocket-powered cycle across the famous **Snake River Canyon** at Twin Falls, about 500 feet deep.

AN IDAHO ALMANAC

State Birthday: Idaho joined the Union on July 3, 1890, becoming the 43rd state in the nation.

State Capital: Boise

State Dimensions: Idaho is 483.5 miles long at its tallest point, and varies from 45 miles wide at the tip of the Panhandle to 310 miles along the southern border. Its area is 83,557 square miles, making it the 13th largest state in area.

State Population: 1,341,131, according to the 2002 resident population estimate

State High Point: Borah Peak (12,662 feet), in the Lost River Range near Mackay

State Low Point: Lewiston (738 feet), at the point where the Snake River flows into Washington

State Motto: *Esto Perpetua,* meaning "It Is Forever." The motto adorns the state seal, which was designed in 1891 by Emma Edwards Green. It's the only state seal in the country designed by a woman.

State Song: "Here We Have Idaho," written in 1931 by Albert J. Tompkins, McKinley Helm, and Sallie Hume Douglas

State Flower: the syringa, which explodes into bloom like delicate white fireworks

State Tree: the western white pine, once abundant north of the Clearwater River. You can still see specimens of the hulking trees along the White Pine Scenic Byway (Highway 6 between Potlatch and St. Maries), but logging and disease have taken a severe toll on the once mighty stands.

State Bird: the mountain bluebird, found throughout the West

State Gemstone: the star garnet, which is found only in Idaho and India. The "star" in the name comes from rays within the garnet—normally four, sometimes six.

State Horse: the Appaloosa, proud horse of the Nez Perce. Horse lovers will want to visit the Appaloosa Museum in Moscow.

State Folk Dance: the square dance

State Insect: the monarch butterfly

State Fish: the cutthroat trout, named for a red or orange slash on the bottom of its lower jaw

State Fossil: the Hagerman horse, discovered in the 1920s near Hagerman

After passing through rapid-ridden Hells Canyon along the state's western border, the Snake rolls into Lewiston—an inland seaport—then on into Washington, eventually linking up with the Columbia River and the Pacific Ocean near Portland, Oregon.

The state's other famous river is the **Salmon River,** one of the country's longest free-flowing watercourses. It begins high in the Sawtooth Valley and flows through the Frank Church–River of No Return Wilderness before joining the Snake River in Hells Canyon. The Salmon was nicknamed the River of No Return early in the history of Euro-American exploration; because of its powerful rapids, explorers could float down the

river but they could never boat back up. Today, jetboats defy this rule on parts of the main Salmon. The Salmon's largest tributary, the **Middle Fork Salmon River,** is another prime whitewater run, even more remote and wild than the main Salmon.

South Idaho Waters

Other rivers beginning in and around the high peaks of the Sawtooths flow into southwest Idaho. The **Boise** and **Payette Rivers** both offer water recreation very near Boise, making them chock-full of boaters in summer. On the South Fork Payette you'll find some of the most spectacular whitewater in the state—a kayaker's heaven. Farther west, the **Weiser River** irrigates the farmlands of Hells Canyon rim country.

In the far southwestern corner of the state, the **Bruneau, Jarbidge,** and **Owyhee Rivers** cut deep, rugged canyons into the desert, far from civilization. The rivers draw rafters and kayakers to their remote reaches in spring, as well as a few hardy canyon hikers year-round.

In south-central Idaho, the **Big Wood River** flows down from the heights north of Sun Valley to rendezvous with the Snake at the bottom of Malad Gorge. Along the way it's joined by the **Little Wood River,** which is fed by **Silver Creek.** All three draw anglers; Silver Creek is among the state's three most famous trout streams. East of the Little Wood, the **Big and Little Lost Rivers** and **Birch Creek** flow down from high valleys and disappear into the lava of the Snake River Plain, later to emerge at **Thousand Springs** along the Snake River in Hagerman Valley.

Down in the state's southeastern corner, **Bear Lake** boasts surreal turquoise-blue waters well used by water-skiers and anglers.

North Idaho Waters

Two of the finest whitewater rivers in the country, the **Lochsa** and **Selway,** begin high along the Continental Divide and race their way down in furious rapids, coming together to form the more placid **Clearwater River,** an important spawning ground for anadromous salmon and steelhead. Farther north, through the southern reaches of Idaho's Panhandle, the **St. Joe** and **St. Maries Rivers** flow through big-timber country into the south end of **Coeur d'Alene Lake.** The lake is also fed by the **Coeur d'Alene River,** a historic waterway through the heart of Silver Valley mining country, and is drained by the **Spokane River,** which flows west into Washington state.

Sandpoint, farther north up the Panhandle, lies on the shores of **Pend Oreille Lake,** the state's largest body of water. The lake is so deep, the U.S. Navy uses it to test submarines. Others prefer to boat on the surface of the water, and marinas dot the shoreline. The lake is fed by the **Clark Fork River** and drained by the **Pend Oreille River.** A tributary of the Pend Oreille, **Priest River** flows south out of **Priest Lake,** the state's

most northerly major lake and one of its most beautiful. Tall mountains ring the shore and wildlife is abundant in the area.

The **Kootenai** and **Moyie Rivers** drain the northernmost reaches of the state along the Canadian border.

CLIMATE

Idaho's varied topography, ranging in elevation from 738 to 12,662 feet, and large size—the state spans seven degrees of latitude and six degrees of longitude—make for a complicated climate. Generally speaking, the state enjoys a relatively temperate, maritime-influenced climate that is drier than Washington and Oregon and milder than Montana and Wyoming. Also generally speaking, the north half of the state is lower, warmer, cloudier, and wetter than the south half.

Humidity is not much of a problem anywhere in the state. In the hottest months, humidity is generally a comfortable 25 percent or lower. Other weather woes you'll seldom see in Idaho include dense fog, tornadoes, and hailstorms—though high winds are common on the Snake River Plain.

Boise

Boise's climate is warm and dry in summer, cold and dry in winter. In July, highs average around 90°F and overnight lows drop to around 59°F. Hot spells with temperatures over 100°F usually occur every summer, but are short-lived. About 90 percent of July days are sunny, and the city usually gets only about a quarter inch of rain that month. Fall in Boise offers stable, pleasant weather. Average high temperatures are around 78°F in September, 65°F in October, and 50°F in November, with average overnight lows of 50°F, 40°F, and 30°F, respectively.

In winter, temperatures remain relatively mild. January is the coldest month, with an average high temperature of around 37°F and an average overnight low around 22°F. Extended cold spells with high temperatures of 10°F or lower are not uncommon. Sunny days drop to around 40 percent in December and January. January is also the city's wettest month, although Boise is a dry place; average January precipitation is around an inch and a half. Winds are relatively calm in winter, keeping windchill problems low.

Winds pick up a bit in spring in time for the city's kite festival. Spring has the most changeable weather and the biggest temperature swings. Daytime high temperatures average around 50°F in March, rising to 61°F in April and 71°F in May. Spring is also a relatively wet season in Boise, with precipitation averaging more than an inch a month all season.

Southwest Idaho

Most of this region's sizable population lives in the relatively low-lying areas along the Snake River Plain and the valleys of the Boise, Payette, and Weiser Rivers. Elevations here range from around 2,000 feet along the Snake River to more than 5,000 feet in McCall. As in the southwest Idaho city of Boise, summers here are toasty and winters are mild. Winter brings freezing temperatures only a couple months of the year, in December and January. The state's reporting station at Swan Falls, on the floor of the Snake River Canyon south of Boise, records the highest annual mean temperature in Idaho, 55°F.

At **Parma** along the Boise River at an elevation of 2,215 feet (about 600 feet lower than Boise), July days run around 93°F on average, while January days come in around 38°F. Up in **McCall,** elevation 5,025 feet, the altitude makes for cooler temperatures; look for July highs around 80°F and January highs around 30°F. Rain and snow also begin to be a factor once you get up off the dry Snake River Plain. McCall receives 28 inches of precipitation a year, in contrast to Boise's 11, and snow sometimes lingers into spring. As in Boise, January is the wettest month and July the driest.

South-Central Idaho

This part of the state also shows a wide range in elevation. Its lowest stretches along the Snake River are the warmest year-round. In **Twin Falls,**

elevation 3,690 feet, July daytime highs average around 90°F, while overnight lows drop to around 55°F. January in Twin Falls brings daytime highs around 40°F and lows around 20°F.

From Twin Falls east up the Snake River Plain, freezing temperatures generally last from around December through February. Daytime high temperatures in **Burley,** about 500 feet higher in elevation than Twin Falls, average 88°F in July and just 36°F in January. Precipitation in south-central Idaho is heaviest in May, followed in no particular order by December, January, April, and June.

Southeast Idaho

Eastern Idaho may have the most complex weather in the state. Farthest from the reaches of the Pacific maritime storms, this region is influenced partially by pooped-out westerlies, partially by southerly storms pushing north from the Gulf of Mexico, and partially by disturbances from every other direction as the surrounding mountains swirl and break storms into any number of tracks. Precipitation patterns here are the opposite of what you'd expect in the west and north parts of the state. Rainfall is heaviest in spring and summer, when thunderstorms are common. The region also has the widest temperature variations from season to season. Winter storms here are among the coldest in the state, so it's no surprise that Grand Targhee Ski Area, in the Tetons just outside Driggs, Idaho, offers the state's lightest powder.

Pocatello, on the Snake River Plain at an elevation of 4,454 feet, sees July highs averaging 89°F and January highs right around the freezing mark of 32°F. In July, **Idaho Falls,** elevation 4,730 feet, stays just a couple of degrees cooler than Pocatello, but its January highs average a frigid 28°F. Both cities are wettest in May and June. The **Island Park** area, elevation 6,300 feet, can see brutal cold: on December 17, 1964, the mercury dipped to -51°F. Temperatures aren't usually that severe, however. January highs average 25°F, July highs a pleasant 79°F.

> *Generally speaking, the state enjoys a relatively temperate, maritime-influenced climate that is drier than Washington and Oregon and milder than Montana and Wyoming.*

The High Country

High altitudes mean lower temperatures, which makes the high country a great place to be in summer and a bitterly cold spot in winter. The National Weather Service reporting station near **Stanley,** at an elevation of 6,780 feet, holds the record for the state's lowest annual average temperature: a nippy 35.4°F. Much of the high country's precipitation comes as snow, a great boon to Sun Valley's reputation as a premier ski destination. December and January are the wettest months in Sun Valley, with high temperatures right around freezing. Spring comes late to the mountains; snow covers the high peaks and meadows until well past summer solstice. Look for wildflowers in June at the earliest, and not till July in many places. In summer, Sun Valley enjoys high temperatures in the 70s and low 80s, and minimal precipitation.

East of Sun Valley in the rain shadow of the high peaks, the Lost River, Pahsimeroi, and Lemhi Valleys are among the state's driest regions, receiving an average of just over eight inches of precipitation annually.

North-Central Idaho

North-central Idaho is unique for its deep canyons—Hells Canyon of the Snake River, Salmon River Gorge, and the canyons of the Clearwater River and its tributaries. Towns on the floors of these canyons have the lowest elevations in the state and are sheltered from the wind, giving them the state's warmest temperatures. In summer, you'll definitely want air-conditioning in places like **Lewiston, Riggins,** and **Orofino,** where average temperatures hover around 90°F and periods of 100-degree temperatures are not uncommon. On the plus side, in winter, none of these cities has a mean temperature below freezing. Lewiston golfers play year-round, and a lush spring comes to town in March and April, when blossoms explode into color.

Up out of the canyons, on the prairies of north-central Idaho, higher elevations and increased wind make for cooler temperatures year-round in places like Moscow and Grangeville. Daytime high temperatures in **Moscow,** elevation 2,660 feet, average 84°F in July and 35°F in January. Precipitation in Moscow averages 23 inches annually, with winter the wettest season.

The Panhandle

North Idaho's maritime-influenced climate derives from prevailing westerlies that carry warm, wet storms from the Pacific and Gulf of Alaska across the Northwest. The Washington Cascades wring some of the moisture from these storms, but the Columbia River Gorge ushers other storms right on through, to drop rain and snow on the Panhandle's mountains. Consistent with maritime weather patterns, winters here are cloudy and wet, while summers are clear and relatively dry. July is the prime travel month in the Panhandle, with precipitation reliably lower than in other months. Temperatures are more moderate year-round than at corresponding latitudes on the east side of the Continental Divide.

In the Silver Valley town of **Kellogg,** elevation 2,290 feet, look for July highs in the mid-80s, January highs in the mid-30s, and about 30 inches of rainfall a year. Farther north in **Sandpoint,** elevation 2,100 feet, July highs generally average 80°F, and January brings highs right down to freezing. Sandpoint receives an average of 34 inches of precipitation a year.

Flora

DESERT AND SHRUBLAND

Sagebrush Country

Before the arrival of settlers and their irrigation practices, southern Idaho was largely an arid desert covered in heat- and drought-tolerant grasses and shrubs. Dominant among them is **sagebrush**—genus *Artemisia*—which comes in at least 23 different species in Idaho. One of the most common is big sage *(Artemisia tridentata)*. In addition to the pleasant, pungent aroma characteristic of all sages, big sage can be readily identified by its silvery sheen and the three rounded teeth on its leaftips. Most sage species are small shrubs, but one variety, basin big sage, can grow to the size of a small tree.

In sage-dominated areas, you'll likely also encounter **antelope bitterbrush,** a favorite browse of antelope, deer, elk, and domestic livestock. Occasional particularly alkaline soils in the sagebrush zone support a number of salt-loving shrubs—botanists call them halophytes—including **greasewood, winterfat,** and **shadscale.**

Alongside the streams and rivers that slice benevolently through this barren landscape, larger, lusher vegetation flourishes. The *bois* that gave the Boise River its name were magnificent stands of **black cottonwood.** These impressive trees can grow to more than 100 feet tall and eight feet in diameter, and they light up bright yellow in fall. Black cottonwood is the state's largest native broadleaf tree, found along every major river in the state. Another native species, **narrowleaf cottonwood,** grows principally in southeast Idaho; look for it along the South Fork of the Snake River, downstream from Palisades Reservoir.

Another common plant along Idaho riverbanks is **willow.** About 30 species inhabit the state, making *Salix* the largest genus in Idaho. Willows range in size from shrubs to large trees. Their bitter bark is the source of salicylic acid, a proven headache remedy. Perhaps this explains why the bark is a favorite food of the perennially busy beaver. In winter, the yellows and oranges of the plant's leafless stems brighten drainages across the state. While shrub-size willows are most common in the wild, the large **golden weeping willow** *(Salix alba,* var. *tristis)* is a popular tree-size ornamental.

Juniper Highlands

In the high-desert areas of southern Idaho, you'll find occasional tracts of juniper. These evergreens are too small for commercial lumber production but are widely used across southern Idaho for fenceposts and firewood. The tiny, spherical, pale-blue cones are frequently called "berries," and they're responsible for giving your gin its just-so flavor. The berries, along with the tree's scaly leaves, make the juniper easy to identify.

Near the Utah border on I-84, you'll pass through a large area of **Utah juniper** that supports a population of ferruginous hawks. To the east are occasional woodlands of **Rocky Mountain juniper,** the most common species in the state, while to the west stretch vast areas dominated by **western juniper,** the largest of the three species found in Idaho. The Owyhee County Backcountry Byway passes through a particularly large and absolutely stunning forest of western juniper.

A couple of pines are commonly found growing in and around juniper woodlands, primarily in the southern reaches of the state. The hardy **limber pine** ordinarily prefers higher elevations but has established a community among the juniper woodlands around Soda Springs, as well as atop the lava fields of Craters of the Moon National Monument. **Singleleaf piñon** also enjoys the company of junipers, in and around south-central Idaho's City of Rocks. The piñon is an anomaly in many ways. It's a Great Basin species most commonly found farther south in Nevada—the City of Rocks community is the northernmost tip of its range and its only foothold in Idaho. It's also the world's only species of pine growing single needles akin to a fir; all other pines grow needles in bundles of 2 to 5. And unlike other pines, the piñon bears extra-large seeds called pine nuts, a food enjoyed and often relied upon by Native Americans.

Mountain Shrub Zone

As you head up into Idaho's southern hills, the sagebrush-dominated desert vegetation gives way to a habitat of predominantly broadleaf shrubs. The most common species of this zone is **curlleaf mountain-mahogany.** It's no relation to the exotic Southeast Asian mahogany prized for fine woodworking, but its dark wood is similar. Deer and elk love the stuff and tend to keep it trimmed down to shrub size. You can identify mountain-mahogany by its narrow and leathery one-inch-long green leaves, and by the unique two- to three-inch-long feathery tails emerging from its seed pods. Other common shrubs in this zone include **black chokecherry,** found throughout the state in warm, relatively low-altitude locations; **antelope bitterbrush,** whose range extends down into the sagebrush zone; and **western serviceberry,** one of Idaho's most ubiquitous plants.

A number of relatively small native trees also inhabit this zone, including **interior box-elder** and **bigtooth maple.** The latter lights up like a blowtorch in fall, all dark reds and oranges. It's the state's largest color-changing tree.

FORESTS

Botanists classify Idaho's forests under the umbrella heading of **Rocky Mountain montane,** a biome that includes most of the forest lands of the Rockies, extending from British Columbia in the north, through Idaho, and on down to New Mexico in the south. Several different specific forest types make up this biome.

Ponderosa Pine Forest

On sunny slopes at lower elevations (1,000–3,500 feet), the **ponderosa pine** is king. It's the most wide-ranging and common pine in North America, and one of the grandest as well. A large ponderosa can reach over seven feet in diameter and be as tall as an 18-story building.

Mature ponderosas have thick, platelike bark that provides protection from forest fires; the bark is colored so intensely golden-orange it

seems to glow in the sunshine. As a result, many foresters call them "punkins." The tree's thirsty root system sucks up nutrients to such a degree that no other trees or even shrubs of consequence can grow within a wide radius of the trunk. This makes the ponderosa look like a solitary loner and accentuates its magnificence.

Ponderosa pine needles are 4–8 inches long and grow three to a bundle, but unless you're looking at a young tree that hasn't developed its characteristic bark or size, you probably won't need to get up so close for identification. The best place in Idaho to see these beautiful trees is, not surprisingly, along the state's **Ponderosa Pine Scenic Byway,** Highway 21 between Boise and Stanley.

Douglas Fir Forest

Above the ponderosas at a cooler and wetter altitude is the Douglas fir zone. Douglas fir is named after David Douglas, a 19th-century naturalist who named and catalogued many of the trees found in the Pacific Northwest. This tree is a little harder than ponderosa pine to identify from a distance. No particular distinguishing features are apparent until you get up close and personal. Look at the cones. Odd paper-thin bracts—each forked like the hind end of a horseshoe crab—protrude from behind the normal woody cone scales. Most of central Idaho—millions of acres—is covered with Douglas fir. It's the most important fodder for Idaho's timber industry, and you can find it across the state. The biggest one, a 209-foot-tall skyscraper nearly six feet in diameter, rules the woods southeast of Clarkia.

Cedar-Hemlock Forest

Given an even cooler, wetter environment than the Douglas fir zone, things start to get interesting. Where the ponderosa pine rules essentially alone, and the Douglas firs have but one or two interlopers keeping them company, the cedar-hemlock zone is shared by three climax species and several other prominent hangers-on. Here the woods can take on the dark, wet, fecund feel of a rainforest.

The three climax species in this zone are **grand**

fir, **western red cedar,** and **western hemlock.** Southern Idaho is too dry to support these trees, so this zone is found primarily in maritime-influenced west-central and northern Idaho.

Grand fir prefers the zone's drier ranges, usually equating with either lower altitudes or lower latitudes. Like all true firs, its cones stand upright on the branches and its needles grow singly from the twigs.

Western red cedar generally is a little thirstier, quenching that thirst either by growing higher within the zone or by hunkering down near streambeds. Western red cedars have a different family tree, so to speak, than pines and firs. They're in the juniper family *(Cupressaceae)* and, like junipers, their leaves are scalelike rather than needlelike. Their foliage looks distinctly ferny from a distance. They're the giants of this zone, not so much in height—all three climax species in this zone top out around 170 feet—but in bulk. The biggest western hemlock is about six feet in diameter, the biggest grand fir a foot wider, but the biggest western red cedar measures over 18 feet in diameter. This goliath can be found in Giant Cedar Grove, north of the hamlet of Elk River in Clearwater County.

The western hemlock thrives in the wet and stormy high-altitude end of the zone. Forests dominated by this tree have an enchanted, primeval quality, giving you the impression that if you took a short nap on the forest floor, you might awaken covered by a blanket of lush ferns and mosses. Head for Priest Lake State Park to see what the western hemlock forests are all about.

Another prominent inhabitant of this zone is **western white pine,** Idaho's **state tree.** This massive tree is the battleship of the state's arboreal fleet. Its hulking, gray trunk rises straight as an arrow off the forest floor, reaching heights of nearly 200 feet. The biggest white pine in Idaho is nearly seven feet in diameter. The species is very valuable to the timber industry. Between the chainsaws and the dreaded white pine blister rust—a fungus lethal to these leviathans—it's lucky Idaho has any specimens of its state tree left standing. At least one narrow corridor is preserved for tourists; check out the **White Pine Scenic Byway,** Highway 6 north of Potlatch in north-central Idaho.

One more resident of the cedar-hemlock zone is worth a mention. Scattered throughout the wetter areas of the Panhandle and densely concentrated in the mountains around Elk City is the **Pacific yew.** This tree has attracted a lot of attention in recent years since the discovery that its bark contains taxol, a compound that slows the growth of cancerous tumors. The yew is a relatively small tree with flat, one-inch-long leaves and thin, reddish bark.

Subalpine Forests

The highest forests of Idaho—ranging in elevation from around 5,000 feet right up to the timberline—are the airy realm of **Engelmann spruce, subalpine fir,** and **mountain hemlock.** Both Engelmann spruce and subalpine fir have steeply peaked crowns; the latter is especially pointy on top, looking almost surreally cartoonish. The two trees are usually found growing together as neighbors. If you can't tell them apart by their shape, look at the cones: the fir's stand up on the branches, while the spruce's hang down.

The third climax species of the subalpine forests is the exquisitely elegant mountain hemlock, John Muir's favorite tree. You'll have no trouble recognizing this one—just look for the graceful, droopy crown. These trees require a cool, wet climate, and as a result, are found only in the high mountains of Idaho's Panhandle, and then usually on the wettest north-facing slopes.

Several other trees also prefer life in the subalpine zone. **Limber pine** is found at subalpine heights in the sunny east-central and southeast portions of the state, and has been known to grow occasionally at lower elevations, too. Look for it in the lava fields at Craters of the Moon National Monument. **Whitebark pine** is a gnarly denizen of the craggy timberline reaches, ranging from the high country of central Idaho north to the Panhandle. It's almost never found lower than the subalpine zone. Grizzly bears like to chow down on whitebark pine nuts in fall, so it's not a bad idea to know what the tree looks like if you're hiking in bear country. Both the limber and whitebark pines have short needles that come five to a bundle. Male whitebark cones are easy to identify—they're purple. **Subalpine larch** is another high-altitude habitué. It requires a cold but sunny climate and is found above 8,000 feet in the Sawtooths, and above 7,000 feet in the Selkirks. Like all larches, its needles turn brilliant gold in fall.

Two More Ubiquitous Trees

A prolific deciduous tree counts as one of the regulars in Idaho's forests. The splendid **quaking aspen** provides a delicate counterpoint to the deep green of surrounding conifers. Its albino bark and shimmering leaves—light green in spring, brilliant gold in fall—light up the woods across much of the state. The South Hills' Rock Creek Canyon is a veritable Jackson Pollock of aspens and cottonwoods in autumn.

Unfortunately, the bark of this beautiful tree is often defaced. Aspen bark is a favorite food of beavers, so streambank aspens are frequently chewed up. Less justifiable are the initials, hearts, four-letter words, and other symbols carved into aspen trunks in the high country by thoughtless humans. This tradition probably started with bored Basque sheepherders and was picked up by modern-day campers and four-wheel-drive ex-plorers. The scars last the life of the tree, a sad reminder of the inability of our species to just leave the earth alone.

Another tree found widely across Idaho is the **lodgepole pine.** It's easy to identify: the trees' long, straight trunks, once used by Native Americans as lodge poles, are covered with a thin, pale, distinctively pebbly bark.

The lodgepole's clever reproductive strategy has led to its ubiquity. The tree produces two types of cones. Some of the cones open and drop normally, allowing the tree a chance to reproduce in any openings in the understory. Others remain closed and tightly sealed with resin until fire sweeps through. The flames melt the resin, freeing the seeds and allowing them to get started on the open, sunlight- and nutrient-rich burned-out slopes. Thanks to this unique trait and a fast-growing nature, lodgepoles tend to come back first and dominate forests charred by fire. The lodgepole isn't too picky about its habitat. It'll grow anywhere from the Doug fir zone up to the subalpine zone, but it does prefer cold temperatures. You'll find good examples of lodgepole forest at Harriman State Park near Island Park, a very cold place in winter that was burned out many summers ago.

Fauna

THREATENED AND ENDANGERED SPECIES

Wolves

Largest of the wild dogs, the wolf stands close to three feet tall at the shoulder, stretching as long as six feet from nose to tail tip. An average adult male weighs around 100 pounds. Wolves are intelligent, playful, social animals with one unfortunate character trait that has made them pariahs in their homeland. Although wild deer and elk form the mainstay of their diet, they've also been known to eat livestock. Humans do this in mass quantities and think nothing of it, but when wolves do it, it's an outrage to those who make their livelihood off Big Macs and Whoppers. The wolves' taste for steak tartare has caused some of the most heated debate in the Northwest and probably more than a few fistfights over the years in saloons across rural Montana, Wyoming, and Idaho.

For many years, ranchers killed the animals with abandon. Once the most numerous large predator in the United States, wolves were virtually exterminated from the American Rockies by the 1930s—trapped, shot, and poisoned by ranchers and bounty hunters. In 1988, the gray wolf population in Boise National Forest was estimated at between four and nine.

In 1973, Congress passed the Endangered Species Act, designed to identify and protect endangered species and nurse their populations back to self-sustaining levels. As originally written, the act required the U.S. Fish and Wildlife Service to take positive action to reintroduce endangered species to their former habitat, at the same time placing severe penalties on anyone attempting to harm those species in any way. When it came the wolves' turn for protection under the law, it set off a major political battle in the West, pitting ranchers against the government and environmentalists, who pushed for the act's full implementation on behalf of the beleaguered wolf.

More than a decade of political wrangling ensued, as the powerful Western ranching interests and their allied representatives in Washington—both elected and nonelected—attempted to overthrow the Endangered Species Act. At last a deal was reached that seemed to please no one—probably the sign of a good compromise. The act was not overturned, and the U.S. Fish and Wildlife Service (USFWS) proceeded with efforts to reintroduce wolves to the West. But the Act was amended to allow reintroduction of the wolves as "nonessential, experimental" populations south of I-90, which removes the strictest protective measures of the federal government from such populations. (North of I-90, where there isn't much ranching, the wolves received regular endangered species status.)

The compromise appears to have worked. Fifteen gray wolves were released into central Idaho in 1995, and by 2002, the state's wolf population had climbed to more than 250 in an estimated 19 packs. In the broader Northern Rockies region—including Idaho, Montana, and Wyoming's Yellowstone National Park, where wolves were reintroduced in the mid-1990s—there were an estimated 664 wolves in 44 packs by 2003. These numbers helped lead the USFWS in March 2003 to reclassify gray wolves as a "threatened" species. But wolves remain controversial. Ranchers still harbor a loathing for the animals that borders on obsession, and there's talk throughout the Northern Rockies about bringing back sanctioned wolf hunts.

Grizzly Bears

At one time this biggest and most powerful of North American mammals was widespread across the West. But that was before Lewis and Clark

set the stage for human encroachment on grizzly habitat. In the lower 48 states, a population once estimated at tens of thousands of animals was reduced by humans—either directly by hunting, or indirectly by habitat loss—to about 1,200 today. In 1975, grizzlies were given threatened status under the Endangered Species Act, and today Idaho is one of only four states in the country where *Ursus arctos*, the grizzly bear, still lives. (The others are Washington, Montana, and Wyoming.)

Not that Idaho harbors vast numbers of the bear. Chris Servheen, grizzly bear recovery coordinator for the U.S. Fish & Wildlife Service, estimates there may be 100 griz in Idaho at any given time. Unless you go backpacking in a few specific areas of the state and get extremely lucky, you'll never see a grizzly. They roam the northern tip of the Panhandle north of Sandpoint, particularly in the Selkirk Mountains; the Bitterroot Range from Clark Fork south to the headwaters of the St. Joe River; and along the Wyoming border from near Henry's Lake south to Alpine.

The grizzly is immense. A full-grown adult male averages 450 pounds and can weigh up to 500 pounds. Just coming across a fresh grizzly print in the mud is enough to set the adrenaline flowing as the scale of this beautiful beast becomes apparent. No matter how big and bad you think you are, you're a wimp compared to the griz.

Grizzlies are far larger than black bears, but at a distance, it might be difficult to gauge an animal's size. You can't tell a black bear from a grizzly by color alone—grizzlies can appear black and black bears can be brown. Look for the dish-shaped head profile and the telltale Quasimodo shoulder hump.

During the Clinton administration, the U.S. Fish & Wildlife Service studied plans to reintroduce more grizzlies into Idaho, but the plan was suspended once George W. Bush came to power. (The state of Idaho also filed suit to stop the effort, basically pleading that Idaho today is a far different place than when the bears roamed wild 200 years ago.) The issue is far from resolved, however, and you can expect more debate surrounding grizzly bears in years to come.

COURTESY OF THE IDAHO TRAVEL COUNCIL

With some luck, you might see a grizzly.

Salmon

Idaho was once home to literally millions of anadromous fish—in other words, fish that are born in fresh water, migrate downstream to the sea, grow into adults there, then return upriver to their birthplace to spawn and start the process all over again. Idaho is at the headwaters of the great Columbia River Drainage; historically, the total run of adult fish to the Columbia River has been estimated at 8 to 16 million fish, of which the Snake River may have produced 1.5 to 3 million. Salmon and steelhead once made their way annually from the Pacific up the Columbia to the Snake River, and up the Snake River to prime spawning grounds on the Salmon and Clearwater Rivers and their tributaries, a journey of up to 900 miles. Redfish Lake in Idaho's Sawtooth Mountains gained its name from the first settlers to the area, who found the lake colored red with the bodies of thousands of sockeye salmon each spawning season. Idaho's Native Americans relied on the salmon as a staple in their diet for centuries.

Then the dams came; humans harnessed the waters of the Columbia for cheap electricity. Between 1938 and 1973, 12 dams were constructed on the Columbia, Snake, and Clearwater Rivers.

The main-stem dams were equipped with fish ladders to help adults get upstream to spawn, but provided no help for offspring making their way back to the sea. The fish were sucked into dam turbines and killed, died of disease exacerbated by the warmer temperature of the slower-moving water, or succumbed to increased predation during the journey. Before the dams, the young smolts made it to the Pacific in 7 10 days. After the dams, it took two months or more, for those who made it at all.

Three species of salmon—the coho, chinook, and sockeye—once spawned in Idaho waters, along with the steelhead, an anadromous rainbow trout. The coho was officially declared extinct on the Snake River in 1986. The sockeye may be next; from 1991 to 2003, only 16 wild sockeye have returned from the ocean. All sockeye that return are captured and placed in a captive-breeding program in an effort to save the species. Wild chinook salmon were declared a threatened species when returns declined to a few thousand adults in the early 1990s, and wild steelhead were listed as threatened under the Endangered Species Act in 1997. Although artificial production (hatchery) programs produce millions of smolts every year and provide some surplus fish for fishing, the once-abundant wild and natural runs remain at a tiny fraction of the historical numbers. None of the mitigation measures attempted, including capturing smolts above the dams and barging or trucking them to the sea, has worked to restore natural spawning and wild salmon runs.

Environmentalists have urged the breaching of four dams on the Lower Snake River, but the idea hasn't gained political traction, and the salmon issue remains mired in legal maneuvering. Dams *are* a primary culprit in the salmon's fate, but the issue is more complex than simply "dams versus salmon." Water withdrawals for 3 million acres of irrigated Idaho cropland, the Northwest's continuing population boom, highway and home construction that fragment salmon habitat, and insatiable demand for cheap electricity—all are contributing to the salmon's decline. When it comes down to it, we can have our modern, ultra-consumptive lifestyle, or we can have wild salmon, but we probably can't have both.

Bull Trout

Back in 1949, a world-record 32-pound bull trout was pulled from Pend Oreille Lake. But the bull trout—actually not a trout at all, but a char—hasn't been doing so well in recent years, and it's now listed as threatened. A predator fish that prefers the coldest waters, bull trout are also sometimes called Dolly Varden.

Woodland Caribou

Two small herds of Selkirk Mountains woodland caribou cling to a precarious existence in the Panhandle's Selkirk Range and neighboring eastern Washington and British Columbia. Populations had declined to around 25 animals in the early 1980s. Today, after extensive management efforts to strengthen populations, there are still only around 35 to 40 animals left. Habitat loss and low birthrates have inhibited their comeback. Wildlife biologists have proposed establishing a third herd, hoping to keep the gene pool strong and avoid catastrophic loss of animals from disease. The caribou, a medium-size member of the deer family, has a broad muzzle, large hooves, and impressive antlers with shovel-like brow tines.

MAMMALS

Black Bears

Common and numerous throughout Idaho and the West, the black bear *(Ursus americanus)* is much more likely to be encountered by Idaho hikers and backpackers than its larger cousin the grizzly. The black bear was once a shy, nervous creature of little threat, but continued human-bear encounters have left it less afraid of humans and more likely to be trouble. Black bears are smaller than grizzlies, have straight (as opposed to dished) head profiles, and lack the grizzly's trademark shoulder hump. Also note that unlike grizzlies, many black bears are adept at climbing trees.

Wild Dogs and Cats

The wolf's little cousin, the **coyote** *(Canis latrans),* is alive and well in Idaho. This survivor plays a leading role in many Nez Perce legends; he's a cagey prankster who always seems to have a lesson to teach. **Mountain lions** inhabit remote parts of Idaho but are so shy and elusive they are seldom seen by humans. Other cool cats found in Idaho include the **bobcat** and the **Canada lynx.**

Horns and Hooves

Elk were found across the country when European explorers first arrived. By 1900 the New World's new residents had killed off 99 percent of them. The rest were found almost entirely in Yellowstone National Park. Today Idaho supports several herds. Don't miss the wintertime elk-viewing Hap and Florence Points Memorial Sleigh Rides in Donnelly, or the summertime evening browsing at Burgdorf Hot Springs near McCall.

White-tailed deer and **mule deer** are plentiful, as is the largest member of the deer family, the **moose.** Priest Lake in the Panhandle is a possible spot to spot a moose, as are the Caribou National Forest of southeast Idaho and along the North Fork of the Payette River near McCall.

Mountain goats can often be seen on the high cliffs of central Idaho, while **bighorn sheep** share the arid southwestern deserts and highlands with **pronghorn.** Owyhee County also is home to small herds of **wild horses.**

Small Mammals

Beavers have become popular helpers in restoring rangelands eroded by cattle. Dams built by the 50-pound, paddle-tailed rodents create wetlands, slow fast-moving storm water before it can do erosion damage, and catch eroded topsoil before it's washed downstream. **River otters** inhabit many of the state's waterways. I've seen them right by the falls in Idaho Falls, and on the South Fork of the Snake near Ririe. **Marmots** and **pikas** inhabit rocky areas, usually above timberline. The pika's sharp whistle is familiar to high-country backpackers.

Life isn't so good these days for the **Northern Idaho ground squirrel,** a species found only in a 20-mile by 61-mile area in Adams and Valley Counties. In the mid-1980s, there were about 5,000 such squirrels; today, there are fewer than 500, and they're listed as threatened. Ground squirrel populations have declined mainly due to habitat loss and fragmentation.

BIRDS

Raptors

Southwest Idaho provides the focal point of human efforts to preserve raptors, or birds of prey. On the outskirts of Boise you'll find the World Center for Birds of Prey, and, farther south, the Birds of Prey National Conservation Area. The latter preserve protects a stretch of the Snake River and the surrounding clifftops where, in spring, the world's densest concentration of nesting raptors can be found—more than 700 pairs, of 14 different species.

A cruise down just about any rural road in the region will provide close-up looks at big birds of prey perched on power lines or soaring on thermals. One day while I was getting lost near Eden in the south-central part of the state, I happened on a farmer's plowed field where I had to stop and rub my eyes in disbelief. Scattered across the field—perhaps the size of a couple of football fields put together—were literally scores of hawks, looking like so many crows in a wheatfield.

But Idaho's incredible cast of raptors—including **red-tailed hawks, Swainson's hawks, ferruginous hawks, goshawks, northern har-** riers, peregrine falcons, prairie falcons, bald eagles, golden eagles, short-eared owls, great horned owls, ospreys,** and others—aren't just found in southern Idaho. For example, bald eagles, whose populations have recovered from near extinction and have been downlisted from endangered to threatened status under the Endangered Species Act, can be found across the state in winter, from Boise to Coeur d'Alene, fishing in open waters. Ospreys seem to particularly like the southeast shores of Coeur d'Alene Lake, around Harrison, while ferruginous hawks congregate in the Juniper Valley near the Utah border. And the ubiquitous **vulture** will carry on wherever there's carrion.

Waterfowl

Eastern Idaho lies along a major avian migratory route, and its lakes and wetlands become mass staging areas for hundreds of thousands of **ducks** and **geese** in spring and fall. **Sandhill cranes** flock to Gray's Lake National Wildlife Refuge in some numbers; if you're lucky, you might catch a glimpse of the endangered **whooping crane** there as well. The largest of all North American waterfowl is the rare **trumpeter swan,** which weighs 30–40 pounds and has a wingspan of up to eight feet. Hunting and habitat loss had reduced their numbers to as few as 200 at the turn of the century. Though they are still rare, the trumpeter population is now about 3,000. Trumpeters migrate through the Henry's Fork area; look for them at Harriman State Park in winter.

FISH

Trout

Many consider the anadromous steelhead trout to be the state's premier game fish. Unfortunately, these beauties are threatened with extinction in Idaho, so all fishing for them is catch-and-release only. Adult steelhead weigh 10–15 pounds and are found in the Snake, Salmon, and Clearwater Rivers and their tributaries.

True trout species in Idaho include **rainbow, cutthroat, brook, brown,** and **lake trout**, this last also known as mackinaw. Also in the trout family are Idaho's **kamloops** and **kokanee.**

Sturgeon

For sheer size, the king of Idaho's piscine population is the bottom-feeding white sturgeon. These giants live about as long as people—100-year-old individuals have been reported, although the oldest fish officially documented by state biologists was 65. Today these fish grow to lengths of 11 feet and more, and weigh upwards of 300 pounds. In the old days, before commercial fishing and the construction of the Snake River dams, individuals up to 20 feet long and weighing more than 1,000 pounds were reported (and yes, photographed for posterity). But populations have declined steadily since the turn of the 20th century. Commercial sturgeon fishing has been banned since 1943, and today all sport sturgeon fishing is catch-and-release only. In 1995, sturgeon fishing on the Kootenai River was closed completely. The strongest remaining sturgeon populations are found today on two stretches of the Snake River: between Bliss Dam and C. J. Strike Dam, and between Hells Canyon Dam and Lewiston.

Warm-Water Fish

Idaho's lakes harbor a number of species prized by anglers, including largemouth and smallmouth **bass,** three different species of **catfish,** and **perch, crappie,** and **tiger muskie.** The **Bonneville cisco** is a rare sardine-like fish living only in the waters of Bear Lake, in Idaho's southeastern corner.

History and People

THE EARLIEST INHABITANTS

The earliest people to roam the state on a more-or-less continuous basis probably came into the area some 14,000 years ago. Luckily not yet clear on the concept of no-trace camping, these nomadic hunters left remnants of their existence behind. At the bottom of Wilson Butte Cave near Dietrich in south-central Idaho, archaeologists have discovered bones of a prehistoric horse, camel, and sloth dating from 13,000 B.C., and a spear point dated to 12,500 B.C.—one of the oldest conclusive bits of evidence of human habitation in the country.

Native Americans

Before the arrival of the Lewis and Clark expedition in 1805, the Northwest, including the future Idaho, was inhabited by numerous tribes of indigenous peoples. The **Kootenai** tribe roamed the territory now comprising southern British Columbia, northeastern Washington, the Idaho Panhandle, and northwestern Montana. They fished for salmon and sturgeon in the rivers; hunted deer, elk, and caribou; and gathered wild vegetables, roots, and berries. The **Coeur d'Alene** tribe lived around Coeur d'Alene Lake. They, too, hunted deer and fished in the lake and its feeder rivers. To catch salmon they trekked to Spokane Falls, which blocked salmon migration to Coeur d'Alene Lake and the upstream rivers.

Eastern Oregon's Wallowa Valley, parts of southeastern Washington, and Idaho's Clearwater River Valley were once the home territory of the **Nez Perce** tribe. They fished for salmon in the Clearwater River, hunted deer, elk, moose, bighorn sheep, and bear, and gathered camas roots from the vast field on the Camas Prairie around Grangeville.

Southwestern Idaho was part of the territory wandered by the **Shoshone** and **Paiute** tribes of the Great Basin, a vast area spanning parts of southeastern Oregon, northeastern California, southwestern Idaho, and northern Nevada. Tribal cooks in this desert landscape had an entirely different list of ingredients to choose from; hunters brought in pronghorn, sage grouse, squirrels, rabbits, and prairie dogs, as well as deer. Some bands found pine nuts; some searched for seeds and berries. Bands were small, and the people peaceful.

The Shoshone people coexisted in south-central and southeastern Idaho with the **Bannock** people; the two tribes had distinct languages but shared similar hunter-gatherer lifestyles.

The Spanish introduced horses to North America in their forays into Mexico and today's southwestern United States, and by around 1700 the horse reached the Native Americans of Idaho. It was seized on by the various tribes, whose migratory lifestyles suddenly got much easier. Soon many tribes made forays across the Continental Divide into what is now Montana and Wyoming. There they found great herds of buffalo that would sustain them until the white man came and wiped out the herds. The trails blazed by the Idaho tribes crossing east to the buffalo-hunting grounds were the same trails later used in the opposite direction by explorers, fur trappers, and pioneers.

THE GRAND ADVENTURES OF LEWIS AND CLARK

The Corps of Discovery

Even before the April 1803 brokering of the Louisiana Purchase gave the U.S. title to most of the West, President Thomas Jefferson secretly began planning an exploratory expedition to find a viable northern route between the Mississippi River and the Pacific Ocean. Jefferson looked to his personal secretary, a young Virginian named Meriwether Lewis, to lead the mission. Lewis had been a captain in the Virginia state militia. Much of his duty had been west of the Alleghenies, and he had considerable experience dealing with indigenous Native Americans.

Lewis chose fellow Virginian William Clark as his co-commander. Clark also had considerable military experience. He was known as a skilled negotiator with Native Americans, as well as a qualified mapmaker. He also recruited many members for the expedition. By the winter of 1803–04, Lewis and Clark and their party of about 40 men were camped at the confluence of the Missouri and Mississippi Rivers near St. Louis. Lewis was 29; Clark, 33.

In May 1804, the expedition, known as the Corps of Discovery, set out west. Their mission: to follow the Missouri River to its headwaters in the Rocky Mountains, cross the Rockies, and find the nearest navigable waterway to the Pacific Ocean. The first summer was marked by several meetings with Indian nations and by Lewis and Clark's careful recording—via their journals and sketches—of many plants and animals unknown in the Eastern United States.

By October 1804, the expedition had reached North Dakota. They wintered there near a village of Minnetaree (Hidatsa), Mandan, and Amahami people. There they picked up their famous guide, a teenage Shoshone woman named Sacagawea. As a girl, Sacagawea had lived with her people in the Lemhi Valley near present-day Salmon, Idaho. But on a hunting expedition into Montana, her band had been attacked by the Minnetarees. Sacagawea, about age 12, was captured and taken east, to be traded among the Indians like so much legal tender. She ended up as the property and wife of French trapper Toussaint Charbonneau. When Lewis and Clark reached the Minnetaree village, they hired Charbonneau as an interpreter, at least in part with the hope that Sacagawea might be able to help them find her people and negotiate for horses to cross the Rocky Mountains. So when the Corps of Discovery resumed its westward journey in May 1805, Sacagawea, Charbonneau, and the couple's two-month-old baby joined the expedition.

Scouting the Bitterroots

A small advance party led by Lewis crossed the Continental Divide on August 12, 1805, becoming the first whites to lay eyes on the land that would become Idaho. Lewis recorded the day's events:

At the distance of four miles further, the road took us to the most distant fountain of the waters of the mighty Missouri, in search of which we have spent so many toilsome days and restless nights. Thus far I had accomplished one of those great objects on which my mind has been unalterably fixed for many years; judge then of the pleasure I felt in allaying my thirst with this pure and ice-cold water which issues from the base of a low mountain. . . . Here I halted a few minutes and rested myself. Two miles below, McNeal had exultingly stood with a foot on each side of this little rivulet and thanked his god that he had lived to bestride the mighty and heretofore deemed endless Missouri.

It was the last piece of the American jigsaw puzzle to be filled in by white eyes and the beginning of the end for the region's Native American inhabitants. The explorers' route across the Continental Divide is today commemorated by the **Lewis and Clark National Backcountry Byway,** which connects Montana's Highway 324 with Idaho Highway 28 at Tendoy. It can be negotiated in summer by a sturdy passenger vehicle or a trusty Appaloosa.

The party continued down the western side of the pass and soon surprised a small group of Shoshone women. After being assured of the party's peaceful intentions, the women led the group back to their main encampment, where the whites were received with open arms. In a twist of fate, Sacagawea and a Shoshone woman saw each other and gleefully embraced. It seems Sacagawea had found her people at last—the Shoshone woman was a childhood friend. Later that night, the two groups celebrated with a reunion feast. But it was a bittersweet reunion for Sacagawea, who learned that most of her family was dead.

Lewis told the Shoshone chief, Ca-me-âh-wait, of his plan to navigate the Lemhi River downstream, eventually to the Columbia. The chief advised against it, telling Lewis that not far to the north, past a major confluence (with the Salmon River), the river cascaded through steep, impassable canyons.

Lewis suspected the chief was exaggerating and decided to forge ahead with the plan.

Continuing West

On the morning of August 17, 1805, Clark and a small party began to scout a route down the Lemhi River. Not far past the confluence of the Lemhi and Salmon Rivers, the steep route along the Salmon was judged impassable, exactly as Chief Ca-me-âh-wait had told Lewis. Clark dispatched a messenger relaying the word to Lewis, who agreed that the expedition should abandon the Lemhi-Salmon Rivers route and instead attempt the Nez Perce route—the Lolo Trail—which crossed the Bitterroot Mountains far to the north. Lewis and the rest of the expedition set out immediately, crossing Lemhi Pass and catching up with Clark once again. Sacagawea bade a

sad farewell to her people and, along with the rest of the Corps, headed north.

They doggedly worked their way up the Continental Divide, first along the west side via the North Fork of the Salmon, then across to the Montana side near **Lost Trail Pass** (Highway 93 today) and down into the Bitterroot River Valley, where they camped with a party of 400 Salish people.

Over the Bitterroots, Barely

After camping for a few days at the junction of the Bitterroot and Lolo Creek, the party proceeded west up the creek along a traditional Nez Perce hunting trail. On September 13, 1805, they crested **Lolo Pass** and dropped back into Idaho. They camped in present-day Packer Meadows near Lolo Pass and along the Lochsa River near what's now the Powell Ranger Station. Game was scarce, and they had to kill a horse for meat. On September 15, the party set off up Wendover Ridge to gain the Nez Perce trail to the north. It began to snow. In his entry for September 16, Clark wrote:

> *Several horses slipped and rolled down steep hills which hurt them very much. . . . The one which carried my desk and small trunk turned over and rolled down a mountain for 40 yards and lodged against a tree, broke the desk, the horse escaped and appeared but little hurt. . . . After two hours delay we proceeded on up the mountain, steep and rugged as usual . . . when we arrived at the top, . . . we could find no water and concluded to camp and make use of the snow . . . to cook the remains of our colt and make our soup. . . . Evening very cold and cloudy. Two of our horses gave out, poor and too much hurt to proceed on [they were] left in the rear. . . . Nothing killed today except two pheasants. From this mountain I could observe high rugged mountains in every direction as far as I could see.*

It snowed all the next day, obscuring the trail and slowing progress even further. Clark was "as wet and as cold in every part as I ever was in my

LEWIS AND CLARK BICENTENNIAL

By Julie Fanselow

Idaho and other states along the Lewis and Clark Trail are commemorating the bicentennial of the expedition through 2006. Note the word "commemorating": Organizers of this event, heeding lessons learned from the 1992 quadricentennial of Christopher Columbus' voyage to America, are avoiding the word "celebration." As a result, many of the Native American tribes Lewis and Clark encountered, including Idaho's Nez Perce, are using the occasion to share their view of the story.

In June 2006, the Nez Perce—who call themselves Nimiipuu ("The People")—will host one of the 15 bicentennial "signature events" on and around their reservation in north-central Idaho. "Among the Nez Perce" will focus on the tribe's hospitality toward the expedition and on the strong horse culture that thrives even today. For more information on the event, call 208/843-2253 or see www.nezperce.org.

Meriwether Lewis

Although the Nez Perce event will probably draw the most national attention, many Idaho communities are making plans to recognize the explorers' 1805–1806 trek through what's now Idaho. Among them are Salmon, the homeland of Sacagawea's people, the Lemhi Shoshone or Agai-Dika ("Salmon Eaters"), which honors its native daughter at a festival each August; Weippe, where the expedition finally left the Bitterroot Mountains and found help from the Nez Perce; and Lewiston, where an annual Lewis and Clark Symposium and Discovery Faire takes place each June.

Several Idaho towns also plan to host the the national traveling exhibit "Corps of Discovery II: 200 Years to the Future" during the bicentennial years. The show, coordinated by the National Park Service, includes interactive exhibits and a "Tent of Many Voices" featuring diverse

William Clark

speakers and performers. Tentative plans call for Corps II to be in Idaho in Salmon (August 2005), in Kamiah (September 2005), in Boise (May 2006), and on the Nez Perce Reservation near Lewiston (June 2006).

One note: Because the Lemhi Shoshone tribe prefers the spelling Sacajawea, pronounced Sac-a-ja-WEE-a, for the young woman who accompanied the expedition, that's the spelling you'll see most often used in Idaho. Nationally, however, most historians use the spelling Sacagawea (pronounced Sa-cah-ga-WEH-a), so that's the one used in this book unless a site's proper name dictates otherwise.

For more information on Lewis and Clark Bicentennial events and attractions across Idaho, see www.lewisandclarkidaho.org or contact state bicentennial coordinator Keith Petersen at 208/792-2249.

life, indeed I was at one time fearful my feet would freeze in the thin moccasins which I wore." It's a wonder they didn't lose anyone to hypothermia. The early-season storm had driven the game out of the mountains to lower, warmer elevations, making food scarce for the expedition. They shot another horse for dinner that night and huddled around campfires trying to get warm.

By September 18, the expedition had run out of spare horses to fricassee. (Picture yourself on a remote mountain trail in 1805, in stormy weather, with no Gore-Tex, no road, no car, no ready-made food, and no idea what lay ahead. It's safe to say that the expedition was running on hope at this point.) Clark and a party of six hunters went on ahead to find, kill, and bring back food. Two days out they sighted the Weippe Prairie—a welcome, easily traversable bench unlike the steep canyons they'd been crossing. There, they met the Nez Perce. Although some discussed killing the white strangers, Nez Perce oral history says they were stopped by a woman named Watkuweis who—like Sacagawea—was kidnapped when she was younger and had been helped by white people. The agreeable Nez Perce gave Clark's party dried salmon and camas flour, some of which Clark sent back to Lewis and the rest of the expedition with one of his men. Clark and his hunting party accompanied the Nez Perce to their main encampment farther downriver at present-day Orofino. Lewis and the rest of the expedition straggled in later.

Among the Nez Perce

Now all were safe and in good hands with the friendly Nez Perce. They established their own camp, called Canoe Camp, just west of the Nez Perce camp, near today's Ahsahka—where they recuperated from their difficult mountain crossing.

Besides being a place to recuperate, Canoe Camp was important for another reason. When Lewis and Clark saw the Nez Perce paddling up and down the river, they knew that they could now safely do the same. The expedition members began cutting down ponderosa pines to fashion into canoes, and by October 6, 1805, five canoes were finished and preparations were made to get under way. Under cover of darkness, the ex-

pedition members dug a secret hole and buried all their saddles. Then they branded their remaining horses and left them with the Nez Perce, intending to pick them up on their return trip the following spring.

The next day they floated and loaded their canoes and said goodbye to their hosts. Nez Perce Chief Twisted Hair gave Lewis and Clark a map of what lay downriver, and a couple of Nez Perce offered to come along as guides. At last they shoved off. The river's rapids proved difficult, and twice canoes were damaged. But the expedition reached the confluence of the Clearwater and Snake Rivers (site of present-day Lewiston, Idaho, and Clarkston, Washington) on October 10, and paddled on into Washington.

Epilogue

The expedition continued down the Snake to the Columbia and then down the Columbia to the Pacific Ocean in mid-November 1805. They built Fort Clatsop near present-day Astoria, Oregon, and stayed for the winter. On March 23, 1806, they began their return journey by essentially the same route they had come. They picked up the horses and saddles they'd left with the Nez Perce at Orofino. The Indians once again treated them warmly, and the explorers camped near present-day Kamiah for nearly a month while they waited for the snow to melt from the Bitterroots.

Lewis and Clark arrived in St. Louis to a hero's welcome on September 23, 1806. Most people had long since given them up for dead. Lewis served as governor of Louisiana Territory for two years and died under mysterious circumstances—either murder or suicide—in Tennessee on his way to Washington, D.C., in 1809. Sacagawea died in 1812 (but not before she and Charbonneau tried homesteading near St. Louis circa 1809–11). Clark became Superintendent of Indian Affairs for Louisiana Territory and later served as governor of Missouri Territory. He maintained a lifelong trusted relationship with the West's Native Americans and negotiated many Indian treaties before his death in 1838.

The expedition had been a success on many fronts. It had carried out its mission while losing only one man—Charles Floyd, whose appendix ruptured three months into the trip. It had proved an overland route to the Pacific was possible, mapped the land and cataloged its flora and fauna, and established friendly relations with the indigenous peoples. But all those accomplishments contributed to the subsequent flood of white immigrants to the West, an unstoppable wave that would wash away Native American culture and have a profoundly pernicious effect on the land and resources of the Northwest.

THE FUR TRAPPERS

David Thompson

Two years after Lewis and Clark passed through Idaho on their way back home, British fur trappers began working their way into the territory from Canada. One of the first to arrive was geographer David Thompson, an Englishman working for Britain's venerable Hudson's Bay Company. Thompson—today widely considered one of the greatest geographers in history—was an explorer at heart, who used fur trapping as a convenient way to fund his true passion. He had come to Canada as a teenage apprentice for Hudson's Bay, and by the time he arrived in Idaho in 1808, he had vast experience in mapmaking and dealing with indigenous peoples. He had also jumped ship, so to speak, leaving Hudson's Bay Company for its Montreal-based British archrival, the North West Company.

In 1809, Thompson and his crew built a log house, the first permanent structure built by whites in Idaho, near the present-day town of Hope on Pend Oreille Lake. They named it Kullyspell House after the area's Kalispel Indians—a goodwill gesture guaranteed to grease the wheels of trade with the locals. In the four years Thompson stayed at Kullyspell House, he and his colleagues sent bushel upon bushel of beaver pelts back to London, where beaver-fur hats were all the rage. Also during that period, Thompson explored and mapped much of the Panhandle, established good relations with the Native Americans, and surveyed the passes that would later allow railroads into the area. In doing so he set the stage for further white expansion into the Panhandle.

Andrew Henry

Not to be outdone by the Brits, American interests soon raced west to reap their share of the wealth. First to the scene were members of the St. Louis-based **Missouri Fur Company**. In 1809, Pennsylvania native Andrew Henry, a former lead miner, became a partner in the enterprise. In the fall of the following year, Henry led a party of the company's trappers across the Continental Divide into southern Idaho. There he discovered a big, beautiful lake and encouraging prospects for trapping. Deciding to settle in the area for the winter, Henry headed downstream from the lake several miles and built a fort. What he didn't know was that the area sees some of the coldest, most severe winter weather in the West. The winter of 1810–11 was no exception. The local deer and antelope hightailed it out of there early to go play on a warmer range, leaving little for Henry's party to hunt and eat. The men were forced to fry up their own horses to survive. As soon as the first spring thaw came, Henry decided Missouri wasn't such a bad place after all. He returned home posthaste. While the trip hadn't yielded much in the way of beaver pelts, Henry did get immortality out of it: the big beautiful lake and the river below it are now called **Henry's Lake** and **Henry's Fork,** respectively.

Wilson Price Hunt

The same winter that Andrew Henry huddled shivering and homesick in eastern Idaho, 28-year-old greenhorn Wilson Price Hunt was holed up in South Dakota, leading an expedition for John Jacob Astor's **Pacific Fur Company.** After winter let up, Hunt's party continued west. That fall they made it to Jackson Hole, where they came upon three impressive mountain peaks stacked against the horizon. The sight inspired a couple of understandably horny French Canadians to name the impressive peaks Les Trois Tétons—"The Three Breasts." Today we know the beautiful mountains as the Grand Tetons.

The party continued over Teton Pass into Idaho, arriving at abandoned Fort Henry in October 1811. There they made the mistake of leaving their horses behind and attempting to ride the Snake River west. The eastern Snake is a relatively placid affair, today floated by novices. But the flat waters become cantankerous downstream. The expedition portaged around Idaho Falls and American Falls with little difficulty. But then they came to the Milner Reach—a section that, even today, is run only by experts and fools.

The Hunt party lost a man and equipment on the upper Milner Reach, but the worst was yet to come. Soon they came to a spot so ferocious, so impossibly unforgiving, they named it **Caldron Linn,** or Witch's Caldron Falls. From a safe vantage point today, you can feel some of what Hunt and his men felt. The innocuous river rounds a corner and suddenly—far too suddenly—funnels down a tight rocky gorge, thundering into a frothing white madness. The falls spark respect, if not outright fear, in your heart. And remember, today the flow is regulated by Milner Dam upriver. When Hunt's party first saw Caldron Linn, the water was racing unbridled down from the Continental Divide. It must have been horrifying. The expedition abandoned thoughts of floating to the Columbia River and began an overland trek along the banks of the Snake. They pressed on forlornly, reaching Fort Astoria at the mouth of the Columbia River in mid-February 1812.

As a footnote, the next year some of the group retraced their route from Astoria to the confluence of the Snake and Boise Rivers, where they intended to set up a trapping base. They might have succeeded, but two years later, in 1814, all but three were killed by Native Americans. It was the first wholesale murder of whites by Native Americans in Idaho.

Are Those Bagpipes I Hear?

One of the surviving members of the Hunt expedition was an enormous Scotsman, a Highlander named **Donald Mackenzie.** With flaming red hair and a bulk of over 300 pounds, he must have been an impressive sight.

Mackenzie worked the Snake River and its tributaries for years. His 1818 expedition met with some bad luck that ended up contributing to Idaho's geographic lexicon. In those years, it was common to find Hawaiians among the members of trapping expeditions. When Cap-

tain James Cook discovered what he christened the Sandwich Islands in 1778, his interpretation of the name the islanders gave themselves was "Owyhees." Subsequently, English vessels working the Pacific would bring these Owyhees to the Northwest to work as laborers. A few of them could usually be found on Mackenzie's expeditions, and the 1818 trip was no exception. At one point, Mackenzie assigned three of them to trap along an unnamed, unexplored river south of the Boise River–Snake River confluence. The men never returned; presumably they were killed by Native Americans. The remaining members of the expedition named the unexplored river after the unfortunate islanders. Today on the map of Idaho you'll find not only the **Owyhee River** but the Owyhee Mountains as well. Both are in Owyhee County.

Another Scotsman, seasoned trapper **Finan McDonald,** led an 1823 Hudson's Bay Company expedition from Spokane east into Montana, then back into Idaho over Lemhi Pass. On the upper Lemhi River the expedition was ambushed by a party of Blackfeet. Outnumbered almost three to one, McDonald and company fought a smart battle—the battle of their lives—and miraculously defeated the Blackfeet, losing only six men in the process. The Blackfeet lost 68 of their 75 warriors in the skirmish, which put an irremediable dent into their control of the area. When McDonald got back to Spokane, he vowed never to return to that part of the country. But by vanquishing the Blackfeet, McDonald had succeeded in opening the door to the upper Snake River country for trappers and those who followed.

A New Breed

By the time Canadian **Peter Skene Ogden** took charge of the Hudson's Bay Company Snake River operations in 1824, the Idaho fur-trapping scene had changed drastically from the days of David Thompson's Kullyspell House. Increased numbers of white trappers in the territory were coming into more frequent conflicts with Native Americans, particularly the Blackfeet and Bannock, who were by now well armed. And competition between British and American trappers had increased as the beaver populations had decreased. Ogden's marching orders were to trap out the Snake River country, leaving not a single beaver behind for the Americans. Easier said than done. Although Ogden led profitable expeditions annually until 1830, the regimented bureaucratic machine of the HBC was giving ground to an American cadre of loosely associated "freelance" trappers well versed in the changing ways of the West.

The earliest trappers had succeeded because they were good explorers, but by the 1820s different skills were needed to succeed in the fur trade. With the land now extensively mapped and traveled, it was more important to be handy with a rifle than a compass. Flexibility and mobility were advantageous when seeking the isolated areas where beaver remained plentiful. The profitability of HBC's thoroughly planned, expensive, and massive expeditions—the 1824 brigade numbered 140 persons and 392 horses—was challenged by American frontiersmen who could roam freely and relatively easily throughout the territory. But how to organize these independent mountain men into a single economic unit?

William Henry Ashley was among the first to tackle this problem. Ashley hooked up with Andrew Henry and brought together some of the most skilled young mountain men of the day, among them **Jedediah Smith** and **Jim Bridger.** They sent the men out trapping in small teams, with instructions to rendezvous at a later date to exchange pelts for payment and new supplies. This strategy proved to be enormously successful, and the **Snake River rendezvous** played a memorable part in Western lore.

Imagine a kind of Wild West Mardi Gras—an anything-goes three-day drunk full of white trappers and Native Americans from a number of different tribes, all singing, dancing, gambling, fighting, competing at this or that, and carrying on well into the wee hours of each night. Such was the scene at the many rendezvous that took place nearly annually between 1825 and 1840. Presumably the participants managed to get a little trading done, too. A favorite rendezvous location was the Teton Valley, which they called "Pierre's Hole," after "Old Pierre"

Tevanitagon, an Iroquois trapper once associated with Hudson's Bay Company.

"The Trees! The Trees!"

It may sound like something out of *Fantasy Island,* but it was actually the men of an 1832–34 expedition led by **Captain Benjamin Louis Eulalie de Bonneville** who uttered those famous words. Well, not those words exactly. The men were French Canadians, so it came out "Les bois! Les bois!"

Bonneville was from a Parisian family that came to America in 1803 after Napoleon took control of their homeland. Young Bonneville graduated from West Point and became an army officer. When he decided to mount his own expedition to the West, the army graciously gave him some time off to do so.

In 1832, the 110-man expedition left Fort Osage, Missouri, and made it to the Salmon River headwaters before winter set in. The following spring they moved to southeast Idaho, and the year after that, in 1834, they followed the dry and dusty north bank of the Snake River west. After miles and miles of this desert landscape, they topped a small rise and saw to the west a river valley filled with trees, lush and verdant in the distance. The French Canadians could hardly contain themselves and blurted out the aforementioned cries of joy.

Today you can drive to the site where they saw the trees—it's just north of I-84—and read a plaque that will tell you that it was the Bonneville expedition's ecstatic French Canadians who gave the Boise River its name. It's a nice story, but actually, the name had at that point been used by trappers on that river for more than 20 years.

Bonneville got an Idaho county, a prehistoric lake, and a modern-day Utah salt flat named for him, but he never really amounted to much as a trapper. You can read all about him in Washington Irving's book *The Adventures of Captain Bonneville,* published in 1837.

The Fur Forts

The year 1834 also saw the establishment of two permanent fur-trading forts on the Snake River:

Fort Boise in the west, at the confluence of the Snake and Boise Rivers near present-day Parma; and Fort Hall in the east, near present-day Blackfoot. Both forts were successful and important for two reasons. First, they led to the eventual end of the rendezvous system by creating what were essentially permanent, year-round rendezvous sites. Then too, their strategic placement at either end of the Snake River Plain would make them important way stations along the emigrant trails soon to be established.

Fort Boise (not to be confused with the U.S. Army fort of the same name in today's city of Boise) was built by the Hudson's Bay Company and run by a jolly French Canadian trapper named François Payette. The portly Monsieur Payette was well known for the hospitality he lavished upon visitors to his fort, setting out feasts for his guests and regaling them with tales of his past adventures. The Payette River was named after him.

Fort Hall was built and run by Nathaniel Wyeth, a Boston entrepreneur who had been trying unsuccessfully to wring a profit out of the West for some years. The fort was christened with a raucous party on August 5, 1834. Wyeth must have had high hopes that day. Unfortunately, the venture here proved only marginally lucrative. After just two full seasons, he sold the fort to the Hudson's Bay Company and moved back to Boston. One might suspect Wyeth's financial disappointments were caused by a lack of business acumen, but for this venture he just had bad luck and bad timing. Although Fort Hall remained in use by the Hudson's Bay Company until 1856, out West, the times, they were a-changing.

> Hollywood couldn't have written a better script. Henry was enamored of Narcissa, but Narcissa dumped him and married Marcus. Henry married Eliza. In 1836, the four Presbyterians loaded up their Bibles and set out West together. You don't suppose there was any tension on that wagon train.

Silk Hats and Wagon Roads

Ah, the fickle finger of fashion. Not long after Fort Hall was built, beaver hats became passé in London and on the East Coast of America. Now silk hats were all the rage. Meanwhile, over on the east side of the Mississippi, the population of the United States kept increasing. Over the years, trappers had opened up many passes across the Rockies and had established well-worn trails—including the framework for the Oregon Trail—that could be navigated by wagons.

Forts Boise and Hall changed roles, from fur-trading outposts to roadside rests for Oregon Trail pioneers. The same year that Nathaniel Wyeth headed back to Boston, two emigrant missionary couples—Henry and Eliza Spalding, and Marcus and Narcissa Whitman—stopped at first Fort Hall, then Fort Boise on their way west.

EARLY MISSIONARIES

When Idaho's indigenous peoples first encountered whites, they must have been amazed at the odd things the pioneers carried with them: guns, medicines, Christianity. The white man had powerful things; did he have powerful mojo, too? One can understand Native American curiosity about white religion.

In 1831, the Nez Perce decided to send a party of emissaries back to St. Louis to visit their old friend William Clark. After the success of the Corps of Discovery expedition, Clark had taken an assignment with the U.S. government as head of Indian affairs for the West. The Nez Perce may have intended to ask Clark to send them someone to teach them reading, writing, and farming—or they may have sought spiritual assistance in exploring Christianity. Whichever their motivation, word soon spread of the Nez Perce sending representatives all the way to St. Louis in search of a Christian god, and the challenge was quickly taken up.

Henry, Narcissa, Marcus, and Eliza

An enormous new territory, full of heathens and now open to whites: it was the proverbial apple tempting proselytizing Christians to head West and show natives the path of righteousness. Among the first on the scene were Henry Spalding, Narcissa Prentiss, Marcus Whitman, and Eliza Hart. Hollywood couldn't have written a better script. Henry was enamored of Narcissa, but Narcissa dumped him and married a doctor, Marcus. Henry married Eliza. In 1836, the four Presbyterians loaded up their Bibles and set out West together. You don't suppose there was any tension on *that* wagon train.

Narcissa and Eliza were the first white women to cross the Rockies. That the two women had made the journey and appeared to be faring well was a significant milestone on the road to westward expansion. As long as the Wild West was inhabited only by wild men, it wasn't seen as a place a family could live. But now women had made the trek, survived, and were planning to settle down. The West took on a new stature, as a place one might conceivably call home. Americans back east began to eye the West with more interest.

The two couples eventually went their separate ways. Marcus and Narcissa continued on to Washington Territory near today's Walla Walla, where they established a mission among the Cayuse people. There the good doctor took in and doctored both sick whites and sick Native Americans. When a wagon train of settlers infected with the measles showed up, Whitman's big medicine healed the whites, but failed on the Native Americans, who had never before been exposed to the disease. Many Cayuse died under Whitman's care, and the Native Americans understandably concluded that Whitman was killing them. In 1847, the Cayuse raided the mission and killed both Marcus and Narcissa, along with 12 other white workers.

The Lapwai Mission

Meanwhile, Henry and Eliza had ended up in Idaho, where they built a mission among the Nez Perce at the confluence of Lapwai Creek and the Clearwater River. By all accounts, the Spaldings were quite a couple. Eliza learned to read and write the Nez Perce language, and soon was teaching locals of all ages to do the same. Word of her successful school reached a Protestant mission in Hawaii, which sent Eliza a print-

ing press so she could print her lessons. In 1838 Eliza had a baby (also named Eliza), the first white child born in Idaho.

Henry was equally busy. First he built a cabin and outbuildings, then taught the locals farming. They got a sizable garden up and sprouting and built a gristmill, sawmill, and blacksmith shop. Soon they were up to their ears in corn, and up to their eyes in potatoes. The Nez Perce were sufficiently intrigued by the idea of farming to settle around the mission and begin cultivating their own plots. In 1839, Henry put in an irrigation system, the region's first.

Things went well for a few years, but soon the novelty wore off for the Nez Perce. The Spaldings were unable to supply the Native Americans with much in the way of firearms or magic medicinal remedies, and Henry became a strict disciplinarian who was sometimes harsh with the locals. When word got to the Spaldings that Marcus and Narcissa Whitman had been killed, Henry and Eliza decided to leave Lapwai. With a friendly Nez Perce escort to protect them from the Cayuse, they moved to the Willamette Valley and took up farming. Eliza died there in 1851. Henry moved back to Lapwai in 1863. He died there in 1874 and both he and Eliza are buried there. The site of the Spaldings' Lapwai mission is today part of Nez Perce National Historic Park, easily visited off Highway 12 east of Lewiston.

The Catholic Contingent

Protestants weren't the only ones actively attempting to convert Idaho's indigenous peoples. The first Catholic missionary on the scene was the Belgian priest **Father Pierre Jean de Smet,** who arrived in Idaho's Coeur d'Alene country in 1841. De Smet laid the groundwork for the Mission of the Sacred Heart, which was constructed in its final form and location by **Father Antonio Ravalli** in the early 1850s. The mission was built entirely without nails and still stands today, the oldest extant public building in Idaho. It boldly crowns a hillock along the Coeur d'Alene River, east of the city of Coeur d'Alene. The disastrous floods of early 1996 inundated much of the Panhandle, but the old mission stayed high and dry—a credit to Father Ravalli's site selection.

WESTWARD BOUND
South Pass: Gateway to the West

By the 1840s, the reports of Lewis and Clark, fur trappers, the Spaldings and Whitmans, and naval explorers off the Pacific coast all confirmed Oregon Country was not a desert wasteland. Rather, it was a bountiful region of good water and rich soil, ripe for cultivation and settlement. But how to get there? Lewis and Clark, following the Missouri River and its tributaries, had struggled over the Continental Divide at Idaho's Bitterroot Range. Clearly, settlers' wagons could never negotiate the passes that had almost defeated the Corps of Discovery.

The key that unlocked the West to settlers existed but had gone all but unnoticed. In 1824, the great mountain man Jedediah Smith had led a party of trappers working for William Henry Ashley across the Rockies at Wyoming's South Pass. Unlike Idaho's paths across the Rockies, South Pass hardly seems a pass at all. It arcs gently up and over the Continental Divide like a rolling swell on a calm sea. South Pass was reached not by following the Missouri River to its headwaters in Montana, as Lewis and Clark had done, but by following the Missouri to its confluence with the Platte River (near present-day Omaha, Nebraska). From there, the emigrants followed first the Platte, then the Sweetwater River, west to the latter's headwaters in Wyoming's Antelope Hills, just east of South Pass.

It wasn't until 1841, however, that the first bold party of pioneers hell-bent on settling the West set out from Missouri, headed for South Pass. The group of 70 hopefuls was led by Thomas Fitzpatrick, who had helped found the Rocky Mountain Fur Company in 1830, and John Bidwell, who split off with about half the settlers at Soda Springs and made his way to California. Among the 70 emigrants was Jesuit Father de Smet, the early Panhandle missionary. Their journey was successful.

The following year, one of the country's great explorers, **John C. Frémont,** headed to Wyoming as a member of an official government survey expedition. The survey party crossed South Pass, and Frémont's rich, prosaic reports made the crossing seem like a walk in the park. The following year, Frémont took the trail all the way to Oregon Country. With the benefit of an immensely talented ghostwriter—his wife, Jessie—Frémont described the whole route from St. Louis

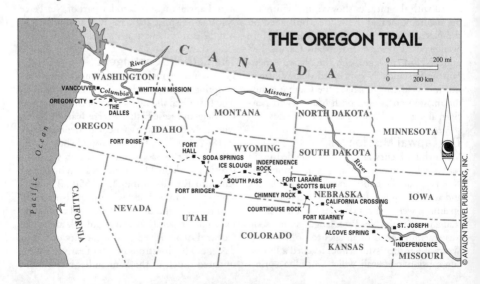

THE OREGON TRAIL

to Oregon in an enthusiastic and detailed report that was published by Congress and found its way into the hands of many an American contemplating the trek. The route Frémont described—one capable of being negotiated by settlers' wagons—came to be known as the Oregon Trail.

The Great Migration

In 1843, a combination of favorable reports from the West, malaria outbreaks in the Mississippi and Missouri River valleys, and perhaps a desire to participate in history prompted the first major wave of emigrants to pack their wagons. About 1,000 hopefuls set out from Independence, Missouri, that spring. The schedule for the crossing was tight. They couldn't leave the Midwest before the spring grasses had sprouted—they needed the new growth to feed their livestock. Yet they had to be safely across the mountains of Oregon before the first snowfall. The average trip took five months.

The "trail" the pioneers followed was seldom a single set of tracks but rather a braid of parallel trails. Only in the narrow passes and canyons did the various parties funnel into the exact path of their predecessors; in those places, even today, you'll find deep wagon ruts.

Along the way, the Oregon Trail emigrants crossed through the territories of many different indigenous nations between Missouri and Oregon. Some of the Native Americans were friendly, some more hostile. The emigrants were understandably worried about Native American attack, but that proved the least of their worries. Most who died succumbed to accidents or disease.

Along the Snake River

After crossing South Pass, the original Oregon Trail entered today's southeast Idaho—at the time part of Oregon Territory—near Bear Lake and headed north to Fort Hall, Nathaniel Wyeth's old fur fort on the upper Snake River. In 1837, Wyeth had sold Fort Hall to the Hudson's Bay Company. The British managers, fearing they'd be driven out by Americans flooding into Oregon, customarily tried to discourage settlers from continuing west. They exaggerated the difficulty of the route, telling emigrants that the rest of the trail to Oregon was impassable by wagons. As a result, many pioneers here traded their oxen and wagons for horses for the remainder of the journey.

Like bookends, Fort Hall in the east and Fort Boise in the west were the only two safe harbors along Idaho's stretch of the Oregon Trail. Leaving Fort Boise, the trail followed the south side of the Snake River west through hot, dry, and treeless desert and lava country. Occasionally emigrants might sight the tantalizing waters of the river, usually out of reach at the bottom of steep, rocky canyons.

At Three Island Crossing, near today's Glenns Ferry, they were faced with a choice: brave the river crossing to easier going on a shorter route down the north side, or continue the long way down the hot and dry south side. Much of the decision depended on how high the Snake was running when they got there. The Snake's south side can be pretty miserable during the dog days of August, even for today's motorists. Imagine what the pioneers felt like, tromping through the dust day after day, with no air-conditioned car or motel room to offer respite. Reaching Fort Boise and the legendary hospitality of François Payette must have felt very good indeed, especially knowing that they were nearing Oregon.

Between 1841 and 1848, most westward-bound pioneers followed this route to Oregon; a far smaller number turned off the trail and headed south to California. Those proportions were reversed dramatically following the discovery of gold in California in 1848. Between 1849 and 1860, about 42,000 pioneers followed the Oregon Trail west to fertile farmland in Oregon's Willamette Valley, while some 200,000 others staked their future on easy money and headed to California, the "Golden State."

The California Trail and Hudspeth's Cutoff

Those pioneers choosing California as their destination followed the Oregon Trail west from Fort Hall only as far as the confluence of the Snake with the Raft River. There they turned south up the Raft River Valley, crossed the divide at City of Rocks, and continued south into

Nevada and across the Sierras to the promised land. This route was used primarily until 1849. That year, a group of emigrants led by Benoni Hudspeth tried a shortcut similar to the original route followed by John Bidwell in 1841. From Soda Springs, they turned directly west, crossed four separate north-south-trending mountain ranges, and rejoined the California Trail midway up the Raft River Valley. This route turned out to be 25 miles and two days shorter than the previous route via Fort Hall. After word got out of Hudspeth's successful cutoff, the longer route through Fort Hall was dropped like a hot Idaho potato, even by those settlers headed for Oregon. In 1855, the Hudson's Bay Company's Brits packed up the Union Jack and left Fort Hall for good.

Other Routes

In 1859, the federal government got on Jim Bridger's bad side. It commissioned engineer Frederick Lander to build a new wagon road from Wyoming's South Pass directly west to Fort Hall. The **Lander Road** took 100 miles off the length of the Oregon Trail. It also bypassed Fort Bridger, depriving the fort's great mountain-man proprietor of a large chunk of business.

In 1862, another mountain man, Tim Goodale, pioneered a new route from Fort Hall to Fort Boise. Instead of following the hot, dry Snake River Plain west, **Goodale's Cutoff** headed northwest from Fort Hall to the base of the Pioneers. Hopping west from river to river at higher elevations than the routes to the south, Goodale's followers made their way across the Camas Prairie near present-day Fairfield before rejoining the Oregon Trail some 75 miles east of Fort Boise.

The Wood River Valley town of Hailey is named for John Hailey, who pioneered a stagecoach route from Salt Lake City to Boise City in 1869. The **Kelton Road** left Kelton, Utah, passed through the major pioneer-trail intersection at City of Rocks, continued northwest to the little oasis at Rock Creek, then crossed the Snake River and followed the north side of the river into Boise. This was the most important mail and freight route across southern Idaho until the Oregon Short Line railroad was completed in 1883.

CULTURES CLASH

With settlers pouring into age-old Native American territories—including traditional hunting grounds and sacred sites—and competing for often meager resources, tensions were bound to arise. Native American attacks accounted for less than four percent of the emigrant deaths on the Oregon Trail. Nevertheless, such attacks made sensational headlines in the eastern newspapers, fueling the cause of jingoist politicians and business leaders who believed in manifest destiny at any cost.

More than one commentator has noted that when whites killed Indians, the press typically reported the skirmish as a "battle," but when Indians killed whites, it was a "massacre." Such was the case with the three most famous conflicts between settlers and Native Americans in Idaho.

The Ward Massacre

On August 20, 1854, a wagon train of emigrants led by Missourian Alexander Ward was 25 miles east of Boise when it ran into trouble. One of the emigrants caught an Indian horsethief in the act and shot him. Soon the wagon train was attacked full force by the rest of the tribe. Of the 20 people in the wagon train, 18 were killed in a particularly brutal fashion. The Native Americans stole all the livestock and valuables belonging to the unfortunate emigrants, then apparently went on a shooting spree. A half dozen or more whites in the general area were killed, presumably by the same tribe. Troops were dispatched from Fort Boise, and the perpetrators were hunted down. Three were shot, three hanged, and others jailed. As the episode appeared to involve just one local renegade band, the matter ended quickly.

The Utter–Van Orman Massacre

In September 1860, Owyhee County was the scene of another famous emigrant–Native American conflict. The eight-wagon, 44-person Utter–Van Orman Train was making its way west when it was attacked by Shoshones. Four Fort Hall soldiers came to the rescue, but couldn't help much. The initial fight lasted two days. Nine emigrants were killed and the covered wagons were torched. Some of the emigrants tried to escape and were killed by the Shoshones. The soldiers tried to ride out for help. Two were killed. When it was all over, 23 immigrants were dead, and four children had been kidnapped by the Native Americans. Eighteen survivors were left stranded with no food or supplies and tried to walk out of the desert to the north. When a rescue party finally reached them, only 12 were still alive. They had been reduced to dining on their dead.

One of the army officers sent out to look for the kidnapped children tried to keep the situation in perspective. Major John Owen, quoted in Brigham D. Madsen's *The Bannock of Idaho*, summed up succinctly and prophetically the nature of the entire "Indian problem":

These Indians 12 years ago were the avowed friends of the White Man. I have had their young men in my employment as hunters, horse guards, guides, etc. I have traversed the length and breadth of their entire country with large bands of stock unmolested. Their present hostile attitude can in great measure be attributed to the treatment they have received from unprincipled White Men passing through their country. They have been robbed, murdered, their women outraged . . . and in fact outrages have been committed by White Men that the heart would shudder to record.

The Battle of Bear River

The worst slaughter of Native Americans by U.S. troops in the nation's history took place on the morning of January 29, 1863, about 12 miles north of Franklin. Earlier that winter, a party of miners near Bannack, Montana, had been attacked by Shoshone-Bannocks. One of the miners was killed. Troops from the army's Camp Douglas, near Salt Lake City, rode north to bring the attackers to justice. Led by Col. Patrick E. Connor, the troops came upon a band of more than 400 Shoshones camped near the icy Bear River. The army charged in firing, but the band was determined to fight back and the battle was bloody. After several hours, the Shoshones realized they were losing. They tried to escape but were brutally cut down. Connor lost 22 men in the battle, while his troops wiped out somewhere between 200 and 400 Native Americans, including an estimated 90 women and children. Connor was promoted to brigadier general as a result.

This battle had an effect on the big picture of the relationship between Native Americans and whites in a large part of the West. It broke the spirit of the Native Americans to the extent that most tribes accepted the futility of fighting and resigned themselves to treaty-created reservations. Only one last major conflict occurred in Idaho after the Bear River Massacre, but it was a doozy: the Nez Perce War of 1877.

MORMON INFLUX
Salmon River Mission

Not to be outdone by the early missionary work of the Presbyterians and Catholics, the Latter-day Saints arrived in Idaho in 1855. That year, Brigham Young sent 27 Mormon men to the Lemhi Valley to work with, and hopefully convert, the local Native Americans. While it lasted, the farming outpost they established—just north of present-day Tendoy, very near where Lewis and Clark crossed into Idaho—was the state's first white agricultural settlement.

wagon train on Oregon-California Trail

Brigham Young

The missionaries had selected the site because it was the summer hunting and fishing site for three different tribes—Bannock, Shoshone, and Nez Perce. This very aspect that the Mormons saw as favorable led to the mission's undoing. Although the missionaries succeeded in establishing good relations with all three tribes separately, each tribe came to resent the attentions the Mormons paid to the other two tribes. In the end, many tribe members turned against the Mormons. The mission's horses and cattle were stolen, and a few men were killed. The mission was abandoned in April 1858.

Franklin and Beyond

In April 1860, a group of Mormons once again came north from Salt Lake City, this time founding a settlement just across the Idaho border. They built an irrigation system and began farming the Cache Valley. Before long, a sawmill, fort, and cabins went up. In June, Brigham Young

himself paid a visit, naming the town Franklin after Mormon apostle Franklin Richards. By the end of the year, the town had a population of over 100. Until an official government survey in 1872, the settlers thought they'd built their town in Utah. As it turned out, they'd founded the first town in Idaho.

The Mormons grew onions, potatoes, and wheat, which they shared freely with the area's Native Americans in hopes of ensuring peaceful relations. This strategy was successful for a time. But as more settlers came to town, claimed land, and built cabins, the native people began to feel threatened. The Mormons lost increasing numbers of horses and cattle to thievery, and incidents of violent confrontation escalated. The Mormons were prepared to flee the valley when Colonel Connor and his men came through looking for a fight with the Native Americans. When the Battle of Bear River was over, the settlers helped care for the wounded and frostbitten soldiers and surviving Shoshones alike.

After the battle, the Shoshones signed the Treaty of Box Elder with the government, promising peace in exchange for government help. The government never came through with its side of the bargain. But by that time Connor and the bluecoats were installed at a new fort in nearby Soda Springs, making raids a riskier proposition for the Shoshones. The Fort Hall Indian Reservation was established in 1867, and most of the beleaguered Cache Valley Shoshones resignedly moved onto the reservation. The area was now wide open for white expansion, and the Mormons quickly took advantage of the opportunity. With a religious doctrine encouraging large families, the Latter-day Saints soon expanded their empire across Cache Valley and southeast Idaho. Much of the productive green farmland that today covers vast tracts of Idaho's dry southeast is a result of hard, tenacious work by early Mormon settlers.

GOLD FEVER

Before 1848, the Oregon Trail was the major highway and the California Trail a smaller spur. Then James Marshall discovered gold at Sutter's

Fort and the two trails swapped places in importance. Gold fever built throughout the West, as strikes were made in British Columbia, Nevada, and Colorado.

The first find in Idaho was made by E. D. Pierce in 1860. Pierce was an Irish immigrant who had been a captain in the Mexican War. In 1852, while trading in north-central Idaho's Nez Perce country, he heard stories of gold in the area. He caught gold fever, but he didn't start prospecting there. News of Canada's Fraser River strikes reached him and he raced north, apparently meeting with little success.

In 1855, the Nez Perce signed a treaty with the U.S. government that created the Nez Perce Reservation. Pierce returned to Idaho's Nez Perce country in 1860 to find that whites were no longer welcome on the lands he had seen. He asked the tribe to let him do some prospecting on the reservation, but the Nez Perce understandably refused. Not to be deterred, Pierce and 10 other men snuck onto the reservation without permission and began searching for riches on the north fork of the Clearwater River. The Nez Perce eventually discovered the miners but restrained themselves from throwing the trespassers out. That fall, one of the Pierce-party miners, Wilbur Bassett, found some very fine gold—*oro fino* in Spanish—in a shovelful of dirt. The Idaho gold rush was on.

The Clearwater Mines and Boise Basin

Soon the Orofino Mining District was formed and miners rushed into the area. By the summer of 1861, some 3,000 people had moved in; by the following summer, 10,000. Pierce City and Orofino were founded as the Nez Perce looked on helplessly. The miners spread out, and new mining towns sprouted: Elk City, Newsome, Florence. Some $3 million worth of gold dust was carried out of the area by the steamships plying the Snake and Columbia Rivers to and from Lewiston.

Named for Meriwether Lewis of Corps of Discovery fame, Lewiston became the rip-roaring supply center for the Clearwater District. Outlaws and vigilantes ran unchecked by any active judicial system. Idaho's first newspaper, *The Golden Age*, was started up in Lewiston, and mail service was

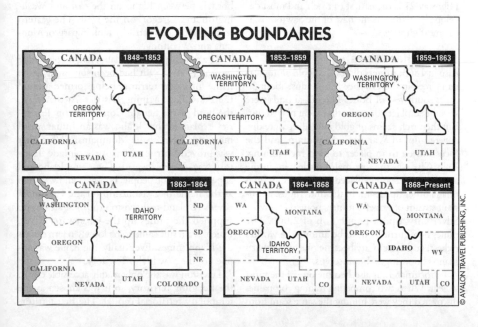

EVOLVING BOUNDARIES

instituted; the mail was carried on foot between Lewiston and Pierce City, a 10-day trip.

In August 1862, a group of miners discovered gold in the Boise Basin, 30 miles north of today's city of Boise. Idaho City, Placerville, Centerville, and nearby Rocky Bar and Atlanta sprang up to support the hordes of money-hungry hopefuls. Because these communities supported a substantial population of white folk, the government decided it needed a fort in the area to protect the miners and their families from hostile Native Americans. The army selected a site at the foot of the mountains along the Boise River and dedicated Fort Boise on July 4, 1863. (This fort was not connected with the Hudson's Bay Company's famous fur fort of the same name, at the confluence of the Boise and Snake Rivers some 40 miles to the west.) A town was platted around the army post and grew quickly as the major supply center for the Boise Basin mines.

The Boise Basin mines yielded an estimated $66 million in gold. Today the basin's boomtowns are ghost towns, relying not on mining but on tourism to keep them alive. Idaho City on Highway 21 is the easiest to reach and most developed; Atlanta, at the base of the Sawtooths, is the most ghostly.

The Owyhee Mines

Also in 1863, miners discovered gold along Jordan Creek in the Owyhee Mountains, about 50 miles southwest of Boise. The initial finds were streambed placer deposits that soon played out. But then rich seams of gold and silver were discovered up on War Eagle Mountain, and the focus shifted from placer to hard-rock mining. Ruby City was the first major settlement in the area but was soon replaced by Silver City two miles farther upstream. In the mid-1860s, a constant stream of hopeful miners poured in, giving Silver City a peak population of 2,000. The mines here turned out to be among the world's richest, and Silver City became one of southern Idaho's boomingest boomtowns.

Unfortunately, it also became one of the most violent. When two competing mining companies discovered they were mining the same seam from opposite directions, an underground mining war broke out. One company's foreman was killed by gunfire deep in the shafts, while mining magnate J. Marion More died when an argument on the porch of the Idaho Hotel in Silver City got out of control and shots were fired. The territorial governor sent in troops from Fort Boise to quell the disturbance, which ended with no further bloodshed. The Owyhee unrest was a portent of even greater troubles to come in Idaho's mining history.

Idaho Territory

During the Clearwater, Boise Basin, and Owyhee mining booms, this part of the country was part of Washington Territory, headquartered in Olympia. Fearful that the wealth and population explosion that mining was bringing to the eastern part of the territory would result in a shift of governmental power away from them, Olympians began lobbying to separate the mining districts in a new territory. On March 4, 1863, President Abraham Lincoln signed into law the act creating Idaho Territory. The western boundary of the territory corresponded to today's borders between Idaho on the east and Washington and Oregon on the west. The eastern reaches of the new territory took in parts of Montana and Wyoming.

The territory's name, Idaho, had no particular meaning. In 1859 it had been suggested as the name for a new territory being formed around the Pike's Peak Mining District. At that time, the head of the Senate Committee on Territories explained that Idaho was an Indian word meaning "Gem of the Mountains." When that was proved untrue, the name Colorado Territory was chosen instead. The name Idaho still appealed to some people, however, and was used as the name of a steamship on the Columbia River's Portland-to-Lewiston run. The steamship supplied the mines up the Clearwater River, which as a result came to be loosely referred to as the Idaho mines. Eventually, the name was applied to the new Idaho Territory.

Lewiston was the only readily accessible city in the fledgling territory, so it was chosen as the temporary territorial capital. The first territorial governor, William Wallace, was a close personal friend of Abe Lincoln. Wallace took office in Lewiston on July 10, 1863, and immediately faced his first crisis. It seems Lewiston wasn't technically in Idaho Territory, but instead squarely on the Nez Perce Reservation, as delineated by the 1855 treaty. The Nez Perce had allowed whites a primitive staging and supply camp at the site, located at the confluence of the Clearwater and Snake Rivers. But the inch given had turned into a mile taken, and Lewiston had become a full-fledged town in the process. When Wallace and the federal government approached the Nez Perce, asking the Native Americans to once again negotiate away more of their land, including Lewiston, the Nez Perce were divided. One group resigned themselves to a reduced reservation and signed a new treaty; the other group refused. The "nontreaty" Nez Perce didn't make trouble then but 14 years later precipitated the Nez Perce War of 1877.

Just five months after taking office as Idaho's governor, Wallace was elected as a territorial delegate. He resigned as governor and moved to Washington, D.C., in December 1863. His replacement, Caleb Lyon, arrived in Lewiston in August 1864. Lyon soon found himself in the middle of a heated debate over where to put the territory's capital. Since the formation of the territory, the mines served by Lewiston had begun to play out and most of the miners had moved south to the Boise Basin, where mines were beginning to boom. In December 1864, the territorial legislature met in Lewiston and voted to move the capital to Boise City, supply center for the Boise Basin mines and protected from trouble by the U.S. Army's Fort Boise. Lewiston's residents were furious, and Governor Lyon was on the hot seat. Under the pretense of going duck hunting, he fled across the Snake River to Washington and didn't return for a year. In the meantime, territorial secretary C. DeWitt Smith arrived in Lewiston and, with the aid of federal troops, forcibly took possession of the territorial seal and archives and took them south to Boise. From that point on, Boise was entrenched as, first, territorial and, later, state capital.

THE NEZ PERCE WAR

Those bands of Nez Perce who refused to sign the 1863 treaty reducing the size of their reservation continued to live as they had before, roaming their traditional homelands. One of these bands, led by Old Joseph, called eastern Oregon's Wallowa Valley home. As the 1860s progressed, more whites began encroaching on Joseph's territory. Since Joseph's band of Nez Perce had not signed the 1863 treaty, and had remained peaceful toward white settlers, U.S. President Grant signed a proclamation that formally assigned the Wallowa Valley to the Nez Perce. But lobbyists in Washington, intent on developing the region for themselves, raised such an outcry that Grant rescinded the order two years later. On his deathbed, Old Joseph instructed his son Joseph never to give up the Wallowa Valley to the whites. Young Chief Joseph took that request to heart.

Joseph's band lived in the Wallowa Valley until 1877, when continued pressure from whites led the Bureau of Indian Affairs in Washington, D.C., to order all nontreaty Nez Perce onto the Lapwai Reservation by June of that year. At a meeting in Lapwai between the Nez Perce and the Army, the Nez Perce argued to no avail that they had not signed the treaty and were not bound by it. Toohoolhoolzote, the Nez Perce's spiritual leader, was defiant. The military man in charge of the U.S. Army's Columbia River district, Gen. Oliver O. Howard, grew frustrated with Toohoolhoolzote's refusal to capitulate. "We do not wish to interfere with your religion," said Howard, "but you must talk about practicable things. Twenty times over you repeat that the earth is your mother, and about chieftanship from the earth. Let us hear no more, but come to business at once." When Toohoolhoolzote responded contemptuously, "What person pretends to divide the land and put me on it?" Howard lost his temper and had Toohoolhoolzote locked up. He was later released, but his arrest angered the Nez Perce. Many young warriors immediately wanted to fight, but Joseph restrained them. The chief faced an agonizing decision. As a man of peace, he sought no bloodshed. But his father had specifically asked him to never give up the Wallowa Valley homeland.

Joseph chose the path of peace and resigned himself to moving onto the reservation. Returning to Oregon, he gathered his people and moved across the Snake River to the Camas Prairie, in preparation for checking in with the army at Lapwai. Joseph would never again live in his beloved Wallowa Valley, and would not set eyes on it again for more than 20 years.

The First Confrontation

On June 2, 1877, the nontreaty bands of Joseph and Whitebird were camped at Tolo Lake near present-day Grangeville for a last rendezvous as a free people. Over the course of the next 10 days, frustration and anti-white sentiment grew within the ranks, particularly among the young warriors. One young man from White Bird's band had seen his father murdered by a white settler on the Salmon River. Others had also suffered at the hands of the whites but had not sought revenge. As emotions in camp built to a fever pitch, a handful of young warriors broke ranks and went on a rampage, killing several settlers who had treated the Nez Perce poorly. Word got back to General Howard at Lapwai, providing him with a convenient excuse for overreacting. Howard sent two cavalry units racing toward Tolo Lake. The Nez Perce leaders at Tolo Lake, warned of the impending attack, held a meeting. Facing the superior numbers and firepower of the U.S. Army, the leaders knew they had to fight or flee—or both.

The Nez Perce bands moved down to the bottom of White Bird Canyon and prepared for the first assault. The unlucky commander of the cavalry units, Captain David Perry, led his troops down White Bird hill right into a Nez Perce ambush. Thirty-four of Perry's 100 troops were killed; the rest fled back to Fort Lapwai. The Nez Perce packed up and went on the move again. Perry's resounding defeat was a personal affront to General Howard, who now took charge of the Nez Perce problem himself.

Joseph and White Bird led their group across the Salmon River to the west, then doubled back across the river farther north and sped across the Camas Prairie to hook up with Chief Looking Glass's band near Kooskia. General Howard tried to follow but was unable to make the second

crossing of the Salmon and had to retrace his steps, losing several days in the process.

The nontreaty band of Chief Looking Glass, camped near Kooskia, had wanted no trouble. Their land was already on the smaller reservation, so they wouldn't be forced to move. Nevertheless, a contingent of bluecoats and civilian volunteers attacked Looking Glass's camp. The attack was unsuccessful but enraged Looking Glass into joining Joseph and White Bird in the fight. Soon all three Nez Perce bands linked up on the South Fork of the Clearwater River, south of Kooskia. There they devised a plan to cross the Bitterroots and enter Crow territory, hoping to receive support from their traditional allies. Howard and his now all-out force of 600 men at last caught up with the Nez Perce. Despite being severely outnumbered, the Nez Perce again managed to hold off Howard's troops and fled—men, women, children, and a whole herd of ponies— east into the Bitterroots. Their superior knowledge of the terrain allowed them to outdistance the army. When Howard realized the Nez Perce were out of his grasp, he telegraphed General William Tecumseh Sherman and requested Sherman to send a force to cut the Nez Perce off.

The Flight to Canada

After crossing the Bitterroots, Joseph and White Bird knew they were days ahead of Howard, so they stopped to rest at Big Hole, Montana. They didn't know, however, about the telegraph sent by Howard, and didn't know that now Colonel John Gibbon and a large force of bluecoats were galloping toward them at full speed from Fort Shaw, Montana. Gibbon and his troops surprised the Nez Perce in a dawn attack at Big Hole. Both sides sustained heavy casualties. Amazingly, the Nez Perce turned the tables on the army, forcing them to retreat and pinning them down while the surviving Nez Perce quickly packed up and once again fled south.

Still heading for Crow country, they crossed the Bitterroots again, and moved south through Lemhi Valley and east to Henry's Lake. Howard soon caught up to the recuperating Gibbon and formulated a new plan. Figuring the Nez Perce would turn east through Yellowstone National

Park (established in 1872) and head for the plains, Howard devised a scheme to trap the Nez Perce in the park. He was delayed along the way, however, when a party of Nez Perce retraced their steps, snuck into Howard's camp in the night, and stampeded the army's mules before catching up with the main party. By this time, word of the bravery and incredible evasionary tactics of the Nez Perce had made the news back East. Most of the country was following the unfolding drama in the daily papers; no doubt many were rooting for the underdog Nez Perce. When the news that the Nez Perce had run Howard's mules right out from his camp, Howard became the laughingstock of the country. And his embarrassment was not yet over.

Despite the setback, Howard pursued his plan to trap the Nez Perce in the park. The Nez Perce suffered a psychological setback of their own when they found out that Crow scouts were working for General Howard. Now, they realized, their last hope was to turn north and head for Canada, where they believed exiled Sioux chief Sitting Bull would welcome them and take them in. They entered Yellowstone, frightening a party of tourists and actually taking them hostage for a time so they couldn't set Howard on their trail.

Using the telegraph to speed communication, Howard ringed the park's major geographical exits with troops. This time the Nez Perce embarrassed not only General Howard but Colonel Samuel D. Sturgis as well. Sturgis had been assigned to cover the park's northeastern exit along the Clark Fork River. When the Nez Perce didn't show up in his area, Sturgis got impatient and decided that the Nez Perce were instead going to come out to the south, on the Shoshone River. He sent scouts up to find out. The scouts sighted the Nez Perce and watched them apparently head in the direction of the Shoshone, as Sturgis thought they would. When the scouts returned with the news, Sturgis left his assigned post and took his troops south. At the Shoshone River, he headed upstream expecting to find the Nez Perce coming down, defeat them, and reap the glory. But the Nez Perce, after being seen by Sturgis's scouts, doubled back and turned down a narrow side canyon headed for the very Clark Fork area that

Sturgis had left. They escaped the park scot-free. Sturgis continued all the way up the Shoshone with no sight of the Nez Perce. General Howard, who had been trailing the Nez Perce and thought he was driving them into Sturgis's waiting trap, was now ahead of Sturgis. Clearly Colonel Sturgis would have some explaining to do.

When the press got ahold of this news, some papers called for Howard's removal. Others just laughed at the army and cheered on the Nez Perce, now seen as heroic by much of the nation.

The Nez Perce thought they had once again evaded trouble. Tired of running, and thinking themselves days ahead of Howard, they slowed down. But General Howard's boss, General William Tecumseh Sherman, was not pleased. He ordered the ambitious Colonel Nelson Miles to speed northwest from his base at Fort Keogh, Montana, and intercept the Nez Perce before they could reach safety at the Canadian border. Clearly the Nez Perce were headed for Canada, where they would be no threat to the Americans. Why didn't Sherman just let them go? It was part ego—for the Nez Perce had made fools of the U.S. Army not once but several times—and part personality. Sherman was an unequivocally ruthless, heartless man who had helped win the Civil War for the north by marching across Georgia burning everything in his path. And it was Sherman who, in 1867, said of the country's Native American peoples, "The more we can kill this year, the less will have to be killed the next war, for the more I see of these Indians, the more convinced I am that they all have to be killed or be maintained as a species of paupers."

Last Stand at Bear's Paw

Miles and his troops found the Nez Perce camp at Bear's Paw, southeast of Havre in north-central Montana, less than 40 miles from the Canadian border. They rushed headlong into an attack, with losses on both sides—among them Toohoolhoolzote. But the army was unable to defeat the Nez Perce immediately and was forced into a siege of the camp. It was September 28, and the first storms of the season had already descended, leaving the camp cold and covered in snow. Miles was worried, correctly, that in the initial attack, a few Nez Perce might have escaped to get help from Sitting Bull. On October 4, General Howard and his troops arrived, making the Nez Perce situation all the more desperate. Joseph, Looking Glass, and White Bird held a council to determine their course of action. By messenger, first Miles, then Howard, had assured the Nez Perce that if they surrendered, they would not be punished and would be returned to the Northwest, though Joseph would not be permitted to resettle in the Wallowa Valley. Joseph saw this as a draw with the army, not a defeat. But Looking Glass and White Bird didn't trust Howard and decided to try to make a break for Canada and Sitting Bull's camp. Shortly after the meeting was over, Looking Glass was shot in the head and killed by one of Miles's scouts. That was enough for Joseph. On October 6 at 2 P.M., Joseph mounted his horse, rifle across his lap, and rode out to the army to surrender. He handed his rifle to Miles, and spoke to General Howard through an interpreter:

> Tell General Howard I know his heart. What he told me before, I have it in my heart. I am tired of fighting. Our chiefs are killed. Looking Glass is dead. Toohoolhoolzote is dead. The old men are all dead. It is the young men who say, "Yes" or "No." He who led the young men [Joseph's own brother, Ollokot] is dead. It is cold, and we have no blankets. The little children are freezing to death. My people, some of them, have run away to the hills, and have no blankets, no food. No one knows where they are—perhaps freezing to death. I want to have time to look for my children and see how many of them I can find. Maybe I shall find them among the dead. Hear me, my chiefs! I am tired. My heart is sick and sad. From where the sun now stands I will fight no more forever.

As the surrender commenced, most of the Nez Perce came out of their camp, giving their rifles to the army in exchange for food and blankets. The army now treated their foes as respected adversaries who had fought a good battle. After dark,

White Bird and his band snuck out of camp and hightailed it for Canada. Along the way they encountered a war party sent by Sitting Bull and told them that it was too late, Joseph had surrendered. They continued on to Sitting Bull's camp and remained in Canada, where White Bird died in 1882.

Alvin M. Josephy Jr. sums up the war in his book *The Nez Perce Indians and the Opening of the Northwest*:

> The Nez Perces, leaving Idaho with approximately 750 persons, including women, children, and sick and old people, with all their baggage and a huge horse herd, had conducted an unprecedented 1,700-mile retreat, fighting almost all the way. . . . At least 120 of their people had been killed . . . and they had slain approximately 180 whites and wounded 150. Man for man, they had proven themselves better fighting men and marksmen than the soldiers or volunteers, many of whom were poor shots and had no stomach for combat. . . .
>
> . . . The Nez Perce survivors of the struggle, once a rich and self-sufficient people, were made destitute and thereafter they became burdens to the American taxpayer. The Indians had lost their horses, cattle, guns, personal possessions, savings of gold dust and cash, homes, freedom—everything but their honor. With their defeat the history of the Nez Perces as an independent people came to an end.

The Bitter End

Despite the promises of Howard and Miles, the Nez Perce were not permitted to return to the Northwest; General Sherman vetoed that idea. Only public sympathy for the Nez Perce kept Sherman from ordering Joseph executed. Instead the Nez Perce were loaded onto trains and taken to a malarial swamp near Fort Leavenworth, Kansas. They were subsequently shuffled several times to various undesirable spots in the Midwest, many dying of disease at each location. Sher-

each "civilized" Indian was allotted a private plot of land on their reservation. Any land left over after all the plots had been allotted was thrown open for purchase by white homesteaders.

The act was supported by anti-Indian land-grabbers as well as do-gooders who believed it was in the Native Americans' best interest to become fully integrated into white society. After the allotment process, the Nez Perce people ended up with less than 200,000 acres, down from seven million acres under the 1855 treaty, and down from their original home territory spanning 10 million acres or more. More important, perhaps, the forced relinquishment of the tribal way of life amounted to nothing short of cultural genocide. Subjugation was now complete; "the Indian problem" was solved.

BOB RACE

Chief Joseph

man's intended genocide was coming to fruition, albeit more slowly than he might have wished.

After the war's end General Howard sided with Sherman against any leniency for the Nez Perce, but Colonel Miles constantly advocated for Joseph and his people, probably feeling guilty that his promises to them had been broken. Between Miles's efforts and public outcry, in May 1885 the 268 Nez Perce who were still alive were finally allowed back to the Northwest. The Looking Glass and White Bird followers were returned to Lapwai, while Joseph and his followers were sent to the Colville Reservation in eastern Washington. There Joseph continued his efforts to reclaim his treasured Wallowa Valley homeland, but to no avail. His pleas were refused at every turn, and he died on the Colville Reservation on September 21, 1904. The reservation physician listed the cause of death as a broken heart.

The Dawes Act

With Idaho's Native Americans forced into submission on reservations, the U.S. government came up with one more nail to hammer into the native peoples' cultural coffin. In 1887 Congress passed the Dawes Act, also known as the Allotment Act or the Severalty Act. Under the act,

THE IRON HORSE
Idaho's First Railroad

With the driving of the golden spike at Promontory, Utah, on May 10, 1869, the Union Pacific and the Central Pacific Railroads were linked, and a transcontinental rail line became a reality. The rail line passed north of Salt Lake City, but that was no problem for Brigham Young and the Mormons; they formed the Utah Central Railroad and built their own spur north to the Union Pacific Line at Ogden, completing the link in 1870. The following year, the Mormons organized the **Utah Northern Railroad,** planning to build a narrow-gauge line north from Ogden to the gold mines of western Montana. This rail line reached Franklin on May 2, 1874. Here it temporarily ran out of steam, but not before it had become the first railroad into Idaho Territory.

Franklin grew into a major freight center for wagons shipping goods back and forth from the Montana mines, which lay due north over Monida Pass (the route of today's I-15). With all this commerce on the route, it was inevitable that someone would succeed in pushing a rail line through. A new company loosely affiliated with Union Pacific, the **Utah and Northern Railway Company,** grabbed the honor, completing a connection between Franklin and the Northern Pacific line at Garrison, Montana, in

1884. This line had a profound effect on south-east Idaho, as settlements of predominantly Mormon colonists sprang up all along the route. Between 1879 and 1889, many new towns appeared in the region, among them Menan, Rexburg, Rigby, Sugar City, and Victor.

Tracks Along the Oregon Trail

Scouts for the Union Pacific had investigated possible railway routes along the Oregon Trail as early as 1867. By 1881, the company was ready to build the line. All it needed to do was sidestep government regulations that prohibited it from doing so. Another "loose affiliate" of Union Pacific was formed, and work on the new **Oregon Short Line Railway** began. Construction began off the main Union Pacific line at Granger, Montana, and headed northwest to Montpelier, Pocatello, and Shoshone, where a spur was constructed up to the Wood River Valley mines. The line was completed through to Huntington, Oregon, on November 17, 1884, and hauled both passengers

© DOVER PUBLICATIONS INC.

railroad handcar

and freight. With transfers at Granger and Huntington, passengers could make an Omaha-to-Portland trip in three and a half days. The iron horse had made the country smaller.

The line also eased development of the Snake River Plain, as irrigation equipment, seeds, harvested crops, cattle, and laborers could now cross the plain easily and connect with markets across the country. Pocatello, junction of the Oregon Short Line and the Utah and Northern, became an important rail hub, and in 1893 was named the seat of Bannock County.

Northern Routes

Railroad builders in northern Idaho were also hard at work in the 1870s and 1880s. In 1883, the **Northern Pacific Railway** connected eastern Washington with Missoula, Montana, via Sandpoint, resulting in a through line from St. Paul, Minnesota, to Portland, Oregon. In 1887, a branch line was extended up the South Fork Coeur d'Alene River; by 1891 it had crested Lookout Pass and connected through to Montana along the route of today's I-90. This line was later taken over by the Northern Pacific. In 1892, the **Great Northern Railway** connected St. Paul and Seattle via Bonners Ferry, Sandpoint, and Spokane. The Great Northern was owned by James J. Hill, known as the Empire Builder. Today's Amtrak train by that name follows Hill's old Great Northern route.

Finally, in 1909, the odd **Chicago, Milwaukee, St. Paul, and Pacific Railroad** pushed into Idaho from Montana south of Lookout Pass. Odd because a 438-mile segment of the line over the Continental Divide was handled by electric-powered trains. Numerous tunnels and trestles were built to get the trains down from the pass to Avery, Idaho, on the St. Joe River. The now-abandoned railroad grade has become the Route of the Hiawatha, one of the West's coolest mountain-biking trails.

In addition to these main lines, a whole web of spur lines connected all parts of the region in a relatively short time. The timing was fortuitous, because the biggest mining boom in the state's history—the country's history, for that matter—took place in north Idaho at the very same time.

SILVER STRIKES

Wood River Mining District

Gold was the initial draw bringing miners into present-day Idaho, but it was silver that created the state's longest-lasting, most lucrative boom. Miners first discovered galena ore—rock rich in silver, lead, and zinc—in the Wood River Valley in 1879. Almost immediately, the boomtown mining camps of Ketchum, Hailey, Bellevue, and others sprouted. By 1880 some 2,000 mining claims had been filed in the valley. The biggest mine in the district, the Minnie Moore, was in the hills west of Bellevue.

In May 1883, the Oregon Short Line spur was completed up the Wood River Valley from Shoshone, allowing major mining equipment to be brought in, and the face of mining began to change. The days of the lone prospector heading out to pan gold in remote creeks were fading. With easy access to the mines provided by the railroad, investors seized the opportunity to bring in modern technology and reap exponentially larger rewards. Professional mining engineers, geologists, and metallurgists replaced grizzled old sourdoughs, while mining corporations replaced individual mine owners. Concentrators and smelters were built right in the Wood River Valley, allowing more wealth to stay in the area. The valley became a prosperous place. In 1883, Hailey got the first telephone system in Idaho. Ketchum's smelter enjoyed electric lights. Newspapers, saloons, and social clubs flourished. By all accounts, the Wood River Valley was an orderly and pleasant place in those days. But trouble was on the horizon.

The advent of the mining corporation had turned the average miner from an independent contractor into nothing more than a day laborer, working for wealthy absentee owners. In 1884, in the face of declining lead and silver prices, the Minnie Moore Mine tried to cut wages. The mine's workers went on strike in protest. The mine brought in scabs to replace the strikers, which enraged the townsfolk. A battle broke out, and fighting was stopped only when the territorial governor sent in federal troops from Boise. The mines continued to operate with the scab employees, the price of silver continued to decline, and the mines eventually played out. By 1893, the valley's mining boom had gone bust. But the troubles experienced here foreshadowed worse times to come for Idaho's mining industry.

Noah Kellogg's Lucky Ass

The saga of what would become one of the world's most profitable mining districts began with prospector A. J. Pritchard's discovery of gold along the North Fork Coeur d'Alene River in 1878. Pritchard tried to keep his find quiet, but word got out. By 1883, the rush was on, with Murray and Eagle City the destinations du jour. In contrast to the relatively civilized social scene of the Wood River Valley, the North Fork was a wild, rambunctious place full of drinking, gambling, and prostitutes such as the locally legendary Molly B'Damn.

The easy gold played out by 1885 and the bang came off the North Fork boom. With the resultant slowdown in construction, 60-year-old carpenter Noah Kellogg found himself unemployed and destitute. Rumors of galena finds across the mountain on the South Fork had circulated through Murray for years. Kellogg figured he'd check them out. He nagged a contractor friend, O. O. Peck, and a doctor named J. T. Cooper into giving him a prospector's grubstake. In this common practice of the day, financiers supplied a prospector with food, tools, and other supplies in exchange for a share of anything the prospector found. Peck and Cooper agreed to give Kellogg a barely adequate grubstake, more to be rid of him than in hopes he might find anything. Kellogg resented the cheapskate stake, but he took it, loaded it on a donkey, and headed for the South Fork.

What happened next is part legend, part mystery. The legend says that while Kellogg was camped up a tributary of the South Fork, near present-day Wardner, his donkey wandered off. When Kellogg found the animal, it was transfixed, staring at a huge glittering outcropping of a prospector's dream-come-true: high-grade galena ore. This makes a nice mythical story, and engendered the former motto of the town of

Kellogg: "Discovered by a jackass and inhabited by its descendants." But experts agree that any outcropping of galena ore wouldn't have been shiny, but dull and red-streaked from oxidization. There is no doubt, however, that Kellogg had stumbled onto something big.

The mystery involves the chronology of events. Kellogg returned to Murray claiming failure, got another grubstake from a different group of rowdy miner friends, then headed out into the hills again. Did he actually make his find on the first trip or on the second? It seems likely that his first trip produced the find, and Kellogg, resentful of Cooper and Peck's halfhearted support, lied about his "failure" so he could get better terms from a new set of partners. That's certainly what Cooper and Peck thought. They sued Kellogg and were eventually awarded an illogical 25 percent interest in Kellogg's find. As it turned out, the find was a mother lode, and Kellogg and company's Bunker Hill and Sullivan Mine became one of the most profitable mines in world history.

The Coeur d'Alene Mining War of 1892

Almost overnight, every inch of the hills surrounding the valley of the South Fork of the Coeur d'Alene—today called the Silver Valley—swarmed with miners. Shafts were sunk at an incredible pace, and the valley's lush forests were cut down for mine timbers and boomtown buildings. Big mining corporations bought up nearly all the mines and, as they had done in the Wood River Valley, brought in the expensive smelters, mills, and mining engineers necessary to take best advantage of the underground riches.

But the labor strife that had plagued the Wood River Valley also followed the trail to the Coeur d'Alenes. Many of the same miners who had been involved in the Wood River Valley troubles migrated to the Silver Valley and formed a union in 1886. The mine owners responded by forming their own organization in 1889. In 1892, the two groups began to butt heads. Low silver and lead prices, coupled with an increase in freight rates, led the mine owners to ask the miners to accept a pay cut. The miners refused, and in

January 1892 the owners shut down the mines, throwing hundreds of miners out of work in the dead of winter.

In spring, the mines attempted to reopen using scab labor. The first efforts were unsuccessful, as the townspeople threw the strikebreakers out. But the mine owners retaliated, hiring 54 armed "security guards" out of Lewiston and Moscow to keep the mines open with scabs, and they even employed an agent from the famous Pinkerton Detective Agency to infiltrate the union and work toward its undoing. The mines resumed operation, albeit at a reduced pace.

That summer, the union miners took action. They blew up an abandoned mill, seized a nonunion mine and held the crew hostage, and threatened to dynamite working mills and concentrators. The mine owners appealed to Washington, and President Benjamin Harrison sent in federal troops. The soldiers rounded up all the union miners involved in the incident and temporarily imprisoned them in a large outdoor pen. The nonunion miners went back to work, while the union men regrouped for another day.

History Repeats Itself

In 1899, a replay of the Coeur d'Alene mining disputes took place. By this time, the strong Western Federation of Miners had been formed and the union movement had gained strength. The mine owners nevertheless refused to recognize the unions, employing both union and nonunion workers at the same scale.

Union workers marched on the Bunker Hill Mine on April 24, 1899, demanding a uniform $3.50 daily wage for all underground workers and an end to the employment of nonunion miners. The mine owners refused the demands, and some mines ceased operations.

On April 29, the union miners resorted to violence once again. They hijacked a Northern Pacific train in Burke, up Canyon Creek, loaded it with stolen dynamite, and headed for Kellogg. All along the way, miners joined in the procession. When they reached Kellogg, the miners blew up the Bunker Hill offices and an adjacent mill, then reboarded the train and drove it back to Burke. Word reached Idaho governor Frank Steunenberg, who in turn called President William McKinley. Once more federal troops were dispatched. Before they could get there, one of the Bunker Hill employees was shot to death by a miner. At that point, Governor Steunenberg declared martial law.

The troops arrived and again rounded up the union men, arresting about 1,000 of them and incarcerating them in the "bull pen" as before. Steunenberg brought in high-powered lawyers—including William Borah and James Hawley—to prosecute the union leaders, and on July 27, scapegoat and union secretary Paul Corcoran was convicted of second-degree murder in the death of the Bunker Hill man and sentenced to life imprisonment. He was pardoned two years later. Most of the bullpen prisoners were eventually released without trial, and although martial law remained in effect for a year and a half, peace returned to the Silver Valley.

FAMOUS IDAHOANS

Among famous natives or transplanted residents who have called Idaho home:

Arts and Entertainment
Gutzon Borglum—sculptor of Mount Rushmore
Mariel Hemingway—actor
Lana Turner—actor
Bruce Willis—actor

Business
Joseph Albertson—founder of Albertson's supermarkets
Nephi and Golden Grigg—founders of Ore-Ida Potato Products, Inc.
Harry Morrison and Morris Knudsen—cofounders of Morrison-Knudsen civil engineering firm
J. R. Simplot—potato king, the richest man in Idaho

Literature
Carol Ryrie Brink—Newbery Award–winning novelist
Edgar Rice Burroughs—creator of the *Tarzan* series
Vardis Fisher—novelist and director of the WPA-era Federal Writer's Project
Mary Hallock Foote—pioneer novelist
Ernest Hemingway—Nobel Prize–winning novelist
Ezra Pound—poet

Politics
Cecil Andrus—four-term governor (1971–77, 1987–94) and Secretary of the Interior in the Carter administration (1977–80)
William Borah—six-term senator, serving 1907–40
Frank Church—four-term senator, serving 1957–81
George Shoup—first state governor, 1890 (resigned to become U.S. Senator)
William Wallace—first territorial governor, 1864–65

Sports
Stacy Dragila—Olympic pole vaulter, gold medalist, 2000
Harmon Killebrew—home-run champ for the Minnesota Twins, played 1954–75
Walter Johnson—record-setting pitcher for the Washington Senators, played 1907–27
Picabo Street—Olympic skier, gold medalist, 1998

A Tragic Epilogue

Six years after he had ordered troops in to squelch the 1899 Coeur d'Alene mining war, former governor Steunenberg was killed by an assassin's bomb outside his home in Caldwell. The trail of evidence led to Harry Orchard, one of the miners who had been involved in the bombing of the Bunker Hill offices, and a man with high contacts in the Western Federation of Miners. Orchard supposedly confessed to the crime and implicated union officials in a conspiracy to kill Steunenberg. The officials were arrested and their subsequent trial made national headlines. Two of the greatest American lawyers of the time were pitted against one another: William Borah prosecuted the case, and Clarence Darrow defended the miners. Orchard was convicted and spent the rest of his life in the Idaho Territorial Penitentiary at Boise. The union leaders were acquitted, but even many union miners believed the union brass had somehow been involved. The unions lost credibility among the workers and were dormant for a long time thereafter.

MODERN TIMES

Statehood

Oregon gained statehood in 1859, Nevada in 1864, Washington and Montana in 1889. By 1890, the movement was afoot to either make Idaho Territory a state or apportion it among neighboring states. The rivalry between the former and the current capital cities, Lewiston and Boise, had continued unabated since C. DeWitt Smith had "stolen" the territorial books out of Lewiston in 1865. Lewiston residents wanted nothing more than to separate themselves from Boise. Nevada was looking to annex southern Idaho. Northern Idaho residents were split; Palouse farmers and many others wanted to annex the north state to geographically and economically aligned Washington, while Silver Valley miners preferred annexation to Montana, which they perceived as a more mining-friendly state. Boise politicians fought to retain a unified Idaho with Boise as the capital. Finally, southern Idaho threw northern Idaho just enough of a

bone to keep it from seceding: plans for a university in northern Idaho, at Moscow. Northern Idaho agreed to the deal and got behind the push for Idaho statehood. President Benjamin Harrison signed the bill creating Idaho, the 43rd state, on July 3, 1890, and Idaho's star was officially placed on the nation's flag the following day, July Fourth. Emma Edwards Green designed the state seal in 1891, the University of Idaho opened in Moscow on October 3, 1892, and Idaho granted women the right to vote in 1896, becoming the fourth state in the union to do so.

The Growth of Agriculture

Idaho's population nearly doubled between 1890 and 1900, and more than doubled between 1900 and 1910. The reason? Agriculture. First the timber barons—men such as Frederic Weyerhauser, who had made a fortune wiping out the forests of the Great Lakes region—came west and discovered the great pine forests of Idaho. The U.S. government had given much of Idaho's forest lands outright to the railroads, supposedly to encourage westward expansion. Given the cozy relationship between the era's politicians and business leaders, one suspects their motives were rather less principled and more self-serving. The timber companies snapped up this land for a song, since the railroads knew their trains would haul the logs out of the forests. It was a classic case of mutual back-scratching. Loggers flooded into the state to partake in the conversion of green to gold.

Next, dry farmers turned the Palouse into a profitable sea of green. Between the fertile farmland there and the new university, the population of north-central Idaho swelled. But the biggest factor in increasing Idaho's population after the turn of the century was the development of irrigation on the Snake River Plain. A whole network of privately financed canals laced southwest Idaho by 1900, and settlers rushed in to try their luck at farming. These canals made use of the region's many tributaries of the Snake River. But the mass volumes of water held in the Snake River itself weren't fully exploited until the completion of major government-sponsored irrigation projects in the early 1900s.

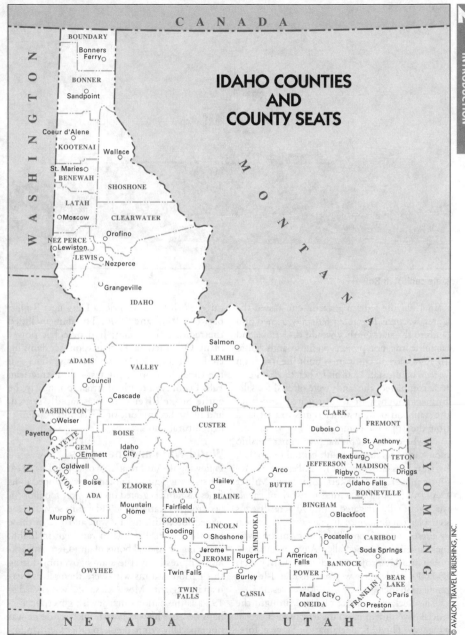

IDAHO COUNTIES
AND
COUNTY SEATS

CANADA

WASHINGTON

BOUNDARY

Bonners
Ferry

BONNER

Sandpoint

Coeur d'Alene

KOOTENAI   Wallace

St. Maries

BENEWAH   SHOSHONE

LATAH

Moscow   CLEARWATER

Orofino

NEZ PERCE
Lewiston

LEWIS

Nezperce

Grangeville

IDAHO

MONTANA

Salmon

LEMHI

ADAMS   VALLEY

Council

Cascade

Challis

WASHINGTON   CUSTER

Weiser

Payette   BOISE

PAYETTE   Idaho
GEM   City

Emmett

Caldwell

Boise   ELMORE   CAMAS

ADA

Hailey

Murphy   Mountain   Fairfield   BLAINE
Home

GOODING
LINCOLN
Gooding   Shoshone

MINIDOKA
Jerome
JEROME   Rupert

OWYHEE   Twin Falls
Burley

TWIN   CASSIA
FALLS

CLARK   FREMONT

Dubois   St. Anthony

Rexburg   TETON
JEFFERSON   MADISON   Driggs

Arco   Rigby
BUTTE   Idaho Falls

BONNEVILLE

BINGHAM

Blackfoot

Pocatello   CARIBOU

Soda Springs

American
Falls   BANNOCK

POWER   BEAR
LAKE

Malad City   Paris
ONEIDA   FRANKLIN   Preston

WYOMING

NEVADA   UTAH

OREGON

CANYON

© AVALON TRAVEL PUBLISHING, INC.

state capitol in Boise

In 1894 the federal government passed the Carey Act, which granted federally owned arid lands to the states if they would undertake and complete irrigation projects on those lands within 10 years. Private companies built the irrigation systems on the state land, and when those systems were completed, the lands were offered for sale. Farmers bought parcels of irrigated land from the state and bought water rights to that land from the irrigation companies.

Nowhere was this public-private partnership more successful than in south-central Idaho. Led by Twin Falls entrepreneur Ira B. Perrine, the region's movers and shakers completed Milner Dam in 1905, along with a network of canals that eventually irrigated 244,000 acres. Farms soon blanketed the once dry, desert region, which as a result of its incredible transformation was nicknamed the Magic Valley. Along with subsequent similar projects under the Carey Act, 850,000 arable acres were created, and Idaho's population increased by 50,000 as a result.

The Reclamation Act of 1902 brought the federal government in on the irrigation efforts in a big way. The U.S. Reclamation Service, forerunner of the Bureau of Reclamation, built huge, earth-filled Minidoka Dam near Rupert between 1904 and 1906. The dam included the region's first major hydroelectric power plant. Other federal Reclamation Act dams included Arrowrock Dam on the Boise River—at the time the world's highest—and American Falls Dam. As a result of irrigation, nearly the entire Snake River Plain was rapidly settled, and Idaho became one of the country's premier agricultural states.

World War I and the 1920s

Following the outbreak of World War I in 1914, the state's agricultural potential was tapped to its fullest as farmers geared up to supply food for Allied troops. Nearly 20,000 Idahoans served in the armed forces during the war, and 782 of those lost their lives. Patriotism ran high in Idaho, spawning occasional bouts of anti-German backlash. Interestingly, the state's governor during this period and his wife were themselves German immigrants. Moses Alexander was elected in 1914 as the nation's first Jewish governor. Perhaps because he was Jewish, or because he was not especially sympathetic to other German immigrants enduring suspicion bordering on persecution in the state, Alexander's loyalties were considered above reproach.

At the end of the war, returning GIs brought home victory but also a particularly virulent strain of influenza dubbed the Spanish flu. The virus swept through the population of the United States. A half million Americans died from the disease, and Idaho was not exempt. The epidemic lasted until spring 1919.

The Roaring '20s didn't do much roaring in Idaho. After the war, agricultural exports tapered off as European farmers returned to their fields. The resultant farm-commodity surplus sent prices plummeting down; many farmers suddenly found themselves struggling. In a prelude to the Great Depression, small independent banks that dealt virtually exclusively in loans to farmers began to go under, as farmers found it increasingly difficult to make their loan payments. Labor groups like the radical-socialist Industrial Workers of the World, cofounded by Big Bill Haywood of Coeur d'Alene Mining War fame, tried to take advantage of the economic downturn by organizing strikes and advocating labor control of industry. But conservative Idahoans would have none of it. They had seen Russia's Bolshevik Revolution of 1917 and its aftermath, and feared that the Wobblies, as the IWW members were known, were working to overthrow the U.S. government.

Highways and automobiles made steady inroads into Idaho during the 1920s. The Prohibition era came, along with the "talkies." But worsening economic conditions caused a population exodus from the state.

The Great Depression

No sooner had Idaho dug itself out from the economic trough of the 1920s than the whole country was thrown into the Great Depression of the 1930s, precipitated by the stock market crash of October 1929. With drought exacerbating dried-up markets, Idaho's farm economy hit the basement. Farm prices dropped to their lowest point in a century, and between 1929 and 1932, the state's total farm income dropped 65 percent. Farmers lost their farms to foreclosure; bank runs caused many banks to fail. Firefighters in southwest Idaho deliberately set fires to provide themselves with employment; Idaho's governor had to call out the national guard and close off all public access to the forests. Drought had stricken the Midwest as well, bringing refugees into Idaho and other Western states in search of work and better conditions. But conditions weren't any better in Idaho, and the influx of economic refugees added to the burden of the state's relief agencies.

Soon after his inauguration in 1933, President Franklin D. Roosevelt initiated his New Deal program of federal spending in an effort to jump-start the nation's economy. Many of the New Deal programs aided Idaho greatly. The Civilian Conservation Corps (CCC) put young men to work in Idaho's expansive national forests. They helped control the blister rust devastating Idaho's vast tracts of white pine; fought forest fires; planted trees; built roads, trails, and fire-lookout towers; and constructed public facilities such as those in Heyburn State Park. The Rural Electrification Administration strung power lines across the state, benefiting schools, industries, and residences. The Public Roads Administration improved some 1,650 miles of Idaho road ways. The Works Progress Administration, whose name was later changed to the Work Projects Administration, constructed bridges, water supplies, sewer systems, and recreational facilities. A similar program, the Public Works Administration, helped build roads in and near Idaho's national forests, develop the state's infrastructure for irrigated agriculture, and construct dozens of school buildings. And the Federal Writers Project, led in Idaho by Vardis Fisher, produced the WPA *Guide to Idaho,* the first of the WPA state guides. A total of $331 million in New Deal aid money went to Idaho.

In the meantime, some entrepreneurs found ways to succeed without federal help. Harry Morrison and Morris Knudsen started their famous civil engineering firm in 1912; it went on to become one of the biggest such companies in the world. And in 1936, railroad baron and sometime statesman W. Averell Harriman founded his Sun Valley Ski Lodge, which enjoyed immediate success as an escape from the trials and tribulations of the era and spawned the world's first chairlifts for skiers.

World War II

Roosevelt's New Deal spent somewhere in the neighborhood of $24 billion over seven years in an attempt to bolster the American economy. But then Hitler invaded Poland on September 1, 1939, the opening foray of World War II, and the coffers of the U.S. Treasury really opened up. In the first year of its involvement in the war alone, the United States spent more than double that amount.

After the Japanese bombed Pearl Harbor on December 7, 1941, defense spending skyrocketed. Idaho benefited in several areas. The Defense Department kept Morrison-Knudsen busy building airfields and roads in the Pacific theater. The navy built Farragut Naval Training Center on the shores of Pend Oreille Lake in the Panhandle and used it to train recruits for submarine duty. Construction of the base put 22,000 men to work nearly round-the-clock. Pocatello got an ordnance plant, Boise an airfield for bombers. Mountain Home's airbase was built, and Sun Valley Lodge was taken over by the navy as a hospital.

Of the 60,000 Idahoans who served in World War II, nearly 1,800 died, eight were declared missing in action, and 31 were captured as prisoners of war. As it had in World War I, Idaho's agricultural industry provided much of the food the GIs ate during the conflict; the war started Idahoan J. R. Simplot on the road to riches when he began dehydrating potatoes and selling them to the military. In addition, as more high-tech armaments were developed, Idaho's supplies of strategic minerals were tapped. Cobalt, tungsten, and antimony mines worked overtime to satisfy defense-industry requirements.

A POW camp for German prisoners was established at Farragut Naval Base. And following the Japanese attack on Pearl Harbor, Japanese-Americans living on the West Coast were rounded up and incarcerated at several concentration camps farther inland, including one near Minidoka. Between September 1942 and October 1945, this "relocation center" was the eighth-largest "city" in Idaho, holding about 10,000 internees. Morrison-Knudsen built the camp, the construction of which helped pull south-central Idaho out of the Depression.

The war had exacted a horrible price in human lives but, as elsewhere in the country, had gotten the state's economy back on track.

Postwar Growth

Following World War II, mining for strategic metals continued to enjoy defense-industry support as the Korean, Cold, and Vietnam Wars raged on. Other industries that had fueled the war effort turned their knowledge and experience to civilian uses. J. R. Simplot went from selling dehydrated potatoes to the military to selling french fries to McDonald's.

The U.S. Departments of Defense and Energy established the National Reactor Testing Station in Idaho in 1949. Here physicists and nuclear engineers developed the world's first nuclear power plant, EBR-1, and first sent fission-produced electricity through the wires to provide electricity for municipal needs, supplying the town of Arco for a couple of hours on July 17, 1955. The site also developed fission reactors for America's nuclear navy.

Entering a New Century

The last part of the 20th century saw Idaho transitioning from its traditional, natural resources–based economy. While agriculture remains strong, and pockets of mining and timber activity continue, technology and tourism have become increasingly important.

Idaho has embraced advanced technology in a big way. Hewlett-Packard established a Boise division in the 1970s, and Micron Technology—a semiconductor company begun in the capital city in 1978—is now the state's largest private employer. In 2002, computer giant Dell established a customer service call center in Twin Falls, and countless small technology companies have gone into business around the state. Although economic fallout in the early 21st century meant tech-industry layoffs, especially in Boise, Idaho's pro-business climate means good long-term prospects for the industry. The state's recreational riches, meanwhile, have proven a drawing card both for tourists and for entrepreneurs who like to mix business and leisure.

PEOPLE AND POLITICS

Idaho's population breaks down as follows: white, 87 percent; Hispanic, eight percent; Native American, one percent; all others, four percent. Following is a brief look at some of the ethnic groups that spice up the stew.

Hispanics

Traveling through some parts of Canyon County, you might think you were south of the border in Mexico. The fields of the Treasure Valley are worked chiefly by migrant farm workers, most of them of Mexican descent; nearly 20 percent of the county's residents are Hispanic. If you're a fan of Mexican food, you'll find restaurants in Nampa and Caldwell that are some of the most authentic and delightful in the country.

Native Americans

After relegating Idaho's native peoples to reservations, the federal government gave them only minimal aid. Unemployment and poverty became epidemic, forcing the tribes to look for income in nontraditional places. When they hit upon gambling, they struck the mother lode. Today, revenues from tribal bingo halls, casinos, and Indian lotteries bring in large sums of money to the tribes, helping turn the tables on poverty. In 2003, Idaho voters approved a measure allowing expanded Indian gaming, despite strong opposition that was rooted—no surprise here—in south-central Idaho, a region closely aligned with the border-town destination of Jackpot, Nevada.

The **Coeur d'Alene** tribe is setting aside a percentage of the profits from its gaming operations to reacquire land that was first granted and then taken away by successive treaties with the whites. The tribe is also putting substantial amounts into both remedial action and court fights to clean up and gain control of the waters and shores of Coeur d'Alene Lake—waters ravaged by heavy-metal pollution from a century of mining. The Coeur d'Alene Reservation is in north-central Idaho, surrounding the south side of Coeur d'Alene Lake.

Other Indian reservations in the state include the Shoshone-Bannock **Fort Hall Reservation** in southeast Idaho; the Shoshone-Paiute **Duck Valley Reservation,** straddling the Nevada border in southwest Idaho; and the **Nez Perce Reservation,** in north-central Idaho, home to the headquarters of Nez Perce National Historic Park.

The Kootenai tribe doesn't have its own reservation, but it owns the **Kootenai River Inn** in Bonners Ferry. You can support the descendants of Idaho's indigenous Kootenai and learn a little about their culture by staying at the inn on your way through the area.

Basques

Their homeland is in northern Spain, but many Basque immigrants make their home in Idaho. Boise has the largest Basque population in the West and offers plenty of opportunities for the visitor to learn about this unique culture. You can eat Basque food at a number of restaurants across the state—try Boise's Bar Gernika, where chances are good you'll overhear the unusual Basque language being spoken while you eat. Boise is also the site of the annual Festival of San Inazio and the once-every-five-years Jaialdi, an international blowout that draws Basque people from all over world.

Republicans

Idaho is one of the most Republican states in the country. George W. Bush won all but one county (Blaine, home of Sun Valley) in 2000, and the state legislature is overwhelmingly GOP. *Idaho Statesman* columnist Dan Popkey recalls how, during the era of U.S. Senator Frank Church and Governor Cecil Andrus (the 1960s through the 1980s), Democrats "shared power in Republican Idaho through force of intellect and personality." But these days, the only areas where Democrats prevail are Sun Valley, Pocatello, and Boise; the latter elected former Democratic state legislator Dave Bieter as mayor in 2003 in a four-way race in which Bieter polled more than 50 percent. Democrats also made some gains in the 2002 state legislature elections, but Dems remain very much the minority party.

Many Idahoans are firmly entrenched in the mindset of the Sagebrush Rebellion: "It's our land to do what we want with, and the federal government should mind its own business." (Unless the feds want to give them money—then it's okay.) You can count on Idaho's elected representatives in Washington to rubber-stamp all pro-mining, pro-logging, pro-ranching, and pro-business legislation and to fight all pro-environmental bills that would get in the way of anyone making money in Idaho. Liberal-minded travelers may find it frustrating to see such a beautiful land governed by people with so little interest in conservation. On the other hand, if you don't talk politics, you'll find the people of Idaho universally friendly and welcoming, even in the smallest rural nooks and crannies.

On the Road

Land. Big, beautiful land. That's the state's number-one sightseeing highlight. No matter where you go in Idaho, you'll see expansive land—from the vast sagebrush deserts of the Snake River Plain to the densely forested mountains of central Idaho to the crystal-blue lakes of the Panhandle. More than two-thirds of the state is owned by the public in the form of national forests, BLM lands, and state parks. In that sense, it hardly matters where you travel in Idaho—virtually all roads are scenic. But let's take a quick tour of the state and see what stands out, area by area.

Boise

The state capital and surrounding Ada County hold around nearly a quarter of Idaho's population and offer a delightful mix of urban amenities and outdoor fun. Here you can put on your tuxedo for a symphony performance at **Morrison Center for the Performing Arts,** which boasts near-perfect acoustics and draws heralded performers from around the country; rock out at the **Big Easy Concert House,** anchor of Boise's superlative rock and alternative music scene; or head to the open-air **Idaho Shakespeare Festival,** which presents the Bard's classics each summer under Boise's star-filled skies. For recreation, try a run or ride on the **Boise River Greenbelt,** a tree-lined jogging and bike path that follows the Boise River from one end of town to the other.

The greenbelt is just one of many parks and open spaces that make Boise a thoroughly livable city.

In winter, skiers make the short drive up to **Bogus Basin,** a first-rate alpine and Nordic ski center. In summer, the foothills at the edge of town, known as the **Boise Front,** draw scads of mountain bikers out for scenic trail riding just minutes from downtown.

Southwest Idaho

Although **Ada and Canyon Counties** comprise the state's most densely populated region, Southwest Idaho has pleasing rural vistas and abundant wild country ready for exploration. The state's highest concentration of **wineries** can be found between Nampa and Caldwell; most offer tours and tasting. You'll also find roadside **fruit stands** and excellent **Mexican restaurants** throughout the Nampa-Caldwell region.

History buffs can check out the former mining stronghold of **Silver City** in the Owyhee Mountains. Once a mining boomtown, the "Queen of the Owyhees" was the site of a mining war that cost the life of J. Marion More, one of the biggest mining magnates in the state's early history. More was gunned down on the front porch of the **Idaho Hotel.** He died, but the creaky old Idaho Hotel clings to life; today you can get a room there.

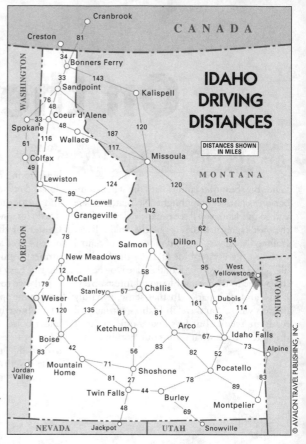

Off-pavement adventurers won't want to miss the **Owyhee County Backcountry Byway,** which circles around behind the Owyhee Mountains from Grand View to Jordan Valley, Oregon. Along the way you'll get sweeping views of rolling juniper forests and pass idyllic creekside campgrounds that you'll probably have all to yourself even during the peak of tourist season.

Farther north, the Snake River Plain gives way to lush valleys and mountains. Folks come from all over the world to Weiser each summer to participate in the world's greatest **Old Time Fid-** dle Festival. At Cambridge, you can turn west to meet the Snake River at the point where it enters **Hells Canyon,** the deepest river gorge in North America. Each summer, whitewater rafters and kayakers come here in droves to challenge the big-water rapids and enjoy this magnificent Wild and Scenic stretch of the Snake.

Whitewater fans also flock to another southwest Idaho watercourse, the **Payette River,** in search of the wet and wild. Take Highway 55 north from Boise to see paddlers in brightly colored kayaks and rafts challenging the cascades in summer. East of the Payette River lies one of the biggest gold-mining districts in Idaho history, the **Boise Basin.** Take Highway 21 out of

Boise to reach the largest of the old mining camps here, **Idaho City.** Here you can walk down wooden-plank sidewalks, past buildings now haunted by the ghosts of old sourdoughs, or wander through **Pioneer Cemetery.**

Highway 55 continues along the Payette River to the Cascade-Donnelly-McCall area. A major new resort near Donnelly, **Tamarack,** will unveil its downhill skiing in 2004–05 and golf in 2005. **McCall** ranks among the most fun towns in Idaho. Its young, outdoor-oriented populace thrives on hiking and mountain biking in the Payette National Forest and skiing up at **Brundage Mountain.** The town hosts the blowout **Winter Carnival** each year, either in late January or early February. McCall is also home to **Ponderosa State Park,** one of Idaho's best state parks. Covering a peninsula jutting out into Payette Lake, the park is a haven for campers in summer and for cross-country skiers in winter.

South-Central Idaho

If ever there was a place to get off the interstate, this is it. All the best of this portion of the state lies off the main drag. Get off I-84 at Bliss and take Highway 30 through **Hagerman Valley.** This route holds one highlight after another, including one of the world's most important fossil beds; a Frank Lloyd Wright house overlooking the Snake River; the oldest pottery in Idaho; the Thousand Springs area, where the Snake River Plain Aquifer pours out of basalt cliffs in a miles-long stretch of cascading springs; and a crazy, huge rock that defies gravity—maybe it'll topple when you're there!

Twin Falls is the region's population center. The city was named for a falls on the Snake River, but the namesake falls plays second fiddle as a tourist attraction to **Shoshone Falls,** just downstream. Often compared to Niagara Falls, Shoshone Falls is most impressive in spring when the water is flowing at maximum volume. Nearby is the **Evel Knievel Jump Site,** where the famous daredevil tried, and failed, to jump the Snake River Canyon on a rocket-powered motorcycle. The canyon itself is a marvel, especially from **Centennial Waterfront Park** beneath the Perrine Bridge.

Southeast of Twin Falls, the **South Hills** are far more impressive than they appear from a distance. This playground for Twin Falls–area residents offers great panoramic views, as well as alpine and cross-country skiing in winter, and hiking and mountain biking in summer. North of Twin Falls, out across the desolate lava-strewn Snake River Plain, lies one of the two or three sites in Idaho most worshipped by fly-fishing enthusiasts: **Silver Creek.** Near the town of Picabo, this spring creek flows at a constant temperature through a high-desert meadow. The big, smart trout inhabiting the creek challenge anglers from around the world.

South of Burley, the site of today's **City of Rocks National Reserve** marked an important crossroads for westward-bound emigrants; several trails converged here where a "cityscape" of rock towers juts into the desert sky. Some of the rock

COURTESY OF THE IDAHO TRAVEL COUNCIL

The canyon at Twin Falls is almost 500 feet deep—Evel Knievel made a famous attempt to jump across it on a motorcycle.

towers are hundreds of feet high, a fact that today has made the reserve and neighboring **Castle Rocks State Park** internationally known centers for **rock climbing.**

Southeast Idaho

Each of this region's two largest cities, **Pocatello** and **Idaho Falls,** has about 51,000 people, and they're forever jockeying for third and fourth place in the census (behind Boise and Nampa). This is also potato country; across much of southeast Idaho you'll see vast fields planted with Idaho's famous spuds.

Pocatello is home to **Idaho State University** and is also the gateway to **Lava Hot Springs,** a funky little resort town built around an area rife with crystal-clear, sulfur-free hot springs. Indigenous Native Americans and westward-bound emigrants enjoyed soaking here; modern-day sightseers will, too.

The state's farthest southeast corner is the land of the **Mormon pioneers.** The little town of Franklin—the oldest permanent white settlement in Idaho—was founded by members of the church in 1860. Today, many of the original historic buildings remain. Farther east, **Bear Lake** is a sight to behold. The huge lake—half in Idaho, half in Utah—holds dissolved limestone particles in suspension, coloring the lake a surreal turquoise blue. Nearby are the **Paris Tabernacle,** a stunning example of early Mormon architecture, and **Minnetonka Cave,** one of the country's few federal show caves.

Idaho Falls attractions include a good zoo and the recently renovated and renamed **Museum of Idaho.** It's also home to most employees of the **Idaho National Engineering and Environmental Laboratory** (INEEL), a federal facility devoted to nuclear research. On its tract of desolate rangeland west of the city lie 52 nuclear reactors, including **EBR-1,** the world's first atomic power plant. Today you can tour this decommissioned reactor; everyone who does so gives glowing reports.

West of INEEL, **Craters of the Moon National Monument** preserves an eerie wonderland of volcanic features—including lava "bombs" and lava-tube "caves"—all caused by the same

volcanic hotspot that today fuels the geysers and boiling mudpots of Yellowstone National Park.

To the east and north of Idaho Falls, you'll find some of Idaho's wildest country. Anglers head for the **Henry's Fork** or **South Fork Snake River,** both of which offer blue-ribbon trout fishing. Numerous guides and fishing lodges in the area cater to fly-fishers. From across the region, the mighty **Teton Range** dominates the eastern horizon. Although these jagged peaks are technically in Wyoming, their western flanks are accessible only through Idaho. To get there, you'll head up into **Teton Basin.** Once a favored site for the mountain-man rendezvous in the fur-trading days, today the basin is best known as the gateway to **Grand Targhee Ski and Summer Resort,** which enjoys the Northwest's finest powder skiing.

North of Teton Basin, Idaho borders and even holds a narrow strip of **Yellowstone National Park.** To get to the park proper, you'll head north through the scenic **Island Park** area into Montana, then east into Wyoming. But you can also take back roads east from **Ashton** in through the little-visited Bechler region, Yellowstone's "back door," with the park's highest concentration of waterfalls.

The High Country

Thanks to Sun Valley and, to a lesser extent, Stanley, this is the most well known part of the state. **Sun Valley,** grande dame of American ski resorts, was the brainchild of Union Pacific railroad tycoon Averell Harriman, who wanted to create a world-class ski area rivaling those of the Alps. Today, it's one of the biggest ski resorts in the country, and arguably *the* most luxurious. Surrounding the resort are the twin towns of Ketchum and Sun Valley, playgrounds for the rich and famous and full of expensive homes and fancy restaurants.

Stanley, just over the hill from Sun Valley, still clings to its Wild West heritage. Once a mining supply camp, today Stanley is a base camp for those heading into the **Sawtooth Range,** Idaho's most famous and beautiful mountain range and a wilderness area closed to all mechanized vehicles. In summer, the dusty little town fills up with whitewater rafters, who float down the **Salmon**

River, which runs right through town, or the **Middle Fork Salmon River,** which begins in the high country just northwest of town. Mountain bikers head for the nearby **White Cloud Peaks,** a lofty realm with miles of trails open to bicycles.

East of Stanley, two high-country valleys separated by massive peaks provide a classic example of basin-and-range geology. Highway 93 runs down the **Lost River Valley,** past an active earthquake fault and past **Borah Peak,** the state's highest mountain, at an elevation of 12,662 feet. Farther east, Highway 28 descends Lemhi Valley at the edge of the **Continental Divide.** Along this route, you can take a side road up to **Lemhi Pass** on the Montana border, where on August 12, 1805, Lewis and Clark became the first whites to set eyes on the territory that would later become the great state of Idaho.

North of Stanley, occupying a huge chunk of the center of the state, the **Frank Church–River of No Return Wilderness** tempts explorers into the largest wilderness area in the lower 48 states. Larger than Rhode Island and Delaware combined, this wilderness provides virtually limitless terrain for hikers. The Salmon River and its Middle Fork flow right through the heart of it, past herds of bighorn sheep and mountain goats, past hot springs and early Native American rock art, past hermits' cabins and a few remote guest ranches.

North-Central Idaho

North of McCall, Highway 95 follows alongside the Little Salmon River to its confluence with the main Salmon at **Riggins,** a town that lives for whitewater. The town's small main street is lined with companies offering guided float trips on the Salmon, either upstream—in or near the Frank Church–River of No Return Wilderness—or downstream, through Lower Salmon Gorge to the confluence with the Snake in Hells Canyon. Just west of Riggins, **Hells Canyon National Recreation Area** encompasses the Snake's Wild and Scenic run through Hells Canyon, as well as the impressive **Seven Devils Range** that separates the Salmon and Snake south of their confluence. The Seven Devils provide great backpacking opportunities and some of the best views in all of Idaho; from **Heaven's** Gate Lookout you can look down toward the Snake River, more than a vertical mile below.

At **Lewiston** the Snake flows out of Idaho at the state's lowest point. Here at Idaho's only seaport, the Snake River meets the Clearwater River, and Highway 95 meets Highway 12. Known as the Lewis and Clark Highway, Highway 12 follows the Clearwater east up to its headwaters on the Continental Divide. Along the way it passes the headquarters of **Nez Perce National Historic Park,** where a visitor center explains the past and present of the Nez Perce people. Before the coming of white miners, the Nez Perce freely roamed this area. Their resistance to being forced onto a reservation led them into battle with the U.S. Army—a battle they very nearly won.

Farther east on Highway 12, the Selway and Lochsa Rivers meet to form the Clearwater. Both the Lochsa and Selway are world-class whitewater runs. The Lochsa flows alongside Highway 12, allowing the passing motorist to watch the thrilling rides of rafters and kayakers on the raging water below. The Selway begins in the high country of the Frank Church–River of No Return Wilderness and flows down to its confluence with the Lochsa through the **Selway-Bitterroot Wilderness,** Idaho's second-largest wilderness area. Numerous campgrounds in the area draw RVers in summer, while the backcountry beckons with hot springs and alpine lakes.

North of Lewiston, Highway 95 climbs onto a fertile tableland called the **Palouse.** The biggest city on the Palouse is **Moscow,** home of the **University of Idaho.** The fun college town offers coffeehouses and brewpubs, and hosts the annual **Lionel Hampton Jazz Festival,** drawing many of the world's finest jazz musicians to the UI campus each February. North and east of Moscow once stood the largest stands of white pine in the West. Disease and the logging industry combined to devastate their numbers, but a few can still be found here and there.

Once prime fishing grounds for the indigenous Coeur d'Alene people, the southern tip of Coeur d'Alene Lake now is the site of **Heyburn State Park,** the oldest of Idaho's state parks. Here you'll find good camping, hiking, and boating, as well as a small interpretive center devoted to the

COURTESY OF THE COEUR D'ALENE CHAMBER OF COMMERCE/JOEL RINER

chairlifts on Silver Mountain

Coeur d'Alene people, their legacy, and their current efforts to protect Coeur d'Alene Lake for future generations.

The Panhandle

Idaho's northern reaches are largely unspoiled and lushly green. **Coeur d'Alene,** the unofficial capital of the Panhandle, is a sparkling gem of a city on the shores of beautiful Coeur d'Alene Lake. Water sports on the lake are huge here in summer, as is **Silverwood,** a theme park with several big coasters and a water park.

East of Coeur d'Alene, **Old Mission State Park** preserves an exquisitely elegant mission built by Jesuit priests beginning in 1847. I-90 then climbs through the Silver Valley, once the world's most profitable mining district. In Kellogg, the alpine ski resort of **Silver Mountain** boasts the world's longest gondola. Farther east, the old mining town of **Wallace** is so well preserved the whole town is listed on the National

Register of Historic Places. This region also is home to two outstanding bike trails, the **Route of the Hiawatha** and the paved 72-mile **Trail of the Coeur d'Alenes.**

North of Coeur d'Alene, Highway 95 takes you to **Sandpoint,** a onetime art colony with much to offer the visitor. The town enjoys a magnificent setting on the shores of Idaho's largest lake, **Pend Oreille.** Boating, bicycling, and sunbathing on the city's beautiful sandy beach provide opportunities for summer fun, while in winter everyone heads up to **Schweitzer Mountain,** one of Idaho's top ski and summer resorts. Sandpoint is also a gastronome's heaven, offering many fine restaurants and brewpubs.

Northwest of Sandpoint, on the other side of the Selkirk Range, lies **Priest Lake,** a lightly developed, out-of-the-way gem favored by anglers and outdoor enthusiasts. Wildlife abounds here; people don't. From Priest Lake, it's but a hop, skip, and a jump to the Canadian border.

Recreation

WILDERNESS AREAS

What is a wilderness? Many definitions come to mind. For the purposes of this book, wilderness is defined as those areas of the state officially designated as such by the U.S. Congress, pursuant to the Wilderness Act of 1964. That act reads, in part, "A wilderness, in contrast with those areas where man and his own works dominate the landscape, is hereby recognized as an area where the earth and community of life are untrammeled by man, where man himself is a visitor who does not remain."

With few exceptions, no mechanical vehicles are permitted in wilderness areas. That not only means no motor vehicles, but also no mountain bikes. Basically, that leaves feet and pack stock. Idaho holds six federally designated wilderness areas, each of which is briefly described here.

Frank Church–River of No Return Wilderness

Big enough to be a state in itself, the 2.3 million-acre Frank Church–River of No Return Wilderness is the largest wilderness area in the country outside Alaska. It was established by Congress in 1980 and encompasses parts of four national forests and six ranger districts, as well as two of the country's most famous whitewater rivers—the Salmon River and its Middle Fork, both designated Wild and Scenic.

Visitors who venture into this wild realm might be lucky enough to spot a gray wolf; 15 were released into the Frank Church in 1995, and they've managed to reproduce despite the wishes of local ranchers. A few grizzly bears may also inhabit the area.

For more coverage of the Frank Church wilderness, please see the High Country chapter. For general information on the wilderness, contact the **Salmon-Challis National Forests Supervisor's Office**, 50 Hwy. 93 S., Salmon, ID 83467, 208/756-2215, www.fs.fed.us/r4/sc.

Selway-Bitterroot Wilderness

The Magruder Road forms the northern bound-ary of the Frank Church–River of No Return Wilderness. Step across the road, over to the north side, and you'll be in the nearly contiguous Selway-Bitterroot Wilderness, another 1.3 million acres of wild preserve. Together, the two areas are bigger than Connecticut. If you're looking to get away from it all, you're in the right place.

The Selway-Bitterroot Wilderness is named after its two defining features: The Wild and Scenic Selway River—one of the state's ultimate wilderness raft trips—and its tributaries drain the southern half of the wilderness, while the ramparts of the mighty Bitterroot Range line the wilderness on the east. Within its boundaries are peaks to climb, rivers and lakes to fish, wildlife to watch, hot springs to soak in, and vast lonely horizons to clear the troubles from your mind.

Trailheads providing access to the Selway-Bitterroot Wilderness are found along Highway 12 on the north; the Selway River Road out of Lowell (FR 223) on the west; Red River Hot Springs on the southwest; and the Magruder Road on the south.

For more information about the Selway-Bitterroot Wilderness, contact the Forest Supervisor, **Nez Perce National Forest,** Rt. 2 Box 475, Grangeville, ID 83530, 208/983-1950, www.fs.fed.us/r1/nezperce, or the Forest Supervisor, **Clearwater National Forest,** 12730 Hwy. 12, Orofino, ID 83544, 208/476-4541, www.fs.fed.us/r1/clearwater.

Sawtooth Wilderness

Idaho's handsomest peaks are protected from mechanized intrusion and commercial development by the 217,000-acre Sawtooth Wilderness. Waters flowing from this wilderness feed three major Idaho rivers—the Payette, Boise, and Salmon—and the high granite walls draw rock climbers from across the country. The wilderness is part of the much larger Sawtooth National Recreation Area, which provides plenty of terrain for mountain bikers outside the wilderness boundaries.

From time to time, you'll hear the idea

AN OUTDOOR STATE OF MIND

Every so often I head for Sun Valley, Idaho, because I have friends there, and because Idaho contains large quantities of nature. The problem is that my friends are never content to sit around with a cool beverage and look at the nature from a safe distance, as nature intended. No, my friends want to go out and interact with the nature in some kind of potentially fatal way.

Dave Barry

He wasn't exaggerating. A 2003 report by the Outdoor Industry Foundation showed that Idahoans rank tops nationwide in going outside to have fun, with nearly 87 percent of state residents taking part in at least one outdoor pursuit.

Idahoans led the nation in two activities, with 32 percent taking part in single-track bike riding and 42 percent who described themselves as car campers. The state's residents ranked second in birdwatching; third in dirt road bicycling, hiking, fly-fishing, and rafting; and fourth in backcountry camping and ice climbing. Idahoans also ranked in the top third for bicycle touring (paved), canoeing, natural and artificial rock climbing, recreational and touring kayaking, cross-country skiing, and snowshoeing.

The report demonstrated Americans' insatiable desire for outdoor recreation. "It is amazing to see that as participation in outdoor recreation grows, federal support for public lands decreases," Myrna Johnson, director of Outdoor Industry Foundation's Business for Wilderness program, said when the report was released. "Outdoor recreation and all the benefits it brings the American people is entirely dependent on protecting and preserving our public lands."

Idaho's neighboring states—Wyoming, Utah, Montana, Oregon, and Washington—ranked second, third, fourth, seventh, and 14th, respectively. The West in general ranked tops for all regions, with 73 percent of the population into outdoor activities. Mississippi was in last place among the states, with just 44 percent participation.

broached to create a national park here, but the idea never gets very far. Mostly, folks figure if it ain't broke, don't fix it.

Common trailheads into the wilderness are found on the west side of Highway 75 from the Sawtooth Valley to Cape Horn and on the east side of the wilderness at Grandjean and Atlanta. For more information, contact the **Sawtooth National Recreation Area,** Headquarters Office, Star Route (Highway 75), Ketchum, ID 83340, 208/727-5000 (business) or 208/727-5013 (visitor information), www.fs.fed.us/r4/sawtooth.

Gospel-Hump Wilderness

The odd name of this preserve is an amalgam of the two high points that bracket the area: Gospel Peak on the west and Buffalo Hump on the east. Surrounding the high ridgeline between the two is a 206,000-acre wilderness closed to motor vehicles, mining, and other hallmarks of modern man. More than 200 streams and 35 lakes cover the area, making it a favorite haunt of backpacking anglers. Elevations on the wilderness range from 2,000 to almost 9,000 feet. North of the Gospel-Hump divide, the terrain is lush and densely forested. South of the divide it's drier and sparsely vegetated. Elk, deer, black bear, cougars, moose, mountain goats, and bighorn sheep will be some of the creatures watching you plod down the dusty trail.

Commonly used trailheads into the wilderness can be found out Salmon River Road, east of Riggins; at the top of Slate Creek Road (FR 354), east of Slate Creek Ranger Station off Highway 95, north of Riggins; and at the end of Buffalo Hump Road (FR 223) southwest of Orogrand, off Highway 14 near Elk City. For more information, contact the Forest Supervisor, **Nez Perce National Forest,** Rt. 2 Box 475, Grangeville, ID 83530, 208/983-1950.

Hells Canyon Wilderness

At just over 200,000 acres, Hells Canyon Wilderness is modestly sized, but it's a gem. From the floor of Hells Canyon along the banks of the Snake River, the wilderness extends up onto both rims, reaching a high point atop 9,393-foot He Devil Peak, highest peak in Idaho's Seven Devils Range. That 8,000-foot elevation differential in a relatively short distance makes for interesting hiking. At certain times of year, a hike from rim to river could find you plowing through waist-deep snow in the morning and sweltering in relentless sunshine in the afternoon. It also makes for a unique biome; several species of plants here aren't found anywhere else. For common trailheads and further information, see The Hells Canyon Corridor in the North-Central Idaho chapter.

Craters of the Moon Wilderness

Idaho's smallest wilderness area is unique. This 43,000-acre spread is covered not with high peaks, alpine lakes, and pine forests, but by vast fields of lava. The wilderness stretches south from Craters of the Moon National Monument, taking in parts of the Great Rift. Water is scarce, and temperatures on the black lava can be baking in summer. Late spring and fall are the best times for extended trips here. Most visitors begin their explorations from the national monument visitor center, where they can pick up the required permit for entry into the wilderness. For more information contact **Craters of the Moon National Monument,** P.O. Box 29, Arco, ID 83213, 208/527-3257, www.nps.gov/crmo.

STATE PARKS

Each of Idaho's 26 state parks highlights a different Idaho natural wonder. But they all feature well-kept facilities, and many offer outstanding interpretive programs. Most parks charge a $4 motor vehicle entry fee (no charge for walk-ins or bike-ins). For $25, you can buy a calendar-year pass that provides unlimited entry to all the state parks that year (it doesn't include camping fees, however, and campers must now pay the day-use fee as well); a second vehicle can be covered for just $5 more. Another pass, the $49 Visit Idaho Playgrounds (VIP) annual pass, covers admission to all the state parks plus all Park N' Ski areas, Craters of the Moon National Monument, and select Forest Service, Bureau of Land Management, and Bureau of Reclamation day-use areas. The VIP passes are good for the calendar year, with next year's passes going on sale each November. To buy one, call 800/847-4843 or go to www.idahorec.org.

Many of the parks are designed for camping. You'll generally find RV-suitable campsites with water and electric hookups for $16 a night, or water only for $12 a night. If sewer hookups are available, they cost an extra $2. An extra vehicle that can fit completely within the first site costs an extra $5. The first-rate restroom facilities are kept clean, and most parks have showers as well; noncampers can use the showers for $3. In 2003, several parks built camper cabins that sleep up to six people and rent for $35 a night. The cabins have electricity and heat, and a cooking grill outside. You'll also find larger cabins at Harriman, Heyburn, and Ponderosa, as well as year-round yurts at Harriman, Ponderosa, and Winchester State Parks. Pets are allowed on a leash at most parks but must be kept enclosed within your RV or tent at night.

Reservations are taken for some campsites and cabins; the reservation fee is $6. Call the park of your choice, or go to www.reserveamerica.com. (A link to reservable Idaho state park campsites and cabins is also available from www.idahoparks.org.) Some parks offer campsites on a first-come, first-served basis.

Following is a brief rundown on the state parks, chapter by chapter. The day-use-only parks are specified, and the rest provide campgrounds. For more information, see the listings in the corresponding chapters, or contact the **Idaho Department of Parks and Recreation,** 5657 Warm Springs Ave., P.O. Box 83720, Boise, ID 83720-0065, 208/334-4199.

Boise

Just west of town near Eagle, **Eagle Island** makes a great summer destination for the kids. It's a day-use park on the Boise River, with a water slide that'll keep the little guys busy for hours. Big lawns make for great picnicking or Frisbee golf, while the Boise River offers cool splashing and warm beaches. East of town off Highway 21, **Lucky Peak** offers day-use facilities scattered around Lucky Peak Reservoir, a popular watersports area where Boiseans go to escape the summer heat.

Southwest Idaho

South of Mountain Home, **Bruneau Dunes** shows off the country's largest single-structured sand dunes and also holds Idaho's largest observatory. Farther east, near Glenns Ferry, **Three Island Crossing** marks the spot where the Oregon Trail pioneers faced a challenging ford of the Snake River. North of Boise up Highway 55, **Cascade** features good fishing and water sports on big, beautiful Cascade Reservoir. A bit farther north in McCall, **Ponderosa** lies on a peninsula jutting out into beautiful Payette Lake. This must-see park is covered with massive ponderosa pine trees and offers plenty of hiking and biking trails through woods and past meadows.

South-Central Idaho

Right off I-84 east of Bliss, **Malad Gorge** day-use park highlights geology in action. The Malad River thunders down through the narrow gorge, slowly eroding away the volcanic canyon walls. Down the highway near Wendell is primitive **Box Canyon** State Park, which protects a huge natural spring and a gorgeous wildlife-filled canyon. A new park, **Billingsley Creek,** in the Hagerman Valley, is a great place to see wildlife. At **Niagara Springs/Crystal Springs** near Buhl, the Snake River Plain Aquifer gushes forth from the lava. Northeast of Rupert, **Lake Walcott** offers camping, fishing, and easy access to good birding at nearby Minidoka National Wildlife Refuge. Near the Utah border between Oakley and Almo, the state shares management of **City of Rocks National Reserve** with the

National Park Service. It's a historic spot, but the big draw now is rock climbing, as it is at the new **Castle Rocks.**

Southeast Idaho

Between Rupert and American Falls off I-86, **Massacre Rocks** combines history, geology, scenic beauty, and a fantastic interpretive program in one neat package. Don't miss it. Way down in the southeasternmost corner of the state, **Bear Lake** State Park is relatively primitive, but right on the shores of the beautiful turquoise-blue lake. No showers or interpretive programs. North of Ashton on the way to West Yellowstone, Montana, you'll pass **Harriman,** offering great hiking, cross-country skiing, and up-close looks at endangered trumpeter swans; and **Henry's Lake,** an angler's favorite.

The High Country

Sawtooth National Recreation Area takes up much of the public land in this chapter's area, but the state chips in with the unique **Land of the Yankee Fork** State Park, between Challis and Sunbeam off Highway 75. The day-use interpretive park has ghost town sites and a visitors center that detail the mining operations that once were the focus of life here.

North-Central Idaho

On the Camas Prairie between Lewiston and Grangeville, **Winchester Lake** is a small but peaceful park offering fishing, hiking, and—when the snow's deep enough—cross-country skiing. In Lewiston, **Hells Gate** lies at the lower gateway to Hells Canyon. Some rafters take out here, and jetboaters often use the park marina to begin their sorties up into the famous canyon. East of Lewiston, near Orofino, **Dworshak** lies on the shore of Dworshak Reservoir, offering a great place to ditch the family while you boat off in search of piscatorial pleasure.

Just north of Moscow, off the west side of Highway 95, the day-use **McCroskey** State Park offers great views and very few people. Farther north, **Heyburn** is the oldest and largest of Idaho's state parks, not counting the enormous, jointly run City of Rocks. The park guards the southern reaches of Coeur d'Alene Lake. No entrance fee is charged.

The Panhandle

Coeur d'Alene Parkway is a greenbelt along the north shore of Lake Coeur d'Alene. **Coeur d'Alene's Old Mission,** east of Coeur d'Alene off I-90, preserves the beautiful mission built by Jesuit priests and indigenous Coeur d'Alene people in the early 1850s. It's also the headquarters of the new **Trail of the Coeur d'Alenes,** a 72-mile paved path that crosses the Panhandle from Mullan to Plummer. The 4,000-acre **Farrugut** State Park lies on the southwest shore of Pend Oreille Lake, on the site of a WWII–era naval base. Troops once trained here for duty in submarines, and the lake is still used for submarine research and development. South of Sandpoint, **Round Lake** is a small park perfect for a leisurely afternoon of fishing, or a quick cross-country-ski workout in winter. Finally, up in the Panhandle's northwest corner, **Priest Lake** offers three different units around the lake of the same name. Wildlife abounds, the scenery is magnificent, and the crowds are minimal to nonexistent.

NATIONAL FORESTS

Idaho encompasses all or part of 13 different national forests, which together cover most of the state. So it's no surprise that national forest campgrounds are the most numerous of any type in Idaho. The big, popular ones with developed drinking water sources are usually managed by private companies under contract with the Forest Service. At these campgrounds, you'll typically find a campground host who keeps the place picked up and collects fees from campers. Fees commonly run $11–13 per site per night for up to two vehicles. Some of these campgrounds are on a **central reservation system;** make reservations for these campgrounds by calling ReserveAmerica's National Recreation Reservation Service (NRRS), 877/444-6777, or reserve on the Web at www.reserveusa.com. The reservation fee is a steep $9. For a complete list of USFS campgrounds in Idaho (which also specifies which campgrounds are reservable), call the USFS Intermountain Region office in Ogden, Utah, at 801/625-5306.

Other, free Forest Service campgrounds are scattered throughout the state. These are usually found in less popular or more remote areas either too small for practical fee collection or lacking potable water. At these campsites, you'll usually find an outhouse, picnic tables, and fire rings or grills, but you'll often be on your own for drinkable water. As a good many of these campgrounds are found along lakes or streams, this is not much of a problem for anyone with a water filter.

At most USFS campgrounds, you are permitted to stay a maximum of 14 days at one spot before moving on. Some have shorter stay limitations. Many campgrounds charge fees only during the summer and are free the rest of the year. These won't be plowed in winter, however, and any piped water supplies will be shut off.

One other Forest Service option is available: rental guard stations and lookout towers. Air surveillance today has largely replaced the staffed lookouts, so the Forest Service offers the buildings to the public as backcountry accommodations. Almost by definition, these will have terrific views and be ensconced in remote and wild landscapes. The rentals are by and large primitive, and sleep anywhere from a pair of cozy friends to a whole college football team. Many are accessible only on skis or snowmobiles in winter. For more information, see the individual listings found throughout the book.

BLM LANDS

Most of the 12 million acres of BLM land in Idaho are found on and around the Snake River Plain in the southern portion of the state. BLM campgrounds are generally free, primitive, minimally maintained, and minimally used. Depending on your perspective, that could be good or bad. They tend to be near areas offering recreation opportunities, like rivers, lakes, remote hiking areas. The BLM maintains a number of district offices in Idaho; for more information, see Internet Resources.

ON THE ROAD

SUMMER SPORTS

Whitewater Rafting and Kayaking

Idaho ranks as king of the lower 48 states when it comes to wild whitewater, boasting about 1,000 more whitewater miles than runner-up California. The Snake River through Hells Canyon, the Salmon River and its Middle Fork, and the Lochsa, Selway, and Payette are the state's most notorious rivers. The Snake and the main Salmon offer big-water thrills; the Lochsa and Payette offer challenging runs through narrower gorges; and Middle Fork and the Selway provide a wilderness experience par excellence. Many more rivers await Idaho's whitewater enthusiasts, however, ranging from the remote desert canyon run of the Jarbidge near the Nevada border to the lushly forested run of the Moyie near the Canadian border.

If you go with a commercial guide service, you won't need to worry about a permit. Otherwise, you must obtain a permit from the Forest Service for private, noncommercial trips on the Middle Fork of the Salmon, the main Salmon, the upper Selway, and the Snake River through Hells Canyon. Only a limited number of permits, awarded through the Four Rivers Lottery, are issued each season. You need to fill out an application form, available October 1 for the next summer, and get it in between December 1 and January 31 for the following season. You can specify your preferred rivers and launch dates. For Middle Fork permits, contact the **Middle Fork Ranger District,** Hwy. 93 N., P.O. Box 750, Challis, ID 83226, 208/879-4101; for main Salmon permits, contact **North Fork Ranger District,** Hwy. 93, P.O. Box 780, North Fork, ID 83466-0180, 208/865-2725; for Selway permits, contact the **West Fork Ranger District,** 6735 West Fork Rd., Darby, MT 59829, 406/821-3269; for Snake permits, contact **Hells Canyon National Recreation Area,** P.O. Box 699, Clarkston, WA 99403, 509/758-1957. Applications can also be downloaded online at www.fs.fed.us/r4/sc/recreation/4rivers.htm, but you must mail or fax them in before January 31.

Other Water Sports

With lakes and reservoirs scattered from one end of the state to the other, you'll never be too far from **water-skiing** and **windsurfing.** Especially popular for the latter are the windy reservoirs of the Snake River Plain, notably American Falls Reservoir and Lake Walcott. Others take their boards up to Redfish Lake in the Sawtooths, where the winds can be erratic but the views are world-class. In the state's southeastern corner, Bear Lake is popular with water-skiers, as are Lakes Coeur d'Alene and Pend Oreille in the Panhandle, and Payette Lake at McCall. **Sailing** is best on Payette, Coeur d'Alene, and Pend Oreille Lakes. **Scuba diving** is a limited proposition in Idaho; check out Brownlee Reservoir in spring. It's on the Snake River west of Cambridge.

Mountain Biking

For mountain bikers, Idaho is nirvana. Look at all that national forest land, with all those national forest roads ripe for the pedaling. Yes, mountain biking's big up here, virtually everywhere. Here are some suggestions for places to try.

In Boise, the **Boise Front** is practically right behind the state capitol — head out 8th Street and just keep going. At **Bogus Basin,** ride up the hill and take off on the forest roads.

If you're in southwest Idaho and ready for multiday solitude, head for the **Owyhee County Backcountry Byway;** if you'd rather go out for the day and come back to a brew, head up to McCall and explore the **Payette National Forest** or the lift-served trails at **Brundage Mountain.**

In the south-central area, head southwest from Twin Falls to the **South Hills** for high and scenic biking; or for a quick jaunt close to town, explore the **Snake River Rim Recreation Area** on the north side of the Snake River, heading east from Perrine Bridge.

There's lots to choose from in the southeast. The **Mink Creek** trails outside Pocatello make for a good workout; or try the lift-served biking at **Grand Targhee.**

The high country is total mountain biker heaven. Just about anywhere in the **Wood River Valley,** you'll find dirt roads heading off into the mountains. Or cross over Galena Summit and bike into the **White Cloud Peaks,** an airy realm of sheer craggy summits and wildflower-filled meadows.

INTERNATIONAL SCALE OF RIVER DIFFICULTY

Class I: Very Easy. Small regular waves and riffles. Few or no obstructions. Little maneuvering required.

Class II: Easy. Waves up to three feet. Wide, clear channels that are obvious without scouting. Low ledges; small rock gardens. Some maneuvering required.

Class III: Medium. Rapids with numerous high, irregular waves capable of swamping an open canoe. Strong eddies. Narrow passages that often require complex maneuvering. May require scouting from shore.

Class IV: Difficult. Long difficult rapids with powerful, irregular waves, dangerous rocks, boiling eddies, and constricted passages that require precise maneuvering in very turbulent waters. Scouting from shore is necessary and conditions make rescue difficult. Generally not possible for open canoes. Boaters in covered canoes and kayaks should be able to Eskimo roll.

Class V: Very Difficult. Long, violent rapids with wild turbulence and highly congested routes that must be scouted from shore. Rescue conditions are difficult and there is significant hazard to life in event of a mishap. Ability to Eskimo roll is essential for paddlers in kayaks and covered canoes.

Class VI: The Limits of Navigation. Difficulties of Class V carried to the extreme limits of navigability. Nearly impossible and very dangerous. For teams of experts only, after close study and with all precautions taken. Rarely run and a definite hazard to your life.

If water temperature is below 50°F, or if the trip is an extended trip into a wilderness area, the river should be considered one class more difficult than normal.

rafting on the Middle Fork of the Salmon River in central Idaho

ON THE ROAD

In the north-central area, **McCroskey State Park** north of Moscow is a little-known state park used more by mountain bikers than by cars. The park offers sweeping views of the Palouse. When you're done there, head east to Harvard and up into the **Palouse Range,** where mighty forests of white pine once covered the land and where you still might ride past a big tree or two.

For Panhandle biking, first try the **Route of the Hiawatha** near Lookout Pass, for thrills negotiating the tunnels and trestles of an abandoned railroad grade. After that, head for **Priest Lake,** where you can ride from the northwest edge of the lake all the way to Canada if you'd like.

Road Biking

Although many Idaho roads are narrow, with little or no shoulder, paved trails are popping up all over. The **Boise River Greenbelt** offers a beautiful traffic-free path long enough to give the average cyclist a workout. The **Wood River Valley** makes the list, for its extensive network of bike paths. The **Palouse,** east of Moscow, offers gently rolling terrain and bucolic vistas around Princeton, Harvard, Deary, and Bovill. But the best road-biking experience of all is the 72-mile **Trail of the Coeur d'Alenes,** a recent rails-to-trails conversion that is tied with Minnesota's Willard Munger State Trail for the longest continuous paved bikeway in North America. It crosses the Idaho Panhandle from Mullan in the east to Plummer in the west.

Fishing

You'll need to purchase an Idaho state fishing license before you head out to try your luck. Idaho residents pay $23.50 adults, $12.50 youths 14–17. Nonresident anglers pay $74.50 for a season, or $10.50 for the first day, $4 each additional consecutive day. You can get a license at sporting goods stores, many convenience stores, or any office of the Idaho Department of Fish and Game.

Old fly-fishers never die, they just find heaven in Idaho at **Silver Creek,** in south-central Idaho, and at **Henry's Fork** and the **South Fork Snake** in the southeast. Fishing lodges in these parts are sometimes booked years in advance. Mean-

while, the Rambo types among the angling crowd prefer to wrestle the enormous, primeval-looking **sturgeon,** which inhabits the lower Snake River. Others find **steelhead** fishing on the Clearwater River to hold the biggest thrills.

To find out up-to-the-minute information on the fishing conditions in various parts of Idaho, you need only pick up the phone and dial **800/ASK-FISH** (800/275-3474). The state is one of many in the country that participate in this fishing-information hotline system, which is offered by the Sportsfishing Promotion Council and funded by the Sportfish Restoration Fund. A small percentage of the sales price of fishing tackle, motorboat fuel, and fish finders goes to the fund. The recorded hotline information will tell you all you'll ever want to know, and maybe even more. For example, anglers up in the Panhandle might or might not enjoy knowing that the region's abundant perch are biting on "Swedish pimples bathed with maggots, cut bait, or perch eyes." Yum. Information is also available on licensing and regulations.

For more information, contact the **Idaho Department of Fish and Game,** 600 S. Walnut St., P.O. Box 25, Boise, ID 83707, 208/334-3700, www2.state.id.us/fishgame.

Golfing

At last count, Idaho held about 100 golf courses. Many courses in southwest Idaho and south-central Idaho stay open year-round. Linksters will find many modest, nine-hole courses in small towns throughout the state, as well as several world-class megacourses. Among the most impressive courses are the Robert Trent Jones Jr. courses in the Sun Valley area and the luxurious Coeur d'Alene Resort course with its novel floating green. Statewide, prices range from around $12 to well over $100 a round.

Hiking and Backpacking

With all that public land at their disposal, hikers will find no shortage of trails to explore. Start with the wilderness areas for a pristine experience free from exhaust fumes and chain saws. For sheer scenic beauty, it's hard to top **Sawtooth Wilderness,** which offers peaks and lakes galore. Nevertheless, the **Hells Canyon Wilderness,** with its exquisitely beautiful Seven Devils Range, gives the Sawtooths a run for their money. If you really want to get lost for a couple of weeks, head out into the vast **Frank Church–River of No Return Wilderness** or the adjacent **Selway-Bitterroot Wilderness.** Both take you about as far from the madding crowd as you can get in the state.

Those looking for the ultimate Idaho trek can attempt the 1,200-mile **Idaho Centennial Trail,** which runs the length of the state, south to north. The trail starts near Murphy Hot Springs on the Nevada border and follows the Jarbidge and Bruneau Rivers north, crossing I-84 near Glenns Ferry. It works its way into the Sawtooths, then traverses both the Frank Church and Selway-Bitterroot Wildernesses, crossing Highway 12 near the Lochsa Historical Ranger Station. From there it bears east to the high Bitterroots, following the Continental Divide along the Idaho-Montana border for a time, before sliding off the divide to head west into the Cabinet Mountains and over to Priest Lake. At Priest Lake, the trail makes a short hop, skip, and jump north to the Canadian border. Signage of the trail is nearing completion; for more information, contact the **Idaho Department of Parks and Recreation,** 5657 Warm Springs Ave., P.O. Box 83720, Boise, ID 83720-0065, 208/334-4199.

Backpackers should be prepared to shell out fees for parking at some trailheads. The USFS has been experimenting with the user-fee system, so its status is not yet permanent. But then, do fees ever stop once they're started? At many trailheads on the Sawtooth National Forest, one-week passes ($5) or annual passes ($15) have been required. Passes are generally available from ranger stations and trailhead-area merchants.

Horsepacking and Horseback Riding

If backpacking seems like too much work and you'd rather hire horses to haul you and your load, you'll find a number of guide services in the state offering horsepacking trips. The **Sawtooth National Recreation Area** is a focal point for the Idaho horsepacking businesses, although trips are available in all parts of the state.

If you don't know how to communicate with Old Paint, you might consider spending a week learning to ride at one of Idaho's numerous guest ranches. It's hard to beat the programs offered by **Hidden Creek Ranch,** 11077 E. Blue Lake Rd., Harrison, ID 83833, 208/689-3209 or 800/446-3833. Dozens of others can do the job as well. For other options and information, contact the **Idaho Outfitters and Guides Association,** P.O. Box 95, Boise, ID 83701, 208/342-1919 or 800/847-4843.

Hot Springs

Thanks to its geology, Idaho is blessed with more hot springs by far than any other state in the West. The lion's share lie in the state's central mountains, in an area bounded roughly by Highways 12 and 20 on the north and south, and Highways 95 and 93 on the west and east. No matter what your style—developed or primitive, clothing-mandatory or clothing-optional, easy access or remote—you'll find a hot spring here to suit you. Many of the springs taunt the nose with that characteristic sulfur smell; many do not. True hot-springs believers come to appreciate the smell and can follow their nose to hot-soaking delights.

> *Thanks to its geology, Idaho is blessed with more hot springs by far than any other state in the West.*

The best developed family hot springs in Idaho is the state run **Lava Hot Springs** resort, in the laid-back little resort town of Lava Hot Springs, southeast of Pocatello. The facility is immaculate, the setting beautiful, and the fumes sulfur-free. My vote for a middle-of-the-road hot springs resort, developed but rustic, goes to **Burgdorf Hot Springs,** outside McCall. Here you can soak in a sand-bottomed pool, stay in a rustic old pioneer's cabin, and watch elk feed under the stars. For a personal spiritual retreat, head for **Murphy Hot Springs.** Whatever problems you have in your life will seem trivial when you tap into the power of the universe out here. It's remote, quiet, magical—out in the middle of nowhere in Owyhee County. If your head is in the right space, Murphy Hot Springs can't be beat.

ON THE ROAD

Idaho holds so many undeveloped natural hot springs, it's beyond the scope of this book to describe each and every one. Whole books are devoted to the topic (see Suggested Reading). A couple of favorites: **Chattanooga Hot Springs** in Atlanta, and **Elk Bend Hot Springs,** south of Salmon off Highway 93. The award for the most social natural hot springs goes to **Jerry Johnson Hot Springs,** off Highway 12 east of Lowell. You'll just about always find good conversation with your soaking companions here.

Rock Climbing and Mountaineering

Rock jocks will find world-class climbing centers at **City of Rocks/Castle Rocks** in south-central Idaho, a massive area of rock towers up to 600 feet high; in the **Sawtooth Range,** on sheer granite spires and big-wall faces; and in the Panhandle's **Selkirk Range,** which climbers share with grizzlies and woodland caribou.

Mountain ranges literally cover most of the state. There's no end to the peak-bagging possibilities. Highest peak in the state is **Borah Peak,** elevation 12,662, in the Lost River Range near Mackay. It's an easy Class 2–3 climb, but airy in places; it makes a comfortable solo for the experienced mountaineer and a great place to take your neophyte partner for his or her first big summit. Borah isn't a particularly impressive peak to look at, but others in the range are.

Ketchum, in close proximity to the Soldiers, Smokies, Pioneers, Boulders, Sawtooths, and White Clouds, is the hub of a strong mountaineering scene. The area holds enough peaks to keep you busy well into your next life. Among the biggest: **Castle Peak** in the White Clouds tops out at 11,815 feet; **Hyndman Peak** in the Pioneers juts up into the thin air at 12,009 feet.

WINTER SPORTS

Alpine Skiing

In a state with so many mountains, ski resorts are understandably ubiquitous. Sixteen alpine ski areas dot the state, from Magic Mountain in the extreme south to Schweitzer Mountain in the extreme north. Powderhounds should take Idaho's climatology into consideration; for better powder, go higher or drier. The best powder skiing in the state isn't even in the state but just across the border in Wyoming at **Grand Targhee,** accessible only through Driggs, Idaho. Here, continental weather patterns produce colder, drier storms than the maritime-influenced storms of the more northerly and westerly resorts.

Sun Valley is the West's oldest, grandest ski resort, offering a zillion fast lifts up a big mountain and luxurious pampering at every turn. It's also the state's priciest resort. **Schweitzer Mountain** outside Sandpoint, **Silver Mountain** at Kellogg, **Brundage Mountain,** near McCall, and **Bogus Basin** outside Boise are medium-size areas offering lots of fun skiing at reasonable prices. Schweitzer enjoys a beautiful base lodge/hotel; Silver Mountain boasts the world's longest gondola; Brundage offers some of the best kids' facilities in the state and the liveliest ski-town atmosphere; and Bogus Basin has killer night skiing. Downhill skiing debuts in 2004–05 at **Tamarack,** a major new resort near the town of Donnelly.

Smaller than those resorts, but offering good skiing at a budget price, are several locals-oriented areas, including **Pomerelle, Soldier Mountain,** and **Magic Mountain** (South-Central); **Pebble Creek, Kelly Canyon,** and **Lost Trail Powder Mountain** (Southeast); and **Lookout Pass** (Panhandle).

Rounding out the list are three T-bar-and-rope-tow sorts of places where you can slide around for a pittance—if there's any snow on the ground, and if anyone's around to run the place. All tend to have short seasons and tend to be open only on weekends. These resorts are **Bald Mountain, Cottonwood Butte,** and **Snowhaven** (all North-Central).

Snowcat Skiing and Heli-Skiing

Snowcats—large tracked vehicles that can paddle their way over and through the snow—can haul a number of skiers up the powdery slopes to steep, untracked bowls. Brundage Mountain, Grand Targhee, and Soldier Mountain all offer this service. **Sun Valley Heli-Ski,** 260 1st Ave. N. in Ketchum, P.O. Box 978, Sun Valley, ID 83353, 208/622-3108 or 800/872-3108, offers the ultimate skier fantasy—a chopper flight to virgin powder on untracked backcountry peaks and bowls.

Nordic Skiing

Across the state, from Boise to Bonners Ferry, you'll find **Park N' Ski areas** established by the Idaho Department of Parks and Recreation. To use the Park N' Ski areas, you must first buy a permit, which costs $25 for an entire season or $7.50 for a three-day permit. Theoretically, this is supposed to get you plowed trailhead parking and groomed trails. But grooming can be sketchy at some areas. For more information on the Park N'

Ski areas, contact the Idaho Department of Parks and Recreation, 5657 Warm Springs Ave., P.O. Box 83720, Boise, ID 83720-0065, 208/334-4199, www.idahoparks.org/rec/ccskiing.html.

Most of Idaho's privately operated Nordic areas offer well-groomed trails—many absolutely immaculate—for about $10 a day. Best of the bunch: McCall's **Little Ski Hill; Grand Targhee;** and the crème de la crème, **Galena Lodge.**

In a class by themselves are the public/private partnership **Wood River Valley** trails. Two separate systems in the lower and upper parts of the valley offer a vast network of meticulously groomed trails. The lower valley system is free, courtesy of Blaine County. The North Valley trails require a $9 daily permit (or $25 a week, $80 a season), which is easily worth three times as much. The North Valley system culminates in the trails at Galena Lodge, the ultimate intimate cross-county skiers' chalet.

Snowshoeing

Most of the state's Nordic areas welcome snowshoers, too. Just be careful not to step on the groomed tracks. But the great thing about snowshoeing is you don't need a trail—you can just set off across any snowy patch of land. Some ski areas and other parklands offer guided snowshoe treks, which can be a great way to learn animal tracks and other winter ecology.

Yurts

Nordic skiers who'd like to combine two days of cross-country skiing with an overnight stay in the backcountry will find several comfortable yurt systems in Idaho's mountains. Among them: the **Portneuf Range** yurts near Pocatello, reserved through Idaho State University's Wilderness Rental Center, 208/282-2945; the **Sawtooth Range** yurts near

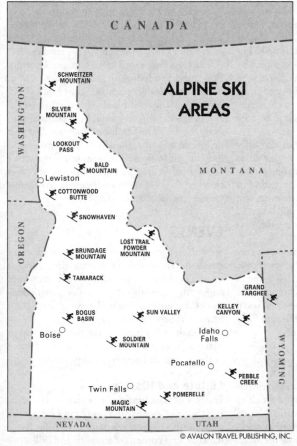

ALPINE SKI AREAS

CANADA

SCHWEITZER MOUNTAIN

SILVER MOUNTAIN

LOOKOUT PASS

BALD MOUNTAIN

Lewiston

COTTONWOOD BUTTE

SNOWHAVEN

LOST TRAIL POWDER MOUNTAIN

BRUNDAGE MOUNTAIN

TAMARACK

GRAND TARGHEE

BOGUS BASIN

SUN VALLEY

KELLEY CANYON

Boise

SOLDIER MOUNTAIN

Idaho Falls

Pocatello

PEBBLE CREEK

Twin Falls

POMERELLE

MAGIC MOUNTAIN

WASHINGTON

OREGON

MONTANA

WYOMING

NEVADA

UTAH

© AVALON TRAVEL PUBLISHING, INC.

ON THE ROAD

Stanley, reserved through one of the local guide services such as Sawtooth Mountain Guides, 208/774-3324; and the **Galena Lodge** yurts high in the Boulder Mountains, reserved through Galena Lodge, 208/726-4010.

Ice Fishing

Some guys'll do anything to get out of the house—like bundle up in more layers than they can possibly move in, go outside in the dead of winter when it's roughly a thousand below zero, cut a hole in a frozen lake, and drop a line for perch. Perch! Yeesh.

In any case, popular ice-fishing holes include just about any lake with a surface that freezes sufficiently solid in winter, among them **Cascade Lake** at Cascade and **Cocolalla Lake** south of Sandpoint.

Arts and Entertainment

PERFORMING ARTS

Boise's not exactly New York City, but it is home to the excellent **Boise Philharmonic, Boise Opera, Boise Master Chorale,** and **Ballet Idaho,** as well as the premier **Idaho Shakespeare Festival.** In addition to performances by those groups, the city's comedy club, rock 'n' roll clubs, country-music emporiums, and small (but growing) jazz scene make for an entertainment calendar busy enough to satisfy all but the most ardent city-dweller.

Most of Idaho's other major cities also offer community orchestras, and both major cities and many small towns harbor community theater groups. The quality is usually first-rate, and what you lose in cutting-edge talent and training, you more than make up for in down-home heart. In Idaho, people take pride in performing for their friends and neighbors.

Look for plentiful student performances and active nightlife scenes at Idaho's college towns: Boise, home of Boise State University; Moscow, home of the University of Idaho; and Pocatello, home of Idaho State University. On those campuses, you'll likely find a film club screening great foreign films and independent fare at budget prices.

VISUAL ARTS AND CRAFTS

Mountain landscapes, wildlife, and Western themes dominate the subject matter of much of the state's two-dimensional artwork. Native American crafts—beadwork and leatherwork, primarily—are also widespread across the state.

Visitors to the big Shoshone Bannock Indian Festival and Rodeo, at Fort Hall the second week in August, will be faced with an enormous array of craftworks to choose from. Also watch for the superb Thousand Springs Festival in the Hagerman Valley the last weekend of September.

The biggest art towns in the state are Ketchum, Boise, and Sandpoint, in that order. Ketchum is a gallery prowler's paradise; some blocks have several galleries, all filled with quality work. Boise's galleries run the gamut from traditional to avant-garde, while Sandpoint's venues display a delightful mix of regionally famous artists and local hopefuls. **Boise Art Museum** is the state's premier public art repository. The museum hosts traveling shows of merit and houses a respectable permanent collection.

EVENTS

Something's going on somewhere in Idaho every weekend, year-round. If you're traveling through an area of the state and want to find out what's happening, consult the particular travel chapters of this book; many major events have been listed in the appropriate city sections.

If, on the other hand, you're planning a trip to Idaho around a big event, here's a list of some of the biggest and best events, by activity.

Culture and History

Festival of San Inazio: Boise, last weekend in July. Boise's Basque community pulls out all the stops for this cultural celebration; look for food, dancing, and contests of strength and skill.

Three Island Crossing Reenactment: Glenns Ferry, second weekend in August. Watch wagons, cowboys, and oxen ford the Snake River in a recreation of the historic Oregon Trail crossing.

Shoshone Bannock Indian Festival and Rodeo: Fort Hall, second week of August. One of the biggest powwows in the West, drawing Native Americans and visitors from all over the continent for dancing, drumming, rodeo, and arts and crafts.

Music

Lionel Hampton Jazz Festival: Moscow, late February. How can this many jazz masters show up in one place at the same time? Don't miss it.

National Oldtime Fiddlers' Contest: Weiser, third full week of June. The finest fiddlers in the country compete, and a party atmosphere prevails day and night.

Festival at Sandpoint: Sandpoint, late July through mid-August. Performances by big-name jazz entertainers, many outdoors by the lake, along with street dances and a fun crowd.

Rodeo

Dodge National Circuit Finals Rodeo: Pocatello, mid-March. All the big names show up for the country's second-largest points-qualifying rodeo.

Snake River Stampede: Nampa, mid-July. A venerable southwest Idaho institution and one of the country's top 25 rodeos, this one draws upwards of 40,000 spectators.

Caldwell Night Rodeo: Caldwell, mid-

August. My inside source says the Snake River Stampede may be bigger, but this one is the most rip-roarin' fun.

Sports

Boulder Mountain Nordic Ski Classic: Ketchum, early February. Idaho's biggest Nordic ski race, held on the Wood River Valley's magnificent Boulder Mountain Trail.

Race to Robie Creek: Boise, mid-April. Thousands of legs thrash madly up and over Adalpe Summit in the Northwest's toughest half-marathon.

Sun Valley Ice Show: Sun Valley, mid-June through September. All the big names perform on the ice at the ritzy Sun Valley Lodge.

Payette Whitewater Roundup: Banks, July. Idaho's largest kayak competition features scores of brightly colored boats and competitors from all across the country.

General Fun

Winter Carnival: McCall, late January or early February. The state's funnest winter carnival in the state's funnest town—snow monsters, ice sculptures, sleigh rides, and a parade.

Western Days: Twin Falls, early June. Downhome festival with one of Idaho's biggest parades, a carnival, food booths, and music.

Summer Fest: Driggs, July 4 weekend. Brightly colored balloons speckle the sky with the Tetons in the background. How scenic can you get?

Accommodations and Food

HOTELS

The list of top-drawer luxury hotels in Idaho is short. **Coeur d'Alene Resort** perennially shows up on *Condé Nast Traveler*'s Gold List of the country's best lodgings. Its over-the-top amenities include a golf course with a floating green and a penthouse suite with a glass-bottomed swimming pool. **Sun Valley Lodge** boasts a blue-blood heritage, and renovations have kept the posh, upper-crust atmosphere alive and well.

Boise offers a few quality hotel options: the **Owyhee Plaza** and **Statehouse Inn** have a bit more class than the chains. The **Grove Hotel** is another option—it enjoys a great location, but suffers from inexplicably thoughtless design.

MOTELS

By far the greatest number of Idaho lodgings fall into this category. Chain lodgings dominate all but the lowest end of the price spectrum. Prices

and amenities vary widely from chain to chain and are usually directly proportionate to price. You pretty much get what you pay for.

The beauty of staying at one of the links in a motel chain is that you always know what to expect. While minor variations may exist between one Motel 6 and the next, the old saying, "if you've seen one, you've seen them all," is close enough to the truth. Another benefit of staying at a chain is that all have centralized reservations systems, accessed by one toll-free telephone call.

Idaho is primarily a rural state, and most chains have locations only in larger cities; don't go looking for a Hilton in Grangeville or Tendoy. Rates are generally highest during summer's peak travel season and lowest between Labor Day and the Christmas holiday season. Motels in resort ski towns usually have twin peak seasons: summer tourist season and Jan.–Feb. peak ski season. Some of the chains commonly found in Idaho are listed below, along with their toll-free numbers.

Low-Priced Chain
Motel 6, 800/4MOTEL6 (800/466-8356), www.motel6.com, holds down the low-priced end

PROVIDED BY THE COEUR D'ALENE RESORT

the award-winning Coeur d'Alene Resort

of the national-chain spectrum. Many Idaho locations are now about $50–55 in summer, a bit less the rest of the year. Count on your room to be Amish-ly plain but spotlessly clean—no dust bunnies under the bed, torn window screens, or moldy grout in the shower. Likewise, no plush terrycloth robes, mini-shampoos, or room service. The single, thin blanket on each bed will probably be sufficient for you most of the year, but if you're traveling in winter, you'll want to ask for a couple of additional ones. Towels are also thin, just substantial enough to do the job, but no more. Rooms are small but not cramped, and the bathrooms all have showers but no tubs. All locations offer free local calls, no motel service charge on long-distance calls, and color TV with HBO and ESPN. Nonsmoking rooms are available, kids 17 and under traveling with an adult family member are free, and AARP members get 10 percent off. All the Idaho locations have seasonal swimming pools. Not a bad deal, all things considered. You'll find Motel 6s in Boise, Coeur d'Alene, Idaho Falls, Pocatello/Chubbuck, and Twin Falls.

Medium-Priced Chains
All the **Super 8 Motels,** 800/800-8000, www .super8.com, offer complimentary morning coffee, alarm clocks or wake-up calls, and some nonsmoking rooms. Other amenities vary from location to location. Rates are usually in the $50–75 range.

The Sleep Inn, Comfort Inn, Quality Inn, and Clarion Inn chains are all owned by Choice Hotels International, www.choicehotels.com. At all, most rooms are in the $50–100 range; rooms can be reserved at 800/4CHOICE or www.choicehotels.com. The **Sleep Inn** chain is the budget choice among the four. Amenities include credit card–style room keys, two-story lobbies, data ports for computers and fax machines, coffee bars with complimentary coffee and doughnuts and *USA Today* newspapers, and adequately sized, clean, and pleasant (if a bit institutional) rooms. **Comfort Inns** offer much the same style and amenities as Sleep Inns, and add a complimentary deluxe continental breakfast. **Quality Inns** are a step up, usually offering pools, on-site restaurants, complimentary full breakfasts, and other extras. **Clarion Hotels** 800/CLARION (800/252-7466) are the upscale motels in the group. Members of the Choice group are found throughout Idaho. Choice Hotels also include the Econolodge and Rodeway chains, which tend to have fewer amenities but lower rates, too. Econolodge properties often rival Motel 6 for the lowest chain-motel rates in town.

Holiday Inn Express, 800/HOLIDAY (800/465-4329), www.hiexpress.com, is another popular choice in the midprice category, with most rooms priced $55–95 and one of the best breakfast buffets in the business. Other chains with Idaho locations and rates near the top of the medium price range include Hampton Inn, Fairfield Inn, and Courtyard by Marriott.

High-End Chains

At this level, you'll find noticeably larger rooms, full-service amenities, and good locations. Rates will usually be in the $80–130 range. **Shilo Inns,** 800/222-2244, www.shiloinns.com, are generally well-kept, though quality varies; some fit more in the midrange category in both price and ambience. **Red Lion Hotels,** 800/RED-LION (800/733-5466), www.westcoasthotels.com, likewise have some deluxe properties among their nine Idaho hotels (Lewiston is a good example), and others that are more moderate in price and style. **Holiday Inns,** 800/HOLIDAY (800/465-4329), feature prime real estate, swimming pools, and on-site restaurants. The region's nicest chain is probably the **Ameritel Inns,** 800/600-6001, www.ameritelinns.com, with seven amenity-filled locations. Prices and quality are both on the high side.

Best Westerns

The Best Western group of lodgings, 800/528-1234, www.bestwestern.com, isn't really a chain so much as a co-op. It's an association of independently owned and operated lodgings that have voluntarily joined together for marketing purposes. To be a member lodging, each establishment must conform to certain standards. Membership entitles the establishment to the benefits of national marketing, use of the Best Western name, and the Best Western–logoed wrappers around those little bars of soap.

Locations are more numerous and widespread than with the true chains, and prices vary more widely. But the minimum standards keep the risk of a bad experience low, and you might appreciate the variety in character from one to the next—they're not cookie-cutter accommodations. As with the chains, the consumer also gets the advantage of the centralized toll-free reservations line, listed above.

HOSTELS

Hostels provide dorm-style accommodations and, usually, shared use of cooking facilities for very low prices. You lose a bit of privacy in the deal, but gain the opportunity to meet new people and make new friends. Idaho currently has three Hostelling International–affiliated hostels: one on the outskirts of Boise, in Nampa; another in the tiny way-north-Idaho town of Naples; and the Lucky 13 Guest Ranch & Guest House, which opened for business in 2003 near Salmon and North Fork.

GUEST RANCHES AND FISHING LODGES

Most of Idaho's 20 or so guest ranches provide a bit of Old Western adventure with their accommodations. Typically rustic and remote, these lodgings put an emphasis on outdoor activities such as fishing, hunting, swimming, and horseback riding. Rates are usually based on stays of a week and generally include all meals and recreation. Some are working ranches; some operate summers only, while others are open year-round.

Also usually offering weeklong packages, but replacing horseback activities with guided fishing, are Idaho's numerous fishing lodges. Most of these are found along the Henry's Fork and the South Fork Snake River in southeast Idaho.

Many guest ranches and fishing lodges are members of the Idaho Outfitters & Guides Association, P.O. Box 95, Boise, ID 83701, 208/342-1919, www.ioga.org. Contact the association for more information.

ON THE ROAD

RURAL BAR ETIQUETTE

Idaho has a great many rural taverns frequented by local ranchers, farmers, and loggers who consider it their moral obligation (and good fun) to test the mettle of any stranger who walks in the door. Generally speaking, the smaller the town, the more difficult this test will be. Upon entering, all conversations will cease and all eyes will turn upon you. If you give yourself away as a city slicker, an environmentalist, a Californian, or—god forbid—all three, you fail. If you come off as just one of the guys, passing through town on a hay-hauling trip from Leadore to Grasmere, you pass. With practice, you should be able to pass at least long enough to down a brew or two and be on your way. Here are some handy tips to help you get through those first awkward moments after you walk in the door:

• Always wear a baseball cap. The cap here is not considered an article of clothing so much as a part of the head. Therefore, it is not necessary to remove it when you enter the bar. It should be worn forwards, not backwards. And, for pete's sake guys, get a short haircut.

• Swagger through the doors with a grimace on your face and a bow-legged stride, both of which suggest that you have spent the better part of the day on your horse and now need something to kill the pain.

• Be as taciturn as possible. When you get up to the bar, the bartender will look at you and silently throw a coaster down on the bar in front of you. He or she will under no circumstances say, "Hi, how ya doin'?" and neither should you. At this point, you should utter only one word—namely the brand of beer you want.

• Never ask what kind of beer is available, and never, ever, order an import or a microbrew. As a rule of thumb, it's best to order the cheapest beer they have. Budweiser is not always the cheapest, but it's universally available and therefore a safe bet. You can probably get away with ordering a Coors if you'd prefer, but if you do, remember that Coors rhymes with furs, not boors. Given a choice, draft is more acceptable than a can, which is more acceptable than a bottle.

• Don't say anything else for at least another five minutes, or unless you're spoken to first, which you won't be. Don't smile, don't look around, just stare down at the bar.

• If, by now, the rest of the bar patrons are ignoring you and are back in their own conversations, you've probably passed. If the bartender returns to ask if you want another one, congratulations, you're in there! Now you may finally utter a few more words if you so desire, such as "Where's the bathroom?" Whatever you say, be exceedingly polite. Always say "yes, sir," "no, ma'am," and "thank ya kindly."

• Don't push your luck—stay away from the jukebox.

BED-AND-BREAKFASTS

Idaho's B&Bs fall into two camps. Many are converted residences, where you'll be sharing a family's home and living space with them. Others are more like small motels, designed as guest accommodations from the ground up and generally offering more privacy at higher prices. Breakfasts are included in the rates, but if it makes a difference to you, be sure to inquire what sort of breakfast is served; a few B&Bs offer only a light, continental breakfast.

ACCOMMODATIONS PRICE CATEGORIES

It's a futile proposition trying to provide exact price information in a travel guide. Between the time the guide is written and the time it finally makes its way onto the bookstore shelves, the prices at lodgings (and all other establishments, for that matter) might have changed several times. For that reason, this guide uses accommodations price categories to give you a rough idea of how much you'll be paying for a room for the night.

The categories used in this book are: Under $50; $50–100; $100–150; $150–250; and Over $250. Many lodgings offer a wide range of accommodations, from a dark broom closet for cheap to a penthouse suite for more than you make in a month. In these cases, the accommodation will be listed in the category where most of its rooms fall. You may be able to pay a little less if you ask the proprietor nicely (and don't mind that broom sticking you in the ribs all night) and, at least at the fancier places, you'll likely be able to pay a whole lot more for something luxurious if you want. The categories, however, give you a good idea whether a given establishment is superfine or superfunky, and they allow you to easily compare price levels around town.

The rates used to categorize the various lodgings are the peak-season rack rates, based on double occupancy. Many lodgings run specials and offer travel-club and other discounts. And if an accommodation's prices straddled the category break at the time of writing, it was placed in the higher category. All this means you might be pleasantly surprised to pay less than you're expecting, and you probably won't be unpleasantly surprised at having to pay more than you were expecting.

RV PARKS

You'll seldom have a problem finding an RV park in Idaho. Most ubiquitous is the **KOA** (Kampgrounds Of America) chain, 406/248-7444, www.koakampgrounds.com. KOA's seven Idaho locations tend to be well-kept and full of amenities, though priced a bit higher than non-chain campgrounds. Most KOA locations also offer Kamping Kabins in addition to full-hookup RV sites. The shedlike cabins are about the size of a basic motel room, with electricity and heat but no bathrooms. They run about $35–55 a night.

Good Sam parks are part of a nationwide membership chain, sort of like the Best Westerns of the RV world. You can join the club on your first visit to one of the member parks. The token membership fee gets you a card good for a discount on subsequent stays at all Good Sam parks across the country.

FOOD AND DRINK

Idaho is a meat-and-potatoes state. Steak houses are standard, but particularly in rural areas, vegetarians will make good use of grocery stores. The larger cities all provide a range of fare. In Boise, you can get nearly every ethnic food you could dream of, and in nearby Canyon County you'll find some of the best Mexican restaurants this side of Los Angeles. As Idaho has a large Basque population, many towns (particularly in the southwest) have Basque restaurants. And cowboy cooking is dear to the heart of many Idahoans; Dutch-oven cookouts and barbecued steaks are the prime offerings of many tourist resorts and excursion providers.

Southwest Idaho holds the state's best vineyards, while microbreweries producing excellent beer dot the state.

ON THE ROAD

Transportation

BY AIR

Major Airlines

No international flights serve Idaho directly. Boise is the state's largest airport and is served by **Alaska Airlines,** 800/252-7522, with nonstop service to and from Seattle; **America West,** 800/235-9292, which flies to and from its Phoenix hub; **Delta Air Lines,** 800/221-1212, regionally based in Salt Lake City; **Frontier,** 800/432-1359, with service to and from Denver; **Northwest,** 800/225-2525, offering direct flights to Minneapolis/St. Paul with worldwide connections from there; **Southwest Airlines,** 800/435-9792, which offers direct flights between Boise and many western U.S. cities; and **United,** 800/241-6522, which flies direct to and from San Francisco, Chicago, and Denver.

Travelers headed into and out of southeast Idaho generally book flights through the airport in Salt Lake City, Utah, 161 miles south of Pocatello. Those headed for the Panhandle book flights into Spokane, Washington, 33 miles west of Coeur d'Alene.

Commuter Airlines

Once you've arrived in Idaho, you can avail yourself of smaller airlines of the turboprop sort to fly you to and among the smaller cities. **Horizon Air,** 800/547-9308, an affiliate of Alaska Airlines, maintains an extensive route system across the Northwest and California. From Boise, Horizon/Alaska flies to about a dozen cities around the West. Delta-affiliated **Skywest Airlines,** 800/453-9417, also serves Idaho Falls, Pocatello, Sun Valley, and Twin Falls with nonstop service from Salt Lake City. **Big Sky,** 800/237-7788, flies nonstop between Boise and Billings and Missoula, Montana. **Salmon Air,** 800/448-3413, has weekday flights from Salmon to McCall and Boise.

Backcountry Charters

To fly into one of Idaho's many rural burgs, or to remote airstrips in the state's expansive backcountry, you'll need to hire an air taxi service. A number of companies do a booming business shuttling rafters, backpackers, and anglers into the wilderness. For starters, try **McCall Aviation,** 800/992-6559, which offers branches in Mc-

McCall planes flying over Payette Lake

© McCALL AVIATION INC.

Call, Stanley, and Salmon; or **Sawtooth Flying Service,** at Boise Airport, 800/798-6105.

BY TRAIN

Train service in Idaho is now limited to Amtrak's **Empire Builder,** which runs between Chicago and either Portland or Seattle via Wisconsin, Minnesota, North Dakota, Montana, north Idaho, and Spokane, Washington. The route's name was the nickname of James Jerome Hill (1838–1916), a Canadian-born railroad magnate who founded the Great Northern Railway; the Great Northern's line between St. Paul, Minnesota, and the Pacific opened up the Northwest at the turn of the 20th century. Today's Amtrak train makes one run daily in each direction. Its only Idaho stop is in the Panhandle at Sandpoint, where it creeps through in the middle of the night (11:49 P.M. westbound, 2:47 A.M. eastbound). Sample one-way coach fares (advance purchase) are: Sandpoint to Seattle or Portland, $84; to Glacier National Park, Montana, $80; to Chicago, $374. For Amtrak information and reservations, call 800/USA-RAIL (800/872-7245). Web users can look up Amtrak at www.amtrak.com.

BY BUS

Greyhound, 800/231-2222, goes most everywhere, and tickets don't cost much. **Northwestern Stages/Trailways,** 800/366-3830, connects Boise with McCall, Lewiston, Grangeville, and Spokane, Washington. Look them up in the local phone book of whatever city you're in, or call them in Boise at 208/336-3300. **Sun Valley Express,** 877/622-VANS, offers service between Boise Airport and Sun Valley. **Rocky Mountain Trailways,** 208/656-UTAH, 800/356-9796 outside southeast Idaho, offers daily van shuttle service between Salt Lake City and the Idaho communities of Rexburg, Rigby, Idaho Falls, Blackfoot, and Pocatello.

BY CAR

Driving is the easiest and most efficient way to make your way around Idaho, but with some caveats. Except in and around major cities and on the interstates, all Idaho highways are two-lane and undivided. To make matters worse, few, if any, are equipped with "Botts Dots"— those bumpy, reflective lane markers that wake you up if you drift out of your lane. This can make driving a challenge, particularly on dark, rainy nights. If you can't see the lanes clearly, slow down. All the major national car-rental companies are represented in Idaho, including at the state's major airports.

Traffic Laws

Here are a few of the common Idaho traffic laws you ought to know before you start the car. First, you'll need to possess and carry a valid driver's license from your home state or country, or a valid international driver's license. You must also possess and carry proof of liability insurance in the following minimum amounts: $25,000 for injury or death of one person, $50,000 for injury or death of two or more people, $15,000 for property damage. Your vehicle must also be currently registered. Finally, before you turn the key, buckle up—it's the law; you must wear your seat belt in Idaho. All children under 40 pounds must be strapped into a car seat.

Once out on the road, a couple of rules are worthy of special mention. First, in America, you drive on the right side of the road. Unless posted otherwise, you are permitted to make a right turn on a red light after coming to a complete stop. You can also make a U-turn at a controlled intersection if no sign specifically prohibits it, and then only if you can do so safely, in one continuous movement (no three-point turns). Unless posted otherwise, the maximum speed limit on city streets is 35 mph. And be careful of horses; horseback riders are permitted on most public roads.

A special note for you RVers: Idaho law requires you to pull over if you are holding up three or more vehicles.

Drinking and Driving

The drinking age in Idaho is 21. And the state has a double standard for drunk drivers. If you're 21 or over, you're considered legally drunk if your blood-alcohol level is .10 percent. But if you're under 21, you're considered drunk and subject to arrest with a blood-alcohol level as low as .02. If you're under 21, don't even think of driving if you've had anything whatsoever to drink.

Penalties for a first drunk-driving conviction are up to six months in jail, up to a $1,000 fine, and mandatory license suspension for at least 30 days and up to 180 days—up to one year if you're under 21.

Winter Driving

Old Man Winter is always ready to get you if you don't watch out, so just say "slow." You'll see plenty of signs warning of **frost heaves,** places where water beneath the pavement has frozen and expanded, buckling the road. Hitting one of these at too high a speed on a rain- or snow-slickened road can throw you instantly out of control. Note that there is absolutely no truth to the rumor that in spring when the frost heaves melt out and dry up, they are then known as the "dry heaves."

The weather in Idaho can be unpredictable, and much of the state gets at least some snow in winter. You'd be wise to carry chains in your trunk between October and April. Also in the trunk should go a short-handled shovel, so you can dig yourself out of that snowbank, and blankets, a sleeping bag, and extra food and drinking water, just in case you get stranded. Winter and summer, carry emergency flares and a flashlight or headlamp. If you do break down in a snowstorm, stay with the car. Don't try to walk for help unless you can see that it's very close; many people have died of hypothermia in the attempt.

Summer Driving

Much of the state swelters in summer—particularly at low elevations on the Snake River Plain and in the canyons of western Idaho. Make sure your radiator is in good working order, and carry a couple of extra gallons of coolant in the trunk. As in winter, also carry extra food and water in

Half the fun of exploring the state is leaving the highway behind and heading out into the desert or deep into the mountains. Special precautions apply, since often these roads will take you a day's hike or more away from the nearest other human being.

the trunk, in case you get stuck out in the middle of nowhere. And even in summer, carry blankets. Idaho summer days may get hot, but nights can still get plenty cold in many parts of the state, even in mid-July. If you're renting a car, make sure it has a functioning air conditioner—you'll need it. As in winter, keep emergency flares and a flashlight or headlamp handy at all times.

As summer opens up many roads into high mountain country, roadside encounters with wildlife become more common. In your travels through the state, you'll see far too many dead deer and other animals on the roadsides. Only rarely should there be any excuse for this. Never outdrive your headlights at night, use your high beams whenever possible, and immediately slow down as soon as you spy any animal even remotely close to the road.

Getting Off the Pavement

Half the fun of exploring the state is leaving the highway behind and heading out into the desert or deep into the mountains. Special precautions apply, however, since often these roads will take you a day's hike or more away from the nearest other human being. Four-wheel-drive vehicles are really in their element here, but if you go slowly enough, most of Idaho's dirt roads are passable in the family sedan.

Southern Idaho's deserts are especially desolate—plan on being on your own. If ever a case could be made for carrying not one but two spare tires, this would be it. Make sure your jack works and you know how to use it. Two jacks could even come in handy. Carry a shovel to dig yourself out of the sand or mud, and some boards—two-by-fours or whatever you can fit in the trunk—to put under your stuck wheels for traction.

In the mountains, you'll have to contend with **logging trucks,** which often barrel down narrow one-lane roads and around blind corners at high speed with seeming disregard for everything in their path. The best advice is to just stay out of areas being actively logged; stop at the nearest ranger station to find out where these areas are. If you must enter an active area, it helps to have a CB radio. Usually, a communication channel is posted on the entrance to every logging road where a tourist might wander in. If you have a CB, tune to the posted channel and let everyone know you're on that road, or at least listen in to find out who else is out there.

Further Information

To find out the current status of the roads along your intended route, call the Idaho Transportation Department's 24-hour recorded **road conditions** report at 208/336-6600 or 888/432-7623 (in Idaho). RVers can obtain a list of RV **dump stations** in the state by contacting the RV Program Supervisor, Idaho Department of Parks and Recreation, 5657 Warm Springs Ave., P.O. Box 83720, Boise, ID 83720-0065, 208/334-4199.

Other Practicalities

HEALTH AND SAFETY

Emergencies

If your honey is choking on an Idaho potato, find a phone and **dial 911** to summon emergency help. The 911 system is installed almost universally throughout Idaho, although a few backwaters aren't hooked in yet. If 911 doesn't work, dial 0 (zero) for the operator, who will patch you through to either the ambulance or coroner's office, as appropriate.

Plants to Avoid

A few plants in Idaho can cause discomfort if they come into contact with your skin. **Poison ivy** is common in the state; look for small white-to-yellow berries and large, waxy, ternate (three to a bunch) leaves. Poison ivy likes water, so be especially careful on overgrown trails around creekbeds. **Stinging nettle** has broad, coarse-toothed leaves, and also grows near water. Unlike with poison ivy, you'll know you've encountered stinging nettle soon after contact. Yes, it stings. If any of these plants contact your skin, wash the area with soap and water and try not to scratch. Easier said than done, no doubt. Once the area is thoroughly washed, you can't spread the rash by scratching, but you can scratch the skin open, inviting infection. Calamine lotion or mud packs may offer some relief.

Giardia

The *Giardia lamblia* intestinal parasite has spread throughout the backcountry of the West in the past 20 years, lurking in streams and lakes, just waiting for the thirsty, unsuspecting hiker to come along. You should assume *all* water in the backcountry to be contaminated, no matter how crystal clear and pure it may appear.

Once inside you, the giardia parasite attaches itself to the intestinal wall, causing symptoms including severe fatigue, cramps, nausea, diarrhea, and gas. To ensure that none of the little buggers gets inside you, you'll have to boil (10 minutes minimum at sea level; longer at altitude), chemically treat (iodine, halazone, or other water-purification tablets), or filter your water. If you go with a filter, be sure to get one with a pore size of less than one micron (one millionth of a meter) in diameter. That's the maximum width that will safely filter out *Giardia*.

Schistosomes

Shallow waters at the edges of lakes commonly harbor the larvae of these parasitic flatworms. The larvae can penetrate human skin, and after doing so will die, but not before causing **swimmer's itch.** The itchy red spots or welts will go away after about a week. Some people are more susceptible than others for some reason, but who wants to find out into which camp you fall? To avoid the possibility of contracting the bug, swim in water away from the shore and towel off as soon as you get out of the water.

Ticks

These creepy crawlers cling to brush and hop a

ride on any warm-blooded animal that happens by. Inserting their barbed mouth parts into the skin, the ticks clamp on tight and begin sucking merrily away. Contrary to commonly held misconception, you do not remove a tick by unscrewing it, burning it out, or covering it with nail polish or petroleum jelly in an attempt to suffocate it. Instead, get a pair of tweezers and grab it as close to the head as possible, then pull it out with slow, steady pressure. Wash the area with soap and water and check to see if any part of the tick broke off under the skin. If so, best check with your doctor or at least monitor your condition closely for any signs of illness. Ticks have been linked to the spread of Lyme disease and Rocky Mountain spotted fever, but such cases are rare. Ticks are most prevalent in late spring and early summer. To avoid them, tuck your shirt into your pants and your pant legs into your socks or boots. Wearing a DEET-based insect repellent would be an additional safeguard. Check your clothes often during your hike, and do a thorough body check when you get back to your home base.

Mosquitoes

The joke about mosquitoes being the state bird could apply in some parts of Idaho, though the dry Snake River Plain doesn't seem to get as many. With lots of wild backcountry holding lots of water, Idaho grows 'em big and bountiful. Summer is prime time for skeeters; a hike in the woods in mid-July or August will invite a bloodthirsty bombardment. Repellents containing DEET work the best.

Yellow Jackets

The picnickers' pariah, these unwelcome intruders inevitably will crash your plein air party, buzzing around your soda can, your sandwich, and you. They're incredibly persistent, and the more agitated you get, the more persistent they seem to become. The best advice may be just to ignore them. Or you can try creating a "sacrifice area" by opening a couple of cans of soda and making a really gooey ham sandwich with lots of mustard, then setting it all out at some distance from your table. If you're lucky, the yellow jackets will go for the easy grub and leave you alone. Of course, if you're allergic to their sting, you should just retreat to the safety of the Buick rather than risk anaphylactic shock. In the end, you just can't win with these buggers.

Rattlesnakes

These venomous pit vipers inhabit Idaho, generally at elevations below 5,000 feet, but you'll probably never see one. They crawl into cool places under rocks and logs in the heat of day, and even if they're out and about they'll generally avoid humans if possible. Your greatest chance of encountering one along the trail would be in early morning or evening, or in turning over the wrong rock. Scrambling up rocks is also risky, as you tend to grab above your head in places you can't see. If you do get bitten, the current medical consensus seems to be to get to a doctor as soon as possible, rather than trying the incision-and-suction method formerly recommended. It seems many people did more damage than the snake by slicing themselves or their friends open incorrectly. The best advice is to be cautious and avoid contact in the first place. If you come around a bend in the trail to find one staring you down and rattling at you, just back off a safe distance and wait for it to crawl away. And never invite trouble by poking at a rattler with a stick or otherwise harassing it. If you do, you'll get what you deserve.

Mines

One place you might indeed encounter a rattlesnake at midday is a place to be avoided for other reasons as well. Idaho is full of old abandoned mines. Rattlers come in for the cool darkness. You come in to explore and wind up getting bitten by the snake, falling down a hidden shaft, getting knocked unconscious by a falling rotten timber, and buried alive in the ensuing cave-in. What do you think you're going to find, anyway? Golfball-size gold nuggets lying on the ground? Right. Just stay out.

Viruses

Idaho is a low-worry state with no high per-capita rates of any particular diseases. The state is not immune, however, to a couple of problematic viruses found nationwide.

Hantavirus attracted a lot of attention several years ago after a major outbreak in the Four Corners area of the Southwest. It can be fatal, and is worth mentioning because it is spread by the deer mouse and other rodents common to Idaho. The virus is found in the animals' urine, saliva, and feces. You can get it by handling contaminated materials, being bitten by a rodent, or, most commonly, by breathing in the virus in contaminated dust or airborne mist from urine. Household disinfectants such as bleach and alcohol will kill the virus. If you rent a backcountry cabin and find telltale signs of rodent habitation, the safest course of action would be to spray the area down with bleach, then mop it up. Don't sweep mouse droppings up without spraying them with disinfectant first. And don't invite rodents into your camp by leaving food out carelessly or intentionally attempting to feed them. Cases of Hantavirus infection in humans are fortunately rare.

As of this writing, **West Nile virus** hadn't become a widespread problem for humans in Idaho, though wearing mosquito repellent with DEET is a good idea.

Crime

Idaho's relatively small population makes for a relatively low crime rate. Homicides and other violent crimes are thankfully rare and still make front-page news, even in Boise. Part of this, I suspect, is that Idaho also has a strong sense of community. People know their neighbors here more than in many other parts of the West. You needn't go out of your way to invite crime—as elsewhere in the world, don't leave your valuables in plain sight on the front seat of your parked car. But you needn't be overly concerned, either.

SPEAKING IDAHONIAN

So many names of places and things in Idaho are pronounced differently than you'd expect, it sometimes seems as if the whole state is engaged in a plot to confound and humiliate the outsider. Here is a list of the most common odd pronunciations found in the state. Many of them result from their origins as Native American or French words, reflecting the state's multilingual history. Memorize them or risk being branded a tourist.

Boise: "BOY-see," not "BOY zee," and certainly not the French "bwah-zay"
Coeur d'Alene: a butchered French "core-duh-lane"
creek: with one exception, it always rhymes with "sick." The one exception is the Sandpoint catalog company and retailer Coldwater Creek (rhymes with "seek").
Dubois: "doo-boyce" (from Fred), not the French "due-bwah" (from the woods)
Kamiah: "KAM-ee-eye"
Kooskia: "KOO-skee"
Kootenai: "KOOT-nee"
Lochsa: "LOCK-saw"
Montpelier: "mahnt-PEEL-yer," never the French "moan-pale-yay"
Moscow: "MOS-coe"
Moyie: "MOY-yay"
Nez Perce: "nezz purse," never the French "NAY-pare-SAY"
Owyhee: "o-WHY-hee"
Pend Oreille: close to the original French, here it's "PON-der-ray"
root: unfortunately for the author, always rhymes with "foot"
Sawtooths: never "Sawteeth"
Weippe: "WEE-yipe"

INFORMATION AND SERVICES

Media

Best of the state's mainstream newspapers are Boise's *Idaho Statesman,* 208/377-6370, www.idahostatesman.com, the largest-circulation paper in the state, and Lewiston's *Lewiston Morning Tribune,* 208/743-9411, www.lmtribune.com. The Spokane-based *Spokesman-Review* also offers comprehensive coverage of North Idaho; www.spokesmanreview.com.

Also in the state capital, the *Boise Weekly* stands out as a highly credible liberal rag featuring excellent reporting and writing. The *Weekly* is available free around Boise, or by subscription; call 208/344-2055.

NPR junkies will find **National Public Radio affiliates** in Boise at KBSU 90.3 FM, KBSX 91.5 FM, and KBSU 730 AM; in Cottonwood at KNWO 90.1 FM; in McCall at KBSM 91.7 FM; in Moscow at KRFA 91.7 FM; in Rexburg at KRIC 100.5 FM; and in Twin Falls at KBSW 91.7 FM.

Money

Automatic teller machines (ATMs) are found at most Idaho banks and at many grocery stores and other locations; with the appropriate debit or credit card, you can get cash at any time of day or night. If you need to deal with a human, you'll find that most banks are open longer hours than they once were; typically 9 A.M.–5:30 P.M., with some open later in the evening and on Saturdays as well.

Standard Business Hours

You can generally expect most stores to be open Mon.–Sat. 9 A.M.–5 P.M. Many stores are open longer hours and on Sunday. Businesses do not close for a midafternoon siesta. Stores in and near major shopping malls are usually open seven days a week. These stores usually don't open until 10 A.M., but they stay open until 9 P.M.; Sunday hours usually shorter.

Postal Services

The U.S. Postal Service will get a standard letter from any point A in the country to any point B in the country, in less than a week, for just $.37, or just $.23 for a postcard. Give it two weeks between countries. Express Mail service can expedite delivery of domestic mail to usually between one and three days, but it costs almost as much as the private delivery services.

Post office sales counters are generally open Mon.–Fri. 8:30 A.M.–5:30 P.M. Some of the larger cities offer Saturday hours as well, usually in the mornings only. Almost all offices have lobby areas that stay open 24 hours, with self-serve stamp machines and mail drops in them. Mail gets picked up from the post offices on Saturdays, even if there's no counter service.

The post office accepts general delivery (poste restante) mail, but only holds it for around 10 days. After that, it gets returned to sender or disappears off the face of the earth. You'll need to have ID with you to pick it up.

If you need to send something somewhere fast and have a pretty decent guarantee it'll get there, you'll probably want to spend the bucks for a private delivery service. The two most notable services are **FedEx** and **United Parcel Service** (a.k.a. UPS). Either one can get whatever you're sending to wherever you're sending it, overnight. Rates depend on the size of the package, its weight, and where it's going.

Other private businesses will sell you envelopes for your letters and boxes for your souvenirs, and even wrap items for shipping, for a fee. These businesses, such as the chain Mail Boxes Etc., are often also scheduled UPS or FedEx pickup points, so when you get your package packaged you can just leave it for pickup. The convenience will cost you an extra buck or three but save you some running around.

Power Supplies

The United States uses a standardized 120 VAC, 60 Hz power supply. Modern sockets accept a three-prong plug with two flat main prongs and a more rounded grounding prong. Older sockets (including many in Idaho) generally do not accept the ground prong. Adapters are readily available that will convert a three-prong plug into a two-prong, but don't neglect to ground your appliance by screwing the adapter into the wall socket

IDAHO PASSPORT

As part of its commemoration of the Lewis and Clark Bicentennial, Idaho has printed "Corps of Discovery" passports. The idea is to visit—and have your passport stamped in—each of the state's 44 counties by December 31, 2006.

There are between two and six stamping stations in each county; all county sheriff's offices have stamps, too, in case you swing through an area after regular business hours. Each passport holder is also entitled to one "free pass" stamp from one county they missed in their travels. Claim yours in the governor's office at the State Capitol in Boise.

The passports are available free at visitor centers across the state, or you can get one by calling 800/443-2461. People who bring or mail their completed passports to the governor's office will receive a personalized certificate of achievement and a replica Lewis and Clark peace medal. Completed certificates can be mailed to: Idaho Passport, Governor's Office, State Capitol, Boise, ID 83720.

using the eye on the adapter and the screw on the socket. Adapters converting European appliances to American standard sockets are not as readily available in the United States, although you can find them at some consumer electronics stores in major cities. Best to bring your own from home.

Telephones

Here's a relief to visitors from other areas of the country where new area codes seem to be spawning faster than cockroaches. **The telephone area code for all of Idaho is 208.** That means that when you're calling someplace in Idaho that is distant from where you are, you must dial 1-208 before the standard seven-digit telephone number you're trying to reach. If you're calling someplace

near where you are, you need only dial the seven-digit number. If you're not sure how "distant" your intended number is, just dial the seven-digit number. If it's too far away, a disembodied voice will tell you to try it the other way.

You'll notice many numbers in this book listed with an 800, 888, 877, or 866 area code. These are toll-free area codes—no charge to you. You'll need to dial a 1 before the area code.

For telephone **directory assistance** (in other words, to find out someone's telephone number when you don't know it) call 208/555-1212.

Time Zones and Systems

Idaho is shared by two different time zones. Northern Idaho is on **Pacific time.** Down around Riggins, the time zone changes to **Mountain time,** an hour ahead of Pacific time. As with most places in the country, Idaho follows the daylight-saving convention. In spring (the first Monday in April), daylight saving time goes into effect and everyone sets their clocks an hour ahead. In fall (the last Monday in October), the clocks go back an hour to standard time. Remember the ditty: "spring forward, fall back."

Idaho and the rest of the United States use a 12-hour, not a 24-hour, time system. Times from 0001–1159 are labeled A.M., while times from 1201–2359 are labeled P.M. Some examples for you 24-hour habitués: 0030 is 12:30 A.M.; 0100 is 1 A.M.; 1100 is 11 A.M.; 1200 is noon; 1230 is 12:30 P.M.; 1300 is 1 P.M.; 2300 is 11 P.M.; 2400 is midnight.

Tourism Information

If, heaven forbid, you can't find the answer to your question somewhere in this book, contact the **Idaho Department of Commerce/Idaho Travel Council,** 700 W. State St., P.O. Box 83720-0093, Boise, ID 83720, 800/VISIT-ID (800/847-4843), www.visitid.org.

ON THE ROAD

Boise and Vicinity

In the early 19th century, French fur trappers crossing the arid Snake River Plain discovered an oasis of greenery here. After days and weeks of relentless sun and sagebrush, they suddenly found themselves surrounded by trees, big trees, and lots of them—cottonwoods, willows, alders—growing on the banks of a cool, clear-flowing river. The French trappers called the water Rivière Boisée (Wooded River), and the particularly pleasant spot where they lingered awhile came to be known as Les Bois (The Woods). Today it's called Boise (BOY-see to locals, BOY-zee to tourists), and it's still an oasis, both physically and culturally, in the middle of the desert that dominates southern Idaho.

Boise is the state capital and the state's most populous city. But this is Idaho, not New York or California. Boise's total population—about 185,000—is probably lower than the number of licensed cabbies in Manhattan. As a result, people here have yet to suffer the madness that overcrowding has induced in many larger American cities. When you walk down the street, folks here tend to look you in the eye and smile, not look down and try to ignore you.

The crime rate is low. You'll rarely see graffiti;

you probably won't get panhandled. You can walk the streets well past last call without feeling the need to keep looking over your shoulder—and people do stroll the streets late at night, especially on balmy late spring and summer evenings.

The city's climate provides seasonal change but is mild enough to be enjoyed year-round. Boiseans live as much outdoors as in—every spare moment is spent on the river, on the ski slopes, in the mountains. The foothills rising behind downtown provide wide-open land for hiking and mountain biking just minutes from the urban core. And bicycles are the preferred mode

of daily transportation for a large percentage of the local population.

The beautiful Boise River flows right through the heart of the city. Anglers angle and tubers tube the river all summer long, and the city's prized Greenbelt—winding along the riverbank from one end of town to the other—is a well-used, car-free highway for skaters, joggers, and cyclists. Although the river is a bit too tame for the city's whitewater rafters and kayakers, a new whitewater park may be in place by the time you read this, and the wild Payette River offers thrills, spills, and chills just outside town. In winter, Bogus Basin provides a first-class

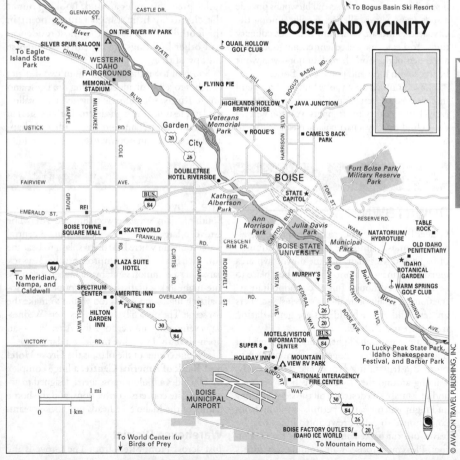

BOISE AND VICINITY

© AVALON TRAVEL PUBLISHING, INC

alpine ski resort and many miles of Nordic trails, all close enough to the city for the truly dedicated skier to enjoy on a long lunch hour.

But the city's decidedly outdoorsy populace also makes time for the genteel trappings of modern civilization. Boise supports an array of urban cultural amenities on par with any city in the Northwest. The Boise Philharmonic is more than a century old and still going strong, while ballet, opera, and Shakespeare alfresco also grace the city's cultural calendar. For those whose tastes run to the more avant-garde, Boise's rock 'n' roll clubs support a strong stable of local musicians and draw fine touring bands. Coffeehouse society thrives in dozens of caffeineries, and several brewpubs provide a suds scene par excellence. Finally, among the city's restaurants are some truly first-class culinary finds. You can enjoy excellent ethnic food from all corners of the world here. Fear not—you won't be stuck with meat and potatoes in Boise.

However much time you've budgeted to spend in Boise, you'd better double it. Just like those early-19th-century fur trappers, you too will no doubt find the city a particularly pleasant spot to linger awhile.

The Lay of the Land

Boise lies at 43° 34' N latitude, roughly the same as Boston, Marseilles, and Sapporo. It's situated on the north shoulder of the Boise River Valley at an elevation of about 2,800 feet. The Boise Mountains rise just north of the city, beginning in foothills right behind town and peaking at about 8,000 feet. The Boise River begins in the high mountains to the northeast and flows through town on the way to its confluence with the Snake River, about 40 miles west of Boise. The river has always supported lush vegetation along its banks, but early settlers built canals that turned the whole valley green for miles around. Looking out at the city today from a high vantage point in the foothills, you'll notice that most residences and other buildings are obscured by a dense canopy of trees.

South of town the land climbs in two distinct benches to a low divide separating the Boise and Snake Rivers. Outside the irrigated river valley, the land resumes the high-desert characteristics of the Snake River Plain, and sagebrush and chaparral species regain dominance.

Sights

DOWNTOWN

Greater Boise sprawls out to the west, merging almost seamlessly into the fast-growing suburbs of Eagle and Meridian. But the downtown area remains distinct—vibrant, alive, the best place to be in Boise. Although full of cosmopolitan attractions, it retains a small-town feel; skyscrapers are few, and many buildings are gems dating from the early 20th century.

Traffic is generally light, although the grid of one-way streets can make getting from point A to point B a frustrating experience. Fortunately, walking around the city center is both practical and pleasurable. Pedestrians fill the sidewalks day and night when weather permits, strolling from coffeehouse to café, brewpub to blues bar. So leave your car parked and check out the area on foot. Pleasant surprises wait around every turn.

The Grove

South of Main Street between 8th and 9th is The Grove, a large brick plaza surrounding a central water fountain where kids often splash to beat the summer heat. By day, impromptu hackeysack games are a common sight; by night, benches serve late-night folk guitarists, cooing couples, and socializing high-school kids too young to make the bar scene. The plaza fills with revelers every Wednesday evening in summer for Alive After Five—an open-air festival with live music and dancing.

On one corner of the plaza is the **Grove Hotel and Bank of America Centre,** a huge complex that includes a multipurpose arena designed to accommodate concerts, conventions, and the home games of the Idaho Steelheads pro hockey team.

Warehouse District

Just across Front Street from The Grove is the

8th Street Marketplace. In the early 1900s, this was part of the city's warehouse district; today, it's one of Boise's best shopping and entertainment districts. You'll find the **Big Easy Concert House** and **Funny Bone Comedy Club** here, and ongoing renovations promise a multiplex theater, hotel, and shops.

World Sports Humanitarian Hall of Fame

Jocks don't have any trouble winning glory for their athletic achievement, but this unusual museum honors the efforts of "those who go beyond the game." Founded in 1994 and recently relocated to more spacious quarters at 855 Broad St., 208/343-7224, www.sports humanitarian.com, the hall of fame showcases such benevolent sports stars as Arthur Ashe, Roberto Clemente, Mary Lou Retton, and the Harlem Globetrotters. Two or three newcomers are inducted each year. Hours are Mon.–Fri. 9 A.M.–4 P.M., Sat. noon–4 P.M. Suggested donation is $3 adults, $2 seniors, $1 students. The Hall of Fame is affiliated with Boise's annual post-Christmas Humanitarian Bowl football showcase.

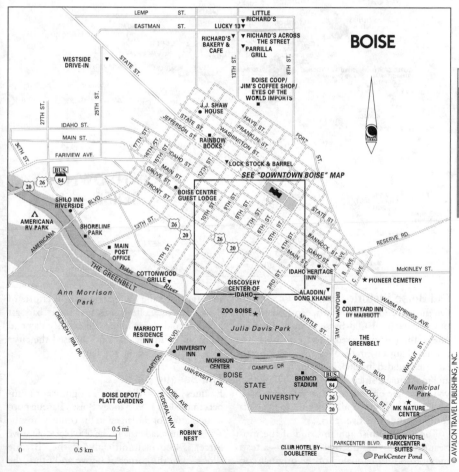

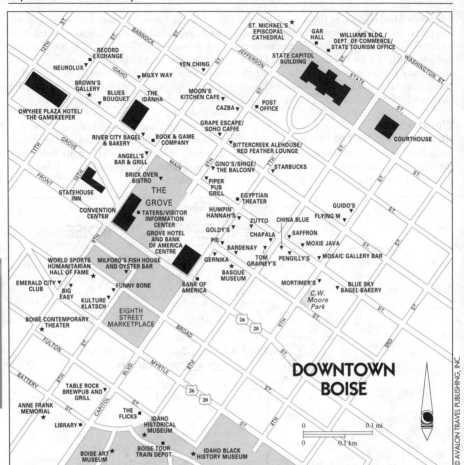

ST. MICHAEL'S EPISCOPAL CATHEDRAL
GAR HALL
WILLIAMS BLDG./ DEPT. OF COMMERCE/ STATE TOURISM OFFICE
STATE CAPITOL BUILDING
WASHINGTON ST.
BANNOCK
12TH ST.
ST.
JEFFERSON
STATE ST.
RECORD EXCHANGE
NEUROLUX
IDAHO
MILKY WAY
YEN CHING ST.
BROWN'S GALLERY
BLUES BOUQUET
THE IDANHA
MOON'S KITCHEN CAFE
POST OFFICE
OWYHEE PLAZA HOTEL/ THE GAMEKEEPER
CAZBA
COURTHOUSE
GRAPE ESCAPE/ SOHO CAFFE
ST.
11TH
GROVE
RIVER CITY BAGEL & BAKERY
BOOK & GAME COMPANY
BITTERCREEK ALEHOUSE/ RED FEATHER LOUNGE
ANGELL'S BAR & GRILL
MAIN
8TH
GINO'S/SHIGE/ THE BALCONY
STARBUCKS
FRONT
10TH
BRICK OVEN BISTRO
THE GROVE
PIPER PUB GRILL
EGYPTIAN THEATER
GUIDO'S
ST.
STATEHOUSE INN
CONVENTION CENTER
TATERS/VISITOR INFORMATION CENTER
HUMPIN' HANNAH'S
ZUTTO
CHINA BLUE
FLYING M
GROVE HOTEL AND BANK OF AMERICA CENTRE
GOLDY'S
PIE
CHAPALA
SAFFRON
9TH
BARDENAY
MOXIE JAVA
WORLD SPORTS HUMANITARIAN HALL OF FAME
MILFORD'S FISH HOUSE AND OYSTER BAR
GERNIKA
TOM GRAINEY'S
PENGILLY'S
MOSAIC GALLERY BAR
EMERALD CITY CLUB
BIG EASY
FUNNY BONE
BANK OF AMERICA
BASQUE MUSEUM
MORTIMER'S
BLUE SKY BAGEL BAKERY
KULTURE KLATSCH
C.W. Moore Park
BOISE CONTEMPORARY THEATER
EIGHTH STREET MARKETPLACE
BROAD
26
20
5TH
ST.
FULTON
8TH
6TH
MYRTLE
BLVD.
DOWNTOWN BOISE
3RD
BATTERY
TABLE ROCK BREWPUB AND GRILL
26
20
4TH
ANNE FRANK MEMORIAL
CAPITOL
THE FLICKS
IDAHO HISTORICAL MUSEUM
0   0.1 mi
LIBRARY
0   0.1 km
BOISE ART MUSEUM
BOISE TOUR TRAIN DEPOT
IDAHO BLACK HISTORY MUSEUM

© AVALON TRAVEL PUBLISHING, INC.

Old Boise Historic District

On the east end of downtown, centered around 6th and Main, is Old Boise Historic District, one of the best-preserved, most enjoyable "old towns" of any city in the West. Shortly after the city was founded in 1863, its premier commercial and residential district developed here. Back then you could hop on a streetcar that ran down Main Street and out Warm Springs Avenue to the Natatorium. Adult fare: five cents.

Today Old Boise remains one of the most beautiful and vital districts in town—a testimony to both the quality of the original construction and the loving restoration efforts of Boise's citizens. Coffeehouses, restaurants, bars, art galleries, and shops hum with activity day and night, in buildings that once housed the city's pioneer businesses and residents.

The Basque Block

Basques began settling here in significant numbers in the late 1890s; today Boise's Basque population is one of the largest in the country (see the sidebar "Euskera Ikazi!"). The 600 block of Grove Street is known unofficially as the "Basque Block." On the corner of Grove and 6th is the

The Basque Block is an area with restaurants, shops, a museum, and a community center dedicated to Basque culture.

Basque Center, built by Basques for Basques in 1952. The building serves as a center for Basque dancing, language, and cooking classes. It's also a social center for older Basques who play cards and converse in their native tongue. This is their space. If you're Basque, you can come in, say *"kaixo!"* and have a drink. If you're not Basque, you won't be kicked out, but this really isn't the place for you. Go to the museum or Gernika down the street instead.

The **Basque Museum and Cultural Center,** two doors down at 611 Grove St., 208/343-2671, www.basquemuseum.com, is adjacent to and includes the Cyrus Jacobs-Uberuaga House, Boise's oldest surviving brick building. The house was built in 1864 by Cyrus Jacobs, an early Boise merchant who eventually became mayor. Later it was purchased by Jose Uberuaga, a Basque who turned the residence into a boardinghouse for Basque sheepherders. Famous Idaho statesman William Borah, a longtime friend to the Basques, married Mamie McConnell, daughter of Governor William J. McConnell, here on April 21, 1895. The museum's exhibits, including musical instruments, crafts, and other items unique to the Basques, provide a historical overview of the Basque culture in their homeland and in America. Hours are Tues.– Fri. 10 A.M.–4 P.M., Sat. 11 A.M.–3 P.M.; closed holidays. Donations are gratefully accepted.

On the end of the block is **Gernika,** one of Boise's classic pubs. It's a great place to get a taste of Basque cuisine and culture; non-Basques are always welcome.

C. W. Moore Park

Canadian-born Christopher W. Moore came to Boise in 1863, the year of the city's founding. He became a successful merchant, opened First National Bank of Idaho—one of the first banks in the West—and was known as a generous philanthropist. In 1916, shortly before his death, he gave the city two lots he owned between 4th and 5th Streets north of Grove Street. The conveyance stipulated that the lots be used for a park.

The park's designers incorporated memorabilia from Boise's early days into the small community park, including a large waterwheel that pulls water from the Grove Street Canal, lifting it up to a hill where it runs in a small stream down through the park and back into the canal. Waterwheels such as

EUSKERA IKAZI!

Euskera ikazi! means "learn Basque!" in the native tongue of the Basque people. If you spend much time in Boise, you'll be wanting to do just that. Idaho is home to about 12,000 Basque-Americans; a large percentage of them live in Boise. A Basque bar, Basque restaurants, Basque dancers, and a Basque block add cultural spice to Idaho's capital city.

Euskadi, the Basque homeland, lies in northeastern Spain and southwestern France. The region straddles the Spanish-French border from around Bilbao in the west to Bayonne in the east. To the south, the Basque country spreads into the Pyrenees Mountains and the foothills on either side. The seven Basque provinces—four in Spain, three in France—hold about 2.5 million Basques. Populations of emigrant Basques can be found throughout the world, with the largest populations being in North and South America and Australia. In the United States, most Basques live in the Western states of California, Nevada, Wyoming, Oregon, Utah, and Idaho.

The Basque language, Euskera, is unique. Hard as they try, linguists are unable to relate it to any other language in the world. As a result, some have suggested that the Basques might be the survivors of the Lost Continent of Atlantis, although a less fanciful theory holds that the Basques compose a unique evolutionary branch that split off from the Cro-Magnon tree some 10,000 years ago.

Although Basque territory was invaded at different times by different peoples, the Basque language and culture have survived intact, perhaps due to the Basques' noted courage and strength in defending their homeland. The *irrintzi,* a Basque war cry likened to an eerie cross between a wolf howl and a horse whinny, was reputedly enough to send all but their fiercest enemies running in the opposite direction.

Besides their skill at raising livestock and farming, Basques established a reputation early on as premier shipbuilders and mariners. As early as the 14th century, Basque fishermen and whalers pulled a harvest from the Bay of Biscay and crossed the Atlantic to pursue their catch off the Grand Banks; they probably landed on the coast of North America about a century before Columbus. A Basque named Lokotza was Columbus's navigator, while another named Elcano took over and completed Magellan's circumnavigation of the earth after Magellan died en route.

Basques first began coming to Boise soon after the city was founded; by 1910, the city's Basque population was sizable. In traditional Basque culture, only one child inherits all the family wealth.

this once were found every 50–100 feet along the canal, which was known as the Grove Street Ditch. The water irrigated the lawns and trees of Boise. Today the canal is mostly hidden underground.

Other bits of history presented at the park include an etched brass map depicting the city at the turn of the 20th century, some of the cast-iron streetlights that lit the city until the 1950s, and a variety of old cornerstones.

THE CAPITOL AREA

Idaho State Capitol

Just after the turn of the 20th century, prominent Boise architect J. E. Tourtelloutte was commis-sioned to draw up plans for the state capitol. He came up with a neoclassic design modeled after the U.S. Capitol, albeit on a smaller scale. Construction began in 1905 and was completed in 1920 at a cost of around $2.3 million. It's the only capitol in the country heated with geothermal hot water.

Outside, the building doesn't gleam white like its inspiration in Washington, D.C., but is instead a rather drab tan, thanks to the exterior use of Boise sandstone; multiton blocks were quarried behind the old Idaho State Penitentiary and hauled to the site by convicts. Inside, however, the impressive rotunda sports vast amounts of marble from Alaska (gray), Georgia (red), Vermont

The others—drawn by stories of goldfield bonanzas and high wages—made their way to the western United States. Many found work as miners, others as ranchhands. A large number became sheepherders, though it wasn't their experience back home that got them that job. Some of them had never tended sheep before; others had run small herds in their homeland, but nothing the size of the operations common to Idaho and the West. But it was a job that they could get without needing to speak English, and that few others were willing to take because of its solitary nature. The Basque shepherds quickly gained a reputation for hard work and reliability.

Out on the range for up to six months at a stretch, with only a trusty *txakurra* (sheepdog) and the crackle of a campfire to keep them company, the Basque sheepherders must have missed their homeland. The high-desert chaparral of the West was nothing like the Basque country's verdant forests, rich farms and pastures, and beautiful ocean shores. Yet they endured, many hoping to save their money and return home some day. When they made their occasional forays into town, they would stay and pick up their mail at Basque boardinghouses, which served as social centers where Basques could share the language, music, food, and camaraderie of their homeland. Though the boardinghouses no longer serve as such, some still stand. The **Cyrus Jacobs–Uberuaga house** on Grove Street's **Basque Block**—next to and part of the Basque Museum—is one example.

Basques eventually assimilated into American culture and today are found throughout Boise's establishment. Famous Basques in history include painter Francisco Goya (1746–1828); Simon Bolívar (1783–1830), the "George Washington of South America," who helped the countries of Venezuela, Colombia, Ecuador, Panama, Peru, and Bolivia win their independence from Spain; and legendary modern-day bicycle racer Miguel Indurain, five-time winner of the Tour de France.

In Boise today, you can taste Basque cuisine at **Bar Gernika** or Oòati; see traditional Basque dances performed by the **Oinkari Basque Dancers;** and get an overview of the unique culture at the **Basque Museum and Cultural Center.** If you're in town for the annual **Festival of San Inazio** at the end of July, you can get a full-blown introduction to Basque life. And if that suits your fancy, make plans to attend the next **Jaialdi,** in the year 2005—it's an international Basque cultural festival held in Boise every five years. For more information, call the Basque Museum at 208/343-2671, or check online at http://jaialdi.com.

(green), and Italy (black). Sixty-foot-high faux-marble pillars support the dome, the very top of which is painted on the underside with 43 stars—Idaho was the 43rd state in the union—against a blue background.

Around the four-story interior are changing exhibits put together by many state agencies and special-interest groups, and several sculptures, most of which are works by Idahoans. An exception to the latter is a replica of the *Winged Victory of Samothrace,* prominently displayed just inside the main entrance. It was a gift from the French following World War II. The first floor holds a portrait gallery of Idaho's territorial governors—beards were apparently in vogue back

then—while the fourth floor displays tapestry murals depicting elements of the state's history and culture. Also on the fourth floor are the entrances to the House and Senate galleries, where you can watch Idaho's lawmakers in action when the legislature is in session. The second and third floors house the executive-branch offices and the legislative chambers, respectively.

Back outside, a circuit of the grounds turns up some interesting finds. Across Jefferson Street stands a bronze statue of former governor Frank Steunenberg, who was assassinated in 1905, supposedly in retaliation for his use of federal troops to squelch the Silver Valley mining riots some six years earlier. On the front steps of the capitol is a replica of the Liberty Bell, sans crack, while to the west is a seacoast cannon of the type used by the Confederacy in the Civil War. Legend has it that before the state plugged the cannon with concrete, some enterprising Boise youths actually managed to pack it with shot and gunpowder and light it off, blowing out all the windows in the building across the street.

Botanical highlights on the grounds include the presidential trees (an oak tree planted by Benjamin Harrison in 1881, a maple planted by Teddy Roosevelt in 1903, and an Ohio buckeye planted by William Howard Taft in 1911); an offspring of the Tree of Gernika, brought here from the Basque country in 1981; a maple tree planted in 1985 in honor of Martin Luther King Jr.; and, on the west side of the capitol, a small flower garden planted in the shape of the state.

The capitol is open Mon.–Fri. 8 A.M.–5 P.M., weekends 9 A.M.–5 P.M. Guided tours are available at 10 A.M. and 1:30 P.M. daily in summer, and by appointment the rest of the year; call 208/334-5174 (April–Dec.) or 208/332-1008 (Jan.–March). A self-guided walking-tour brochure is available from the visitor information counter on the first floor.

Around the Capitol

If you're done touring the capitol but aren't ready to get back in the Buick, take a walk around the neighborhood, past the expansive, freshly mowed lawns and large, predominantly government buildings in the vicinity.

The 1897 **Moses Alexander House** is at 304 W. State St. Alexander served at various times as mayor of Boise and governor of Idaho; he was the nation's first Jewish governor. His beautiful Queen Anne residence here was built at a cost of just $3,200. The state renovated it in 2001, and plans call for turning it into a museum of the state's governors.

The **Idaho Supreme Court Building,** 451 W. State St., features opulent touches such as travertine-limestone walls and granite-chip floors, which brought the price of the building to just under $2 million. Critics of such extravagance refer to the building as the "Palace of Justice."

It's hard to miss the **Joe R. Williams Office Building,** 700 W. State St. Its mirrored glass windows reflect the capitol dome, creating a perfect photo opportunity. Inside is the Idaho Department of Commerce, where you can pick up **tourism information** on all parts of the state. Continuing west on State, the tiny 1892 **GAR Hall,** 714 W. State St., once held meetings of the Grand Army of the Republic—the bluecoat veterans of the Civil War.

NORTH END AND HYDE PARK

Some of Boise's most appealing architecture is found in the city's quiet north end, between State Street and the foothills.

Between 8th and 14th Streets, and Hays and State Streets, numerous churches vie with one another for eye appeal. Seemingly around every corner a different spire draws the eye toward heaven, and nearly every house of worship is a uniquely beautiful work of art. The ivy-covered sandstone walls of English Gothic **St. Michael's Episcopal Cathedral,** 518 N. 8th St. (at W. State St.), draw a congregation that was first organized in 1864, just after the city itself was established.

At 10th and State, the beautiful redbrick arches of **First United Presbyterian Church** come into view. The State Street sanctuary holds some of the original church furnishings brought to the city by covered wagon in 1878. **Congregation Beth Israel Synagogue,** among the West's oldest, was recently moved from 11th and State Streets to Latah Street near Morris Hill Cemetery, southwest of downtown. At 13th and W. Washington, the bright red and white **First Baptist Church** is a relative newcomer; services began in 1948, but the steeple wasn't erected until 1960.

The magnificent **First United Methodist Church,** at 11th and W. Franklin, is sometimes called the "Cathedral of the Rockies." The modern Gothic steeple and its ornate stonework can be seen from some distance in all directions, and it's an impressive edifice from any angle. Across 11th Street, the **Bush Mansion,** 1020 W. Franklin, was built for James Bush, a Boise hotelier and businessman. When it was built in 1892, it was considered one of Idaho's finest homes. The price tag? A whopping $6,000.

Continuing east to 9th and W. Washington, you'll see the octagonal dome of **Central Christian Church,** dating from 1910; heading north and east from there you'll come to **St. John's Catholic Cathedral,** 804 N. 8th St. Built in 1921, it's the spiritual center for Boise's Basque population. The interior of the sandstone cathedral features vaulted ceilings, marble floors, and beautiful stained-glass windows. Behind the cathedral, a 1905 Tudor house now serves as the church rectory. Finally, around the corner to the northeast is the Immanuel Evangelical Lutheran Church, most of which consists of a relatively modern and unremarkable brick edifice. But next to it, at 701 Fort St., is the church's handsome **Augustana Chapel,** an old stone-and-shake affair dating from 1906.

Between 8th and 14th Streets, and Hays and State Streets, numerous churches vie with one another for eye appeal. Seemingly around every corner a different spire draws the eye toward heaven, and nearly every house of worship is a uniquely beautiful work of art.

Boise's coolest "neighborhood," **Hyde Park** lies farther north, up 13th Street—a nice long walk from downtown, or you can hop a bus (Route 18). Hyde Park simply exudes charm. Its main drag—N. 13th Street between Alturas and Brumback—is just about two blocks long, but harbors a concentration of interesting restaurants, coffeehouses, and antique shops.

JULIA DAVIS PARK AND VICINITY

Thomas Jefferson Davis was one of Boise's earliest pioneer settlers. He and his brother homesteaded 360 acres here in 1863, raising vegetables that they sold to the Boise Basin mining communities. On July 7, 1863, Davis and a handful of men got together in Davis's log cabin to lay out the city of Boise. In 1871, Davis married Julia McCrum of Ontario, Canada. The new couple's agricultural empire grew over the years, and they continued to add to their real estate holdings in the valley. Just before the turn of the 20th century, when the couple was enjoying a comfortable retirement, they offered the city about 40 acres along the river for a park. It took a while to settle

the arrangements, but in 1907, Tom Davis saw Julia Davis Park become a reality. Julia died shortly thereafter; Tom died the following year. Their simple graves can be seen today in Pioneer Cemetery along Warm Springs Avenue. Today, the park is the queen of Boise's park system, holding many of the city's major attractions and plenty of open space.

Boise Art Museum

Beautiful inside and out, the Boise Art Museum, 670 S. Julia Davis Dr. (facing Capitol Blvd.), 208/345-8330, www.boiseartmuseum.org, is growing in reputation, with major exhibitions of sculptures by Edward Degas and landscape paintings by Georgia O'Keeffe on the calendar. Its permanent collection includes the Glenn C. Janss collection of American realism, featuring some absolutely amazing photorealist works. Museum admission has doubled in recent years, but so have BAM's offerings and its spunk. A small store sells arts and crafts, art-related books, and art postcards. In addition to providing Boiseans a visual feast, the museum also hosts events year-round, plus the big Art in the Park festival each September.

Hours are Tues.–Wed. and Fri.–Sat. 10 A.M.–5 P.M., Thurs. 10 A.M.–8 P.M. (until 9 P.M. the first Thursday of the month), Sun. noon–5 P.M.; closed Mondays and holidays. Admission is $8 general, $6 seniors and college students, $4 youths 17 and under, free to members and kids under six, and half-price for everyone on the first Thursday of every month.

Idaho Historical Museum

Stories of Idaho's people and progress—from ancient times to modern—are illuminated in grand style at the Idaho Historical Museum, also in Julia Davis Park at 610 N. Julia Davis Dr., 208/334-2120, www.idahohistory.net/museum.html. Artifacts illustrate the lives of Idaho's indigenous peoples, and the fur traders, prospectors, and pioneer settlers who later claimed this land as their own. The exhibits will give you a better understanding of the state's ethnic diversity, particularly of the Native American, Basque, and Chinese cultures still glimpsed today throughout the state. Outside the museum, in the Pioneer Village, are some of the earliest structures built in Boise. The Coston and Pearce cabins were built in 1863, the year of the city's founding. The Mayor Logan Adobe was built in 1865 for Boise's four-term mayor, Thomas E. Logan. The museum is open May–Sept. Tue.–Sat. 9 A.M.–5 P.M., Sun. and holidays 1–5 P.M. April–Oct., it's open Tue.–Fri. 9 A.M.–5 P.M., Sat. 11 A.M.–5 P.M.; closed Thanksgiving, Christmas, and New Year's Day. Admission is $2 adults, $1 for kids ages 6–18.

Boise Tour Train

Just east of the Historical Museum you'll find the little "depot" where tickets are sold for the Boise Tour Train, 208/342-4796, www.boisetourtrain.com. It's actually not a train but a rubber-tired tram, pulled by a miniature replica of an 1890s steam locomotive. No matter; it'll take you around Boise for a one-hour narrated tour, introducing you to Julia Davis Park, the historic Warm Springs neighborhood, Old Fort Boise, the capitol area, and the downtown business district. An informative narration reels off the history and fun facts of the city. Perhaps even more interesting is the number of Boise residents, young and old alike, who wave to the tourists on the train as it makes its way around town. This is one friendly city. Tours run five times daily from late May through Labor Day with a reduced schedule Apr.–May and Sept.–Oct. Adults pay $7, seniors $5, kids 4–12 $4. In summer, tour train patrons can add a gentle one-hour float on the Boise River; the combination price is $26 adults, $21 seniors, $16 children 12 and under. Holiday light tours are held in December.

Idaho Black History Museum

Think of it as a big fat laugh in the face of Idaho's reputation as a state where minorities are unwelcome. This museum, 508 Julia Davis Dr., 208/433-0017, housed in a former church, celebrates the achievements of African Americans in Boise and beyond. Open in summer Tue.–Sat. 11 A.M.–4 P.M.; Sept.–May, Wed.–Sat. 11 A.M.–4 P.M.

Zoo Boise

Zoo Boise, 355 N. Julia Davis Dr., 208/384-4260, is no threat to the preeminence of the San Diego Zoo, but if you enjoy zoos, it's worth a stop. The 70 species here include Amur tigers, penguins, zebras, and birds of prey. The zoo is open daily 10 A.M.–5 P.M.; closed Thanksgiving Day, Christmas, and New Year's Day. Admission is $4.80 for ages 12 and up, $2.30 for ages 4–11, $2.55 for seniors, and free to members and kids age 3 and under. On Thursday, all adults get in for $2.55, children 4–11 $1.30.

Discovery Center of Idaho

On the park's northern fringe is the Discovery Center of Idaho, 131 Myrtle St., 208/343-9895, www.dcidaho.com. More than 100 wild, wacky, and amazing hands-on exhibits—a bicycling skeleton, magnetic sands, and an infinity mirror, to name just a few—fill this huge, mad-scientist-in-training's classroom. Sound, light, fluids, electricity—who needs a stuffy old book to learn about these things when you can come here and experience the phun of physics phirsthand. Kids love this place, and adults like it a whole lot.

The Discovery Center is open June–Aug. Mon.–Sat. 10 A.M.–5 P.M., Sun. noon–5 P.M.; Sept.–May Tues.–Fri. 9 A.M.–5 P.M., Sat. 10 A.M.–5 P.M., and Sun. noon–5 P.M. It's closed Monday and on Thanksgiving Day, Christmas, and New Year's Day. Admission is $6 general, $5 seniors, $3.50 children 3–12; free to members and children under three.

WARM SPRINGS AVENUE

This was one of early Boise's most prestigious addresses, and home after stately turn-of-the-20th-century home can be seen as you cruise down the shady, tree-lined avenue. The street didn't get its name for nothing: Boise's abundant geothermal resources were developed early in the city's history. Today, many of the homes here continue to be heated with naturally hot water.

Pioneer Cemetery

Boise founders Julia Davis and Thomas Jefferson Davis, early Idaho governor George Shoup, and pioneer notables and nobodies alike share this final resting place near the intersection of Warm Springs and Broadway Avenues. The simple, poignant graves remain unadulterated by modern historical plaques or keep-away-from-the-history barriers. It's a nice spot for a picnic, amid the ghosts of Boise's forefathers and foremothers.

MK Nature Center

Squirrels chatter in the trees, rainbow trout cruise sheltered pools, birds practice avian arias, and brightly colored flowers face the sun to shout off the morning dew. It's all at the MK Nature Center—a miniature, 4.6-acre wildlife preserve and botanical garden a couple of blocks south of Warm Springs Ave. at 600 S. Walnut St., 208/334-2225 or 208/368-6060 (recorded information). Trails lead past rushing stream and tranquil glade to unique exhibits like the fluvarium—a cutaway, glass-walled stream where you can watch many of Idaho's native fish species cavorting in their underwater realm. The trails are free and open sunrise to sunset. A visitor center holds additional exhibits and is open mid-March–Oct. Tues.–Fri. 9 A.M.–5 P.M., Sat.–Sun. 11 A.M.–5 P.M.; the rest of the year Tue.–Fri. 9 A.M.–5 P.M., closed Sat.–Mon. Admission is free.

Natatorium and Hydrotube

Well, it used to be a natatorium (indoor pool), and a fancy one at that. The big, elaborate building, from 1892, had removable flooring over the pool, and dances and social functions were often held there. But in 1934 one doozy of a storm blew it apart. Now it's an outdoor pool, open summers Mon.–Sat. 1:30–5:30 P.M. and 7–9 P.M., Sun. 1:30–5:30 P.M. You'll find it at 1811 Warm Springs Ave., 208/345-9270. Admission to the pool is $3.25 adults, $2.25 ages 12–18, $1.75 ages 11 and under. A family package costs $6 for one adult and two kids. The hydrotube, a waterslide popular with kids of all ages, costs $7 for an all-day pass, or you can get a book of 10 tickets for $6; season passes are available that reduce the price somewhat.

Old Idaho Penitentiary

The Old Pen, 2445 Old Penitentiary Rd., 208/368-6080 (recorded information) or 208/334-2844, is one of only four U.S. territorial prisons still standing. It was built in 1870 and remained in use for more than a century. Among its famous tenants: Harry Orchard, convicted for the 1905 assassination of Governor Frank Steunenberg; and Lyda "Lady Bluebeard" Southard, convicted of killing her fourth husband for insurance money, and suspected of doing away with the first three as well.

It's hard to imagine that a 19th-century cellblock with no internal plumbing ("night buckets" were used) served inmates until the 1970s. Not surprisingly, the antiquated conditions led to a riot in 1973 that resulted in the gutting of a couple of buildings. That event helped convince the powers that be to move the prison to a new facility more appropriate to the 20th century. The Old Pen was shut down. Now you can tour this State Historic Site, pondering Sartre in "Siberia" (solitary confinement) and smelling the roses in the prison rose garden, where the original prison gallows once sent unfortunate convicts to their final resting place. The self-guided walking tour here takes approximately 90 minutes. This prison is certainly more interesting architecturally than its famous cousin, Alcatraz. While the latter resembles nothing so much as a WPA project gone to seed, the Old Pen looks like something from another time—part Wild West hang-'em-high hoosegow, part medieval castle.

In 2002, the Old Pen added the J. Curtis Earl Memorial Exhibit featuring 5,000 years of arms and weaponry. The artifacts, dating as far back as 3500 B.C., were accumulated over some 60 years by the late J. Curtis Earl, a part-time Boise resident. You'll see daggers and arrow points from the Bronze age, medieval arms and armor, Civil War artifacts, and an 1883 Gatling gun on its original carriage. Admission is included in the Old Pen entry price, which is $5 adults, $4 seniors, and $3 children 6–12, under 6 free. The Old Penitentiary is open daily 10 A.M.–5 P.M. in summer, noon–5 P.M. the rest of the year; closed on state holidays during fall, winter, and spring.

The **Idaho Mining and Geology Museum,**

Built of hand-cut sandstone, the Old Pen is now on the National Register of Historic Places.

208/368-9876, is a treasure trove for rockhounds. There's a self-guided tour, and volunteers are happy to answer questions. It's in an outbuilding outside the prison walls, just uphill from the main entrance to the prison; donations are welcome. Open April–Oct. Wed.–Sun. noon–5 P.M.

Idaho Botanical Garden

Adjacent to the Old Pen you'll find the Idaho Botanical Garden, 2355 Old Penitentiary Rd., 208/343-8649. One species or another here will be in bloom from late April to mid-October. A humble labor of love relying heavily on memberships and volunteer efforts, the gardens provide an always-welcome oasis of tranquil greenery. Various trails snake around the grounds, with picnic tables and benches strategically placed here and there. Special events include Thursday-evening concerts in summer and Winter Garden aGlow during the Christmas holidays. The gardens are open year-round Mon.–Fri. 9 A.M.–5 P.M. (until 8 P.M. Fri. in summer), Sat.–Sun. 10 A.M.–6 P.M. (May–Oct.) and noon–4 P.M. (Nov.–April). Admission costs $4 general, $3 seniors, $2 students 6–12, free to children under five.

BOISE STATE UNIVERSITY

More than 18,400 students pursue undergraduate and graduate degrees at this 153-acre campus lining the Boise River, making BSU the state's highest-enrollment university and one of the West's fastest-growing schools. It's also a hub of activity for students and city residents.

Parking

Metered parking is available all around campus, and pay parking lots for visitors are available in front of the Administration Building (at Joyce and University) and by the Student Union Building. More information is available at the **Parking Office,** 1001 Lincoln Ave., 208/426-1681. The BSU campus is a short walk from downtown, and the city transit system operates a shuttle bus around campus.

Campus Highlights

On the west end of campus along the river is **Morrison Center for the Performing Arts,** 208/426-1609 or 208/426-1110 (tickets). Considered one of the country's most acoustically perfect performance halls, the award-winning

Morrison Center hosts musical and cultural events year-round. Tours of the 2,000-seat facility are offered by advance arrangement.

The **Hemingway Western Studies Center,** 208/426-1999, contributes to a small university publishing endeavor focusing on the works and study of Western writers. The center also holds Hemingway memorabilia, including pictures of Papa's Ketchum home and a magazine article reprinting a letter Hemingway wrote to his editor, grousing about young wannabe writers dropping by uninvited and interrupting his work. A small art gallery presents exhibits related to the West. The center is open Mon.–Fri. 8 A.M.–5 P.M. Admission is free.

Centennial Amphitheater is a delightful, open and grassy 800-seat amphitheater within earshot of the Boise River. If you brought a sack lunch with you, this would be a great spot to stop and devour it. The adjacent road heading away from the river into the heart of campus leads to the huge, orange-sided **BSU Pavilion.** A variety of events—from BSU Broncos basketball games to concerts by name entertainers—are staged in this 12,000-seat arena. Looking east from the pavilion, you can't miss **Bronco Stadium,** on the east edge of campus. For better or worse, this 30,000-seat stadium is known throughout the Northwest not only as the home of the BSU Broncos football team, but for its bright blue Astroturf (affectionately known as "Smurf Turf"). For ticket information for both venues, call 208/426-4737.

The **Student Union Building,** the on-campus social hub, contains the university bookstore (208/426-2665), an art gallery, cafeterias, pool tables, and even a bowling alley. Adjacent is the **Special Events Center,** a small, 435-seat theater also used for seminars and meetings, and across the parking lot from there, on the first floor of the Liberal Arts Building, you'll find the **BSU Art Gallery,** open daily during the school year, admission free.

In 2002, BSU opened its brand-new, 86,000-square-foot recreation center, 1515 University Dr., 208/426-5641. Unfortunately, most of it is open only to Boise State students, employees, and alumni—though there are exceptions, such as the climbing gym.

Tours and Information

Tours leave the New Student Information Center in the Student Union Building Mon.–Fri. at 10:30 A.M. and 1:30 P.M. in the spring semester, 1:30 P.M. only in fall semester. The center, 208/426-1820, can also provide you with campus maps and further information about the university. Sept.–May, it's open Mon.–Fri. 8 A.M.–5 P.M.; in summer, Mon.–Thurs. 8 A.M.–5 P.M., Fri. 8–11 A.M.

To reach the various campus departments and facilities, call the main **University switchboard,** 208/426-1011. For more information, look up the school on the Web at www.boisestate.edu.

OTHER SIGHTS

Idaho Anne Frank Human Rights Memorial

In 2002, Idaho dedicated this moving tribute to the teenager whose family hid from the Nazis during World War II. A statue of Frank is accompanied by the entire United Nations Universal Declaration of Human Rights, as well as powerful quotes from human rights advocates throughout history. The monument is accessible from the Greenbelt between Capitol Boulevard and 9th Street, or by walking behind the Log Cabin Literary Center at 801 S. Capitol Blvd.

Boise Depot/Platt Gardens

The city of Boise owns the beautiful old Union Pacific Depot at the south end of Capitol Boulevard, at 2603 Eastover Terrace, 208/384-9591. The Amtrak route that once stopped here was abandoned in 1997. The depot's Great Hall holds railroad memorabilia and is open Mon.–Fri. 10 A.M.–noon and 1:30–3:30 P.M.; admission is $1.50 adults, $1 seniors and students, under 12 free. Climb up into the bell tower for a great view of the capitol and downtown. Outside the depot you'll find some railroad cars on exhibit, as well as Platt Gardens, a small landscaped hillside with fountains, ponds, and trees.

National Interagency Fire Center

Call it "Forest Fire Central." Forest fires throughout the country are monitored and firefighting efforts coordinated at this facility adjacent to Boise Airport at 3833 S. Development Ave., 208/387-5512. It's a joint operation of eight federal agencies. Each year at the height of the season, more than 400 dispatchers, pilots, and communications specialists essentially move in here, working nonstop, while 56 smoke-jumpers—parachuting firefighters—are based here. High-tech equipment such as a computerized lightning-detection system, remote weather stations across the West, and infrared mapping gear can identify a trouble spot quickly, while a fleet of planes—from small OV-10 Bronco lead planes to huge C-130 tankers—can be in the air in minutes and headed toward the flames.

In addition to being a command center, the facility also maintains the largest cache of federal firefighting equipment in the country: 5,000 hand-held radios; an arsenal of Pulaskis, shovels, hoses, pumps, and other tools of the trade; and ancillary equipment such as generators, sleeping bags, and emergency fire shelters. The gear is shipped out as needed to firelines across the country.

Free tours are available but must be arranged in advance and are not given during summer's peak fire season.

Peregrine Fund World Center for Birds of Prey

The World Center for Birds of Prey, 208/362-3716 (business office) or 208/362-8687 (interpretive center), www.peregrinefund.org, lies six miles south of I-84 at 5666 W. Flying Hawk Ln. (take S. Cole Road south to the end and continue straight ahead a bit farther). It's on a hilltop only 15 minutes from the city but a world away—worth the trip just to experience the wind blowing across the sage and grasses, unimpeded by gas stations and shopping malls.

The Peregrine Fund started in 1970 from efforts to save the peregrine falcon, whose populations were on the decline due to rising concentrations of the human-made pesticide DDT in the food chain. DDT has since been banned in the United States, and overall, the Fund's efforts have been successful. More than 4,000 peregrines were bred and released into 28 states, and the peregrine was

removed from the endangered species list in August 1999. The Peregrine Fund continues its work to restore viable populations of other endangered raptors worldwide.

The Velma Morrison Interpretive Center here is open daily 9 A.M.–5 P.M. (Nov.–Feb. 10 A.M.–4 P.M., closed Thanksgiving, Christmas, and New Year's Day). Admission is $4 adults, $3 seniors, $2 children 4–16. Outside are several caged eagles, all incapable of surviving life in the wild for one reason or another. Inside, slide presentations fill you in on the status of endangered raptors worldwide, as well as the Fund's efforts to preserve them. You'll see a couple of individuals up close and personal, perhaps a harpy eagle headed for the jungles of South and Central America, or a huge California condor. Highly recommended.

Snake River Birds of Prey National Conservation Area

South of Boise along an 81-mile stretch of the Snake River is a 483,000-acre birds of prey preserve holding the world's densest concentrations of nesting raptors. Hiking and boating opportunities in the reserve can get you within binocular distance of the birds, among them hawks, eagles, owls, peregrine falcons, and large numbers of prairie falcons. For more information, call the preserve office at 208/384-3300.

SCENIC DRIVES

Boise is such a great outdoors city, it'd be a shame not to get out of your car and take advantage of this. But it's possible to get a flavor of the city from behind the windshield. Drive up to **Table Rock,** on the northeast edge of town, for an aerial view. More like a table mountain than a rock, this natural feature can be seen from many parts of Boise. To get there, take Reserve Road northeast from Fort Street, turn right on Shaw Mountain Road, and follow it up the hill. At the top of the hill, bear right onto Table Rock Road when the road forks. Continue past the end of the pavement about a half mile to the top. The road is a little bumpy but passable in the family sedan.

A couple of Boise's original avenues show off the trees that gave the city its name, and also provide a glimpse of some fine old homes. **Warm Springs Avenue** is the commonly cited example—you'll drive down it on your way to the Old Pen and Botanical Garden. Perhaps even more beautiful than Warm Springs, thanks to a wide green median divider planted with pear trees, is **Harrison Boulevard,** which takes you out to Bogus Basin Road. The quiet, residential streets on either side of Harrison hold many tidy, well-cared-for old homes. Another good view of the city can be had from **Crescent Rim Drive,** which curves along the lip of the Boise Bench above Ann Morrison Park. From here the park and the city spread out before you, and behind them the hills and mountains of the Boise Front rise steeply. The snow-covered peaks up at Bogus Basin provide the icing on the cake in winter.

SIGHTSEEING TOURS

Around Downtown
The **Boise Tour Train,** 208/342-4796, is a reasonable way to get an overview and background on some of the key parts of the city.

Flightseeing
Several air charter companies based at Boise Airport fly sightseeing tours by advance reservation.

SP Aircraft, 4105 Wright, 208/383-3323, will take a minimum of two passengers up in a Cessna 172 on a 40-minute air tour for $25 per person. **Sawtooth Flying Service,** 3591 Rickenbacker, 208/342-7888, specializes in transporting hunting and fishing parties to remote backcountry airstrips and ranches. But they'll be happy to fly you over Boise, too. Rates are $200 an hour for up to three passengers in a Cessna 180 or $240 an hour for up to five passengers in a turbo Cessna 206.

Boise River Tours
Retired Idaho Department of Fish and Game biologist John Heimer leads enlightening half-day tours, 208/333-0003, www.boiserivertours.com, of the little-floated stretch of the Boise River between Glenwood Avenue and the town of Eagle. You'll seldom see other boaters on these gentle trips, which are suitable for all ages. Heimer has engaging stories galore about the river, its inhabitants, and the genuinely amazing fact that this wildlife-rich river flows through one of the fastest-growing cities in the United States. The trips also include a tasty riverside snack midway through the float. Tours typically start at 8:45 A.M. in the summer months, but other arrangements can be made. Cost is $40 for adults, $30 for children.

Recreation

This is an outdoor-oriented town. As soon as the spring rains end, Boise's hills come alive with a profusion of wildflowers and the sounds of ratcheting derailleurs. Mountain bikers are everywhere—up on the Boise Front, along the Greenbelt, in the streets downtown. Warm spring and summer evenings find the streets crowded with walkers and joggers, getting after-work exercise or just enjoying the City of Trees. And come the dog days of summer, the Boise River and local reservoirs draw water-sports enthusiasts by the thousands. You can float the Boise right through downtown, past park after verdant park. Or go whitewater rafting on the Payette River less than an hour outside town. When winter snows blanket the Boise Mountains, the skis come out of the

closets, bound for Bogus Basin Ski Area. Both alpine and Nordic skiing there are close enough to get to after work or even on a long lunch hour.

CITY PARKS

No matter which part of town you're in, you'll almost certainly be near one of the 90 parks maintained by the City of Boise. The parks range in size from the grand Julia Davis and Ann Morrison Parks to smaller pocket parks dotting the city. Several of the most popular parks are described below. For a complete list of parks and their respective facilities, contact the Boise Parks and Recreation Department, 1104 Royal Blvd., 208/384-4240, www.cityofboise.org/parks.

All city parks are open sunrise to sunset. Dogs must be kept on a leash and are not allowed at Municipal Park off Warm Springs Avenue or at Platt Gardens adjacent to the Boise Depot. (Dogs can play off-leash in a designated dog park at Fort Boise Park, as long as they're under your control.) Beer and wine are permitted in the parks, except where expressly prohibited. Hard alcohol is not permitted, nor are glass beverage containers. Finally, the Parks Department asks that you not feed the ducks, geese, elephants, or any other wildlife you might encounter.

Boise River Greenbelt

The beautiful, modestly sized Boise River flows through the heart of the city. Its lushly lined banks have been preserved as the city's signature park, the 25-mile Boise River Greenbelt. Paved trails on either side of the river wind along the banks, drawing strollers, bicyclists, joggers, and skaters. Several small piers jut out into the river in places, some half hidden by luxuriant greenery, while benches overlooking the water provide ideal places for quiet contemplation.

Wildlife also enjoys this riparian oasis. You'll see abundant waterfowl, and if you get lucky, you might spy a bald eagle, blue heron, great horned owl, muskrat, beaver, deer, or fox. At some points along the trails, the downtown skyline comes into view, reminding you just how close this tranquil escape is to the urban core. The Greenbelt runs from Garden City in the west (with plans to expand onto Eagle Island) to the Discovery Unit of Lucky Peak State Park in the east. Other major access points include Veterans Memorial Park, Ann Morrison Park (enter from Americana Boulevard), and Julia Davis Park, off Capitol Avenue. But head down to the river anywhere in town and you should be able to find the Greenbelt trails with no difficulty.

Ann Morrison Park

This 153-acre spread lines the south side of the Boise River between Americana and Capitol Boulevards. It's mostly level and grassy, suitable for kite-flying and pickup soccer games. There's also an 18-hole disc golf course, plus nice picnic areas and a big playground. Tubers generally haul out here after floating down from Barber Park.

Julia Davis Park

This is the "sights" park, home of Zoo Boise, the Boise Art Museum, Idaho Historical Museum, Idaho Black History Museum, a rose garden, and a band shell. The tennis courts here see a lot of use, as do the pedal boats you can rent for a cruise around the park's pond. Also of note, the Boise Tour Train (actually a tram) takes sightseers around the city from its "depot" here near the Historical Museum. The park is bounded by Capitol Avenue on the west, Front Street on the north, Broadway Avenue on the east, and the Boise River on the south.

Kathryn Albertson Park

You can't miss the entrance sign for this tranquil, 40-acre wildlife preserve just across Americana Boulevard from Ann Morrison Park; its name is chiseled into 11 huge boulders that look like something straight out of *The Flintstones* or *Jurassic Park*. Paved trails wind around ponds, where many species of birds and other animals can be seen. The park was specifically designed to encourage wildlife—if you're quiet and lucky, you might find yourself within mere feet of a great blue heron or other waterbird. This park is a great spot for quiet meditation, a relaxing picnic, or an outdoor wedding. Swimming and fishing are prohibited, and dogs must be kept on a leash.

At the "rookerie" gazebo is recorded a quote from naturalist Aldo Leopold that seems especially relevant in Idaho today. It reads:

There are some that can live without wild things and some who cannot. Like the winds and sunsets, wild things were taken for granted until progress began to do away with them. Now we face the question whether a still higher standard of living is worth its cost in things natural, wild, and free. For us of the minority, the opportunity to see geese is more important than television; and the chance to find a pasque flower is a right as inalienable as free speech.

COURTESY OF THE BOISE CONVENTION AND VISITORS BUREAU

Kathryn Albertson Park

Camel's Back Park and Reserve

North of Hyde Park out 13th Street, Camel's Back Park has two components. The corner lot at 13th and Heron offers an expanse of green grass with a soccer field, tennis courts, trees, and a large children's play area with some neat equipment. Behind this area is the camel's back itself—a couple of humps of hills rising up about 100 feet. I like up to the top for a great view of the city; this is a popular place to watch fireworks. On the other side of the humps, trails continue down to the 8th Street trailhead.

Fort Boise Park and Military Reserve Park

Fort Boise was built in 1863 as a base from which the U.S. 9th Cavalry could protect Oregon Trail emigrants from attack by hostile natives. The guardhouse at 5th and Fort Streets is the original sandstone structure; the O'Farrell Cabin at 4th and Fort was built by Boise pioneer John O'Farrell for his 17-year-old bride and was the site of the first Catholic mass in town. In addition to the many original buildings, a number of newer government buildings have been added, including Veterans' Hospital and the Idaho Veterans'

Home. This also is the hub of Boise Parks & Recreation activities. The **Fort Boise Community Center,** 700 Robbins Rd., 208/384-4486, houses the city recreation office, a community weight room and gym, an art center, and lots more. Fort Boise Park also has a skate park, tennis courts, and ball fields. The Boise Little Theater, 100 E. Fort St., 208/342-5104, is here, too.

Military Reserve Park encompasses 466 acres of brush-covered foothills behind Fort Boise Park. Only a few dirt roads cross the park, but dozens of hiking and biking trails lace the hills here. It's a quick-access wild area just three blocks from the city. Sagebrush scents and some great city views make the park a good place for a day hike, a trail run, or quality time with Fido, who can run off leash.

ParkCenter Pond

This eight-acre pond amid the hotels and offices of ParkCenter is a favorite spot for float-tube fishing and windsurfing. Sand volleyball courts and picnic tables round out the offerings.

Municipal Park

Your basic picnic venue, Muni Park holds large

grassy areas that make it a natural for family re-unions or employee get-togethers. But anyone can enjoy the shade and tranquility. Off Warm Springs Avenue, it's near the MK Nature Center.

Veterans Memorial Park

As schizophrenic a park as ever there was, the front half of Veterans Memorial holds neatly trimmed lawns, stately evergreens, a small amphitheater, and a solemn memorial to Idaho's fallen veterans. But head down to the back half and the park turns wild. The river flows through it, bringing swamps and riverine jungles that attract would-be Huck Finns with fishin' poles, as well as bicyclers and joggers who work up a sweat running laps on the cool, quiet trails. A large lake separated from the river by a narrow isthmus provides calm water for swimming or floating around on a raft. The park is a freebie, west of town at 36th and State Streets. It's open sunrise to sunset.

COUNTY AND STATE PARKS

Barber Park

On Eckert Road off Warm Springs Avenue east of town, 87-acre Barber Park draws tubers in summer for the six-mile float down the Boise River to Ann Morrison Park. You can rent tubes and rafts here, 208/343-6564, in the summertime. In addition, the park offers fishing access, trees and grass, and shaded picnic areas. A $4 parking fee is charged in the summer floating season to offset the cost of keeping this tidy, well-maintained Ada County park in such good shape. The park is on the Greenbelt bike path and makes a nice destination for a half-day bike ride out from downtown. For year-round info, phone 208/343-1328.

Lucky Peak State Park

Lucky Peak Reservoir, about a 15- to 20-minute drive east of downtown, is Boise's premier place to escape the heat of summer. A day-use-only park, it's made up of three different units. Two of the units are not on the reservoir itself but downstream from Lucky Peak Dam. All are fully operational between Memorial Day and Labor Day.

Coming from downtown Boise, take Warm Springs Avenue east. Eventually it turns into

Highway 21. The first park unit you'll get to, about eight miles from town, is the **Discovery Unit.** The beautiful grassy park along the riverbank offers plenty of sun or shade, picnic tables, and some barbecue grills. No lifeguards are on duty here, and some tricky currents in places make swimming potentially dangerous and certainly not recommended for small children.

Take the kids instead a bit farther upstream to the 25-acre **Sandy Point Unit,** right below the dam. The park, 208/334-2679, is open 7 A.M.–9 P.M. daily in summer, with lifeguards on duty between 11 A.M. and 6 P.M. A calm cove here surrounds a fountain and makes a great place to float around on tubes or rafts, both of which can be rented from the concessionaire. Sunburning on the beaches is the most popular summer activity, but you'll also find abundant grass for Frisbees or hackeysacks. A snack bar means you can leave the picnic basket at home if you so desire, but picnickers will find plenty of tables to further their experiments in ant- and yellow jacket–attraction techniques. Don't bring Spot—no pets are allowed. Fishing is also prohibited here.

You may find it a little creepy to be loafing in the sun right below a dam that is holding back several bazillion gallons of water, but if you set up your lawn chair facing downstream, this won't bother you at all. The day-use fee at both the Discovery and Sandy Point Units is $4.

Finally, the **Spring Shores Unit** is nine miles farther up the highway toward Idaho City and the only unit on Lucky Peak Reservoir itself. The road curves over Highland Pass, past hillsides blanketed with arrowleaf balsamroot—brilliantly yellow in spring—and then drops down to the reservoir (turn right off the highway just across Mores Creek Bridge). This is the boaters' unit of the park—water-skiers, jet-skiers, bassboaters, sailboarders, and even a few sailboaters come here to do their thing in the high-desert lake rimmed by mountains. Anglers try their luck at pulling trout, smallmouth bass, kokanee, perch, and whitefish from the glimmering waters. The large **marina,** 208/336-9505, offers numerous slips and a boat-launching ramp. The concessionaire also runs a small grill (burgers and such), sells boating supplies, and rents multipassenger personal watercraft ("spud tubs"). The marina is open from May 1 to Memorial Day on weekends from noon to 8 or 9 P.M. After Memorial Day until fall, it's open daily from 11 A.M. weekdays, and from 8 A.M. weekends. If it rains, all bets are off. A few picnic tables line the shore. It'll cost you $4 to use the park or launch a boat here.

For more information on any of the units of Lucky Peak State Park, call the Idaho Department of Parks and Recreation at 208/334-4199.

Eagle Island State Park

Summer brings something for everyone at this tidy little state park about eight miles west of Boise at 2691 Mace Rd. in Eagle, 208/939-0696. A 15-acre lake makes a good swimming hole, and a nice sandy beach draws sun worshippers. Kids head right to the waterslide (open weekends noon–8 P.M.), while picnickers will find expansive grassy areas and numerous picnic tables to lay out the spread. The park boundaries extend far to the east—only 26 of the park's 546 total acres have been developed. Walk-in visitors get in free, but it'll cost you $4 to drive the Buick in. The waterslide costs $4 for 10 rides or $8 all day. No pets are allowed in the park, but you can bring a horse; there are 5 miles of equestrian trails.

SPORTS

Bicycling

Boise is a great bicycling town. In addition to the **Greenbelt,** the "Ridge to Rivers" trail system, www.ridgetorivers.org, provides for on-road and off-road cyclists alike and continues to expand under municipal planning efforts. Boise also has plenty of bike lanes to offer cyclists an added margin of safety and comfort by keeping them a little farther away from traffic.

Mountain biking claims the biggest niche of the sport here, and no wonder. Just north of the city lies the **Boise Front,** a vast tract of foothill wilderness—part BLM, part Forest Service land—laced with both primitive roads and single-track trails. You can ride right from downtown and in minutes be out in the sage and rabbitbrush with no other sound than the wind whistling through your ears. This is an immensely popular after-work and weekend destination for Boiseans, and the heavy use is beginning to result in some erosion problems in the area's fragile soil. With the increased bike traffic, collisions at blind corners are not unheard of; ride responsibly.

To get there from downtown, head north on 8th Street and just keep going. Other access points in the same general area include Crestline Road (off Brumback) and Bogus Basin Road just past the Highlands Hollow brewpub. A little farther south, Military Reserve Park, Rocky Canyon Road (at the end of Shaw Mountain Road), and Table Rock Road are other gateways to the Front's trail system. Military Reserve Park has many trails that are well used in summer.

A couple of Boise's bike laws are worth a mention. Bicyclists must slow down and use caution at stop signs, but need not stop if it isn't necessary for safety. Bicyclists must stop at all red traffic lights. Also, it's legal to ride on the sidewalks unless specifically prohibited by signs; pedestrians have the right-of-way, however.

Fishing

How many cities of this size—how many state capitals—offer good fishing right within the city limits? Start with the **Boise River** that flows through town. Its cold waters hold rainbow and brown trout and whitefish. Popular access points include (west to east) Glenwood Bridge, Veterans Park, Capitol Bridge, and Barber Park. The river is stocked with rainbows monthly.

In addition to the river, many urban ponds are frequently stocked. Near the Glenwood Bridge, **Riverside Pond** holds rainbow trout and bluegill. **Veterans Park Pond** holds rainbows, largemouth bass, crappie, bullhead, and bluegill. **ParkCenter Pond** provides a home to rainbow trout, largemouth bass, crappie, bluegill, bullhead, and channel catfish. The ponds make ideal spots for youngsters to try their first fishin'.

A couple of reservoirs not far from town also draw anglers. Large **Lucky Peak Reservoir,** full of rainbow trout and kokanee, is eight miles east of Boise on Highway 21. Summer smallmouth bass fishing is reportedly good as well. Other species inhabiting the reservoir include perch and whitefish, as well as small populations of

BOISE SPORTS OUTFITTERS

The great outdoors is at your doorstep in Boise, and you'll want to get out there and enjoy it. Here's a list of some outfitters that rent the gear you'll need. First look up the type of gear you'll be wanting to rent in the chart on top, then match the numbers listed there to the outfitter list following.

Backpacks: 2, 6, 10
Bikes: 3, 6, 8
Canoes: 7
Inner tubes: 1
Kayaks: 4 (inflatable), 7
Rafts: 1, 4, 7
Rock-climbing shoes: 2, 6, 10
Skates: 8, 9

Skis:
    Alpine: 5, 8
    Cross-country: 2, 6, 8, 10
    Telemark/backcountry: 2, 6, 10
Snowboards: 3, 5, 6, 8, 9
Snowshoes: 2, 3, 5, 6, 8, 9, 10
Tennis rackets: 8
Tents: 2, 6, 10

1. **Barber Park Raft and Tube Rental** at Barber Park on Eckert Road (upstream end of the Greenbelt), 208/343-6564; open Memorial Day to Labor Day
2. **The Benchmark,** 625 Vista, 208/338-1700
3. **Bikes2Boards,** 3525 W. State St., 208/343-0208, www.bikes2boards.com
4. **Boise Army-Navy,** 4924 Chinden, 208/322-0660
5. **Gart Sports,** 1301 N. Milwaukee, 208/378-9590
6. **Idaho Mountain Touring,** 1310 W. Main, 208/336-3854
7. **Idaho River Sports,** in Hyde Park at 1521 N. 13th, 208/336-4844
8. **McU Sports,** 822 W. Jefferson, 208/342-7734; and 2314 Bogus Basin Rd., 208/336-2300, www.mcusports.com
9. **Newt & Harold's,** 1021 Broadway, 208/385-9300
10. **REI,** 8300 W. Emerald (at Milwaukee), 208/322-1141

Boise State University's Outdoor Program, located in the Student Recreation Center, 1515 University Dr., has a mind-boggling selection of four-season rental gear. If you're a BSU student, staffer, or alum, or if you're attending a BSU conference, you qualify to rent gear here. For more information on equipment rentals or eligibility, call 208/426-1946.

bull trout and chinook. Finally, 19 miles east of town you'll come to **Indian Creek Reservoir,** on the south side of I-84. Here you'll find an array of fishables, including cutthroat trout, largemouth bass, bluegill, bullhead, channel cats, and the ubiquitous rainbow trout.

For more information on fishing the waters in and around Boise, pick up the Idaho Department of Fish and Game's angler's guide, *Fishing Urban Boise.* It's available at the Fish and Game office, 600 S. Walnut St., 208/334-3700.

Or you can drop into one of several fishing supply stores in town, among them **Anglers,** 7097 Overland Rd., 208/323-6768; **Idaho Angler,** 1682 Vista Ave., 208/389-9957; and **Stonefly Angler,** in The Benchmark mountain-sports shop at 625 Vista Ave., 208/338-1333.

Golf

Several courses in the vicinity keep Boise golfers swinging year-round, weather permitting—usually about 325 days a year. All the major courses offer club and cart rentals.

Boise Ranch Golf Course, 6501 S. Cloverdale

Rd., 208/362-6501, is an 18-hole, par-71 course with staggered tees providing course lengths of between 5,206 and 6,574 yards. Seven manmade lakes provide water traps galore. Greens fees run $22–28. To get there, take Victory Road west from Cole Road to Cloverdale and turn left (south).

A perennial local favorite for its course, pro shop, and 19th hole is **Shadow Valley Golf Course,** 15711 Hwy. 55, 208/939-6699. Length for the 18-hole, par 72 course runs 5,514–6,433 yards. Many Boise golfers pick Shadow Valley's short, scenic, and unforgiving hole two as the best in town. Also look out for holes 13 and 14 on the back nine. Hole 13 is a 525-yard, par-five dogleg with what many consider the most difficult drive in the city, while 14's green has water on either side and both water and trees behind it. Greens fees run $23–30. To get there, take State Street northwest from downtown and turn right on Highway 55 toward McCall.

In the vicinity is **Eagle Hills Golf Course,** 605 N. Edgewood Lane in Eagle, 208/939-0402. The 18-hole, par-72 course runs 4,922–6,517 yards and is known for its immaculate condition year-round. If you're not careful, you might need your bathing suit to play hole five here—its large water trap is notorious. Greens fees run $15–30.

On the north side of town you'll find **Quail Hollow Golf Club,** 4520 N. 36th St., 208/344-7807. Hole one at this challenging 18-hole course sets the tone for what could be a very long afternoon; it's a 293-yard, par-four nightmare that seems to be made up of equal parts sand, water, and grass. Hole seven provides a great view of the city. Course length here runs 4,557–6,394 yards; par 70. Greens fees run $25–30.

On the east side of town at 2495 Warm Springs Ave. is **Warm Springs Golf Course,** 208/343-5661. One side of the picturesque municipal course runs alongside the beautiful Boise River—also known as "Old Man Watertrap" to those who hook left on hole two. The 18-hole, par-72 course runs 5,660–6,719 yards. Greens fees run $21–25.

Boise's nine-hole courses make for good inexpensive practice rounds. Try the **Golf and Recreation Club,** 3883 S. Orchard St., 208/344-

2008; **Indian Lakes Golf Club,** 4700 S. Umatilla Ave., 208/362-5771; or **Pierce Park Greens,** 5812 Pierce Park Lane, 208/853-3302.

Hiking

Most bike trails in the Boise Front are open to hikers as well as bikers, and the **Hull's Gulch National Recreation Trail** is open to hikers exclusively. Of the two Hull's Gulch trailheads, the lower one is 3.5 miles from the end of the pavement at the north end of 8th Street; the upper is three miles farther up the road. The primitive road is easily traversed in the Oldsmobile; just take it slowly. Both trailheads are on the right and well marked. From the lower trailhead, the 3.5-mile, BLM-developed foot trail rounds a ridge and drops into Hull's Gulch—a deep, brushy canyon sliced down its center by the proverbial babbling brook. In spring, the wildflowers and butterflies try to outdo each other for your attention. (Watch out for ticks, though, who'd just as soon you *didn't* notice them.) The gradually ascending trail eventually reaches the lower limit of the pines, where a few magnificent ponderosas inhabit the sunny slopes.

All along the way, BLM signs identify some of the common botanical species and offer some basic ecology lessons. Among the plants you'll see: willow, rabbitbrush, Rocky Mountain maple, chokecherry, and syringa, the state flower. In spring, wildflowers brightening the gulch include arrowleaf balsamroot, phlox, lupine, and larkspur. Among the animals you might catch a glimpse of: rabbits, lizards, porcupines, badgers, and coyotes. A 2.5-mile loop at the top lets you come back a slightly different path, or you might want to leave the gulch behind at the upper trailhead and just hike back down the dirt road. This route doesn't have quite the same wilderness feel, but it's atop the ridge and provides great views of Boise, the Owyhee Mountains, and a large chunk of southwestern Idaho. For more information on the Hull's Gulch Trail, contact the BLM's Boise District office, 3948 Development Ave., 208/384-3300.

Hot-Air Ballooning

Dawn over the Treasure Valley, the perfect desert

stillness broken only intermittently by the blast of a propane burner lighting off a couple of feet over your head. Ah, the magic of ballooning. Several companies in the area offer rides. Try **Footelights,** 11269 W. Reutzel Dr., 208/362-5914, or **Idaho Hot Airlines,** 4049 W. Plum, 208/344-8462.

Rock Climbing

Good boulder fields are scarce in the Boise area, but several climbing gyms in town and a good top-rope area out near Lucky Peak help keep the local climbers in shape. On the **BSU campus,** you'll find a state-of-the-art climbing gym in the new Student Recreation Center, 1515 University Dr., across from the Student Union. It's usually open Sun.–Thurs. 6:30–10 P.M., except over school holidays. Admission is $5 for nonstudents; equipment rental is available. Climbers must pass a mandatory belay test; free belay classes are offered periodically throughout the week. For more information on hours and access, call 208/426-1946.

The outdoor-equipment supermarket **REI,** 8300 W. Emerald (at Milwaukee), 208/322-1141, offers a single wall open Tuesday nights 6:30–8:30 P.M., with REI employees doing the belaying. It's free.

Both the **West Family YMCA,** 5959 N. Discovery Place, 208/377-9622, and the downtown **Boise Family YMCA,** 1050 W. State St., 208/344-5501, have climbing walls.

The most popular outdoor climbing area in the vicinity is **Black Cliffs,** a one- to two-pitch basalt outcropping on the north side of Warm Springs Avenue/Highway 21, across from the Diversion Dam. You can't miss the roadside cliffs a little less than a mile past the Beaver Dick and Oregon Trail twin historical markers, about seven miles east of downtown. Other popular areas include the old quarry behind the Old Pen, and Rocky Canyon—a small but scenic area north of Table Rock. To get to Rocky Canyon, take Reserve Road to Shaw Mountain Road just as if you were going to Table Rock, but at the Y at the top of the hill, bear left on Shaw Mountain Road. A blue sign at the Y reads "To Rocky Canyon Road." Follow the road to the end of the pavement and continue about another quarter mile on a good gravel road.

Running

The city is full of great places to go jogging. Start with the Greenbelt, where you can enjoy a car-free workout of up to 25 miles, past the rushing waters and lushly vegetated banks of the Boise River. At any time of year, you'll find Boiseans out for exercise on the Greenbelt's paths. All the major parks would be great places to run. You could loop through Ann Morrison Park, using the Greenbelt for one side of the loop and the park's walkways for the other side. Or head over to Veterans Memorial Park on the west end of town—trails there wind down to the Boise River and around a marsh and a large pond.

Racers will find an event scheduled almost every weekend from April to October. This is a runner's town. Among the best-known races in Idaho is mid-April's **Race to Robie Creek,** a brutal 13.1-mile ordeal from Fort Boise Park up Rocky Canyon and over Aldape Summit. That may sound like self-inflicted punishment to you, but upwards of 2,000 masochists have taken up the challenge in recent years.

Scuba Diving

Well, Cozumel it ain't, but Boise's divers enjoy exploring the area's ponds and rivers; in spring before the algae bloom, Brownlee Reservoir on the Snake is reportedly a favorite. The folks at **Boise Water Sports,** 2404 S. Orchard, 208/342-1378, can direct you to Idaho's most popular dive spots, as well as help with dive instruction and equipment rental.

Skateboarding

On weekends, boarders and in-line skaters head to **Rhodes Park,** a concrete slab under The Connector freeway (between 15th and 16th on Front Street, next to Reel Foods Fish Market). The park is the brainchild and labor of love of retired contractor Glenn Rhodes, who thought the kids of Boise needed a safe and secure place to skateboard, away from the streets of downtown and away from the inevitable complaints of stuffy city merchants. Rhodes created this veritable haven for youth, which is absolutely free. The park holds quarter pipes, a half pipe, and rail slides, as well as basketball hoops. **Fort Boise Skate Park** is another option, located off Reserve Street past the baseball field.

Board shops in town include **The Board Room,** 2727 W. State St., 208/385-9553, and **Newt & Harold's,** 1021 Broadway, 208/385-9300.

Skating
The hard-core in-line skaters go to **Rhodes Park,** 15th and Front Streets, to fly up the quarter pipes just like the skateboarders. **Fort Boise Skate Park** and the **Greenbelt** are prime skating territory, too.

Those who prefer skating on thin (or thick) ice can head to **Idaho Ice World,** at Boise Outlet Mall, 208/331-0044. Public skating sessions are held daily; call for times. Admission is $6.50 adults, $5.50 for those 12 and under and 60 and over. Skate rentals are $2 and lessons are available.

Skiing
See Bogus Basin Recreation, below.

Skydiving
You'll have to drive out of town a ways to indulge your adrenaline lust in this fashion. **Snake River Skydiving,** 4005 N. Can-Ada Rd. in Star, 208/377-8111, charges first-timers $149 for a four- to five-hour class followed by a static-line jump. If you're too chicken to go alone, you can piggyback with one of their instructors in a tandem jump for $139 during the week, $149 on weekends. Experienced jumpers with their own gear pay $18 for a flight up to 10,000 feet; gear rental is an additional $20. The company can also take videos of your jump for you.

Swimming
The Boise River and Lucky Peak Reservoir are suitable for summer swimming, but Boise offers a number of swimming pools, too. For indoor swimming, the **Boise Aquatic Center** at the West Family YMCA, 5959 N. Discovery Place, 208/377-9622, has a 50-meter pool for lap swimming, as well as a children's pool, waterslide, and hydrotherapy pool. Admission is $7.25 adults, $3.25 kids, with family rates available.

Outdoor city swimming pools can be found during the summer months at Borah Park, 801 Aurora, 208/375-8373; Fairmont Park, 7929 W. Northview, 208/375-3011; Ivywild, 2250 Leadville Ave., 208/384-1697; Lowell School, 1601 N. 28th St., 208/345-7918; South Junior High, 921 Shoshone, 208/345-1984; and the Natatorium/Hydrotube, 1811 Warm Springs Ave., 208/345-9270. Admission varies from pool to pool, but plan on $3–3.50 adults, $2–2.50 ages 12–18, $1.50–2 ages 11 and under.

A little farther out, the waterslide at **Eagle Island State Park** provides a fun way to cool off. It costs $4 for 10 slides or $8 for a whole day. You'll also pay $4 per vehicle to drive into the park. For more information, call the park office at 208/939-0696.

See the Southwest Idaho chapter for information on Meridian's **Roaring Springs Water Park,** the area's largest.

Tennis
Tennis courts are located in about two dozen of the city's numerous municipal parks, including Ann Morrison off Americana Boulevard; Camel's Back at 13th and Heron; Fort Boise at Fort and Reserve Streets; Julia Davis at 700 S. Capitol Ave., and the Willow Lane Sports Complex at 4650 Willow Ln. in west Boise.

Tubing and Floating
Each summer, some 300,000 people start at Barber Park and float their way down the Boise River to Ann Morrison Park, a 6-mile trip that takes about an hour and a half. You can bring your own gear (air is available at Barber Park 10 A.M.–7 P.M. daily), or rent it (tubes, $5; rafts, $30–42) at the park. The rental office is open in summer Wed.–Fri. 11 A.M.–5 P.M., weekends and holidays 11 A.M.–6 P.M. No reservations are taken. A shuttle bus ($2 per person per trip) leaves Ann Morrison Park every hour on the hour and Barber Park every hour on the half-hour; hours are 1–8 P.M. weekdays and 1–9 P.M. weekends and holidays. Neither the rental office nor the shuttle operates if forecast temperatures fall below 80 degrees.

Walking

One nice aspect about walking in Boise: by and large the city is flat. The **Greenbelt,** Boise's premier walking path, meanders along the lush banks of the Boise River, providing plenty of spots along the way for quiet contemplation of the natural beauty. It also connects a string of parks from one end of town to the other and passes by Boise State University. BSU students often park off-campus and walk to class on the Greenbelt. You can pick up the path just about anywhere—just head for the river—but Julia Davis Park and Ann Morrison Park are two of the most popular access points.

One particularly wonderful spot on the Greenbelt for a stroll is at the east end, off ParkCenter Boulevard at River Run Drive. Here you'll find the **Greenbelt Wildlife Preserve,** which is open *only* to pedestrians and wildlife. You can't park at the access point, which is in a residential area. So park on ParkCenter somewhere, or just budget enough time to mosey on down the Greenbelt from points farther west.

Downtown itself is generally a safe and pleasant place to walk, day and night. Evenings are especially nice here, after all the business traffic has migrated back to suburbia and the setting sun casts a warm glow on the numerous beautiful buildings.

Whitewater Rafting and Kayaking

The **Payette River,** less than an hour outside Boise, drops down out of the mountains in world-class whitewater that draws thrillseekers from all over the country. Summer weekends see hundreds of rafters and kayakers on the river. The rapids here range from moderate Class IIIs all the way up to unrunnable Class VIs. See the Whitewater Madness section of the Southwest Idaho chapter for more info on outfitters.

Boise Parks & Recreation hopes to create an in-town paddling park sometime over the next few years. Call 208/384-4240 for updates.

BOGUS BASIN RECREATION

Skiing and Snowboarding

Boise skiers are spoiled by a superb ski resort just 16 miles north of town. **Bogus Basin Ski Resort,** 2405 Bogus Basin Rd., Boise, ID 83702, 208/332-5100, 800/367-4397, or 208/342-2100 (snow report), www.bogusbasin.com, has a base

night skiing above the Boise city lights

elevation of 5,800 feet and rises to a peak of 7,582 feet—high enough to provide featherweight powder when a cold front blows through. On the resort's 2,600 acres are two quad chairs, a triple chair, four double chairs, and a rope tow, serving 52 trails with a maximum vertical drop of 1,800 feet and a longest run of a mile and a half. Not bad for Boise's "local hill." Snowboarders are welcome anywhere on the mountain, and a separate snowboard park offers a mogul field, halfpipes, quarter pipes, and rail slides. There's also a lift-served tubing hill.

Night skiing here is one of the resort's highlights, with 165 acres open nightly Wed.–Sun. Weather can often be better at night than during the day, and a peaceful, uncrowded feeling settles over the area. The views on a clear night are something special.

Down near the lower day lodge, a **cross-country ski area** offers both skating and traditional tracks more than 12 miles of developed trails. Many trails offer great views of a major chunk of southwestern Idaho, from the Boise Front foothills in the foreground, out across the Snake River Plain, to the Owyhee Mountains in the background. Backcountry telemarkers who don't mind some hiking should ask the staff about Mores Mountain. Trail fees are $10 for adults, $5 for children 12 and under. Rentals and lessons are offered.

The resort's skier-service facilities include two day lodges, cafés, rental and retail shops, a ski school, a racing program, ski programs for children and physically challenged skiers, and day care.

The season here usually starts around Thanksgiving or early December and continues through the end of spring break. Lifts open at 9 A.M. on weekends, 10 A.M. on weekdays, and close Mon.–Tue. at 4:30 P.M. and Wed.–Sun. and holidays at 10 P.M. Full-day lift tickets at Bogus Basin run $32 Mon.–Tues. and $40 Wed.–Sun., $20 kids 7–11, free for seniors 70 and up and kids 6 and under. Half-day adult tickets cost $20 after 4 P.M.

> *Boise skiers are spoiled by a superb ski resort just 16 miles north of town. Bogus Basin Ski Resort has a base elevation of 5,800 feet and rises to a peak of 7,582 feet— high enough to provide featherweight powder when a cold front blows through.*

Buses serve the mountain from Boise and some neighboring communities. Cost is $8 roundtrip or $5 one-way. Call 208/459-6612 for routes and schedules.

Sleigh Rides and Trail Rides

In winter, **Bogus Creek Outfitters**, 1015 Robert St., Boise, ID 83705, 208/336-3130 or 888/264-8727, will bundle you up in wool blankets and take you for a horse-drawn sleigh ride from the Bogus Basin Nordic Area to a cozy cabin a mile deep in the woods. There you'll be served hot drinks by a roaring fire, followed by a cowboy-gourmet meal of soup, steak and prawns, vegetables, and dessert. The two-and-a-half hour evening costs $62.50 per person. The dinner rides are offered twice every evening at 6 and 8:30 P.M., from December through mid-March.

In summer, the outfit offers a similar chuckwagon dinner for the same price. Instead of the sleigh, you'll ride in on horseback or in a covered wagon. Live Western music and mock gunfights contribute to the atmosphere.

Apart from the dinner programs, the company also leads summer trail rides in the area; they're $24 for one hour, $42 for two hours.

Mountain Lodging

Sure it's only a half-hour drive back to Boise, but to guarantee first crack at that untracked powder, you might want to book a room in the **Pioneer Inn** condominiums, 208/332-5200, www.pioneercondos.com, which lie at midmountain, just steps from the slopes—you could ski right to your door if you wanted. Many of the plush yet unpretentious units offer fireplaces, with kindling and firewood provided. A hot tub and sauna can work après-ski wonders on those knots in your quads. Other amenities include a free laundry and free transportation to the lower base area in ski season. The condos are immediately adjacent to Pioneer Lodge—the upper day lodge of the alpine ski area—where the bar and grill is open until 11 P.M. nightly.

Two sizes of units are available: one-room efficiencies ($75–200, depending on the day) and two-room suites ($100–225). Two- or three-night minimum stays may apply; ask for details. The condos are available at reduced rates in summer.

ATHLETIC CLUBS

YMCAs

Boise has two YMCAs, both open to the public for a day-use fee of $12.50 adults, $6.50 youths age 7–18. Here's a hot tip for road warriors on a tight budget: the Y charges just $1.35 for use of its showers.

The extensive facilities at the **Boise Family YMCA,** downtown at 1050 W. State St., 208/344-5501, include pools, basketball and racquetball courts, cardio equipment and free weights, a climbing wall, and child care. It's open Mon.–Fri. 5 A.M.–10 P.M., Sat. 7 A.M.–6 P.M., Sun. noon–6 P.M. The pool closes a half-hour early.

The **West Family YMCA,** 5959 N. Discovery Place (south of W. Chinden Blvd., west of Cloverdale Rd.), 208/377-9622, has racquetball courts, a gym, a teen center, a climbing wall, a child-care center, basketball and volleyball courts, and an indoor running track. In addition, the facility houses the Boise Aquatic Center, which has a 50-meter pool with one- and three-meter diving boards, a children's pool, a waterslide, and a hydrotherapy pool. It's open Mon.–Fri. 5 A.M.–11 P.M., Sat. 7 A.M.–8 P.M., Sun. noon–6 P.M. Aquatic center–only rates are $7.25 adults, $3.25 kids, with family rates available.

Other Clubs

Several other athletic clubs are also open to the public for a day-use fee. **24 Hour Fitness** offers full gyms at two locations: ParkCenter, 555 W. ParkCenter Blvd., 208/343-2288, and Court House, 7211 Colonial (in the Boise Towne Square area), 208/377-0040.

Boise Racquet & Swim Club, 1116 N. Cole Rd., 208/376-1052, has indoor and outdoor tennis courts, a fitness center (with exercise bikes, Nautilus equipment, and free weights), an out-

door heated pool, and saunas, a spa, and suntanning facilities.

Health clubs exclusively for women include **Curves for Women,** 911 W. Jefferson St., 208/433-0141, and **Total Woman,** 670 S. 15th St., 208/342-2110.

SPECTATOR SPORTS

Baseball

Memorial Stadium, 5600 Glenwood (adjacent to the fairgrounds), is home of the Single-A **Boise Hawks,** a farm team of the Chicago Cubs. The season runs mid-June through early September. Tickets range $5.75–10.25. Call 208/322-5000 or visit www.boisehawks.com for tickets or more information.

BSU Sports/Humanitarian Bowl

Boise State University fields intercollegiate athletes in seven men's sports and eight women's sports, most competing in the Western Athletic Conference. Of course, **BSU football** is the big draw, with autumn games at the 30,000-seat Bronco Stadium. The BSU athletic ticket office, 208/426-4737, www.broncosports.com, is on the south end of Bronco Stadium.

The annual **Humanitarian Bowl,** 208/426-4737, www.humanitarianbowl.org, is Boise's single biggest sports event, held at Bronco Stadium during the post-Christmas football bowl season. The bowl game draws its name from the Boise-based World Sports Humanitarian Hall of Fame, which champions athletes' involvement in the community as well as on the field. Tickets (about $15–55) are available through the BSU ticket office or Select-A-Seat, 208/426-1494, www.idahotickets.com, a major local ticket broker with outlets at all Albertsons stores.

Hockey

The **Idaho Steelheads,** affiliated with the Dallas Stars, bring hockey action to Bank of America Centre between October and March. Tickets range around $17–25 for adults, $9–17 for kids. For more information, call 208/424-2200; for tickets call 208/331-8497 or see www.idaho steelheads.com.

Horse Racing

Thoroughbreds and quarter horses race at **Les Bois Park** beginning in late April or May and continuing until August. Post times are Wednesday and Saturday at 5:30 P.M., Sunday and holidays at 2 P.M. Boise homeboy and *Seabiscuit* actor Gary Stevens started his career as a jockey here—a career that reached a stellar high point in 1995 when he rode 25-to-1 longshot Thunder Gulch to victory in the 121st Kentucky Derby.

General admission to the track is $2; add $2 for box seats, $3 for the clubhouse, and $5 for the turf club. Both the clubhouse and the turf club have full restaurants, video monitors, and their own wagering windows. Minimum wager is $2. On non-race days and all through the offseason, diehards can come for satellite wagering, when admission is free to the clubhouse and turf club. The track is at 5610 Glenwood (at Chinden) at the Western Idaho Fairgrounds. Call 208/376-3985 for satellite race schedules and reservations at the clubhouse and turf club, or 208/376-7223 for other information.

FOR THE KIDS

Boise has been called one of the best places in the United States to raise children, and visiting families will have a ball, too. In addition to all the inexpensive things to do at the parks listed in this chapter, you'll find great attractions throughout the metro area.

Planet Kid, 1875 Century Way, 208/375-8923, on the south side of the interstate off S. Cole Road, is an incredible indoor soft playground for kids 1–10. Its agenda is appealing: no arcade or video machines, no silly tickets or prizes, no mall traffic. Part of the Wings Center complex, Planet Kid stresses fitness and fun. Kids can challenge themselves mentally and physically on such play elements as the Rings of Infinity, Cyborg Swing, and Trapdoor Transporter. It's open Mon.–Thurs. 10 A.M.–8 P.M., Fri.–Sat. 10 A.M.–9 P.M., Sun. noon–6 P.M. (closed Sunday in summer). Admission is $7.25 for kids 2–12, $3.25 for toddlers under 2. Wings Center also holds regular "Parents' Night Out" events; your kid (ages 5–12) can play from 6–11 P.M. for $19 while you and your honey have a quiet night out together, maybe at the nearby Boise Spectrum restaurant-and-cinema complex. Call for dates.

Pojo's, 7736 Fairview Ave., 208/376-6981, is another huge (20,000 square feet) fun center, holding indoor bumper cars, high-tech interactive games, redemption games, a nickel arcade, kiddie rides and games for the toddler set, and a café. Admission is free, but it's pretty easy to go through a mess of quarters here. Hours are Mon.–Thurs. 10 A.M.–11 P.M., Fri.–Sat. 10 A.M.–midnight, Sun. 11 A.M.–10 P.M.

Golf & Recreation, 3883 S. Orchard, 208/344-2008, offers batting cages, a par-3 golf course, bumper cars, and a go-kart track.

Tilt in Boise Towne Square Mall, 208/375-5054, has dozens of video games and more. It's open during mall hours. Mon.–Sat. 10 A.M.–9 P.M., Sun. 11 A.M.–7 P.M.

Also see the Southwest Idaho chapter for details on the Boise suburb of Meridian, which hosts **Roaring Springs Water Park** and **Boondocks Fun Center.**

Arts and Entertainment

PERFORMING ARTS

Tickets for many Boise-area performing arts events, especially those at Boise State University's Morrison Center and Pavilion, are available through **Select-A-Seat.** Call 208/426-1494, reserve online at www.idahotickets.com, or stop at any of the dozens of outlets, which include the BSU Student Union Building (1700 University Dr., open Mon.–Sat. 10 A.M.–6 P.M.) and Albertson's stores across southern Idaho and eastern Oregon.

TicketWeb is another major purveyor, online at www.ticketweb.com.

Boise Philharmonic

One of the Northwest's premier symphony orchestras, the Boise Philharmonic is the state's largest performing-arts organization and the oldest as well, dating back more than a hundred years. Symphony season runs mid-September through mid-April, with performances at both the Morrison Center for the Performing Arts on the BSU campus (Saturday nights) and Swayne Auditorium at Northwest Nazarene University in Nampa (Fridays). Numerous internationally acclaimed guest artists perform with the symphony each year.

Ticket prices range between $9–48. Those on a budget will want to take advantage of the "Finishing Touches" open dress rehearsals, held on every concert Saturday in Boise; tickets are $10, $5 students and seniors. For more information, call 208/344-7849 or 888/300-7849, stop by the Philharmonic office in the Esther Simplot Performing Arts Academy at 516 S. 9th St., or see www.boisephilharmonic.org.

Opera Idaho

See Madame Butterfly get the shaft! See Don Giovanni meet his just reward! Opera Idaho performs two masterworks each year, one each in fall and spring. Boise performances usually take place at the Morrison Center. Tickets run $22–59. Call 208/345-3531 for more informa-tion, or come by the opera office, in the Esther Simplot Performing Arts Academy at 501 S. 8th St., Ste. B.

Other Musical Organizations

The 110-member **Boise Master Chorale,** 100 W. State St., 208/344-7901, performs several times a year at various venues during its Sept.–May season. Tickets cost around $12–15. The **BSU Music Department** has a busy schedule of recitals, master classes, concerts, and more. For the schedule and performance venues, call 208/426-3980 (recorded information) or 208/426-1596.

Ballet Idaho

Squeeze into those toe shoes and plié on down to the Morrison Center for a performance by Ballet Idaho. The season runs from October to April; tickets are $17–39. The company teams up with the Boise Philharmonic in December for the perennial holiday favorite, *The Nutcracker.* For more information, write or come by the company's office in the Esther Simplot Performing Arts Academy, 501 S. 8th St., Ste. A, Boise, ID 83702, or call 208/343-0556 (office) or 208/343-0556 ext. 24 (ticket orders).

Oinkari Basque Dancers

The story of the Oinkari Basque Dancers starts in 1949 with Basque Boisean Juanita "Jay" Uberuaga Hormaechea, who could dance the *jota* like a house afire. She decided that all Basque-American children should have the chance to learn the dances of the Old Country and began teaching them.

In 1960, a group of her students went to the Basque Country to see the homeland firsthand. In San Sebastian they met and studied with a local troupe named Oinkari, loosely translated as "check out those flying feet!" The two groups danced together a few times a week, developing close personal and professional bonds in the process. When at last the Boiseans were ready to return to America and form their own troupe, the San Sebastian Oinkaris asked the Boiseans to do them the honor of naming the fledgling American troupe Oinkari as well, in effect creating sister dance companies on either side of the Atlantic.

Boise's Oinkari dancers went on to perform at four World's Fairs and in the rotunda of the nation's Capitol in Washington, D.C. Today the company performs at the international Jaialdi festival, at the annual Festival of San Inazio, and at other times throughout the year. Members wear traditional Basque costumes and dance the *jota*—a quick-step dance that has been around in one variation or another since the 12th century—and other traditional dances. The company remains a vital part of Boise's Basque community; dancers must be of Basque descent to join the troupe. For performance schedules or further information, call 208/336-8219.

Idaho Shakespeare Festival

Boise's bard-based troupe ranks among the city's shiniest cultural gems. From mid-June through September, Will's works and other dramatic delights come alive in an outdoor amphitheater along the river, east of downtown at 5657 Warm Springs Ave. Season tickets are available; individual ticket prices run $18–26 on weeknights, $23–30 on weekends, $18–22 for preview performances. No children under 6 are admitted except on family nights, when kids of all ages pay just $10. The festival grounds are a wonderful place to picnic before the show; bring your own or sample fare from the Shakespeare Café. For more information, contact the festival office, 520 S. 9th St., 208/429-9908 or 208/336-9221 (box office).

Other Theater Troupes

Boise now has about 10 professional and community theater groups, so drama fans often have several playbills from which to choose each week. The venerable **Boise Little Theater** company was organized in 1948. Performances take place between September and June at the Boise Little Theater in Fort Boise Park, 100 E. Fort St., 208/342-5104. Tickets typically cost $9. **Stage Coach Theatre,** 5296 Overland Rd., 208/342-2000, plays mid-September through June. Shows generally run Thurs.–Sat. nights and Sunday afternoons. Tickets run around $8–10.

As its name implies, **Boise Contemporary Theater** presents fare by such current-day playwrights as David Sedaris and Steve Martin, as well as classics by the likes of Lanford Wilson and Samuel Beckett, all in an intimate "black box" environment at the Fulton Street Theater, 854 Fulton St. Figure on four productions October through May. For tickets, call 208/466-8499 or www.ticketweb.com; for info, 208/331-9224 or www.BCTheater.org.

Giggles are guaranteed at the family-friendly shows put on by **Prairie Dog Productions,** 208/336-7383, www.pdplayhouse.com, which performs at the Alano Theater, 3820 Cassia St., up on the Boise Bench. Goofy fare, often tied in with pop culture and holidays, is the troupe's specialty. Tickets ($10 adults, $8 seniors and students, $6 kids 12 and under) are available by calling 208/336-7383, or via www.ticketweb.com.

Also of note, the Hailey, Idaho–based **Company of Fools,** 208/788-6520, www.company-offools.org, brings its productions to the Fulton Street Theater several times each year.

VISUAL ARTS

For information about the Boise Art Museum, see the Sights section earlier in this chapter.

Galleries

Gallery open houses take place on the first Thursday of every month. **Brown's Gallery,** 1022 W. Main St., 208/342-6661, is one of Boise's more established galleries. It carries a mix of Western art, landscapes, and some good local artists. Nothing here will shock or upset you—it's a comfortable gallery for comfortable Boiseans.

At the other end of the art-world spectrum is **Basement Gallery,** in the basement of the old Idanha Hotel, 928 Main St., 208/333-0309. This gallery features the youngest, freshest artists in town, in a gallery with great cutting-edge energy. Other commercial galleries are clustered at the east end of Main Street, in and around Old Boise.

Boise State University has several galleries scattered around campus, including one in the

BOISE PUBLIC ART

One of the treats of exploring Boise is the discovery of art where you least expect it. Boise has about three dozen pieces of public art in an ever-growing collection that spans the city from the airport to downtown nooks and alleys.

The Grove is a good place to start looking. *Great Blues* (David Berry, 1990) is a bronze rendering of the magnificent Idaho-native birds, one of which is captured in mid-flight. You'll find it on the south side of the Brick Oven Bistro. Just to the east is a nostalgic local favorite—*Keepsies* (Ann LaRose, 1985)—depicting a trio of innocent youngsters playing marbles on the plaza. Shades of Ozzie and Harriet. One day I walked by this sculpture and someone had updated it by sticking a cigarette between the lips of one of the kids. Perfect.

On the same side of the plaza, but up on the landscaped perimeter of the West One skyscraper, *1867* (Bernie Jestrabek-Hart, 1984) depicts an old sourdough panning for gold. It was made from 700 pounds of barbed wire.

Homage to the Pedestrian (Patrick Zentz, 2002) is an interactive walkway where mo-

© JULIE FANSELOW

Sidney's Niche, Capitol Terrace

tion detectors set off sounds. It's on the west side of The Grove. Across 9th Street in front of the Statehouse Inn, *Grove Street Illuminated & Boise Canal* (Amy Westover, 2003) offers some glimpses into local history through silkscreened vintage photos and engraved text that observers can see as they walk amid steel and cast-glass circles.

Leaving The Grove and crossing Main Street to the Capitol Terrace complex, you'll find *Sidney's Niche* (Rick Thomson, 1992) on the side wall of the escalator ascending to the 'Piper Pub. Sidney the giant whimsical rat is exposed as the driving force behind the escalator.

Across the street from 168 9th St. is *Spring Run* (Marilyn Lysohir, 1994). Here in a perfect picnic spot, you'll be joined by a school of salmon swimming across a wall. Bring a sandwich, but watch out for the hungry bears.

Also on 9th Street, hidden in an alley between Bannock and Idaho Streets, is *Alley History* (Kerry Moosman, 1992), which incorporates old advertisements and modern embellishments into a pastiche of Boise's commercial life.

If you've flown to Boise, don't leave the airport without seeing some of the impressive art in the new terminal. Huge fish seem almost to jump out of a six-sided lenticular lightbox mural near the baggage claim. (The art was produced for the Idaho Trout Company by Fresno, Calif.–based Big3D.com.) Meanwhile, the ticketing area boasts a gorgeous 50-foot mural by Idaho artist Geoffrey Krueger, who portrays a Boise River scene with the Boise Front foothills rising behind. It's a fitting send-off to passengers, whether they live here or hope to visit again soon.

Liberal Arts Building, one in the Student Union, and another in the Hemingway Center. For current shows, see www.boisestate.edu/art.

Cinema

The Flicks, 646 Fulton (near Capitol and Myrtle), 208/342-4222, www.theflicksboise.com, is Boise's art house. Its four screens show independent and foreign films, as well as some of the more intelligent first-runs. In addition to the theater, a deli-style café here serves dinner nightly and lunch on weekends. You can get a microbrew or glass of wine from the café and take it out onto the patio or even into the theater with you. Tickets are $7.50 general, $5.50 for shows before 6 P.M. and for seniors, children 12 and under, and students with ID. You'll also find a good collection of art and foreign videos for rent in the video shop here, 208/342-4288.

The restored **Egyptian Theater,** 700 W. Main, 208/345-0454, is the city's most historic and beautiful movie house. Built in 1927, its Egyptian design was inspired by the discovery of King Tut's tomb not long before. Check out the ornamental sphinxes up near the roof. In addition to first-run films, the Egyptian regularly screens black-and-white classics, and there are live music concerts here, too. Elsewhere downtown, the old 8th Street Market Place multiplex was torn down in 2003 to make room for a new 10-screen theater planned on the site for late 2004 or early 2005.

Hands down, the biggest Boise-area movie emporium is the **Edwards Boise Stadium 21,** 208/377-1700, in the Boise Spectrum entertainment complex at Cole and Overland just off I-84. Reserve tickets ($8.25 adults, $6 matinees, $5.50 kids and seniors) online at www.edwards cinemas.com.

NIGHTLIFE

For information on pubs and bars, see the listings under Food and Drink.

Music and Dancing

The local music scene in Boise is undeniably rich. The town has a lot of musicians and a lot of places for them to play. Boise fervently supports its homegrown musicians, to the extent that many locals can actually support themselves with their music. It's not uncommon for local bands to draw bigger crowds at the clubs than the nationally famous touring bands that come through town. And cutting-edge out-of-town bands show up in Boise with some regularity.

The **Big Easy Concert House,** 416 S. 9th St., 208/466-TIXX, is the top live-music venue in town, with touring acts about four nights a week and a DJ most Saturdays. The variety here is amazing; one recent month saw shows by Shelby Lynne, Queens of the Stone Age, Lisa Marie Presley, Ted Nugent, and Insane Clown Posse. See upcoming events at www.bravobsp.com.

Blues Bouquet, 1010 W. Main St., 208/345-6605, is another great spot for live music from occasional touring bands and local stars like $oul Purpo$e, a funk and disco outfit that always packs the dance floor. Open nightly.

Neurolux, 111 N. 11th St., 208/343-0886, is a small, intimate, and loud club where you can hear and dance to the vanguard of Boise's young talent, as well as excellent touring rockers. The crowd tends to be 20s and interesting. Open nightly; small cover charge.

China Blue, 100 S. 6th St, in Old Boise, 208/338-0664, is perhaps Boise's poshest dance club, the sort of place to go when you want to dress up a bit. (No jeans, jogging suits, cargo pants, or ball caps allowed.) With lots of boxy black furniture; a champagne bar in the women's room; and a $1,000-a-year members'-only Electrolounge, this is as swank as Boise gets. Below China Blue, the **Diggy Bass Room** offers a downscale alternative with thumping R&B and hip-hop music and fish tanks for tables. Both clubs are open Wed.–Sat., with a cover of about $5.

Tom Grainey's, 109 S. 6th St., 208/345-2505, has a pair of bars, upstairs and down (Toad's Lounge, open Wed.–Sat.), featuring dancing to lots of live rock. Nearby is **Hannah's,** 621 W. Main St., 208/345-7557, Boise's quintessential just-barely-21-something meat market. Lots of inconsequential junk decorates the walls to provide a busy decor, and the multilevel interior holds numerous nooks and crannies that you and your lust-object *du soir* can grope your way to. Hours are Mon.–Sat. 3 P.M.–2 A.M. **Bogie's,** 1124 Front St., 208/342-9663, offers a mix of DJ dancing and live folk and rock bands.

The city's biggest gay club, the **Emerald City Club,** 415 S. 9th St. (entrance around the back), 208/342-5446, draws a fashionable, mostly 20-something crowd—mixed male and female, mostly gay but some straights. The club is open every day of the year, 10 A.M.–2:30 A.M. Expect a reasonable cover charge.

The Balcony, 150 N. 8th St., 208/336-1313, is another club popular with both gays and straights (and everyone in between), with near-nightly DJ music. From its second-floor perch in the Capitol Terrace, it overlooks what surely is Boise's most fabulous block—even if there is a gaping hole in the landscape where the long-on-hold Boise Tower project languishes.

The 'kickers go to the **Silver Spur Saloon,** 5467 Glenwood (across from the fairgrounds), 208/375-0373, where you'll find country-western music and dancing nightly.

Comedy

Boise's sole comedy club is **Funny Bone,** 405 S. 8th St., 208/331-2663. It's for ages 21 and over only. Various headliners do two- to four-night stints. It's open Wed.–Sun. nights, and tickets usually run $7–11, though special shows occasionally are booked with higher ticket prices. The club offers a full bar with no required drink minimum and serves a selection of finger foods to go with your drinks.

EVENTS
Year-Round

Boise is a party town. One event or another happens just about every weekend, year-round. On the first Thursday of every month 5–9 P.M., the delightful **First Thursday** series turns downtown Boise into a street fair. Galleries hold open houses, musicians play on the sidewalks, seemingly all of Boise is out strolling downtown and milling about, and the city garages provide free parking 4–9 P.M. For more information, call the Downtown Boise Association at 208/472-5200 or see www.downtownboise.org.

Spring

Tiny kites, huge kites, noisy kites, stunt kites, box kites, bat-wing kites—they all come out in force, along with pilots of all ages, for the **Boise Kite Festival,** held in Ann Morrison Park around the last weekend in March. Bring your camera. For more information call the Boise Parks and Recreation Department at 208/384-4240.

Also in late March, just in time to cure spring fever, the **Boise Flower & Garden Show** comes to the Boise Centre on the Grove. The four-day event includes gardening seminars, an orchid show, landscaping ideas, and vendors offering outdoor-living solutions. Call 800/888-7631 for more dirt.

In early April, the **BSU/Gene Harris Jazz Festival** pays tribute to the late, great Idaho jazzman. For more information call 208/426-1203. Mid-April brings upwards of 2,000 runners to the **Race to Robie Creek,** 208/368-9990, a 13.1-mile test of strength and will that starts in Fort Boise Park and climbs Rocky Canyon up and over Adalpe Summit, a gain of 2,000 vertical feet followed by a loss of more than 1,000. A spring tradition in Boise since the 1970s, it's considered the toughest half-marathon in the Northwest.

In late April or early May, fans of the Sport of Kings flock to Les Bois Park for the opening of **horse racing** season. The ponies keep running until mid-August, at which point they are very tired and thirsty. The track is at the Western Idaho Fairgrounds on Chinden Boulevard, 208/376-7223. In late May, look for the **Great Potato Marathon,** running from the Discovery Unit of Lucky Peak State Park to Ann Morrison Park. Don't forget to carbo-load on spuds the night before—and no couch potatoes, please.

You know summer's on the way when **Alive After Five** kicks off at The Grove in mid-May. Every Wednesday evening from 5 to 7:30 P.M., The Grove becomes a city party. Crowds pack the outdoor plaza to sample microbrews and food from local restaurants, while listening or dancing to live bands. Also in mid-May, **Zoo Daze** comes to Zoo Boise in Julia Davis Park, with reduced admissions and lots of special events for kids.

The first weekend in June is the annual **Greek Festival** sponsored by Saints Constantine and

Helen Greek Orthodox Church. More Greek food than you can possibly imagine—*dolmathes, souvlaki, spanakopita*—will be spread out by Boise's Greek community, while Greek dancing and revelry continue all weekend. It's held at St. Helen's Church Park, behind the church at 27th and Bannock. For more information, call 208/345-6147.

Summer

For more than a decade, Boise's biggest annual event was the Boise River Festival, but tough economic times forced organizers to call it quits after the 2003 edition. Many Boiseans hope to see it resurrected in some form; others are relieved it's over and that Boise will no longer become one huge clot of rambunctious revelers and motorcoach tourists each June. In any case, with all the recreation close at hand, there's still plenty to do here in summer, topped by playing on the Greenbelt, floating the Boise River, and partying at Alive After Five, which continues each Wednesday evening on The Grove until late September.

Boise celebrates **Independence Day,** July 4th, with fireworks and a parade. The last weekend of July, Boise's Basque community comes out in force for the **Festival of San Inazio of Loyola;** St. Ignatius, a native of Spanish Basque country, died July 31, 1556. The festivities include a performance by the Oinkari Basque dancers, Basque athletic contests, and an abundance of local Basque food and drink. For more information, call the Basque Museum at 208/343-2671.

Fans of chit'lins, fried catfish, black-eyed peas, and sweet-potato pie won't want to miss the Treasure Valley Intercultural Association's **Soul Food Extravaganza,** early August in Julia Davis Park. In addition to great food, look for music, storytelling, and fun for the kids.

The **Western Idaho Fair** comes to the fairgrounds (Chinden and Glenwood) for 10 days in mid-August, bringing with it a carnival midway, livestock shows, eclectic exhibits, fabulous food, and entertainers by the stageful. For more information, call 208/376-3247.

Fall

Autumn brings colorful trees and the opening of a colorful cultural calendar as the Boise Philhar-

monic, Ballet Idaho, and Opera Idaho open their seasons. For information on the Philharmonic, call 208/344-7849; for the Ballet, call 208/343-0556; for the Opera, call 208/345-3531.

The weekend after Labor Day brings **Art in the Park,** one of Idaho's largest and most elaborate arts and crafts shows. Hats, drums, candles, toys, fine arts, and lots of food—you name it, it's here. The "gallery" for this event is beautiful Julia Davis Park. For more information, contact Boise Art Museum, 208/345-8330.

One of the coolest neighborhood bashes in the Northwest can be found mid-September at the **Hyde Park Street Fair,** a weekend full of live music, kids' activities, and community conviviality. It's at Camel's Back Park in the city's North End.

In late September, look for the **Women's Fitness Celebration,** which brings the largest road race in Idaho and the second-largest women-only run/walk in the country. More than 8,000 women and girls typically participate. Call 208/331-2221 for more information.

November finds Santa trying to catch up on shopping for the big night. You might find the Jolly Old Fart at Boise Art Museum's **Beaux Arts Société Holiday Sale.** It runs one long weekend mid-month, and proceeds benefit the museum. For more information, call 208/345-8330.

Thanksgiving may mean turkey to some, but to others it means it's time to break out the skis. Bogus Basin Ski Area typically opens around Thanksgiving, as soon as the white stuff covers Shafer Butte. To find out if the resort is open yet, call 208/332-5100 or 800/367-4397.

The **Festival of Trees** helps kick off the holiday season with a display of ornately decorated Christmas trees. It takes place at The Grove around Thanksgiving weekend. For information, contact the St. Alphonsus Special Events Committee, 208/367-2797.

Late November through January, the Idaho Botanical Garden's **Winter Garden aGlow** features thousands of twinkling lights decked artistically amid the garden grounds, along with bonfires and hot beverages. Call 208/343-8649.

Winter

Kids and adults alike will enjoy the collaborative

efforts of Ballet Idaho and the Boise Philharmonic in bringing performances of Tchaikovsky's masterpiece *The Nutcracker* to Morrison Center. Call 208/426-1110 for schedule and ticket information. Christmas shoppers might find **gift shows** at the fairgrounds and The Grove early in December. And if you're lucky, you might hit The Grove at the right time for **Tuba Christmas,** where upwards of 61 tuba and baritone horn players oom-pah-pah their way through traditional Christmas music and more. Check out www.tubachristmas.com for this year's date.

Other holiday-time events downtown typically include carousel rides, visits with Santa, and a one-day public skate at the Bank of America Centre. To find out what's on the calendar, call the Downtown Boise Association at 208/336-2631 or see www.downtownboise.org. For information on the city's many holiday-related arts events, check with the Boise City Arts Commission at 208/433-5670.

January through March are slow months on the Boise events calendar as winter settles in over the city. Look for a spate of shows at the fairgrounds: an **RV Show** the second weekend in January; a **boat show** the second weekend in February (now there's some wishful thinking); and a **gem show** during the last weekend of February. The four weekends of March at the fairgrounds bring a **Sports and RV Show, Roadster Show, Home and Garden Show,** and an **Antique Show,** in that order.

Accommodations

HOTELS AND MOTELS

Boise has an abundance of hotels and motels, most toward the high end of the $50–100 price range. The major hotel areas are: downtown; around the university; around the airport; and the ParkCenter business district. The downtown places are mostly upscale, though a few less-expensive independents are available there as well. The university area is close to downtown and both Ann Morrison and Julia Davis Parks, though most of the lodgings here tend to be along busy thoroughfares. The airport area is convenient to the interstate and is where most of the national chain motels, including Motel 6 and several other budget places, are located, but it's not within walking distance of downtown. The ParkCenter area is hoofable from downtown for those with time and a reasonable fitness level, and it's close to the Boise River. If you have a favorite chain, call its 800 number; chances are it'll have a place in Boise. A number of possibilities are listed below.

Under $50

It's worth noting that although Boise doesn't have a hostel within the city limits, there's one close by, on the outskirts of Nampa—close enough to call itself **Hostel Boise.** See the Southwest Idaho chapter for details.

Right at the top end of this price range, on the fringe of downtown, is **Boise Centre Guest Lodge,** 1314 Grove St., 208/342-9351, www.guestlodge.com. It's basic, but the rates are reasonable. Amenities include cable TV (with HBO and Showtime) and a small outdoor heated pool. Both smoking and nonsmoking rooms are available. Rates include continental breakfast. No pets.

$50–100

Downtown, the **Owyhee Plaza Hotel,** 1109 Main St., 208/343-4611 or 800/233-4611, was built in 1910, but renovations have kept it up to modern standards. The exterior won't win any awards for architecture, but the interior is elegant. This is a full-service hotel popular with visiting dignitaries and executives. Amenities include shoeshine, valet, barber/beauty shop, a courtyard pool, and one of the city's premier restaurants, the Gamekeeper. Children under 18 are free with parent.

The **Statehouse Inn,** 981 Grove St., 208/342-4622 or 800/243-4622, is one of the finer hotels downtown and is conveniently located right across the street from Boise Centre and The Grove. All rooms in the modern, six-story building have desks and modem hookups. On-site food and drink are available—the Skylight Restaurant offers good views of downtown. There's no pool, but whirlpool tub suites are available. Ask about weekend bed-and-breakfast packages.

The best thing about staying at the somewhat scruffy **Shilo Inn Riverside,** 3031 Main St., 208/344-3521 or 800/222-2244, is its location right on the Greenbelt. Avid walkers and cyclists will have no trouble making it downtown or to BSU from here. (By car, give it 5 minutes.) Amenities include a big indoor pool and a small continental breakfast.

In the university area, options include **University Inn,** 2360 University Dr. (at Capitol Blvd.), 208/345-7170, which offers 84 rooms, including some suites. Amenities include cable TV with premium channels, an outdoor pool and spa, and a restaurant and lounge. No pets. On the other (east) side of campus and across Broadway is **Courtyard by Marriott,** 222 S. Broadway Ave., 208/331-2700 or 800/321-2211. It's a big, newish place about a mile from downtown, and it has an indoor pool, hot tub, and fitness center.

In the ParkCenter area, you'll find **Club Hotel by Doubletree,** 475 W. ParkCenter Blvd., 208/345-2002 or 800/444-CLUB (800/444-2582), and **Red Lion Hotel ParkCenter Suites,** 424 E. ParkCenter Blvd., 208/342-1044 or 800/325-4000, both modern places with tons of amenities particularly oriented to business travelers (many big corporate offices are in this area).

A bazillion places in this price range are out by the airport. Most are branches of the big chains, so they're predictable, comfortable, and entirely unremarkable. Among them: **Inn America—A Budget Motel,** 2275 Airport Way, 208/389-9800 or 800/469-4667, offering rates at the low end of this category; **Best Western Airport Motor Inn,** 2660 Airport Way, 208/384-5000 or 800/528-1234; **Best Western Vista Inn,** 2645 Airport Way, 208/336-8100 or 800/727-5006; **Comfort Inn,** 2526 Airport Way, 208/336-0077 or 800/228-5150; **Motel 6,** 2323 Airport Way, 208/344-3506; **Shilo Inn Boise Airport,** 4111 Broadway, 208/343-7662 or 800/222-2244; and **Sleep Inn,** 2799 Airport Way, 208/336-7377.

Near the airport, but across the highway (at

THE IDANHA

Although you can no longer stay here, the grande dame of downtown buildings remains the 1901 **Idanha Hotel** (pronounced "EYE-din-ha"), 928 W. Main St., whose tall corner turrets are an impressive sight from blocks away. Famed architect W. S. Campbell designed the French château-style masterpiece, Idaho's first six-story building and the first in the state to have an electric elevator. When completed at a cost of $125,000, it was considered the finest hotel west of the Mississippi and featured bay windows, clawfoot tubs, and the finest furnishings. In the hotel's glory days, Teddy Roosevelt, John and Ethel Barrymore, Buffalo Bill, William Borah, and Clarence Darrow all spent the night here. The Idanha's rooms were recently converted to apartments, but the ground-floor Rodizio restaurant and Bartime lounge are open to the public.

exit 53) on and around Vista Avenue, are several other motels. The large **Holiday Inn Boise—Airport,** 3300 Vista Ave., 208/344-8365 or 800/465-4329, has 266 rooms, all with cable TV with free premium stations, as well as pay-per-view movies; some rooms have desks and phones with modem ports. Restaurants on-site include a dining room/lounge and a poolside deli. The pool is part of an indoor recreation center that also offers a Jacuzzi, saunas, mini-golf, and a play area for kids.

Other chain motels in the airport area include **ExtendedStay America,** 2500 S. Vista Ave., 208/363-9040 or 800/EXT-STAY (800/398-7829), with kitchenette studios; **Fairfield Inn,** 3300 S. Shoshone St., 208/331-5656 or 800/228-2800; **Hampton Inn,** 3270 S. Shoshone St., 208/331-5600 or 800/HAMPTON (800/426-7866); **Holiday Inn Express,** 2613 S. Vista Ave., 208/388-0800 or 800/465-4329; and **Super 8,** 2773 Elder St., 208/344-8871 or 800/800-8000.

One of the best bets in this price range is out in the Boise Towne Square mall area. **Plaza Suite Hotel,** 409 S. Cole Rd., 208/375-7666 or 800/376-3608, bills itself as a boutique business

BOISE AND VICINITY

hotel, but leisure travelers will enjoy it, too. A central atrium with an indoor pool and abundant foliage give the place a resort-like feel, as do the bathrobes in each room—even in this price range.

$100–150

The **Grove Hotel,** 245 S. Capitol Blvd., 208/333-8000 or 800/426-0670, has the best location in town, right on The Grove, sort of, but this high-rise, high-profile hotel is a remarkable design failure, especially given its prize real estate. Granted, it was an ambitious project, turning a plain asphalt parking lot into a luxury hotel *and* the Bank of America Centre—a medium-size arena holding an ice skating rink. But what could the architect have been thinking? The plain brown slab of the upper floors could *almost* be forgiven, but the ugly blockhouse look of the two street sides of the building ignores modern architectural considerations of pedestrian friendliness. An expensive sculpture tacked onto the corner seems like a tacky afterthought. The design separates, rather than integrates, The Grove and the Basque block. And on top of that, the building provides no easy access between the hotel and The Grove. To reach The Grove, guests must either navigate a narrow passageway—often locked—into the arena and out to The Grove from there, or walk outside and essentially around the block. All things considered, it seems incredibly disappointing to see brand-new buildings show such lack of consideration and grace in this modern age. That said, the rooms are pleasantly decorated and the lobby is luxe, with plenty of seating, a cocktail lounge, and Emilio's, a decent restaurant. Rates have come down since the hotel's opening, too; some rooms will occasionally slide over the $150 mark, but most are in this range, or even a bit less on weekends.

On the west side of Capitol Boulevard, backing up against Ann Morrison Park, is **Marriott Residence Inn,** 1401 Lusk Ave., 208/344-1200 or 800/331-3131. Its 104 suites are more like apartments than motel rooms; all have full kitchens, and many have fireplaces and living rooms. For an additional $10 per night you can bring your pet. The nicely landscaped complex sits just far enough off Capitol Boulevard to be quiet. Amenities include cable TV with HBO; videocassette movie rentals; and an outdoor pool, spas, and sport court. A large complimentary

interior of the Grove Hotel

COURTESY OF THE GROVE HOTEL

breakfast buffet (just about everything but eggs) is served in the spacious lobby, and if that doesn't fill you up, you can head for Elmer's pancake and steak house next door, where you can charge a meal to your suite. Add to the complimentary breakfast a complimentary evening dessert, as well as in-room coffee, popcorn, and candy all restocked daily. The staff will even go grocery shopping for you if you wish.

The **Doubletree Hotel Riverside,** 2900 Chinden Blvd., 208/343-1871 or 800/222-TREE (800/222-8733), has good Greenbelt access west of downtown, in the same area as the Shilo Inn in the previous price category, but catering to a higher-end business clientele. (In fact, weekday rates sometimes top $150.) This is Boise's largest hotel, with 304 rooms. Amenities include a nice outdoor pool and fitness center. Bikes are available for rent, too. The old Chart House restaurant in the complex has been replaced by **Joe's Crab Shack,** possibly Boise's loudest dining experience.

The Boise Spectrum entertainment complex south of I-84 Exit 50, about seven miles from downtown, has a pair of newer upscale hotels worth a mention: **AmeriTel Inn—Boise Spectrum Center,** 7499 W. Overland (at Cole), 208/323-2500 or 800/600-6001, and **Hilton Garden Inn Boise Spectrum,** 7699 W. Spectrum St., 208/376-1000 or 800/HILTONS (800/445-8667). Both have 24-hour indoor pools and are steps away from a 21-screen multiplex and nearly a dozen restaurants.

BED-AND-BREAKFASTS

All the following B&Bs are priced at the top end of the $50–100 range or the low end of the $100–150 range, depending on the room.

The **Idaho Heritage Inn,** at 109 W. Idaho, Boise, ID 83702, 208/342-8066, www.idheritageinn.com, more than lives up to its name. It's an exquisitely lovely lodging in a turn-of-the-20th-century home that once belonged to Governor Chase Clark and later was the residence of his daughter Bethine and son-in-law Senator Frank Church. How's that for heritage? Needless to say, the inn is listed on the National Register of Historic Places. The location can't be

beat, within walking distance of Old Boise, the 8th Street Marketplace, and the capitol; to help you extend your explorations, mountain bikes are available for rent. The inn's six rooms all have private baths, queen-size beds, a/c, and in-room phones. A full gourmet breakfast is included in the price, as is an evening glass of wine; weather permitting, either may be enjoyed out on the shaded courtyard. No smoking or pets are allowed. Airport pickup service is available by prior arrangement. The only possible drawback here is the inn's proximity to St. Luke's Regional Medical Center—you're bound to hear the occasional ambulance siren. But that shouldn't get in the way of enjoying your stay here. It's a popular place, so make your reservations well in advance.

Another early-20th-century gem, the 1907 **J. J. Shaw House** enjoys a great North End location at 1411 W. Franklin St., 208/344-8899 or 877/344-8899, www.jjshaw.com. The quiet neighborhood and beautiful house and grounds almost guarantee you'll unwind fast. Each of the five rooms (plus a separate guest cottage with kitchenette) has a phone, private bath, and a/c. The romantic third-floor suite, Shaw's Retreat, features its own private staircase and a shower built for two. Rates include full breakfast. Smoking outdoors only; no pets or children eight or younger.

Another historical gem, **Robin's Nest,** 2389 W. Boise Ave., 208/336-9551 or 800/717-9551, began life in 1892 over on Warm Springs Avenue as one of the first homes in Boise to be heated by geothermal hot water. The house was moved to its current location near BSU in 1991. Each of the four rooms has a private bath, TV, and telephone. Two are Jacuzzi suites—one split-level. Rates include a full breakfast. The house is furnished throughout with valuable, well-preserved antiques. Consequently, small children are discouraged, and pets and smoking are not permitted.

RV PARKS

Boise has some good in-town options for RV campers, though tenters will find slimmer pickings, with only one area park currently accepting them. Unfortunately, the nearby state parks are day-use only. Bruneau Dunes State Park, about an hour southeast of Boise via I-84, is the closest state park campground.

The closest private campground to downtown is the delightful **Americana RV Park,** 3600 Americana Terrace., 208/344-5733, hidden away in a tranquil little pocket between the freeway and busy Americana Boulevard (Exit 49 off I-184 to River Street, then cross the river on Americana Blvd.; the park will be on your right). You'll hear the constant whoosh of the freeway nearby, but it's not in your face—the noise is less bothersome here than at some of the other parks. A small canal runs alongside the park, attracting ducks and Canada geese. A central greensward holding a couple of magnificent willow trees makes a nice picnic area. The 107 spaces go for around $20–25 a night, with discount for Good Sam members. No tents. The small laundry and shower facilities are kept spotless. This campground is within a few easy-walking blocks of downtown and virtually right next door to Ann Morrison Park; highly recommended.

Fiesta RV Park, six miles west of downtown at 11101 Fairview, 208/375-8207, has 142 spaces with hookups for $23–32 a night in summer, less in the offseason. It no longer has tent sites. Discounts available to RV- and travel-club members. The park is neat and tidy. It's a bit noisy, however, thanks to its location right on busy Fairview Avenue; sites on the back (south) side are a little quieter. Facilities include a pool, playground, laundry room, showers, and dog-walking area. Propane refills are available.

Tenters are welcome at **On the River RV Park,** 6000 N. Glenwood, 208/375-7432 or 800/375-7432. The 215 spaces here go for $25 a night,

with Good Sam and AARP discounts. Tent sites are $20. Amenities include a Greenbelt location, high-speed wireless Internet access, and a neat laundry and shower building. The park abuts the Western Idaho Fairgrounds and the baseball stadium where the Boise Hawks play, so expect a bit of noise when games or other fairground events take place.

United Campground, 7373 Federal Way, 208/343-4379, is a humble but friendly park sandwiched between Federal Way and the interstate. Sites are $20 a night with full hookups; no tents allowed. Facilities include a playground, a laundry, showers, and a small store.

Down by the airport is **Mountain View RV Park,** 2040 Airport Way, 208/345-4141. It seems like an odd place for an RV park—squeezed in between the airport and the interstate—but it has the advantage of easy freeway access and easy maneuvering within the park itself; all of the park's 63 spaces are pull-throughs. Facilities include laundry and showers. Sites cost $24 a night with full hookups; discounts available.

Hi Valley RV Park, 208/939-8080, is on the way out of town (heading toward McCall) at 10555 Horseshoe Bend Rd. (Hwy. 55), one mile north of Highway 44 (State Street). That puts it about eight miles from downtown Boise. The big park has 194 spaces with full hookups for about $25 a day; discounts for AAA and Good Sam members. No tents allowed. The clubhouse has a large-screen TV, full kitchen, spacious shower rooms, a laundry, and a billiard room. Golfers would enjoy staying here, too, since it's within a five-minute drive of two courses (Shadow Valley and Eagle Hills).

Food and Drink

FINE DINING

Right downtown under the One Capitol Center building at 999 Main St., 208/342-4900, **Angell's Bar & Grill** has a unique layout—you walk from street level down an amphitheater-like grassy slope to the subterranean but open, not basement-like, restaurant. A patio outside offers some of the city's most enjoyable alfresco dining. Inside, the atmosphere is elegance à la Idaho; wood and green tones frame a gallery of wildlife art along the walls.

Your meal might begin with an appetizer of escargots baked in mushroom caps, or a smoked duckling salad layered with mandarin oranges and mango slices. Entrées have included such delectables as filet mignon, charbroiled and topped with sautéed shiitake mushrooms in black bean sauce; and salmon broiled over sugar maplewood coals and complemented with a cognac-laced marionberry coulis. Pasta dishes and surf 'n' turf combos are available, as are fine wines, by the bottle or glass. Dinner entrées are mostly in the $17–27 range. Angell's is open at 11:30 for lunch Tues.–Fri. and for dinner from 5 P.M. nightly.

On the ground floor of a modern office building, **Cottonwood Grille,** 913 W. River St., 208/333-9800, hides its charms from passersby. Inside, you'll discover that the dining room backs right up onto the Greenbelt and the Boise River. In summer, the large patio, replete with pond and waterfall, offers a great place to dine in a natural setting (mist-makers keep alfresco diners cool in the dog days of summer). The extensive menu offers veggie dishes, soups and salads, pastas, seafood, and all the usual upscale meat dishes. Lunch selections are mostly $7–11; dinner entrées range around $14–24. Open for lunch (11 A.M.–4 P.M.) and dinner (5–10 P.M.) daily, plus Sunday brunch.

As might be expected by the name, **The Gamekeeper,** 1109 Main St. in the Owyhee Plaza Hotel, 208/343-4611, is not a vegetarian restaurant. The menu features a zooful of mammals—cow, calf, sheep, pig, and deer—backed up by fowl, fish, and shellfish recipes. Entrées, which start at about $18 and climb high from there, might include rack of lamb in dijon herb crust, broiled filet mignon carved at your table and served with sauces béarnaise and bordelaise, or sliced and sautéed tenderloin of veal stuffed with prosciutto and mozzarella cheese and covered with Marsala wine sauce. You'll want a really rich dessert after all that, won't you? Perhaps the bananas Foster—banana halves sautéed in butter, banana liqueur, and rum with a hint of cinnamon, served over vanilla ice cream.

At meal's end, you'll be relaxing over the last few sips from your $39 bottle of cheap California cabernet about the time the piano man launches into an optimistically upbeat version of "Strangers in Paradise," at which point you know it'll be time to head off into the night, another day of your life irretrievably behind you. The Gamekeeper is open for lunch 11:30 A.M.–2 P.M. Mon.–Fri. and for dinner 5:30–10 P.M. Mon.–Sat.; make reservations.

Prime rib is the claim to fame at popular **Lock Stock & Barrel,** downtown at 1100 W. Jefferson, 208/336-4266. But a variety of other steaks, seafood dishes, and surf 'n' turf combos add to the menu. All dinners include a trip to the salad bar, a bowl of clam chowder, and hot bread. If you still have room for dessert, try the LS&B variation on the traditional mud pie: the cow pie. Most entrées are in the $15–18 range. The casual wood-and-brick decor with low lights and candles is suitable for dates and good conversation. Open for dinner from 5 P.M. Mon.–Sat., from 4 P.M. Sunday.

Milford's, 405 S. 8th St. in the 8th Street Marketplace, 208/342-8382, has a good reputation for fresh fish. The menu changes daily, depending on the catch, but might include fresh Idaho rainbow trout, fresh Alaskan king salmon, halibut, mahi mahi, marlin, cod, red snapper, sole, ahi—if it has gills and scales, chances are Milford's has it. Surf 'n' turf lovers can add the steak of their choice to any entrée. The average entrée price falls in the $17–27 range. A nice bar with fine wines and microbrews looks out on the Marketplace comings and goings. Non-smokers have their own section, but the smoke can find its way in. Milford's is open from 5 P.M. daily for dinner.

Boise diners are thanking their lucky stars for **Milky Way,** especially in its new and improved location in the Empire Building at 10th and Idaho, 208/343-4334. The food is upscale home-style heaven. Entrées (like grilled chicken and ricotta raviolis in a basil cream sauce topped with pine nuts) run $15–24; smaller plates cost $7–10. Open daily for lunch and dinner, with seating until midnight on Friday and Saturday.

Entering **Mortimer's Idaho Cuisine,** 110 S. 5th St. (at Main, downstairs in the Belgravia Building), 208/338-6550, is like descending into a cool, quiet grotto. The rough-cut stone walls and intimate size help give the restaurant the at-mosphere of a cozy, romantic hideaway, and the food here is some of Boise's most acclaimed, at very reasonable prices given the quality and craft involved. Chef Jon Mortimer strives to use the freshest local ingredients possible, and his pic-turesque meal presentations make dining here a truly special thing. Entrées run $17–25, or try the six-course tasting menu for about $40.

Murphy's Seafood & Steak House, 1555 Broadway Ave., 208/344-3691, is a longtime local favorite. Appetizers like oysters Rockefeller or a pound of steamers start things off. Salads come with fresh-baked sourdough and garlic butter. Fresh seafood entrées might include At-lantic salmon mesquite broiled and basted with rosemary, sage, and thyme butter, or barbecued Copper River salmon. Other seafood, chicken, and steak entrées are available. Prices range $12–30, with most around $18–19. Desserts like Mile High Mud Pie and Murphy's Ice Cream Potato (vanilla ice cream rolled in cocoa with hot fudge, topped with whipped cream and nuts) are sure to please. Murphy's is open from 11 A.M. for lunch Mon.–Sat., for dinner nightly, and for brunch on Sunday starting at 10 A.M.

Yes, it's a bar, but the **Red Feather Lounge**'s consistently creative cuisine catapults this multi-level pleasure palace, 250 N. 8th St., 208/429-6340, into the top echelon of Boise dining

experiences. And an experience it is, with Idaho's largest lava lamp, animal-print accents, and hip but friendly staff. Lunch ($7–12) and dinner ($12–25) feature lots of inspired dishes with Northwestern, Southwestern, and even Asian influences. Also look for breakfast Sat.–Sun. (8:30 A.M.–1:30 P.M.; $5–12), featuring every-thing from homemade granola and cinnamon rolls to spicy Mexican chorizo–black bean burritos.

Richard's Across the Street, a bright, spa-cious and universally popular bistro at 1520 N. 13th St., 208/331-9855, brings haute cuisine to Hyde Park. Here you might start with an appe-tizer of butternut squash–filled ravioli in a brown butter sage sauce, then move on to maple-glazed quail stuffed with a wild-mushroom risotto. En-trées range $18–28. Fine wines are available by the bottle or glass. Sit inside or out on the big patio overlooking Hyde Park's hippest corner. Open for lunch 11:30 A.M.–2 P.M. Mon.–Sat., for Sunday brunch 9:30 A.M.–1:30 P.M., and for dinner nightly from 5:30.

ETHNIC FARE

Brazilian

One of Boise's most senior chefs, Peter Schott, has been cooking in the Idanha Hotel for years. His latest venture is the meat-oriented **Schott's Rodizio Grill,** 928 Main St., 208/336-9100. For $16 ($8 children ages 7–12, $5 ages 6 and under), you can feast till you're full on a variety of meats brought to your table on three-foot skew-ers, plus salads and side dishes at a buffet. Open Mon.–Sat. 5–10 P.M. No reservations are taken, so you might have to wait on weekends. Satur-day-evening strollers can grab a plate full of Rodizio fare outside the Idanha for $5.

Chinese

The best Chinese food in town is at **Yen Ching,** 305 N. 9th St., 208/384-0384. The exterior—painted a drab monochromatic tan that would've garnered Mao's approval—hardly hints at what's in-side. Upscale wooden tables and chairs and fine art on the walls provide an atmosphere of casual el-egance. The menu looks standard enough, but just wait until the food comes. It practically jumps off the plate with freshness and flavor. The vegetables are lightly cooked, and the hot and spicy Hunan dishes are the real thing—by the time you're done, you'll have a runny nose. The restaurant also serves exotic cocktails, wines, the requisite Tsing Tao beer, and a microbrew or two. Most entrées range $8–12. It's open daily for lunch and dinner.

Another Chinese restaurant in town, **Twin Dragon,** 2200 Fairview Ave., 208/344-2141, is worth noting for its late-night hours. It's open until 2 A.M. Friday and Saturday, till midnight Sunday.

Egyptian

The unassuming storefront **Aladdin,** 111 Broadway, Suite 115, 208/368-0880, offers some of Boise's best global cuisine. As you walk into the restaurant, Egyptian music greets your ears, and Egyptian-themed murals surround you. Owner-chef Ibrahim A. Ebed was born in Cairo and worked in some of the finest restaurants in New York City, including the U.N.'s Ambassador Grill, before giving up the rat race and moving to Idaho.

Start with an appetizer such as *baba ghanouj* (mashed eggplant and sesame tahini with garlic) or *ful m'dammas* (fava beans seasoned with garlic and fresh herbs, served with tomatoes), accompanied by a homemade unleavened pita bread that's a wonder in itself. Entrées include vegetarian items such as *mahshi* (a plate of stuffed vegetables in a tomato-garlic sauce) and grilled items like *shish taouk* (marinated chicken grilled on a skewer with vegetables and served with rice, hummus, and salad). Seafood dishes, soups, salads, and sandwiches are also on the menu, but save room for dessert—the *baklava* is outrageous, while the bird's nest is a delightful pistachio-filled, nest-shaped pastry. Don't forget to order a Turkish coffee with your dessert—the cardamom brew is nothing like espresso. It's the final taste treat in a meal full of them.

The restaurant is open Mon.–Sat. for lunch ($5–8) and nightly for dinner ($6–17). Belly dancers perform on Fri.–Sat. nights.

Greek

Cazba Mediterranean and Greek Restaurant,
211 N. 8th St., 208/381-0222, is the place to go for shish kabobs, gyros, and baklava. Try the appetizer sampler plate, which includes falafel, baba ghanouj, hummus, feta cheese, Kalamata olives, tomatoes, cucumbers, tzatziki sauce, and warm garlic-herb pita bread. The restaurant has an elegant interior, as well as tables out on the sidewalk. Entrées run $10–16. Open daily for lunch and dinner and weekends for breakfast. The owners of Cazba recently took over the bar next door (the legendary Interlude, long a favorite with state politicos).

Italian

At **Gino's Italian Ristorante,** 150 N. 8th St., in Capitol Terrace, 208/331-3771, you'll find Gino himself in the kitchen, whipping up delicacies inspired by his parents' cooking back in Napoli. Pass on the tables up front and head for the back room, where the atmosphere is a well-done re-creation of Old Italy. Dinner entrées range around $10–18. Fine wines are available by the bottle or glass, and Italian beer lovers can get either Moretti or Peroni. Open weekdays for lunch and Mon.–Sat. for dinner. Gino's recently added a second restaurant, **Gino's Gelato Pizzeria,** 208/331-0475, just across the top of the escalators at Capitol Terrace. It specializes in real Italian-style, thin-crust pizza (about $14–15) and 16 flavors of gelato (Italian-style ice cream).

Japanese

Local sushi lovers are divided in their loyalties between **Zutto,** 615 W. Main St., 208/388-8873, and **Shige Japanese Cuisine,** downtown in Capitol Terrace, 100 N. 8th St., Suite 215 (between Gino's and the 'Piper Pub), 208/338-8423. Service at Zutto can be slow, but fans say it's worth the wait. The tiny eatery is open weekdays for lunch, Mon.–Sat. for dinner. Shige offers sushi as well as dinners like tempura with prawns and vegetables. It's open Mon.–Sat. for lunch and dinner.

Mexican

Finding good Mexican food in Boise is something of a challenge. Most dishes and salsas you'll find are so bland, they'll have even the most recalcitrant WASP trying to figure out how to say *más picante, por favor.*

The venerable **Chapala,** 105 S. 6th St., 208/331-7866, has good food and outstanding service—neither obsequious nor indifferent. You'll have to make a special request for the death-paste salsa. Dinner entrées range $7–12. Open daily for lunch and dinner. There are five other locations around southern Idaho.

Tiny **Roque's,** 2870 W. State St., 208/343-7211, is also popular, for good reason. The flavors are fresh and frisky. Entrées range $6.50–13. Or come for Taco Tuesday, when delicious soft tacos, in your choice of beef, chicken, or pork, are just $.95 each. Wash 'em down with a Tecate beer for another $1.50. *¡Que bueno!* Open Mon.–Sat. for lunch and dinner.

Pan-Asian

Saffron, once a big hit on the Basque Block, took a brief hiatus before reopening in a new Old Boise location, 106 N. 6th St., 208/426-9990. The menu hasn't changed much: Look for creative Asian cooking with Chinese, Thai, and Vietnamese influences.

Vietnamese

Dong Khanh, 111 Broadway (near Main, in the same mini-mall as Aladdin), 208/345-0980, offers Vietnamese staples such as *cha gio* (bean-thread noodles, pork, and vegetables wrapped in rice paper and deep-fat-fried, served with lettuce, cucumber, and fish sauce) and *bun thit nuong* (marinated sliced pork with lemongrass and sesame oil, grilled and served on rice noodles with fresh bean sprouts, cucumber, and lettuce). Most dinner entrées run $6–10. Open for lunch Mon.–Sat. and for dinner daily.

PIZZA

One of the best pizza places in the world is right here in Boise. **Flying Pie** is perfect. Its Zambini is generally acknowledged to be the spicy-hottest pizza in town, endowed as it is with jalapeños, Italian sausage, onions, fresh garlic, Roma tomatoes, and pesto sauce. Vegetarians can order one of six different veggie concoc-

tions. The thin-style crust is available in white, wheat, or sourdough, and all toppings are fresh and delicious. A good selection of imports and microbrews is available to quench the Zambini-burn, and a selection of fine wines is offered, too; the staff can even make recommendations on which wine goes best with which pizza. Prices range $8–21. Flying Pie has two locations: 4320 State St. (near Collister), 208/345-8585, and 6508 Fairview (near Liberty), 208/376-3454. They're both open at 11 A.M. daily with slices for lunch; last call is 10:30 P.M. Mon.–Thurs., 11:30 P.M. Fri.–Sat. Tuesday is all-you-can-eat Gourmet Night, with a smorgasbord of unusual and traditional pizzas offered; price is $6.25 adults, less for kids under 12.

Boise's newest pizza joint, **Pie,** 612 Grove St., 208/426-8400, caters to a college/20something crowd with build-your-own 12-inch pizzas for $11.95. Some popular combos include the veggie-heavy String Cheese Incident and Thai a Yellow Ribbon, with chicken, peanut sauce, and fresh mango. Save room for ice cream—Pie has just about every flavor Ben & Jerry's makes. There's frequent live music, too, as well as a trendy oxygen bar in back. Open daily from 4 P.M.

Guido's, 235 N. 5th St., 208/345-9011, serves New York–style pizza—thin crust, light cheese—by the whole pie (from $9) or by the big slice ($1.60 and up). The atmosphere is casual and cozy, and you can sit outside and chow down in a nice, relatively quiet part of downtown. Open daily for lunch and dinner.

Part of the charm of **Lucky 13,** 1602 N. 13th, 208/344-6967, has to be that you get to eat outdoors in Hyde Park—a very pleasant place to be on a late spring or summer's eve. The crowd is 20–30ish, hip, and fun. Lots of mountain bikers stop here for R&R on their way back from the Front. Of the eight named varieties of pizza, five are vegetarian, including the Viva Las Vegan and the Zucchini Meanie. The crust here is less remarkable than at Flying Pie, and about a hundred times thicker than Guido's. Still, this is good pizza, a league above the chain/franchise varieties. Prices range $9–20. Open 11 A.M. to 9 or 10 P.M. daily.

BREAKFAST, BISTROS, AND LIGHT BITES

Goldy's Breakfast Bistro, 108 S. Capitol Blvd. (right downtown), 208/345-4100, is the gourmet breakfast place in town. The small but chic restaurant is very popular; you may have a wait to get in on weekends. On the menu are sausages such as andouille Cajun and pesto smoked turkey and chicken; egg scrambles with your choice of ingredients, including curry, ham and chutney, and swiss chard and sausage; and a variety of scrumptious frittatas. The fresh-squeezed orange juice tastes straight off the tree, and you can have it plain or in a mimosa. Best of all, the prices are incredibly reasonable given the quality; you can get a superb breakfast here for $5–10. Open Mon.–Fri. 6:30 A.M.–2 P.M., Sat.–Sun. 7:30 A.M.–2 P.M. Goldy's also has a location in Hyde Park.

Moon's Kitchen Cafe, 815 W. Bannock, 208/385-0472, is a Boise institution. It started in 1955 in the back of Moon's Gun & Tackle Shop, quickly gaining a loyal following and a reputation for having the world's finest milk shakes. The milk shakes and the loyal following remain, but the Gun & Tackle Shop has given way to a gift and card emporium. The restaurant section can't have changed much over the years; its walls are a veritable tapestry of kitsch, hung with an eclectic array of tacky memorabilia. Just walking into this place raises your cholesterol level. The menu offers typical greasy-spoon fare: breakfasts of eggs, omelettes, pancakes, and various combinations ($4–8). And, yes, truly wonderful milk shakes. Open daily for breakfast and lunch.

Another longtime diner with an avid local following is **Jim's Coffee Shop,** 812 Fort St., 208/343-0154, on the fringe of Boise's hip North End. The prices don't exactly recall the 1950s, but you'll still find plenty of stuff on the menu for under $3. Open Mon.–Fri. 7 A.M.–4 P.M., Sat.–Sun. 8 A.M.–2 P.M.

Two downtown bagel joints offer quick, inexpensive breakfasts and are also nice for a more leisurely lunch. Look for either **River City Bagel & Bakery,** 908 Main St., 208/338-1299, or **Blue Sky Bagel Bakery,** 407 Main St., 208/388-4242. At both spots, you'll find a good variety of freshly baked bagels and toppings, as well as other light fare. River City has tons of well-spaced tables and reading nooks beneath its high ceiling; Blue Sky has outdoor seating.

The **Brick Oven Bistro** is something of a legend in town. The former Brick Oven Beanery, on 8th and Main Streets at The Grove, 208/342-3456, has served up good, hearty food at reasonable prices for more than a decade. The menu is down-home with style; you've got to admit, a dish such as wild rice meatloaf with burgundy-mushroom gravy and horseradish sauce shows panache. Dinner entrées run around $7–9; sandwiches, salads, soups, and stews are virtually all under $7. A kids' menu, desserts, soda-fountain specials, and a variety of good beers and wines round out the offerings.

The cafeteria-style establishment—you get a tray at one end of the food line and pay at the other—has a warm and comfortable atmosphere of brick, wood, and green-and-white checkered tablecloths. Eat outside when the weather's fine. Open Sun.–Thurs. 11 A.M.–9 P.M., Fri.–Sat. 11 A.M.–10 P.M.

Fresh burritos, wraps, jambalaya, and inventive breakfast fare are on the menu at **Parrilla Grill,** 1512 N. 13th, 208/323-HOTT (208/323-4688), a lively Hyde Park neighborhood hangout. This is fast food, made to order, with plenty of local atmosphere and seating inside and out. Try the BBQ smoked chicken wrap ($6.25 large; $5 smaller) or the Sidewinder (carbonara fettuccine tossed with parmesan, eggs, and bacon; $4). Talk about something for everyone: There's peanut-butter-and-honey tacos for the kids and, on Sunday, 25-cent beers for the adults. Live music sometimes, too. Open daily 8 A.M.–10 P.M.

Here's a concept: a gourmet drive-in. **Westside Drive-In**'s owner-chef, Louis Aaron, has a background in haute cuisine, and it shows. Where else can you get a delicious Caesar salad, Cajun chicken, or fettuccine with broccoli at a fast-food place? Louie also offers burgers, shakes, and malts, all with gourmet flair. Weird, but it works. The drive-in is at 21st and State Sts., 208/342-2957. Open Mon.–Thurs. 6:30 A.M.–10 P.M., Fri. 6:30 A.M.–10:30 P.M., Sat. 7 A.M.–10:30 P.M.; Sun. 11 A.M.–9 P.M.

PUBS AND BARS

Gernika (gair-NEE-ka), 202 S. Capitol Blvd. (on the Basque Block, next to the Basque Museum and Cultural Center), 208/344-2175, is named for the small Spanish city that's the political capital of the Basques. But you don't have to be Basque to enjoy this pocket-sized pub overflowing with character. Inside you'll find a small reproduction of Pablo Picasso's famous painting of the Gernika tragedy, as well as some old black-and-white photos that provide glimpses of early Basque life in Boise. Everything on the menu of typical Basque foods—*solomos, chorizos, croquetas*—costs $8 or less. Basque-country wines and great Northwest microbrews complement the great food. The atmosphere is warm and jovial, and if you're lucky, you might hear owner Dan Ansotegui speaking Basque with the locals. Highly recommended. Open daily from 11 A.M. until late; closed Sun.

It's all about art at **Mosaic Gallery Bar,** 500 W. Main St., 208/338-5006, from the changing exhibits on the walls to the tastefully prepared small plates: tapas ($3–11) and racions (larger tapas; about $10–15). Lunch is good, too, with some of the best clam chowder in Boise. Look for a top-notch wine list (always) and live jazz on Saturday nights. Open Mon.–Fri. 11 A.M.–2:30 P.M. and nightly 4–10:30 P.M.

On the second floor of the Capitol Terrace parking garage-cum-mall-ette, the **Piper Pub,** 150 N. 8th, 208/343-2444, puts you just high enough off terra firma to get an aerial perspective on downtown. Outside, a broad terrace with tables allows you to enjoy your afternoon or evening alfresco, while inside, a gorgeous wooden bar holds the Piper's awesome collection of 33 Scotch whiskeys. Drink your glass of 18-year-old Macallan single malt and wonder why that adolescent nightmare you and your spouse conceived couldn't be as agreeable at that age. Good beer and wine is available, and the food menu is creative, too: look for such fare as mango chicken and soba noodles or sandwiches of herb-crusted, farm-raised elk, with most items $5–13. The Piper is open for lunch and dinner, Mon.–Sat. and for brunch Sat.–Sun.

The fun, often crowded **Table Rock Brewpub and Grill,** 705 Fulton St. (across Capitol Blvd. from Julia Davis Park), 208/342-0944, makes superb beer. The samplers here cost $.75 each, a bargain to acquaint yourself with the string of house brews. Five year-round beers top the list, accompanied by various seasonals. Beer aside, this is a very popular place for food. The all-purpose lunch/dinner menu is as extensive as the beer list and includes everything from soft pretzels to gourmet fare. Hours are Mon.–Sat. 11:30 A.M.–midnight, Sun. noon–10 P.M.

The bland exterior of the **Highlands Hollow Brewhouse,** 2455 Harrison Hollow (Bogus Basin Rd.), 208/343-6820, conceals a warm, lively interior centered around a big, circular Swedish fireplace. Outstanding year-round brews and occasional seasonals await patrons here. The bartenders are knowledgeable and can guide you to a beer you're sure to like—or try a sampler, since they're free. The food menu offers appetizers, soups and salads, burgers, inspired sandwiches (everything from sage sausage to halibut), and entrées such as pepper steak on soba noodles. The kitchen is open Mon.–Sat. 11 A.M.–10 P.M., Sun. 11 A.M.–9 P.M. As Highlands Hollow is right on the way back from Bogus Basin, it makes an irresistible après-ski stop.

Bittercreek Alehouse, 246 N. 8th St., 208/345-1813, serves around 25 of the Northwest's finest microbrews, including offerings from Full Sail, Pyramid, Widmer, Red Hook, and others. The wide-ranging food menu includes burgers, sandwiches, salads, and specials ranging from salmon with hazelnut butter to fish and chips—most in the $7–9 range. The large interior features a wood floor and industrial ceiling—somehow it works—but the outside patio is the place to be, especially when cigar smokers are in the house. Open Mon.–Thurs. 11 A.M.–midnight; Fri.–Sat. 11 A.M.–2 A.M.

A civilized wine bar and shop, **Grape Escape,** downtown at 800 W. Idaho, Suite 100, 208/368-0200, is a great place to sample wines from Idaho, California, and other parts of the world. Its corner location at the busy intersection makes it an ideal people-watching spot (very popular at lunchtime) and a great place to kick back with a good chardonnay or pinot noir. The price of a glass of wine varies depending on what's being poured—about $5.25 for the low end, on up to around $8. The glasses are generously sized. Delicious appetizers cleanse the palate; figure about $6–8 each. The lunch menu offers sandwiches and salads ranging around $7–9. It opens at 11:30 A.M. daily and closes whenever the last patron leaves (2 A.M. at the latest).

You've heard of a restaurant brewing its own beer on the premises, but how about one that distills its own gin, rum, and vodka? **Bardenay,** 610 Grove St. on Boise's Basque block, 208/426-0538, does exactly that, in a beautiful German-made copper-and-brass still that sits behind a glass partition at the back of the restaurant. This new idea was three years in the planning, which including convincing all sorts of government regulators that it was a socially acceptable endeavor. Bardenay produces highest-quality spirits both for use at its bar and for bottling for retail sale. If you don't like hard liquor, you can choose from a wide and well-chosen assortment of fine wines (the wine list is like a mini-encyclopedia, providing copious details about each selection) and microbrew beers. And even if you don't drink at all, come for the food and atmosphere. The food goes the extra mile at every step, using the finest freshest ingredients in extremely creative and successful ways (according to the bartender, the lamb-and-beef meatloaf "kicks ass"). Entrées run $7–13; salads and sandwiches are mostly $6–9. And the lively atmosphere in the converted old brick-and-beam warehouse is jovial and trendy, if a little on the loud side. Open daily 11 A.M.–2 A.M.

When you walk into the Boise institution **Pengilly's,** 513 W. Main St., 208/345-6344, the first thing you'll notice is the exquisite expanse of rich wood, steeped in the smoke of several decades' worth of fine Havana cigars. Cozy wooden booths along one side speak of secret deals and scandalous trysts. If the walls could talk! Across the room, the wooden, vintage-1880 Brunswick back bar recalls days when the workings of the nation's government and economy took place as much in front of bars like this as inside the state houses. Old brass chandeliers—their globe lights adorned with handpainted roses—cast a soft glow across the scene. And check out the ornate 1910-vintage National Cash Register. On the back wall, those blown-up old black-and-whites are family photos belonging to bar owner and family patriarch John Pengilly. One's his mother on a buggy, back in Louisiana; another is of his dad in front of a wood-burning steam locomotive. Both photos date to the early 1900s. One thing's for certain: This place has history. Light live music is offered some nights.

COFFEEHOUSES

The big comfortable **Flying M,** 500 W. Idaho St., 208/345-4320, features funky-chic decor: old grade-school tables and chairs, black-and-white linoleum, beat-up couches, a chandelier in the phone booth. It's popular with locals as a place to meet friends, read, study, or just hang out. The menu holds the usual array of coffeehouse concoctions, as well as light breakfast and lunch fare. Expansive windows make for a bright interior and good weather/people-watching. Part of the coffeehouse is given over to an artsy gift shop selling local crafts; this is home to the Northwest's first Art*O*Mat vending machine, where, for $5, you can buy a piece of original art in a cellophane-wrapped, cigarette-pack-sized box. Cool! Hours are Mon.–Thurs. 6:30 A.M.–10 P.M., Fri. 6:30 A.M.–11 P.M., Sat. 7:30 A.M.–11 P.M., Sun. 7:30 A.M.–6 P.M. Live acoustic music is presented on weekend nights.

Stark modernism is the style at the small **SoHo Caffe,** 802 W. Idaho, Suite 114 (in the Mode Building with Noodles, the Grape Escape, and other stores), 208/344-3121. All the furnishings look as if they might've come direct from the Bauhaus—consciously designed, not merely functional. Good views, good brews, and comfortable, too. Very hip. It's open Mon.–Fri. 6:30 A.M.–9 P.M., Fri.–Sat. 6:30 A.M.–11 P.M., Sun. 8 A.M.–6 P.M.

On the corner of the busy intersection of Bogus Basin and Hill Roads, the classy and comfortable **Java Junction,** 2302 Bogus Basin Rd., 208/343-5282, is right on the way to or from Bogus Basin Ski Area, making it an ideal avant- or après-ski spot to warm up in winter. Open daily

7 A.M. until 8 P.M.; until 9 P.M. on Tuesday, when live music is presented.

The **Kulture Klatsch** caffeinery, established in 1979, advertises itself as Boise's original coffeehouse. It's at 409 S. 8th St., in the 8th Street Marketplace, 208/345-0452. The brick walls hung with good modern art, funky low ceiling, and parquet floor create a denlike atmosphere, cozy rather than airy; it's spacious and comfortable but not the place for people-watching. Bring letters to write. During the day, the crowd is a mix thick with upscale shoppers and businesspeople. Friday and Saturday nights, live acoustic music brings in a younger crowd.

In addition to gourmet coffee in both its standard and espresso varieties, you can get breakfast and lunch. All food is prepared from fresh, unprocessed foods, and vegetarian dishes are the rule rather than the exception. A number of Idaho and California varietal wines grace the wine list, and microbrew aficionados can slurp their way through more than a dozen different varieties, not one of which is brewed by Anheuser-Busch. Hours are Mon. 7 A.M.–3 P.M., Tues.–Thurs. 7 A.M.–10 P.M., Fri. 7 A.M.–11 P.M., Sat. 8 A.M.–11 P.M., Sun. 8 A.M.–3 P.M.

A nationwide chain with 20 Treasure Valley locations, **Moxie Java** serves reliably good coffee and always draws an eclectic clientele. Some think the mochas here are the best anywhere, thanks to their preparation with premixed Nestle's chocolate milk instead of chocolate powder. Others think the mochas here are the worst for the same reason. In Old Boise, Moxie's is at 570 W. Main St., 208/343-9033, a prime people-watching locale. The small store has fishbowl bay windows in front for seeing and being seen, and crowds linger at outside tables in good weather.

Yep, **Starbucks** has finally invaded Boise. One occupies a prime corner downtown in the cool 1906 Adelmann Building at Capitol and Idaho, 208/345-4437. Another particularly comfortable location is out of the fray at 1797 W. State St., 208/367-0781.

Out in fabulously funky Hyde Park, you can choose your caffeinery. **Richard's Bakery & Cafe,** 1513 N. 13th St., 208/368-9629, offers delicious muffins, scones, sticky buns, and more, all baked from scratch daily. You can sit inside or at one of a couple of tables out on the sunny sidewalk. Open daily 7:30 A.M.–9 P.M. **Little Richard's,** 1630 N. 13th St., 208/336-5122, also serves yummy espresso concoctions and light food, or the alcoholic beverage of your choice. Open daily at 6 A.M.

GROCERIES

The **Boise Co-op,** 888 W. Fort St., 208/472-4500, is the biggest natural food store in town. In addition to organic produce, soy milk, vitamins and supplements, and other staples of a healthy diet, you'll find a large selection of cheeses, a deli offering great whole-grain-and-organic-veggie sandwiches, and Boise's best selection of wines and microbrews. The staff alone makes coming here a pleasure—they're all so friendly and, well, healthy. Open Mon.–Sat. 9 A.M.–9 P.M., Sun. 9 A.M.–8 P.M. Highly recommended.

Shopping

MALLS

The **Boise Towne Square mall,** 350 N. Milwaukee, 208/378-4400, is off I-84 at the Franklin Road exit. Sears, JCPenney, and Bon-Macy's are the anchor tenants, and in between you'll find a plethora of clothing stores, places to eat, jewelers, shoe stores, sporting-goods stores, ATMs, book and music stores, and much, much more. Bring a compass. It's open Mon.–Sat. 10 A.M.–9 P.M., Sun. 11 A.M.–7 P.M.

Boise Factory Outlets, 208/331-5000, is east of town past the airport—take Exit 57 off I-84 at Gowen Road. The mini-mall offers dozens of stores selling name-brand merchandise at 30–70 percent off—Adidas, Bugle Boy, Corning/Revere, Van Heusen, and more. The mall is open Mon.–Sat. 10 A.M.– 8 P.M., Sun. 11 A.M.–6 P.M.

8th Street Marketplace, at 8th and Front Streets, 208/344-0641, is a converted warehouse complex that is one of downtown's public-activity hubs. Here you'll find Kulture Klatsch, Milford's Fish House, the Big Easy Concert House, and Funny Bone comedy club. More shops, restaurants, a multiplex theater, and a hotel are set to open during 2004–2005.

Old Boise provides a plethora of shops and restaurants in a compact area on Main between 4th and 6th Streets, while **Capitol Terrace,** on 8th Street between Main and Idaho, has additional places to spend your life savings.

BOOKS

The **Book & Game Company,** 906 W. Main St., 208/342-2659 or 800/824-7320, is the new incarnation of what once was The Book Shop. The book selection has been winnowed, but it's still big—and there's a tremendous array of magazines and all manner of games, too. Drop in Wednesday evenings 7–10 P.M. for Game Night.

Rainbow Books, 1310 W. State St., 208/336-2230, stocks an inventory of more than 20,000 used books.

Comic-book aficionados can try **King's Komix Kastle,** 1706 N. 18th St., 208/343-7142, where you might find the answer to the burning question: Will Spiderman defeat his enemies before the Scarlet Spider discovers the truth behind the man called Kaine and the entire city is destroyed by rogue symbiote aliens?

Finally, don't forget you're in a college town. The **BSU** bookstore, 208/426-2665, carries textbooks and a whole lot more. It's in the Student Union building on campus and open Mon.–Tues. 8 A.M.–7 P.M., Wed.–Fri. 8 A.M.–5:30 P.M., and Sat. 10 A.M.–5 P.M. year-round.

LIQUOR, BEER, AND WINE

For the hard stuff, you'll need to go to one of the dozen **Idaho State Liquor Stores** in town. Check the phone book's *white* pages under "Liquor Stores" for the list. The best retail beer and wine selection in town is at **Boise Co-op,** 888 W. Fort St., 208/472-4500.

MAPS

Idaho Blueprint & Supply, 619 Main St., 208/344-7878, stocks a wide variety of topographic and other maps. **REI,** 8300 W. Emerald, 208/322-1141, stocks USGS topographic maps of the more popular hiking and backpacking areas, while **The Benchmark,** 625 Vista Ave., 208/338-1700, has a cool machine (co-designed by the USGS and National Geographic Society) that lets you custom-design a 3D-like, shaded-relief topo map for any destination you choose.

SPECIALTY SHOPS

Eyes of the World Imports, 804 W. Fort St., 208/331-1212, sells "cool stuff from cool places"—handcrafted items from around the world.

The goodies produced by **Kastle Chocolate,** 610 N. Orchard, 208/385-7300, are rich in highest quality cocoa butter and lack wax and hydrogenated oils. Chocoholics shouldn't come anywhere near here without a lot of money and a designated driver.

Nick's Shoe Store, 1008 W. Main St., 208/342-9747, has been around since 1946. Its clientele includes many statehouse bigwigs.

The Record Exchange, 1105 W. Idaho, 208/344-8010, occupies the corner of the funky block that also holds Neurolux. It's the oldest music seller in town. You'll find new and used CDs, as well as friendly, knowledgeable folks who can fill you in on the latest chords in the Boise music scene.

Taters, in The Grove, 208/338-1062, is the place to go for Idaho souvenirs, specialty food items made in the state, and lots of kitschy potato-related stuff.

Information and Services

TOURIST INFORMATION

The **Boise Convention and Visitors Bureau,** 312 S. 9th St., 800/635-5240 (outside ID), 208/344-7777, www.boise.org, is open Mon.–Fri. 8:30 A.M.–5 P.M. Two **visitor information centers** provide racks and racks of free literature. One's in Boise Centre next to The Grove, 850 W. Front St., 208/344-5338, open in summer Mon.–Fri. 10 A.M.–5 P.M., Sat. 10 A.M.–2 P.M., and in the off-season Mon.–Fri. 9:30 A.M.–4 P.M. The other one is near the airport, at 2676 Vista Ave., 208/385-0362. Its summer hours are Mon.–Fri. 9 A.M.–5 P.M., Sat.–Sun. 9 A.M.–2 P.M.; off-season Mon.–Fri. 9 A.M.–4 P.M., Sat.–Sun. 10 A.M.–1 P.M.

Boise's **Chamber of Commerce** is downtown at 250 S. 5th St., 208/472-5200. The **Idaho Department of Commerce,** 700 W. State St., 208/334-2470, www.visitid.org, offers tourism information for all parts of the state.

RECREATION INFORMATION

The **Boise Parks and Recreation Department** is at 1104 Royal Blvd., 208/384-4240, www.cityofboise.org/parks. The **Idaho Parks and Recreation Department** is east of town a few miles at 5657 Warm Springs Ave., 208/334-4199. The **Idaho Fish and Game Department** is off Warm Springs Avenue at 600 S. Walnut St., 208/334-3700. The Idaho **Outfitters and Guides Association** is at 711 N. 5th St., 208/342-1919.

Boise National Forest headquarters is at 1249 S. Vinnell Way, 208/373-4100. The **BLM Idaho Headquarters** is at 1387 S. Vinnell Way, 208/373-4000. The office has a large public room with exhibits, free literature, and natural history books and recreation guides for sale. Also at this address is the **U.S. Fish and Wildlife Service,** 208/378-5243. The **BLM Lower Snake River District** office is out by the airport at 3948 Development Ave., 208/384-3300; some pamphlets are available here with information on local BLM-managed lands. The **National Weather Service** is nearby at 3833 S. Development Ave., 208/334-9860; call 208/342-6569 for a local forecast.

MEDIA

The *Idaho Statesman,* 1200 N. Curtis Rd., 208/377-6200, is part of the Gannett chain, and is the largest-circulation daily in Idaho. Particularly interesting are its Thursday Rec supplement; the outdoor page in general, particularly for Pete Zimowsky's excellent columns; the humorous and human-interest columns of Tim Woodward; and the Scene entertainment supplement on Fridays. The Statesman also has a weekly magazine called *Thrive* that offers still more entertainment, outdoors, and lifestyle features. The *Boise Weekly,* 109 S. 4th St., 208/344-2055, is a high-quality liberal rag that acts as a watchdog on the establishment; it'll also direct you to the heart of Boise hipness. Bill Cope's columns are consistently outstanding. *The Arbiter,* Boise State's student newspaper, is available in many locations around town as well as on campus.

KBSU, the city's NPR affiliate, has three signals: classical music and performance at 90.3 FM, NPR news and information at 91.5 FM, and jazz at 730 AM. For local and national talk radio, dial up **KIDO** at 580 AM or **KBOI** at 670 AM.

LIBRARIES

The main branch of the **Boise Public Library** is at 715 S. Capitol Blvd. (across from the Boise Art Museum and Julia Davis Park), 208/384-4114 (recorded information) or 208/384-4238 (administration), www.boisepubliclibrary.org. Hours are Mon.–Thurs. 10 A.M.–9 P.M., Fri. 10 A.M.–6 P.M., Sat. 10 A.M.–5 P.M.; and Sun. noon–5 P.M. The library also has a branch at the Boise Towne Square mall, 208/375-5020. Boise State's **Albertsons Library** is on campus at 1910 University Dr., 208/426-1204 (circulation desk) or 208/426-1816 (recorded information), http://library.boisestate.edu. The **Idaho State Library** is at 325 W. State St., 208/334-2150.

POST OFFICES

The **main post office** is at 770 S. 13th St., and the **downtown branch** office is in the old Federal Building at 750 W. Bannock. All mail addressed to General Delivery, Boise, goes to the main office. For postal information, call 800/275-8777.

Transportation

GETTING THERE

By Air

Boise's airport is on the southeast edge of town at 3201 Airport Way (I-84 Exit 53, Vista Avenue), 208/383-3110, www.boise-airport.com. Its spacious and airy new terminal building opened in 2003.

Airlines serving the city include **America West,** 800/235-9292, which flies to and from its Phoenix hub; **Delta/Skywest,** 800/221-1212, which offers flights just about everywhere through its Salt Lake City hub; **Frontier,** 800/432-1359, with service to and from Denver; **KLM/Northwest,** 800/225-2525, offering direct flights to Minneapolis/St. Paul with connections to Amsterdam; **Southwest,** 800/435-9792, offering direct flights between Boise and Salt Lake City, Portland, Reno, Las Vegas, Oakland, and Spokane; and **United,** 800/241-6522, with direct flights to and from San Francisco, Chicago, and Denver.

Horizon Air, 800/547-9308, is a commuter service affiliated with Alaska Airlines; together, the carriers fly nonstop between Boise and the Idaho cities of Idaho Falls, Lewiston, Pocatello, and Sun Valley (Hailey), plus Denver, Los Angeles, Oakland, Portland, Sacramento, San Diego, San Jose, Seattle, and Spokane. A smaller regional carrier, **Big Sky,** 800/237-7788, has flights to and from Billings and Missoula, Montana.

The airport itself offers the usual restaurants and lounges, as well as a business center with phones, fax machines, photocopiers, and both FedEx and UPS courier drops.

Car-rental companies with offices in the airport include **Avis,** 208/383-3350 or 800/331-1212; **Budget,** 208/383-3090 or 800/527-0700; **Dollar,** 208/345-9727 or 800/800-4000; **Enterprise,** 208/381-0650 or 800/736-8222; **Hertz,** 208/383-3100 or 800/654-3131; and **National,** 208/383-3210 or 800/227-7368; and **Thrifty,** 208/342-7795 or 800/847-4389.

Those heading directly from Boise's airport to Sun Valley can catch the **Sun Valley Express** bus here. The route operates year-round. Adult fare is $54 each way, advance purchase. For more information, call 208/342-7750 or 877/622-8267.

Many Boise hotels and motels run free shuttle buses to the airport. You can catch a cab out front if need be; cab fare to downtown should cost about $10. The budget alternative is the city bus; Route 13 connects the airport with downtown for a mere $.75. Call 208/336-1010 for bus schedules and information.

By Bus

Intercity bus service in Boise centers around the Greyhound terminal at 1212 W. Bannock, 208/343-3681. Three **Greyhound** buses daily connect Boise with Portland, Oregon ($39 each way, 10-day advance purchase), and Salt Lake City ($39 each way, 7-day advance purchase). Sharing the Greyhound terminal is **Northwestern Stage Lines/Trailways,** 208/336-3300, which offers one bus daily to McCall, Grangeville, Lewiston, and Spokane (with onward connections to Seattle). One-way fare to Spokane is $36. Buy tickets for both bus lines at www.greyhound.com.

See **Sun Valley Express** in the Airport section above for information on service from Boise to Sun Valley.

By Car

I-84 runs east-to-west across southern Idaho, connecting Boise with Portland to the west and Salt Lake City to the southeast. Highway 55 leaves Boise headed north to New Meadows, where it joins up with Highway 95, the only north-south route traversing the entire state. South of Boise, Highway 55 rejoins Highway 95 for its run across the desert to Winnemucca, Nevada. For 24-hour **road conditions** in Idaho, call 208/336-6600.

GETTING AROUND
Driving and Parking

Driving around downtown Boise could give you fits; the one-way streets always seem to go the wrong way. It's best to just find a place to park and hoof it or bike around town. Both those nonpolluting modes of transportation are safe and practical downtown.

Municipal pay-parking lots are scattered throughout downtown; many downtown merchants validate parking. Metered spaces line the streets, and empty ones aren't too difficult to find, even in the heart of downtown. Look for a blue button on some meters; press it, and you'll get 20 free minutes, which makes those quick trips much less of a hassle. And although the information printed on the meters says they operate 8 A.M.–6 P.M. daily except Sundays and holidays, actually you don't need to plug them on Saturdays either (trust me—that's straight from the men and women in blue). Finally, as odd as it may seem, mind the sign: it *is* illegal to park on Main Street opposite the Owyhee Plaza Hotel

on Friday and Saturday nights. This is intended to discourage young, loud rowdies from encamping there and disturbing hotel guests. The police monitor this block closely, and violators will be ticketed.

Bicycling

Bicycling isn't just a Boise passion—it's probably the most efficient mode of transportation here. The city, even out to the limits of the greater urban area, is still small enough to get around by bike without requiring a major time commitment. In the downtown area, biking (or even walking) is often faster than driving for most trips. Many streets are designated bike routes, with wide lanes marked specifically for cyclists. Even better than the bike lanes is the Boise Greenbelt, a multiple-use, car-free path that follows the beautiful Boise River from one end of the city to the other. Using the Greenbelt and the bike trails, you can get around town in a jiffy.

City Bus

Boise Urban Stages (a.k.a. the BUS) operates 20 bus routes radiating out from the downtown transit mall bordered by Capitol Boulevard, 9th Street, Main Street, and Idaho Street. Among the most potentially useful routes (counterclockwise from downtown): Route 18 goes north to the bottom of Bogus Basin Road; Route 23 heads west all the way out Chinden to Cloverdale, passing the fairgrounds and Les Bois Park (horse races); Route 5 goes southwest to the Boise Towne Square mall (with an extension on Route 26 to the Spectrum entertainment area); Route 13 will take you to the airport, Route 33 to Boise Factory Outlets; Route 20 heads for the Park-Center area; and Route 1 will take you out Warm Springs Avenue toward the Old Pen and Botanical Gardens.

Adult fare is $1, youths (ages 6–18) $.65, seniors and disabled $.50. Transfers are free. For more information call 208/336-1010.

Southwest Idaho

Southwest Idaho is roughly bisected by the broad Snake River on its course between the Oregon border and Glenns Ferry. North of the river lie four of the state's 10 largest cities—Boise, Meridian, Nampa, and Caldwell. South of the river lies a whole lot of nothing—vast, sparsely populated Owyhee County.

Beyond the metropolitan areas north of the Snake, the high desert gives way to foothills, then the pine-forested Boise Mountains. From their origins high in these mountains, the Payette and Boise Rivers rush south and west to meet the Snake, which turns north and snakes up the state's western border through legendary Hells Canyon. All three of these rivers provide whitewater thrills for rafters and kayakers, as well as water to irrigate the farmlands on the Snake River Plain. Onions, alfalfa, mint, apples, peaches, and pears grow in abundance here. Emmett is famous for its cherry orchards, while Canyon County's Sunny Slope area near Nampa is home to a number of fine vineyards.

South of the Snake, the land has not been so easily tamed. It's still primarily desert—a great place for explorers to get away from the crowds to find their own private Idaho. Several desert

To Lewiston

HELLS CANYON DAM
Hells Canyon

Hells Canyon National Recreation Area

Burgdorf

Warren

Hazard Lakes

BRUNDAGE MOUNTAIN

Upper Payette Lake

Big Creek

Cuprum

New Meadows

Payette Lake

Yellow Pine

Frank Church - River of No Return Wilderness

Ponderosa State Park

McCall

To Pendleton

Brownlee Reservoir

Council

Cascade State Park

Donnelly

Cascade Reservoir

Warm Lake

Cambridge

Indian Valley

TAMARACK SKI AREA

Cascade

Midvale

MANN CREEK RECREATION AREA

To John Day

Weiser

Smith's Ferry

To Salmon (The High Country)

Stanley

Sawtooth National Recreation Area

Payette

Banks

Garden Valley

Lowman

Payette River

Fruitland

New Plymouth

South Fork

Atlanta

Ontario

Parma

Emmett

Horseshoe Bend

Idaho City

North Fork Boise R.

To Burns

Homedale

Caldwell

Eagle Island State Park

Eagle

BOGUS BASIN SKI AREA

Boise

Arrowrock Reservoir

SOLDIER MOUNTAIN SKI AREA

Meridian

Nampa

Lake Lowell

Lucky Peak State Park

Lucky Peak Reservoir

To Idaho Falls (Southeast ID)

Marsing

Givens Hot Springs

Murphy

Snake River Birds of Prey National Conservation Area

Fairfield

Silver City

MOUNTAIN HOME AIR FORCE BASE

Mountain Home

Glenns Ferry

Gooding

Wood R.

Grand View

Bruneau

Bruneau Dunes State Park

To Burns

Buhl

SOUTHWEST IDAHO

Grasmere

To Twin Falls (South-Central ID)

OREGON
IDAHO

0   20 mi
0   20 km

51

DUCK VALLEY INDIAN RESERVATION

IDAHO
NEVADA

To Elko

© AVALON TRAVEL PUBLISHING, INC.

SOUTHWEST IDAHO

rivers—the Bruneau and Jarbidge, among others—carve deep gorges through Owyhee County, offering challenging whitewater to boaters during spring runoff and interesting canyon hiking year-round. The major mountain range south of the river, the Owyhee Mountains, was named for an unfortunate expedition of Hawaiian trappers who disappeared here; Owyhee is an archaic spelling of Hawaii. The Owyhees are visible across most of the region, remaining snowcapped until well into summer.

Mining played a big part in the history of the region. Idaho City in the Boise Mountains was the site of the state's biggest goldfields. Silver City in the Owyhees was once the state's biggest boomtown. Today they're both fun places to poke around, calling up the spirits of those who struck it rich and those who struck it out.

West of Boise

The population of Canyon County has exploded in recent years, as the Boise area becomes a megalopolis slowly filling in from the capital city west. Houses are displacing farmland here at a rapid rate, but agriculture remains important.

An elaborate irrigation system initiated by the pioneers around the turn of the 20th century transformed Canyon County from an arid sagebrush plain into the state's most productive agricultural county. Among the 70 different cash crops grown in the county are alfalfa, beans, wheat, barley, corn, onions, and potatoes. Two other big crops offer extremes of olfactory stimulation to passersby: Nampa is home to a sugar-beet refinery that may snap you out of your roadtrip stupor to frantically roll up the windows and turn on the a/c; at the other end of the spectrum, fields of mint will pleasantly tickle your nosebuds as you cruise by on the interstate. And down along the Snake River, the Sunny Slope area is Idaho's premier wine-growing region; numerous vineyards offer winetasting opportunities for visitors. The county also ranks first in the state in livestock production and second in the dairy business.

Two side benefits of Canyon County's agricultural focus are a boon to travelers. Roadside vegetable and fruit stands are plentiful, offering cheap, fresh produce in abundance. For a guide to the county's fruit and vegetable stands and U-pick orchards, obtain a copy of the *Farm to Market Agricultural Tours* pamphlet from the Nampa Chamber of Commerce, 1305 3rd St. S., Nampa, ID 83651, 208/466-4641. And thanks in part to the large numbers of migrant farm workers in the area, you'll find a preponderance of authentic Mexican-food restaurants in both Nampa and Caldwell.

North of Canyon County is quieter Gem County, surrounding the county seat of Emmett. This is also ag country, but here fruit crops take center stage. The county supports thriving orchards—Emmett's annual Cherry Festival in June is one of the region's highlights.

MERIDIAN

The first town you come to driving west of Boise on I-84, Meridian shot from fewer than 10,000 people in 1990 to 39,067 in 2002. The suburb is largely a mess of strip malls and subdivisions, but it's also home to two of the Boise metro area's most popular family fun spots. You really can't miss 'em, since they sit smack-dab next to the interstate.

Roaring Springs Water Park

Southern Idaho can get brutally hot in the summer, so Roaring Springs, 400 W. Overland Ave., 208/884-8842 or 877/420-7529, www.roaringsprings.com, is understandably a huge draw, especially for kids. The park has a wave pool, a kids' play place, and a river for tubing—plus thoroughly gonzo attractions like the U-shaped Avalanche, described by a 9-year-old fan like this: "They put you on a raft on this little platform at the very top, and then they push you down the slope backwards and you're practically flying. You hit the top of the slide and it feels like you're going to fly off and die. You keep doing that until you finally slow down."

All-day admission is $22 general and $18 for kids ages 4–13. Admission after 3 P.M. is $16 for all ages. Open daily 11 A.M.–8 P.M. June through late August and weekends (until 7 P.M.) in late May and early September.

Boondocks Fun Center

Right next door to Roaring Springs, Boondocks, 1385 S. Blue Marlin Ln., 208/898-0900, has two miniature golf courses (one sporting a replica of Utah's Delicate Arch), bumper boats, batting cages, and go-karts outside, plus laser tag and a huge arcade indoors. Prices vary; packages are available starting at $12.75. Open daily 10 A.M.–11 P.M. (Sundays until 8 P.M.).

Food

Like most everything else in Meridian, **Whitewater Pizza & Pasta,** 1510 N. Eagle Rd., 208/888-6611, is in a strip mall (at the corner of Eagle Road and Fairview Avenue), but the vibe here is decidedly non-chain. The menu and decor are inspired by river sports—so, for example, you can chow down on Class VI Pizza ($13 for a 12-inch) or an appetizer of "throw ropes" (cheese-topped sourdough breadsticks, $4) while admiring the kayaks, canoes, and rafts mounted overhead. The bulletin boards by the bathrooms are a good source of Idaho paddling information. Open Sun.–Thurs. 11 A.M.–9 P.M., Fri.–Sat. until 10 P.M., with patio dining and longer hours in summer.

Epi's, 1115 E. 1st St., 208/884-0142, offers outstanding traditional Basque fare in a bright, tidy, and very friendly atmosphere. Basque music fills the air, and Basque art and family photos line the walls. You can choose from such unique dishes as tongue (in a pepper-tomato sauce) or baby squid in a sauce of its own ink. Or stick with something a little less adventurous but equally wonderful, like the sublime lamb stew. Entrées range $11–17. This small restaurant is very popular; reservations (and the restaurant itself) are highly recommended.

Information

For more information on Meridian, contact the Meridian Chamber of Commerce, 215 E. Franklin Road, 208/888-2817, www.meridianchamber.org.

NAMPA AND VICINITY

Since its founding in 1886, Nampa (population 60,300) has seen its share of ups and downs. Once an Oregon Short Line rail stop, the site attracted the attention of Colonel William Dewey, a wealthy mining magnate with great dreams for the city. In 1901 he built a grand hotel here to start the ball rolling; the luxurious Dewey Palace was constructed for a then-astronomical $243,000 and occupied a whole city block. In 1963 the deteriorating hotel was torn down to make way for a plain-vanilla bank and a tire store.

Nampa struggles to make its mark in Boise's shadow, but—unlike Meridian—it's had a chance to grow slowly and develop its own character. The downtown area, though hardly lively, features many beautiful old buildings, shaded benches, and free parking. Meanwhile, out by the freeway, the Idaho Center is a major concert venue, and one of Idaho's only hostels is just a mile north of that.

Hispanic Cultural Center of Idaho

Get an eyeful here. Not only is the vibrant-hued building, 315 Stampede Dr., 208/442-0823, www.hispanicculturalcenter.org, a real architectural standout, it houses an impressive array of work by contemporary Hispanic artists. Check the website for upcoming events, or simply drop by weekdays 9 A.M.–5 P.M.

Warhawk Air Museum

Fans of WWII-era aviation will enjoy this museum, 201 Municipal Dr., 208/465-6646, where you'll find two Curtiss P-40 fighters used in the movie *Pearl Harbor,* along with many other vintage aircraft. Surrounding the planes are aircraft engines, armaments, uniforms, old photos, and other World War II memorabilia. Admission is $5 general, $4 seniors 65 and up, and $3 ages 4–9. Open Tue.–Sat. 10 A.M.–5 P.M., Sun. 11 A.M.–5 P.M.

Canyon County Historical Society Museum

Some dusty old historical museums are exciting only to dusty old historians. But the Canyon County Historical Society Museum, 1200 Front

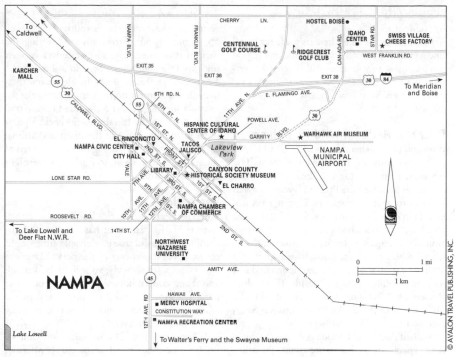

St., 208/467-7611, is a great stop. The history begins with the building itself: the museum is housed in the beautiful old Oregon Short Line Depot, built in 1902 for $30,000. Its architecture is unique and impressive—an ornate design in dark brick with white trim. The building was abandoned in 1972 but saved and restored a year later. It's now listed on the National Register of Historic Places. Inside you'll find railroad memorabilia, old newspapers dating back to 1881, photographs from as early as 1891, and pictures of the old Dewey Palace Hotel in its glory days. Admission is free, though donations are accepted. Hours are Tues.–Sat. 1–5 P.M.

Northwest Nazarene University

NNU, 623 Holly St., 208/467-8011 or 800/852-2978, is a top-rated four-year Christian liberal-arts school subscribing to the Wesleyan doctrines of the Church of the Nazarene, one of which is, "That man is born with a fallen nature, and is,

therefore, inclined to evil, and that continually." No keg parties here, I guess. The campus lies south of downtown on the east side of Highway 45/12th Avenue Road (at Lake Lowell Avenue).

Swiss Village Cheese Factory

Low-fat cheese, high-fat cheese, cheese puffs, cheese balls, grated cheese, yellow cheese, white cheese, blue cheese—it's all here at Swiss Village Cheese Factory, east of town at 4912 Franklin Rd., 208/467-4424. To get there, take Exit 38 off I-84 (Garrity Boulevard) and turn right on Franklin; follow Franklin about 1.5 miles to the factory, at the corner of Star Road.

The factory produces more than 35 different varieties of cheese. You can watch the work in progress from an upstairs gallery, which also contains some exhibits of old tools of the trade, a cheesemaker's album of black-and-white photos, and some interesting explanations of the origins and stories behind several different varieties of cheese (did you know Roquefort was created by accident?).

Also upstairs is a café where it's a safe bet you'll find a grilled cheese sandwich on the menu; you can order it with your choice of cheeses. Downstairs is a retail outlet. Swiss Village Cheese Factory is open Mon.–Sat. 8 A.M.–7 P.M., Sun. 10 A.M.–5 P.M.

Deer Flat National Wildlife Refuge

Birds and birdwatchers alike flock to this 11,430-acre refuge four miles southwest of town. The refuge, managed by the U.S. Fish and Wildlife Service, is a stop on the Pacific Flyway, an avian highway for migratory species. During peak migration in early December roughly 12,000 geese and 100,000 ducks honk and quack their way around the refuge's two units. The first unit—artificial 8,800-acre Lake Lowell—was part of a 1906 irrigation project, and was designated as a national wildlife refuge by President Theodore Roosevelt in 1909. The second unit comprises the 107 islands in the Snake River between Swan Falls and Farewell Bend, Oregon.

Mallard ducks and Canada geese are the dominant species here, but more than 200 other species have been observed on the refuge, among them loons, grebes, pelicans, cormorants, bitterns, herons, egrets, ducks such as the northern pintail and the cinnamon teal, raptors—including bald eagles, red-tailed hawks, and peregrine falcons—and eight different species of sandpipers. A complete birding checklist is available at the visitor center.

Birding is just one of the many forms of recreation available here. Boating, swimming, waterskiing, fishing, horseback riding, mountain biking, cross-country skiing, and ice skating can all be enjoyed at one time of year or another, with certain restrictions in place to protect the refuge's winged inhabitants. No boating is allowed on Lake Lowell October 1 to April 14, and fishing from the shores of the Snake River islands is prohibited February 1 to May 31, when the geese are nesting.

The refuge headquarters and visitor center, 13751 Upper Embankment, 208/467-9278, is in the middle of the northeast shore of Lake Lowell,

near the intersection of Lake and Lake Lowell Avenues. Lake Avenue turns south off Highway 55, on the way out of town toward Marsing; the turnoff is marked. The visitor center is open mid-April through September Mon.–Fri. 8 A.M.–4 P.M. and Sat. 9 A.M.–4 P.M. Inside are informative exhibits focusing on the natural history of the refuge. Outside, a short self-guided nature trail winds down to the lakeshore and back; a pamphlet introduces some of the plant and animal species commonly seen along the way. The rest of the refuge is open dawn to dusk. No overnight camping is permitted.

Recreation

Lakeview Park, at Garrity Boulevard and 16th Avenue N., isn't large but has a lot to offer, including a beautiful rose garden splashing bright colors across one corner of the park. Elsewhere you'll find softball fields; volleyball, basketball, and tennis courts; horseshoe pits; a pool, water park, playground, and duck pond; and picnic tables. The park also provides the venue for many of Nampa's annual events.

Nampa's year-round **Centennial Golf Course,** 2600 Centennial Dr., 208/467-3011, offers an 18-hole, par-72 course stretching over 6,655 yards. The hilly course lies right next to I-84 at Exit 36. Take Franklin Road south one block, turn left onto Industrial Road, left onto 11th Avenue, and left again on Centennial Drive. Greens fees run $12–19. Right across the street is **Ridgecrest Golf Club,** 3730 Ridgecrest Dr., 208/468-9073, offering another 27 holes in the form of an exceptional 18-hole Scottish-links-style course and a nine-hole par 3–4 course. Greens fees on the main course are $15–27; at the beginner-friendly Wee-9 they're $12.

For a budget alternative to Roaring Springs, consider an outing at the **Nampa Recreation Center,** 131 Constitution Way (off 12th Ave. S.), 208/465-2288, www.namparec. The massive (135,000 square feet) building provides opportunities for swimming, basketball, racquetball, running, aerobics, dance, gymnastics, and more. The six different pools include a huge lap pool, play pool, kiddies' wading pool, diving pool, hydrotherapy pool, and Jacuzzi.

Near the pools you'll find a steam room and sauna. The aerobics area offers an indoor running track, weight machines, NordicTracks, exercycles, treadmills, and Stairmasters. A large wall-climbing area offers more than 50 routes for all ability levels; climbers must provide their own belay, and rental equipment is available. Day-use rates are $6.25 adults, $4.25 ages 12–17, $3.25 ages 6–11, $1 ages five and under. The center is open Mon.–Fri. 5:30 A.M.–10 P.M., Sat. 8 A.M.–8 P.M., Sun. 11 A.M.–6 P.M.

Entertainment

Nampa's Idaho Center, 16200 Can-Ada Road, 208/468-1000 information, 208/442-3232 tickets, www.idahocenter.com, includes both an indoor arena and an outdoor amphitheater where major sports and entertainment events are held. The arena is home to the Idaho Stampede pro basketball team and the big Snake River Stampede pro rodeo.

The 1,500-seat Swayne Auditorium at Northwest Nazarene University's **Brandt Center** hosts periodic performances by the Boise Philharmonic during the symphony's Sept.–April season.

Nampa's Civic Center complex, 311 3rd St. S., 208/465-2252, www.nampaciviccenter.com, includes a convention center and performing-arts complex. Its 648-seat auditorium boasts state-of-the-art acoustics and lighting and is the venue for a variety of concerts, art shows, and other entertainment throughout the year. **Frontier Cinema,** 210 12th Ave. S., 208/467-7469, is a budgeteer's dream—all seats $2 every night.

Events

The weekend before Memorial Day, look for the big **Parade America,** a decades-old patriotic tradition in Nampa and one of the larger parades in the Northwest.

The **Snake River Stampede** bucks into Idaho Center in mid-July. The PRCA-sanctioned Stampede is one of the country's top 25 rodeos, attracting some 500 world-champion pros competing in bareback and saddle bronc riding, bull riding, steer wrestling, individual and team roping, and barrel racing. Even the rodeo clowns compete here, in a "bullfight" competition,

while kids 5–7 compete in Mutton Busting. Tickets run $10–15. The week kicks off with one of the West's largest horse parades and a buckaroo breakfast. For more information, call the Snake River Stampede Rodeo Headquarters at 208/466-8497.

Hostel Boise

With a country setting just a mile north of the Idaho Center, **Hostel Boise,** 17322 Can-Ada Road, 208/467-6858, www.hostelboise.com, is a friendly and inexpensive base for exploring the area. A clean kitchen, peaceful back patio, and comfortable living room make guests feel at home, as does owner Elsa Freeman, who's practically made it her mission to bring this hostel (the region's only one, and a Hostelling International affiliate) to Southern Idaho. Bunks in the four-bed dorm rooms cost $14 for HI members, $17 for non-members. A private room for up to three people costs $31 for one person, $35 for two, and $40 for three. Check-in is between 5 and 10 P.M.; check out by 9:30 A.M. Reservations are advised.

Food

Mexican food—the real thing—is almost reason enough to come to Nampa. Word of mouth for the best Mexican *cocina* in town goes to **El Charro,** 1701 1st St. N., 208/467-5804. Others swear by **El Rinconcito,** across the tracks at 824 1st St. S., 208/466-6963, where the corn tortilla chips taste like fresh corn and are accompanied by blazing salsa that fires up the taste buds for the meal to come; open Tues.–Wed. 11 A.M.–9 P.M., Fri.–Sun. 9 A.M.–10 P.M., closed on Mondays and Thursdays.

Tacos Jalisco, 219 11th Ave. N., 208/465-5788, is not just a Mexican restaurant, it's a cheap vacation to Jalisco, the Mexican state and native homeland of owners Atanacio and Guadalupe Arroyo. Mexican radio hits your ears as soon as you walk in, your eyes falling upon an interior straight out of Guadalajara. Sombreros and serapes adorn two walls, while a wreath of dried chiles and a braid of garlic cloves hangs on another. A crucifix watches over the front door, and what looks like a small shrine perches above the doorway leading to the restrooms. Mexican flags hang here and there, and about half the clientele is Mexican. A Tacos Jalisco calendar by the register boasts *"Le ofrece la mejor y más auténtica comida Mexicana del area de Nampa."* True enough. Tacos Jalisco is smoke-free and open Tues.–Fri. 11 A.M.–9:30 P.M., Sat. 9 A.M.–9:30 P.M., Sun. 9 A.M.–8 P.M.

Information and Services

The **Nampa Chamber of Commerce** is at 1305 3rd St. S., 208/466-4641 or 877/20-NAMPA (877/206-2672), www.nampa.com. The 1919 **Nampa Carnegie Library**, 101 11th Ave. S. (at 1st St. S.), 208/465-2263, is beautiful and comfortable; the upstairs tables along the window-lined north wall make particularly fine places to read one of the library's 79,000 volumes. Hours are Mon.–Thurs. 10 A.M.–8 P.M., Fri. 10 A.M.–6 P.M., Sat. 10 A.M.–5 P.M.

The **Idaho Department of Fish and Game** maintains an office at 3101 S. Powerline Rd., 208/465-8465. Inside you'll find a few wildlife and nature exhibits, and right nearby are some stocked fishing ponds and a trout hatchery. The Nampa **Parks and Recreation Department** is in the Rec Center at 131 Constitution Way, 208/465-2215.

If you can't find what you're looking for in any of the shops downtown, head over to **Karcher Mall**, at 1509 Nampa-Caldwell Blvd., 208/465-7845. It was Idaho's first indoor mall and offers about 70 shops, including anchor tenant The Bon Marche.

Walter's Ferry

Highway 45 drops like a plumb line from 12th Street in Nampa south to the Snake River at Walter's Ferry. John Fruit and a partner established a ferry crossing here in 1863, and had they not sold out five years later to Lewellyn and Augusta Walter, we might be calling the town Fruit's Ferry today. The crossing here was the pioneer-days equivalent of a major freeway interchange. Oregon Trail travelers who hadn't crossed to the north bank of the river at Three Island Crossing came down the south side of the river and crossed here. Stage lines ran from Walter's Ferry north to Boise and the Boise Basin

mines, and south to the Owyhee mines and on to California. For a short time after 1866, the steamship *Shoshone* plied the Snake River between here and Olds Ferry (west of Weiser). It proved unprofitable, however, and after just a few trips, the 136-foot, 300-ton vessel was taken for a wild ride down through Hells Canyon and back to Lewiston.

Turn in at Ferry Service and continue down the road—past a hillside full of whirligigs, bird-houses, and even a parade of tricycles—to the **Swayne Museum.** The word "museum" must be used loosely in describing this odd mixture of historical center, animal farm, botanical garden, religious retreat, and amusement park. Whatever you choose to call it, it's fun, tranquil, and definitely unique. The museum was begun by local resident Pappy Swayne (1887–1976) and carried on after his death by his widow, Cleo. You enter to peacocks strutting free around the grounds and a menagerie of other caged fowl and waterfowl including chickens, turkeys, and a pair of swans in a small pond. A nature trail winds along the wooded river-bank past fake wildlife, real lizards and squirrels slithering and scampering about, statuettes of gnomes, and an "enchanted forest" full of smiley faces with legs. The trail loops back past Pappy's grave, a shrine, and a meditation/prayer garden. A sign posted in several places reads: "This Place Was Built as a Vibrant Faith Adventure. You Are My Special Friend and Visitor Today. Please Keep It Free From Harm." A "vibrant faith adventure" sums this place up as well as anything. Admission is free, though donations are accepted.

East of the highway lie the town of Melba and the county's Celebration Park, both of which are adjacent to the Snake River Birds of Prey Natural Conservation Area, covered in the Kuna and the Snake River section later in this chapter. From Walter's Ferry you can work your way west down the river on back roads past several vineyards, then head north on Highway 95 through the small farming communities of Wilder and Parma. If you cross to the south side of the river at Walter's Ferry, Marsing, or Homedale, you'll enter Owyhee County.

CALDWELL

Caldwell (population 29,500) was known as Bugtown when it served as a campsite for workers on the Oregon Short Line Railroad. Today, though it remains the state's ninth-largest city, Caldwell is mostly a drab and humorless place— a workingman's nine-to-five grind kind of town. Jon Katz captured its vibe (or lack thereof) in his 2001 book *Geeks: How Two Lost Boys Rode the Internet Out of Idaho*. All is not lost for Caldwell, however, since it is home to Albertson College, which ranks among the finer liberal arts schools in the West.

Albertson College of Idaho

Albertson College, 2112 E. Cleveland Blvd., 208/459-5011 or 800/224-3246, www.albertson.edu, enjoys a solid reputation, and alumni who include two former governors, a Pulitzer Prize–winning historian, an Academy Award–winning musician, and many Rhodes Scholars. It's also the state's oldest four-year college, founded by the Wood River Presbytery in 1891. It was known as the College of Idaho until the Albertson grocery family gave it a pile of cash in the early 1990s.

Among the buildings on the 43-acre campus are the 850-seat **Jewett Auditorium,** which hosts concerts, lectures, and meetings; the 54,000-square-foot **Langroise Center for the Performing and Fine Arts,** housing the college's music, drama, dance, and visual arts departments; the **Rosenthal Gallery of Art,** which presents a half dozen exhibitions each academic year and also serves as a venue for poetry readings and performance art; and the **Orma J. Smith Museum of Natural History,** containing a sizable collection of animal and plant specimens, minerals, fossils, and Native American artifacts.

Recreation

At **Luby Park,** off Illinois Avenue on the north side of Exit 28, you'll find ballfields, hoops, and tennis courts, as well as the city's beautiful rose garden, which in full bloom presents a kaleidoscope of colors. Look for the **Greenway** along the Boise River on the west side of town; a jogging path and an Oregon Trail

monument highlight the site, just west of the interstate at Exit 27.

Many golfers consider **Purple Sage Golf Course,** 15192 Purple Sage Rd., 208/459-2223, one of the state's finest courses. The 18-hole, par-71 course spreads over 6,754 yards. Greens fees are $14–16; cart rental is available. Open year-round. To get there, take I-84 Exit 25, turn east off the off-ramp (Highway 44), go north on Highway 30, then east on Purple Sage Road to the course. Nine-hole **Fairview Golf Course,** 816 Grant St., 208/455-3090, provides a challenge with small greens and many trees. Greens fees for the 2,572-yard, par-35 course range $10–13 for nine holes. The course is open daily; no tee times needed.

Entertainment and Events

A variety of cultural arts performances are presented at Albertson College's Jewett Auditorium, 20th and Fillmore Streets on campus. Caldwell Fine Arts sponsors a **concert series** at the auditorium, Oct.–April. Past performances have included Latin American dance, American Indian theater, and music ranging from the Aspen Wind Quartet to jazz pianist Marian McPartland. For more information call Caldwell Fine Arts at 208/459-3405 or 208/454-1376.

In early May—Cinco de Mayo to be exact— Caldwell's large Hispanic population stages its annual **Fiesta Cultural** in Memorial Park. Several thousand people typically turn out to see brightly colored Mexican skirts swirling to strains of mariachi bands, or taste *platos típicos* such as *menudo* (tripe soup) and *albondigas* (meatball soup).

In late June, look to the skies for the **Caldwell Air-A-Fair,** an air show attracting upwards of 40,000 spectators annually to Caldwell Industrial Airport. The **Canyon County Fair** comes the last week of July to the fairgrounds at Blaine Street and 22nd Avenue, 208/454-7498. Look for livestock shows, cook-offs, carnival rides, pie-baking and milk-drinking contests, a tractor pull, and other daily entertainment.

The **Caldwell Night Rodeo** is one of the country's top 20 PRCA-sanctioned rodeos, drawing almost 40,000 fans to the rodeo grounds for a weeklong run in mid-August. For more

IDAHO'S WINE COUNTRY

COURTESY OF THE IDAHO TRAVEL COUNCIL

The tasting room of Ste. Chapelle has the airy feel of La Sainte Chapelle in Paris with its high, bright cathedral and stained glass windows.

Conditions along the western Snake River Plain are excellent for growing wine grapes. Long days, cool nights, temperatures moderated by the river, and volcanic-ash soils combine to produce grapes exhibiting a naturally high acidity and strong fruit flavor. The Sunny Slope area is Idaho's premier winemaking district. To reach it, head west of Nampa (toward Marsing) on Highway 55.

Ste. Chapelle Winery, 19348 Lowell Rd., Caldwell, 208/453-7830, www .stechapelle.com, is the largest of Idaho's wineries. Available varietals include chardonnay, fumé blanc, gewürztraminer, chenin blanc, Johannisberg riesling, cabernet, and a variety of sparkling wines. A beautiful grassy amphitheater provides the venue for a **Jazz at the Winery** concert series in summer. The Sunday afternoon concerts are set among vine-covered slopes, with views out across the Snake River Plain. Dancing on the grass and sipping good wine makes for an undeniably rich summer afternoon. Bring a blanket, sunscreen, and picnic basket. Gates open at noon, and concerts begin around 1 P.M. Tickets run $5–20. The winery is open in summer Mon.–Thurs. 10 A.M.–5 P.M. (until 7 P.M. Fri.–Sat.) and Sunday noon–5 P.M.; in winter Mon.–Sat. 11 A.M.–5 P.M. and Sunday noon–5 P.M. Tours available.

Koeing Distillery & Winery, a five-minute drive from Ste. Chapelle at 20928 Grape Lane, Caldwell, 208/455-8386, produces both wines (including chardonnay, cabernet sauvignon, pinot noir, merlot, and a semillon-chardonnay blend) and brandies. Its three-story headquarters includes a handcrafted still from Austria and a wine-tasting room (open Sat.–Sun. April–Dec., noon–5 P.M.).

Hells Canyon Winery, 18835 Symms Rd., Caldwell, 208/454-3300 or 800/318-7873, founded in 1985, produces chardonnay, merlot, syrah, and cabernet sauvignon. Winetastings are available weekends noon–5 P.M. A bed-and-breakfast at the winery has rooms starting at $95.

South of Nampa off Highway 45, **Sawtooth Winery,** 13750 Surrey Ln., 208/467-1200, sits atop a ridge overlooking Hidden Valley and the Owyhee Mountains to the south, Treasure Valley and the Boise Mountains to the north. The winery's 20-acre vineyard produces chardonnays, cabernets, merlot, pinot gris, syrah, and other varieties. The tasting room grounds are neatly landscaped with bright flowers, trim lawns, and a few old wine barrels scattered about to good effect. A small gift shop sells wine-related paraphernalia. Every Mother's Day the winery puts on a big bash here with food, entertainment, and, of course, plenty of wine. To get there, follow the signs west off Highway 45, about midway between Nampa and Walter's Ferry. Hours are Fri.–Sun., noon–5 P.M., or weekdays by appointment.

Idaho has about 20 wineries statewide. For more information, contact the **Idaho Grape Growers and Wine Producers Commission,** 1123 12th Ave. S., Nampa, ID 83651, 208/467-4999 or 888/223-WINE, www.idahowine.org.

information, call the Caldwell Chamber of Commerce at 208/459-7493.

Food

As is true of its neighbor city, Nampa, authentic Mexican food is easy to come by in Caldwell. If you're really hungry, head down to the 400 to 600 blocks of N. 5th Avenue—deep in the heart of Caldwell's Mexican-American community—and hit several Mexican restaurants in one day. Knowing Spanish helps here.

Cilantro's, 417 N. 5th Ave., is a low-key Mexican deli that doubles as a *carnecería* (meat market). The food is cheap, plentiful, and delicious, and you'll find the place doing a good business with the local Mexicanos. The Mexican jukebox here is an added plus.

Also in the area is **Tacos Michoacan,** 605 N. 5th Ave., 208/454-1583, which sports a wildly arty paint job. The chips and salsa here are excellent, and the menu features a wide range of meat dishes, including tacos filled with *adobada* (spiced, grilled beef), *carne asada* (steak), *lengua* (tongue), or even *sesos* (brains). Among the more substantial entrées are *menudo* (tripe) and *camarones con arroz* (shrimp with Mexican fried rice).

At any of the aforementioned restaurants you can enjoy *cervezas Mexicanas,* and you'll hear more Spanish than English spoken by the staff and customers. On your way back toward downtown, you'll pass right by the **Casa Valdez tortilla factory,** 502 E. Chicago St., 208/459-6461, where you can pick up a dozen *tortillas de harina* (flour) or *maíz* (corn), *para llevar* (to go).

Information

The **Caldwell Chamber of Commerce,** 914 Blaine St., Caldwell, ID 83605, 208/459-7493, stocks literature about the area, including a self-guided driving-tour pamphlet to the region's agricultural lands.

EMMETT AND VICINITY

North of Canyon County, Emmett (population 5,000) is the Gem County seat. Travelers heading north into town on Highway 16 will get their first view of the verdant Valley of Plenty, as early

settlers called it, from the top of **Freezeout Hill,** about seven miles southeast of town. From this spot today, the modern highway will take you safely down into Emmett without a worry. But in 1862, when mountain-man Tim Goodale led the first party of Oregon Trail pioneers along this route, they had to descend the long, steep hill without the aid of a ribbon of asphalt. It was one of the more hair-raising parts of their journey.

When the pioneers reached the valley floor, many of them found the bottomland along the banks of the Payette River to their liking. The soil was fertile, and the climate conducive to growing a variety of fruits and vegetables. A ferry was built across the Payette to serve traffic along the Oregon Trail, and a settlement was established nearby in 1864. After the discovery of gold in the area's mountains, the settlement became an agricultural supply center for the mining communities.

For a number of years in the early 1860s, valley residents were plagued by a band of robbers and horse thieves who holed up in "Pickett's Corral," a steep-walled box canyon on the east side of town. Finally, the good people of the valley decided they'd had enough. In 1864 they formed a vigilante group that succeeded in rousting the villains. Among the victorious vigilantes was William "Poker Bill" McConnell, later governor of Idaho.

In 1870, the first postmaster, Thomas Cahalan, named the settlement Emmettsville after his young son (the name was shortened to Emmett in 1900). The town was platted in 1883 and soon thereafter its irrigation canals were constructed, rendering more than 26,000 acres of the valley arable. A lumber mill began operations in 1886. Orchards produced more peaches, apples, apricots, and cherries than local residents and passing travelers could possibly consume. Exporting the fruit out of the valley was a problem until a branch of the Oregon Short Line Railroad (a Union Pacific affiliate) linked the town to Nampa in 1902. With the railroad in place, the town boomed—by 1928 it was the largest shipping point in Idaho on the Union Pacific line. Besides fruit, the town boasted a booming ice industry, and also exported lumber and livestock. Another local industry, salmon fishing, ended abruptly in 1924 when construction of Black Canyon Dam blocked the spawning route up the Payette River. A couple of old salmon gigs in the Gem County Historical Museum attest to the past presence of the once-prolific fish.

Besides fruit growing, a Boise-Cascade sawmill and plywood plant fuels the town economy today.

Gem County Historical Museum

One of the finest regional historical museums in Idaho, the Gem County Historical Museum, at 501 E. 1st St. (at Hawthorne), relates its large collection of historical artifacts to the people who actually used them.

The old country doctor's examination chair isn't just any old chair: it belonged to Doc Reynolds, who practiced medicine in Emmett and the surrounding area from 1906 to 1954. In 1914 Doc Reynolds purchased the second car driven in the Emmett Valley; for years thereafter, it was the only car in town that could make it up Freezeout Hill.

And that old lace dress isn't just any lace dress: it's the dress worn by local resident Kathryn Tyler Hunt to the coronation of Queen Elizabeth. Hunt's maternal great-grandmother, Betsy Barker Tyler, was born in 1755 into a family of well-to-do Bostonians, relatives of the 10th U.S. president, John Tyler. Betsy's daughter Jane scandalized her upper-crust parents when she married rough-and-ready Westerner John Maynard and moved to Idaho. Her parents came to accept the marriage, however, and sent a few things—furnishings and such—to the couple so Jane would have some familiar items in her home. The furnishings were shipped around Cape Horn to San Francisco, then freighted by wagon to Idaho. Some of these family heirlooms are on view at the museum.

The museum is open June–Sept. (possibly longer, depending on the budget), Wed.–Fri. 10 A.M.–4 P.M. or by appointment; 208/365-9530 or 208/365-4340.

Squaw Butte

This high, solitary peak is visible from much of southwestern Idaho. A decent road leads right to the top, where you'll find a BLM lookout, antennas galore, and incredible views. The summit area is a popular launching spot for **hang gliders.** To get there, take Highway 52 (Washington Avenue) north out of downtown and up onto the Emmett Bench. When the highway makes a 90-degree right turn at a major intersection, continue straight instead, onto Van Deusen Road. A ways down Van Deusen, turn right onto Butte Road, then make a left at well-marked Lookout Road, which climbs seven miles to the summit.

Black Canyon Reservoir

Pursuits of choice at this large reservoir behind Black Canyon Dam include **swimming, boating, fishing,** and **water-skiing.** The Bureau of Reclamation maintains day-use areas along the lakeshore. **Black Canyon Park** is the westernmost, offering boat-launching ramps, a swimming area, shaded picnic area, and sandy beach. **Triangle Park,** to the east, features a boat-launching ramp and dock. **Wild Rose Park,** on the downstream side of the dam, has a gazebo by a rose garden. All areas charge a small day-use fee. For more information, contact the Bureau of Reclamation's office at Black Canyon Dam, 208/365-2682 or 208/365-2600.

Golf

The nine-hole **Emmett City Golf Course,** 2102 Salesyard Rd., 208/365-2675, offers a 2,910-yard, par-36 challenge with narrow fairways and many water traps. Greens fees range $10–13. The course is closed Dec. 1–Feb. 1.

Events

Speed demons head to Firebird Raceway, seven miles south of Emmett on Highway 16, 208/344-0411, for **drag racing.** The quarter-mile drag strip hosts National Hot Rod Association events during a season extending April–Oct.; about 45 race dates a year. When the orchards come into bloom in April, Emmett encourages visitors to come and take a look on **Blossom Sunday.** Freezeout Hill, overlooking the valley, is a great place to see the sea of flowers.

Emmett's **Cherry Festival,** running the second

full week of June in Emmett City Park, is one of the town's annual highlights. Locals celebrate this prized crop with a number of events, which can include hot-air balloon races, pie-eating contests, cherry-pit-spitting contests, a carnival, parades, square dancing, the Miss Gem County competition, and lots and lots of food.

Also in June, entrants in the **Black Canyon Canoe Race** paddle posthaste from Horseshoe Bend to Emmett, while the **International Women's Challenge** bicycle races feature fabulously fit femmes pedalling around a circuitous road course that begins in Emmett and ends with a brutal hill climb up old Horseshoe Bend Road.

Emmett's **farmers' market** runs June–Sept., Saturday 8 A.M.–noon in Railroad Park at N. Washington and Park Streets; given the quality produce in the area, this is a sure bet for great groceries, as well as flowers and crafts. Mid-July's the time for the popular **Cruise Night,** which brings out classic cars and 1950s fashions for a night of cruising the city streets.

In early August the **Gem County Fair and Rodeo** comes to town. And as the summer season fades and the air starts getting crisp, it's time for the **Harvest Festival,** which celebrates the valley's bountiful crops with food-related events like a Dutch-oven cookoff. The event is scheduled in late September or October.

For more information on any of these events, contact the Gem County Chamber of Commerce, 127 E. Main, Emmett, ID 83617, 208/365-3485.

Accommodations
$50–100: Emmett features a B&B that makes a fun and fascinating lodging alternative. **Frozen Dog Digs,** 4325 Frozen Dog Rd., 208/365-7372, perches up near Pickett's Corral in the eastside foothills. In this sports-oriented lodging, you'll find many handmade furnishings inspired by items of sporting gear—from the Claes Oldenburg–style giant baseball-mitt sofa to the hockey-stick curtain rods. Darts (the board comes straight from Canterbury, England), a snooker table, and a large-screen TV provide entertainment options for guests, who may also sip on a se-

lection from the well-stocked wine cellar. Also here are a cozy and comfortable living room, a library, and a racquetball court.

Upstairs, each of the three bedrooms is furnished with a queen-size bed, phone, and satellite TV. All rooms have exclusive-use baths; two are assigned separate baths, one room has attached bath. Outside you'll find three pitch-and-putt golf greens, a self-contained, four-room Asian-themed honeymoon cottage, and a landscaped terrace with a Japanese garden, waterfall, and spa.

The complimentary breakfast includes fresh-squeezed juice, fresh fruit in season, and the chef's whim entrée. Rates all fall in the $50–100 range except for the four-room cottage, which rents for $189 April–Sept., $169 the rest of the year.

No smoking, children, or pets. To reach the B&B, take E. Main Street east to Plaza Road, turn left on Plaza, then right on Frozen Dog Road.

Food
The Timbers, 300 Hwy. 16, just east of Washington St., 208/365-6915, is the locals' fancy-food favorite. At lunchtime look for sandwiches and burgers in the $5–7 range; dinnertime brings primarily steak and seafood (with prime rib Fri.–Sat.) for $8–17. The Southwest-influenced decor is clean and bright. Open for lunch and dinner Mon.–Fri., dinner only on Saturday.

Roe-Ann's, 929 S. Washington, 208/365-5911 or 208/365-9926, is the '50s-style diner that started the Cruise Night tradition in Emmett. Carhops, malted milk shakes, teenie boppers—you get the picture.

Information
The **Gem County Chamber of Commerce** dispenses information at 127 E. Main, Emmett, ID 83617, 208/365-3485.

Around Gem County
Between 1894 and 1910, **Pearl** was the center of Gem County's gold-mining boom. Today it's a ghost town with nothing left of its glory days but a few mysterious mine entrances and a clutch of dilapidated buildings overgrown with wild roses. It's a beautiful drive, however, from

Highway 16 over to Horseshoe Bend via Pearl on a gravel road easily navigable in the family sedan. Coyotes romp through cow pastures here, and wildflowers blanket the hillsides. To get there, turn east on Jackass Road, just across the street from the top of Old Freezeout Road.

Heading east of Emmett along Black Canyon Highway (Highway 52) you'll come to a turnoff where you can head north to Ola or south to **Montour,** a onetime stage stop on the route to the Boise Basin mines. In the early 1900s the railroad connecting Emmett and McCall was built through town, and Montour flourished. The prosperity lasted until the Great Depression, when Montour fell victim to the effects of Black Canyon Dam. The dam was built in 1924; upon completion water came creeping into town. The landowners sued the government, prompting the Bureau of Reclamation to buy them out in 1976. The area was turned into **Montour Wildlife/Recreation Area,** an 1,100-acre riparian wildlife preserve home to a variety of waterfowl, upland game birds, raptors, and mammals. Hunting, fishing, and wildlife photography are popular pursuits here. The small, quiet **Montour Campground** (17 grassy sites, fee) includes picnic benches, barbecue grills, and restroom. For more informa-

tion on the Montour WRA, call the area project manager at 208/365-2682.

North of Montour, across Black Canyon Highway (Highway 52), the Ola Highway climbs north up beautiful Squaw Creek Valley. This was once an important stage route supplying the Thunder Mountain mines. The valley is marked by fields and ranches, by old barns and one-room schoolhouses. Nearly every resident of these parts can tell you the history of every dwelling in the area.

At the bottom of the valley, **Sweet** is a blink-and-you'll-miss-it kind of town. A small park near the roadside commemorates a spring where stage horses once watered. If you're looking for something besides spring water, you might find it at the adjacent Sweet Service store.

Continuing north up the panhandle of Gem County, the road climbs alongside Squaw Creek to **Ola,** the county's northernmost outpost. A small store and an old church next to the local cemetery frame the little ranching community, where the silence is deafening and the passage of time tangible. Beyond Ola you can continue on Forest Service roads another 60 miles northwest to Council, or turn off at **Gross** (rhymes with toss) and head east to Sagehen Reservoir and Highway 55.

Highway 95: Hells Canyon Rim Country

Highway 95 intersects I-84 just east of the Snake River, which here constitutes the Idaho-Oregon border. South of the interstate, Highway 95 passes through the little farm towns of Parma and Wilder before crossing the Snake into Owyhee County and continuing south toward Nevada. North of I-84, Highway 95 parallels the Snake as it slithers down into and through Hells Canyon, the deepest river gorge on the continent. Payette, Washington, and Adams Counties, flanking the river, survive on an uneasy mix of farming, logging, and tourism, none of which fill the coffers. Drought has taken its toll on crops in recent years, and Boise-Cascade closed its Council mill in 1995. Yet visitors flock to Weiser each year for a famous fiddle fest, and

locals and tourists alike enjoy recreation in Payette National Forest.

Travelers entering Idaho from Oregon on I-84 will find the **Snake River View Visitor Center** just across the border. It's open year-round, daily 9 A.M.–5 P.M., providing plenty of tourist information as well as the usual rest-stop facilities.

PARMA AND WILDER

Parma

About 13 miles south of I-84, the little town of Parma plays up its pioneer-days historical significance; just outside town at the confluence of the Boise and Snake Rivers once stood Fort Boise, the famed Hudson's Bay Company fur fort run by jolly Frenchman François Payette. Fort Boise, in use between 1834 and 1855, was one of the two primary fur-trading forts bookending the Snake River in Idaho, the other being Fort Hall near present-day Pocatello. Trappers, traders, westward-bound pioneers, and local Native Americans all enjoyed Monsieur Payette's legendary hospitality. Today a beautiful and very British stone monument marks the site of the Hudson's Bay Company endeavor. The monument sits in the center of the 1,500-acre **Fort Boise Wildlife Management Area,** a popular fishing and bird-hunting area managed by the Idaho Department of Fish and Game. To reach the site, take Old Fort Boise Road west off the highway, just north of town. For more information contact the WMA office at 30845 Old Fort Boise Rd., Parma, ID 83660, 208/722-5888.

Although the original Fort Boise long ago succumbed to the elements, a re-creation has been built along the highway in downtown Parma. The new old fort contains a museum and a pioneer cabin. It's open June–Aug. Fri.–Sun. 1–3 P.M., other times by appointment. Come in June for **Old Fort Boise Days,** featuring a parade, crafts fair, period costumes, and chili cookoff. For further information or an off-season appointment to see the re-created fort, contact **Parma City Hall,** 305 N. 3rd St., 208/722-5138. **Fort Boise RV Park,** right outside the re-created fort, offers eight sites with hookups for $13 a night, plus $7 tent sites. The park includes restrooms, showers, and dump station.

Wilder

Continuing south you'll come to the small agricultural hub of Wilder (pronounced like wild and wildest), a center for the farming of onions, wheat, barley, corn, sugar beets, and potatoes. But the most interesting crop you'll see are the hops strung up on tall trellises all along Highway 95 north of town.

Wilder golfers drag the clubs down to **River Bend Golf Course,** 18539 Fish Rd., 208/482-7169, an 18-hole, par-72 course stretching over 6,432 yards. Greens fee is $11 for nine holes, $16 for 18; cart rental is $10 and $18, respectively. The course is open when weather permits,

usually March–November but some years nearly year-round.

FRUITLAND, PAYETTE, AND NEW PLYMOUTH

These three communities, cozied up to one another along the north side of I-84, suffer from their proximity to Ontario, Oregon, just a few miles to the west. Oregon doesn't levy a sales tax, so Idaho consumers cross the border to save some bucks. In addition, big chain motels along the interstate in Ontario draw overnighters away from the independents on the Idaho side of the river. As a result, Fruitland and Payette in particular have an odd lifelessness about them—one foot in the grave and the other on a banana peel. New Plymouth (population under 2,000) doesn't have quite the same feeling of impending doom—it just feels small. The entire county is an agricultural area, and those looking for a scenic drive need only turn off the highway and tootle along back roads through orchards and fields.

Recreation

Local golfers head to **Scotch Pines Golf Course,** 10610 Scotch Pines Rd., 208/642-1829, a challenging, hilly 18-hole course. Greens fee is around $20. Take 7th Avenue N. east off Highway 95, turn left on Iowa Avenue and right on Scotch Pines Road. The course is sometimes closed in winter. Payette's **municipal pool** is in Kiwanis Park, S. 7th St. at 3rd Ave. S, 208/642-6030.

Anglers try their luck on **Paddock Valley Reservoir;** take Little Willow Road off Highway 52, northeast of Fruitland or southeast of Payette. According to the Idaho Department of Fish and Game, the reservoir is renowned for quality crappie fishing. Isn't that an oxymoron? You'll find a boat-launching ramp at the end of the road, on the south edge of the reservoir.

Events

The **Apple Blossom Festival and Great Payette Balloon Classic** runs for two weeks from the end of April to mid-May. Hot-air balloons speckle the skies, while on the ground you'll find a parade, arts and crafts, a carnival, and entertainment.

The **Payette County Fair and Rodeo** comes to the fairgrounds in New Plymouth in mid-August. Look for an ICA rodeo, agriculture and livestock exhibits, and food, food, food. For more information on these and other events, call the Payette Chamber of Commerce at 208/642-2362.

RV Park

RVers passing through the area will find **Neat Retreat** at 2701 Hwy. 95 in Fruitland, 208/452-4324. Full-hookup sites at this pleasant, well-kept RV park cost $23 a night. Amenities include a laundry, restrooms, and showers. It's a quiet park with no pool or playground, and full of retirees with little enthusiasm for boisterous kids; family campers would be better off elsewhere. No tenters are permitted.

Food

One restaurant in downtown Fruitland gets good reviews. **Nichols Steakhouse,** 411 S.W. 3rd St., 208/452-3030, is open Tues.–Fri. for lunch, Tues.–Sun. for dinner.

Information and Services

For more information, contact the **Payette Chamber of Commerce,** 711 Center Ave., Payette, ID 83661, 208/642-2362; the **New Plymouth Chamber of Commerce,** 301 N. Plymouth Ave., P.O. Box 26, New Plymouth, ID 83655, 208/278-5338; or the **Fruitland Chamber of Commerce,** 412 S. Pennsylvania, P.O. Box 408, Fruitland, ID 83619, 208/452-4350.

WEISER AND VICINITY

The seat of Washington County, Weiser lies just north of the confluence of the Snake and Weiser Rivers. North of here the Snake rolls northwest toward its drop through Hells Canyon, while the highway bears north and east, climbing slowly up the Weiser River watershed.

Weiser, both river and town, were named for Peter Weiser, a Revolutionary War veteran and cook for the Lewis and Clark expedition of 1804–06. In May 1806, the Corps of Discovery reached the confluence of the Snake and Clearwater Rivers (site of today's city of Lewis-

ton), and Weiser and two others were dispatched on an exploratory mission up the Snake. When they reached the Snake's confluence with the Salmon, they traveled up that river another 20 miles, becoming the first white men to see the Lower Salmon Gorge. Clark subsequently named one of the Snake's tributaries for Weiser, perhaps in fond remembrance of his chef's particularly savory salmon steaks.

Weiser was once home to famed pro baseball player Walter "Big Train" Johnson, who pitched for the Washington Senators of the American League. Over the course of his 21-year pro career, Johnson won 666 games, making him the second-winningest pitcher in history behind Cy Young. Johnson also holds the record for the most career shutouts (110).

Snake River Heritage Center

This museum at 2295 Paddock Ave., 208/549-0205, was gutted by fire in 1994 and is still undergoing restoration. It's in Hooker Hall, an impressive 1920 building that once housed a Christian-oriented vocational prep school. The museum's exhibits provide an eclectic taste of regional history. It's open weekends noon–4 P.M.; admission by donation.

Historic Buildings

Weiser's early wood-framed commercial district was rebuilt in brick after an 1890 fire reduced much of the town to ashes. Before the fire, the town core had been farther east, but rebuilding efforts centered the new downtown around the **Oregon Short Line Depot.** The Queen Anne–style depot at the south end of State Street was built in 1906–07. At Commercial and E. 1st Streets, the building that now houses **Matthews' Grain & Storage** was once a house of ill repute known as the Clinton Rooms (no Democrat jokes, please). According to local legend, a mailman delivering a C.O.D. package to the Clinton Rooms was one day offered payment in services instead of cash.

A Welsh castle in southwest Idaho? Strange, but true. The local Knights of Pythias began building the storybook **Pythian Castle** in 1904, modeling it after a chateau in Wales. The stone blocks of the facade were quarried north of town, hauled here by wagon, and cut on site. You'll find the castle on E. Idaho Street, between State and E. 1st Streets. For a guide to these and other historic buildings downtown, pick up a free walking-tour pamphlet at the Chamber of Commerce office, 8 E. Idaho St.

Parks and Recreation

Mountain bikers, hikers, and cross-country skiers can get out on the **Weiser River Trail,** which follows an abandoned Pacific and Idaho Northern Railway right-of-way for 84 miles from Weiser up to New Meadows. Some parts flank civilization, others sections are blissfully remote. And some sections are in better shape than others; trail building and maintenance are ongoing.

At **Walter Johnson Park,** Hanthorn and 3rd Sts., you'll find a baseball diamond, naturally, as well as tennis courts, picnic tables, barbecues, and a small stage. Weiser's **municipal pool** is adjacent to the park: admission is $2 ages 13–59, $1 seniors 60 and up, $1.50 kids 12 and under. For more information on the pool or city parks, call the **Weiser Recreation Department** at 208/549-0301.

Rolling Hills Golf Course, 50 W. Indianhead Rd., 208/549-0456, sits at the top of the hill on the north end of town. The tree-lined, 18-hole course ranges over 6,090 yards. Greens fee is $15. Cart rentals available. The course restaurant serves lunch Mon.–Fri. and dinner Tues.–Sat.

Historic Watering Hole

It's just a dive beer joint now, but the **Crescent Bar** building, on State Street between E. Idaho and Commercial Streets, retains perfume-scented memories of its 1930s heyday. Back then, the Shamrock Rooms upstairs housed ladies of uncertain virtue and their transient gentlemen callers.

National Oldtime Fiddlers' Contest & Festival

Each year during the third full week of June, Weiser is occupied by an army of fiddlers and their fans, here to participate in the most prestigious fiddle festival in the United States. All week long, all over town, the strains of fiddles, guitars, and banjos waft through the air. Schoolyards become makeshift campgrounds where hundreds of RVers circle the wagons, pull out their instruments, and play all day and into the night.

The competition itself is staged in the high school gym, on W. 7th Street at Indianhead Road. Each contestant has four minutes to play a hoedown, a waltz, and a third tune of the contestant's choice. The competitors, ranging from preteen to octogenarian, are judged in a number of age categories.

Some of the oldest senior-senior players have played oldtime fiddle since the Wilson administration and are predictably masterful. But in a wander through the warm-up rooms and campgrounds, what may impress you more are the kids. I chanced upon a young girl of about 10 who played with all the passion, longing, and fury of a grizzled pioneer woman remembering a lifetime of hardship on the dry Western plains. The music that sprang from her bow was clean, clear, and, in a word, divine.

Tickets to the daytime rounds are $2 adults, $1 children, while the nighttime rounds run $6–14. A full-week pass (good for everything but the Saturday finals) is available for $35 adults, $20 kids 12 and under. For more information, contact the National Oldtime Fiddlers' Contest & Festival, 309 State St., Weiser, ID 83672, 208/414-0255 or 800/437-1280, www.fiddlecontest.com.

Fiddlers' Hall of Fame

If you missed the fiddle festival on your way through town, you can still stop in at this museum at the Weiser Community Center, 8 E. Idaho St., 208/549-0452. Inside are photos and fiddle memorabilia from the olden days to the present. The museum is open year-round Mon.–Fri. 9 A.M.–5 P.M. Admission is free; donations accepted.

Accommodations

Under $50: Two motels flank the center of town. On the north side, up near the high school and therefore within walking distance of the fiddle festival, is the 13-room **State Street Motel,** 1279

State St., 208/549-1390, while just east of the city center on the highway is the 24-room **Colonial Motel,** 251 E. Main, 208/549-0150. Both are basic but decent.

Indianhead Motel & RV Park, 747 Hwy. 95, 208/549-0331, on the west side of the highway as you head north out of town, offers eight nonsmoking motel rooms. No pets.

RV Parks

Indianhead Motel & RV Park, 747 Hwy. 95, 208/549-0331, has 12 RV spaces with water and electricity hookups for $21 per night. Amenities include a laundry, picnic area, showers, horseshoe pits, and a golf-practice cage. Tent camping is not allowed. The RV park closes in winter.

Just a little farther north, **Monroe Creek Campground,** 822 Hwy. 95, 208/549-2026, charges $20 a night for RV sites with full hookups. Tent campers pay $13 per night. The park is open April 1–Oct. 31 and offers a small store, horseshoe pits, a hot tub, and volleyball court.

Food

For a hearty breakfast, lunch, or dinner, head to **Homestead Cafe,** 813 State St., 208/549-3962. The prices are right and the grub is good. It's open Mon.–Fri. 6 A.M.–9 P.M., Sat. 6:30 A.M.–9 P.M., Sun. 6:30 A.M.–8 P.M. Another option is **Beehive Family Restaurant,** 208/549-3544, on E. 7th Street/Highway 95 heading south out of town. It's open Sun.–Thurs. 6 A.M.–10 P.M., Fri.–Sat. 6 A.M.–midnight. If you prefer *huevos rancheros* to scrambled eggs, try **La Tejanita,** 260 E. 7th St. (Hwy. 95 on the south end of town), 208/549-2768. This Tex-Mex restaurant also offers fast lunches to go and a Mexican minimart.

You can get your espresso fix—Starbucks, no less—at **Huckleberry Coffee Company,** 438 State St., 208/549-3365. The local favorite lunch spot is **Fawn's Classic Candies,** 449 State St., 208/549-2850. Fawn's started out as a homemade candy store, but keeps growing into new areas of culinary expression. Now its deli sandwiches make it a town favorite for an inexpensive lunch. Save room for dessert in the form of a piece or two of scrumptious handmade chocolate. Fawn's is smoke-free.

Information and Services

The **Weiser Chamber of Commerce,** 8 E. Idaho St., Weiser, ID 83672, 208/549-0452, can tell you more about the town and provide you with literature on the area. Contact the Payette National Forest's **Weiser Ranger District,** 851 E. 9th St., 208/549-4200.

North of Weiser

Between Weiser and Midvale, a signed exit to the west leads to **Mann Creek Recreation Area,** which includes Mann Creek Reservoir and Mann Creek Wildlife Management Area. A Bureau of Reclamation campground on the reservoir is a convenient base for fishing, swimming, or birdwatching. Continuing farther up FR 009, you'll eventually climb out of the dry chaparral into the pines, where you'll find good camping at several spots, including the well-maintained USFS **Lower Spring Creek Campground** (14 sites, fee).

Back out on Highway 95 and continuing north toward Midvale, you'll crest a grade and drop down to a rest area on the west side of the highway. Today it may be but a rest area, but 3,000 to 5,000 years ago this was the site of an **ancient quarry** where the local people found raw obsidian blocks for their arrowheads and other tools.

Down in little Midvale you can beat the summer heat with a swim in the **city pool** on Depot Street, just across the railroad tracks by the city park. For a lot more water, head southeast of town on Old Highway 95 and Crane Creek Road to **Crane Creek Reservoir,** a large, isolated lake where you can camp on the shore with no company other than the place's namesake white cranes. Two primitive BLM camping areas with boat ramps but no other facilities bracket the reservoir on the east and west ends. Fishing is excellent for crappie, largemouth bass, bullhead catfish, and even cutthroat trout. It's a great spot to chill out and work on your tan in peace.

CAMBRIDGE

Cambridge once served as a supply center for the Seven Devils Mining District, where copper and silver mining flourished between 1880 and 1905. Today it's primarily a ranching and farming town, although some logging still takes place in the Payette National Forest to the west. Cambridge also rings up a fair amount of tourist revenue, thanks to its location at the intersection of Highways 95 and 71—the latter leading to the big Snake River reservoirs and to Hells Canyon Dam, a popular put-in point for whitewater raft trips down the Snake.

Historical Museum

The **Cambridge-Hells Canyon-Salubria Valley Museum,** 15 Superior St., 208/257-3485 or 208/257-3571, offers numerous exhibits covering pre-town Native American residents, fur trappers, the town's early days, the Seven Devils Mining boom, and local farming and logging history. The museum is open May 15–Sept. 15 Wed.–Sat. 10 A.M.–4 P.M., Sunday noon–4 P.M.; other times by appointment. Admission is free; donations appreciated.

Events

The first weekend in June, Cambridge celebrates **Hells Canyon Days** with an all-you-can-eat breakfast, barbecue, and horse-and-tack sale. The first full week of August brings the **Washington County Fair,** with a parade, rodeo, and big Saturday night dance. For more information, call Cambridge City Hall at 208/257-3318.

Accommodations

Under $50: Moderately priced motel rooms are available—some in this price range, some in the next—at **Hunters Inn Motel,** 10 S. Superior St. (Hwy. 95), 208/257-3325; and **Frontier Motel & RV Park,** 240 S. Superior St., 208/257-3851. The latter also has RV sites (call for availability) at $15 a night with full hookups, including cable TV, as well as restroom, shower, and laundry facilities.

$50–100: The pleasant **Cambridge House B&B,** 10 Superior St. (Hwy. 95), 208/257-3325, is run by the Hunters Inn and offers B&B rooms in a beautifully restored Roaring '20s roadhouse. After ordering a Starbucks caffe mocha at the in-house espresso bar, you can enjoy it inside— where racks of antlers and stuffed game provide a hunting-lodge ambience—or take it outside to one of the tables in front.

HIGHWAY 71 TO HELLS CANYON DAM

West from Cambridge

Across from Bucky's Cafe in Cambridge, Highway 71 heads northwest to the south end of Hells Canyon and a connection with Oregon Highway 86. This is the main route to the Hells Canyon Dam complex, a series of three dams and reservoirs that together constitute one of the recreation highlights of southwest Idaho. State residents trek here in droves in summer for fishing, boating, swimming, hiking, camping, whitewater rafting, and even scuba diving.

If you're heading out Highway 71 toward the reservoirs and aren't in a hurry, try the enjoyable long-cut of **West Pine Creek Road** (FR 031). Continue west where the highway jogs north, about four miles outside town. After passing through several miles of relatively flat farmland, the road begins to climb alongside West Pine Creek. Soon you'll find yourself high in the pines on the shoulder of Sturgill Peak (elevation 7,589). You might be thinking that in winter, the steep slopes here would make a good place for a ski resort. Forget it: it's been tried and didn't make it; Hitt Mountain Ski Area has been defunct for years. A little higher you'll pass some cattle ranches, then reach a ridge crest on the flanks of dramatic Sturgill Peak. A lookout atop that peak would make an ideal day-hike destination, offering panoramic vistas of Oregon's mighty, snowcapped Wallowa Mountains across the Snake River to the west.

The road bends north and descends along Middle Brownlee Creek (numerous spots to splash, best at the lower end), rejoining Highway 71 just south of the USFS **Brownlee Campground** (11 sites, fee). The campground, 1.5 miles up FR 044, sits at the base of Cuddy Mountain, a huge wall of rock named for early pioneer John Cuddy (1834–99), an Irishman who started a lumber and flour mill in Weiser in 1870.

Hells Canyon Dam Complex

After Idaho Power Company completed three dams here on the Snake River in 1959, efforts to usher anadromous fish around them failed. In exchange for hydropower, we forever lost salmon and steelhead runs upriver on the Snake, and by consequence on the Weiser, Payette, and Boise Rivers as well. In the late 1950s, some 40,000–55,000 salmon spawned upstream. Today, none do.

As Cort Conley writes in *Idaho for the Curious:*

> *The tri-dam complex represents one response to energy demand. But the dams were built with a number of costs never computed by accountants or engineers, and such costs must be balanced against the benefits. On one hand, a peak generating capability in excess of a million kilowatts an hour, 39 permanent jobs, some recreation facilities and flood control, and $10,000 a year in taxes for the state of Idaho. On the other hand, thousands of acres of ranch land and wildlife habitat were lost forever, as were a town, salmon and steelhead runs, archaeological sites, and singular whitewater recreation. In addition, sand entrapment and daily flow fluctuations destroyed beaches, waterfowl habitat, and spawning beds for 60 miles of river below Hells Canyon Dam—with no mitigation whatsoever.*

Idaho Power maintains a series of campgrounds around the reservoirs. All but two are developed and offer potable water, restrooms with showers, and picnic tables. From April to October, the developed sites cost $10 a night for RVs, $6 a night for tents. The rest of the year, the sites cost $5 a night for RVs, $3 for tents. Two undeveloped sites on Oxbow Reservoir are a little cheaper—$2 for RVs, $1 for tent sites. Each of the three reservoirs is covered below. For more information about the dams, reservoirs, or campgrounds, call Idaho Power's toll-free recorded reservoir recreation report at 800/422-3143.

Brownlee Reservoir

The southernmost of the three reservoirs making up the Hells Canyon complex, Brownlee is also the largest—15,000 acres, 58 miles long—and the favorite of anglers. In 1993 a record-setting black crappie was caught here, and in 1995 a couple of Idaho women landed a record 58-pound eight-ounce flathead catfish. Bass, perch, bluegill, and, in winter, rainbow trout also inhabit the reservoir. Not to throw a damper on your fishing pleasure, but don't eat too many fish out of Brownlee—they've been found to hold elevated levels of methylmercury. One other note: Scuba divers say the diving here is good for a brief period of time in spring, when the water starts to warm and before the algae blooms cloud visibility. Burgers, boat rentals and inexpensive motel rooms are available at **Gateway Lodge,** 4330 Hwy. 71, 208/257-3531, from about February through mid-November, depending upon the descent of winter and the coming of the thaw.

Woodhead Park is the biggest and newest Idaho Power campground on the Hells Canyon reservoirs. Four separate campground loops wind around the east shore of Brownlee Reservoir. In addition to potable water, restrooms, and showers, you'll find several docks and a couple of large boat-launching ramps. A fish-cleaning station here bears witness to the campground's primary clientele. Those staying onshore will find gazebo-shaded picnic tables and ample grassy areas for sunning or laying out a lunch spread.

Oxbow Reservoir

The next reservoir north of Brownlee is Oxbow, a narrow strip of water running between Oxbow Dam in the north and Brownlee Dam in the south. Although more anglers head for Brownlee, Oxbow contains its share of crappie. At the south end of the reservoir just below Brownlee Dam is Idaho Power's **McCormick Park.** It's right along a wooded bank, but aside from the natural greenery the landscaping is minimal. The undeveloped **McCormick Overflow** area outside the developed campground is a big dirt lot with no facilities.

Highway 71 crosses to the west side of the reservoir and continues north. Soon you'll come to **Carter's Landing,** the other unimproved campsite on the reservoir. This is a far nicer spot than McCormick Overflow.

COURTESY OF THE IDAHO TRAVEL COUNCIL

Snake River in Hells Canyon

Hells Canyon Reservoir

This is the farthest north of the three reservoirs, the last one before the river is once again allowed to run free. North of Hells Canyon Dam, rafters and jetboaters navigate the Wild and Scenic stretch of the Snake through Hells Canyon and down to Lewiston.

On the west shore of the reservoir in Copperfield, Oregon, is Idaho Power's **Copperfield Camp.** Of all the Idaho Power campgrounds this is the closest to civilization. It's tidy and beautifully landscaped, but also the busiest of the bunch.

At Copperfield Camp, Idaho Highway 71 becomes Oregon Highway 86 and hairpins back to the southwest en route to Baker, Oregon. Hells Canyon Road crosses the river back into Idaho and continues up the east shore of the reservoir. About seven miles up the east shore you'll come to the nicely landscaped and relatively quiet **Hells Canyon Park.** Here Klein-

schmidt Grade begins its climb up the canyon wall to Cuprum, from where you can continue on back roads all the way over to Council.

No more Idaho Power campgrounds are between Hells Canyon Park and the end of the road, but you'll pass a couple of spots along the river that are suitable places to pull off and camp. The biggest of these is **Big Bar.** The bar was settled in the 1890s by John Eckels, who grew fruits and vegetables to supply the miners in the Seven Devils Mining District at the top of Kleinschmidt Grade. It's said the miners found his award-winning strawberries especially delightful.

A bit farther north you'll pass **Black Point,** providing a great panorama of the river and canyon. Finally you'll come to Hells Canyon Dam itself. The road actually continues right across the dam to the Oregon side of the river and downstream about half a mile to road's end at **Hells Canyon Creek Interpretive Center,** sponsored jointly by Hells Canyon NRA and the Wallowa-Whitman National Forest. Here whitewater rafters put in for float trips through Hells Canyon and rangers provide NRA information. The center, 541/785-3395, is open Memorial Day weekend to early September daily 8 A.M.– 4 P.M., Pacific time.

Boating Hells Canyon

The float trip through Hells Canyon is a prized notch in the belt for Idaho whitewater devotees. This is big water, with monster waves and powerful hydraulics that can eat boats for lunch. Even veteran raft guides respect the power of the Class IV Wild Sheep and Granite Rapids. The toughest section of the river lies between the put-in just below Hells Canyon Dam and Pittsburg Landing, a 32-mile, two-day trip. From here on down to Hells Gate State Park at Lewiston are 73 miles dotted with a number of Class III bumps. Permits are required for any boating above Heller Bar, about 30 river miles above Lewiston; for more information, contact the Snake River administrative office of **Hells Canyon NRA,** 2535 Riverside Dr. in Clarkston (do not send mail to this address) or P.O. Box 699, Clarkston, WA 99403, 509/758-1957 (float

SOUTHWEST IDAHO

information), 509/758-0270 (power-boat information), 509/758-0616 (general canyon information). The office is open in summer daily 8–11:30 A.M. and 12:30–4 P.M.; in winter it's open those same hours but Mon.–Fri. only.

Note that both jetboats and rafters are permitted to run the canyon. If you're into peaceful solitude, make sure you go on a trip during one of the nonmotorized periods, when only paddlers are permitted. Those periods are Mon.–Wed. of every other week (except Fourth of July week) starting the first full week in June and continuing through the end of August.

Outfitters

Among the raft companies running trips through Hells Canyon are **Holiday River Expeditions of Idaho, Inc.,** P.O. Box 86, Grangeville, ID 83530, 208/983-1518; **Hughes River Expeditions, Inc.,** P.O. Box 217, Cambridge, ID 83610, 208/257-3477 or 800/262-1882; **Idaho Afloat,** P.O. Box 542, Grangeville, ID 83530, 208/983-2414 or 800/700-2414; **Northwest Voyageurs,** HC2 Box 501, Pollock, ID 83547, 800/727-9977; and **River Odysseys West (ROW),** P.O. Box 579, Coeur d'Alene, ID 83816, 208/765-0841 or 800/451-6034.

Expect to pay around $1,350 for a five-day raft trip, $885 for a three-day run.

INDIAN VALLEY AND THE WEST MOUNTAINS

Up the Little Weiser River

Highway 95 heads east out of Cambridge for about 10 miles before resuming its northward course. Along the way you'll pass the turnoff to Indian Valley. The town itself is just a store amid hundreds of square miles of farmland, but traveling through Indian Valley will take you to small **Ben Ross Reservoir,** where you can enjoy fishing and primitive camping. Continuing south past the reservoir you'll reach the junction where Little Weiser River Road (FR 206) turns east and follows the Little Weiser River all the way to its headwaters high in the West Mountains.

The Little Weiser River is the quintessential babbling brook, its banks lined with sweet-smelling syringa, its cool waters inviting for a summer splash. Local equestrians head out for trail rides from many places along this road. Up the road you'll come to the USFS **Big Flat Campground** (13 sites, fee), an idyllic spot on the banks of the river. Site 13, all the way around the loop, is the biggest and best. Some bluffs in the area make good, view-filled day-hike destinations, and the campground is a perfect spot to drop a line in the water and see what bites.

Up the Middle Fork Weiser River

Back out on Highway 95 and continuing north you'll soon pass the turnoff to the residential hamlet of Mesa; just beyond you'll come to Middle Fork Road (FR 186), which follows the Middle Fork Weiser River east into the mountains. About nine miles up the road, look for a small trail marker on the left. Trail 203 leads two miles up the hill through wooded rangeland to **Laurel Hot Springs.** It's an easy enough trail, in good shape except for the copious amounts of cow excrement. If you're unlucky, you may have to chase cattle out of the way—and as the wooded slopes on either side of the trail aren't easy for the bovines to manuever in, they'll probably just keep fleeing up the trail in front of you all the way to the hot springs. Once there, you and the cud-chewing beasts will probably have the springs all to yourselves. The water is hot but the pools are shallow. A good campsite area perches just above the springs.

Farther up the Middle Fork on FR 186 is USFS **Cabin Creek Campground** (12 sites, fee), a small, popular spot next to the river, though not nearly as nice as Big Flat Campground to the south. From here you can continue east on FR 186 past **White Licks Hot Springs** to the Long Valley towns of Cascade, Donnelly, and McCall, just on the other side of the West Mountains.

COUNCIL

The Adams County seat, Council got its name from the fact that various bands of Native American tribes once gathered around council fires here for peace talks, tribal games, and trading. The area was settled by whites circa 1878.

The little town is struggling to stay alive after the big Boise-Cascade mill closed in 1995. Fittingly, the town cemetery is beautiful. If you're in town the third full week in July, look for the **Adams County Fair and Rodeo.** For more information, call Council City Hall at 208/253-4201.

Historical Museum

Don't miss the **Charles Winkler Memorial Museum** in the old city hall at 100 S. Galena St., 208/253-4201. The story of the Winkler family paints as good a picture as any of the history of Council and environs from the turn of the century on. George and Elizabeth Winkler came to Idaho by covered wagon in 1889; they were the fourth family of pioneers to settle in Council Valley. The Winklers had six sons: George Jr., Lewis, William, Mark, James, and Charles. William became a lawman, sheriff of first Washington County, then Adams County. Lewis was a skilled blacksmith. Pharmacist Charles turned to politics, serving seven consecutive terms in the Idaho state legislature.

With America's entry into World War I, Charles and George Jr. were called upon to serve. Their photos are on display in the museum's remarkable photo collection: Charles looks rugged and brash, George quite dapper in his civvies. Also in the picture are the Ingram brothers, Alta and Alva. I wonder what ever became of Alta—he looks sensitive and a bit sad. These dashing, strapping, handsome and confident young men who crossed the Atlantic to fight the good fight—they're all dead now. If the mustard gas didn't get them, time eventually did. Their offspring are pictured in a second set of photos, those of the area's veterans of World War II. More Winklers here: Henry a private in the 11th Division, 42nd Armored Regiment based at Camp Polk, Louisiana, and George M. (no clue to the nature of his assignment). Traveling back and forth between the World War I and World War II photos provides a fascinating and poignant glimpse at the generations of Winklers, Andersons, Fullers, Hams, and Lakeys of this part of Idaho.

Other exhibits are equally mesmerizing. There's the pocket-size Civil War diary of private Lewis Kester, uncle of George Lewis of Indian Valley.

The date on the cover reads 1863. It's behind glass—what do you suppose is written inside? There's a camp ax once owned by Craig "Pinky" Baird, an Indian fighter and scout in the 1870s; the inscription tells us Pinky's family was "ambushed by Indians coming across the Plains and the rest of his life he avenged their deaths." Nearby you'll find a pair of buckskin moccasins once worn by Chief Eagle Eye, the last chief of a renegade band of mixed Indians. "Their is no dought," the inscription reads, "but what Uncle Pinky took this Indian's scalp." Then there's the first bottle of whiskey sold in Council following the repeal of Prohibition. It's empty, of course, and the accompanying tag tells us the contents were "sampled by Fred Weed, J. L. Johnson, Troy Perkins, Jamie Fisher, and C. A. Phillips." A night to remember, no doubt.

The museum is open Memorial Day–Labor Day, Tues.–Sun. 10 A.M.–4 P.M.

Golf

Council Mountain Golf Course, 1922 Hwy. 95 S., 208/253-6908, offers nine holes over 3,236 yards, par 37. On weekends, the greens fee is about $15; on weekdays about $12. Club and cart rentals are available, and a restaurant and small pro shop are on-site. The course is closed in winter.

Accommodations

Under $50: The small, neatly landscaped **Starlite Motel,** 102 N. Dartmouth (Hwy. 95), 208/253-4868, offers rooms with a/c, cable TV, and phones.

Information

For more information about Council, contact the **Council Visitor Center,** adjacent to the Forest Service office on Highway 95 at the north end of town, 208/253-0161. It's open late May through late October, 8 A.M.–noon and 1–5 P.M. daily. If it's not open when you're in town, try **Council City Hall,** 501 N. Galena, 208/253-4201, where you can almost always dig up somebody. For information about recreation in the surrounding Payette National Forest, contact the **Council Ranger District,** 500 E. Whitely Ave., at the north end of town, P.O. Box 567, Council, ID 83612, 208/253-0100.

TO HELLS CANYON VIA KLEINSCHMIDT GRADE

From Council, Hornet Creek Road heads northwest up into the Cuddy Mountains past beautiful high-country ranchland and into the heart of the Seven Devils Mining District. This area once was a bustling silver and copper mining center. Today it's home to a number of Forest Service campgrounds and a couple of old mining towns still clinging tenuously to life.

Hornet Creek Road eventually becomes Council-Cuprum Road (FR 002) and soon leads to USFS **Lafferty Camp** (eight sites, fee). The camp occupies a gorgeous site on the Crooked River, and offers picnic tables, a barbecue grill, and magnificent ponderosa pines. Continuing down the road you'll follow Crooked River for a while, past several pullouts that will tempt you to stop and walk down to the water for a cooling splash. Eventually you'll come to an intersection where FR 002 veers left to Cuprum and FR 105 continues north. Following FR 105, you'll pass the hamlet of **Bear**—consisting of a pay phone, an old one-room schoolhouse, a few cabins, and not much else—and, farther up the road, two more Forest Service campgrounds. **Huckleberry Campground** (six sites, fee) is on FR 110 just past the FR 105/110 junction, while undeveloped **Bear Creek Campground** (six sites, free) lies just down FR 130 off FR 110, where the road crosses Bear Creek. Three miles down FR 110 past Huckleberry Campground you'll find a trailhead providing access to the Rapid River roadless area.

Continuing about a mile up FR 105 past the FR 110 junction, you'll come to another major intersection. A right turn onto FR 112 takes you north on an often marginal road, past the **Smith Mountain fire lookout** (great views of the Seven Devils) to Black Lake and the USFS **Black Lake Campground** (four sites, free). This is the southern gateway to the Seven Devils Range and the Hells Canyon Wilderness, and another trailhead for a descent into the Rapid River roadless area.

For more information on the Seven Devils Range and the Rapid River roadless area, see The Hells Canyon Corridor in the North-Central Idaho chapter.

If instead of turning right onto FR 112, you continue straight on FR 105, you'll eventually wind up in Cuprum. But first you'll pass the junction with FR 108, which leads to **Horse Mountain Lookout, Kinney Point Overlook,** and **Sheep Rock Overlook.** All three offer panoramic views of Hells Canyon and the Wallowa Mountains. At Sheep Rock—approximately nine miles of rough road down from the turnoff at FR 105—a half-mile **nature trail** leads past 21 interpretive stations and the overlook. Pick up the interpretive trail guide at the Council Ranger District office in Council.

Cuprum was a boomtown when the mines were in full swing. Now it's just a cough and a wheeze away from a ghost town. From just outside town, **Kleinschmidt Grade** drops steeply southwest to the Snake River. This road was built by the enterprising Kleinschmidt brothers in the boom days, as a route to haul ore from their two mines down to the river. From there they ferried the ore across and up the river to a railroad terminus at Huntington, Oregon. Kleinschmidt Grade is not for the faint of heart. Although it's easily passable in your Buick Electra, it's only wide enough for one vehicle along most of its length, and the dropoffs into Hells Canyon are precipitous. Only a handful of strategically placed guardrails prevent the motorist from becoming a Wile E. Coyote dustcloud thousands of feet below. To make matters worse, big ore trucks still use the road; common sense will tell you to plan your descent outside of normal working hours.

NEW MEADOWS

At New Meadows, Highway 95 meets Highway 55. Turn left on Highway 95 to head north to Riggins; continue straight on Highway 55 to reach McCall. The original town of Meadows was a thriving burg west of the present town. But when the Pacific & Idaho Northern Railroad arrived from Weiser in 1911, the company pulled the typical railroad shenanigans. Rather than bring the tracks into town, they brought the town to the tracks. The company bought a large tract of land outside town, built a lavish $30,000 depot on it, then sold lots around it. The population made the shift. New Meadows grew, very profitably for the railroad, and old Meadows faded away. The railroad ran until 1979, hauling Meadows Valley cattle and lumber to market.

Zim's Hot Springs

The biggest attraction in the New Meadows area is Zim's Hot Springs, P.O. Box 314, New Meadows, ID 83654, 208/347-2686, which draws a sizable crowd of regulars up from Mc-Call for nighttime après-ski soaks. The developed hot springs resort lies west of Highway 95 in Meadows Valley, four miles north of town; watch for signs along the highway. An artesian well pumps sulfur-free hot water continuously through the 90–96°F swimming pool and 105°F soaking pool. The daily rate is $6 for ages 13 and up, $5 seniors, $4 kids under 12. You can also camp at Zim's; $16 a night for an RV site with water and electricity hookups, $8 for no hookups or a tent site. Zim's is open Tues.–Sat. (and major Monday holidays) 10 A.M.–10 P.M. in summer. The lodge building includes a rec hall, video games, snack bar, and pool tables.

Golf

Also north of town is **Meadow Creek Golf Resort,** 1 Meadow Creek Ct., 208/347-2555, which offers an 18-hole par-72 course stretching across 6,696 yards. Greens fees range $30–35.

Accommodations

$50–100: The **Hartland Inn and Motel,** Hwys. 95 and 55, New Meadows, ID 83654, 208/347-2114 or 888/509-7400, offers 11 motel units and five B&B rooms in a 1911 mansion. A hot tub awaits your après-ski arrival.

Camping

Meadows R.V. Park, 2.5 miles east of town on Highway 55, P.O. Box 60, New Meadows, ID 83654, 208/347-2325 or 800/603-2325, features spaces with full hookups for $17. The quiet, tidy park includes showers and a laundry. Nearby you'll find **Packer John Park,** a former state park now owned by the county. It has a few modest campsites with no facilities ($5 a night), as well as Packer John's old cabin, which is well on its way to being reclaimed by the earth.

Information

For information about the area, check in at the Payette National Forest's **New Meadows Ranger District,** 700 Virginia (a half mile east of town down Highway 55), P.O. Box J, New Meadows, ID 83654, 208/347-0300.

Highway 55: Payette River Country

Highway 55 heads north from the west side of Boise, eventually joining Highway 95 at New Meadows. At the little town of Horseshoe Bend the highway meets the Payette River, which it follows all the way to McCall. This incredibly scenic drive takes the traveler through the heart of whitewater country. The Payette River isn't particularly long, at least not compared to Idaho's famous Snake and Salmon Rivers, but it's steep and powerful. And its proximity to Boise makes it the state's most heavily used whitewater. By and large, the towns along the Payette—Horseshoe Bend, Banks, Smith's Ferry, Garden

Valley—are small in population, but ever so large in river lore.

WHITEWATER MADNESS
Main Payette

Between Banks and Horseshoe Bend the main Payette offers up the tamest water on the river. Which isn't to say it's placid; three Class III rapids and several easier ones make for a thrilling ride, especially for whitewater neophytes who might be a little nervous about offering themselves up to the river goddess. The river's highest

The Payette is one of Idaho's most popular rivers for float or whitewater rafting trips.

flow rates are found here, peaking at around 8,000 cfs in June. That can make for some big waves. But the river is widest here as well, which tempers its ferocity. Between the rapids you'll find plenty of time for relaxation, on sandy beaches or in good swimming holes.

The South Fork

At Banks, the two major forks of the Payette meet. The South Fork, coming in from the east, is the most prized stretch of the river for most boaters. The **Lower South Fork,** between the Deer Creek put-in and Banks, offers a five-mile thrill ride through three Class III rapids, the Class III+ Bronco Billy rapid, and the awesome waves of the Class IV Staircase. In high water, Staircase will put you into adrenaline overload. Think of your blender on frappé. You'll need plenty of speed and concentrated paddling to make it through the string of waves nearly a boat-length high. And when it's all over and you're safely back in Banks, you'll thank your lucky stars you came through in one piece—then beg to do it again. The great thing about the Payette is you *can* do it again. Access is easy, as Highway 17 (Banks-Lowman Road) parallels the river. And the stretch is

short, so you can run it three times a day if you have the necessary stamina.

Above Deer Creek you come to the **South Fork Canyon** stretch, between the put-in at the Deadwood River confluence and the takeout at Danskin Station. Even more challenging than the lower South Fork, this stretch of river drops 475 feet in 13 miles. Along the way you'll have the chance to soak in a riverbank hot spring, portage around a 40-foot waterfall, and paddle for all you're worth through a slew of Class IV crunchers. Scenery is outstanding as you find yourself closed in by the canyon's steep granite walls.

Other boatable stretches on the South Fork include a relatively easy float between Danskin Station and Garden Valley, and the Grandjean stretch, way up near the headwaters in the alpine realms on the flanks of the Sawtooths. The Deadwood River, a tributary of the South Fork, is an experts-only river not run commercially.

The North Fork

Continuing north up Highway 55 past Banks, the North Fork of the Payette puts on quite a show. Incredible amounts of water funnel through the tight, rock-filled canyon in a raging flow no wider than a Winnebago. From just south of

Smith's Ferry to Banks, the North Fork is for all intents and purposes just one long Class V rapid. Needless to say it's not run commercially. In fact, just looking at the river from the highway fills you with wonder that this river has ever been run at all. It has. Can you say *"cojones grandes?"*

Above Smith's Ferry, the river returns to a descent once again suited to mere mortals. The **Cabarton run** from Cabarton Bridge to Smith's Ferry makes a popular day trip through a canyon with some healthy but not too intimidating rapids. A bonus on this stretch is the abundant wildlife along the river, including bald eagles, ospreys, and deer.

Guides

Many companies offer guided trips on the Payette, among them **Bear Valley River Co.,** next to the Banks Store & Cafe, 208/793-2272 or 800/235-2327, which guides all the Payette's major runs, as well as the Grandjean Stretch on the upper South Fork; **Cascade Raft Company,** 7050 Hwy. 55, RIO, Horseshoe Bend, ID 83629, 208/793-2221 or 800/292-7238, which offers all the major runs plus a kayak school; **Headwaters River Company,** P.O. Box 1, Banks, ID 83602, 208/793-2348 or 800/800-7238, also offering all the major runs plus kayak lessons; and **Idaho Whitewater Unlimited,** P.O. Box 570, Garden Valley, ID 83622, 208/462-1900, which also rents and sells rafting equipment. Expect to pay around $35–40 per person for a half-day trip, $75–100 for a full-day trip including lunch.

Information

For more information on boating the Payette, contact the Boise National Forest's **Emmett Ranger District,** 1805 Hwy. 16 #5, Emmett, ID 83617, 208/365-7000.

BACK ON TERRA FIRMA

Thunder Mountain Line

Horseshoe Bend is home depot for the **Thunder Mountain Line** excursion railroad. Three basic trips are offered: The *Horseshoe Bend Express,* a 2.5-hour tour from Horseshoe Bend to Banks and back; the *Cabarton Flyer,* a 2.5-hour round trip from Cascade to Smith's Ferry; and the *Cascade Limited,* a five-hour trek from Horseshoe Bend to Cascade and back. Other offerings include murder mystery trains, "river and rails" train-rafting combos, wine-tasting trips, and more. Tickets for the basic trips cost $24.50 adults, $23 seniors 60 and up, $15 kids 4–12. Tickets for the five-hour trip are $60/55/45. Reservations are advised; for schedules and reservations, call 208/793-4425 or 877/432-7245 or see www.thundermountainline.com.

Banks

Even if you're not a boater, it's fun to sit out on the back deck of **Banks Store & Cafe,** 208/793-2617, and watch the brightly colored rafts and kayaks make their way downstream. A little of the river life is sure to rub off on you. Breakfast is served all day and the pie is homemade. Summer hours are 7:30 A.M.–8:30 P.M. daily; shorter (and variable) hours the rest of the year.

Up the Middle Fork

Eight miles east of Banks, Route 17 crosses the Middle Fork Payette River. Turning left up the Middle Fork will take you to Crouch, a small supply center for area cabins. If you arrive in time for dinner, try the **Longhorn Saloon & Restaurant,** 208/462-3108, a 50-year-old establishment serving steaks, seafood, and salads. Summer hours are Sun.–Thurs. 7 A.M.–10 P.M., Fri.–Sat. 7 A.M.–11 P.M. (It closes an hour earlier the rest of the year.) Prime rib specials are offered on Friday and Saturday night.

Past Crouch up Middle Fork Road (FR 698) you'll enter the heart of Boise National Forest and find a number of hot springs and Forest Service campgrounds. Between Crouch and the Trail Creek Junction lie **Tie Creek Campground** (seven sites, fee), **Hardscrabble Campground**

> *The Cabarton run from Cabarton Bridge to Smith's Ferry makes a popular day trip through a canyon with some healthy but not too intimidating rapids. A bonus on this stretch is the abundant wildlife along the river, including bald eagles, ospreys, and deer.*

SOUTHWEST IDAHO

(six sites, fee), **Rattlesnake Campground** (10 sites, fee), and, right at the junction of Forest Roads 698 and 671, **Trail Creek Campground** (10 sites, fee). About 1.5 miles upriver from Hardscrabble Campground, across the river from the road, you may see the steam rising out of **Rocky Canyon Hot Spring.** If you decide to soak, be careful fording the Middle Fork.

If you turn right up FR 671 at Trail Creek Junction, you'll eventually come to USFS **Silver Creek Campground** (five sites, fee) and a trailhead, from where Trails 27 and 26 lead east to Deadwood Reservoir; Trail 44 leads north toward Stolle Meadows and Warm Lake.

A left on FR 698 at Trail Creek Junction reveals in less than a half mile a spur leading off to the left; take it down to the river and **Fire Crew Hot Springs,** a good place for a soak after the peak spring runoff has passed. Seven miles or so farther north on FR 698 you'll find **Boiling Springs Campground** (seven sites, fee) and **Boiling Springs Guard Station,** a Forest Service cabin rented through the NRRS, 877/444-6777. The cabin is available Memorial Day weekend through the end of October and rents for $35 a night. Next to the cabin is **Boiling Springs,** which may not boil but is plenty hot; mix the spring water with river water for a comfortable soak.

From the trailhead at Boiling Springs Campground you can follow trails north to Stolle Meadows and Warm Lake. Along the way **Moondipper, Pine Burl,** and **Bull Creek Hot Springs** invite further exploration. The first two lie along Middle Fork Trail 033; the latter is on Bull Creek Trail 102. Continuing on FR 698 takes you to FR 671, where you can turn left and loop back to Trail Creek Junction.

In winter, a cross-country ski trail is set and groomed from Crouch to Boiling Springs.

Garden Valley

From the Middle Fork turnoff, Route 17 continues east through Garden Valley, a beautiful, wide, and flat stretch of land fronting on the South Fork Payette. The bucolic valley is filled with farms and corrals, and flanked by mountains on either side. Eventually the road leads to Lowman and Highway 21.

A few miles east of the village of Garden Valley, the USFS **Hot Springs Campground** offers eight fee sites surrounded by ponderosa pine and adjacent to a hot springs. Sites are reservable; call 877/444-6777. The campground is usually open April to late September.

North Fork Campgrounds

Several USFS campgrounds line the North Fork between Banks and Smith's Ferry. Heading upriver you'll come to **Swinging Bridge** (11 sites, but the swinging bridge is long gone), **Cold Springs** (five sites), and **Big Eddy** (four sites). All are open May 15–Sept. 30, and all charge a fee. The North Fork offers good fishing for rainbow trout and whitefish.

Smith's Ferry and Vicinity

Smith's Ferry is 55 miles north of Boise and 17 miles south of Cascade on Highway 55. **Cougar Mountain Lodge,** 9738 Hwy. 55, 208/382-4464, is a cozy roadhouse restaurant—a nice place to duck in out of the weather. Rooms are available; cross-country skiing no longer is.

West of Smith's Ferry, small but scenic **Sagehen Reservoir** lies in a forested, 4,800-foot-high basin; from Highway 55 at Smith's Ferry, take Forest Roads 644, 626, and 614. Forest Service campgrounds ring the lake, which offers good fishing for stocked trout. Small boats are permitted on the reservoir; Antelope and Sagehen Creek Campgrounds offer docks and ramps.

Counterclockwise around the lake from the southeast shore, campgrounds include **Hollywood** (six sites), **Eastside** (six sites), **Sagehen Creek** (15 sites), and **Antelope** (20 sites). All are fee sites, open mid-May to mid-September. Reservations are taken for Antelope and Sagehen sites; call 877/444-6777. The others are first-come, first-served. Also here at the west side of the reservoir is the **Sagehen Dam Picnic Area,** charging a small day-use fee.

Hikers will find a trail (Joe's Creek Road, then Joe's Creek Trail 137) between Sagehen Creek and Antelope Campgrounds that leads north up Joe's Creek about five miles to great views at the top of West Peak (elevation 8,086 feet). In early summer, hikers should keep their eyes peeled for morel mushrooms, which grow profusely in the area.

Forest Service Rental

Northwest of Sagehen Reservoir, at the foot of the West Mountains on Third Fork Squaw Creek, Boise National Forest rents **Third Fork Cabin** between May 25 and October 31 for $30 a night. From the south side of Sagehen Reservoir, take FR 626 west to a major junction and continue west onto FR 618. That road soon makes a right turn; the cabin is about five miles farther. To make reservations, call 877/444-6777.

Information

For more information on recreation opportunities in Payette River country, contact the Boise National Forest's **Emmett Ranger District,** 1805 Hwy. 16 #5, Emmett, ID 83617, 208/365-7000.

CASCADE AND VICINITY

Cascade was named for a falls on the North Fork Payette River that lost its thunder in 1948 to Cascade Dam. The resulting 30,000-acre Cascade Reservoir, though long plagued with water-quality problems, is one of the state's most popular fishing holes. Perch are the most numerous fish in the lake and are sought by both boating anglers in summer and ice-fishers in winter. Cascade is the Valley County seat, its economy fueled by a large lumber mill. Look for big changes in the next decade or so as the Tamarack resort near Donnelly opens phase by phase.

Bicycling

About eight miles south of town, Clear Creek Road (FR 409) intersects Highway 55 and climbs a gentle grade to the northeast. The narrow road winds through tall pine forest and alongside babbling Clear Creek. Add occasional vistas and potential wildlife sightings and you've got an easy and ideal bicycling adventure. Bring a picnic lunch. Those looking for a little more challenge can continue up the road, over Clear Creek Summit and Railroad Pass and down Curtis Creek to Warm Lake Road for a pleasant loop trip.

theater marquee, Cascade

© JULIE FANSELOW

Golf

The nine-hole **Cascade Golf Course,** 117 Lakeshore Dr., 208/382-4835, lines the east shore of Cascade Reservoir. Greens fee is $15 on weekdays, $18 on weekends. Lessons, cart rentals, and a small pro shop are offered; the course's restaurant and lounge overlook Cascade Reservoir. It's closed November–March.

Park N' Ski Areas

Just north of town, Warm Lake Road turns east off Highway 55. Five miles up Warm Lake Road is **Crawford Park N' Ski;** three miles farther on you'll find **Scott Valley Park N' Ski.** The latter is the better of the two, with seven miles of well-marked trails. The northside trail heads into the woods and follows the ridge north, climbing slightly and providing open views of the valley. The south side of the loop crosses a wide-open, treeless field, where you'll feel like Diane Keaton skiing across Finland in *Reds.* If you can't find your glide here, it's hopeless.

SOUTHWEST IDAHO

Events

Look for **Thunder Mountain Days** over July Fourth weekend, featuring a rodeo, parade, buckaroo breakfast, and barbecue. The **Valley County Fair** comes to town the first week in August; lumberjack competitions and a rodeo are among the fair's highlights.

Cascade's main street—Highway 95 through town—is at its best during the year-end holidays, when it's all lit up with Christmas lights. The lights stay up until the end of McCall's Winter Carnival—a welcoming sight to travelers coming into town on a blustery winter's night.

For more information on these events, call the chamber of commerce at 208/382-3833.

Accommodations

The new **Ashley Inn,** 500 N. Main St., 866/382-5621, www.TheAshleyInn.com, looks a bit out of place along the highway north of downtown Cascade. You can bet the owners wish they had a piece of lakeside property. Still, it's by far the nicest place in town, with lots of art, an indoor pool, and fireplaces in each of the 67 rooms. Rates ($85–215) include a breakfast buffet featuring fresh fruit, biscuits and gravy, and pastries.

Camping and RVing

The beautiful **Water's Edge RV Resort,** at the north end of town along Highway 55, P.O. Box 1018, Cascade, ID 83611, 208/382-3120 or 800/574-2038, lies along the bank of the Payette River. Amenities include bathroom and laundry facilities, beach volleyball courts, horseshoes, free kayaks and canoes for guest use, and evening campfires. Rates are $20 for full hookups, including cable TV.

On the northeast shore of Cascade Reservoir you'll find a cluster of Forest Service and Bureau of Reclamation fee campgrounds. Several others ring the southern reaches of the reservoir. From Cascade, take Cabarton Road (FR 17A) south and turn west on West Mountain Road (FR 422).

Information

The Cascade Chamber of Commerce is at 113 Main St., P.O. Box 571, Cascade, ID 83611,

208/382-3833. For Payette National Forest recreation information, contact the **Cascade Ranger District,** 540 N. Main St., P.O. Box 696, Cascade, ID 83611, 208/382-4271.

WARM LAKE

East of the highway, Warm Lake Road leads up into the mountains to the South Fork of the Salmon River and the community of Warm Lake. This is wild country, near the west edge of the Frank Church–River of No Return Wilderness. The owner of Warm Lake Lodge once saw a wolf investigating his Dumpster, and the Forest Service has recorded wolf sightings in this area since the early 1980s—well before reintroduction.

Hot Springs

Hot springs lovers could spend a whole weekend exploring the many hot pools in the Warm Lake area, among them **Molly's Tubs, Vulcan Hot Springs, Penny Hot Spring,** and **Trail Creek Hot Spring.** Molly's Tubs and Vulcan lie along or just off FR 474, 1.3 and 6.5 miles, respectively, south of Warm Lake Road. Penny Hot Spring is 4.5 miles north of Warm Springs Road off FR 474, across from the former Penny Campground. Trail Creek is west of Warm Lake, a half mile east of mile marker 61 on Warm Lake Road For more information, check out Evie Litton's *The Hiker's Guide to Hot Springs in the Pacific Northwest* (see Suggested Reading), or consult the rangers at the **Cascade Ranger District,** 540 N. Main St. in Cascade, 208/382-4271.

Horseback Riding and Horsepacking

Juniper Mountain Outfitters Inc., 21292 Simplot Blvd., Greenleaf, ID 83626, 208/454-1322, offers trail rides and horsepack trips from the Stolle Meadows trailhead south of Warm Lake. Stolle Meadows is near the headwaters of the South Fork Salmon River, and if you're around in July and August you can watch chinook salmon spawn in the river.

Accommodations

$50–100: Warm Lake's two mountain lodges are both open year-round. In winter, either would make a good base camp for cross-country skiing in Boise National Forest. **Warm Lake Lodge,** Warm Lake, ID 83611, 208/632-3553, has been around since 1911. Its rustic cabins line the shore of Warm Lake and range in size from a small unit with a single double bed to a hot tub–equipped unit sleeping 10 (these two would be on either side of this price category). Some units have kitchenettes. Campsites are available for $15 a night. Other facilities at the resort include a restaurant and lounge, store, post office, and boat dock. Pets are discouraged.

North Shore Lodge, 175 N. Shoreline Dr., Cascade, ID 83611, 208/632-2000 or 800/933-3193 (reservations), offers cabins of various sizes, all with kitchenettes. Other facilities include a restaurant and lounge, store, gas and oil sales, canoe and boat rentals, horseshoe pits, volleyball courts, and docks. Pets okay but must be leashed.

Forest Service Campgrounds and Cabin Rental

Boise National Forest campgrounds in the Warm Lake area include **South Fork Salmon River** (14 sites, fee), **Shoreline** (25 sites, fee), and **Warm Lake** (10 sites, fee). In addition, the **Stolle Meadows Guard Station** is available for rent year-round except April; winter access is by cross-country skis or snowmobiles only. The cabin sleeps up to five at a rate of $30 a day. For reservations, call the NRRS, 877/444-6777.

YELLOW PINE

Out past Warm Lake, past Landmark, past Halfway Station, and past Johnson Creek, you'll finally come to Yellow Pine, one of the state's most remote communities. The tenacious outpost once supplied the Big Creek mining district; today it's home to the **Yellow Pine Harmonica Contest,** an annual blow that draws reasonably large crowds, considering the effort it takes to get out here. The contest takes place in early August.

Accommodations

Over $250: In the Yellow Pine vicinity you'll find **Wapiti Meadow Ranch,** HC 72, Cascade, ID 83611, 208/633-3217, an Orvis-endorsed

lodge catering to fly-fishers. It lies between the South and Middle Forks of the Salmon River and is surrounded by nine different lakes in close proximity. The big stone lodge is the center for a variety of activities, including horseback riding, hiking, fishing, snowmobiling, and skiing. After pursuing your favorite recreational pastime you can soak under the stars in the outdoor spa. The small dining room serves gourmet meals. Six-night fly-fishing packages cost $2,500 per person for all lodging, meals, horseback riding, use of fishing gear, and guide service. If you're not hooked on fishing, you can enjoy a six-night package offering horseback riding instead ($1,750 per person), or if space is available, you can stay and just hang out six nights for $1,200, meals included. The lodge can also arrange horsepack trips and whitewater-rafting trips. A 15 percent service charge and 7 percent in taxes are added to your bill; gratuities to staff are not expected.

Camping

North of Yellow Pine and north of Wapiti Meadows on FR 340, the USFS **Big Creek Campground** (four sites, fee) lies between two trailheads providing access into the Frank Church–River of No Return Wilderness.

DONNELLY

Tamarack

Trying to steal some thunder from Brundage to the north, **Tamarack,** 208/325-8409, www.tamarackidaho.com, bills itself as "the first ski, golf, and lake resort to be built in the United States in more than 20 years." That sounds like a tall claim, but Tamarack does have ambitious plans ($1.5 billion in spending over 15 years) that are coming together one piece at a time.

For now, there's cross-country skiing, snowshoeing, and guided snowcat skiing in winter and a mountain bike park in summer, including several miles of model trails designed and prepared by members of the International Mountain Biking Association. Rentals and lessons are available for both skiing and biking. There's also a small café serving sandwiches, quesadillas, and such, with most fare in the $6–8 range. Downhill skiing starts in the winter of 2004–2005, followed by the opening of a Robert Trent Jones II 18-hole golf course in 2005. To get to Tamarack from Donnelly, look for the Stinker Station, then turn west on Roseberry Road and follow the signs.

Elk-Viewing

Many years ago, local ranchers Hap and Florence Points started putting out hay for a herd of elk that came down from the heights to winter in Long Valley. The idea was to create a single feeding ground that would draw the herd and keep them from getting into the hay supplies of every rancher in the valley. The plan was successful; the herd came to know Points Ranch as an easy meal and stayed out of trouble elsewhere. Eventually it occurred to the couple to use this regular feeding ground for another purpose as well—to provide an opportunity for the public to see these magnificent animals up close. Points started bringing along paying customers on his wintertime sleigh rides to feed the herd. Neighbors Joe and Vicki Eld took an interest in the operation and began helping Hap with the feedings. After Hap and Florence passed away, Joe and Vicki determined to keep the Points's efforts alive. Today the Elds continue to offer the elk a safe haven from winter hardship and hunters. When the herd comes down, Joe and Vicki select two stately shires from their stable, hitch them to the sleigh loaded with hay, and carry the hay and hayriders out to the elk.

The **Hap and Florence Points Memorial**

Sleigh Rides are a not-to-be-missed experience. After climbing aboard the sleigh with your fellow passengers and a motley crew of the most lovable pooches you've ever seen, Vicki gives the word and the shires begin their purposeful plodding out to the feeding grounds. The sight of the first few elk is exhilarating; then you come to the body of the herd. Large numbers of elk—cows and big-antlered bucks alike—come over to the sleigh and start chowing down on the very hay bales you're sitting on. Occasionally you might have to duck to avoid the rack of antlers attached to a hungry bull.

Some people originally were concerned the elks' exposure to people would make them less wary of humans and an easier target for hunters when they left the safety of the ranch. But according to Vicki, studies show the opposite to be true—apparently the regular contact with humans allows the herd to better recognize human scent and therefore avoid contact with our species everywhere but on Points Ranch. The Idaho Department of Fish and Game supports the venture, buying the hay to feed the herd.

The rides are offered at least once daily when the elks' club convenes, usually mid-December through March. The fee is around $15 adults, $10 for teens, $5 children 12 and under. Reservations are required; when you call to make them, Vicki will give you directions to the ranch and fill you in on the procedures to be followed when you get there. It's important to follow her directions explicitly to avoid spooking the elk. Call 208/325-8876 for reservations and information.

McCall and Vicinity

With an ideal location on the shore of beautiful Payette Lake, surrounded by millions of acres of National Forest land, it's not surprising McCall (pop. 2,000) is a recreation center. More than that, however, it's one of the state's most unabashedly fun towns. McCall knows how to have a good time. Its young, outdoor-oriented populace enjoys practically out-the-back-door skiing at Brundage Mountain, boating on the lake, and hiking in expansive backcountry. When

the locals aren't outdoors, you'll find them having a good time with friends at The Pub or dancing the night away down at the Yacht Club. Tourism drives the economy—vacation homes dot the lakeshore, and thousands of visitors pour in on summer weekends and for Winter Carnival, the town's biggest annual event. Yet McCall seldom feels too crowded; if you come in the offseason, you'll think you've discovered your own private paradise.

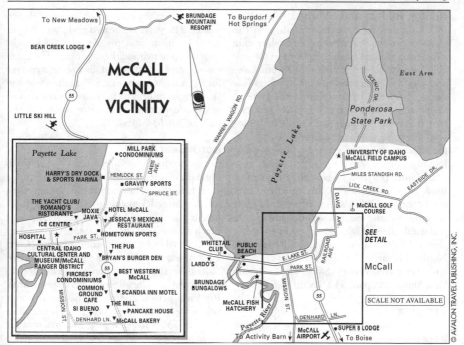

To New Meadows

BRUNDAGE MOUNTAIN RESORT

To Burgdorf Hot Springs

BEAR CREEK LODGE

McCALL AND VICINITY

East Arm

55

LITTLE SKI HILL

Ponderosa State Park

Payette Lake

WARREN WAGON RD.

SCENIC DR.

Payette Lake

MILL PARK CONDOMINIUMS

HARRY'S DRY DOCK & SPORTS MARINA

HEMLOCK ST.

DAVIS AVE.

GRAVITY SPORTS

SPRUCE ST.

THE YACHT CLUB/ ROMANO'S RISTORANTE

MOXIE JAVA

HOTEL McCALL

JESSICA'S MEXICAN RESTAURANT

ICE CENTRE

HOMETOWN SPORTS

HOSPITAL

PARK ST.

CENTRAL IDAHO CULTURAL CENTER AND MUSEUM/McCALL RANGER DISTRICT

THE PUB

BRYAN'S BURGER DEN

55

BEST WESTERN McCALL

FIRCREST CONDOMINIUMS

COMMON GROUND CAFE

SCANDIA INN MOTEL

SI BUENO

THE MILL

PANCAKE HOUSE

MISSION ST.

DENHARD LN.

McCALL BAKERY

WHITETAIL CLUB

PUBLIC BEACH

LARDO'S

BRUNDAGE BUNGALOWS

McCALL FISH HATCHERY

E. LAKE ST.

PARK ST.

RAILROAD AVE.

DAVIS AVE.

UNIVERSITY OF IDAHO McCALL FIELD CAMPUS

MILES STANDISH RD.

LICK CREEK RD.

EASTSIDE DR.

McCALL GOLF COURSE

SEE DETAIL

McCall

SCALE NOT AVAILABLE

MISSION ST.

55

DENHARD LN.

Payette River

To Activity Barn

McCALL AIRPORT

SUPER 8 LODGE

To Boise

© AVALON TRAVEL PUBLISHING, INC.

PONDEROSA STATE PARK

Considered by many the crown jewel of Idaho's state park system, Ponderosa State Park, P.O. Box A, McCall, ID 83638, 208/634-2164, occupies a 1,000-acre peninsula jutting into Payette Lake, two miles northeast of downtown McCall. The peninsula was never logged in the early days, so the old-growth ponderosa pines here—up to 400 years old and 150 feet tall—are big and abundant. Lodgepole pine, Douglas fir, and grand fir tower over the park, and wildflowers brighten the meadows and forest floor. Besides conifer forest, marshes and arid sagebrush flats provide habitat for a wide variety of species, including woodpeckers, muskrats, ducks, foxes, ospreys, and, in summer, big, hungry mosquitoes. Summer visitors can hike or bike through the park, or head for the park's beaches to play in the waters of Payette Lake. In winter, the park becomes especially quiet and serene under a blanket of snow. Cross-country ski trails lead the visitor to views overlooking frosty Payette Lake and the mountains beyond. Summer or winter, here it's possible to get far enough away from civilization to feel alone in the wilderness—an impressive achievement for Idaho's most popular state park.

Visitor Center

Most of the visitor facilities are on the south and west sides of the peninsula. Immediately upon entering the park and paying the usual $4 per vehicle state park entry fee, you'll come to the visitor center. Rangers are on hand here to answer your questions, provide you with a park map, and fill you in on the park's interpretive-program schedule. Something takes place at the park amphitheater just about every night all summer long, and rangers lead guided hikes many mornings. Also ask about the junior ranger program, designed to keep youngsters happy and maybe expand their minds a bit, too.

SOUTHWEST IDAHO

Hiking, Biking, and Skiing

Pick up a park trail map from a ranger at the visitor center. Road bicyclers will enjoy the scenic paved loop road down the peninsula to Osprey Cliff, which affords great views of Payette Lake and McCall. Hikers and mountain bikers will find a seven-mile system of dirt trails more to their liking. The off-pavement trails also lead from the visitor center out to the tip of the peninsula, offering loops of several different lengths. All the trails are open to hikers, and two are open to mountain bikers as well.

In winter the trails lie beneath a blanket of snow, over which easy- to intermediate-level cross-country ski trails are set. Most of the trails are groomed and include skating lanes where trail width allows. **Lighted night skiing** is available 6–11 P.M. on the wide and relatively flat Northern Lights trail. Skiing at the park is free if you have a valid Park N' Ski sticker or a State Park Annual Passport, $4 a day otherwise.

Camping

The park proper holds 137 campsites in three loops just west of the visitor center. Each loop includes bathrooms and showers, and in the vicinity you'll find a volleyball court, beaches, boat docks, and a day-use picnic area with boat ramp. Another 84 campsites lie in the adjacent Lakeview Village Unit, 208/634-5280, a former private RV park south of the park's main unit. Lakeview Village is more densely crowded than the park's main unit, offering a boat ramp, boat dock, volleyball court, horseshoe pits, showers, and laundry.

Campsites at either unit cost $16 a night with water and electricity, $12 a night water only. Those rates are for a single vehicle; each extra vehicle costs $5 a night more. Written campsite reservation requests are accepted by mail after January 1 each year for the following summer season. Reservations must be made and paid for 15 days or more prior to the requested date; phone reservations are taken after March 31. A nonrefundable $6 reservation fee is charged and is not applicable to the camping fee.

Other Accommodations

The park has some yurts available for rent year-round—especially nice for ski-in overnights in winter. The yurts are heated and cost $35 per night for up to four people, plus $4 a night each for up to two additional persons. The Lakeview Village campground also rents a cottage for $75 a night in summer, $55 in the off-season (two-night minimum). For reservations and more information on these options, call the park at 208/634-2164.

North Beach Unit

On the north edge of Payette Lake, this annex to the park is intended to remain in a primitive state. Facilities are limited; no official campsites, just one large RV parking area. The big draw here is a long sandy beach—the longest public beach on the lake—used by visitors arriving by boat as well as by car. In addition, the North Fork Payette River above the inlet here is a no-wake zone; the placid waters are perfect for canoeing and kayaking. Rent watercraft from **Silver Pig Enterprises,** 208/634-4562, on the west side of the beach. Canoes cost $9 an hour, $25 a half day, $50 a full day. Single kayaks rent for $7 an hour, $21 a half day, $42 a full day. Double kayaks are available, too. Silver Pig is open daily in summer, 10 A.M.–6 P.M.

To reach the North Beach Unit, follow Warren Wagon Road 9 miles from the west edge of McCall up the lake's west shore.

OTHER SIGHTS

Central Idaho Cultural Center and Museum

On the corner of State and Lake Streets, this center, 208/634-4497, comprises several restored CCC buildings that house local-history exhibits and offices of community organizations. It's open Mon.–Fri. 10 A.M.–4 P.M.

University of Idaho McCall Field Campus

Practically right next door to Ponderosa State Park, this 11-acre, pine-covered campus offers UI Moscow's forestry students a spectacular setting in which to study flora and fauna, ecology, and related topics. Nonstudents can attend periodic extension courses in environmental education and natural-resource management, as well as related topics such as nature drawing and wilderness literature. On-campus lodging and dining are available to course participants at extremely reasonable prices. The annual McCall Folk Music Festival is also held here. For more information on the field campus, contact program manager Rose Poulin, P.O. Box 1025, McCall, ID 83638, 208/634-3918 (May–Oct.) or 208/634-8444 (Nov.–April).

Fish Hatchery

The kings of their genus, chinook salmon can grow to be five feet long and weigh well over 100 pounds. The Columbia, Snake, and Salmon Rivers once were honeymoon highways leading from the Pacific Ocean over 700 miles inland to the royal spawning grounds on the Salmon's South Fork and other high-mountain tributaries. But then came the dams, and logging-induced siltation, and there went the salmon. Returning spawners dwindled to disastrously low levels. To help compensate for declining chinook populations, the Idaho Department of Fish and Game raises chinooks at the **McCall Fish Hatchery,** 300 Mather Rd., 208/634-2690. Hatchery personnel trap spawning fish near Warm Lake on the South Fork, then perform massive artificial insemination at the hatchery. More than two million juvenile salmon are raised and released annually, hopefully to make their way downriver to the sea. With luck, maybe one-tenth of 1 percent will someday return to the spawning grounds. Self-guided tours are possible year-round, 8 A.M.–5 P.M. daily.

McCall Smokejumper Base

Some 80 Forest Service smokejumpers are based at the McCall airport facility, 605 S. Mission St., 208/634-0390. Sanity apparently isn't a job requirement for these fearless men and women who suppress and manage wildland fire, both lightning- and person-caused. After parachuting out of planes into burning areas, they haul 100-pound packs—filled with chainsaws, Pulaskis, and the like—out to the nearest pickup point, sometimes miles and miles away. Couch

potatoes need not apply. Smokejumpers from McCall are regularly dispatched to fires all over the country, including Alaska, and make an average of 600 jumps on 160 fires each year. In summer, hour-long tours of the McCall facility are available at 11:30 A.M. and 2:30 P.M. daily, unless all the crews are out on fires. Tours often include a video and a tour of smokejumper facilities and aircraft.

Sightseeing Flights

The isolated ranches in the mountains east of town get their mail delivery by skiplane in winter. You can tag along with the mail carrier/pilot on the two- to three-hour **mail-run flights** for $60 per person. For more information, contact McCall Aviation, 208/634-7137 or 800/992-6559, www.mccallair.com. Flights leave from the company's office at McCall Airport, 300 Dienhard Ln., Monday and Thursday at around 8:30 A.M., depending on the weather. **Breakfast flights** to backcountry guest ranches are also popular. For details and reservations, call **Arnold Aviation,** 208/382-4844.

RECREATION

Brundage Mountain

McCall owes much of its high fun factor to Brundage Mountain, a first-rate ski and summer resort just outside town. In winter, the resort's 1,300 acres and 1,800-foot vertical drop are served by a high-speed quad chair, two triple chairs, and two surface lifts. From the top of the mountain at 7,640 feet, you'll enjoy sweeping views of the Payette Lakes, Salmon River Mountains, and the impressive Seven Devils Range.

Powderhounds will want to avail themselves of the resort's snowcat skiing as well, which will take them to untracked runs far from the crowds. And parents will appreciate Brundage's Kids' Center, which offers the finest kids' programs and facilities of any ski resort in Idaho; your little Picabo-in-training will feel special at the separate, well-designed children's lodge opening right out onto the bunny slope. Day care is available.

Full-day adult lift tickets cost around $34; juniors 12–18 and seniors 65–69, $27; kids ages

7–11, $18. Kids age 6 and under and seniors age 70 and up ski free. The lifts operate daily 9:30 A.M.–4:30 P.M.; reduced-price lift tickets are offered after 1 P.M. Both ski and snowboard rentals and lessons are available.

A bus runs from McCall to the mountain daily during winter; fare is $4 round-trip, $3 one-way (free to people staying at the motels where it stops).

Snowcat skiing costs around $225 per person per day, $135 per person for a half day, including off-piste skis, lunch, and snacks. Die-hards will opt for the overnight cat-ski adventure, including a stay in a backcountry yurt; around $550 per person. Reservations are required for all cat skiing; call 208/634-7462 or 208/634-4151.

In summer, the resort runs a chairlift to the top of the mountain for mountain bikers and sightseers. From the top, bikers can access a 15-mile single-track trail system built especially for mountain bikes. The lift runs Fri.–Sun. from late June to Labor Day. A full-day lift pass is $20; a single-ride pass costs $9 adults, $5 kids 7–12 and seniors 65 and older. Mountain-bike rentals are available; an introductory package costs $30, including bike, helmet (required), and single-ride lift pass.

If biking isn't your sport, perhaps rafting is. The resort's summer offerings include guided whitewater trips on the Salmon River; adult rates are around $49 per half day; $75 per full day, including lunch; $299 for a two-day trip covering some 39 river miles; and $770 for a four-day trip that couples a 55-mile run on the lower Salmon with a 20-mile run on the Snake River through Hells Canyon. Reservations required; call 888/889-8320. Trips begin from the Brundage Mountain Adventures office in Riggins.

Also in summer, the resort's amphitheater becomes an alpine concert venue extraordinaire. Look for a bluegrass festival in mid-August and an end-of-summer concert in early September. Bring a lawn chair and your picnic basket. All in all, Brundage is a fantastic place to play any time of year.

To reach the resort, take Highway 55 east toward New Meadows, and watch for the signed turnoff to your right about eight miles outside town. For

catching some air at Brundage

more information, contact Brundage Mountain, P.O. Box 1062, McCall, ID 83638, 208/634-4151 or 800/888-7544 (business office), 208/634-7462 (ski area), or 208/634-7669 or 888/255-7669 (recorded snow report), www.brundage.com.

Little Ski Hill

This dual alpine and Nordic area lies about three miles northwest of town on Highway 55, 208/634-5691. The nonprofit operation run by Payette Lakes Ski Club began in 1937, making it the second-oldest ski hill in Idaho after Sun Valley. Although the alpine area—one T-bar serving one hill—is humble, it's also cheap, at $6 a day (including night skiing Fri.–Sat. 5–10 P.M.). The grooming is excellent, and the slope facing the highway is just steep enough to entertain the intermediate skier. The lift is closed on Monday.

The Nordic area is one of the best tracked in the state. The longest loop in the 50-kilometer system passes several side trails, some climbing a ridge to offer speedy-turny descents on the way back. The main trail meanders south through a string of valleys far from the highway. If you have the energy, go all the way to the end—it gets better as you go. The trails are open daily during daylight hours. They're groomed Tues.–Sun. by *real* grooming equipment, not a broken-down snowmobile pulling a sheet of plywood. Both skating and traditional tracks are set, and you don't have to share them with snowmobiles.

Full-day trail passes cost $3. Seniors 65 and up are free. No rentals are available—the closest outfitter is Home Town Sports on Highway 55 on the way out of town toward the ski area. Lessons are available by appointment.

Combined Nordic/alpine season passes run $52 for adults, $26 for kids age 5–12.

A small day lodge along the highway includes a snack bar and some picnic tables for sack lunches. Friday-night telemark races are common, as are cheap BYOB feeds accompanied by live acoustic music.

Other Nordic Ski Trails

About 10 miles of groomed trails loop out to the end of the peninsula and back at Ponderosa State Park. In addition, the city doesn't mind if you cruise **McCall City Golf Course,** as long as you don't trash it. The course is a popular place for local dogs to bring their people, the kind of easy access open space that invites an impromptu game of Frisbee ski-golf. The course is at the end of Reedy Lane off Davis Avenue.

Other Winter Fun

Head out to the **Activity Barn,** on Moonridge Road (take Mission or Deinhard off Highway 55 to Moonridge), 208/634-2222, www.activitybarn.com, for lift-served snow tubing ($7 for one hour, $12 for two hours; family rates available) and more cross-country skiing (by donation). A yurt serves as a warming hut, offering hot drinks and snacks, as well as a wood stove to warm your frozen pinkies by.

Ice Skating

McCall's new pride and joy is the year-round **Manchester Ice & Event Centre,** 200 E. Lake St.,

208/634-3570, www.manchester-icecentre.com. Opened in 2003, the facility is a great place to skate, with huge windows that look out on Payette Lake. Public skating sessions are held at least once daily ($5.50 general, $4 ages 12 and under; skate rental $2); call for current times. This is also the Idaho Steelheads pro hockey team's training facility, and many hockey clinics and camps are held throughout the year. A café opens daily at 10 A.M. for both skaters and spectators.

Day Hikes near McCall

The Payette National Forest surrounding McCall is full of trails, allowing you to plan hikes of just about any length you want, from a couple of hours to a couple of weeks. Stop in at the **McCall Ranger District,** 102 W. Lake St., 208/634-0400, for trail suggestions and a list of the topographic maps you'll need for the hike you choose.

A few short day hikes suitable for all ages and ability levels are described here. **Duck Lake Trail** begins up Lick Creek Road (Forest Highway 48), just past Lick Creek Summit. An overlook at the summit provides panoramic views of the glacier-carved landscape. The trail climbs ever so slightly for about a mile to Duck Lake, making for a pleasant, two-mile roundtrip jaunt. Those looking for a little longer hike can try Trail 083 from Duck Lake up and over a steep ridge to Hum Lake. From Hum Lake the trail loops back to Lick Creek Road; then it's about a two-mile walk down the road back to the car.

Heading up Warren Wagon Road toward Burgdorf Hot Springs, turn off on Josephine Creek Road (FR 316) to reach the trailhead for a steep but short half-mile hike up to cirque-bound **Josephine Lake,** a favorite haunt of fly-fishers.

In the Hazard Lakes area, north of Brundage Mountain on FR 257, the **Upper Hazard Lake Trail** begins at either Hard Creek Guard Station or Hazard Lake Campground and climbs less than 400 feet in elevation for two to three miles to the lake. Along FR 257 in this area, the Lloyds Lake Overlook provides scenic views of Lloyds Lake and Vance Creek Canyon.

Closer to town, don't forget the beautiful trails at Ponderosa State Park.

SOUTHWEST IDAHO

Fishing

Between the Payette Lakes and the numerous streams around McCall, the intrepid angler can catch cutthroat, rainbow, lake, and brook trout, as well as kokanee, kamloops, and bass. Anglers who are also backpackers should know that the Payette National Forest surrounding McCall contains some 300 mountain lakes and 1,400 miles of streams.

Golf

At **McCall Golf Course,** 1001 Reedy Ln., off Davis Ave., 208/634-7200, you can choose between three different nine-hole courses or combine them as you wish. The scenic course, on the east side of town, charges around $32 on weekends and holidays and $28 on weekdays for 18 holes. It's generally closed Nov.–April.

The 18-hole, par-72 **Whitetail Club Golf Course** was designed by Roger Packard and two-time U.S. Open winner Andy North. The lovely course is semi-private, but you can play there if you stay at the high-end lodge that shares its name. Greens fees including a cart are typically $110 Sun.–Thurs., $135 Fri.–Sat., but check the lodge for packages.

Sleigh Rides and Trail Rides

Ya-hoo Corrals, 2280 Warren Wagon Rd., 208/634-3360, offers sleigh rides in McCall's winter wonderland. The company's big draft horses will pull you over hill and dale along snow-covered back roads. Cost is $15 adults, $8 students, $4 children. In summer the Ya-hoos offer carriage rides, barbecue dinner rides, and trail rides, priced $22–50.

Outdoor Outfitters

Gravity Sports, 503 Pine St., 208/634-8530, rents canoes, kayaks, and mountain bikes in summer, and cross-country touring skis, telemark skis, skating skis, snowboards, and snowshoes in winter. **Home Town Sports,** 300 Lenora St., 208/634-2302, rents mountain bikes and water toys in summer; in winter you can rent alpine,

Nordic, and telemark skis, as well as ice skates and snowshoes.

Harry's Dry Dock & Sports Marina, 1300 E. Lake St., 208/634-8605, and 315 N. 3rd St., 208/634-3902, rents ski boats, pontoon boats, fishing boats, canoes, and jet skis in summer, snowmobiles in winter.

ENTERTAINMENT AND EVENTS

Nightlife

Rock 'n' rollers usually wind up at **The Yacht Club,** 203 E. Lake, 208/634-5649, for loud live music and dancing. It's basic—bar, pool table, dance floor—but bands from Boise often make it up here to help patrons boogie the night away. Expect a few-bucks cover charge and expensive beers. Across the street is **Forester's Club,** 304 E. Lake, 208/634-2676, a smoky old dive with a crusty regular clientele.

Events

McCall's **Winter Carnival** is the biggest and best winterfest in the state, and it's not uncommon for more than 20,000 people to pack in on opening day. Motel rooms are booked a year in advance for this party. Fanciful snow sculptures line the streets, and an ice-carving contest brings out world-class artists. Sled dog races, a sledding hill, and an ice-skating rink draw devotees, while everyone enjoys the parades, fireworks, food, and fun. It all takes place around the first week of February.

> *McCall's Winter Carnival is the biggest and best winterfest in the state, and it's not uncommon for more than 20,000 people to pack in on opening day.*

If you're in town in late February or early March, grab your skis and head to the **First Security Winter Games** public ski competition up at Brundage. Racers of all ages and abilities compete in a number of categories.

When all the snow has melted and the summer sun beats down, it's time for the **Payette Lakes Craft and Antique Fair.** Local artisans pull out all the stops for this festival, held on the last weekend in July.

For its size, McCall boasts a rich and diverse music scene. All summer long, Brundage

COURTESY OF THE McCALL CHAMBER OF COMMERCE

McCall Winter Carnival

Mountain hosts concerts and other events. In mid-July, the **McCall Summer Music Festival,** 208/634-7631, formerly the McCall Folk Music Festival, takes place at nearby Roseberry, with three evenings of live jazz, blues, country, swing, and traditional music. Late September typically brings a garage band festival to Art Roberts Park, downtown on the lakefront due north of 2nd Street.

For a complete events calendar, contact the **McCall Area Chamber of Commerce,** 102 N. 3rd St., P.O. Box 350, McCall, ID 83638, 208/634-7631 or 800/260-5130, www.mccall-id-chamber.org. For more information on cultural events in McCall, contact the **McCall Arts and Humanities Council,** 1001 State St., McCall, ID 83638, 208/634-7136.

ACCOMMODATIONS

$50–100

Some of the cheapest digs in town are available at **Scandia Inn Motel,** 401 N. 3rd St., 208/634-7394, which rents doubles at the low end of this price range. It has very reasonable weekly rates, too.

The historic **Hotel McCall,** 1101 N. 3rd St., McCall, ID 83638, 208/634-8105, turned 100 in 2004, but it's been nicely updated to include 26 rooms and five condos at the town's busiest corner, just steps from the lake. Rates include continental breakfast, afternoon wine, cookies and milk at bedtime, and movie rentals. Smoking outside only; no pets. Choose a downstairs room with shared bath, a standard room with private bath, or a condo (in the next higher price category).

Amenities at the **Best Western McCall,** 415 N. 3rd St., 208/634-6300 or 800/528-1234, include an indoor heated pool and hot tub, refrigerators and microwave ovens in almost every room, and remote-control cable TV with HBO. On the south side of town is the newish **Super 8 Lodge,** 303 S. 3rd St., 208/634-4637 or 800/800-8000, a tidy 60-room motel with a breakfast bar, hot tub, guest laundry, and cable TV.

$100–150

Brundage Bungalows, 308 W. Lake St., 208/634-8573, features cute separate bungalow cabins, some at or just below the low end of this category, each with cable TV and VCR and all

SOUTHWEST IDAHO

but one with microwave and refrigerator. Pets okay; no smoking indoors.

South of the lake on Highway 55 downtown, **Fircrest Condominiums,** 300 Washington St., McCall, ID 83638, 208/634-4528, offers studio, one-, and two-bedroom condos at moderate prices. Pets are OK, and it's within walking distance of many shops, parks, restaurants, and bars.

The beautiful **Mill Park Condominiums** sits on the lakeshore just east of downtown. Each of the eight three-bedroom units offers a great view of the lake and features amenities including a Jacuzzi tub, fireplace, cable TV, microwave, washer and dryer, and private garage and boat dock. Smoking outdoors only; no pets. For reservations and information, call 208/634-4151 or 800/888-7544.

Bear Creek Lodge, P.O. Box 970, McCall, ID 83654, 208/634-3551 or 888/634-2327, www.bearcreeklodge.com, lies a few miles northwest of town at mile marker 149 on Highway 55. While this makes it slightly less convenient than in-town lodgings for enjoying McCall's lively social scene, the location also has its advantages—it's closer to Brundage Mountain and the Little Ski Hill and farther from McCall's noise and bustle. The beautiful modern lodge lies alongside Bear Creek on a scenic 65-acre spread. Accommodations include 13 fireplace-and-refrigerator-equipped guest rooms, as well as separate duplex cabins featuring king beds and in-room hot tubs. In the gorgeous dining room you'll be served a complimentary gourmet breakfast buffet. In the evening the dining room is open to guests and nonguests alike for an extra-charge, multicourse, fine-dining dinner. Those who want to splurge will find room offerings in the next higher price range as well.

Over $250

The former Shore Lodge is now the newly remodeled, semi-private **Whitetail Club,** 501 W. Lake St., 208/634-2244 or 800/657-6464, www.whitetailclub.com. Classy comfort is the rule here, with abundant room to ramble through both the public areas and large guest quarters. Rates for the 77 suites usually start at $275 and two-night minimum stays are the rule on weekends, but many packages are available that might make this place worth a special-occasion splurge, especially for avid golfers. For example, a two-night package with two rounds of golf plus breakfasts runs about $580 for two people in the fall.

Property Management and Reservation Services

To rent one of the numerous condos or cabins in the area, get in touch with Jan Kangas at **Accommodation Services,** 1008 N. 3rd St., P.O. Box 1522, McCall, ID 83638, 208/634-7766 or 800/551-8234. The company handles rental properties in a range of sizes and prices. All include full kitchens; most have fireplaces or woodstoves, as well as washers and dryers. **McCall Vacations,** 805 N. 3rd St., P.O. Box 1506, McCall, ID 83638, 208/634-7056 or 800/799-3880, also lists around 90 rental condos, cabins, and homes at a range of prices. **In Idaho Vacation Services,** P.O. Box 2013, McCall, ID 83638, 800/844-3246, can not only find you a room in McCall or anywhere else in Idaho, they can help you plan what to do when you get here (or there) and make all the arrangements for you.

FOOD
Brewpub
The Pub, 807 N. 3rd St., 208/634-1010, has taken over the old McCall Brewing Company digs. A well-worn wood floor, wood paneling, and an open-beam ceiling seem to bring the outdoors in, a feeling heightened by the tabletops, which feature glassed-over topo maps of the area. Pull yourself up to the long copper bar by the brew kettles and choose from a full line of handcrafted ales. Varieties change with the season, but all are excellent. Try a sampler set to find your favorite. The food here is as good as the beer. You'll find not just the usual deep-fried pub grub but a full lunch and dinner menu. Burgers and salads run around $7, fancier entrées $8–19. Open for lunch and dinner daily. In summer the upstairs deck offers great views, great brews, and great people-watching.

Fine Dining

For upscale American traditional, try **The Mill,** 324 N. 3rd St. (on the west side of Highway 55 up the hill from the lake), 208/634-7683, where you can get steaks, seafood, and a variety of other meat and poultry dinners, most priced between $7 and $30 (although the lobster tail claws its way into your wallet for around $45). Open daily at 6 P.M. The restaurant also has a cocktail lounge.

Ethnic Fare

Italian dinners are the specialty of **Romano's Ristorante,** in the Yacht Club Building, 203 E. Lake St., 208/634-4396. Fresh-made pasta dinners average $9–12; other dishes run $12–18. It's open for dinner Tues.–Sun. from 5:30 P.M. Romano's has lakeside dining in season, as does **Panda Chinese Restaurant,** 317 E. Lake St. in the little McCall Mall, 208/634-2266. Panda's lunch specials run about $6, with dinners mostly $8–13. Mexican-food fans like **Si Bueno,** 339 Deinhard Ln., 208/634-2128, open for lunch and dinner.

Breakfast, Burgers, and Light Bites

If your idea of breakfast is a strong cuppa joe, with or without anything else, head to **Moxie Java,** 312 E. Lake St., 208/634-3607. Enjoying a prime location at the busiest corner in town, it's right across the highway from the Hotel McCall and just a short stroll from the lakeshore. Moxie's, a Boise-based chain, is a good place to hang out with a high-test bean brew, reading the paper, chatting with a friend, or watching the goings-on out on the street. A java-embellished version of Claude "French Roast" Monet's *Giverny* water lilies graces the walls. Another good bet for coffee is **Common Ground Cafe,** 303 E. Colorado St., 208/634-2846, which also sells CDs and offers Internet access.

For a full breakfast, head for the **Pancake House,** 209 N. 3rd St. (Highway 55 at the south end of town), 208/634-5849. In addition to pancakes, the place serves homemade cinnamon rolls, omelettes and other egg dishes, and burgers and sandwiches for lunch.

The **McCall Bakery/Sour Dough Lil's Deli,** 112 N. 3rd St., 208/634-2750, offers coffee, doughnuts, muffins, turnovers, croissants, and bagels in the morning, as well as delicious deli sandwiches for lunch. Open Mon.–Sat. 6 A.M.– 5 P.M. Locals say the best veggie burger in town is at **Bryan's Burger Den,** 600 3rd St., 208/634-7964, open for breakfast, lunch, and dinner.

Lardo's, 600 Lake St., 208/634-8191, is a McCall institution. The rambling joint on the west side of town offers a big wooden bar serving microbrews and a restaurant cooking up burgers, sandwiches, salads, and pastas ($7–12) for lunch and dinner daily. You can order more substantial steak, seafood, and chicken dinners for around $10–22. In summer a plant-filled outdoor deck makes a great spot to take a break from the action.

INFORMATION AND SERVICES

Information

The **McCall Area Chamber of Commerce** is at 102 N. 3rd St., P.O. Box 350, McCall, ID 83638, 208/634-7631 or 800/260-5130, www .mccall-idchamber.org. For Payette National Forest recreation information, try the Supervisor's Office at 800 W. Lakeside Ave., P.O. Box 1026, McCall, ID 83638, 208/634-0700; the **McCall Ranger District,** 102 W. Lake St., McCall, ID 83638, 208/634-0400; or, for the east side of the forest, the **Krassel Ranger District,** 500 N. Mission St., P.O. Box 1098, McCall, ID 83638, 208/634-0600.

Transportation

Salmon Air, 208/756-6211 or 800/448-3413, flies between Boise and McCall each weekday ($108 one-way or $172 roundtrip per person). **McCall Aviation,** 208/634-7137 or 800/992-6559, flies rafters, backpackers, anglers, and guest-ranch customers into the backcountry just about anywhere in Idaho.

EXPLORING THE BACKCOUNTRY

McCall is surrounded on three sides by the Payette National Forest, which offers some 2,000 square miles of prime hiking, biking, and horseback-riding country. Pick up a map from the office of the **McCall Ranger District,** 102 W. Lake St., McCall, ID 83638, 208/634-0400.

Burgdorf Hot Springs

This natural hot springs resort, c/o General Delivery, McCall, ID 83638, 208/636-3036, makes a scenic and relaxing day trip from McCall. Take Warren Wagon Road off Highway 55 at the west end of McCall, and follow it north—past Payette Lake, and past Upper Payette Lake. The USFS **Upper Payette Lake Campground** (20 sites, fee) lies on the shore of the lake and offers a boat-launching ramp. Continuing up the highway, you'll pass thousands of acres of lodgepole pines charred in the fires of 1994. Eventually you'll come to the end of the pavement at the junction with FR 246, the road into the hot springs. In winter, the snowplows clear no farther, so you'll have to ski or snowmobile the rest of the way. Turn left on FR 246 and follow it two miles to the hot springs.

The resort has been around since 1865, and the current owners and managers are in the process of restoring an old hotel and several creaky dilapidated cabins on the property. The restored cabins are very rustic—no electricity but lots of character—and rent for $25 per adult, $7.50 per child 5–13. The large, beautiful 50- by 75-foot hot-springs pool has rustic log sides and a sand bottom. It's about five feet deep and fed by a constant flow of 104°F spring water. Admission to the pool is $5 adults, $2.50 kids 5–13. A bonus for wildlife watchers: across the road from the resort is a big open meadow where in summer a large herd of elk comes to browse in the early evening. If you're lucky you might spy a moose here as well. It's a popular show; you'll find the dirt road to the hot springs lined with parked cars and folks peering through binoculars at the numerous animals.

Camping is available right next door at the USFS **Burgdorf Campground** (six sites, free).

Secesh

If instead of turning down the spur to Burgdorf you continue east on Forest Highway 21, you'll come to Secesh, where prospectors still try their luck at hydraulic mining along the Secesh River.

Short for Secessionist, the river's name came by way of Confederate sympathizers among the Civil War–era miners here. Cabins line the river, but the only services in "town" are at **Secesh Stage Stop,** three miles east of the Burgdorf turnoff, 208/636-6789, where you can get a first-rate home-cooked meal in a homey atmosphere. So homey, in fact, you'll feel like you're eating in a stranger's house. Have no fear, the strangers are friendly.

Three miles farther you'll come to FR 378, a short spur that leads to the USFS **Chinook Campground** (nine sites, fee), where you can try your luck fishing in the Secesh or don your pack and head up to Loon Lake on Trail 081.

Warren

Dedicated explorers can continue yet farther east on Forest Highway 21 to the old gold-mining town of Warren, which in the boom days supported more than 2,000 people. According to the Payette National Forest's walking-tour guide to the historic town, "except for occasional bar fights, Chinese tong wars, highway robberies, and a huge 1904 business-district fire, Warren was considered a relatively calm mining camp." Today a handful of century-old buildings still stand, including a former hotel, saloon, and assay office.

If time gets away from you in your explorations of the town, and you don't want to drive back to McCall in the dark, call **Backcountry B&B,** P.O. Box 77, Warren, ID 83671, 208/636-6000. Inside you'll find a rec room with a pool table and TV. Outside you'll find miles and miles of wide-open country for snowmobiling, cross-country skiing, hiking, fishing, or whatever else you might fancy. The B&B ($50–100) is open year-round, but the roads aren't plowed this far, so you might have to fly or snowmobile in. For more Warren information, contact the **McCall Ranger District,** 102 W. Lake St., P.O. Box 1026, McCall, ID 83638, 208/634-0400.

East of Warren out FR 340 lies the remote USFS **Shiefer Campground** (four sites, free), a great place for isolated fishing on the South Fork Salmon River. At this point you're 77 road miles from McCall.

Camping

In addition to the Payette National Forest campgrounds already listed, several others lie to the east and northwest of McCall. **Kennally Creek Campground** (14 sites, fee) offers a horse-unloading ramp and hitching rails at the Kennally Lakes trailhead. Take Highway 55 south from McCall a little over 10 miles, then turn east on FR 388 and follow it 19 miles to the campground.

Three more campgrounds are accessed via Lick Creek Road (Forest Highway 48), which begins east of Ponderosa State Park. **Lake Fork Campground** (nine sites, fee) is nine miles east of McCall, **Ponderosa Campground** (14 sites, fee) lies along the Secesh River 31 miles from

McCall, and **Buckhorn Bar Campground** (10 sites, fee) is on the South Fork Salmon River beneath Sixmile Ridge—continue past Ponderosa Campground and bear right at two forks, first following Forest Highway 48, then turning off onto FR 674.

Northwest of McCall, take Highway 55 past the turnoff to Brundage and turn right on FR 453 to reach **Last Chance Campground** (23 sites, fee). Or do turn up to Brundage and continue past it to **Grouse Campground** (six units, fee) on Goose Lake, or a dozen miles farther to **Hazard Lake Campground** (12 sites, fee), which is near good hiking on the Lava Ridge National Recreation Trail.

Highway 21: The Ponderosa Pine Scenic Byway

If you follow Warm Springs Avenue east from downtown Boise, you'll eventually find yourself on Highway 21, designated by the state as the Ponderosa Pine Scenic Byway. A scenic route it is indeed. You'll pass many big, beautiful ponderosa pines, skirt the old Boise Basin Mining District, climb for a while alongside the South Fork Payette River, then round Cape Horn into Stanley at the foot of the Sawtooths. It's 131 winding miles between Boise and Stanley.

The drive is interesting in a couple of other ways as well. The Lowman Complex fires of 1989 charred 72 square miles and destroyed 26 buildings in and around Lowman. The summer of 1994 was also a bad fire season throughout the West; in the Idaho City area, the Star Gulch and Rabbit Creek fires on the southeast side of Highway 21 blackened more than 100,000 acres of forest. Many interpretive points along the highway discuss the fires and the subsequent regeneration of the forest.

In addition, several stretches of the narrow highway cling to precipitous mountainsides that frequently send down snowslides in winter and rockslides in spring and early summer. When things get bad, road crews close the highway. You'd be wise to check the Idaho Department of Transportation's 24-hour road conditions re-

port, at 208/336-6600 or 888/432-7623 (in Idaho), before setting out.

To find out more about the sites along Highway 21, pick up an audio-tape tour from one of the ranger stations en route. For southbound travelers, that's the Stanley ranger station, on Highway 75 three miles south of Stanley, 208/774-3000. Northbound travelers can pick up a tape in Boise at the Idaho Department of Parks and Recreation office, 5657 Warm Springs Ave., 208/334-4199, or at the Boise National Forest Supervisor's Office, 1249 S. Vinnell Way, 208/373-4100; in Idaho City at the Idaho City Ranger District, on Highway 21 west of town, 208/392-6681; or in Lowman at the Lowman Ranger District, 7359 Hwy. 21 east of town, 208/259-3361.

Arrowrock Reservoir and Middle Fork Boise River

Coming up Highway 21 from Boise, at the upper end of Lucky Peak Reservoir, a turnoff to the right (FR 268) leads along the northern arm of Lucky Peak Reservoir to Arrowrock Dam. Beyond the dam, the road follows the north shore of Arrowrock Reservoir to its inlet and continues up the Middle Fork of the Boise River all the way to the old mining town of Atlanta, at the foot of the Sawtooths. It's a long, long way both to Tipperary and Atlanta, along often bumpy washboard road.

Numerous free Boise National Forest campgrounds are strung out along the route. Heading upstream, these include **Cottonwood** (three sites), **Willow Creek** (10 sites), **Badger Creek** (five sites), **Troutdale** (four sites), and **Ninemeyer** (eight sites). For more information on the campgrounds, contact the **Mountain Home Ranger District,** 2180 American Legion Blvd., Mountain Home, ID 83647, 208/587-7961.

IDAHO CITY

After gold was discovered here in 1862, prospectors came flooding in seeking a share of the wealth. Many found it. More gold was mined from the mountains of this area than from all of Alaska. Along with the miners came gamblers, ladies of the evening, lawmen, and ne'er-do-wells. Looking at Idaho City today, it's hard to imagine that for a while this was the biggest city in the Northwest. By 1864 some 20,000 people inhabited the area, with Idaho City the booming hub. Today the town's population is around 300, and the surrounding area—once full of mining camps—now holds many more ghosts than people.

Historical Sights

Wandering through town on the many wooden sidewalks will take you past one historic "first" after another. Among them: the 1863 building where the *Idaho World*—Idaho's oldest newspaper—was first published; the 1864 **Idaho Territorial Penitentiary,** a handhewn log hoosegow that once held the killer of Idaho City's first marshal; the 1865 **Boise Basin Mercantile,** Idaho's first general store; and the 1867 **St. Joseph's Catholic Church,** successor to an 1863 church that was the state's first Catholic church for white settlers. Out past the west end of town is **Pioneer Cemetery.** Of the first 200 men and women buried there, it's said only 28 died of natural causes. To find out more about the town's Wild West history, visit the **Boise Basin Historical Museum,** Wall and Montgomery Sts., featuring old photos, mining tools, and other artifacts and memorabilia.

Boise Basin Loop

Several old mining camps lie northwest of town in the Boise Basin, once the richest goldfield in Idaho history. You can make a loop trip past several of them in your Buick or, if you're ambitious, on your mountain bike. From Idaho City, take FR 307 up Slaughterhouse Gulch and over the divide down to Grimes Creek. The creek is named for George Grimes, who discovered gold here in 1862 and was killed the same year by someone who wanted it. Turn right on FR 382 and continue a couple of miles to **Centerville,** also founded in 1862 and named for its location halfway between Idaho City and Placerville. A bit farther down the road is **Pioneerville,** another important early mining camp. When you reach Route 17 turn left, head west to Garden Valley, and turn south again on Alder Creek Road (FR 615). Follow this road to **Placerville,** founded by miners from California in December 1862; less than a year later the place boasted a population of 3,200. West of Placerville are **Granite,** site of the basin's first stamp mill, and **Quartzburg,** founded in 1864 around a hardrock mine.

Continuing south from Placerville on FR 307 will take you to New Centerville Junction and on back to Idaho City.

Just between August 1862 and December 1863 the basin yielded more than $6 million in gold dust. By the time the miners were through, they'd reaped a glittering treasure estimated at $250 million. While this loop gives you a good sense of the area's gold-mining boom days, it also reveals the ugly consequences—streambeds obliterated by dredge tailings. You'd be hardpressed to call this a "scenic" drive.

Nordic Skiing

Three Park N' Ski areas lie along Highway 21 between Idaho City and Lowman. Thanks to their proximity to Boise—close enough for a day trip—the areas are the most heavily used and the best groomed in the state Park N' Ski system. Most of the trails are of intermediate level in difficulty. Both traditional and skating tracks are set, usually once a week on Thursday. That puts them in good shape for the weekend. By Wednesday they're usually pretty well thrashed. Park N' Ski permits ($20 a season or $7.50 for three days) are required and sold in Idaho City at Tom's Service, 208/392-4426, and Idaho City Grocery, 208/392-4900.

Eighteen miles north of Idaho City, **Whoop-Um-Up Creek Park N' Ski** offers four miles of marked but ungroomed trails. Two loops are set on the west side of the highway, three on the east side. This is the place to bring Fido, as dogs are not permitted on groomed trails. Another three miles up the highway, **Gold Fork Park N' Ski Area** provides eight miles of marked and groomed trails in loops on both sides of the highway. Finally, 3.5 miles farther north is **Banner Ridge Park N' Ski Area,** where you'll find 16 miles of marked and groomed trails.

The Banner Ridge and Gold Fork systems are connected by a groomed trail, and both trailheads provide access to **Beaver Creek Cabin,** a two-bedroom Forest Service cabin you can rent for $35 a night. Make reservations through the Idaho City Ranger District, P.O. Box 129, Idaho City, ID 83631, 208/392-6681. Telemarkers can also ask at the ranger station for directions to great slopes off the Gold Fork and Banner Ridge systems.

For more information about the Park N' Ski trails, contact the Idaho City Ranger District, west of Idaho City on Highway 21, 208/392-6681. There you can also pick up the brochure *Park N' Ski—Idaho City Area,* which describes all the trails in the three systems.

Accommodations

Under $50: The creaky old **Idaho City Hotel,** 215 Montgomery St., P.O. Box 70, Idaho City, ID 83631, 208/392-4290, was built at the turn of the 20th century. Despite extensive renovations, the hotel's mining camp character has been preserved. Like as not those bumps in the night are the ghosts of grizzled old prospectors, still hell-bent on finding the mother lode. Each of the hotel's five guest rooms has a double bed, phone, cable TV, and private bath with shower. Children under 18 stay free with parents. Across town, the affiliated **Prospector Motel,** 517 Main St., also P.O. Box 70, 208/392-4290, offers six more rooms.

The year-round **Warm Springs Resort,** 1.5 miles southwest of town at 3742 Hwy. 21, P.O. Box 28, Idaho City, ID 83631, 208/392-4437, offers a large campground-and-cabins complex built around a natural artesian warm-springs swimming pool. The pool is heated to 94°F in summer, 97°in winter. Also on the grounds are a volleyball court and horseshoe pits. Day-use swimming costs $5 general, $2.50 ages 2–12. Cabins are available in two sizes, and rates include a couple of swim passes. The 22 RV sites with full hookups run $18, including two swim passes per site. Space in three dry camping areas with no hookups costs $7.50 a site, including up to four swim passes per site. The resort is open May 1 through Labor Day weekend Wed.–Mon. 10 A.M.–10 P.M., the rest of the year Wed.–Sun. noon–9 P.M. Closed Christmas.

Camping

Between Idaho City and Lowman you'll find several Boise National Forest campgrounds. **Grayback Gulch** (12 sites, fee) lies about three miles south of Idaho City on Highway 21. About halfway between Idaho City and Lowman along the highway is a cluster of three fee campgrounds all within a couple of miles of one another: **Ten Mile** (14 sites), **Bad Bear** (eight sites), and **Hayfork** (six sites). Farther north, just past the Whoop-Um-Up Creek Park N' Ski Area, is **Edna Creek** (nine sites, fee).

For more information, contact the **Idaho City Ranger District,** P.O. Box 129, Idaho City, ID 83631, 208/392-6681.

Forest Service Rentals

Three guard stations in the Boise National Forest east of town are available for rent. Closest to Highway 21 is the **Beaver Creek Cabin,** well known to cross-country skiers using the Banner Ridge and Gold Fork Park N' Ski Areas. The cabin sleeps up to six people and costs $30 a night. Well east of the highway in remote hinterlands on the way to Atlanta are the **Barber Flat** and **Deer Park** guard stations. Barber Flat sleeps six and rents for $35 a night. Deer Park sleeps four and costs $30 a night. Both lie along different stretches of the North Fork Boise River.

SOUTHWEST IDAHO

For reservations or more information, contact the **Idaho City Ranger District,** P.O. Box 129, Idaho City, ID 83631, 208/392-6681.

Information

The summers-only **Idaho City Visitor Center,** on the corner of Main Street and Highway 21, 208/392-6040, offers reams of information about the town and the area, as well as a helpful staffperson who can answer your questions. Pick up a walking-tour map here. If you have more questions, try the **Idaho City Chamber of Commerce,** P.O. Box 507, Idaho City, ID 83631, 208/392-4148.

To Atlanta

The old mining town of Atlanta is ensconced at the southern edge of the Sawtooths, a long, long drive east of Idaho City. But then, Atlanta is a long, long drive from anywhere. It's covered under Elmore County in the Southwest Idaho chapter, but the marginally easiest, albeit not the shortest, route to get there begins near the Whoop-Um-Up Creek Park N' Ski Area. From Highway 21, take FR 384 east and south to FR 327; follow FR 327 east and south to FR 268, then FR 268 east into Atlanta.

LOWMAN

The next minuscule burg up the highway is Lowman, where you can turn west toward Garden Valley and Banks, or continue straight toward Stanley. For information about recreation in the Boise National Forest, stop in at the **Lowman Ranger District,** 7359 Hwy. 21, Lowman, ID 83637, 208/259-3361.

Camping

USFS campgrounds in the Lowman area include **Whitewater** (five sites, fee) and **Pine Flats** (27 sites, fee, hot springs), both a short distance west down the Garden Valley Road; **Park Creek** (26 sites, fee), three miles north of Lowman up Clear Creek Road (FR 582); **Mountain View** (14 sites, fee), right in Lowman; and **Kirkham** (16 sites, fee), **Helende** (10 sites, fee), and **Bonneville** (20 sites, fee), all

east of Lowman on Highway 21 heading toward Stanley. Kirkham is right at the roadside Kirkham Hot Springs, while Bonneville is within walking distance of the more secluded Bonneville Hot Springs.

Forest Service Rentals

In winter, Boise National Forest offers two ski-in guard stations for rent. **Warm Springs Guard Station** is near Bonneville Hot Springs, a mile north of Highway 21 at mile marker 91. It sleeps six and is available for $30 a night between November 15 and May 1. The large **Elk Creek Guard Station** lies in gorgeous remote meadowlands west of Cape Horn, on the edge of the Frank Church–River of No Return Wilderness. The complex holds four different rental cabins. Two sleep 2–4 persons for $30 per cabin per night, one sleeps 6–10 for $35, and the fourth could accommodate the Bolivian army, assuming they could scrounge up US$40 for the privilege. The cabins are available Nov. 15–May 15. To reach Elk Creek, continue north on Highway 21 to FR 082, the road to Dagger Falls. Follow the road toward the falls, but at Bruce Meadows, continue straight (west) instead of turning north. Bear right at the next two forks, then continue about 2.5 miles to the station. Elk, deer, and bear (the occasional grizzly sighting has been reported) inhabit the area. For reservations, call the NRRS at 877/444-6777. For more information, contact the Lowman Ranger District, 7359 Hwy. 21, Lowman, ID 83637, 208/259-3361.

GRANDJEAN

A few miles farther up the highway past Bonneville Hot Springs, FR 524 turns off to the east and leads about six miles to Grandjean, named after Emile Grandjean, supervisor of the Boise National Forest from 1906 to 1922. The trailhead here is the back door into the Sawtooth Wilderness.

Recreation

You may see bicycles or cars parked along the shoulder of the road out to Grandjean. Their owners are more than likely enjoying a soak.

The road parallels the South Fork Payette River, where several **hot springs** emanate from the banks.

Affiliated with Sawtooth Lodge is **Sawtooth Wilderness Outfitters,** P.O. Box 81, Garden Valley, ID 83622, 208/259-3408 (summer) or 208/462-3416 (offseason), which offers guided trail rides and horsepack trips into the Sawtooth Wilderness. Trail rides cost $15 an hour, $50 a half day, $85 a full day. Multiday pack trips cost $195 per person per day.

Accommodations

$50–100: Remote **Sawtooth Lodge,** c/o 130 N. Haines, Boise, ID 83712, 208/259-3331 in the Grandjean area or 208/344-2437 from Boise, has been around since 1927, offering rustic but comfortable cabins, RV sites, spectacular views, a sparkling mineral-water swimming pool, a restaurant, and, of course, easy access to the wilderness. Cabin rates don't include meals. RV sites with hookups are available for $15 a night. The lodge is open Memorial Day weekend through mid-October.

Elmore County

MOUNTAIN HOME

You'll be disappointed if you're expecting Mountain Home to be in the mountains. The Elmore County seat lies at an elevation of 3,180 feet on the dry, dusty Snake River Plain. The county has often been plagued by drought.

With farming a shaky prospect, the local economy relies heavily on the presence of Mountain Home Air Force Base, home to the nation's premier air intervention composite wing. As part of its air combat preparedness mission, the 366th Wing trains pilots to drop bombs effectively. Pilots currently use a 100,000-acre training range southeast of Bruneau in Owyhee County, but for years the USAF has been pushing for the establishment of a second range there. That proposal has been opposed at every turn. Wildlife biologists believe the jet noise and small marker charges on the practice bombs will disturb the area's herds of bighorn sheep and pronghorn; the Shoshone-Paiute people of Duck Valley Indian Reservation see the bombing range as an encroachment on their sacred territory. The air force says it's now sending pilots on practice missions to ranges in Nevada, a waste of time and fuel.

The bombing range controversy is a chronic sore spot in these parts, but the 11,500 or so residents of Mountain Home clearly support the air force. The highlight of the town's events calendar is **Air Force Appreciation Day,** held the first Saturday after Labor Day. The event features a fly-by, parade, barbecue, and entertainment. For more information, call the Mountain Home Chamber of Commerce at 208/587-4334.

Accommodations

$50–100: Two upscale chain motels lie right off I-84 at Exit 95. **Best Western Foothills Motor Inn,** 1080 Hwy. 20, 208/587-8477 or 800/528-1234, offers 76 rooms. Its outdoor heated pool is open seasonally. Among other amenities are a spa, sauna, and several premium cable-TV channels. A couple of doors north is **Sleep Inn,** 1180 Hwy. 20, 208/587-9743 or 800/753-3746, where rates include a continental breakfast.

Camping

The most reliable private campground in town is the **Mountain Home KOA,** 220 E. 10th N., 208/587-5111, which has a laundry, rec room, playground, and showers. Its 50 spaces rent for $20 (tents) or $35 (RVs). But Mountain Home is so close to great public-land camping that unless you particularly need to be right in town, there's no point in camping there. Fifteen miles south of town is **Bruneau Dunes State Park** with good camping, while the mountains to the north of town are chock-full of Forest Service campgrounds.

Information and Services

The **Desert Mountain Visitor Center** is at the south side of I-84, Exit 95, at 2900 American Legion Blvd., 208/587-4464. The center's staff dispenses bundles of brochures and information about the area. Hours are 9 A.M.–5 P.M. daily in

SOUTHWEST IDAHO

summer; 10 A.M.–4 P.M. in winter. The **Mountain Home Chamber of Commerce** is at 205 N. 3rd E., 208/587-4334. For Boise National Forest recreation information, stop by the office of the **Mountain Home Ranger District,** 2180 American Legion Blvd., 208/587-7961.

Greyhound Bus Lines stops at the Conoco station at 495 N. 2nd E., 208/587-3416.

NORTH TOWARD ATLANTA

Little Camas Reservoir

Highway 20 starts climbing as soon as you head north out of Mountain Home, and it's not long before the temperature starts to drop. Right along the highway you'll soon come to Little Camas Reservoir, somewhat overshadowed by its bigger neighbor, Anderson Ranch Reservoir, to the north, but nevertheless a beautiful quiet place for fishing or just relaxing. At the end of the road on the north side of the lake, look for **Fort Running Bear RV Park/Resort,** P.O. Box 909, Mountain Home, ID 83647, 208/653-2493. The name may be a little kitschy, but the park is beautiful and well maintained. It's a membership-based park, but facilities are available to nonaffiliated travelers on a short-term basis (like a night or two per year). For nonmembers, one of the 76 sites costs $20 a night, including hookups. Cabins, with satellite TV no less, are also available for under $50. Amenities include a hot tub, pool, rec room, minigolf, laundry, and showers.

Anderson Ranch Reservoir Recreation Area

Southwest Idaho anglers come to this expansive reservoir year-round to fish for kokanee, chinook salmon, rainbow trout, and smallmouth bass. In addition, the **South Fork Boise River** below the dam offers blue-ribbon trout fishing. Water-skiing is popular on the reservoir in summer—you'll find several boat-launching ramps around the lake—as is snowmobiling in winter. Two different roads traverse the east and west shores. To reach the west shore, turn off Highway 20 on FR 134 and you'll soon drop precipitously down to the dam. The road crosses the dam and continues north up the west side of the reservoir.

Fall Creek Resort and Marina, HC 87 Box 85, Fall Creek, ID 83647 (winter mailing address: c/o 6633 Overland, Boise, ID 83709), 208/653-2242, lies at the Fall Creek inlet to the reservoir, eight miles up the west shore from the dam. This is the area's newest resort and a beautiful spot to hole up in. The warm and spacious lounge and restaurant provide views of the cove and the mountains; a downstairs fitness area features a sauna, spa, and exercise equipment. The marina rents paddle boats ($6.50 per hour), sells marine fuel, and maintains a small store for groceries, tackle, and marine supplies. Rooms are available (in the $50–100 category). RV sites cost $10 per day with water and electricity hookups (there's a dump station at the marina); note that the RV facilities are primarily for day use—if you stay overnight you're charged for two days. Other facilities include a game room, gift shop, boat ramp and moorage, and shower rooms.

Continuing up FR 113, the road climbs to beautiful wooded tableland before descending to the lake's main inlet at the little town of **Pine.** Here FR 113 joins the main road along the east shore. No boat rentals are available in the Pine area. **Pine Resort,** 208/653-2323, offers RV sites with full hookups for $15 a day, as well as a gift shop, laundromat, bar, and a café open for three meals a day. **Nester's,** 208/653-2222, sells groceries and fishing tackle and offers six motel rooms ($50–100).

To reach the east shore, continue east on Highway 20 three miles past Little Camas Reservoir and turn left onto FR 152; follow that road down to Forest Highway 61 and make a left. This side of the reservoir is busier than the more remote southwest area where Fall Creek Lodge is. **Deer Creek Lodge,** HC 87 Box 615, Pine, ID 83647, 208/653-2454, offers a café (serving three meals a day year-round), accommodations (under $50), RV sites ($15 a night with hookups), and a few tent sites ($4.50 a night). About two miles north of Deer Creek Lodge you'll meet the west shore road at Pine.

Johnson's Bridge Hot Springs

Forest Highway 61 crosses the South Fork Boise River at Johnson's Bridge, where you'll no doubt see many cars parked along the north side. On the east bank of the river, just downstream from the bridge, a hot spring sends toasty water flowing down into riverside pools suitable for soaking. It's a popular spot with area campers and usually crowded.

Trinity Springs

The crystal-pure water of Trinity Springs flows out of the ground here at 25 gallons a minute after percolating down out of the Sawtooths over the course of 16,000 years. The mineral-rich elixir is bottled here by Trinity Springs Ltd., 208/653-2363, and sold nationwide as a natural dietary supplement. (You won't see the word "water" anywhere on the bottle.) The folks here are friendly and interested in promoting a health-conscious, environmentally friendly way of life. If you can give them a day or so notice, they'll be happy to host you for a tour and free sample. It's worth it just to see the architecturally exquisite bottling facility.

Trinity Mountains

An alpine gem in southern Idaho, the Trinity recreation area holds craggy peaks and numerous small lakes that often remain snowbound into August. Trinity Mountain, elevation 9,451 feet, crowns the area, providing panoramic views of the Sawtooths and Smoky Mountains to the northeast, and the Snake River Plain and Owyhee Mountains to the southwest. If you make it all the way up to the Forest Service fire lookout on top—the highest lookout in the Boise National Forest—say hello to fire spotter John Thornton for me. John hosted me one evening as we watched an amazing hours-long light show of lightning strikes over the Owyhees. Nice.

This is great mountain-biking country. Forest Roads weave through pine woods, aspen groves, and wildflower-filled meadows. One of the best hiking/backpacking trails in the area is the **Rainbow Basin Trail** (Trail 1174). The trail begins at Big Trinity Lake Campground and meanders south for about four miles past short spur trails to nine different alpine lakes holding rainbow and cutthroat trout. It's open to pedestrians only.

Big Trinity Campground (15 sites, fee) lies at the end of FR 129E off FR 129. Other USFS campgrounds in the vicinity include **Little Trinity Campground** (three sites, free), **Big Roaring Campground** (10 sites, fee), and **Little Roaring Campground** (four sites, free). All the campgrounds are open July–Sept. For a bit more comfort, consider renting the Forest Service's **Big Trinity Guard Station.** The cabin sleeps six and rents for $30 a night July 15–Sept. 30. For reservations call NRRS, 877/444-6777. For more information on the guard station or the campgrounds, contact the Boise National Forest's **Mountain Home Ranger District,** 2180 American Legion Blvd., Mountain Home, ID 83647, 208/587-7961.

To reach Trinity Mountain and the Trinity Lakes, take Fall Creek Road (FR 129) north from Fall Creek Lodge on the west side of Anderson Ranch Reservoir, or take Trinity Creek Road (FR 172) west off Featherville Road (Route 61) just south of Featherville.

Featherville and Points East

Featherville is a small Old West–style enclave at the confluence of the small Feather River and the big South Fork of the Boise River. The town is marred by the hideous dredge tailings down on the river. FR 227 heads east out of town and follows the South Fork of the Boise up to its headwaters. Along the way are numerous hot springs and USFS campgrounds, at least one of each is guaranteed to match your style. The following sites are listed from west (Featherville) to east (Big Smoky Creek).

Four small campgrounds (all $2 per vehicle) appear in rapid succession within the first seven miles from Featherville. **Abbott Campground** (seven sites) comes first, followed closely by the like-sized **Chaparral Campground.** A mile and a half farther is five-site **Bird Creek Campground,** followed a couple of miles later by five-site **Willow Creek Campground.** The spur into Willow Creek Campground continues farther up to little-used **Willow Creek Hot Springs.**

Baumgartner Campground, a dozen or so miles from Featherville, is the main destination for most of the campers headed up the South Fork. John Baumgartner was a local miner who died in 1941 and left his mining claims to the federal government for a park. This campground is the result. The big attraction here is the Forest Service–developed hot-springs pool—a deluxe, improved, concrete-lined number. In years past, the pool was a favorite party spot for the area's incorrigible youth, who would come and do the age-old rowdy-teen-beer thing. The Forest Service now closes the pool at 10 P.M. to inhibit such socially unacceptable behavior. Speaking of which, swimsuits are mandatory.

Sites here cost $10 for single-vehicle sites, $20 for double-size, Twinnebago sites; 17 are reservable through NRRS, 877/444-6777. The large, 30-site campground lines the river amid groves of majestic ponderosa pines. A short nature trail starting near the hot pool loops across the hillside above the creek; signs explain aspects of the area's natural history along the way.

Continuing east up the South Fork Boise, you'll pass swampy and unappealing Lightfoot Hot Springs along the shoulder of the road, and continue a while longer to **Bounds Campground.** The 12 sites here cost $6 a night.

Just past Bounds campground you'll come to the private cabins of the Big Smoky area. Here you'll find a Forest Service guard station, as well as Trapper's Inn—a store with ice, bait, and other necessities of life in these parts.

The road forks here. FR 227 crosses Big Smoky Creek and makes its way out of the mountains down to Fairfield (see Fairfield and Vicinity, under North of the Snake River in the South-Central Idaho chapter) or Ketchum (see Ketchum and Sun Valley in the High Country chapter). Continuing straight (FR 072) takes you to **Canyon Transfer Camp,** which has six campsites ($4 per night) with picnic tables and grills, along with facilities for equestrians, but is otherwise unremarkable on its face. Its hidden attribute, however, makes it a fitting grand finale to your sojourn up the river. The campground does double duty as the trailhead for the level, three-mile trail to **Skillern Hot Springs,** where the springs pour in a natural hot waterfall down a cliff, into a cliffside pool.

Over to Atlanta

If you go straight at Featherville instead of veering east, you'll mark yourself as a true adventurer: you'll be headed for the old mining town of Atlanta. You've got your choice of two routes at this point. **Phifer Creek** is the easier and longer of the two, and if you're headed to Atlanta after coming down from the Trinities, this is the road you'll be on. **James Creek** is a lot shorter, but steeper and more demanding. The decision point—in other words, the road junction—is at the ghost mining town of **Rocky Bar.** The right fork is the James Creek route, the left goes via Phifer Creek.

ATLANTA

Although prospectors discovered precious metals around Atlanta in the 1860s, development of the area was hampered by its inaccessibility. Eventually, the logistics problems were solved, and between 1932 and 1936, the Atlanta Mining District held the most productive gold mines in Idaho. Today, only around 40 people live here year-round, which qualifies Atlanta as a ghost town in most people's books. But the setting alone is worth the trip out here. The little village lies at the south end of the Sawtooths, which rise just north of town. Greylock Mountain, elevation 9,317 feet, dominates the skyline, summoning backpackers up into the high reaches of the Sawtooth Wilderness. The wilderness boundary is less than a mile from town.

Atlanta preserves its history in **Community Historic Park,** which holds several pioneer-era buildings, among them the old jail. The town's biggest shindig is **Atlanta Days** in late July, which brings out all the local hermits for a dance, community breakfast, and horseshoes tournament.

Hot Springs

Atlanta is blessed with not one but two hot springs near the center of town. **Atlanta Hot Springs** is up the hill on your right as you drive east from town toward Power Plant Campground. It's basically Atlanta's community bathtub—not a particularly private spot, but skinnydipping is accepted. **Chattanooga Hot Springs** is one of the nicest in the state. It's in a much more secluded spot, unseen from the road, beneath bluffs lining the Middle Fork Boise

River. Here the springs pour out of the bluff in a waterfall, into riverside pools with great views. When you start to get overheated, you're just steps from the cool water of the river. To get to Chattanooga, take a spur road heading north onto a grassy flat just west of Atlanta Hot Springs. Park on the blufftop and descend the steep trail to the springs. Highly recommended.

Accommodations

Under $50: "Fancy" digs are available May 31–Oct. 31 at the USFS **Atlanta Guard Station,** right in "downtown" Atlanta. The cabin sleeps six in relative luxury, as guard stations go; this one has electricity, a living room, woodstove, kitchen with propane stove and refrigerator, an indoor toilet and shower, and indoor drinking water. Such a deal for just $45 a night. For reservations or information, contact the Boise National Forest's **Idaho City Ranger District,** P.O. Box 129, Idaho City, ID 83631, 208/392-6681. In recent years, the cabin has been used for fire crew lodging, so it may not be available every summer.

Though primarily a café, **Beaver Lodge,** 208/864-2132, also offers several rooms for rent, although they usually fill up early with long-term renters who take them for the whole summer.

$150–250: It seems **Pinnacle Peaks Sawtooth Lodge,** P.O. Box 39, Atlanta, ID 83601, 208/864-2168, was originally the private retreat of Herman Coors, the rowdy black sheep of the Coors brewing family. Legend has it the family set him up out here in the boondocks to keep him out of their hair, and that his Prohibition-era parties were wild. The 500-acre spread was bought by Boise merchant Alva Greene in 1965. Greene rebuilt the place over the course of a decade, turning it into a 17,000-square-foot, 18-room luxury inn. Today, Pinnacle Peaks is aimed mostly at family reunion and retreat groups of 10 or more people. If you have a group that size, you can swim in the retreat's hot-spring-heated pool or hot tub; hike, fish, mountain-bike, or cross-country ski; play tennis, volleyball, or horseshoes; or rent an ATV, horse, or snowmobile to explore the surrounding mountains. Rates include all meals; call for details.

Camping

Two USFS campgrounds are in the area. **Riverside Campground** is closest to town and offers seven sites, while **Power Plant Campground** is down the road toward the trailhead and offers 25 sites. Both are free.

Food

In addition to the Beaver Lodge Cafe, food is available at the **Whistle Stop Tavern,** 208/864-2157, a combination bar and grocery store that, according to proprietor Jim Sayko Jr., sells "at least one of just about everything that anyone who comes up the road needs."

GLENNS FERRY

In 1869, Gus Glenn built a ferry across the Snake River here, putting an end to the dangerous ford that Oregon Trail emigrants had been forced to negotiate. By 1879, enough of a settlement had grown up around the ferry that a post office was established, but it wasn't until the arrival of the Oregon Short Line Railroad in 1883 that Glenns Ferry was formally platted into a town.

Three Island Crossing State Park

Here at one of the most historic sites on the Oregon Trail, settlers faced a decision that could have life-or-death consequences. Reaching this point from the south side of the river, they could either brave the ford of the river here—a dangerous undertaking in high water, but one that led to a shorter, easier route to Fort Boise—or continue down the longer, drier, more sparsely vegetated south side of the river. The three islands in the river served as stepping stones for those who attempted the crossing.

At the 513-acre state park, P.O. Box 609, Glenns Ferry, ID 83623, 208/366-2394, you'll find 101 campsites ($16 a night with hookups, $12 without; $35 camping cabins) with all the usual state park amenities; an Oregon Trail interpretive center featuring many historical exhibits about the trail and the indigenous Shoshone people of this area; and an interpretive path leading down to the river, past visible Oregon Trail wagon ruts. Of particular interest at the beginning of the trail is a beautiful, fully restored Conestoga wagon. Rangers offer nightly naturalist programs between Memorial Day weekend and Labor Day weekend. The big event of the year at the park is Three Island Crossing, the annual reenactment of a pioneer crossing.

Glenns Ferry Historical Museum
This museum in the old 1909 schoolhouse, 200 W. Cleveland, 208/366-7706, holds exhibits that provide insight into the town's early history. It's open June–Sept., Fri.–Sat. noon–5 P.M. Admission is free; donations appreciated.

Carmela Vineyards and Golf Course
Vines, wines, and a nine-hole golf course, all on a scenic stretch of the Snake River—Carmela Vineyards makes a great stop. The winery, 795 W. Madison, 208/366-2313 or 208/366-2539, produces seven varietal wines, and a restaurant serves lunch and dinner daily (brunch on Sunday). Dinners range around $12–20.

Vineyard Greens Golf Course at the winery, 795 W. Madison, 208/366-7531, surrounds the vineyard with a par-34 course stretching 2,369 yards. Greens fees (including a cart, if you want one) are Mon.–Thurs. $12, weekends $17. Hardcore golfers can park the RV at **Vineyard RV Park** across the street. Sites cost $12 a night with hookups, no tents allowed, minimal facilities, no reservations.

Events
In late July, the **Elmore County Fair** comes to the Glenns Ferry fairgrounds. Look for a rodeo, 4-H shows, food, and fun. The fair is but a prelude, however, to the big event of the year. On the second weekend in August, southern Idaho history buffs don pioneer garb, saddle up the wagons, and re-create the **Three Island Crossing** of the Snake River here. The crossing was a pivotal moment for westward emigrants following the Oregon Trail. Some pioneers found low water and an easy crossing. Others risked life and limb to cross during higher water, or chose not to cross in favor of a safer but longer and drier route on the south side of the Snake. As a living history demonstration, this one tops them all. The site today doesn't look much different from the way it did back then, and it's easy to believe yourself transported back in time to the days of the great Overland Migration. Don't miss this one. Admission to the festivities is $4 adults, $1 children. A free shuttle bus operates between town and the park. For more information, contact the Glenns Ferry Chamber of Commerce, 103 E. 1st Ave., P.O. Box 639, Glenns Ferry, ID 83623, 208/366-7345.

Kuna and the Snake River

KUNA
A little more than seven miles south of the Boise bedroom community of Meridian (see earlier in this chapter) lies the town of Kuna (pronounced "Q-na"), a last outpost of civilization before the desolate sage-covered expanse of the Birds of Prey National Conservation Area just to the south. The town retains something of an isolated, frontier feel, a peaceful eddy away from the bustling Treasure Valley corridor to the north. Many of the buildings have a jury-rigged look that speaks of independence from strict building codes and overzealous city planning. You'll find a saddle- and shoe-repair store here that does a brisk business without the added draw of an espresso machine. Farms, ranches, and a winery surround the town, making for a wide-open landscape that effectively derails Kuna from the tourist track. For a good meal, head to **El Gallo Giro,** 482 W. 3rd St., 208/922-5169, a local favorite with friendly servers and authentic Mexican food. It's open from 10 A.M. daily; no smoking on weekends.

Kuna Butte, rising from the plain on the south edge of town, is the remnant of one of the old shield volcanoes that once oozed molten lava across the plain for miles around, filling in the Snake River Canyon and forcing the river's path farther west in the process. Today, with a little imaginative navigating, you can find a gravel road that will lead you up onto the butte, where on a clear day you can see west into Oregon. Although the butte isn't within the Birds of Prey area proper, the birds don't seem to care; I saw a couple of burrowing owls up here during midday.

Three miles west of Kuna off Kuna Road is the award-winning **Indian Creek-Stowe Winery,** 1000 N. McDermott Rd., 208/922-4791, where the Stowe family makes fine varietal wines, including pinot noir, chardonnay, white riesling, white pinot noir, and cabernet sauvignon. Their bestseller is the white pinot, which is sweet and delicious. The winery's tasting room is surrounded by the picturesque, 21-acre vineyard; it's open weekends noon–5 P.M. and by appointment. The winery is not the easiest place to find, partially owing to its odd location right on the Ada–Canyon County line (which makes for some weird addressing anomalies). Coming into Kuna from Boise, turn left at the last T intersection by the visitor information booth, right before downtown; then make an immediate right just across the railroad tracks. Follow this road straight west for about three miles. It starts out designated as Avalon Street and later is renamed Kuna Road. Turn right on McDermott and find the winery a short distance down on your right.

SNAKE RIVER BIRDS OF PREY NATIONAL CONSERVATION AREA

The southern border of Ada County is defined by the Snake River, and the river here and the undeveloped high desert surrounding its banks have been designated the Snake River Birds of Prey National Conservation Area. The chaparral along the riverbank is home to large populations of rodents and small mammals that constitute the prime diet for a variety of birds of prey. Among the raptors permanently residing in or just passing through the reserve are short-eared owls, burrowing owls, northern harriers, kestrels, Swainson's hawks, red-tailed hawks, sharp-shinned hawks, golden eagles, and the largest nesting concentration of prairie falcons in the country.

The NCA boundary is three miles south of Kuna on Swan Falls Road. On your way down to the river—another 16 miles farther—you'll pass a couple of noteworthy sights. **Kuna Cave** is an

red-tailed hawk, one of the inhabitants of the Snake River Birds of Prey National Conservation Area

underground lava tube that isn't easy to find, and unless you're a geology buff particularly fascinated by lava tubes, it isn't worth finding in the first place. Its primary role these days appears to be a party spot for area teens, as evidenced by the graffiti-covered walls and plentiful soda-cup-and-straws litter. If you must, turn right onto Kuna Cave Road and follow it down just past the cows to a turnoff marked by a white sign sporting a black arrow. Head south down this dirt road a couple hundred yards to another turnoff to the left. A short distance away you'll spy a rock ring with a fancy ladder leading down into the hole.

Back out on Swan Falls Road you'll see the raised lava butte of **Initial Point** on the east side of the road. In addition to being a great viewpoint over the vast plain and the Owyhee Mountains to the south, the point is significant in that it marked the starting point for Idaho Territory's first official land survey, begun in 1867. The base meridian for the survey ran due north from here, through what would become the town of— you guessed it—Meridian. It's just a short hike up to the top of the butte, which is a tranquil spot for meditation or a picnic (provided the locals aren't using the adjacent hillside for target practice, as they are wont to do).

The road continues down to the canyon rim and a pullout parking area at **Dedication Point.** A quarter-mile nature trail here leads to the edge of the abyss, and interpretive signs provide information about the various birds of prey, flora, and geology of the area.

The road continues southeast for a moment before making a hairpin turn and dropping precipitously into the canyon, to the road's end at **Swan Falls Dam.** The dam was the brainchild of Colonel William Dewey, a pioneering southwest Idaho entrepreneur who intended to use the hydroelectric power generated at the dam to run an electric railway up to his mine near Silver City. His plan never materialized, but the dam did supply electricity to Murphy and, until World War II, to Silver City as well. The dam, built in 1901, was the first hydroelectric project on the Snake River. A grassy picnic area and restrooms make this a good place for a stop.

For more information on the Snake River Birds of Prey National Conservation Area, contact the BLM Lower Snake River district office at 3948 Development Ave. in Boise, 208/384-3300.

MELBA

West of the Birds of Prey Area, just across the Canyon County line, is the hamlet of Melba. To folks in Melba, Kuna is the Big City and Boise might as well be Manhattan. Melba is the very definition of rural, a small community of farmers and ranchers. A couple of bars serve as town halls. The **Palace Bar & Grill** is famous for the humorous Wino Crossing sign out front, but go instead just down the street to **Cook's 2-Hole Bar,** 313 Broadway, 208/495-9784. Order up a $1 draft and check out the gallery of Western art on the walls. That's mustachioed proprietor Lee Cook and his pal Lefty in the photo behind the bar. Here you'll run into a colorful cast of locals and maybe some "out-of-towners," like cowboys Sky and Dennis, over from their 1,200-acre spread outside Murphy (across the river in Owyhee County) because it's Monday and the bar in Murphy is closed. Outside you'll find a sideyard beer garden with horseshoe pits and a barbecue; it's party central on summer weekends and holidays.

CELEBRATION PARK

South of Melba on the Snake River and butting up against the western edge of the Birds of Prey Area is Canyon County's Celebration Park, 5000 Victory Lane, 208/495-2745. The park's site is historic in a number of ways. Some 15,000 years ago, Lake Bonneville broke its banks and sent a veritable tidal wave rushing down the Snake River Plain. The rocks that were picked up, tumbled smooth, and set back down by the raging waters are collectively known as melon gravel; here at Celebration Park is an enormous melon-gravel field.

Thousands of years after the flood, Archaic Indians wintered in the area and doodled all over the melon gravel, creating a huge outdoor art gallery of petroglyphs—artworks etched into the stone. Many of them show similar themes; some have been interpreted, but the meaning of most remains a mystery. When the park was in the process of opening in 1989, Canyon County officials called in representatives of Idaho's Native American tribes to see if any of them recognized the artwork as belonging to their respective tribe's cultural tradition. Each tribe had the same answer: "This rock art is important and must be preserved, but we can't identify it as belonging to our ancestors." Guesstimates date the earliest human habitation in the area to between 7,500 and 12,500 years ago. In addition to the artwork, other structures you might see among the rocks include primitive rock ovens and game walls.

Later, early pioneers settled here and did some of their own rock carvings. A few of these obviously "modern" representational works can be found scattered through the park.

Finally, the park preserves the historic Guffey Bridge, which was built in 1897 to carry Colonel William Dewey's Boise, Nampa and Owyhee Railroad across the Snake River. Dewey had dreams of running the railroad all the way to his mine near Silver City, but the tracks never made it past Murphy. Today the rails are gone, and the lovingly restored bridge is open only to pedestrians, equestrians, and bicyclians. You can use the bridge to access trails on the river's south side. There the town of Guffey once boasted a restaurant, hotel, and post office. No evidence of the town remains today.

A small visitor center here is staffed by naturalists who can answer your questions about this unique area. Guided walks are generally available daily 10 A.M.–2 P.M., and they're well worthwhile, since it's hard to find—much less understand—all the rock art on your own. For those unwilling or unable to explore the park on foot, everything in the park can be seen on a CD-ROM disc on the visitor center's computer. Adjacent to the center are a garden of indigenous flora, an archery range of sorts where you can practice throwing spears with an ancient atlatl, and a small campground offering primitive riverside sites ($5; restroom only, no hookups; three-day limit). The day-use-only fee is $2 per vehicle.

GUIDED BIRDS OF PREY AREA TOURS

While it's possible to experience the Birds of Prey Area on your own, either by boating down the river or hiking through the canyon and along the rim, **Birds of Prey Expeditions/Whitewater Shop River Tours,** 4519 N. Mountain View Dr., 208/327-8903, www.birdsofpreyexpeditions.com, offers expert, interpretive half- or full-day tours of the preserve. Owner Steve Guinn was drawn into his role as one of the Birds of Prey Area's chief spokesmen almost by accident. A former whitewater guide, he bought out a rafting company that had a permit to float the Snake River through the raptor nesting grounds. Boise resident Morley Nelson—a legendary raptor expert and the man most responsible for the establishment of the preserve—heard that Steve had a permit for that section of the river and went to him to arrange a float down the river for 135 members of the National Audubon Society. During the course of the trip, Morley's passion for the birds rubbed off on Steve. The two formed an informal partnership in their efforts to protect the area's raptor residents for future generations. That was almost 20 years ago.

Eventually, Steve got out of the whitewater business altogether and now focuses solely on providing instructional trips through the Birds of Prey area. Morley joins Steve's trips a couple of times a year, providing his personal expertise on the magnificent birds and their habitat. As Steve says of Morley: "He's an eagle trapped in a man's body." If you can get in on a "Morley trip," don't miss it.

Steve starts the full-day tours by giving a short explanation of the area's ecology. He explains the workings of the food chain—how the various species of grasses feed the rodents and other small mammals that feed the hawks, falcons, eagles and other birds of prey. Then he takes you on a bus tour of the area, off the beaten path to hidden nests and favored raptor hunting grounds. After lunch, you'll board a motorized pontoon boat for a cruise up the placid Snake River through the heart of the nesting grounds. All along the way, Steve adds tidbits of historical and cultural information, providing an integrated overview of the land and its significance.

In addition to the regular paying customers, Steve takes more than 1,500 school kids through the area in late April and May, introducing them to the region's beauty and importance. He also joins others in efforts to rehabilitate and release injured birds found throughout southwestern Idaho. Clearly, for Steve the preserve has become as much a mission as a business.

The trips cost around $60 for a half day, $100 for a full day including lunch. Various special tours are occasionally offered; call for updates on schedules and prices.

South of the Snake River

On a lonely stretch of blacktop near Three Creek, sunset fast approaching, I pull the car onto the shoulder and shut off the engine. In front of me, the desolate desert of Owyhee County rolls out to the horizon, silent, empty, lifeless. Or is it? I get out of the car and see something move. It's a short-eared owl, gliding silently just over the top of the sagebrush.

As I take a walk down the middle of the deserted two-lane highway, the sky is working its way through the Crayola box: goldenrod, orange, peach, salmon, mauve, coral, lavender, cranberry, and that delicious, just-before-twilight plum. When I get back to the car, the last faint glimmers of daylight have given way to a dark, moonless night. Before I start the engine, I turn my attention one last time out onto the desert—to the sage, the sand, the silence . . . the silence . . . the silence suddenly broken—no, smashed—by a loud and chilling racket, a Hallelujah Chorus of coyotes. By the sound of it, they're not more than 30 or 40 feet away, out there in the darkness. Had they been watching me the whole time? Their song is over in less than a minute, just a quick overture to welcome the night. The silence returns, but now I can imagine the multitudes of lives being played out in the "empty" landscape of Owyhee County.

MARSING AND VICINITY

Marsing (pop. 940) is one of Owyhee County's "big" cities. The south side of the Snake River here has long been a strategic location on the trade and settler's route connecting the bustling Treasure Valley to the north with Nevada and California to the south. Before the river was spanned in 1921, two different cable ferries—one upstream, one downstream of today's Marsing—hauled travelers back and forth. When the bridge's site was being selected, the cities of Nampa and Caldwell vied for it. Nampa won. As soon as the bridge was completed, Marsing was officially established and grew quickly.

Today it's an agricultural center watched over by dramatic Lizard Butte across the river. **Island Park,** on the upriver side of the bridge, offers a grassy area with picnic tables, barbecue grills, and some resident ducks. Anglers might try dropping a line here in hopes of making the acquaintance of a smallmouth bass or two.

The annual **Flower of the Desert Festival** in May is the town's biggest bash. Also in May is **Fishing Day,** followed by a **Fishing Derby** in June. **Sprint boat races** take place on the river here about once a month throughout summer, while a **Holiday Parade** livens up Main Street in December. For a complete schedule of local events and more information about the town, stop by **Marsing City Hall,** 425 Main St., 208/896-4122.

Food

At **The Sandbar River House Restaurant,** 18 Sandbar Ave., 208/896-4124, in a converted house on the riverbank, you'll find more than the usual burgers and Budweiser. Lunch features several sandwiches (averaging $7), while the dinner menu offers prime rib, lamb, buffalo steak, chicken (teriyaki, or sautéed in wine sauce), and seafood. Entrées range around $11–20. The cool, shaded back patio is the place to be in summer, offering views of the river and Lizard Butte. The Sandbar is open Tues.–Sun. for lunch and dinner.

Dinner reservations are recommended. To get there, head toward the river from downtown and make the last left before you get to the bridge (across from Island Park). The restaurant is down a block on the right.

Highway 95 North

Highway 95 North actually starts out heading west from Marsing before turning north toward the Snake River and I-84. About halfway to the little farm town of **Homedale,** Jump Creek cuts down through the Owyhee foothills, forming a spectacular steep-walled canyon where 60-foot **Jump Creek Falls** plunges into a deep pool. It's an idyllic spot for a cooling summer swim.

The site is managed by the BLM. Primitive camping is possible but there are no developed facilities. To get there, take Jump Creek Road south off Highway 95. At the Y just past the high-tension wires, go right. Just a little farther, at the base of a small ridge, go left. At the next Y you can go either way—from there on out, all roads lead to the parking area. An easy trail leads up about a quarter mile to the falls.

Homedale is on the Snake River, and RVers looking for a riverside spot to stop will find the pleasant **Snake River RV Resort,** Rt. 1 Box 1062-200, Homedale, ID 83628, 208/337-3744, just outside town to the southeast. Follow the signs off Highway 95 at Pioneer Road. Don't let the industrial approach throw you; the 50 grassy sites on the river are beautiful. You'll also find a gazebo with picnic tables and a barbecue, a boat ramp, and a bathhouse with restrooms and shower and laundry facilities. The proprietors are very friendly. Site with full hookups costs $15.50 a night for up to two adults and two kids; tenters pay $10.

HIGHWAY 78 TO MURPHY

Givens Hot Springs

Nomadic native peoples had been using the hot springs here for thousands of years when Oregon-bound Milford and Mattie Givens came upon the spot in 1879. The couple immediately abandoned their journey down the dusty Oregon Trail and set up housekeeping. In 1881 they built a home, and in the 1890s, with the help of their four sons, they added a bathhouse. Alas, marital bliss eluded the settlers and they divorced. Mattie stayed in the family home and remarried, this time to Gus Yanke. Gus helped expand the home into a traveler's oasis that eventually included a hotel, a restaurant, an ice-cream parlor, tree-shaded picnic grounds, a barbershop, and a post office. In 1907, a school was established that apparently doubled as a matrimonial service—three of the four Givens boys married girls who came to teach there.

The resort became known throughout the area and was well used by Oregon Trail pioneers, Silver City miners, and residents of the Treasure Valley. The hotel burned down in 1939 and was never rebuilt. In 1952, a new bathhouse was constructed. Although only a small icehouse today remains of Milford and Mattie's handiwork, the resort is still owned by their descendants, who have renovated the property in recent years.

The present bathhouse holds an Olympic-size pool, private soaking tubs, and a small snack bar. Use of the swimming pool costs $5 adults, $4 seniors, $3.50 kids. The soaking tubs rent for $5 an hour per person. A soak and swim pass costs $7.50. Suit rentals are $1, towels $.50. Outside are picnic areas, horseshoe pits, and areas for baseball, volleyball, and fishing on the Snake River. Campsites are available for $15 a night with hookups, $10 without. Those rates are for one or two people; additional adults are $2 each, kids $1 each. Cabins are also available (under $50).

The resort is right on the south side of Highway 78, 11 miles south of Marsing, 208/495-2000. It's open year-round, noon–10 P.M. daily.

The Blue Canoe

Continuing southeast on Highway 78, 2.5 miles past the Walter's Ferry bridge, you'll find another kind of desert oasis. The Blue Canoe restaurant, 208/495-2269, shines like a brightly painted toenail on the dry, sagebrush-covered foot of the Owyhee Mountains. The large menu features prime rib (Fri.–Sat. night) and crawdads from nearby C. J. Strike Reservoir, with most entrées in the $10–20 range. It's open Fri.–Sat. 4–9 P.M., Sun. 11 A.M.–7 P.M.

Murphy

Although Murphy is the Owyhee County seat, it's not the largest town in the county. In fact, it's one of the smallest. In the mining boom days at the turn of the century, Silver City was the county seat. But when metal prices dropped and the mines began to play out, a new site closer to the Snake River was proposed. At that time, Murphy had the county's only railroad terminal, the end of the line for the Boise, Nampa and Owyhee Railroad. Colonel William Dewey had hoped to build an electric continuation of the railroad from Murphy all the way up to his mine near Silver City, to be powered by electricity from the Swan Falls Dam hydroelectric plant he'd built. But the railroad never made it past Murphy. In the meantime, the county's extensive cattle and sheep industries had turned Murphy into the largest livestock-shipping point in the Northwest. It was this fact that secured the county seat for the town in 1934.

Murphy is semifamous for its single parking meter in front of the courthouse. The meter was originally an unsubtle hint by locals to discourage people from parking in front of the courthouse gate. Now the lone meter highlights the fact that this little hamlet could well be the smallest county seat in the country. Tourist facilities are limited; the town has no motels and just one café.

The **Owyhee County Historical Complex,** on Bassey Street one block south of the highway (look for the sign by the courthouse), 208/495-2319, includes several transplanted structures and a small historical research library. Among the historic buildings are a one-room schoolhouse, a homesteader's log cabin, and the old Marsing depot, outside of which sits a Union Pacific caboose. Much of the museum's exhibit space is devoted to the history of the Owyhee mines and includes a re-created stamp mill. Library archives hold microfilmed newspapers dat-

THE OWYHEE MINING WAR

During Silver City's 1860s heyday, two of the most lucrative mines in the area were the Golden Chariot and the Ida Elmore. All hell broke loose when it was discovered that the two mines were working opposite ends of the same vein. Gentlemanly negotiation and even litigation be damned; this was the Wild West. When the shafts of the two companies eventually met, the miners engaged in a full-fledged war deep underground. Shots rang out night and day, as miners fired blindly in the darkness of the mine shafts. The Golden Chariot's manager led an assault against the Ida Elmore shaft; a bullet through the head dropped him in his tracks. The Owyhee County sheriff declined to get involved, saying it wasn't his duty.

Idaho's territorial governor, David W. Ballard, sent a proclamation to both sides ordering them to cease the battle. A settlement was negotiated. But while the settlement may have stopped the armed conflict, it did little to reduce the personal animosity between representatives of the Golden Chariot and the Ida Elmore. This animosity broke out again in violence on the front porch of the Idaho Hotel, with disastrous consequences.

J. Marion More was one of the early bigwigs of Idaho's mining industry and one of the owners of the Ida Elmore. On the evening of April 1, 1868, More went to the Idaho Hotel for dinner. On the porch of the hotel he encountered Sam Lockhart, a representative of the Golden Chariot. The two exchanged words and the situation became tense. More raised his cane as if to strike Lockhart, who drew his gun and fired, hitting More in the chest. More shots were fired—exactly who fired at whom remains a mystery. One of the shots hit Lockhart. More died the next day and was buried in the Boise Basin mining hub of Idaho City. Lockhart lingered until summer before giving up the ghost. Governor Ballard, fearing war would break out again, ordered troops up to Silver City from Fort Boise. Some 95 soldiers and a cannon arrived, but the town was in no mood for further violence. The troops stayed just a few days before returning to Boise.

ing as far back as 1865, as well as more than 4,000 historic photographs of Owyhee County. The museum complex is open year-round Tues.–Sat. 10 A.M.–4 P.M. Admission is free; donations appreciated. On the first weekend each June, the museum sponsors **Outpost Days,** a festival of folk art, cowboy poetry, country music, parades, food, a Saturday night dance, and the event-culminating Horny Toad races.

SILVER CITY

Silver City lies in a draw on Jordan Creek, 6,200 feet high in the Owyhee Mountains. To get here, you'll have to negotiate a narrow winding road for 23 miles up from Murphy. The gravel and dirt road is usually blocked by snow more than half the year, and even in summer it's not recommended for trailers and large RVs. But if you think it's hard getting to Silver City today, just imagine what it was like trying to get here during the town's heyday, roughly 1860–1900. Back then Silver City had a population of 2,500 people, along with some 75 businesses and 300

on the porch of the Idaho Hotel, Silver City

homes. Its prosperity led to its status as the county seat from 1866 until 1934. By 1874, it boasted the first telegraph office and the first daily newspaper—*The Idaho Avalanche*—in Idaho Territory. Today Silver City's population is listed as six. The difference? While modern-day residents are after nothing more than remote relaxation, the boomtown-era residents came for silver and gold.

Accommodations

The **Idaho Hotel,** P.O. Box 75, Murphy, ID 83650, 208/583 4104, is the gathering spot in Silver City. Built in 1863, the hotel was falling down until Ed Jagels bought it in 1972 and brought it back to life. Jagels has passed away, but the hotel is being kept open by his friends, who are doing even more to shore up the aging structure. Go into the saloon, grab a cold one, and find your way across the sloping floor to a table by the back window. Besides microbrews you'd never expect to see in the boonies, the dining room offers snacks, short-order food, and family-style meals with a week's notice.

You can even rent a room here ($40–80). The Ritz it ain't, but the 130-year-old hotel looks a damn sight better than you will at that age, and it's a fun place to stay.

Besides the hotel, the town holds some rental cabins in various price ranges and various states of entropy. And just downhill from town, the BLM oversees a free, primitive 12-site campground along Jordan Creek.

Events

Events in Silver City include the **Owyhee Cattlemen's Association Rendezvous,** on the last weekend of July; the annual poker tournament on Labor Day weekend; and the town's open house in mid-September, when 10 buildings are open to the public (the $10-per-person fee for the open house goes to the watchperson's wages fund).

GRAND VIEW TO BRUNEAU AND VICINITY

Owyhee Uplands National Backcountry Byway

If you're in need of solitude, the Owyhee Uplands National Backcountry Byway might be just the

SOUTHWEST IDAHO

ticket. From east of Grand View, the gravel road loops out behind the Owyhee Mountains, leading back to Jordan Valley, Oregon, or Silver City. Along the way it passes through varied and spectacular high-desert terrain virtually devoid of humans. The gravel road is easily passable in the Oldsmobile from as soon as it dries out in spring through the first snowstorm of late fall. Most of the land surrounding the road is public (BLM), so unless posted otherwise, you can set up your tent anywhere you want. Several creeks along the way provide an ample water supply, but much of this land is used for grazing cattle; make sure to boil or filter the water, or better yet, bring your own.

Heading south out of Grand View you'll pass through arid ranchlands, then quickly leave civilization behind. Soon you'll reach the Owyhee foothills and begin ascending Poison Creek, where you'll find a small BLM picnic area. The road keeps climbing and it won't be long before you'll have a sweeping, eagle's-eye view of the Snake River Plain. Onward and upward, the higher elevation brings new flora—first hills of mountain mahogany, then high tablelands covered in dense juniper forest. Wildflowers brighten the interspersed grassy slopes until well into July. Keep your eyes peeled for wildlife. Mule deer, pronghorn, bighorn sheep, badgers, and coyotes inhabit this broad-brushed landscape, while, looking skyward, you might see golden eagles, red-tailed and ferruginous hawks, northern harriers, and short-eared owls.

The road continues relatively level for miles through beautiful rolling terrain before suddenly dropping down into the canyon formed by the North Fork of the Owyhee River. A small BLM campground along the river here is a great spot to stop for the day and get wet while you explore the area. Upstream, the river rounds a bend to a hidden valley where large gravel bars along the banks make secluded sunning spots. Downstream, the river enters a dramatic gorge with red rock walls rising vertically hundreds of feet above the water.

Continuing past the campground you'll pass through more cattle country. It's open range out here—there are no roadside fences to keep bovines off the road. Drive carefully to avoid inadvertent steak tartare. You'll pass the little ranch called Cliffs and then descend through irrigated farmland and ranchland into Oregon and the turnoff to DeLamar and Silver City (it's marked with a huge sign for the Kinross DeLamar mine). Continuing straight here will take you into Jordan Valley, Oregon, where you can hook up with Highway 95 and head north back into Idaho. If you head to Silver City from here, you'll have good road up to the DeLamar junction, then rougher road for the last eight miles into Silver City. From Silver City, you can descend the north side of the Owyhee Mountains into Murphy. Don't head up this way if the roads are wet. You might make it up to the top, but coming down the other side is steeper, slipperier, and more treacherous.

The length of the byway from Grand View to Jordan Valley is 103 miles, and you can figure on traveling about 35 mph (or less) en route. The road is well marked with directional signs and the special Backcountry Byway route markers, but obviously there are no services along the way, so make sure to top off the tank before you set out. For more information about the route, contact the BLM's Boise Field Office, 3948 Development Ave., Boise, ID 83705-5389, 208/384-3300.

C. J. Strike Reservoir and Wildlife Management Area

Clifford J. Strike was the president of Idaho Power Co. from 1938 to 1948. The dam named after him, built in 1952, backs up 7,500-acre C. J. Strike Reservoir, a popular fishing hole holding bass, bluegill, crappie, perch, catfish, and even the mighty sturgeon. The reservoir and the land surrounding it make up the 12,500-acre C. J. Strike Wildlife Management Area, protected habitat for migratory ducks and geese in winter. The WMA headquarters is near Jack's Creek, 12 miles east of Grand View on Highway 78. Several BLM camping areas are spread along the southern shore of the reservoir. From east to west: **Jack's Creek** Sportsman's Access Area; **Cottonwood** Sportsman's Access Area; and **Cove** campground, with 26 sites, fishing, swimming, and hiking trails. All are free.

Bruneau

Residents of the little town of Bruneau are up in arms over a snail. Seems strange, but it turns out a certain tiny snail unique to these parts is an endangered species, and federal regulations to preserve it are seen by the locals as putting a serious crimp in their lifestyle.

If you pass through town and continue out Hot Springs Road, it eventually turns into Clover-Three Creek Road and leads to a spur road to the **Bruneau Canyon Overlook.** The Bruneau River has sliced a deep gash in the earth here. You can see the river glimmering down at the canyon bottom, but you can't get down to it here. The river is run by rafters and kayakers, who put in southwest of here across the river near Grasmere.

Continuing southeast on Clover-Three Creek Road, you'll pass through the Air Force's Saylor Creek bombing range and end up at the remote outpost of Three Creek, between Murphy Hot Springs and Rogerson.

Bruneau Dunes State Park

One of the state's larger parks, Bruneau Dunes State Park, HC 85 Box 41, Mountain Home, ID 83647, 208/366-7919, encompasses some 4,800 acres of southwestern desert. Two enormous, interconnecting sand dunes—the tallest nearly 500 feet high—rise from the center of the park. Unlike most sand dunes these don't shift much, thanks to prevailing winds that blow in opposite directions for roughly equal amounts of time. The pristine dunes are closed to motor vehicles, but you can hike right up to the top. There you'll find an interesting crater that the two dunes seem to spiral out of, and great views across the Snake River Plain. Kids, and the more childlike adults among us, won't be able to resist

rolling back down the giant sandhills. Various hiking trails lead around the base of the dunes, past a couple of lakes that attract both wildlife and anglers. Another feature of the park is an observatory holding a 25-inch telescope and several smaller scopes. Public stargazing programs are offered on Friday and Saturday at around 9:30 P.M. March–Oct. ($3).

The park holds a grassy, 48-site campground charging the standard state park fees ($16 a night with hookups, $12 without), as well as rental cabins that can sleep up to five people for $35. Inside the small visitor center, you'll find fossils, mounted specimens of species native to the area, and lots of information about how the dunes came to be.

Highway 51 to Owyhee, Nevada

Miles and miles of wide-open sage-covered landscape greet the eye on the long trek down Highway 51 to Nevada. A bar at the outpost of **Grasmere** is good for a cold one on a hot summer day. Near Grasmere, kayakers turn off the highway and head east into the desert, bound for the put-in on the Bruneau River. The Bruneau is run commercially by **Wilderness River Outfitters,** P.O. Box 72, Lemhi, ID 83465, 208/756-3959 or 800/252-6581. Just past **Riddle,** you'll enter the **Duck Valley Indian Reservation,** home to 1,600 members of the Shoshone and Paiute tribes. The reservation's **Mountain View Reservoir** is stocked with rainbow trout; pick up a reservation fishing permit at the tribal headquarters on the Nevada state line. Camping is permitted for a token fee. For more information, call the reservation office at 702/757-3161.

South-Central Idaho

The south-central segment of the Snake River Plain is known as the Magic Valley, thanks to an act of magic that turned a dry, barren desert into the state's breadbasket. When the Oregon Trail pioneers crossed through here, they suffered one of the bleakest stretches yet faced on their westward journey. But in 1894, Congress passed the Carey Act, under which the government gave away enormous tracts of Western desert to those who could irrigate and cultivate it. A small group of visionaries, looking at the big Snake River, knew that if they could find a way to move that water up onto the desert, they could turn south-central Idaho into a garden of Eden. Looking at the region today, it's clear they succeeded.

Massive engineering projects began shortly after the turn of the century. Milner Dam was completed in 1905. Minidoka Dam followed just a year later. Soon several dams backed up the Snake, and a 2,600-mile canal network spread the stored water across the arid, sage-covered plain. Today, south-central Idaho grows most of the state's sugar beets, as well as bumper crops of barley, beans, peas, and potatoes. The town of Burley is known as Idaho's food-processing capital, while the land surrounding Jerome and

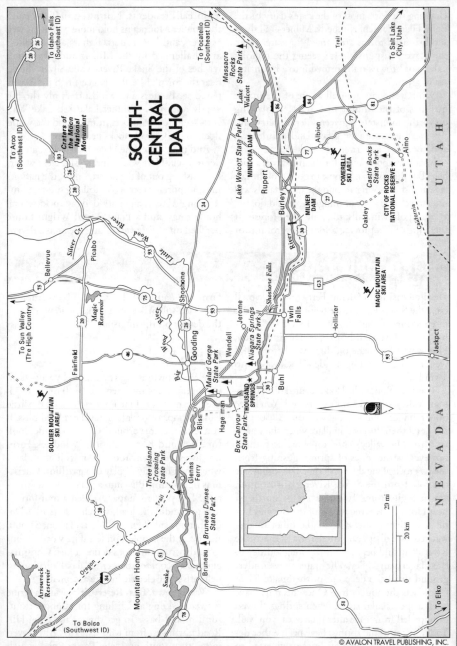

SOUTH-CENTRAL IDAHO

© AVALON TRAVEL PUBLISHING, INC.

Gooding supports most of the state's dairy cattle. Buhl, Filer, Hansen, Kimberly, Milner—all these south-central towns are named for water men, the players responsible for seeing the region's palette of browns transformed into a bountiful sea of green.

While residents are well aware of the magic qualities of their home turf, travelers blasting down the interstate between Glenns Ferry and American Falls see a lot of farmland, a little lava, and not much else. Even the Snake River makes only cameo appearances for the freeway traveler here. But those who take time to get out of the fast lane and start nosing around the hinterlands will find an eclectic array of things to see and do.

South of Twin Falls, the pine-filled forests of the South Hills provide a local playground for Twin Falls residents. Northwest of Twin Falls, the Soldier Mountains hold more woods, as well as rivers and hot springs. Rafters and kayakers are challenged by the Milner and Murtaugh reaches of the Snake River, while Silver Creek, near the town of Picabo, is a certified fly-fisher's paradise. Boaters and windsurfers ply the big windy reservoirs—Milner Lake and Lake Walcott—and rock climbers from around the world flock to the City of Rocks near Almo.

And then there's the Hagerman Valley, a wonder in itself. Here you'll find crystal-clear waterfalls gushing out of the desert; one of the nation's most important archaeological dig sites; an outstanding winery; a gravity-defying rock; several hot springs; and a Frank Lloyd Wright house perched on a cliff overlooking the Snake River.

Hagerman Valley

Heading east from Glenns Ferry on I-84, you'll cross the Snake River twice before arriving at the intersection of Highway 30 at Exit 137. Designated the **Thousand Springs Scenic Byway,** Highway 30 was the old highway before I-84 went in. Today it's a sight-laden "back way" into Twin Falls.

The great Bonneville Flood scoured out Hagerman Valley some 15,000 years ago. You'll see huge rounded boulders that were carried along by the flood then dropped in place when the waters receded. The valley's chief topographic feature, however, is the series of springs gushing from the lava rock along the north rim. The springs are outflow from the Snake River Plain Aquifer, which begins some 100 miles to the northeast near Howe. There the waters of the Big and Little Lost Rivers, Birch Creek, and other smaller watercourses disappear into the lava of the Snake River Plain and begin a century-long journey to the Hagerman Valley. The water flows underground until the deep cut of the Snake River Gorge sets the aquifer free. Once this must have been a spectacular sight, when springs flowed unimpeded from mile after mile of canyon wall. Today, most of the springs have been either despoiled by hydropower facilities or diverted to farmlands and fish hatcheries. Nevertheless, what's left still makes an unusual sight, well worth the detour off the interstate.

BLISS

The first town along the scenic byway—still within earshot of the interstate—is Bliss. In 1833, the Oregon Short Line Railroad named the little hamlet (pop. 185) for local rancher David Bliss. If you're in the area around Christmastime, look for Dick and Karen Elliott's Woodtick Farm northwest of town. You can't miss it after dark, when their holiday display of a **gazillion Christmas lights** turns Bliss into a major tourist attraction. The power company added a transformer just to handle the load, which results in a December power bill for the Elliotts of about $1,500. Each year the couple wonders if it's worth it, but so far they continue, considering it their Christmas gift to the people of southern Idaho. Donations to help offset the electric bill are accepted.

West of town, **Bliss Reservoir** provides a venue for water-skiing and fishing for rainbow trout, sunfish, and bass. To get there, take King Hill Road northwest from I-84 Exit 137. After seven miles, turn south on Idaho Power Road, which leads back under the interstate and a couple more miles down to the reservoir.

Note: Before you head down into Hagerman Valley on Highway 30, you might want to continue another eight miles east along the interstate and check out Malad Gorge State Park. It's covered under North of the Snake River, later.

HAGERMAN

Shoshone people spearfished for salmon on the Snake River here for centuries, until whites showed up and drove off first the Shoshone, then the salmon. The Oregon Trail passed near the site—wagon ruts are still visible across the river from town—which later became a stagecoach stop. Present-day Hagerman began in 1892, when Stanley Hegeman applied for a post office. The Postal Department got Hegeman's name wrong and granted the post office under the present spelling.

Hagerman Fossil Beds
National Monument

The 4,300 acres here are not developed for tourist use, nor will they ever be. That's because the area is one of the world's foremost fossil beds, and indiscriminate tourist trampling could destroy priceless archaeological remains. The digs at the monument have yielded more than 125 full skeletons of a prehistoric, zebralike horse from the Pliocene epoch. Now called the Hagerman horse, *Equus simplicidens* is the earliest known member of the *Equus* genus and has been designated the Idaho state fossil. The bones were first discovered by a local rancher in 1928, and a major archaeological excavation led by paleontologists from the Smithsonian Institution began the following year. Two theories prevail as to why so many of these ancient horses died in one place. One theory assumes the prehistoric watering hole here turned into a mud bog, trapping the animals in sticky goo. The other theory holds that the horses drowned trying to cross the river during a flood. In addition to the Hagerman horse, fossils of more than 140 other species have been unearthed here, including waterfowl, otters, muskrats, and 3.5-million-year-old beavers.

The bulk of the visitor information on this fascinating historical site is found at the national monument visitor center in downtown Hagerman, 221 N. State St., P.O. Box 570, Hagerman,

Stop here to learn about the world's richest known fossil deposits from the Pliocene epoch.

ID 83332, 208/837-4793. The visitor center is open Memorial Day weekend through Labor Day weekend daily 9 A.M.–5 P.M., the rest of the year Thurs.–Sun. 10 A.M.–4 P.M. When funding allows, rangers lead free tours of sites in the monument on weekends in summer; tours leave from the visitor center. Otherwise, a flyer describing a self-guided auto tour (22 miles, two hours) is available here. The best view of the fossil area is from the Bell Rapids Sportsman's Access Area, on the Hagerman side of the river (follow signs off Highway 30). You won't see anything exciting, but your imagination can fill in the picture with thousands of prehistoric beasts.

You can also drive over to the other side of the river for a closer look. Continue south through Hagerman and turn right just after you cross the bridge over the Snake River. Alongside the fossil area you'll find a turnout with an interpretive sign, but you won't see giant dinosaur bones sticking out of the mud. Continue up to the top of the hill for a look—and perhaps a short walk along—some well-preserved Oregon Trail wagon ruts.

Teater's Knoll

Not far from downtown Hagerman, the former home of the late Western-landscape artist Archie Teater overlooks a fast-flowing bend in the Snake River. Teater loved the Hagerman Valley and wanted a house as inspirational as its surroundings. In 1952, he hired an out-of-town architect to design his dream art studio. The architect came up with a bold concept—a 1,900-square-foot, one-bedroom, open-floorplan design based on parallelograms, so that all the house's angles would be set at either 60 or 120 degrees. Local financiers thought the plans were nuts and advised Teater to find a good local architect instead. But the house was completed in 1957 and still stands today. The foundation and walls are stone, the interior is oak and fir. The prow-shaped roofline looks as much a geologic feature as the steep basalt walls of the Snake River Canyon rising behind it. And due to the house's superb design and its location on the tree-covered knoll, it's very difficult to see. Which is unfortunate, because as it turns out, Archie Teater's dream home

is the only house in Idaho designed by master architect Frank Lloyd Wright.

Teater moved to Carmel, California, in the 1970s and died in 1978. The house was sold and today remains a private residence. It's listed on the National Register of Historic Places but is not open to tourists, not even gawkers. One can only hope that someday it will be open to the public. For the whole story of the house, read *Teater's Knoll: Frank Lloyd Wright's Idaho Legacy*, by architect Henry Whiting, a later owner of the home.

Snake River Pottery

On the same road as the Teater house—Old Highway 30 northwest of Hagerman—lies the oldest pottery in Idaho, established in 1947. Snake River Pottery, 555 E. River Rd. (look for the rattlesnake logo), P.O. Box 1110, Bliss, ID 83314, 208/837-6527, sells handmade earthenware, stoneware, and terra-cotta pieces by a handful of regional potters, including founder Aldrich Bowler and resident potter Ned Swisher. It's open year-round daily 9 A.M.–5 P.M., and if you can't make it during those hours, you might swing by anyway—if someone's there, you're welcome to come in. From the beautiful back deck of pottery, overlooking the river, you'll get a good view of the Teater house. This is one peaceful place.

Hagerman Valley Historical Society Museum

Like the national monument visitor center, this small museum, 100 S. State St., 208/837-6288, holds a full-size cast replica of a Hagerman horse skeleton. You'll also find some historic photos of the Hagerman Valley. The museum is open April–Oct. Wed.–Sun. 1–4 P.M.; closed on holidays. Admission is free.

Snake River Boat Tours

Several outfitters conduct guided boat trips down the Snake River through Hagerman Valley. You can cruise up the river on a motorboat, or shoot down the rapids in a raft. Due to the influx of spring water into the river, this section of the Snake can be run nearly year-round.

1000 Springs Tours, P.O. Box 449, Hagerman, ID 83332, 208/837-9006, offers two-hour cruises down the Snake through Hagerman Valley aboard a 30-foot motorized pontoon boat. Along the way you'll see Blue Heart Springs, which gurgle their way up from the riverbed into a crystal-clear pool, and Riley Creek Falls. Tours are offered year-round, weather permitting, but prime season is April through October. Cost is $24 adults, $12 children 12 and under. Reservations are advised. Also available are elegant dinner tours offering a selection of 12 menu items, including prime rib; beer, wine, and cocktails are available. The dinner tour is about $35 per person. All tours leave from Sligar's 1000 Springs Resort, on the river six miles south of Hagerman.

For those who prefer a raft to a motorboat, the Hagerman Reach of the Snake churns through challenging Class II–III rapids—exciting, but not dangerous when you ride with a skilled skipper. Outfitters offering guided trips on the Hagerman Reach include **High Adventure River Tours,** 1211 East 2350 South, Hagerman, ID 83332, 208/733-0123 or 800/286-4123, and **Idaho Guide Service,** 563 Trotter Dr., Twin Falls, ID 83301, 208/734-4998 or 888/73-IDAHO (888/734-3246). Plan on spending about $40–60, with lunch.

Accommodations

Under $50: The 16-room **Hagerman Valley Inn,** State St. at Hagerman Ave., P.O. Box 480, Hagerman, ID 83332, 208/837-6196, is a trim, modern motel on the south side of downtown. Smoking and nonsmoking rooms are available, and amenities include an upstairs deck, downstairs hot tub, cable TV, and a grassy front yard.

$50–100: Billingsley Creek Lodge, 17940 Hwy. 30, P.O. Box 449, Hagerman, ID 83332, 208/837-4822, is on Highway 30 just south of River Road. It's been around since 1928 and boasts a distinguished literary history of sorts: Ernest Hemingway and Vardis Fisher both stayed here at one time or another. Although it's right along the highway, the resort is well landscaped; that and its location on Billingsley Creek give it an air of tranquillity. Choose from six lodge rooms or a couple of private cottages.

RV Park

Hagerman R.V. Village, 18049 Hwy. 30, 208/837-4906 or 208/837-4412, offers 51 sites with hookups (including some phone hookups), as well as a laundry, restrooms, showers, an exercise room, and a sauna. The rate is $17 per vehicle per night; weekly and monthly rates available.

Food

Hagerman's finest dining is at the **Snake River Grill,** State St. at Hagerman Ave., 208/837-6227, which serves breakfast, lunch, and dinner daily and has a nice outdoor patio. Chef Kirt Martin is known to have a way with wild game. Dinner entrées range $11–19. Hours are Monday 6 A.M.–2 P.M., Tues.–Thurs. 6 A.M.–9:30 P.M., Fri.–Sat. 6 A.M.–10 P.M., Sunday 7 A.M.–9:30 P.M.

Information and Services

Hagerman City Hall, 110 W. Main St., 208/837-6636, is the best place to go for town information. It's open Mon.–Fri. 8:30 A.M.–12:30 P.M. Hagerman also has a **chamber of commerce,** but as there isn't much commerce in Hagerman, the chamber is a bit iffy. You can try them at 111 W. Hagerman Ave. (downstairs), P.O. Box 599, Hagerman, ID 83332, 208/837-9131, www.hagerman-idchamber.org.

THOUSAND SPRINGS AREA

Along this stretch of the Snake, a torrent of waterfalls emerges from the black basalt cliffs on the river's north side. This extensive line-up of springs—maybe a thousand, maybe not—gushes forth clean, crystal-clear water at a constant 58°F. The spring water makes an ideal medium for fish-farming; hatcheries in the area raise millions of young trout each year.

Hagerman Wildlife Management Area and Fish Hatcheries

On the north side of the Snake River, two miles south of Hagerman, the Hagerman WMA preserves 880 acres of riverine wetlands as wildlife habitat. Fed by the constant-temperature spring water, the area stays ice-free all year long. This makes it a winter haven for ducks and geese by the thousands, as well as ospreys, peregrine falcons, and bald and golden eagles. The river also supports a healthy population of river otters.

Within the WMA is **Hagerman State Fish Hatchery,** 1060 State Fish Hatchery Rd., 208/837-4892, which raises millions of trout annually to be stocked in waters across Idaho. Six miles of walking trails loop from the hatchery past many lakes and ponds. Anglers find success in many of these waters, but before you cast a line, check with the **Idaho Department of Fish and Game,** 868 E. Main St., Jerome, ID 83338-0428, 208/324-4359, for seasons and possible closures.

Fish-hatchery fans will find a second hatchery, the **Hagerman National Fish Hatchery,** just down the road, RR1 Box 256, Hagerman, ID 83332, 208/837-4896. This federal facility raises 1.5 million steelhead smolts each year. Visit in March and April for the best look.

Nature Conservancy Thousand Springs Preserve

This 400-acre preserve, 1205 Thousand Springs Grade, Wendell, ID 83355, 208/536-6797 or 208/536-5748, is a real challenge to find. From the west side of the river, you can look right across at the power plant and the unbridled springs on either side. But getting over to those springs is quite another matter. To get there from Highway 30, first follow signs to the Hagerman National Fish Hatchery (on the north side of the Snake River bridge, three miles south of Hagerman), then work your way south along the rim. Once you get up on the river's rim, it's easy to get lost. Some roads lead out to the edge of the canyon, only to dead-end. Sometimes you become accustomed to a regular grid of gravel roads, only to find that suddenly the pattern ends and you have to drive miles out of your way before coming to the next intersection. Stock up on patience before you head this way.

The preserve occupies the former Minnie Miller ranch, purchased by businesswoman and dairy farmer Minnie Miller in 1918. For 36 years, Miller steadfastly protected her share of the Hagerman Valley springs from usurpment and development, and upon her death she deeded the property to an equally staunch environmentalist. The property was sold to the Nature Conservancy in 1986. Among the highlights of the preserve are Minnie Miller Falls, which pours forth from the canyon wall and cascades down nearly 200 feet into crystalline pools, and Ritter Island, site of Miller's 1920 home, now the Conservancy office. A quarter-mile trail on the island leads north to the falls, the only totally undisturbed springs along the entire 40-mile width of the aquifer.

Most of the preserve is open daily for exploring. To get there, take a couple of Advil and hope for the best. If you get lost, frustrated, and angry, *Moon Handbooks Idaho* assumes no responsibility; you've been forewarned.

From Highway 30, turn east on either Road 2925 S or State Fish Hatchery Road and then turn south (right) at the first T intersection. This road leads toward the National Fish Hatchery, but first you'll come to a fork. The feds' hatchery is to the right; go left instead. The road will curve up a hill to your left (east). Now you should be on Road 3000 S. Continue straight, past the intersection with Road 1175 E, and turn south on Road 1200 E. A couple of bends in the road around this point will totally confound your sense of direction. A compass would be helpful (no, I'm not joking). If you're lucky, you'll now find yourself heading south on Road 1200 E, which will jog out away from the river and turn into 1300 E. Keep going down 1300 E until you see the graffiti-covered silo at the intersection of 3200 S. Just past the silo, turn right on Thousand Springs Grade and descend past the old dairy barn and the hydropower facility to the preserve.

Commercial Hot Springs Resorts

The first of three resorts you'll come to as you head south down Hagerman Valley is **Sligar's 1000 Springs Resort,** 18734 Hwy. 30, Hagerman, ID 83332, 208/837-4987. Sligar's offers a large, hot-spring-fed indoor swimming pool, hot baths, and an RV park; all are open year-round. Day-use fee for the swimming pool is $5 general, $4 children 6–13, $3 toddlers five and under. Campers get a discount. The hot baths cost $7 an hour for the plain tubs, $8 an hour for the Jacuzzi tubs; tub rates include use of the swimming pool. Campers pay $22 a night with full hookups, $15 a night without; children under age two camp free. The resort charges $2 per night per large pet. Picnickers can drive in and use the grounds for $10 per vehicle per day (from opening until 9 P.M.). The RV park is open daily. The pool facility is open Tues.–Sat. 11 A.M.–9:30 P.M., Sunday noon–8 P.M.

The other two resorts are on opposite sides of the river but share the same turnoff from the highway. Turning left (east) will take you to a T intersection. Turn right and follow Banbury Road 1.5 miles, over a small hill and down to **Banbury Hot Springs,** 1128A Banbury Rd., Rt. 3 Box 408, Buhl, ID 83316, 208/543-4098. The venerable resort offers a crystal-clear outdoor swimming pool fed by continuously flowing hot and cold springs; five hot tubs that are drained, cleaned, and disinfected before each use; and picnic and camp grounds, luxuriously shaded under a profusion of mature trees. A boat-launching ramp ($5 fee) and dock are down on the river, and restrooms, showers, and a laundromat are available for campers. The popular area has a wholesome, family atmosphere. Admission to the pool costs $6 general, $5 kids 6–13, $3 for tykes five and under. Campers get a 50-cent discount. The tubs rent by the hour; $6 per person for the plain tubs, a dollar more for the Jacuzzi versions; kids under 11 pay half price. Tub rental here doesn't include admission to the swimming pool. Campers pay around $15 per night for a tent site and $20–25 for an RV site. The resort is open weekends from Easter until late May, then daily until Labor Day; the pool and office hours are noon–10 P.M.

Finally, **Miracle Hot Springs,** on the west side of the highway, 19073A Hwy. 30, P.O. Box 588, Buhl, ID 83316, 208/543-6002, is small but spunky—a personal favorite. Where else would you find alligators on the grounds? In addition to the regular (first-come, first-served) soaking tubs here are four reservable VIP tubs that are large, private, temperature adjustable, and open to the stars. Rates for the continuous-flow-through swimming pool and regular hot tubs are $6 general, $5 for seniors 55 and up, $3 for kids 3–13, $1 for little ones 0–2, including a

swim diaper. Private tubs are an extra $2–4 per person for one hour, $10–12 per person for two hours. Massage is available by appointment. As with the other two resorts, there's an RV park here. The sites are a little close to the highway but nicely landscaped. Rates are around $10–15. Miracle also has several geodesic domes available to rent. The "dome suite" sleeps two in a real double bed for $48. Two "camping domes" can accommodate up to six people each for $30; bring your own sleeping bags (pads are provided). The relaxed, low-key resort is open year-round Mon.–Sat.

BUHL AND VICINITY

Buhl was founded in 1906 and named after Frank Buhl, a bigwig in the Twin Falls Land and Water Company. It's an agricultural center where you'll find fertilizer stores, tractor lots, Farm Bureau Insurance, Farmers National Bank, and a big Green Giant vegetables plant right in the middle of town. But this is also one funky farm town, with a great arts center, many alternative-health practitioners, and more.

Eighth Street Center

A few blocks off Buhl's main drag, the Eighth Street Center, 200 N. 8th St., 208/543-2888, http://buhlartscouncil.tripod.com, is home to the Buhl Arts Council and a cornucopia of arts classes, performances, and gallery space. Here, "the arts" can mean everything from painting exhibitions to couples massage classes. A permanent labyrinth-butterfly garden is at home outside across the alley from the center. Check out the website to see what else is happening.

Bordewick Sportsman's Access Area

Idaho is chock-full of Sportsman's Access Areas—you'll see numerous signs along every freeway. This one is spectacularly notable for its location on a stunning stretch of the Snake River where several species of large waterbirds nest and congregate. Great blue herons, white pelicans, and Canada geese can often be seen soaring above the riffles and around the many verdant islands. You'll also find good fishing, toe-dabbling, and primitive camping at this beautiful site, or at several other possible campsites along this stretch of the Snake. A little farther down the road is the state's **Magic Valley Fish Hatchery,** 208/326-3230, which raises millions of steelhead from roe to fingerling size for release back into the Salmon River drainage. To get to the access area and the hatchery, head out Clear Springs Road and turn right just before you cross the river.

Clear Springs Foods

The world's largest commercial trout farm is just north of Buhl on Clear Springs Road (turn off Highway 30 at the big Buhl water tower). Clear Springs Foods, 208/543-8217 or 800/635-8211, produces millions of pounds of Idaho rainbow trout each year. Visitor facilities include a picnic area and a fish-viewing pond. The pond holds trout, of course, as well as a couple of big Snake River sturgeon. An underwater viewing window gives you a trout's-eye view of their riverine abode.

Niagara Springs State Park

On the river's north side, across the water from the reaches of the Bordewick Sportsman's Access Area, lies Niagara Springs State Park, 2136 Niagara Springs Rd., 208/536-5522. A National Natural Landmark, the springs gush out of the canyon wall at 250 cubic feet per second.

It's a roundabout route to get there from Buhl, much easier from Wendell to the north. After crossing the river on Clear Lakes Road, the road ascends to the north rim. Turn right on the Bob Barton Highway and continue past one, two, three, four intersections (1600 E, 1700 E, 1800 E, and 1900 E, respectively). The next intersection you'll come to should be with Rex Leland Highway, which does double duty as 1950 E. If you traveled south from Wendell, this is the road you would follow straight down the whole way, without all the confusing rigamarole. Turn right here and follow the road down to the river and the park. It's a steep drop of 350 vertical feet to the canyon floor; the gravel road is not recommended for trailers or motor homes.

Two different areas make up the park. The Emerson Pugmire Memorial Recreation Area offers a picnic area and a campground that has

bathrooms and running water but no hookups; sites are $7 a night. A $2 per car entry fee is charged, but if you camp, that $2 will be included in your $7 camping fee. The area is well maintained and offers a large expanse of grass and a great location on a scenic stretch of the Snake River. Continuing a little farther down the road will take you to the Crystal Springs Area, where you'll find those springs, as well as a small pond for year-round fishing.

Niagara Springs Wildlife Management Area

Just west of Niagara Springs State Park, the Niagara Springs WMA protects 957 acres of habitat for waterfowl and other wildlife. Wildlife viewing and fishing are the two most popular pastimes here. Birdwatchers and others can follow trails both up on the canyon rim and down along the water, where sightings of songbirds and mule deer are common. In winter, waterfowl arrive in large numbers. Anglers can try for rainbow trout in the Thompson-Mays Canal or for trout, catfish, and sturgeon in the Snake River.

To reach the WMA, follow the directions to the state park, above, but after descending to the bottom of the river gorge, turn right to one of several parking areas. Trails follow the river east, past Boulder Rapids and a couple of ponds. For more informaton, contact the WMA in care of the **Idaho Department of Fish and Game,** 868 E. Main St., Jerome, ID 83338-0428, 208/324-4359.

Balanced Rock

This huge question-mark-shaped rock 17 miles southwest of Buhl, west of Castleford, is balanced on a small point and looks as though a strong wind would blow it over. Apparently the thought of that happening scared the county lawyers, since the wondrous natural feature has been reinforced with concrete around the base.

Just down the hill from Balanced Rock is **Balanced Rock Park,** offering picnicking and swimming along Salmon Falls Creek. Rock climbers can find interesting climbing on the area's castle-like hoodoos—the formations that gave the town of Castleford its name. And across the road on the

Balanced Rock

trough, where the road all but disappeared in the grasses. I turned around there and went back the way I came. Only adventurers with 4WD—and more boldness than I—would want to reach the canyon via this route.

The other approach from the north is viable, however. From the intersection of 3300 N and 1000 E Roads, proceed east for "a half block" to 1050 E Road and turn right. This road will eventually take you out to two different spots along the canyon rim. The atlas shows the road continuing through to 2900 N Road and eventually to Highway 93, but it looked like a dead end at the canyon rim to me. Once at the canyon, you're in for a treat. The earth drops away some 600 vertical feet, down to the creek below. Like a miniature Snake River Birds of Prey Area, raptors circle the rim and can be seen in some numbers soaring through space below. Fishing and backpacking down in the canyon are possible, but getting down there is problematic. Be extremely careful—there is absolutely no one out here to come to your aid.

Perhaps the intrepid explorer can find a road on which to continue south to **Cedar Creek Reservoir** and **Salmon Falls Reservoir.** Both reservoirs, however, are reached by paved road from Rogerson, so they are covered in Highway 93 to Nevada under South of the Snake River, later.

river's north side, hot spring water pours out of a pipe, creating a seminatural Jacuzzi.

Salmon Falls Creek Canyon

Head down the lonely roads south of Castleford, and the flat rangeland spreads out before you almost as far as the eye can see. Hidden in this landscape is Salmon Falls Creek Canyon, a spectacular gorge cut by the creek into the surrounding grasslands. Only a thin, dark strip of exposed basalt along the rim gives away the canyon's existence, and then only when you're almost right on top of it. The road there is acceptable for two-wheel-drive passenger cars, though it's overgrown with brush and would be worrisome to those driving a cherry new Park Avenue. After any kind of precipitation, it would definitely be 4WD only.

The DeLorme atlas indicates a road to the canyon extending off the south end of 1400 E Road. I followed this road as far as I could, out across beautiful, empty land to an old cattle

Golf

Clear Lake Country Club, 403 Clear Lake Ln., 208/543-4849, offers a gorgeous 18-hole, 5,895-yard, par-72 course in the Snake River Canyon. The 13th green is shaped like a rainbow trout, and the 14th tee offers commanding canyon views. Greens fees run $24–28; cart rentals available. The course is open year-round. Hard-core hackers can park the Winnie at the club's RV park; sites cost $15 a night with hookups. Non-golfers can go fly-fishing on the Snake or cast a line into the club's own private, no-license pond (also fly-fishing only) for $10 adults, $3.50 kids.

Events

Before irrigation came to the Magic Valley, sagebrush was the dominant crop among the

SOUTH-CENTRAL IDAHO

dirt farmers hereabouts. **Buhl Sagebrush Days** on July 4 weekend commemorates the humble and pungent desert-dwelling shrub. Look for food, fun, and a fabulous fireworks display. For more information, contact the Buhl Chamber of Commerce.

Smith's Dairy
Who started the myth that a good milk shake should be so thick as to deflate your brain cavity when you suck it out through a straw? Smith's

Dairy, 205 S. Broadway, 208/543-4272, is a must-stop for its rich, naturally wholesome, icy cold, and just-thick-enough milk shakes. To give you an idea how homespun this place is, the dairy still employs milkmen—uh, milkpersons—to deliver milk in glass bottles, house to house. The kids'll love it.

Information
The **Buhl Chamber of Commerce** answers visitor inquiries at 716 Hwy. 30 (on the east side of town), Buhl, ID 83316, 208/543-6682.

North of the Snake River

East of Bliss on I-84, you'll pass first Malad Gorge State Park, then two major routes that leave the interstate heading north. Highway 46 passes through Gooding on its way to the Camas Prairie and the town of Fairfield. Highway 93 runs due north out of Twin Falls, passing near Jerome and continuing to Shoshone. There it veers northeast toward fly-fishing nirvana, the Little Wood River and the pristine trout-filled waters of Silver Creek. Highway 75 continues north out of Shoshone on its way to the Wood River Valley (see the High Country chapter).

MALAD GORGE AND BOX CANYON STATE PARKS
The Big Wood and Little Wood Rivers meet near Gooding to form the Malad River. The river would today probably just be called the lower Big Wood if early fur trappers in the area hadn't experienced a culinary catastrophe here. In 1819, Donald Mackenzie's expedition stopped at the river and dined on beaver steak. Many of the men subsequently became ill, leading Mackenzie to christen the river with the French word for sick. Subsequent expeditions in 1824 and 1830 reported similar fates. Before the fur trappers came along, Shoshone Indians had inhabited the area, hunting pronghorn and fishing for salmon; after the trappers, thousands of Oregon Trail pioneers passed by here, many of whom were traveling the Kelton Road. The gorge was a major stop along that route.

When the Malad River reaches 2.5-mile-long Malad Gorge, it gets a boost of spring water flowing into it at 1,200 cubic feet per second. The supercharged river froths and foams in tormented torrents down through the narrow lava-rock chasm. It reaches the height of hellbound fury at Devil's Washbowl, where it plunges over a 60-foot waterfall into calmer waters. Below Devil's Washbowl, the canyon widens. Standing on the rim surveying the scene, you'll be looking about 250 feet straight down to the shimmering river below. Springs pour out from the rim in places, cascading down the cliffs in ribbonlike waterfalls. Rest assured, people cascading down the cliffs would not look nearly as beautiful. Signs warn visitors about getting too close to the edge of the precipice; deep fissures run parallel to the rim, indicating another layer of rock getting ready to slough off into the canyon. It could happen tomorrow, or it might take a thousand years.

Although there is some disagreement among geologists, prevailing opinion seems to have it that the modestly sized Malad River on its own wouldn't have been powerful enough to carve such a deep canyon here. Rather, the gorge is most likely another example of the work of the Bonneville Flood—the apocalyptic wall of water that crashed across the Snake River Plain almost 15,000 years ago, reconstructing the landscape dramatically as it went. Melon gravel seen in the area lends support to this theory.

COURTESY OF THE IDAHO TRAVEL COUNCIL

Malad Gorge State Park

Facilities

The 652-acre **Malad Gorge State Park,** 1074 E. 2350 S., Hagerman, ID 83332, 208/837-4505, is a day-use area on the south side of I-84 at Exit 147. The center of activity is the Devil's Washbowl overlook and interpretive area. Here signs explain the human and geologic history of the site, and a footbridge allows visitors to take a breathtaking stroll out high above the gorge. It's definitely not for acrophobes. As you walk across the footbridge, which is within diesel-sniffing range of the highway, the rumbling of the big rigs roaring by on I-84 shakes the bridge and adds to the excitement. One odd feature here—perhaps engendered by engineering requirements—is the placement of the overlook bridge directly above Devil's Washbowl; you can't actually see the falls well from the bridge. Continue across the decidedly ugly iron bridge and on down the trail for better views of the turbulent cascade.

Elsewhere in the park proper, a green picnic area with restrooms makes a good place to break out the lunch, while a loop road continues down to the Snake River rim, past a couple of "coves" or smaller gorges eroded out of the cliffs. Hiking trails let visitors get off the asphalt and see some of the park's wildlife, including lots of hawks and jackrabbits.

Across the Highway

While the south side of the river holds the park's developed portion, the river's course on the north side of the interstate is at least as interesting. To get there, take the same exit at Tuttle, but turn first north, then immediately west, onto the old road. About 100 yards or so before yet another bridge crossing the Malad, you'll see a dirt road leading off to the right. Follow it to a small parking area; from here the river, narrower than on the other side of the highway, is a just a short walk away. And you can get closer to its power as it cuts down through the lava rock. In a few thousand years, the park viewpoint will probably be up here somewhere, as the Malad River continues its relentless whittling away at the land.

One local story tells of a group of Oregon Trail pioneers who crossed the Malad in this area, using a 16-foot-long wagon box as a bridge. Another party of pioneers came along hot on their heels but was unable to repeat the feat—their party's longest wagon box stretched only 14 feet, a couple feet shy of bridging the gap. If the story

SOUTH-CENTRAL IDAHO

is true, it shows that the Oregon Trail pioneers weren't always motivated by the finest humanitarian principles; the first group, it is said, refused to let the group behind them cross on their jury-rigged bridge.

Box Canyon State Park

This primitive state park protects a 35-acre canyon and the 11th largest spring in North America. The spring and canyon are home to a variety of wildlife, including endangered snail species and the rare Shoshone sculpin. Access is currently limited, but guided hikes are sometimes offered; for dates and directions, contact the rangers at Malad Gorge State Park, 208/837-4505.

GOODING AND VICINITY

Today's Gooding was originally a railroad stop called To-po-nis, a Shoshone word meaning either "Black Cherries" or "Trading Post." Given the absence of orchards in the desert here, one might guess that the latter was the correct translation. The town's name was changed in 1896 to honor local sheep baron Frank Gooding, who went on to become a successful career politician. He was first elected mayor of the town bearing his name, then elected governor of Idaho, then elected to the U.S. Senate, where he served from 1921 until his death in 1928. In 1913, the town of Gooding was designated as the Gooding County seat.

Cities of Rocks

North of town, Highway 46 climbs into the Bennett Hills, passing access roads to two different "cities of rocks"-areas of hoodoo formations carved by eons of erosion. The common mushroom-cap shapes are created because the layer of basalt (lava rock) on top is harder than the rhyolite (consolidated volcanic ash) underlying it and therefore less easily worn away by wind and water.

The first turnoff you'll come to heading north (14 miles north of Gooding) is for **Little City of Rocks.** Four miles farther up the highway is the turnoff for **Gooding City of Rocks.** Their names seem to indicate the latter is the area of choice. Actually, while both are worth exploring, Little City of Rocks is about a mile or less off the highway, al-

lowing quick access to relatively tall, impressive formations. Gooding City of Rocks, on the other hand, lies at the end of a nine-mile dirt road, and once there, the rocks—or those near the road at least—are much more humble in size. But the Gooding City of Rocks area does offer great views of the Snake River Plain, as well as opportunities for extended exploring; the SRMA there encompasses more than 20,000 acres where you might come upon Native American petroglyphs or a herd of desert-dwelling elk. Other residents in the area include deer, black bear, chukars, golden eagles, prairie falcons, red-tailed hawks, great horned owls, and an abundance of those stealthy beasts, range cattle. Glimpses of intriguing Fir Grove Mountain led me to put the area on my list for further exploration.

Make sure to have water with you out here. Both areas are hot and dry, especially on lizard-sizzling summer afternoons. For more information, contact the **BLM Shoshone District,** 440 W. F St. in Shoshone, 208/732-7200.

Recreation

Throw your clubs in the trunk and head a half mile east of town to the nine-hole **Gooding Country Club,** 1951 Hwy. 26, Gooding, ID 83330, 208/934-9977. On weekends, the greens fee is $15 for nine holes, or $19 for 18. On weekdays, it's $12 for nine, $15 for 18. Carts, clubs, and lessons are available, and facilities include a driving range and a restaurant. The course is open March through mid-November.

If tennis is your racket, head to the court at Main and 10th Streets, or the courts at the high school on 7th Avenue W. All are lighted. The **municipal pool** is at 202 14th Ave. E., 208/934-5870.

Events

Gooding boasts a good-sized Basque community, which throws the annual **Basque Picnic** in mid-July. That same weekend is Gooding's **Summerfest,** a street fair with antique cars and hot rods, games and contests, arts and crafts, and lots of good eats. The third week in August, the **Gooding County Fair and Rodeo** kicks up its heels at the fairgrounds on the northwest edge of town; the fair hosts the Miss Teen Rodeo Idaho contest. Also look for the **Spud Festival** in late September. For a complete events calendar, call Gooding City Hall at 208/934-5669.

Accommodations
$50–100: The beautiful old **Gooding Hotel,** 112 Main St., Gooding, ID 83330, 208/934-4374 or 888/260-6656, is listed on the National Register of Historic Places. The building's construction date is unknown, but it was moved here from Ketchum in 1888, and an addition was constructed in 1908. Today the hotel serves as a B&B, actually run by Goodings, descendants of the town's founding family. It offers two rooms with private bath (including one suite) and eight more with shared bath. Rates include a large country breakfast.

Food
For a mean breakfast—or lunch or dinner, for that matter—try **Wyant's,** 222 4th Ave. E., 208/934-9903. Expect good grub at good prices, with a bonus of amusingly surly waitresses. For pizza and subs, head for **Zeppe's,** 215 Main St., 208/934-8890. The locally recommended fine-dining restaurant in town is **Wood River Inn,** 530 Main St., 208/934-4059, which serves steak, seafood, and other dishes in a clean, conservative decor. Entrée prices range $7–15. The restaurant is open for lunch and dinner Mon.–Saturday.

Information
For information about the town, contact the **Gooding Visitor Center,** 308 5th Ave. W., Gooding, ID 83330, 208/934-5669.

FAIRFIELD AND VICINITY

Fairfield is up on the Camas Prairie, named for its vast fields of wild camas lilies. The camas root was a favored food source of the indigenous Native Americans. Today it's a showy subject for photographers in late spring, when the flowers bloom and turn the fields into a sea of violet-blue.

Camas Prairie Centennial Marsh Wildlife Management Area
A variety of waterfowl either live in or stop off at this tranquil marsh southwest of Fairfield. Among the more interesting avian inhabitants on its 3,100 acres are sandhill cranes and great blue herons. Several species of raptors, including golden eagles, prairie falcons, peregrine falcons, and great horned owls, also frequent the area, as do mule deer and pronghorn. The marsh makes a great spot to enjoy the camas blooms in spring. To get there, take Wolf Lane south off Highway 20, 10 miles west of Fairfield.

Skiing
Twelve miles north of Fairfield up Soldier Creek Road, **Soldier Mountain Ski Area,** Fairfield, ID 83327, 208/764-2526 or 208/764-2327, offers a friendly and inexpensive alternative to Sun Valley, which lies some 60 miles to the east. The hill's 1,400-foot vertical drop is served by two double chairs and two surface lifts. All 36 runs are groomed. Tickets are $30 adults and $20 for ages 7–17 and 62–69. Skiers ages 6 and under and 70 and over get in free. Thursday and Friday are buy-one, get-one-free days for lift tickets. Rentals, lessons, and a snowboard park are available, too. At the base lodge, you can chow down for breakfast, lunch, and dinner, or get a beer or a glass of wine. A large, sunny deck provides good views of the slopes.

If you've wanted to try **snowcat skiing,** this is an economical place to do it; the cost is $175 for a full day including lunch, or $75 for a half-day. Snowcat skiing is offered every day all winter, as long as enough people sign up. Call for reservations.

Soldier Mountain's lifts are open Thurs.–Sun. and holidays, 9 A.M.–4 P.M., usually between December and April, depending on snowfall. Fairfield has basic accommodations, camping and food.

North of Fairfield
The Soldier Mountains and Smoky Mountains immediately north of Fairfield are laced with trails of one sort or another, and by and large open to offroad vehicle travel on or off existing roads—it's something of a sacrifice area. Farther north, trails are open to hikers or offroad vehicles on existing roads only. Some hiking-only trails can be found in the area, but these aren't regularly maintained and could prove sketchy in places.

Next to Soldier Mountain Ski Area, the USFS **Pioneer Campground** offers five free sites between June 1 and September 30. Just south of Soldier Mountain Ski Area, FR 094 splits off to the east. It winds its way up into the Soldier Mountains, over Couch Summit (elevation 7,008 feet), and down into the drainage of Five Points Creek. Soon you'll come to the USFS **Five Points Campground** (three sites, free) and, a little farther down the road, the confluence of Five Points Creek and the larger Little Smoky Creek (which is also the junction of FR 094, which ends here, and FR 227). FR 227 (Little Smoky Road) follows the beautifully babbling Little Smoky east to a couple of sites of interest. **Worswick Hot Springs** is an idyllic spot where Worswick Creek flows down to join Little Smoky. Several pools here hold clear, sulfur-free water of various temperatures ranging all the way up to *really hot!* It's a reasonably popular spot and you probably won't be alone, so discretion is called for before shedding your shorts. Past Worswick, the road splits, with FR 227 continuing over Dollarhide Summit and on into Ketchum, and FR 015 heading southeast to the **Little Smoky Winter Recreation Area,** a snowmobile trailhead.

Back at Little Smoky Campground, FR 227 continues down the Little Smoky past **Preis Hot Springs,** an easy-to-miss, and no-sweat-if-you-do, one-person tub along the right side of the road. Eventually the road takes you to the confluence of Little Smoky and Big Smoky Creeks—which in turn feeds the **South Fork of the Boise River.** (The numerous campgrounds and hot springs along Big Smoky Creek and the South Fork of the Boise are covered under North Toward Atlanta in the Elmore County section of the Southwest Idaho chapter.) It's 47 miles from Fairfield to Featherville.

JEROME

The Jerome County seat, this small town is primarily an agricultural service center. Examples of the businesses here: a cheese company, a milk transporter, a potato processor, and a PVC-pipe manufacturer. Jerome began in 1907 as a company town for the Twin Falls North Side Land and Water Company, which was developing the irrigation systems on the north side of the Snake River. Like the neighboring dairy center of Wendell, Jerome was named for a son of W. H. Kuhn, one of the financiers of the Twin Falls North Side Irrigation Project. For more on the town's history, visit the **Jerome County Historical Museum,** 220 N. Lincoln, 208/324-5641. It's open Tues.–Sat. 1–4:30 P.M., year-round. Admission is free; donations appreciated.

Minidoka Internment National Memorial

After the Japanese bombed Pearl Harbor on Dec. 7, 1941, the U.S. government decided that Americans of Japanese ancestry living along the Pacific coast were a threat to national security. Perhaps they would side with their former countrymen. Perhaps they would radio secret military information to incoming squadrons of Zeroes, hellbent on replacing apple pie with sushi on diner menus from Peoria to Pocatello. Some 110,000 Japanese-Americans living on the West Coast were rounded up and herded into one of 10 camps across the West, where they were confined beginning in August 1942. The U.S. Supreme Court later ruled this practice unconstitutional, but it was a moot point by then. The *Enola Gay* dropped her lethal load over Hiroshima on Aug. 6, 1945, and eight days later the war in the Pacific was over. The U.S. government didn't bother to apologize for its internment atrocity until 1988, following years of tireless lobbying by the Japanese-American community.

East of Jerome lies the site of one of these former camps, a place the government named Hunt. It was also called the Minidoka Relocation Center, which has such an innocuous ring to it, compared to "concentration camp." But that's what the 950-acre camp really was. The nearly 7,500 internees here lived a humiliating life in tarpaper barracks, surrounded by barbed wire and armed guards. Many of the young males were summoned out to serve in the U.S. armed forces. Go figure the logic in imprisoning a people and at the same time asking the strongest among them to fight for your cause. Many young Japanese-American men from Hunt died defending America from their ancestral cousins; their names are inscribed on one of the plaques here. In December 1944, the government allowed Japanese-Americans to return to the West Coast; the camp closed in October 1945.

Other than the small memorial area, the rest of what was once the camp is now bucolic farmland betraying no evidence of its shameful history. But the site has been designated as a national memorial, and planning is underway for some additional interpretation. To get to the site, take Highway 25 east from Jerome. The turnoff to the area is marked by a couple of the familiar roadside historical markers. You can also get more information by calling 208/837-4793.

> *Shoshone's architecture is noteworthy for its extensive use of local lava rock. Somehow the pioneer masons learned how to fit the lightweight rocks together into solid foundations and walls—a feat no modern-day builders can duplicate.*

Events

The second weekend in June, the locals come out for **Live History Days,** a celebration of pioneer life. Those old geezers knew a lot of skills. Maybe you'll learn something about farming, cooking, spinning, or weaving. The Jerome Chamber of Commerce has the details.

Information

The **Jerome Chamber of Commerce** is at 1731 S. Lincoln, Suite A, Jerome, ID 83338, 208/324-2711.

SHOSHONE AND VICINITY

Once a rowdy rail hub, Shoshone still seems to delight in its frisky heritage. The chamber of commerce pamphlets fairly gloat when relating the gory details surrounding the town's former brothels and speakeasies. Shoshone's layout also contributes to its Wild West ambience. Railroad tracks split the center of town in two, leaving the two main streets to face off across the tracks like a couple of gunfighters.

Architectural Highlights

The town's architecture is noteworthy for its extensive use of local lava rock. Construction with lava rock is a lost art. Somehow the pioneer ma-

sons learned how to fit the lightweight rocks together into solid foundations and walls—a feat no modern-day builders can duplicate. Adding to the architectural flavor here are flaking signs for businesses long gone, painted on many exterior walls around town.

Right downtown on the north side of the tracks is the McFall Hotel, 230 N. Rail St. W., a faded 1896 beauty. Currently undergoing restoration, the hotel has a guest list that has included Teddy Roosevelt, Ernest Hemingway, Erle Stanley Gardner, and three U.S. presidents. Other fine original structures still standing include the Hotel Shoshone; the Nebraska Bar; the W. H. Baugh Building, now housing the Shoshone Showhouse movie theater; and the Doncaster, once a Prohibition-era speakeasy and now a florist shop.

Accommodations

$50–100: Governor's Mansion Bed and Breakfast, 315 S. Greenwood, P.O. Box 326, Shoshone, ID 83352, 208/886-2858, was originally owned by the brother of Frank R. Gooding, a sheep baron who served as governor of Idaho from 1901 to 1905. The B&B has five rooms (some under $50), and rates include full breakfast.

Food

The **Manhattan Cafe,** 133 S. Rail St. W, 208/886-2142, is a small diner offering character in spades and a mean eggs-'n'-taters breakfast. It's open for breakfast, lunch, and dinner every day of the year except Christmas.

Events

The **Mannie Shaw Fiddlers' Jamboree,** named after the late fiddler Mannie Shaw of Fairfield, is a 30-year tradition in Shoshone. So rosin up the bow and git on down to City Park during the second week in July. Also in July is the **Lincoln County Fair.** For more information on local events, contact **Shoshone City Hall,** 207 S. Rail St. W., 208/886-2030.

Information

Inquire about the highlights of the surrounding high desert at the **BLM Shoshone District,** 400 W. F St., 208/886-2206. The **Shoshone Chamber of Commerce** can be reached at P.O. Box 575, Shoshone, ID 83352, 208/886-2030.

NORTH OF SHOSHONE

Shoshone Ice Cave

North of town up Highway 75 is Shoshone Ice Cave, 208/886-2058, which offers a 40-minute guided tour through a lava tube with a fascinating history and geology. Water seeping into the tube from the Big Wood River, as well as from percolating rainwater, collects and freezes on the floor of the cave here, thanks to air currents that keep the cave perennially icy. The convenient, year-round source of ice was a boon for the early town of Shoshone—especially during the blazing summers. The tour costs $6 general, $5.50 seniors, $3.75 kids 5–14. Outside the cave is a gift shop selling tourist schlock, as well as a museum boasting an impressive collection of gems and minerals. The site is open May 1–Oct 1.

T-Maze Caves

Real spelunkers of the lava-tube variety will no doubt want to come here instead of the aforementioned tourist attraction. These undeveloped tubes are considered by geologists to be the finest examples of the phenomenon in Idaho. One of the 14 different "caves" is the longest mapped in the state. The area is on BLM land near Mammoth Cave. For directions and further information, contact the BLM Shoshone District Office, 400 W. F St., Shoshone, ID 83352, 208/732-7200.

Black Magic Canyon

While you're asking at the BLM office for directions to T-Maze Caves, you might want to inquire about Black Magic Canyon as well. Near the point where Highway 75 crosses the Big Wood River, the Big Wood has carved a stretch of beautiful, unusual formations out of the rock. At one time, Boise's United Mining Corp. wanted to remove rocks from the site to sell for landscaping and decorative purposes. The mining claim was

nullified in court. As the judge put it, "[I]n this case, it is not possible to place a monetary value on the irreplaceable, unique geologic features which would be irretrievably lost if [the company] were permitted to mine this national treasure." A small parking lot and interpretive sign marks the site. Stay out of the canyon if water is flowing through it; it's dry much of the year.

Magic Reservoir

Continuing north on Highway 75, you'll pass two turnoffs to Magic Reservoir, which lies out of sight to the west. The first turnoff, right at the Big Wood River, leads to the west shore, while a turnoff farther north leads to the east shore. Boat ramps and laid-back fishing lodges are available at both areas.

The reservoir is five miles long, 1.5 miles wide, and about 120 feet deep at its deepest. The fishing is good for rainbow trout and perch, and a few brown trout also lurk along the east side's rocky shore. Ice fishing is popular in winter, as is water-skiing in summer. Campers can pitch a tent anywhere around the shoreline, no charge. Lava Point, just north of West Magic, is the most heavily used primitive camping area.

For more information about the reservoir, contact the BLM Shoshone District at 400 W. F St., Shoshone, ID 83352, 208/732-7200.

Silver Creek

Silver Creek is born of crystal-pure alkaline springs in the high desert west of Picabo, and it meanders slowly down to the Little Wood River through wide-open meadows. The wild rainbow and brown trout here can see you coming a mile away, and don't get fooled easily. They're big and strong, and they lure fly-fishers from around the world. To avid flycasters, this is nirvana.

One of the prime fishing areas along the creek is the Nature Conservancy's **Silver Creek Preserve,** P.O. Box 165, Sun Valley, ID 83353, 208/788-2203 or 208/788-8988. It's on the south side of Highway 20, seven miles east of Highway 75 or four miles west of Picabo. The Nature Conservancy works constantly to keep the preserve and the surrounding lands in pristine shape, a difficult task given the ever-increasing usage of the area. At the heart of the 825-acre core area is a small visitor center with interpretive information and a store selling conservation-oriented items to support the preserve. The center is up on a small rise, offering sweeping views of the creek. It's also a trailhead for a half-mile nature trail that loops down to and around the creek. Along the way is a boardwalk that takes you right out over the water, which is so clear you can see every grain of sand and piece of gravel on the bottom. Even if you're not a fishing fiend, this is a peaceful and pleasant place. If you *are* a fishing fiend, you can fish here free—catch-and-release fly-fishing only—but you'll have to sign in at the visitor center first. The preserve relies heavily on do-

nations, so don't hesitate to leave a buck or five while you're there.

Fishing-guide service to Silver Creek is offered by a number of companies, including **Silver Creek Outfitters,** 500 N. Main St., P.O. Box 418, Ketchum, ID 83340, 208/726-5282 or 800/732-5687. For other guide companies, see the fishing information found under Ketchum and Sun Valley in the High Country chapter.

To reach Silver Creek from Shoshone, either head north up Highway 75 and turn east on Highway 20, or take Highway 26/93 northeast through Richfield to Carey, and there turn west on Highway 20. The latter route follows alongside the Little Wood River, also known as a good brown-trout stream.

Twin Falls

Twin Falls (population 35,600), seat of the county of the same name, was founded in 1904 as a hub for Carey Act settlers, who came flooding in to grab up 160-acre parcels for $25 an acre. The huge Snake River irrigation projects of the day turned the desert here into a livable, arable place. Potatoes, sugar beets, and alfalfa are among the crops grown locally, and cattle ranches and dairies also add to the ag scene. Yet Twin Falls is too big to be just a farm town. Diverse services (including a Dell call center that employs hundreds), light industry, and a highly regarded community college contribute to the town's healthy mix of rural character and urban amenities.

The city perches on the rim of the Snake River Canyon, a spectacular gorge that tempted daredevil Evel Knievel in 1974. Knievel attempted to fly a rocket-powered motorcycle across the 1,500-foot gap, but his parachute deployed prematurely, causing Knievel to drift rather anticlimactically into the canyon. The stunt did earn the city a claim to fame, though. Today, the canyon provides ample recreational refuge for residents and visitors.

The twin falls for which the city is named were supposedly once a sight, but dams have dimmed their glory. Just downstream, however, wide, Niagara-like Shoshone Falls has been a tourist des-

tination since the pioneer days and still constitutes the city's prime sightseeing attraction.

Spending a summer day in Twin Falls will give you a clue as to why the westward-bound pioneers were so relieved to get to tree-filled Boise. Here the summer sun reflects off a city covered by mile upon square mile of asphalt and concrete, right up to the canyon rim, buffered by precious little shade. If you declined to get air-conditioning in your Roadmaster, you'll regret that decision when the dog days of summer here push the mercury past 100°F.

SIGHTS

Perrine Bridge and Hansen Bridge

Coming from the interstate, you'll enter Twin Falls over 1,500-foot-long **Perrine Bridge.** It's named for I. B. Perrine, the region's biggest pioneer-era promoter and the man most responsible for bringing about the irrigation projects that turned much of the area green. The bridge ushers traffic across the river, 486 feet above the glimmering waters. The town's main tourist-information center is just across the bridge on the southwest side. From there, you can actually walk out onto the bridge on a pedestrian walkway—not for those with a fear of heights.

BASE JUMPING

By Julie Fanselow

Like Clark Kent ducking into a phone booth and emerging as Superman, the mild-mannered, all-American town of Twin Falls has another side: a top international destination for BASE jumping.

BASE stands for building, antenna, span (bridge), earth—and in the case of Twin Falls, it's all about the "S." BASE enthusiasts say the 486-foot-high Perrine Bridge over the Snake River Canyon is the only one in the United States where it's legal to jump year-round. BASE jumpers travel from around the world to plunge off the Perrine, and on summer holiday weekends, as many as 150 people may be in town for the opportunity. Don Mays, whose Snake River Canyon Tours boat frequently shuttles jumpers from their target landing site beneath the bridge, estimates there have been 30,000 jumps—with two deaths and a handful of serious injuries—since he started his service in 1996.

Of course, people don't just show up and jump. BASE experts say would-be jumpers need to become proficient in sky-diving before attempting BASE jumps. After about 200 jumps from an airplane, parachutists should be ready for the more demanding BASE experience. (It's harder because you're closer to the ground, and there's less room for error.) Would-be jumpers are also urged to take BASE jumping instruction; first-jump courses (many held at the Perrine Bridge) are offered by such manufacturers as Vertigo BASE of Moab, Utah, and Consolidated Rigging of Auburn, California.

BASE jumpers say Twin Falls is exceptionally friendly to their kind. Many jumpers stay at the KOA in nearby Jerome or at the half-dozen or so motels within walking distance of the canyon. Come nightfall, you'll often find BASE enthusiasts swapping stories at restaurants near the bridge, especially the Outback Steakhouse and Johnny Carino's Italian Kitchen.

If you'd like to see BASE jumpers in action, just stand on either end of the Perrine Bridge any fine day with calm winds, and you're likely to spot some. You can also watch jumpers preparing their gear on the lawn at the Buzz Langdon Visitor Center and in the canyon at Centennial Waterfront Park.

COURTESY OF THE IDAHO TRAVEL COUNCIL

BASE jumpers from around the world come to the Perrine Bridge.

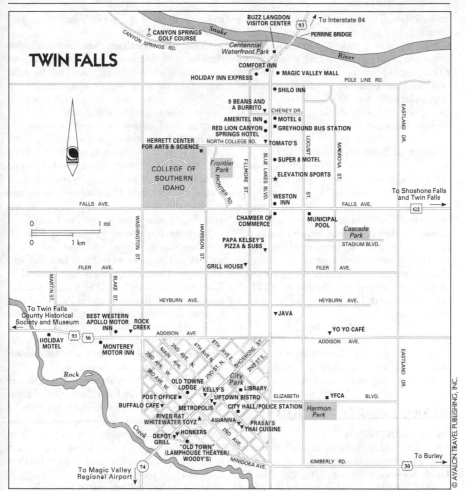

TWIN FALLS

BUZZ LANGDON
VISITOR CENTER
93 To Interstate 84
CANYON SPRINGS
GOLF COURSE
CANYON SPRINGS RD.
Snake
PERRINE BRIDGE
Centennial
Waterfront Park
River
COMFORT INN
HOLIDAY INN EXPRESS
MAGIC VALLEY MALL
POLE LINE RD.
SHILO INN
9 BEANS AND
A BURRITO
CHENEY DR.
AMERITEL INN
MOTEL 6
RED LION CANYON
SPRINGS HOTEL
GREYHOUND BUS STATION
HERRETT CENTER
FOR ARTS & SCIENCE
NORTH COLLEGE RD.
TOMATO'S
LOCUST
SUPER 8 MOTEL
MADRONA ST.
EASTLAND DR.
Frontier
Park
COLLEGE OF
SOUTHERN
IDAHO
FILLMORE ST.
BLUE LAKES BLVD.
ELEVATION SPORTS
FRONTIER RD.
WESTON
INN
ST.
To Shoshone Falls
and Twin Falls
FALLS AVE.
FALLS AVE.
G2
0 1 mi
0 1 km
WASHINGTON ST.
CHAMBER OF
COMMERCE
MUNICIPAL
POOL
Cascade
Park
HARRISON ST.
PAPA KELSEY'S
PIZZA & SUBS
STADIUM BLVD.
FILER AVE.
GRILL HOUSE
FILER AVE.
MARTIN ST.
BLAKE ST.
HEYBURN AVE.
HEYBURN AVE.
To Twin Falls
County Historical
Society and Museum
JAVA
BEST WESTERN
APOLLO MOTOR
INN
ROCK
CREEK
YO YO CAFÉ
ADDISON AVE.
ADDISON AVE.
HOLIDAY
MOTEL
93 30
MONTEREY
MOTOR INN
Rock
2ND AVE. N.
MAIN AVE. N.
4TH AVE. N.
6TH AVE. N.
2ND ST. N.
SHOSHONE ST.
2ND ST E.
EASTLAND DR.
2ND AVE. W.
3RD AVE. W.
OLD TOWNE
LODGE
City
Park
KELLY'S
LIBRARY
POST OFFICE
UPTOWN BISTRO
BUFFALO CAFÉ
METROPOLIS
CITY HALL/POLICE STATION
Elizabeth
YFCA
BLVD.
Harmon
Park
RIVER RAT
WHITEWATER TOYZ
ASIANNA
PRASAI'S
THAI CUISINE
DEPOT
GRILL
HONKERS
2ND AVE.
Creek
"OLD TOWN"
(LAMPHOUSE THEATER/
WOODY'S)
MINIDOKA AVE.
KIMBERLY RD.
30
To Burley
74
To Magic Valley
Regional Airport

© AVALON TRAVEL PUBLISHING, INC.

Hansen Bridge crosses the Snake east of the city. Until 1919, crossings here were made via rowboat. Then a suspension bridge was built, and in 1966, the current bridge was put in. It's a 350-foot drop from the bridge to the river.

Shoshone Falls

This cascade east of town has been called the "Niagara of the West." At 1,000 feet wide and 212 feet high, the horseshoe-shaped falls is 52 feet higher than Niagara. You have to pay $3 per car to get within viewing range of the falls, though they are often a mere trickle, since much of the water is diverted to the region's irrigation system. Spring is usually the best time to see some water going over.

Fortunately, there's more to do here if the falls aren't falling. Twin Falls' 2004 centennial year is celebrated with a new trail leading out of the canyon from Shoshone Falls Park. Also part of the same park complex, **Dierkes Lake** is a favorite haunt of fisherfolk, swimmers, paddlers, and rock climbers. The swimming areas here employ lifeguards in summer, and trails provide some nice hiking opportunities, if you can ignore the obnoxious trophy homes perched on the canyon rim. To get to Shoshone Falls and Dierkes Lake, take Blue Lakes Boulevard to Falls Avenue and go three miles east—to 3300 East Road—and two miles north, following ample signage. The parks are open year-round daily 7 A.M.–9 P.M.

College of Southern Idaho

A two-year community college offering associate and vocational degrees, College of Southern Idaho, 315 Falls Ave., 208/733-9554, enrolls approximately 7,000 students. One highlight for visitors to the 300-acre campus is the free **Herrett Center for Arts & Science,** which boasts a collection of almost 20,000 pre-Columbian artifacts from North and Central America. The museum also holds a gallery of contemporary art and a planetarium (planetarium shows: $4 adults, $3 seniors, $2 children). The center is open year-round, Tuesday and Friday 9:30 A.M.–9 P.M., Wed.–Thurs. 9:30 A.M.–4:30 P.M., Saturday 1–9 P.M. (extended hours in summer). Numerous public events are held in the school's Fine Arts Auditorium, and the rest of the nicely landscaped campus makes a nice spot for a picnic lunch or a stroll.

PARKS AND RECREATION

Guided Recreation

Visitors with a hankering to get out for some serious adventure in the area can contact **Idaho Guide Service,** 563 Trotter Dr., 208/734-4998 or 888/734-3246, which offers guided canoe, raft, and kayak trips, as well as hiking and biking trips. Fishing excursions and powerboat tours are also available.

Parks

Though most of Twin Falls' prime canyon-rim real estate has been claimed by chain stores and tony professional offices, paved paths offer pedestrian and bicycle access much of the way, too. To find one especially nice stretch, take Pole Line Road west from Blue Lakes Boulevard, then north on Washington Street. Park

in the small lot at the end of Washington, and stroll east from there.

Centennial Waterfront Park lies practically at the base of Perrine Bridge and offers a dock and boat ramp in addition to splendid views. It's at the bottom of Canyon Springs Road, a scenic drive in itself past a waterfall gushing forth from the canyon's south rim. Photographers will find this an excellent place to get a shot of the bridge.

City Park was the original central-city park platted by the town founders in 1904. It's still a major venue for events throughout the year, among them summer concerts by the Twin Falls Municipal Band, held Thursday evenings in June and July. The park is bounded by 4th and 6th Avenues E., Shoshone Street, and 2nd Street E.

Harmon Park hosts community baseball games in summer. Its several diamonds are in use day and night by both Little Leaguers and adult teams. Across the street is the **YFCA,** 1751 Elizabeth Blvd., 208/733-4384, a good place for travelers to get a shower. **Frontier Park** also offers baseball diamonds as well as a 2.1-mile fitness trail and lighted tennis courts. It's across from the College of Southern Idaho on Frontier Road, which is off Falls Avenue between Washington Street N. and Blue Lakes Boulevard N.

A bit farther afield are **Shoshone Falls/Dierkes Lake Park** and **Twin Falls Park,** east of town at the namesake Twin Falls, where you'll find a boat ramp, dock, and 10 acres of lawns for Frisbee picnics and other diversions. To get there, continue east on Falls Avenue past the turnoff to Shoshone Falls, to 3500 East Road. A left turn there will take you to the falls.

Across the Snake River, east of Perrine Bridge, is **Snake River Rim Recreation Management Area.** This wild, undeveloped piece of native desert scrubland is ideal for running the dog or taking a long leisurely walk or mountain-bike ride. You'll also have great views across the river to the **Evel Knievel launch ramp,** a giant wedge of dirt still piled up on the south rim. Several pocket canyons along the rim offer good exploring and some interesting rock-climbing terrain; trails can be found to **Devil's Corral,** a lushly vegetated gorge concealing a couple of small lakes and a cave holding Native American pictographs, and to **Vineyard Lake,** to the east, where you'll find a waterfall or two. Call the Parks Department for exact directions. To get to this area from town, cross the Perrine Bridge heading north and make the first right turn.

More relatively undeveloped parkland can be found at **Rock Creek Canyon,** a favorite with mountain bikers. Rock Creek meanders from the southeast outskirts of the city northwest across the edge of town. Paved paths are accessible behind the city parks headquarters building and at Twin Falls County's **Rock Creek Park,** off Addison Avenue W.

The **municipal pool,** managed by the local Y, is an outdoor facility in summer. Come fall, a giant bubble-like cover encloses it for year-round use. You'll find it at 756 Locust St. N., 208/734-2336.

For more information on the city's parks, contact the **Twin Falls Parks and Recreation Department,** 136 Maxwell Ave., 208/736-2265.

Golf

Down in the canyon, offering great worm's-eye views of Perrine Bridge, is 18-hole **Canyon Springs Golf Course,** 199 Canyon Springs Rd., 208/734-7609. The 6,452-yard, par-72 course is laced with rock and water traps. Also here are a driving range, pro shop, restaurant, and lounge. Greens fees run $16–30. The course is open year-round.

Another 18-hole course is **Twin Falls Municipal Golf Course,** on Grandview Drive, two miles west of Blue Lakes Boulevard off Addison Avenue W., 208/733-3326. Greens fees for the 5,234-yard, par-68 course run $15–18.

Candleridge Golf Course, 2097 Candleridge Rd., 208/733-6577, offers a nine-hole par-31 course stretching over 2,005 yards. Greens fees are about $8 for nine holes. From the south side of the Perrine Bridge, go east on Poleline Road 1.5 miles.

ENTERTAINMENT AND EVENTS
Fine and Performing Arts
The **Magic Valley Arts Council,** 132 Main Ave. S., 208/734-2787, www.magicvalleyartscouncil.org, is the clearinghouse for cultural informa-

tion. Its downtown headquarters includes two small art galleries that exhibit and sell quality local artwork. The council also offers an annual **Arts on Tour** series with the College of Southern Idaho, as well as a midwinter **Foreign Film Festival.**

Nightlife
Twin Falls' nightlife scene, such as it is, centers mostly around the Old Town area, south of downtown via Shoshone Street. **Honkers,** 121 4th Ave. S, 208/733-4613, has frequent live music: sometimes rock, sometimes country. **Woody's,** 213 5th Ave S., is a popular sports bar and pool parlor. Unfortunately, a once-successful brewpub that anchored the Old Town scene went out of business in 2003, though there's hope another entrepreneur will revive the business when the economy picks up.

This is a moviegoing town, with about 20 indoor screens and two drive-ins. For the latest in indie and art-house fare, head for **The Lamphouse Theatre,** 223 5th Ave. S., 208/736-8600. Grab a beer or wine from Woody's next door; you can take it right into the movie. The Lamphouse sometimes presents live theater, too, and the onsite video store rents a great selection of quality films.

Twin Falls has quite a jazz scene, owing to a strong music department at the College of Southern Idaho. (CSI also is the home of the Boise State University Radio Network's statewide jazz feed, on the air here at 1450 AM, in Boise at 730 AM, and in McCall at 89.9 FM.) But because there's no jazz club, you'll find trios and quartets playing in such odd places as the local TCBY. To find out who's playing where, keep your eyes open for fliers around town, or call the CSI jazz studies program at 208/732-6765.

Events
The week leading up to the first weekend in June brings **Western Days** to town. You can "howdy pardner" your way from the mock gunfight to the barbecue to the Western dance to the chili cook-off. Naturally, there's a parade. A few weeks later, **Jazz in the Canyon** takes center stage at Centennial Waterfront Park, with a full day of music including a well-known headliner or two.

The **Twin Falls County Fair and Magic Valley Stampede** is held at the fairgrounds in nearby Filer in August or September. In addition to a PRCA points rodeo, you'll find a Miss Rodeo Idaho contest, an ag expo, medium-name entertainment, and the usual carnie scene.

Polkas and beer: an irresistible combination. **Oktoberfest** comes to Twin Falls in early October, so put on those old Frankie Yankovic albums and start practicing now.

For more information on any of these events, call the chamber of commerce at 208/733-3974.

ACCOMMODATIONS

The two major motel districts in town are on the north end of Blue Lakes Boulevard and on the west end of Addison Avenue (Highway 30). Both zones are busy thoroughfares. The Blue Lakes Boulevard accommodations are primarily the bigger chain motels, while the Addison Avenue establishments are mostly older but serviceable independents.

Under $50

The Twin Falls **Motel 6,** 1472 Blue Lakes Blvd. N., 208/734-3993 or 800/4MOTEL6 (800/466-8356), offers 157 rooms, a pool, and guest laundry.

Near the heart of downtown, **Old Towne Lodge,** 248 2nd Ave. W., 208/733-5630, offers basic but inexpensive rooms with cable TV. **Monterey Motor Inn,** 433 Addison Ave. W., 208/733-5151, has 36 rooms—some nonsmoking—with queen and king beds. Amenities include a pool, indoor hot tub, cable TV with HBO, and a guest laundry.

$50–100

Best Western Apollo Motor Inn, 296 Addison Ave. W., 208/733-2010 or 800/528-1234, offers a complimentary continental breakfast, free HBO, a pool, and a hot tub. On the Blue Lakes strip,

Weston Inn, 906 Blue Lakes Blvd. N., 208/733-6095, has 97 rooms (smoking or nonsmoking), an indoor pool, and free continental breakfast. Family suites are available and pets are allowed.

Super 8 Motel, 1260 Blue Lakes Blvd. N., 208/734-5801 or 800/800-8000, offers queen-size beds, nonsmoking and wheelchair-friendly rooms, cable TV, an in-house guest laundry, and free coffee and doughnuts in the morning.

Comfort Inn, 1893 Canyon Springs Rd., 208/734-7494 or 800/228-5150, is near the south rim of the Snake River canyon and the Perrine Bridge. The inn offers cable TV, a free continental breakfast,, and an indoor pool and spa. King-size suites, some with whirlpool tubs, are available. In the same area, **Holiday Inn Express,** 1910 Fillmore St. N. (across Blue Lakes Boulevard from Magic Valley Mall), 208/732-6001 or 800/465-4329, offers 59 business-friendly rooms, each with modem ports, hair dryers, and irons and ironing boards. Other amenities include free continental breakfast, an indoor pool and spa, cable TV with HBO, and an exercise room.

Red Lion Canyon Springs Hotel, 1357 Blue Lakes Blvd. N, 208/734-5000 or 800/RED-LION (800/733-5466), features 112 rooms—all with king or queen beds, irons, hair dryers, and phones with modem ports—a restaurant and lounge, and an outdoor swimming pool.

AmeriTel Inn, 1377 Blue Lakes Blvd. N., 208/736-8000 or 800/600-6001, offers rooms with either one king or two queen beds. Kids 12 and under stay free with parents. The inn's wide-ranging amenities include a complimentary continental breakfast as well as evening fresh-baked cookies, in-room work areas with modem ports, fax and copy service, satellite TV with HBO and Disney Channel, an indoor pool and Jacuzzi open 24 hours, a fitness center, a half-court basketball court, and a guest laundry room. Suites are available, including some with kitchens and some with in-room spas.

Shilo Inn, 1586 N. Blue Lakes Blvd., 208/733-7545 or 800/222-2244, offers an indoor pool, spa, sauna, and fitness center, satellite TV with premium channels, and a guest laundry. Extra amenities in each room include a VCR, microwave, small refrigerator, an iron and ironing board, and a hair dryer. Rates include continental breakfast.

Camping

The **Twin Falls/Jerome KOA,** 5431 Hwy. 93, 208/324-4169, is five miles north of town, just across I-84. RV sites here run $24–28 a night, tent sites $19, Kamping Kabins $34–47. The large campground has a playground, mini-golf, rec room, laundry, café (breakfast and dinner), store, and, in summer, a heated pool and free outdoor movies. Kids have ample opportunity to do their thing, while parents can take a break from them in the adults-only TV lounge or the adults-only indoor hot tub.

One exit farther east is **Anderson's Camp,** on Tipperary Road, I-84 right off Exit 182, 208/825-9800 or 888/480-9400. This large, full-service park offers all the usual park amenities—laundry, showers, playground, barbecue grills, rec hall—and adds a couple of extras like a pool, waterslide, and miniature-golf course. RV sites with full hookups are $24 a night, tent sites $19. You can also rent a covered wagon to sleep in for $33 a night.

Oregon Trail Campground & Family Fun Center, 2733 Kimberly Rd., Twin Falls, ID 83301, 208/733 0853 or 800/733-0853, is on the way out of town heading east on Kimberly Road (Highway 30). The 40-site RV park features a playground, restrooms and showers, a game room, snack bar, and guest laundry (open 24 hours). RV sites with hookups cost $18 a night; tent sites are $15 a night.

FOOD

Twin Falls is clogged with chain eateries, most concentrated along the Blue Lakes Boulevard–Pole Line Road axis on the city's north end. But a few local eateries stand out, both here and closer to downtown.

Rock Creek, 200 Addison Ave. W., 208/734-4154, is a longstanding steak-and seafood place west of downtown. With subdued lighting and a friendly bar, it makes a reliable stop for visitors to Twin, with dinner entrées priced mostly in the $12–20 range. Open for dinner only daily.

Right downtown, **Metropolis,** 125 Main Ave. E., 208/734-4457, is a café and bakery open Mon.–Fri. 7:30 A.M.–6 P.M., Saturday 8:30 A.M.–

1 P.M. (an Internet terminal is available for customers; $2 for 15 minutes).

One of the city's newest breakfast and lunch spots, **YoYo Café,** occupies an old house at 1703 Addison Ave. E., 208/732-0044. Come here in fine weather for some of Twin's only outdoor dining. Sandwiches, salads, and quiche (most $6–8) are the menu mainstays. Closed Sundays.

Ethnic Fare

Many Bosnian people moved to Twin Falls during the 1990s via College of Southern Idaho's refugee resettlement program, so Eastern European food isn't hard to find. Aside from being a gathering spot for the local Bosnian community, the **Grill House,** 561 Fillmore St. in the Campus Commons strip mall, 208/734-3356, serves a good variety of meat and chicken dishes and shish kabobs.

The best Thai food in Twin is at **Prasai's Thai Cuisine,** 428 2nd Ave. E., 208/733-2222. Right next door, **Asianna,** 412 2nd Ave. E., 208/733-0777, has sushi, bento boxes, tempura dishes, and more. Entrées at both are mostly in the $7–13 range.

For fast sit-down Mexican food, locals recommend **La Casita,** 111 S. Park Ave., 208/734-7974, and **9 Beans and a Burrito,** 799 Cheney Dr., 208/736-3773. You can fill up at either spot for well under $10.

Creative and traditional Italian dishes are on the menu at **Tomato's,** 1309 Blue Lakes Blvd., 208/735-9100. Prices are fair (most entrées run $9–12), and portions are huge. **Papa Kelsey's Pizza & Subs,** 637 Blue Lakes Blvd. N., 208/733-9484, has good pizza ($12–16) and oven-baked sub sandwiches ($4–7).

Breakfast

For a good breakfast, **Kelly's,** 110 Main St. N., 208/733-0466, is a real find. Great omelettes bursting with fresh veggies and tasty homefried potatoes with a minimum of grease are among the delights on the menu. The bright and cheery downtown eatery is a no-smoking establishment, and it's also open for lunch. Hours are Mon.–Fri. 7 A.M.–2:30 P.M., Saturday 7 A.M.–2 P.M.

Night owls and insomniacs head to the 24-hour **Depot Grill,** 545 Shoshone St. S.,

208/733-0710—a Twin Falls institution since 1927. The Depot serves breakfast around the clock, and the menu offers a delightful variety of pancakes, including the author's favorite: dollar-size buckwheat cakes. Mom's are better, but beggars can't be choosers. The Depot also serves lunch and dinner. The **Buffalo Cafe,** 218 4th Ave. W., 208/734-0271, is open for breakfast and lunch and makes good omelettes.

Coffee

Like its sister establishments in Hailey, Ketchum, and Coeur d'Alene, **Java,** 228 Blue Lakes Blvd. N. (tucked in behind Blockbuster Video), 208/733-9555, boasts great coffee, food, decor, and people. It's open 6:30 A.M.–midnight, every day of the year except Christmas. The Bowl of Soul is the house specialty, but try the "Keith Richards" if you want to rock 'n' roll all night long.

SHOPPING

The 430,000-square-foot **Magic Valley Mall,** 1485 Pole Line Road E., at Blue Lakes Boulevard just south of the Perrine Bridge, 208/733-3000 or 888/686-6255, holds more than 70 stores including JCPenney, Sears, Shopko, and Bon-Macy's. Most shops are open Mon.–Sat. 10 A.M.–9 P.M., Sunday 11 A.M.–6 P.M. There's a six-screen movie theater here, too.

Gear for all your outdoor adventures is the specialty of **Elevation Sports,** 1170 Blue Lakes Blvd. N., 208/734-6635. For paddle-sports sales, rentals, and know-how, head to **River Rat Whitewater Toyz,** 138 2nd Ave. S., 208/735-8697.

INFORMATION AND SERVICES

Information

The best spot to pick up visitor information is the **Buzz Langdon Visitor Center,** 3591 Blue Lakes Blvd. N., on the southwest side of the

Perrine Bridge, 208/733-9458. If you don't find an answer there, your next stop might be the **Twin Falls Chamber of Commerce,** 858 Blue Lakes Blvd. N., 208/733-3974 or 800/255-8946, www.twinfallschamber.com.

One note on Twin Falls' confusing downtown grid system: The numbered "avenues" run from northwest to southeast. The numbered "streets," which run southwest-northeast, may soon be rechristened with the names of area towns. Also pay attention to the street names' designation of N, E, and W—for instance, there are two 3rd Avenues: 3rd Avenue N. and 3rd Avenue W., and they are parallel and four blocks apart. If and when the renaming happens, ask for an updated map at the visitor center, chamber, or city offices.

For information on local recreation, contact the city **Parks and Recreation Department,** 136 Maxwell Ave., Twin Falls, ID 83303, 208/736-2265. For adventures farther afield into the **Sawtooth National Forest,** call the forest supervisor at 208/737-3200, or stop by the office at 2647 Kimberly Rd. E., east of downtown. That office also serves as the forest's Twin Falls Ranger District headquarters.

Services

Twin Falls' main **post office** is at 253 2nd Ave. W. There's another branch with Saturday hours at 1376 Fillmore St. Both are 800/275-8777. The city's beautiful **public library** graces the corner across from City Park at 434 2nd Ave. E., 208/733-2964.

Transportation

Twin Falls airport is about four miles south of town on Blue Lakes Boulevard, 208/733-5215. Commercial air service is provided by **Skywest,** 800/453-9417, which makes several flights daily to and from Salt Lake City. The **Greyhound Bus Station** is in the Snake River Chevron at 1390 Blue Lakes Blvd. N., 208/733-3002.

South of the Snake River

HIGHWAY 93 TO NEVADA

Between Twin Falls and Buhl, Highway 93 turns south and makes a beeline for the Nevada border, carrying car- and busloads of gamblers through the high rangeland to casinos at Jackpot, just over the state line. Along the way are a couple of points of interest, as well as the turnoff for the route west to Murphy Hot Springs and the old mining town of Jarbidge, Nevada. Keep your eyes peeled for birds of prey as you head south on the highway; they're abundant (and big!) down here.

Nat-Soo-Pah Hot Springs and RV Park

At Hollister, a clearly marked turnoff leads east 3.5 miles to Nat-Soo-Pah Hot Springs resort, Rt. 1, 2738 E. 2400 N., Twin Falls, ID 83301, 208/655-4337. According to the management, Nat-Soo-Pah means "Magic Mineral Water" in the language of the indigenous Shoshone people.

The resort, established in 1926, is well kept and peaceful, offering camping as well as day use of the spring-fed swimming pool with waterslide, spa and soaking pools, and the picnic grounds. The 125- by 50-foot swimming pool and the 10-person spa are kept at 99°F, while the soak pool is hotter—around 105°—and can accommodate up to 25 people. Don't be put off by the bright green water here; a sign explains that the color comes from a deposit of iron pyrite that the water flows over before emerging from the artesian well.

The large, grassy campground holds 75 sites, 29 of which offer full hookups; renters are welcome. Facilities include showers, bathrooms, and a dump station. Picnickers can take advantage of barbecues and horseshoe pits, and kids will like the game room.

The resort is open early May to late August, weekdays noon–10 P.M., weekends 10 A.M.–10 P.M. Day-use rates are $5 for ages 6 and up, $3 for young 'uns 1–5. Campers pay $12 a site for one vehicle and one or two people, $1 each additional person.

Take the plunge at Nat-Soo-Pah.

SOUTH-CENTRAL IDAHO

Rogerson

There's not much to Rogerson beyond a small store with gas and RV sites, the Salmon Dam Saloon, and a dog sleeping in the road. But that's all the town needs to supply the gamblers en route to Jackpot, or the anglers heading for either of the two reservoirs (Salmon Falls and Cedar Creek) west of town. The road to the reservoirs also continues past Three Creek to Murphy Hot Springs and Jarbidge, Nevada; it's paved all the way to the top of the downgrade into Murphy Hot Springs.

Note: You might be tempted to turn east at Rogerson in an effort to find your way down to **Magic Hot Springs.** At last word, the private facility there is not open to the public.

Salmon Falls and Cedar Creek Reservoirs

A marker out on the highway tells the interesting story of Salmon Falls Reservoir. Salmon Falls Dam was built in 1910, but thanks to low area rainfall and the leaky, porous lava rock around the dam itself, the reservoir didn't fill up until 1984. Access to the reservoir is located around the dam west of Rogerson or at the end of a few gravel roads (ranging 3–7 miles in length) that turn west off Highway 93, south of Rogerson. At the dam, a BLM campground (fee) offers a boat ramp and shaded picnic tables. The campgrounds along the east shore of the reservoir are free but primitive, with neither trees nor gazebos to block the scorching summer sun.

Fishing is good in the lake for rainbow and brown trout, as well as kokanee, crappie, bass, perch, and walleye. Ten miles west of Salmon Falls Dam, Cedar Creek Reservoir offers more fishing and primitive camping.

Murphy Hot Springs/Jarbidge

What is it about this place that brings such a sense of mystery, awe, and wonder? Maybe it's the long, straight road to get here—so long and straight that it leads your eye beyond the edge of perception to the portals of your imagination. Maybe it's the stillness—so still you can hear a hawk think, so quiet you can hear the shadows of the wheatgrass dancing across the sage. Maybe it's the light, brilliant and clear, enveloping you like a womb of radiant energy; or the clouds that drift across the sky like pieces of your last broken heart. Maybe it's the wind, carrying with it the eternal voice of the earth and the spirit of every human and animal that ever passed this way. Life is a poem here—a poem written in a language you cannot speak, yet understand in your heart. Even if you have never been down this road before, you sense that you know this place and have been too long away from it.

About 49 miles west of Rogerson via the Three Creek Road, you get to Murphy Hot Springs. Native Americans from the Duck Valley Indian Reservation reportedly recognize this spot, where two forks of the Jarbidge River meet on their way down from the snow-covered Jarbidge Mountains, and where natural mineral water flows from the earth at 106°F, as a magic spot with healing powers. Those less metaphysically minded will appreciate Murphy Hot Springs simply as a remote and idyllic spot with rivers perfect for fishing or splashing, and picturesque canyon walls leading the eye ever upward toward the Jarbidge massif.

Past Murphy Hot Springs, the narrow gravel road continues 15 more miles to Jarbidge. It first descends one fork of the Jarbidge, past several shaded primitive campsites, before turning back on itself and climbing alongside a more westerly fork. At the U-turn in the road is the BLM's **Jarbidge River Recreation Site,** which, when the river is flowing just right, serves as the put-in point for whitewater rafters and kayakers on the river. Primitive campsites are found on both sides of the river around the put-in.

The Jarbidge River offers a Class IV whitewater run in its short spring season, May–June. The normal takeout is 29 miles downstream at the confluence of the West Fork Bruneau, at Indian Hot Springs. This is one of the remotest stretches of whitewater in the state, through steep-walled canyons filled with wildflowers, cactus, and juniper. Of course, the river's also full of rock gardens and the shores are full of rattlesnakes. Those yearning for this kind of adventure can contact **Wilderness River Outfitters,** P.O. Box 72, Lemhi, ID 83465, 208/756-3959 or 800/252-6581, and sign up for a trip. The six-day trip costs around $1,900, including a run down the Bruneau as well. It's expensive due to the difficult logistics and the fact that each raft carries just one guest plus the guide.

On up the road toward the Nevada state line, you'll climb a canyon that's a veritable Rorschach test of phallic hoodoos. Numerous sandy beaches and swimming holes line the river for the next many miles.

At the top of the hill, the canyon opens out into a broader valley, at the head of which sits Jarbidge, Nevada. Once a booming gold-mining town, today it's a remote mountain enclave supporting about 50 residents in summer, maybe 30 in winter. Here you'll find **Tsawhawbitt's Lodge B&B, The Barn Hotel, The Tired Devil Cafe, The Outdoor Inn,** and the "world-famous" **Red Dog Saloon.** The Red Dog boasts a portrait of Diamondtooth Lil, who was something of a "head madame" for the gaggles of working girls who once serviced the gold miners here. Lil would still like the Red Dog today—the saloon advertises half-price drinks for unescorted women on Thursday nights. And down at the Outdoor Inn, make sure to check out the wooden bar. It was hand-carved out of Burmese mahogany in Massachusetts around 1865, shipped around the Horn, and used at the Golden Nugget in Las Vegas before being brought up here 25 years ago. On one end of the bar is a gorgeous mythic-size sculpture of Pan lusting after Diana—a perfect touch after your trip up the naturally erotic canyon below.

For more about Jarbidge, go buy *Moon Handbooks Nevada.*

Jackpot, Nevada
As with Jarbidge, you'll find out all about Jackpot in *Moon Handbooks Nevada.* Hard up against the border, Jackpot rises out of the Nevada desert like a neon oasis for parched Idaho gamblers. Taken together, the casinos here are the second-largest employer in the greater Twin Falls area. And since most of the town's clientele comes from Idaho, not Nevada, the town runs on Idaho's Mountain Time, not Nevada's Pacific Time.

Cactus Pete's Resort Casino, 775/755-2321 or 800/821-1103, is the town's biggest gaming establishment. In addition to the slots and tables, the resort regularly books name entertainment, although Jackpot, Nevada, is not exactly Las Vegas. The acts you'll see here have usually long since vanished from the Letterman and Leno circuit.

SOUTH HILLS
From the vicinity of Twin Falls, the mountains to the south don't look like much. Unlike the mountain ranges farther east or west, no great attention-getting peaks pierce the skyline here. In fact, from a distance, the terrain looks like nothing more than a thick layer of mud caked on the horizon. But don't let nature's clever disguise fool you into driving on past without further investigation. These hills, known locally as the South Hills, harbor beautiful desert canyons, magnificent groves of cottonwood and aspen, one of the state's healthiest mule deer populations, and hundreds of square miles of uncrowded recreation land.

South from Hansen, Rock Creek Road (County Road G3) follows Rock Creek to its source in the heart of the South Hills. The drive up Rock Creek Canyon is sufficiently entertaining in itself to warrant an afternoon's sightseeing and picnicking. Those with more time will find this a great area for extended exploring.

Rock Creek Stage Station
Today the interstate is miles away, but back in the 1860s, when the Rock Creek Stage Station was built by James Bascom and John Corder, it was one of southern Idaho's major transportation hubs, and the first trading post west of Fort Hall. Oregon Trail wagon trains, stage lines, cowboys and Indians—all passed by here on their way to somewhere else. Gone, today, are the horses whinnying in the stables and the rowdy pioneers downing whiskey and carrying on in the saloon. Now the only sounds breaking the pervasive stillness of the Snake River Plain are the babbling waters of the creek and the birds chirping in the willows.

Herman Stricker bought the property in 1875, and he and his wife, Lucy, scratched a life out of the expansive Snake River Plain. If your imagination is in good working order, you might find the scene quiet enough to let you conjure up the ghosts of Herman and Lucy for a guided tour of their home on the range. The old store—the oldest building in southern Idaho—still stands, alongside a couple of sod-roofed underground cellars. The dry cellar was used to store supplies and as protection from Native Americans, while the "wet" cellar housed booze for the saloon. Nearby is the turn-of-the-20th-century house Lucy had built after the Strickers' original home burned down in 1899, as well as a graveyard holding the remains of a dozen or so pioneers. Among the graves are two identified only as "a gypsy woman, 1893," and "immigrant baby, 1897."

The site is a great spot for a picnic, and you'll come away with a feeling for what it must have been like on the Oregon Trail so long ago. Rock Creek Stage Station is five miles south of Hansen, a bit west of County Road G3 (watch for signs), and the buildings are sometimes open for tours. Admission is free; donations are appreciated. For more information or an appointment to tour the home, call either the Idaho State Historical Society at 208/334-2844, or the Friends of Stricker Ranch at 208/423-4000.

Campgrounds

Forest Service campgrounds and picnic areas line Rock Creek Canyon from bottom to top. In ascending order: **Schipper Campground** (seven sites, free), where an incredibly steep trail climbs the bluffs behind camp for a panoramic view of the canyon; Birch Creek picnic area; Harrington Fork picnic area (wheelchair friendly); Third Fork picnic area and trailhead; **Lower and Upper Penstemon Campgrounds** (12 sites, fee); **Pettit Campground** (eight sites, fee); and **Diamondfield Jack Campground and trailhead** (eight sites, free), which, at 7,000 feet, is the highest of the campgrounds and particularly popular with the dirt-bike and ATV crowd.

Penstemon and Diamondfield Jack Campgrounds are kept open year-round. The others open anywhere between April and June, depending on the snowpack, and usually close for the season sometime between mid-September and mid-October.

Nature Trails

An easy, quarter-mile interpretive trail leads up to small but picturesque **Ross Falls,** between the Third Fork and Lower Penstemon sites. The aspen groves and ferns along the trail give the area a lush feeling, contrasting sharply with the sage-covered slopes visible across the canyon. The 2.6-mile **Eagle Nature Trail** loops between the Pettit and Diamondfield Jack areas, taking you on an enjoyable stroll past stands of lodgepole pine, subalpine fir, and quaking aspen. If those trails put you in the mood for something longer, consult your Forest Service map or the Twin Falls Ranger District, 2647 Kimberly Rd. E., 208/737-3200, for the hundreds of miles of trails crisscrossing the Sawtooth National Forest here.

Skiing

Near the crest of the hills, you'll come to small **Magic Mountain Ski Area** (mailing address: 3367 N. 3600 E., Kimberly, ID 83341), 208/423-6221 or 800/255-8946. The area offers 20 runs and 700 vertical feet serviced by one double chair, a poma, and a rope tow. Lift tickets cost around $20; family rates available. The small day lodge and café here are also open in summer.

A short distance beyond the ski hill is the **Diamondfield Jack Snow Play Area,** the end of the plowed road in winter. The trailhead here serves more than 200 square miles of USFS and BLM lands heavily used by snowmobiles in winter and by motorcycles and other ORVs in summer. If you like the social scene created by hordes of happy dirt-bikers, this is your place—camp anywhere in the vicinity. If you're looking for something a little quieter, see Two More Campgrounds, below.

The USFS Twin Falls Ranger District sets several **cross-country-ski trails** in the area. The Magic Trail is an easy half-kilometer loop behind the ski area lodge. Also good for beginners is Centennial Trail, a 1.6-kilometer loop at Penstemon snowplay area, by Lower Penstemon Campground. A bit harder are the Penstemon Trail, which offers two loops of five and 13 kilometers heading north from Upper Penstemon Campground; and the Rock Creek Trail, which offers loops of three and four kilometers heading south, across the road from the ski lodge. The hardest trail, Wahlstrom Hollow, is a 6.5-kilometer loop on the east side of the road about a mile north of the ski lodge. For more information, call the ranger district at 208/737-3200.

Pike Mountain Overlook

Unlike most mountaintop viewpoints, this one is easy to reach in the old Rambler (only in summer, of course—in winter you'll need cross-country skis). The road has been well graded, and the summit (elevation 7,708 feet) is developed for tourist use. A large gravel parking area on top could accommodate a small car dealership, and asphalt paths provide easy wheelchair access. Views are impressive: the South Hills roll hither and yon in every direction, and mountain ranges picket the horizon. It's a nice place for a picnic. Look for the signed turnoff at the south end of the ski area.

Two More Campgrounds

Unlike the campgrounds listed above—which are right on Rock Creek Road and hence very popular—the two described below are found next to each other in a high, remote area that requires some off-pavement driving to reach. But the rewards are worth the extra effort for those who prefer tranquillity to the constant cacophony of motorized on- and off-road vehicles. Pick up a Forest Service map before you set out, at either the Twin Falls Ranger District office, 2647 Kimberly Rd. in Twin Falls, 208/737-3200, or the Burley Ranger District office, 3650 S. Overland Ave. in Burley, 208/678-0430. Armed with the map, you can choose from one of two routes to reach the campgrounds. Take either FR 500 and FR 526, or FR 538, FR 533, and FR 526. The roads are pretty good, though expect to be bounced around a bit and don't attempt them when they're wet.

Fathers and Sons Campground is a small, quiet area with restrooms, picnic tables, water from a pump, and an abundance of wildflowers. **Bostetter Campground** is larger, along Bostetter Spring. Check at the adjacent guard station for an update on the water quality here. The two fee campgrounds hold a total of 37 sites and are a

world away from the moto-madness of the Diamondfield Jack area. You'll still find ORVs here, but the numbers are small enough to preserve a semblance of tranquility. Both campgrounds usually are open between June and mid-September.

To Rogerson

FR 500 heads west from near the ski area, eventually taking you down to Rogerson. Along the way it passes the **Shoshone Wildlife Pond,** a 27-acre enclosure providing secure nesting habitat for waterfowl, and **Bear Gulch Campground,** a 13-site fee area at an elevation of just under 6,000 feet.

Phantom Falls

Think twice before heading off to explore isolated Phantom Falls. The road there from the Diamondfield Jack area is long, and beyond the two campgrounds it's rough going in places. If you're bound and determined to take the mountain roads all the way over to Oakley, you'll pass right by the trail to the falls and might want to check them out. If you're planning on returning down Rock Creek Canyon, the difficulty of the trip to the falls would probably outweigh the interest.

Leaving the Fathers and Sons Campground area, the road winds its way gradually down out of the mountains. The temperature starts to warm up, and the pines give way to high-desert chaparral. The trailhead to the falls is well marked. The hot, dry, and dusty trail climbs alongside Fall Creek. Its gurgling water can be heard all the way to the falls but makes only a few fleeting cameo appearances—most of the way it's hidden from sight by thick streamside vegetation. All the way to the falls, plentiful cow pies mark the area as rangeland. The often goopy and fly-ridden piles can be found right next to the water in many places, making the thought of a refreshing splash in the creek much less appealing.

After 1.5 miles of easy hiking, you reach the falls. Here the creek drops about 50 feet off an impressive overhanging rock face. The cool cascade might tempt the overheated hiker into showering in the spray. It comes down pretty hard, however, and other than this natural shower, there is no way to enjoy the water. You'll find no pool at the bottom to swim or even soak in—just an inch or two of water lapping up against the cowflops.

If you are continuing east to Oakley, you'll find easy going on gravel road from here on out.

UP THE SNAKE RIVER

Murtaugh

The town of Murtaugh is a tiny farming hamlet set off from even the rural stretch of Highway 30 that passes just to the south. Once a railroad town, Murtaugh retains some glimpses of its heritage. Check out the **Iron Rail Bar & Grill,** 109 W. Archer, down by the tracks, 208/432-5657. The 1908 building used to be the railroad depot, and later served as a Model T repair garage and a general store. Today it provides a character-infused stop for those who have come to partake of the numerous recreational opportunities nearby.

Whitewater Rafting

The bridge over the Snake River at Murtaugh is the put-in point for experienced rafters and kayakers attempting the **Murtaugh Reach.** At peak spring flows, this is one of the toughest stretches of whitewater in the state. The 15-mile section of river between here and just above Twin Falls offers a number of Class III and IV rapids. Agricultural diversion in early summer makes for a short season, however. **Idaho Guide Service,** 563 Trotter Dr., Twin Falls, ID 83301, 208/734-4998 or 888/734-3246, and **White Otter Outdoor Adventures,** P.O. Box 2733, Ketchum, ID 83340, 208/726-4331, lead guided day trips on the Murtaugh Reach. Expect to pay around $100 per person, including lunch.

Caldron Linn

Even the worst rapids on the Murtaugh Reach can't compare to what lies just upriver from the bridge: the man-eating falls at Caldron Linn, which early settlers nicknamed the Devil's Scuttle Hole. Linn is the Scottish word for waterfall, and this linn's resemblance to a boiling, bubbling witch's caldron earned the cascade its sinister moniker. On Oct. 28, 1811, Wilson Price Hunt's fur-trapping expedition attempted to navigate the rapids. One of the trappers, Antoine Clappine, drowned in the attempt. A year later, Robert Stuart's Astoria party passed this way and described the scene thusly:

> *[A]t the Caldron Linn the whole body of the River is confined between two ledges of Rock somewhat less than 40 feet apart, and here indeed its terrific appearance beggars all description—Hecate's caldron was never half so agitated when vomiting even the most diabolical spells as is this Linn in a low stage of water.*

To get to the site, cross the Murtaugh bridge and turn east on the other side of the river, following signs down to the falls.

Murtaugh Lake

Those who prefer placid water underneath their boat can cross Highway 30 to the south and head down to Murtaugh Lake, a haven for anglers, water-skiers, and white pelicans in the middle of the arid desert.

Camping is available at either of two areas on the west shore of the lake. **Dean's Cove** is maintained by the Murtaugh Lakes Ski Club and Twin Falls County. The small grassy area is lined with a couple of docks and has tree-shaded picnic tables. The other area, **Murtaugh Lake Park,** is bigger, offering lots of grass, a baseball field, docks, picnic tables and shelters, restrooms, and boat ramps.

Milner Dam and Recreation Area

Milner Dam was completed in 1905, and the newly backed-up waters were diverted into canals that irrigated some 360,000 acres of cropland. Twin Falls, Jerome, and other towns to the west subsequently grew up along the river. Along the south side of Milner Reservoir, history and recreation share the spotlight at the BLM's Milner Historic Recreation Area. The 2,055-acre site provides easy access to the water for anglers, boaters, and water-skiers. It also preserves a stretch of Oregon Trail ruts. At this point the westward-bound OT pioneers had journeyed 1,315 miles from their starting point in Independence, Missouri. A small interpretive gazebo provides more details for trailophiles.

The character of the river changes here compared to points west. The volcanic, basalt cliffs found farther downstream are exchanged for low, verdant banks. Several free, primitive campsites are found along the reservoir's south bank.

Mini-Cassia Country

Before the Snake River was dammed and the volcanic soil of Snake River Plain irrigated, communities such as Oakley and Albion developed along rivers in the higher valleys to the south. After the advent of irrigation, communities developed on the Snake River Plain as well. Rupert and Burley, both founded in 1905, were the biggest of these in this region. Today Rupert is the seat of Minidoka County, which extends north from I-84 out into the lava fields. Burley is the seat of Cassia County, which encompasses the original high-valley settlements and several interspersed mountain ranges south of the interstate. Together, the two are known as Mini-Cassia Country, a combination of the two counties' names.

BURLEY

Burley lies near the crossroads of five pioneer trails. The Oregon Trail ran from east to west about one mile south of town. The California Trail branched off the Oregon Trail and turned south up the Raft River Valley. The Salt Lake City–Oregon Trail route used after 1838 crossed the California Trail near here. And the Salt Lake–California Trail route joined the California Trail just south of the City of Rocks. Finally, the Hudspeth Cutoff, first taken in 1849, came straight west over from Soda Springs.

The town is named after David Burley, an Oregon Short Line Railroad agent who also helped foster the region's potato-farming industry.

Cassia County Historical Society Museum

One of the finer specimens on the historical museum circuit, this one, at E. Main Street and Highland Avenue, 208/678-7172, brings together an impressive collection of artifacts. You'll find a number of re-created rooms, from a doctor's office

to a photo studio to a saloon; collections of saddles, guns, hand tools, sewing machines, dolls, toys, and more; and displays pertaining to the area's sheep, mining, and fur industries. But don't miss the collections of old newspapers and photographs. Among the newspaper articles are some detailing the trials and tribulations of Diamondfield Jack. And my favorite photo records the first auto accident in Burley. The year was 1914. Someone drove their car into a canal! A couple of other beautiful old photos show Shoshone Falls and Twin Falls—*before* the dams were built.

The museum is open April 1–Nov. 1, Tues.–Sat. 10 A.M.–5 P.M., or by appointment. Admission is free, but donations are gratefully accepted.

Recreation

The city's 20 miles of river frontage make for easy access to Snake River recreation. Waterskiing is popular here, with boat landings on the north side of Burley Bridge and adjacent to Burley Golf Course.

Burley Municipal Golf Course, E. 16th St., 208/678-9807, offers 18 holes over 6,500 yards. The scenic par-72 course lies astride the Snake River, and costs $17 on the weekends, $16 during the week. Also here are a driving range, pro shop, and snack bar. Take I-84, Exit 208, to Main Street and turn left; the course will be straight ahead on your left.

Events

On the last weekend of June, speedboats thunder down the Snake River during the **Idaho Regatta.** The event draws powerboat fans out of the woodwork, temporarily doubling the town's population. It's held at the riverfront marina.

The **Cassia County Fair and Rodeo** is a six-day Western wingding in mid-August featuring a rodeo, exhibits, rides, and food. It's held at the fairgrounds on Main Street. The last weekend in July brings the **Spudman Triathlon,** an event that has been covered by ESPN and called one of "20 triathlons not to miss" by *Triathlete* magazine. Some 300 ironspuds compete. For more information on any of these events, call the Mini-Cassia Chamber of Commerce, 1177 7th St. in Heyburn, 208/679-4793 or 800/333-3408.

Accommodations

$50–100: Near the freeway (Exit 208), **Budget Motel,** 900 N. Overland Ave., 208/678-2200 or 800/635-4952, has 140 nicer-than-average rooms, along with a pool, Jacuzzi, cable TV with Movie Channel, and a kids' playground. Family rates available. Right next door, the 128-room **Best Western Burley Inn & Convention Center,** 800 N. Overland Ave., 208/678-3501 or 800/528-1234, offers an outdoor heated pool, a guest laundry, and an on-site restaurant and lounge.

Food

Across from the fairgrounds, small **Charlie's Café,** 615 E. Main, 208/678-0112, puts a Mexican twist on the basic diner; what a welcome change to get *huevos rancheros* for breakfast in-stead of the usual two eggs scrambled with hash browns and toast. The food is good, and you can get an espresso drink to go with it. Hours are Mon.–Sat. 6 A.M.–9 P.M.

Among the ethnic restaurants in town are **Angela's Authentic Mexican Food,** 1198 E. Main, 208/678-9913; **Lee Chop Stick,** 2126 Overland Ave., 208/678-2003, a Vietnamese restaurant; and **George K's East,** 275 E. 3rd N., 208/678-9173, specializing in Chinese food.

Information

The **Mini-Cassia Chamber of Commerce,** 1177 7th St., Heyburn, ID 83336, 208/679-4793 or 800/333-3408, handles inquiries for both Burley and Rupert.

THE CITY OF ROCKS LOOP
Oakley and Vicinity

When the Saints go marchin' in, Oakley is one of the places they go marching in to, the Saints in this case being the Latter-day Saints, or members of the Mormon Church. Mormons settled the town between 1878 and 1880, and remain dominant here today.

Oakley has a nice collection of 1880s-era stone and brick buildings.

SOUTH-CENTRAL IDAHO

City of Rocks

The whole town has been designated a National Historic District, and a number of surviving turn of the-20th-century buildings are listed on the National Register of Historic Places. **Judge Benjamin Howells Mansion,** a Queen Anne–style home built by the judge in 1909, today is a private residence only rarely opened to the public. The nearby 1904 **Howells Opera House** was renovated in the 1980s to once again serve as an entertainment venue. And the Gothic Revival **Marcus Funk/Tanner Residence** was built in 1900 by a Mormon polygamist who intended one floor of the mansion for each of his three wives. The stone evident in much of the local construction—Oakley Stone, a type of quartzite—is still quarried in the area and is shipped worldwide for use in construction and as flagstone.

Oakley's **City Park,** on Main Street, provides a shady green with picnic tables, a playground, and the municipal pool (open June 1 to Labor Day, 1–6 P.M. and 7–9 P.M.). Also in the park is the memorial jail cell that once imprisoned (rightly or wrongly?) the legendary Diamondfield Jack Davis. On Main Street across from the park, the **Daughters of the Utah Pioneers Historical Museum** provides an artifact-filled peek at Oakley's past. It's open summer weekends 2–5 P.M.

Seven miles southwest of town is **Goose Creek Reservoir,** where boating, fishing, and swimming help residents beat the summer heat. The road to the west side of the dam (Trapper Creek Road) continues to Phantom Falls and eventually on up into the South Hills.

City of Rocks National Reserve

Castles of eroded granite, some over 600 feet tall, create a mythic, fairy-tale landscape at this out-of-the-way natural landmark. They also make City of Rocks one of the country's top rock-climbing destinations. As at Yosemite, Joshua Tree, and Smith Rocks, here you'll hear the clinking of climbing gear from sunup until sundown and a host of foreign languages being spoken in the campgrounds that dot the preserve. Rock jocks have put up more than 600 routes, ranging in difficulty from 5.4 up to supposedly a 5.14a.

The 14,300-acre preserve also lies at a major intersection of pioneer trails. What a sight this must have been for those early adventurers! Some of them were moved to record their passage in axle grease on Signature Rock alongside the trail. Today the signatures of these California-bound settlers and miners can still be seen on the rock, between the preserve and Almo.

Another bit of history here concerns a famous heist. In 1878, bandits held up the Overland Stage near Almo. Supposedly they buried their loot somewhere out here in the City of Rocks. But the granite towers remain silent as to its whereabouts.

Among the most impressive rock formations at City of Rocks is Twin Sisters, on the west side of the preserve. The elder sister is composed of granite 2.5 billion years old, while the younger one was born just 25–30 million years ago. The two look similar, however, because for millions of years they've been subject to the same forces of erosion.

The reserve's 78 primitive campsites go for $7 per site per night for up to eight people (plus $5 for a second vehicle). They're reservable, with a $6 reservation fee. For campsite reservations and more information, call the reserve headquarters in Almo, four miles to the east, or see www.nps.gov/ciro. There's no fee to enter the park.

Sawtooth Mountain Guides, P.O. Box 18, Stanley, ID 83278, 208/774-3324, www.sawtoothguides.com, holds climbing classes and guided trips at City of Rocks several times a year and also plans instruction at the new Castle Rocks State Park. Contact the outfitter for more details.

Castle Rocks State Park

Rock climbers are positively giddy over the opening of this, Idaho's newest state park, right next door to City of Rocks. Not only is it the first major new climbing area in the United States to open in the last quarter-century, but it was designed by climbers, for climbers. Once a private ranch, Castle Rocks includes many of the same sort of challenging granite spires as its neighbor. Although crag climbing is the park's reason for being, it's not the only thing to do at the 1,240-acre preserve. Picnic grounds, horseback trails,

> *Castles of eroded granite, some over 600 feet tall, create a mythic, fairy-tale landscape at City of Rocks. They also make this out-of-the-way natural landmark one of the country's top rock-climbing destinations.*

and mountain biking are other attractions, and the wildlife watching is superb, too: You may see mule deer, bighorn sheep, or even mountain lions. Castle Rocks is a day-use-only park, and the usual $4 state park vehicle admission fee applies.

Almo

Almo was founded in 1881 as a stage stop on the Kelton-to-Boise route. Neither the stage route nor any other major thoroughfare passes through town today. Yet down at **Tracy's Merc,** 208/824-5570, you're liable to see license plates from all over the United States and hear foreign languages from all over the world. That's because the town serves as the supply center for the City of Rocks. Tracy's, established in 1894, still uses a turn-of-the-century National Cash Register to tally up the gallons of bottled water and other camping supplies it sells to climbers. On the south end of town you'll find the **City of Rocks National Reserve-Castle Rocks State Park Headquarters,** 3035 Elba-Almo Rd., P.O. Box 169, Almo, ID 83312, 208/824-5519, where you can pick up information about rock climbing or the areas's rich human history.

Cache Peak Area

North of Almo, Highway 77 leads to the community of Elba, where you can turn west and head up into the highest reaches of the Albion Mountains. These are the state's highest mountains south of the Snake River. Here you'll find glacially carved, high-alpine scenery—a rarity in southern Idaho.

The four **Independence Lakes** sit in a high cirque between Mount Independence (9,950 feet) and Cache Peak (10,339 feet). It's a three-mile hike up to the lakes, the lower two of which offer good trout fishing. To get to the trailhead, take FR 548 east from Elba (or west from Oakley) up to the Basin-Elba pass. There, take FR 562 south to FR 728 east. A small parking area is at the trailhead on Dry Creek.

Mountaineers looking to bag Cache Peak

will find a Class 2 route up the northwest ridge—leave from Independence Lakes and head first to the saddle between Cache Peak and Mount Independence.

For more information, contact the USFS **Burley Ranger District,** Rt. 3, 3650 Overland Ave., Burley, ID 83318, 208/678-0430.

BLM Recreation Areas

Back down to Elba, a short jaunt north on Highway 77 brings you to Connor Junction. Here you can continue north back to Burley, or east to the Raft River Valley and beyond to I-84 on its southeasterly run to the Utah border. Three BLM recreation areas are found in this general area.

The **Jim Sage Mountains** lie to your right heading north from Elba, and rise due south of Connor Junction. The mountains are public land and open for exploring but are entirely undeveloped.

East of Connor Junction, on the way to Malta, you'll come to a signed turnoff on your left to BLM's **McClendon Spring Recreation Site.** The gravel road climbs minimally and gradually before turning north and taking a level course to a beautiful, cottonwood-shaded seasonal spring. The spot was used as a campsite by pioneers traveling the California Trail. Today, primitive campsites here offer panoramic views of the Raft River Valley and the Black Pine Mountains beyond. The Black Pine Range, with its distinctive bumpy top—high in the middle and low on both ends—looks to the mind's eye like the back of a giant, sleeping crocodile.

As you continue north from Connor Junction, a signed turnoff to the right leads to **Coe Creek BLM Picnic Area.** The BLM official responsible for designating this site must have been cruising around in the government-issue four-by, contemplating what cruel joke he or she could inflict on the unsuspecting tourist. Not that there aren't some worthwhile reasons to check out this site. But the dirt road to get there climbs three long miles virtually straight up into the Cotterel Mountains—don't even consider bringing the Winnebago. Once you finally get there, you'll find a humble, overgrown, viewless picnic area next to a seasonal spring. The adjacent aspen

grove is nice, but the barbed wire and cow pies aren't. All in all, it's probably not worth the trip for anyone but the most curious adventurer or the duty-bound travel writer. The upside is in the views of Cache Peak, Mount Harrison, and Albion Valley that you'll get on the way back down.

For more information on the BLM lands in this area, contact the **BLM Burley District,** 200 S. Oakley Hwy., Burley, ID 83318, 208/678-5514.

Howell Canyon Recreation Area

This popular area in the Sawtooth National Forest above Albion offers year-round recreation opportunities ranging from camping, fishing, horseback riding, and hiking in summer to skiing and snowmobiling in winter. The road up the canyon takes off from Highway 77 just south of Albion and winds its way up into the mountain heights. A good viewpoint pullout along the way puts the area's landscape into aerial perspective.

Heading up the mountain, you'll first encouter the short spur that leads down to **Bennett Springs Campground,** offering six free sites along an aspen-lined creek. Next up the hill comes the **Howell Canyon Snowmobile Area.** The trailhead parking area here serves 25–30 square miles of trails, mostly on snow-covered Forest Service roads.

A little higher is **Pomerelle Mountain Resort,** P.O. Box 158, Albion, ID 83311, 208/673-5599 or 208/673-5555 (snow report). The 8,000-foot elevation here makes for plenty of fluffy-dry powder on the area's 24 runs, all groomed; five runs are lit for night skiing Tues.–Sat. from the end of December through mid-March. One thousand vertical feet are served by a triple chair, a double chair, and a free rope tow. Snowboarders will like the halfpipe, while skinny-skiers can skate off down the small **cross-country ski** trail system set from the far side of the parking lot. A full-day lift ticket costs $25, youth ages 7–12 pay $17, and kids 6 and under ski free if they ski with a parent at all times. Night passes are $15. Rentals, lessons, and food are available at the base area, and a shuttle bus runs weekends and holidays from Jerome, Twin Falls, Burley, and Rupert. The resort is open daily in season—usually mid-November until mid-April—and open for hiking in summer.

DIAMONDFIELD JACK: A STORY OF FRONTIER JUSTICE

In the late 1880s, great herds of both cattle and sheep grazed the rangelands of southern Idaho. Ranching was then—as it still is—big business. Ranchers prospered and ranching dynasties grew out of the high-desert chaparral. But cattle and sheep don't mix well on the range because of differences in their eating habits. Picture a lawnmower with an adjustable blade. If you set the blade high, you'll cut your grass at the level a grazing cow would. If you set it low, you'll cut your grass at sheep level. Sheep can graze where cattle have previously dined, but not vice versa; once sheep have grazed a meadow, cattle will find the cupboard bare.

For a while, the two ranching factions had a gentleman's agreement worked out, whereby sheep would run the east side of the Goose Creek Divide, cattle the west. But as more and more sheepmen came to the area, they began to push over the divide into cattle country. Not surprisingly, this led to first animosity, then confrontation. One of the biggest cattle dynasties in the region was the Sparks-Harrell Cattle Company. The company tired of sheepmen encroaching on its lands and decided to do something about it.

Jackson Lee Davis, a.k.a. Diamondfield Jack, showed up in Albion one day in 1895. No one knew where the mysterious stranger came from, but soon after his arrival he landed a job as a range rider with the Sparks-Harrell Company. His main duties, it seems, were not in the nature of fence-mending and cowpunching. Instead, he was employed at top dollar to keep shepherds off the ranch—a task he performed quite well by intimidation. He was only about 25 years old at the time, but he was a crack shot with a .45, talked a tough line, and tended to brag and boast loudly about his exploits, real or imagined. Soon he developed quite a reputation as a mean SOB.

In early February 1896, Jack and a man named Fred Gleason saddled up and rode out to tour the vast ranch. On February 17, two young shepherds were found dead in their sheep camp, just east of Rogerson on Deep Creek, 80 miles southwest of Albion. Jack was blamed immediately but was nowhere to be found. A warrant went out for his arrest, and he was finally tracked down in Arizona and returned to Idaho to stand trial.

The sensational trial pitted cattlemen against sheepmen. The two dead sheepers had been Mormons, and Albion was a Mormon town in sheep territory, so things didn't look good for Jack. Both sides hired high-powered attorneys: William Borah for the prosecution, James Hawley for the defense. Sparks-Harrell nearly went broke trying to save Jack from the gallows. Fred Gleason was tried and acquitted in April 1897. Jack was convicted of first-degree murder,

The ski area marks the end of the plowed road in winter. In summer, the road continues higher to **Thompson Flat Campground,** situated near a high meadow filled with wildflowers and some cattle. The campground—in a neighboring lodgepole pine grove—is a fee area for either overnight camping or day-use picnicking, though cattle get in free.

A short distance past Thompson Flat the road forks, with the right fork descending to beautiful **Lake Cleveland.** The cirque lake is flanked on three sides by steep slopes, including some impressive granite walls. The high alpine feel here makes the lake a favorite of Mini-Cassia anglers

and campers. A small campground on the far (west) shore of the lake gets crowded in summer. A larger campground on the near side offers more room and fewer people but isn't right on the lake. Both sites are fee areas for either overnighting or day-use picnicking. You're up at 8,300 feet here—don't look for hookups. Fishing in the lake is good for rainbow trout.

Back at the fork in the road, bearing left will take you up good graded road right to the summit of **Mount Harrison** (elevation 9,200 feet) and the Forest Service fire lookout there. From up here, the irrigated farmlands down on the Snake River Plain stretch out to the northern horizon

entirely on circumstantial evidence, and sentenced to hang on June 4, 1897. His lawyers appealed and Jack received a stay of execution pending appeal. The appeals dragged on for four years, during which time Jack was jailed in Albion. There he became popular with the local townsfolk for his polite manners and jovial demeanor under the circumstances. Parents let their kids talk to Jack through his cell bars.

In November 1900, two cattlemen employed by Sparks-Harrell Co., Jeff Gray and J. E. Bower, confessed to the killing. They said they had gotten in a fight with the two sheepmen and killed them in self-defense, a story most subsequent researchers believe to be true. A corncob pipe found at the scene was identified as Bower's. The two men were tried and acquitted, the jury agreeing with the self-defense argument.

So Jack was set free, right? Wrong. Frontier justice wasn't bound by common sense. The case went all the way to the U.S. Supreme Court, which upheld the lower courts. The hanging would proceed, Jack's final days loomed, and his only hope now was a pardon from the state Board of Pardons.

The hanging was scheduled for July 3, 1901, anytime between sunrise and sunset, at the discretion of the sheriff. Thankfully, the sheriff decided on sunset. Meanwhile, a couple of Jack's allies rode to the telegraph office in Minidoka to await word of a pardon from the Board. There was a telegraph line into Albion, but it would be too risky to rely on that—the sheepmen might cut it.

On the morning of July 3, the Board of Pardons met and commuted Jack's sentence from death to life imprisonment. He was to be transferred to Idaho Territorial Prison in Boise. The telegraph came through to Minidoka and the two riders grabbed it and rode off for Albion at breakneck speed, changing horses twice en route and arriving in Albion with just three hours to spare. When he got the news, the sheriff treated Jack to a sumptuous dinner, and the townspeople gave Jack gifts to send him on his way to Boise.

Jack spent 18 months at the Old Pen. During that time, his friends assembled enough proof of his innocence to convince the Board of Pardons to grant Jack an unconditional pardon and restoration of his good name. He was set free on December 18, 1902. On the day of his release, the state sent a buggy to take Jack from the prison into town. But first he stopped off at the old Natatorium resort on Warm Springs Boulevard and enjoyed drinks with James Hawley, his erstwhile lawyer, who had been elected mayor of Boise.

like a patchwork quilt. To the south, many of the mountains you see lie across the state line in Utah. Mount Harrison is also known as a popular **hang gliding** area; international glider meets are occasionally held here.

Albion

Founded in 1868, Albion was a logging center for the timber taken down from the Albion Mountains that rise just outside town. The town enjoyed county seat status until irrigation of the Snake River Plain drew most of the local populace down the hill. The county seat was moved to Burley in 1919. Albion gained particular notoriety in 1897, when Diamondfield Jack Davis was jailed, tried, and convicted here for the murder of two sheepmen (see the sidebar "Diamondfield Jack").

At the north end of town, a group of impressive old buildings stands abandoned on a hillock. They were constructed in 1893 for the campus of **Albion Normal School,** a state teacher's college that closed in 1951. The campus was taken over by Magic Valley Christian College for a time, but that school, too, closed its doors and moved off to eastern Oregon. Eventually the state sold the 44-acre site and all the buildings to the city of Albion. The city continues its efforts to attract some organization willing to spend the money to bring the buildings back to life. The buildings and the grounds are so peaceful and beautiful, it's a shame to see them fade into oblivion.

For a good meal in Albion, visit the **Sage Mountain Grill**, 255 N. Main St., 208/673-6696. It serves breakfast, lunch, and dinner daily, including fine dining on weekends and outdoor seating when the weather allows.

RUPERT AND VICINITY

Kitty-corner from Burley on the north side of the interstate, Rupert is the Minidoka County seat. The U.S. Bureau of Reclamation laid out the town in 1905, when it was building Minidoka Dam. The downtown area surrounds a beautiful town square, a feature seldom seen in this part of the country.

The town might be named for a Bureau of Reclamation engineer, or it might be named for a pioneer-era mail carrier. To find out which alternative is more likely, check in at the **Minidoka County Museum**, 100 E. Baseline, 208/436-0336, a mile east of town. It's open daily 1–5 P.M.; closed major holidays.

Rupert throws an **Independence Day Celebration** par excellence. The obligatory rodeo is supplemented by food and fireworks. For more information, call the **Mini-Cassia Chamber of Commerce**, 1177 7th St., Heyburn, ID 83336, 208/679-4793 or 800/333-3408. It's open Mon.–Fri. 9 A.M.–4 P.M.

Minidoka Dam and Lake Walcott State Park

With the Reclamation Act of 1902, Congress authorized construction of dams along the Snake River and provided irrigated land to settlers to farm. The farmers would make annual payments to the government for a term, at the end of which they would receive title to the land along with water rights on it. Minidoka Dam was built in 1906, the first of the Reclamation Act projects on the Snake. After the dam was completed and irrigation began to turn the brown plains green, thousands of settlers disembarked at the Minidoka railroad station with hopes of sowing their dreams

in southern Idaho's volcanic soil. Other dams on the Snake followed, eventually irrigating a total of one million acres of dry, high-desert chaparral.

A hydroelectric plant was soon added at Minidoka Dam; seven turbines weighing over five tons each were hauled in by horse-drawn wagon from the Minidoka rail station. Power from the plant—the first federal hydropower project in the Northwest—was used to pump water into the irrigation system, with the remainder delivered to surrounding towns. As a result, Rupert was one of the first towns in the country to be powered by electricity.

During construction of the 86-foot-high, earth-filled dam, crews lived in an adjacent camp. When the dam was completed, their camp evolved into **Walcott Park**, the focal point for recreation on the lake. The park was popular with the region's residents right from the start. On the July 4 weekend in 1912, an estimated 500 revelers celebrated the holiday here. Today the 22-acre park is still popular with boaters, water-skiers, windsurfers, and anglers. The latter might come up with a trout, bass, or perch on the end of their lines. Large expanses of grass and groves of mature shade trees make the park a picnickers' paradise, and beautiful walking or bike paths meander along the shoreline, past cattails, cottonwoods, and willows. The campground offers 23 sites for $16 a night with hookups, as well as two camping cabins that sleep up to five people for $35. For information, call the park office at 208/436-1258.

Note: In order not to disturb migratory waterfowl, the lake is closed to all boating Sept. 30–March 31.

Minidoka National Wildlife Refuge

Lake Walcott is also the centerpiece of the Minidoka National Wildlife Refuge, a 20,000-acre preserve established in 1909. Birdwatchers will have a field day here; in fall, up to a quarter million ducks and geese pass through. You might also spot whistling swans, snowy egrets, and great blue herons. Winter brings bald eagles, ospreys, Canada geese, and mallards. In spring look for tundra swans, common loons, and lots and lots of ducks, including buffleheads, common goldeneyes, and common mergansers. Summertime brings western and Clark's grebes and white pelicans. In addition to the abundant birdlife, the refuge also supports a healthy population of mule deer.

The U.S. Fish and Wildlife Service's refuge headquarters, Rt. 4 Box 290, Rupert, ID 83350, 208/436-3589, is next to Walcott State Park, where you'll find a campground with picnic areas and boat-launching facilities. Anglers heading out onto the water will find the fishing good for perch and rainbow and brown trout. Small populations of crappie and bass are also present.

EXPLORING THE WAPI FLOW AND GREAT RIFT

Confirmed desert rats, spelunkers, and lava lovers will find outstanding exploring opportunities in the barren desert northeast of Rupert. A vast sea of lava here, the Wapi Flow, oozed out of a shield volcano at Pillar Butte only a relatively short 2,100 years ago. The intense volcanic activity in this hot spot also created the Great Rift, a crack in the earth's crust over 800 feet deep in places and stretching northwest from here all the way to Craters of the Moon National Monument. The Great Rift has been designated a National Natural Landmark.

Note that all the sights in this area are found down unimproved dirt roads, impassable when wet, challenging when dry. As Sheldon Bluestein puts it in his book *Exploring Idaho's High Desert* (see Suggested Reading), the roads require "either four-wheel-drive or maximum intestinal fortitude" to navigate. Make sure you have USGS topographic, BLM, or other good maps of the area. Top off your tank before you set out and carry plenty of water with you; if ever a place called for carrying two spare tires, this is it. It's dry and desolate out here, and help is a long way off.

Area Highlights

The three **Baker Caves**—lava tubes, actually—were discovered here in 1985 by local farmer Mark Baker, and subsequently excavated by a team of archaeologists from Boise State University, the Idaho Archaeological Society, and the BLM. The caves Baker discovered held abundant evidence of human habitation dating to about 1,000

years ago. One contained the bones of some 17 bison butchered there. Also found at the site were a few stone pipes, as well as evidence of cooking and the making of beads and reed arrow shafts.

The **Wood Road Kapuka** is an "island" of vegetation surrounded by *pa'hoe'hoe* lava. Here, pioneers cut a road into the kapuka to get to the abundant junipers growing in the area, which they cut down for firewood.

Bear Trap Cave is an impressive gaping mouth in the ground suitable for a role in a Steven Spielberg movie. It's a lava tube, created when an outer skin formed on a stream of lava, cooling and solidifying while the molten magma in the center of the tube flowed right on out. The entry to the cave is a spot where the tube's ceiling collapsed.

Crystal Ice Cave was once a commercial tourist attraction, but the site deteriorated and was closed to the public. The BLM doesn't really want people poking around the ice cave. Unlike the popular tourist attraction Shoshone Ice Cave, this one is not formed in a collapsed lava tube. Rather, it is a part of the Great Rift, a massive fissure in the earth's crust plunging hundreds of feet deep in places. While falling in the wrong place in a lava tube might result in broken bones, a fall into the Great Rift could easily be fatal. As the sign at the site says: VERY DANGEROUS—PLEASE STAY OUT. The lava flows here make for excellent day hiking, however.

Other area points of interest include **Pillar Butte,** source of the Wapi Flow; **Split Butte,** a prominent feature befitting its name; and **Higgins Blow-Out,** a craterlike depression in a butte near the Wood Road Kapuka.

If the foregoing descriptions have tempted you into further exploration of this unique and little-visited area, get directions and more information at the **BLM office** in Burley, 200 S. Oakley Hwy., 208/678-5514, and/or read the aforementioned book by Sheldon Bluestein.

EAST TOWARD AMERICAN FALLS

I-84 to Salt Lake City

East of the Rupert and Burley area you'll soon come to a major interchange where I-84 splits off to the southeast heading toward Ogden, Utah, while I-86 continues the westward journey toward American Falls and Pocatello.

I-84 crosses the Raft River Valley and climbs gradually up the Black Pine Valley, through desolate undeveloped rangeland flanked most of the way by the Black Pine Range to the west and the Sublett Range to the east. Black Pine Valley (also called Juniper Valley) is home to few people but supports significant numbers of ferruginous hawks. These hawks—largest of the North American buteos—nest in the area's widespread stands of Utah juniper. They feast all summer on large local populations of jackrabbits and rodents, then head south to the southwestern United States and northern Mexico for the winter.

After cresting the pass, it's just a hop, skip, and a few gallons of gas to the Utah border, where you'll throw this book into the back seat and reach into the glovebox for *Moon Handbooks Utah.*

One other note at this juncture: if time is not of the essence on your Utah-bound journey, you might consider continuing east on I-86 to the American Falls area, then turning south on one of the more rural and definitely scenic roads that eventually meet I-84 just over the Utah line at Snowville. Highway 37 leaves the interstate west of American Falls and drops through Rockland Valley, intersecting the Arbon Valley Highway

outside Holbrook. The Arbon Valley Highway cuts off the interstate east of American Falls and winds through beautiful wheat fields and through the Curlew National Grasslands on its way to the state line.

Eastbound on I-86

As you cruise east down the interstate, bound for American Falls and the next chapter of this book, you can spot a number of interesting topographical features to either side of the freeway. **Horse Butte** is that big golden beaut to the south just after the freeway splits. The butte is a fault scarp—relatively young in geologic age. Also to the south, you can make out three different mountain ranges along this stretch. The **Raft River Mountains** are the long, low range in the distance that seem to be running parallel to your direction of travel. They're located just across the border in Utah. The range that appears more like a single pyramid is the **Black Pine Range,** while farther east, the low, brown **Sublett Range** starts far to the south and runs north to almost directly in front of you.

On the other, north, side of the freeway, the vast black expanse of the Wapi Flow soon comes into view. The high point that you can see—a long butte with a little raised nipple toward its right edge—is **Pillar Butte,** the shield volcano that was the source of the flow.

Southeast Idaho

Idaho is the number-one potato-producing state in America, and southeast Idaho is the number-one potato-producing region in the state. Across the region you'll see long A-frame potato sheds, as well as miles upon miles of blooming potato fields in summer. Potatoes pervade not only the fields of southeastern Idaho but the culture as well: the mascot of the Shelley High School Russets is a gladiator potato, and the World Potato Expo in Blackfoot—a kind of shrine to *Solanum tuberosum*—holds the world's largest potato chip and other spudobilia.

This corner of the state lays claim to the old-est white settlement in Idaho. Franklin, near the Utah/Idaho border, was established by Mormon pioneers in 1860. These early immigrants thought they were still in Brigham Young's stronghold of Utah, but ended up being Idaho's first settlers instead. The Mormons fanned out from Franklin and today contribute an unmistakable character to the region. A conservative bunch, the Latter-day Saints. Southeast Idaho's nightlife is the state's tamest, and fine-dining opportunities are few and far between.

Pocatello and Idaho Falls are as cosmopolitan as it gets around here. Pocatello is the livelier of

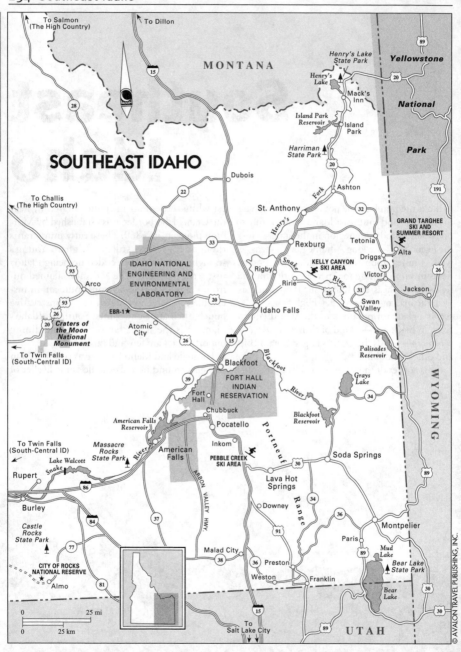

SOUTHEAST IDAHO

the two thanks to its rambunctious railroad heritage and college-town status. Idaho Falls—home to most of the employees of Idaho National Engineering and Environmental Laboratory (INEEL), the state's single largest employer—supports a small urbane contingent that gathers at a handful of popular pubs and coffeehouses. Other noteworthy population centers include the Island Park vicinity, where folks live to snowmobile in winter and fish the Henry's Fork in summer, and the Teton Valley, a rollicking fur-era rendezvous site that has retained a fun-loving spirit ever since.

Those looking to get away from civilization will find plenty of the big wide open here. The landscape can be deceptive, especially in summer. Crossing the Snake River Plain on the interstate might lead you to think you're in low-altitude flatland, but both Pocatello and

Idaho Falls lie at elevations of nearly 5,000 feet, and much of the lava-covered plain sleeps beneath a blanket of snow in winter. Not deceptive, however, are the mountains ringing southeast Idaho—they're unmistakably tall. The most prominent of them, visible across much of the region, are the famed Tetons, rising just across the border in Wyoming. These lofty peaks provide superb slopes for downhill skiers; powderhounds flock to Grand Targhee, on the west side of the range near Driggs, as well as Jackson Hole, just a short drive away to the east.

North of the Tetons, a token sliver of Yellowstone National Park slops over into Idaho. This Idaho-Wyoming border country harbors some of North America's biggest wild animals. More moose live in southeast Idaho's mountains than in any other part of the state, and grizzly bears can still be found in the area's remote highlands and valleys.

Massacre Rocks to American Falls

MASSACRE ROCKS STATE PARK

On August 9, 1862, three small wagon trains were plodding down the dusty Oregon Trail east of here when the first two trains in the line—the Smart and Adams parties—were attacked by a band of Shoshone. Six white emigrants were killed and several more wounded. The next day, 36 men from the third wagon train in the line boldly rode out in pursuit of the Indians. To their profound regret, they actually managed to find the Indian camp and were quickly forced to flee for their lives. Four more of their numbers met their maker in the process. All told, 10 pioneers were killed. Whether that qualifies as a massacre is for you to decide.

The "massacre rocks" themselves—actually not where the skirmishes took place—straddle the interstate just north of Exit 28. The Oregon Trail passed between the rocks, just as the interstate does now. The pioneers on the trail called the narrow passage Gate of Death or Devil's Gate, reflecting their fear of Indian ambush here. The name Massacre Rocks was coined long after the

1862 skirmishes by an enterprising entrepreneur who built a gas station and store here in the 1920s; the catchy name drew tourists in to find out more and perhaps buy a soda or two while there. The roadside stop also became a favorite gathering place for locals. But time eventually took its toll on the structures, which ended up being sold to the federal government and torn down.

Today Massacre Rocks State Park, set amid range grasses and junipers on a tranquil stretch of the Snake River, offers visitors a chance to study the area's Oregon Trail history, as well as the much older history of the land itself. Evidence of the area's volcanic past abounds, as do telltale signs of the great Bonneville Flood, which roared down the river here some 14,500 years ago. Wildlife watchers and flora fans also will be enthralled; the park's 900 acres are home to more than 200 species of birds—including western grebes, white pelicans, and great blue herons—and almost 300 species of desert plants, among them locoweed, tumble mustard, and yarrow.

Geologic History

The Snake River Plain-Yellowstone geologic

province, which includes the park, is a volcanic swath that began to erupt 15 million years ago. Here at Massacre Rocks, the eruptions took place some 6.5 million years ago. The volcanoes weren't the towering, exploding type like Vesuvius, Krakatoa, or Mount St. Helens. Rather they were shield volcanoes, cracks in the earth's skin through which molten lava flowed out like blood from a wound. At Massacre Rocks, as the 2,000°F molten lava rose toward the earth's surface, it came in contact with the water in the Snake River Plain Aquifer. The water instantly turned to steam and created lava geysers, spattering yellow-brown volcanic tuff in all directions. Subsequent flows covered the older ones. The lava rock you see across the river to the north is much younger than that on the south side—only 75,000 years old. By comparison, the youngest flows in Idaho were along the Great Rift, north of Massacre Rocks. There the lava oozed out of the earth just 2,100 years ago.

Long after the lava flows ceased here, another cataclysmic event further altered the landscape. Utah's Great Salt Lake is still fairly large today, but it's just a small remnant of enormous Lake Bonneville, which once covered some 20,000 square miles of Utah, eastern Nevada, and southern Idaho. About 14,500 years ago, the lake overflowed its natural rock dam, which soon collapsed under the force of the rushing water. Some 1,000 cubic miles of water burst through Red Rock Pass, smashing down through today's Marsh Valley, Portneuf Narrows, and Pocatello. The flood lasted about eight weeks and was the second-largest known flood in world history. It held more water than the total annual flow of all the major rivers in North America combined. The floodwaters carved out the Snake River channel, carrying boulders along with it. When the waters finally receded, these boulders were dropped downstream as "melon gravel." The flood also carved out secondary channels that today appear like hanging valleys along the Snake River rim.

Visitor Center

Start off at the park visitor center, where you pay the standard state park $4-per-vehicle entrance fee. The small center overlooks the Massacre Rocks and provides a multipanel route map of the entire Oregon Trail—from Independence, Missouri, to the Pacific Ocean—showing highlights and major stops along the way. This series of panels may befuddle you until you figure out that north is at the bottom, not the top, of each panel. (If you try to read the panels as you would a map, you may come to believe that Lewis and Clark pioneered an emigrant trail to New Jersey.) The visitor center's other exhibits focus on the area's cultural and natural history. Many pioneer-era artifacts are on display. You'll find trailheads for the Geology Exhibit and Yahandeka Trails here as well.

Devil's Garden

A fenced-off area alongside the upper campground loop encloses Devil's Garden, a plot roughly 50 feet square holding numerous small pinnacles, each around six inches high. An interpretive sign theorizes that the pinnacles were formed when escaping gas vented through the volcanic ash,

COURTESY OF THE IDAHO TRAVEL COUNCIL

Massacre Rocks State Park

carrying silica up with it. The silica glued the ash together, creating hardened areas around each vent hole. The softer ash around the vents eventually eroded away, leaving the small pinnacles standing above the surrounding surface.

Register Rock

Along Rock Creek, a few miles west of the park proper, is a shady day-use area once popular with Oregon Trail wagon trains. Register Rock bears the carved-in signatures of dozens of emigrants who passed this way, including "H. Chestnut, Aug 20 1869." Now the rock is surrounded by a vandal-discouraging, seven-foot-high chain-link fence and sheltered by a gazebo. If you didn't pay the $4 entrance fee at the main park entrance, you'll have to pay it here. Mature shade trees and grassy lawns surround the rock, making the site eminently picnickable. To reach Register Rock, cross to the south side of the highway at the Massacre Rocks State Park exit and follow the signs.

Hiking Trails

Six different hiking trails thread their way through the park, one or another taking you down to the river, to high points overlooking the river, or to Oregon Trail ruts on the south side of the freeway. Start with the **Yahandeka Trail,** a quarter-mile, self-guided interpretive trail that loops out from the visitor center. Interpretive signs along the way point out common vegetation in the area and explain some of the park's unique topography. Along any of the trails you're likely to surprise a cottontail bounding through the brush, or see a white pelican or two cruising elegantly through the sky above your head. Also of note is the short **Geology Exhibit** trail starting at the visitor center. The trail climbs up to a great viewpoint of river and rocks, where signs detail the park's volcanic origins and explain how the Bonneville Flood reshaped a large part of southern Idaho.

Interpretive Programs

Park rangers offer a different interpretive program every night of the week from Memorial Day to Labor Day. On most nights, programs are presented in an amphitheater overlooking the Snake River. Common topics include the park's geologic history, the lives of the Oregon Trail pioneers, and the lifestyles of the indigenous Native American peoples. Other nights, guided walks take the place of the amphitheater program.

If you're in the area in early June, you'll be just in time for the **Massacre Rocks Rendezvous;** look for a tepee village and traders' row, as well as contests in black-powder rifle shooting and knife throwing.

Campground Facilities

The park's 52 fee campsites are divided into two loops. The upper loop is less crowded but a little closer to the interstate and therefore noisier. The lower loop is closer to the water, quieter, but more crowded and susceptible to swarms of bloodthirsty bugs. Both loops have some pull-through sites, some double sites, water, and restrooms with showers. All sites have water faucets and power outlets; site 23 is wheelchair-friendly. An RV dump station is available, and boaters can launch their watercraft at the ramp to the west of the interstate exit. The park is open for camping year-round, but facilities are limited in winter. Rates are $16 with power hookups, $12 without. Massacre Rocks also has two new cabins that sleep up to five people for $35.

Information

For more information, write Park Manager, Massacre Rocks State Park, 3592 Park Ln., American Falls, ID 83211, or call the visitor center at 208/548-2672.

AMERICAN FALLS AND VICINITY

Those visitors coming to American Falls in search of the namesake falls will be disappointed—they no longer exist. When American Falls Dam was built in 1925, it provided electricity to the city but obliterated the falls in the process. The reservoir also inundated the original townsite. The whole town was moved first, but when the lake level drops in prime summer irrigation season, you can spy an old grain elevator and other evidence of southeast Idaho's Atlantis.

American Falls sits squarely in potato country, and farming drives its economy. Recreation on the reservoir provides the bulk of the local fun for the town's residents; it's especially popular with windsurfers, who take advantage of the strong winds that regularly rip across the Snake River Plain here. Basic accommodations and food are available. For more information, contact the **American Falls Chamber of Commerce,** 239 Idaho St., American Falls, ID 83211, 208/226-7214.

American Falls Dam and Reservoir

The largest reservoir on the Snake and the second largest in the state, the American Falls impoundment offers water-recreation opportunities of all sorts, including fishing, water-skiing, sailing, and windsurfing. A Bureau of Reclamation **visitor center** on the dam's north side (open May–Oct.) holds historical photos and exhibits relating to the moving of the original townsite and the dam's 1977 reconstruction, as well as information on facilities around the reservoir. You'll also find a boat ramp and picnic areas here.

Two marinas are on the reservoir near American Falls. **Willow Bay Recreation Area** is just north of town at 2830 Marina Rd., 208/226-2688. It offers a boat-launch area, camping, bike paths, picnic areas, ball fields, horseshoe pits, and a burgers-and-fries café. Farther east—take Exit 44 and wind around some dirt roads down to the water, following signs—is **Seagull Boat Club,** 208/226-2086, a small, private marina at which nonmembers are welcome for a small fee.

Just below the dam on the river's south side is the Bureau of Reclamation's **Oregon Trail River Access,** offering boat ramps, docks, and restrooms, but nothing in the way of grass or shade. To get there, take Lincoln Street to Falls Avenue to Valdez Street.

A couple of BLM sites provide water access and allow primitive camping along the Snake River. Both are downstream from the dam. **Pipeline Recreation Area** is farther west, on the south side of the river. Take Exit 36 and follow the road west along the north side of the freeway. A large pipeline crosses the river at the well-marked site. **Snake River Vista** is on the north side of the river. Turn left just after crossing the dam and follow the signs five miles to the area.

Indian Springs Resort

This popular pool, park, and 120-site campground, at 3249 Indian Springs Rd., 208/226-2174, lies just down Hwy. 37 a mile south of I-86 (Exit 36). The expansive, 16-acre grounds include picnic areas, volleyball courts, baseball diamonds, horseshoe pits, a driving range, arcade, showers and laundry, and lots of trees and grass.

Admission to the Olympic-size, spring-fed, 90°F pool costs $5 for adults, $4 for ages 12–17, and $3 kids 3–11. Day use of the entire resort costs $7.50/6/5, respectively. The pool is open Memorial Day weekend through Labor Day weekend, Mon.–Sat. 10 A.M.–9 P.M., Sunday noon–6 P.M.; the rest of September, it's open weekends 10 A.M.–6 P.M. Suit and towel rentals are available. Camping costs $11 a night dry, $17 for full hookups. The campground's main season is also Memorial Day through Labor Day, but camping usually can be arranged the rest of the year by calling ahead.

South to Utah

Two routes beginning on either side of American Falls make excellent alternatives to I-84 for getting down to the Utah border. East of American Falls (Exit 52, then south), the Arbon Valley Highway threads its way between the Deep Creek Range on the west and the Bannock Range and Pleasantview Hills on the east. It's beautiful irrigated farmland the whole way, and you'll have the good, paved road mostly to yourself. As you head south, you'll be watched over first by the pyramid of Bannock Peak (elevation 8,263 feet), then by the massive hulk of Deep Creek Peak (elevation 8,748 feet). Both are west of the road.

Not long after passing Arbon, you'll come upon mile after mile of the proverbial amber waves of grain—wheat is the crop of choice down here. Near the Power-Oneida county line, you cross an all-but-unnoticeable crest separating the Bannock Creek drainage to the north from the Deep Creek drainage to the south. Soon you'll enter the Curlew National Grasslands and come to **Holbrook,** in the midst of the grasslands. The tiny farm town offers a neat little park suitable for a picnic or rest stop. Holbrook is also the junction with Highway 37 and Highway 38, which heads east to Malad City.

South of Holbrook you're in the Curlew Valley, and as you continue your trek toward the Beehive State you come to the USDA's **Curlew Campground,** on Stone Reservoir. Here you'll find picnic shelters, fire grills, a boat ramp, and 11 fee sites without hookups. Stone Reservoir is a popular water-skiing destination and offers anglers a shot at black crappie or planted rainbow trout. Head south, and you'll be in Utah before

you can say "Brigham Young Slept Here." The route joins I-84 at Snowville, Utah, a few miles southeast of the state line.

Highway 37 begins just west of American Falls (Exit 36, then south) and crosses the farmland of Rockland Valley, climbing the Rock Creek drainage between the Deep Creek Range on the east and the Sublett Range on the west. At the southern end of this route you'll find the small USFS **Twin Springs Campground** (five sites, free). This spot was a popular campground and watering hole along the Oregon Trail's Hudspeth's Cutoff.

Pocatello and Vicinity

Pocatello (population 51,200) began in 1864 as a stage stop named after chief Po-ca-ta-ro of the region's Shoshones. Po-ca-ta-ro (translation unknown) and his warriors were a thorn in the side of encroaching settlers in this area until 1863, when the U.S. Army finally forced them into submission. Po-ca-ta-ro signed a peace treaty and ended up on the Fort Hall Reservation, where he died in 1884. His gravesite today can be seen only with scuba gear; it was flooded by the filling of American Falls Reservoir in 1925.

In 1879, the iron horse galloped into town, belching soot and putting Pocatello on the map. The Utah and Northern Railroad extended north from Salt Lake City and Franklin that year. It was followed five years later by the Oregon Short Line, pushing west from Montana on into Oregon. Pocatello became a regional division point and the biggest rail hub west of the Mississippi. By 1920 it had grown into a bustling city of 15,000, with a lively mix of people and commerce that enabled it to become a libertine oasis in the land of the Latter-day Saints.

Today, despite the continued presence of the railroad and the added presence of the university, Pocatello is relatively quiet. Granted, you can actually find bars and coffeehouses here—not always a given in Mormon country—but the street scene after dark is minimal, and the clubs are relatively tame.

One worthwhile activity in Pocatello is watching the summer sunsets. The late-afternoon light comes shooting in low and bright off the northwestern horizon, rolling fast and unfettered down the Snake River Plain. Then it banks off Big Southern, Middle, and East Buttes like a heavenly pinball, slipping through the city's mountainous flippers before disappearing down canyon toward Inkom. Head up to Red Hill on the ISU campus for the best show.

SIGHTS
Historic Buildings

Downtown's historic district, bounded roughly by Garfield Avenue and the railroad tracks, and by Lander and Lewis Streets, holds a number of architectural delights dating back to the 19th century. Among the highlights: the 1898 **Trinity Episcopal Church,** 248 N. Arthur Ave.; the 1916 Valentine building and the 1919 Carlson Building, kitty-corner from each other on the east and west corners of the Arthur Avenue/Center Street intersection; and the 1916 Yellowstone Hotel, 230 W. Bonneville, down by the Old Oregon Short Line/Union Pacific Depot at the east end of W. Bonneville Street.

The most beautiful old building in town is the **Standrod Mansion,** 648 N. Garfield, built in 1901 by Judge Drew W. Standrod. The gorgeous sandstone castle was designed by San Francisco architect Marcus Grundfor in a Classical Revival

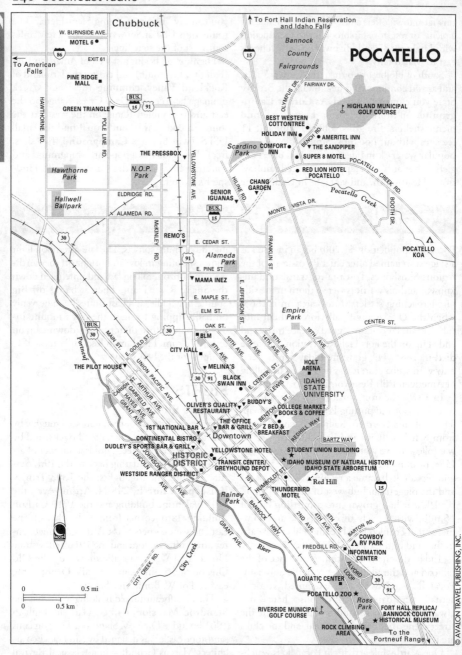

POCATELLO

COURTESY OF THE IDAHO TRAVEL COUNCIL

Standrod Mansion

style; its interior is filled with oak, tile, and imported French marble. The mansion is now home to **The Backroom** furniture store, 208/233-4198.

Ross Park

The town's biggest city park holds a number of attractions worthy of a visit. On the lower level of the park is **Pocatello Zoo,** 2900 S. 2nd Ave., 208/234-6196, which encages a humble menagerie of bears, badgers, bobcats, bison, mountain goats, mountain lions, and more. Kids will like the new petting barn. The zoo is open April 1–June 15, daily 9 A.M.–5 P.M.; June 16 through Labor Day weekend, daily 10 A.M.–6 P.M.; and Saturday after Labor Day weekend until October 31, weekends only 10 A.M.–4 P.M. It's closed Nov. 1–March 30. Admission is $2.25 for ages 12–59, $1.75 for ages 60 and up, $1.50 for ages 6–11, and $.50 for ages 3–5.

Also on the lower level of the park you'll find grassy and shaded picnic areas, horseshoe pits, volleyball courts, baseball fields, a playground, and the city's recently remodeled and expanded **Aquatic Center,** 208/234-0472, which offers lap pools, waterslides, water volleyball, and even inner tubing on a "Lazy River." Admission is $5

adults, $4.50 ages 10–17, $3 ages 4–9, $1.50 tots 3 and under; everybody gets in for half price from 6–9 P.M. Monday and 8–9 P.M. the other evenings. Lockers are available, but you'll need your own lock.

Upper Ross Park, accessed from Alvord Loop off S. 5th Avenue, offers, among other things, the **Fort Hall Replica,** 208/234-1795, a reconstructed version of one of the most important trading posts on the Oregon Trail. Native Americans, fur trappers, and pioneers all congregated at the fort, which stood north of today's city of Pocatello on what is now the Fort Hall Indian Reservation. The reconstruction—re-created from the original plans—allows you a look at life here circa 1830–50. Within the thick adobe walls are blacksmith and carpentry shops, a large Native American exhibit, and exhibits on the fort's history and the Oregon Trail. It's open mid-April through Memorial Day weekend, Tues.–Sat. 10 A.M.–2 P.M.; June through Labor Day weekend, daily 10 A.M.–6 P.M.; the rest of September, daily 10 A.M.–2 P.M. Closed the rest of the year. Admission is $1.50 general, $1.25 for ages 6–11 and 60 and older, and $.50 for ages 3–5. You can often see the zoo's hoofed animals better from the parking lot of the old fort than you can from the walkways inside the zoo itself. Kids can get a free look at the bison, deer, pronghorn, and other ungulates from behind the fence here.

Next to the fort is the **Bannock County Historical Museum,** 3000 Alvord Loop, 208/233-0434. It's open daily 10 A.M.–6 P.M. from Memorial Day weekend through Labor Day weekend, and Tues.–Sat. 10 A.M.–2 P.M. the rest of the year. Admission is $1 general, $.50 ages 6–12.

The cliffs separating Upper and Lower Park are used for **rock climbing** practice. Some 75 recorded single-pitch routes vary in difficulty from 5.7 to 5.12c. About a third of the climbs are bolted. Two different parking areas access opposite sides of the cliffs. To reach the "shady side," head for Lower Ross Park as if you were going to the zoo, but continue past it. Look for a big open parking area close to a pink house. The cliffs are obvious. To get out to the sunny side, head south of town on 5th Street until it joins with 4th to form Old Bannock Highway, then look for the cliffs on your right.

One other note: Visitors to the park will have to leave Fido at home. No dogs are allowed.

Idaho State University

ISU began in 1901 as a two-year community and vocational college. By 1927 it had grown sufficiently large to warrant its designation as the southern branch of the University of Idaho. In 1947 it became Idaho State College, and in 1963 gained its current status and title as Idaho State University. Today its enrollment is about 13,600. The 735-acre campus fronts S. 5th Avenue, with its main entrance at S. 5th and E. Humbolt.

Several buildings on campus are worth a special mention. The **Idaho Museum of Natural History,** S. 5th Ave. at E. Dillon St., 208/282-3317, offers displays focusing on the most important events in Idaho's natural history. This is the best place in the state to learn about dinosaurs and other prehistoric creatures that used to roam Idaho, including the remains of a Columbian mammoth found near Grangeville, which was excavated by ISU museum paleontologists in the mid-1990s. The museum is open Memorial Day through Labor Day weekend, Mon. 4–8 P.M.,

Tue.–Fri. 10 A.M.–5 P.M., and Sat. noon–5 P.M.; the rest of the year, Mon. 4–8 P.M., Tue.–Fri. 10 A.M.–4 P.M., Sat. noon–4 P.M. Closed Sundays and holidays. Admission is $5 general, $4 for seniors age 56 and up, $3 for ISU studemts, $2 for ages 4–11.

At the museum you can also pick up a brochure detailing a guided walking tour to the **Idaho State Arboretum,** a collection of labeled trees and shrubs spread around the museum grounds. Among the 51 botanical species you'll see are syringa, Idaho's fragrant state flower, and its cousin, the mock orange. For more information about the arboretum, call the Museum of Natural History.

Also on campus you'll find **Holt Arena,** 208/282-2831, a large sports, concerts, and events venue; and the **Student Union Building,** which houses a movie theater (208/282-2701), bowling alley (208/282-3335), bookstore (208/282-3237), the ISU Outdoor Program office (208/282-3912), and the Wilderness Rental Center (208/282-2945).

For more information about the school, contact University Relations, Campus Box 8265, Idaho State University, Pocatello, ID 83209, 208/282-3620. For a specific department, call the university switchboard at 208/282-0211.

Fort Hall Indian Reservation

The Shoshone and Bannock tribes of the Fort Hall Reservation were two separate peoples speaking two different languages yet sharing many cultural similarities. Both tribes were hunters and gatherers who roamed the Great Basin region of Nevada, Utah, Wyoming, and Idaho in search of fish and game. When whites arrived, the two tribes were muscled onto the Fort Hall Reservation, which was established by executive order of President Andrew Johnson in 1867. The reservation originally encompassed 1.8 million acres, but 20 years later the Dawes Act took its toll. The act's allotment process reduced the size of the reservation to about 540,000 acres, where many of the 3,900 enrolled tribal members live today.

The reservation is just north of Pocatello up I-5. To learn more about its history and people, head for the **Shoshone-Bannock Tribal Mu-**

seum, just off I-15 at Exit 80, Fort Hall, 208/237-9791. At the museum, you can view exhibits and historical photographs preserving tribal heritage, and buy books, posters, and Native American art. You can also arrange tours of the Fort Hall Bottoms to view both the reservation's buffalo herd and the site of Nathaniel Wyeth's original 1834 Fort Hall trading post. The museum is April–Oct. daily 10 A.M.–6 P.M.; the rest of the year daily 10 A.M.–5 P.M. Closed Thanksgiving, Christmas, and New Year's Day. Admission is $2 adults, $1 seniors, $.50 for youths 6–18.

Across the street from the museum is the reservation's Trading Post complex, with a restaurant, a casino, and a gift shop selling Native American–made goods.

Some of the region's best fishing can be found on the reservation, on a stretch of the Snake in the Fort Hall Bottoms, essentially the inlet waters of American Falls Reservoir. Few anglers compete for the plentiful five- to seven-pound trout here. To fish the Bottoms, you'll need to pick up a permit from the tribe. Permits are available at the TP Gas and Truck Stop at I-15 Exit 80. The fishing season usually runs April–Oct.

The spectacular **Shoshone Bannock Indian Festival and Rodeo** draws Native Americans and interested nonnatives from all over the United States and Canada. Traditional Indian dancing takes center stage—multitudes of dancers and drummers come attired in intricate dress and face paint. In addition, the event features a rodeo, arts and crafts show, and softball tourney. It all takes place the second week of August at the Fort Hall rodeo grounds.

For more information about the festival, the tribes, or the reservation, write Shoshone-Bannock Tribes, Fort Hall, ID 83201, or call the reservation administrative offices at 208/238-3700.

RECREATION

The ISU Outdoor Program website at www.isu.edu/outdoor is an excellent place to learn about recreational opportunities throughout Southeast Idaho.

Hiking and Mountain Biking

The **Gibson Jack Trailhead,** at the top of Gibson Jack Road off Bannock Highway, offers access to one of the nicest hiking opportunities in the Pocatello area. The trail follows Gibson Jack Creek into a Research Natural Area—closed to motorized vehicles. It's about four miles from the trailhead to a gate at the area boundary. You won't find a single head of cattle on this spread, and as a result, the watercourse is in excellent shape. The creek is too small to offer much in the way of a swimming hole, but a couple of "dabbling holes" can cool the peds on a hot summer day.

City Creek is a local favorite for hiking and mountain biking. Following the trail up the creek will eventually take you to the top of **Kinport Peak** (elevation 7,222 feet), a quick fix for local mountaineers when time doesn't permit a road trip to more rarefied realms. To get to the trail, take W. Center Street west to Lincoln Avenue, turn left on Lincoln, and right on City Creek Road.

Mink Creek, south of town, provides a major focus for outdoor recreation in the area. The Bannock Highway, which originates on the southwest side of Pocatello, parallels the hills for several miles before veering right and climbing alongside Mink Creek. The road continues up and over Crystal Summit and down to the Arbon Valley on the other side of the range. Along the way it passes numerous trailheads offering gateways into the Bannock Range. The bottom of Mink Creek can also be accessed from the Portneuf Area exit off I-15 South (Exit 57).

Starting at the bottom of the hill, **Cherry Springs Nature Area** is the first turnout you'll come to. Here you'll find a beautiful nature trail winding through the creekbed vegetation and breaking out onto the slopes on the far side. It's a day-use-only area. Continuing up Mink Creek, you'll pass trailheads to **Slate Mountain, West Mink Creek, Valve House Draw, Corral Creek-South Fork Mink Creek,** and **Porcelain Pot Gulch,** before topping out at Crystal Summit—just under 6,000 feet in elevation. Some of these trailheads serve cross-country skiers and snowmobilers in winter.

Between the Cherry Springs site and the Slate

Mountain trailhead, a road branches left and climbs the East Fork of Mink Creek. This road dead-ends at Scout Mountain Campground and the **East Mink trailhead.** From here, trails connect to Valve House Draw to the west and to the 8,700-foot summit of Scout Mountain to the east. Also here is the **Justice Park Picnic Area,** which offers a pleasant place to break out the chardonnay, brie, and apples. Break out your wallet, too—a small day-use fee is charged.

Alpine Skiing

Pebble Creek Ski Area lies up E. Green Canyon Road, just a short drive south of town on I-15 (follow signs from the Inkom exits), P.O. Box 370, Inkom, ID 83245, 208/775-4452 or 877/524-7669, snow report: 208/775-4451, www.pebblecreekskiarea.com. With 1,100 acres on Mount Bonneville, the small resort offers a not-so-small 2,200 vertical feet, served by two double chairs and one triple chair. Head for Al's Drop to get your adrenaline pumping. Skiing, telemarking, and snowboarding lessons are offered, and rentals are available. Lift tickets cost $30 adults, $17 kids 6–12 and seniors 70 and up, $3 tots 5 and under. Cheaper beginner-lift-only tickets cost $10 for anyone. Day care is available.

The season generally runs mid-December through mid-April, with the resort open Fri.–Sun. in the early and late season (closed Christmas Day), daily Dec. 26 through Feb., and Wed.–Sun. in March. Night skiing is usually offered until 9:30 P.M. Fri.–Sat. Jan–mid-March.

Portneuf Range Yurt System

On Pocatello's eastern flank lies a cross-country skier's nirvana. Wide-open snow-covered wheat fields gradually give way to the high ridges and backcountry bowls of the Portneuf Range—all just minutes from town. And as a bonus, the area is blessed with a public yurt system.

Several canvas-topped, Mongolian-style shelters are spread across the area from just east of town to just north of Pebble Creek Ski Area.

On Pocatello's eastern flank lies a cross-country skier's nirvana. Wide-open snow-covered wheat fields gradually give way to the high ridges and backcountry bowls of the Portneuf Range—all just minutes from town.

Some can be reached by novice skiers, and others require more skiing ability and backcountry savvy to reach. Each is equipped with plywood bunk beds, a woodstove, cook stove, lantern, pots, a shovel, and an axe. You'll need to bring all your own winter-camping gear, as well as mantles for the lantern and Coleman fuel for both the lantern and stove. Most yurts sleep six.

Maintenance of the yurts is overseen by Idaho State University's Outdoor Program, but all users are expected to help keep the huts shoveled out and in good shape. The main office of the Outdoor Program, Box 8128, ISU, Pocatello, ID 83209, 208/282-3912, has maps and more information. Reservations are required and are made through the **ISU Wilderness Rental Center,** 208/282-2945; call for information and current fees, which vary depending on the yurt and night of the week. Weekends tend to book up fast.

Don't let the fact that these yurts were built by public agencies lull you into a false sense of security in the backcountry. Avalanches aren't common but neither are they unheard of, winter navigation is often problematic, and winter temperatures can bring hypothermia and even death to the unprepared. If you have any doubts about your backcountry skills, you would be well advised to enjoy the yurts on an organized, guided tour. Tours are offered periodically by the Outdoor Program, as well as by the Pocatello Parks and Recreation Department, 911 N. 7th Ave., P.O. Box 4169, Pocatello, ID 83201, 208/234-6232.

Other Nordic Ski Areas

The treks to the two lower yurts begin from **Rapid Creek Park N' Ski Area,** 11 miles north of Inkom on Rapid Creek Road, at the junction with McKee Road. Trails here are groomed regularly and include loops ranging from two kilometers to more than two miles in length.

Inman Canyon Park N' Ski, the trailhead to the Inman yurt, is four miles northeast of Inkom, up Rapid Creek and Inman Canyon Roads. The trailhead and some of the area's trail system are shared with snowmobilers, so be alert.

Five Nordic-ski trailheads lie up Mink Creek, 15 miles south of Pocatello on the west side of the Bannock Range. Take Bannock Highway south, making sure to bear right at the Y just before Mink Creek (if you hit the town of Portneuf, you've gone too far). About 15 miles of trails here are marked and groomed periodically and are of beginner to intermediate difficulty. Other ungroomed trails lace the area.

Heading up the creek you'll first pass the turnoff up the east fork. About a mile down this road is the **East Mink Creek** trailhead, shared with snowmobilers. Back out on the main road and continuing up Mink Creek proper you'll pass several trails/trailheads, listed below in order as you head up the canyon. **West Mink Creek** is a very popular, moderately difficult trail that leads through a Research Natural Area for four miles to a warming hut. **Valve House Draw** trail is well suited to beginner skiers. The **Corral Creek/South Fork Mink Creek** trail starts out as moderately difficult, then becomes steeper. It's little used and recommended for advanced skiers looking for solitude. The **Porcelain Pot** trail, up in the nosebleed seats at 6,000 feet, is a well-developed intermediate trail. Finally, the **Parity Trails** begin at Crystal Summit. One loops north to connect with the Corral Creek trail. A second, shorter loop connects with the Porcelain Pot trail; it's rated "More Difficult," entailing a challenging steep grade near Crystal Summit.

ENTERTAINMENT AND EVENTS

Performing Arts

Pocatello is home of the **Idaho State Civic Symphony,** 208/234-1587, which typically presents about nine classical performances between September and April. Concerts are usually held in Goranson Hall on the ISU campus; single-performance tickets are $17 adults, $7 high-school age and younger. In addition to the regular season, a once-a-year pops concert features contemporary works.

Other performing arts groups based in town

include **Theatre ISU,** 208/282-3595; and **Westside Players,** 1009 S. 2nd Ave., 208/234-2654.

Nightlife

The **Green Triangle** (the "Green T" to locals), 4010 Yellowstone Ave. (Chubbuck), 208/237-0354, is the town's biggest bar and gets crowded with cowpokes every night of the week. A mechanical buckin' bronc throws the cowboys on the floor and challenges the cowgirls to outslink Debra Winger's *Urban Cowboy* number. Country bands and country dancing are in the chute nightly (cover charge), and beer (Bud, Coors, etc.) and pool tables provide additional entertainment. A small kitchen gives burgers a home on the range.

Pocatello sports bars include **The Pressbox,** 1257 Yellowstone Ave., 208/237-9957, where you'll find all the big, pay-TV sports specials on the bar's multiple TV screens; and **Dudley's Sports Bar & Grill,** downtown at 150 S. Arthur Ave., 208/232-3541, where you'll find about seven screens, about the same number of microbrews, and an above-average pub-grub menu. Dudley's also sports a cast of regular characters par excellence.

Among other bars downtown, **1st National Bar,** 232 W. Center, 208/233-1516, is a popular rock 'n' roll and blues dance bar where a lot of local bands cut their teeth on the way to the small time. The varied crowd is heavy on the students. Tuesday is karaoke night. **Continental Bistro,** 140 S. Main St., 208/233-4433, offers the highest brow in Pocatello. Here you'll find plenty of good beer—microbrews and imports in abundance—and good wine, as well as live jazz on Wednesday nights. Hours are Mon.-Sat. 11 A.M.–10 P.M. for food, until 1 A.M. for drink.

Just across the tracks from downtown, **The Office Bar & Grill,** 251 E. Center, 208/232-9816, is a popular weekend nightspot offering a clean-cut, low-key meat-market atmosphere.

Events

The **Dodge National Circuit Finals Rodeo** comes to Holt Arena around the third week of March. It's a biggy—the country's second-largest points-qualifying rodeo. Here the top two cowboys from each of 12 circuits nationwide compete for glory and a goodly sum of cash. For more information, contact Dodge National Circuit Finals Rodeo, Box 4541, Pocatello, ID 83205, 208/233-1546. Out at Pebble Creek Ski Area the same time of year, the **Cowboy Classic Slalom and Barrel Race** features rodeo pros riding barrels down the mountain. Yeeeha!

Pocatello is the setting for part of the Idaho International Folk Dance Festival in late July and early August. For more details and a complete events calendar, contact the **Greater Pocatello Chamber of Commerce,** 343 W. Center St., Pocatello, ID 83204, 208/233-1525, www.pocatelloidaho.com.

ACCOMMODATIONS

Under $50

Several lodgings lie on either side of I-86 at the Chubbuck exit (Exit 61). This lodging area is closest to the airport. On the north side of the freeway is **Motel 6,** 291 W. Burnside Ave., 208/237-7880 or 800/4MOTEL6 (800/466-8356). This is one of the cheapest Motel 6s you'll find anywhere (still less than $40 most of the year), and kids 17 and under stay free with an adult family member. Amenities include a seasonal pool, TV with HBO and ESPN, and a coin laundry.

The **Thunderbird Motel,** 1415 S. 5th Ave., 208/232-6330 or 888/978-2473, www.thunderbirdmotelid.com, is just across the street from the ISU campus and close to Ross Park and downtown. It has an outdoor pool in summer and a guest laundry year-round, and some rooms have refrigerators and microwaves. Pets are welcome for a small extra charge.

$50–100

Clustered up against the hill on the east side of town (Exit 71 off I-15) are most of the city's upscale chain motels. Among the lowest in this category but pretty ritzy for the money is **Super 8,** 1330 Bench Rd., 208/234-0888 or 800/800-8000, which offers 80 rooms. King rooms with in-room Jacuzzis are available. Kids 12 and under stay free.

Red Lion Hotel Pocatello, 1555 Pocatello Creek Rd., 208/233-2200 or 800/RED-LION (800/733-5466), offers a restaurant and lounge, an indoor pool, Jacuzzi, and sauna, and a small exercise room. Pets are okay with a deposit; nonsmoking rooms and a guest coin laundry are available.

AmeriTel Inn, 1440 Bench Rd., 208/234-7500 or 800/600-6001, offers 110 rooms, 70 percent of which are nonsmoking. Among the rooms are a number of suites, some with kitchenettes, some with king beds and in-room spas. All rooms have cable TV with free HBO and desks including phones with modem ports. Other amenities include an indoor pool, spa, and fitness center open round-the-clock; complimentary continental breakfast and fresh-baked desserts in the evenings; and a free airport shuttle.

A little farther up the hill is **Best Western Cottontree Inn,** 1415 Bench Rd., 208/237-7650 or 800/528-1234. King beds, kitchenettes, and family rates available. Some 60 percent of the rooms are nonsmoking. Amenities include a pool, hot tub, cable TV with Showtime, a guest laundry, and an onsite Frontier Pies restaurant. Pets are permitted on a limited basis.

Holiday Inn, 1399 Bench Rd., 208/237-1400 or 800/200-8944, has 190 rooms. With its Holidome indoor recreation area (including a pool complete with waterfall) and kids-eat-free restaurant policy, this is a good place for families. Other amenities include a guest laundry, game room, and fitness center.

At **Comfort Inn,** 1333 Bench Rd., 208/237-8155 or 800/228-5150, rates include a complimentary continental breakfast and amenities such as remote-control cable TV (with Showtime), indoor pool and whirlpool, and phones with modem ports. Kitchenettes, nonsmoking rooms, and a king suite are available.

Z Bed & Breakfast, 620 S. 8th Ave., 208/235-1095 or 888/235-1095, is in a great location near the ISU campus and right by the ever popular College Market coffeehouse/bookstore. The restored 1915 Colonial Revival home has three guest bedrooms with private baths. Rates include a full breakfast. No pets, no smoking.

$150–250

The **Black Swan Inn,** 746 E. Center, 208/233-3051, www.blackswaninn.com, offers more than a dozen "Fantasy Theme Suites." Examples include the Caveman Suite, the Pirates Suite, the Jungle Falls Suite—log onto the website for pix of the whole place. The Sea Cave Suite is home to a lovely mermaid—though only in southeast Idaho will you encounter a mermaid wearing a bikini top. It's a fine line between "fantasy" and "cheese"—up to you to decide on which side of that line this place lies. The weekend rates for most of the suites are in this category; weekday rates are less expensive.

CAMPING
RV Parks
Pocatello KOA, 9815 W. Pocatello Creek Rd., 208/233-6851, is up Pocatello Creek Road past the cluster of motels and restaurants by the interstate. The campground offers 85 sites for $20 dry, $25 for full hookups; tents $18.50. A dump station is free to guests; fee for nonguests. Facilities include showers, a laundry, game room, playground, and a small grocery store that also sells gasoline and propane.

Cowboy Mobile Home and R.V. Park, 845 Barton Rd., 208/232-4587, on the south end of town near Ross Park, offers 41 sites with full hookups (including cable TV) for $?? plus tax. Facilities at this Good Sam park include showers and laundry. No tent camping.

If no event is taking place at the **Bannock County Fairgrounds,** Chubbuck and Bench Rds., 208/237-1340, and all other local parks are full, you can park your RV there for $20 a day, including hookups, showers, and restrooms. If an event is taking place, all are welcome at $10 a day, whether or not the other parks in town have room.

Forest Service Campground
Caribou National Forest supervises **Scout Mountain Campground** (27 sites, fee) perched at 6,500 feet on the shoulder of 8,700-foot Scout Mountain. Nearby is the East Mink trailhead, from where trails crisscross the mountains. To get to the campground, head south of town, either on Bannock Highway or on I-15 South (exit at the "Portneuf Area Recreation" sign, Exit 63). About five miles up the hill from the Bannock Highway/Portneuf Road junction, the East Fork road turns off to the left. Follow the road to the campground at the end. Tightwads might prefer one of the free, unofficial campsites found in several places along the East Fork, along the road to the campground.

For more information, contact the Caribou National Forest's **Westside North Ranger District,** Suite 187, Federal Building, 250 S. 4th Ave., Pocatello, ID 83201, 208/236-7500.

FOOD
Fine Dining
Continental Bistro, 140 S. Main, 208/233-4433, offers artfully prepared continental meals in an upscale bistro atmosphere. The gourmet fare and casual, elegant (for Pocatello) atmosphere give the place a good vibe. The average entrée price is around $15, and the desserts are downright decadent. Accompanying the menu is an extensive list of fine wines from all over the world—many available by the glass and an ever-changing array of 16 beers on tap, including microbrews and fine imports. Enjoy live jazz with your meal Wednesday nights year-round; in summer, the musicians set up on the big back patio. Open Mon.–Sat. for lunch and dinner.

The Sandpiper, 1400 Bench Rd., 208/233-1000, is part of a small regional chain that serves up reliably comfortable atmosphere and reliably excellent food and drink at all of its locations. The menu emphasizes steak and seafood, but chicken, pork, and lamb dishes and first-rate salads are also available. Entrées range $15–30. An extensive list of microbrews and fine wines, by the bottle or glass, complements the dinner menu. Open for dinner daily from 4:30 P.M.

Asian
If you're in the mood for Chinese or even Vietnamese food, **Chang Garden,** 1000 Pocatello Creek Rd., near the motels, 208/234-1475, is a good choice. Chow down at the bountiful buffet (at lunch Mon.–Fri., dinner Fri.–Sat.), or order

off the menu. It's all good. Open daily for lunch and dinner.

Italian

A couple of Italian restaurants with different styles both offer excellent meals. **Remo's,** 160 W. Cedar, 208/233-1710, is often cited as one of the city's best restaurants. Appetizers like roasted garlic on a baguette, and carpaccio—thin slices of filet mignon with capers, sliced red onions, and dijon sauce—start things off. Most entrées run $12–17 and feature steak and seafood with an Italian emphasis; pastas like garlic chicken fettuccine alfredo; poultry dishes like chicken parmigiana; and even a rack of New Zealand lamb marinated in cabernet and fresh spices. The food is excellent and the wine list is among the best in town, including more than a dozen Italian reds. Many excellent wines are offered by the glass, and microbrews and imported beers are available. In summer you can dine alfresco on the nice front patio-cum-bar—a pleasant spot on all but the hottest days. Remo's is open Mon.–Sat. for lunch and dinner.

Buddy's, 626 E. Lewis St., 208/233-1172, is the place to go for delicious pizza and down-home Italian food. It's unpretentious, inexpensive, and fun. Buddy's salads are excellent, and you'll find the restaurant's bottled dressing available for sale throughout Idaho. Open Mon.–Sat. for lunch and dinner.

Mexican

Señor Iguanas, 961 Hiline Rd., 208/233-4422, doesn't drench its food in cheese the way many other Mexican restaurants do. The chiles rellenos, tamales, and enchilada dishes are consistent favorites. If you do crave lots of cheese, head instead to **The Pilot House,** 1628 N. Arthur Ave., 208/233-2332.

All the small regional Mexican chains are represented in Pocatello. **Mama Inez,** 390 Yellowstone Ave., 208/234-7674, serves big portions at reasonable prices, as does **Melina's,** 714 N. 5th Ave., 208/232-0014. **Eduardo's,** 612 Yellowstone Ave., 208/233-9440, is another local favorite, but the atmosphere is gaudy and the salsa didn't even begin to draw a sweat—though

the wide selection of Mexican beers helps the medicine go down.

Breakfast and More

Oliver's Quality Restaurant, 130 S. 5th, 208/234-0672, is an American-style diner with a twist. The menu includes a full complement of vegetarian dishes at breakfast, lunch, and dinner daily, and a sign announces that the restaurant uses all-natural potatoes grown locally with no pesticides or herbicides. It's still a smoky diner, but at least it shows a health-conscious side. The service is excellent, the coffee endless. It's the place to go for a full eggs-and-potatoes or pancakes breakfast.

Coffeehouses

College Market Books & Coffee, 604 S. 8th Ave., 208/232-3993, occupies a handsome brick building in a quiet neighborhood near the university. An eclectic student scene makes for great people-watching. Pick up an espresso and one of the store's offbeat books or magazines and take them out to a table on the front porch. College Market is open daily 7 A.M.–7:30 P.M.

Another option is **Main Street Coffee & News,** 234 N. Main St., 208/234-9834, which is open Mon.–Fri. 7 A.M.–9 P.M., Sat. 7 A.M.–6 P.M., Sun. 9 A.M.–4 P.M. The shop sells a good selection of magazines and some out-of-town newspapers, including the *Wall Street Journal* and Sunday's edition of *The New York Times*.

INFORMATION AND SERVICES

For more information about the city, contact the **Greater Pocatello Chamber of Commerce,** 343 W. Center St., P.O. Box 626, Pocatello, ID 83204, 208/233-1525 or 877/922-7659, www.pocatello.com. A **Tourist Information Center** is near Ross Park at 2695 S. 5th Ave., 208/234-7091. Open year-round, Mon.–Sat. 9 A.M.–6 P.M., Sun. 9 A.M.–2 P.M.

Recreation information is provided by the **City of Pocatello Parks and Recreation Department,** 911 N. 7th Ave., 208/234-6232; Caribou-Targhee National Forest's **Westside North Ranger District,** 415 S. Arthur Ave., Pocatello, ID 83204, 208/236-7500; and the

BLM Pocatello Resource Area, 1111 N. 8th Ave., 208/236-6860.

The big mall in town is **Pine Ridge Mall,** 4155 Yellowstone Ave. (Chubbuck), 208/237-7160, home to the Bon-Macy's, JCPenney, ZCMI, and a couple of dozen other stores to supply your every need.

TRANSPORTATION

Pocatello Regional Transit, 215 W. Bonneville, 208/234-2287, www.pokytransit.com, operates city bus service in town. Fare is $.60 for adults, $.30 for students (and $.30 for everyone on Saturdays). All the buses have bike racks. **Greyhound Bus Lines,** 208/232-5365 or 800/231-2222, also uses the Transit Center at 215 W. Bonneville as its Pocatello terminal. Buses run south to Salt Lake City, northeast to Idaho Falls, and west to Burley.

Pocatello Airport, 208/234-6154, is west of town off I-86. It's served by **Skywest,** 800/453-9417, with flights to Salt Lake City, and **Horizon Air,** 800/547-9308, with flights to Boise and Spokane. Car rental companies at the airport include **Avis,** 208/232-3244 or 800/831-2847; **Budget,** 208/233-0600 or 800/527-0700; and **Hertz,** 208/233-2970 or 800/654-3131.

South to Utah

HEADING DOWN I-15

Leaving Pocatello heading south on I-15, you'll flow like lava past the by-now-familiar basalt cliffs betraying the Snake River Plain's volcanic history. Mountains flank the highway to either side—the Portneuf Range on your left, the Bannock Range on your right. Straight ahead in the distance, the unique summit ridge of Oxford Peak kisses the sky like a giant pair of lips.

Those entering Idaho on I-15 instead of leaving will find the **Gateway Southeast Idaho Visitor Center,** 208/766-4788, at the Cherry Creek Rest Area, seven miles north of the border. The center is well stocked with tourist brochures covering all parts of the state.

Mormon Canyon Campground

At I-15 Exit 47, Highway 30 takes off east toward Lava Hot Springs and Soda Springs, while the road to the west leads into the Bannock Range and the BLM's primitive Mormon Canyon Campground. To get to the campground, turn west at the off-ramp and follow the road to its T junction with Marsh Creek Road. Turn left on Marsh Creek, then right on Green Road almost immediately thereafter. Follow Green Road straight up to the campground on the eastern edge of the Caribou National Forest.

The site is actually in Goodenough Canyon, along Goodenough Creek. But Goodenough Canyon is a box canyon, while Mormon Canyon, just over a small ridge, provides access via a hiking/ORV trail up into the Bannocks—all the way to Scout Mountain, Mink Creek, and Pocatello if you so desire. The Mormon Canyon Trail crosses Goodenough Creek to the south. Alternatively, a trail straight up Goodenough Creek leads past several primitive, secluded, creekside campsites. This dead-end trail would make for a great day hike. To the north, a third trail leads to Bell Marsh Creek and from there either up to Scout Mountain or back out to Marsh Creek Road. This latter trail in particular is great for relatively easy mountain biking; the Mormon Canyon trail is more difficult. A loop trip could connect the two trails nicely.

The campground here is quiet and idyllic. Shade abounds under a magnificent mix of trees, and Goodenough Creek babbles beautifully. Best of all, it's free.

Indian Rocks State Park

If your map shows this once-upon-a-time state park right off the interstate at Exit 47, disregard it. The site had some Native American rock art that the state once thought worth preserving. But attempts to keep the park afloat ran aground, as low visitor turnout didn't justify the cost of

M

SOUTHEAST IDAHO

upkeep. The park was abandoned and the site turned over to the Boy Scouts for use as a camp.

Summit Campground

As you continue south on I-15, you'll cross the Bannock Range at Malad Summit, where a bridge spans the highway. That's the road you'll need to be on to get to the USFS Summit Campground, but there's no off-ramp there. Instead, you'll have to continue down the interstate several miles to Exit 22. There you'll cross under the highway in seemingly the wrong direction, loop back north past Devil Creek Reservoir, and cross the highway once again on the aforementioned bridge.

The 12-space campground is a fee site on Mill Creek, near two trailheads. The first, for the Wright Creek National Recreation Trail, you passed about a half mile back. It leads up and over the Elkhorn Mountains, a subrange of the Bannocks, passing Wakley Peak (elevation 8,801 feet) along the way. Farther up the road past the campground is Summit Canyon Trailhead, from where you can tap into a number of trails lacing the Elkhorns. To get high, take the trail to Elkhorn Peak (elevation 9,095 feet).

Devil Creek Reservoir

Anglers fish for planted rainbow trout and kokanee salmon at this small impoundment seven miles north of Malad City. Primitive camping is available along one end of the west shore, and an RV park with a boat ramp is at the other end, nearest the freeway exit.

MALAD CITY AND VICINITY

French trappers named the Malad River in the 1830s, after eating some local beaver meat that didn't agree with them—*malade* is the French word for "sick." In 1843, a party led by John C. Frémont passed through the area and encountered a small band of emaciated Indians. Frémont noted that since the establishment of Fort Hall in 1834, trappers and buffalo hunters using the fort as a trading center and home base had devastated the Malad Valley's once-prolific buffalo herds, much to the dismay of the local Native American population.

On his first sight of the Malad River Valley in 1854, Brigham Young didn't think much of the area. Perhaps he spoke French. But in 1856, Young nevertheless sent 15 families here to try to add another settlement to the Mormon empire. They found good land with plentiful grass for livestock, numerous streams full of fish, and abundant game in the vicinity. They also found Chief Pocatello camped in the area, so they built a fort. But growth escaped the settlement until Henry Peck came to town.

In 1864, Peck—an entrepreneur and the town's first would-be chamber of commerce president—came to Malad in hopes of turning the valley's grasslands into a lucrative business. He planned to sell hay to the stage lines and freight wagons passing through the area, as feed for their livestock. Peck also began encouraging construction and growth in the valley. At that time, the county seat for Oneida County was at Soda Springs, but Peck pushed for removal of the seat to Malad. In 1866, he went so far as to travel to Soda Springs, swipe the county records, and bring them back to Malad. History is unclear whether he had legislative authority for this action. In any case, from that point on Malad took over as county seat.

Today the town holds about 2,000 residents, some of whom are kids who find the town's slow pace boring. "There's nothin' to do," said one. "It sucks," said another. Ah, the impatience of youth. Others a little longer in the tooth might find the town the perfect antidote to the rat race. Basic accommodations and food are available.

Recreation

Several reservoirs on the outskirts of town make good fishing holes. **Daniels Reservoir,** 18 miles northwest of town out Bannock Street, offers camping, a dock, and plenty of trout. **St. John Reservoir** is the local kids' pond three miles northwest of town. It's full of bluegill, bass, perch, and rainbow trout. **Crowther Reservoir,** on the edge of town to the north, is stocked with rainbows. **Pleasantview Reservoir,** west of Malad out Lower St. John Road, offers two lakes and fishing for bass, rainbow trout, and tiger muskies. In town, you can cool your wheels in the **La**

THE LEGEND OF THE IRON DOOR

Thar's gold in them thar hills! Or at least there might be. One tale of treasure—in this case stolen, not mined—persists in the annals of Malad City folklore. Back when the stagecoach ran from Malad to Montana, holdups on the route were common. At some point during this era, three strangers showed up in a Utah town that had just been gutted by fire. The three men found a heavy iron door—off a bank vault, perhaps—among the ashes. They bought the door, loaded it on a wagon, and rode off to the north. Turns out the trio was a gang of stage-robbin' desperados. They found a cave somewhere near Malad, installed the iron door over the mouth of the cave, and kept their considerable booty securely locked within.

As legend has it, the three of them had a falling out. Their disagreements led to a gunfight that ended with all three of them wounded in the cave. One of them got out, locked the other two inside, and crawled to a nearby ranch for help. Alas, the grim reaper was closer than the nearest doctor. Knowing he was on his deathbed, the gunman with his dying breath told the rancher the tale of the iron door. But he died before he revealed the door's location. People have been looking for it ever since.

Supposedly the door was discovered one day by the late Glipsy Waldron, a rancher from Samaria. But he found it during a storm and couldn't relocate it when he returned. Others also found the door and tried to mark it for their return; one sheepherder supposedly tied a sheep to the door, in hopes that the animal's bleating would lead him back to it. No such luck.

In more recent times, Malad Valley miner Leo D. Williams and his partner, an Ogden doctor, found what looked like an old, abandoned mine shaft covered by rock and dirt. They had a hunch they might find the remains of the iron door inside, fallen to the bottom of the shaft. After digging a ways down, they found some humanlike bones; that jibed with the story of the two gang members who supposedly died inside the "cave." The doctor loaded the bones into his truck, intending to take them to Weber College for positive identification. But that same week he fell ill and died, and somewhere along the way the bones were lost. The mystery continues.

Grande Aqua Plunge (no phone), the county-owned community swimming pool. It's on N. Main Street, a couple doors down from the Dude Ranch Cafe, and open Mon.–Sat. 1–8 P.M. in summer.

Information

For more information about Malad, contact **Malad Area Chamber of Commerce**, 208/766-5323. For information about backcountry recreation in the Targhee-Caribou National Forest, contact the **Westside South Ranger District**, 75 S. 140 E., P.O. Box 146, Malad, ID 83252, 208/766-4743. The **BLM Malad Field Station** office is at 195 S. 300 E., 208/766-5900.

Highway 36 to Weston

This route heads southeast from just north of Malad, passing three reservoirs suitable for fishing.

After turning off I-15, you'll come to **Deep Creek Reservoir**, where anglers try to hook planted rainbow trout, native cutthroat trout, or bass. The reservoir has a boat ramp and docks. Nearby, trails lead from the USFS **Third Creek Campground**—a reservable group site on FR 231/Third Creek Road—up Third Creek into the Bannock Range, the high point of which is Oxford Peak (elevation 9,282 feet). To get there, turn off the highway a couple miles south of the reservoir. **Weston Reservoir,** about six miles farther down Highway 36, is known for its perpetually hungry yellow perch. Trout and bass are other possible catches. The lake is stocked annually.

Soon the canyon narrows into a gallery of granite outcroppings. As you round a corner, **Standing Rock** suddenly comes into view. This impressive granite tower sheered off the steep canyon wall and dropped to its present location astride the highway. The rock was named by John C. Frémont when his expedition found this pass through the mountains on August 29, 1843. It looks as though Frémont's expedition must have preferred Hamm's Ice as their beer of choice—the empty blue Hamm's boxes in the midden here outnumber empty Busch boxes by a wide margin.

Dry Canyon Campground

The Targhee-Caribou National Forest manages this small, primitive campground (three sites, free). Look for the turnoff on the south side of the highway between Weston Canyon and Weston. Look hard; for some reason, the sign marking the turnoff has been placed about 100 feet off the highway. Near the highway, Dry Canyon seems most aptly named. Up toward the rim, however, Douglas fir groves provide a cooler, less arid feel.

The free campground is quiet and beautiful. But as is infuriatingly typical of almost every USFS campground in southern Idaho, you'll be sharing this one with cattle. Walk up the small creek a short way to see the riparian nightmare caused by irresponsible grazing. Not only do herds of hoofprints in the soft, wet ground turn a beautiful brook into a stagnant swamp, but the area is a cattle sewer as well. If humans urinated and defecated in mountain streams, society wouldn't tolerate it. So why do we tolerate it of cattle? The Forest Service map says that drinking water is available here, but bring your own.

HIGHWAY 91

Cherry Creek Campground

Hikers, ORVers, and cow-pie collectors alike flock to this small campground located high on the slopes of Oxford Peak. The trail to the top of the 9,282-foot peak starts near here. Par for the course, as soon as you rumble over the cattle crossing at the national forest entrance, you'll likely find yourself face to face with a bovine or 20, who will flee your arrival and run down to the creek and purge a steamy load into it. Really makes you think twice before taking a cooling summertime dip in publicly owned but privately despoiled Cherry Creek. The small USFS camp-

ground is free but has just five sites. To get there, take Malad Valley Road (Highway 191) southwest out of Downey and turn south on Aspen Creek Road, which soon turns into Cherry Creek Road (FR 047). Follow the road straight up the creek for another six miles to the campground.

Downata Hot Springs

This popular, full-service resort, 25900 S. Downata Rd. (3.5 miles south of Downey along Highway 91), Downey, ID 83234, 208/897-5736, offers volleyball courts, horseshoe pits, picnic areas, wagon/sleigh rides, B&B rooms, a restaurant, a campground, and more. But the big draw here in the arid reaches of Bannock County is the water. The resort's pure, 113°F natural hot springs feed a beautiful 300,000-gallon, Olympic-size swimming pool, a whirlpool tub, and a couple of hydrotubes. Summer is prime time—between Memorial Day and Labor Day, the pool is open Mon.–Fri. 11 A.M.–9 P.M., Sat. 10 A.M.–10 P.M., Sun. 11 A.M.–7 P.M. The rest of the year, pool operating hours are limited; call first. But the B&B and hot tub remain open year-round. Use of all the facilities costs $9 general, $7 kids 4–9. Lower specials and limited-use rates are available.

RV sites cost $18 a night with hookups (electricity and water), $14 without. Tenters pay $11 a night. Other accommodations include a ranch house that can sleep up to 12 people for $200 a night; a bunk house with room for seven people ($100 a night); and some bed-and-breakfast rooms for two ($50).

Red Rock Pass

Though not especially impressive to look at today, Red Rock Pass, on Highway 91 at mile marker 30.1, marks the spot where ancient glacial Lake Bonneville finally overflowed its banks and sent a torrent of water crashing through the Snake River Valley. Over time, the lake all but disappeared; Utah's Great Salt Lake is the last remnant.

Bear River Massacre Site

During the settling of the West, the U.S. Army several times annihilated whole bands of Native Americans in a single battle. The army killed 130 Cheyenne at Sand Creek, Colorado, in 1864;

173 Piegan at Marias River, Montana, in 1870; and, in the most infamous attack of all, 146 Lakota men, women, and children at Wounded Knee, South Dakota, in 1890. But here in Idaho, U.S. Army Col. Patrick E. Connor assured his place in hell by leading the single biggest massacre of Native Americans in the country's history.

At dawn on January 29, 1863, Connor's California volunteers—assigned to put down Native American resistance in the area—launched a surprise attack on a village of Northwestern Shoshone. An estimated 400 Shoshone were asleep that morning in Battle Creek Canyon when the thundering hooves of Connor's cavalry descended upon the camp. A few Native Americans managed to escape by diving into and floating down the ice-choked Bear River. The rest—up to two-thirds of them women and children, even babies—were slaughtered. Only 14 bluecoats lost their lives in the one-sided battle.

Plans are afoot for a bigger, better memorial to the tragic event. At present, all you'll find at the site, on Highway 91 a few miles north of Preston, are two historical signs. The older one—erected by the Daughters of the Utah Pioneers—takes a pro-white perspective. The newer sign provides an account more sympathetic to the Shoshone.

PRESTON

The Franklin County seat, Preston was founded by Mormon pioneers in 1866. Originally called Worm Creek, it was later renamed for Mormon leader William B. Preston. Today it's a hub of area farming; primary local crops include grains, hay, beans, and corn. You'll also see a number of dairy farms in the area.

Several beautiful examples of pioneer-era architecture still grace the town, among them the **Oneida Stake Academy,** 151 E. 2nd St. S., an early Mormon school; and the **Mathias Cowley home,** 100 S. 100 E., built for an early Mormon leader.

Entertainment and Events

The **Worm Creek Opera House,** 70 S. State St., 208/852-0088, screens movies and hosts live community-theater productions. Summer is prime season for the local thespian troupe.

Two annual events make for fun times in town. The **Preston Night Rodeo** at the very end of July features PRCA rodeo action and a carnival. The **Festival of Lights** opens on Veterans Day with a parade, then shines on through the end of the year with one of the state's best holiday lights displays. For more information or a complete events calendar, call the Preston Chamber of Commerce.

Food

On the way up to the Bear River Range, the **Deer Cliff Inn,** eight miles up Cub River Canyon (turn off Highway 91 about five miles southeast of town), 208/852-0643, lies right along the road at the base of impressively sheer Deer Cliff. The rustic restaurant offers gourmet dinners May–Oct., Mon.–Fri. from 5 P.M., Saturdays and holidays from noon. It's closed Sundays. Live entertainment livens the place up on Friday and Saturday nights 7–10 P.M. Cabins are also available.

Bear River Range Recreation

The moose may be the largest member of the deer family, but it's certainly not the most graceful. One August evening I drove around a corner in the Bear River Range, above Preston on the way to Mink Creek. Much to my surprise, and no doubt to their far more profound surprise, I came upon two moose—mother and child—loitering in the roadway. Their panicked flight looked like something right out of the cartoons. Mom charged off the road right into a dense thicket, thrashing through it with far more noise than necessary. Junior attempted to follow her but tripped over his own feet and fell flat on his face. I thought it was hilarious, but I'm sure it wasn't funny to them.

Two national forest fee campgrounds can be found in the area. Closest to Preston, at lowest elevation, is **Albert Moser Campground,** offering nine sites along the Cub River. Farther up the road is the turnoff to **Willow Flat Campground,** which occupies a beautiful spot in a steep-walled box canyon. Here the Cub River meanders over riffles and through pools, much to the delight of anglers. From the campground, a hiking trail leads to Willow Spring and Bloomington Lake, and an unimproved 4WD road crosses the range east to the Bear Lake region.

Just back down the road from the Willow Flat campground is Thomas Spring, once a popular stop on the Shoshone Indian trail between Cache Valley and Bear Lake. The Shoshone Trail was used as a mail route for many years. In summer, it was probably a cush route for the intrepid mail carriers. But in winter, they must have cursed the glue right off their stamps as they slogged the mail over the mountains on snowshoes.

Information

For more information about the town, contact the **Preston Chamber of Commerce,** 70 S. State St., Preston, ID 83263, 208/852-2703.

FRANKLIN

On April 14, 1860, 13 Mormon pioneers arrived on the banks of the Cub River here and immediately went to work establishing a townsite. They had come north from Salt Lake City on the advice of Brigham Young and were under the mistaken impression that they were still in Utah. An official boundary survey in 1872 revealed that instead of founding just another Utah town, these pioneers had founded the very first town in Idaho. Later Franklin enjoyed the first telephone and telegraph connections in Idaho, and in 1874, the first railroad line into the state. Many buildings remain from the pioneer days, making for an interesting walking tour for students of history, Mormon history in particular.

Historical Buildings

The log-cabin-style 1937 **Relic Hall** is what most towns would call a historical museum.

Old portraits of the forefathers and -mothers line the walls, most glaring down on the visitor with dour expressions. Another interesting photo, for Mormon-history buffs at least, shows the jail in Carthage, Illinois, where Joseph and Hyrum Smith were murdered by an angry mob. Old pioneer tools and artifacts fill the rest of the building. It's open May–Sept. 10 A.M.–noon and 1–5 P.M. Admission is free; donations accepted.

Next door is a stone building dating from the 1860s that once housed the **FCMI store.** The FCMI, or Franklin Cooperative Mercantile Institution, was one of the early branches of the Mormon ZCMI department store chain that thrives to this day. Now the FCMI building holds a collection of pioneer-era furniture.

Just down the street is the 1872 **Bishop Hatch House,** also constructed of locally quarried sandstone artfully carved by immigrant English stonemasons. Lorenzo Hill Hatch was the town's second Mormon bishop and its first mayor. Before settling in Franklin he served in the Utah legislature, and after his move to Idaho he became the first Mormon elected to the Idaho legislature. His house in Franklin was the largest in town when it was built. It had to be big to accommodate the good bishop along with his three wives and 24 children. The Hatch home also became a popular guesthouse for visitors, including Brigham Young himself. Some say the house is the finest example of Greek Revival architecture in Idaho. It was purchased by the Idaho State Historical Society in 1979 but has not been fully restored and is not open to visitors.

For more information about the Relic Hall or Hatch House, contact the **Idaho Pioneer Association,** Franklin, ID 83237, or the **Idaho State Historical Society, Historic Sites Division,** 2445 Old Penitentiary Rd., Boise, ID 83712, 208/334-2844.

Highway 30 to Bear Lake Country

LAVA HOT SPRINGS AND VICINITY

Today the natural hot springs alongside the Portneuf River draw tourists to this small resort town. But long before the first whites arrived, the Shoshone and Bannock tribes gathered here to partake of the waters. The tribes may have had their differences, but they considered the waters a gift of the Great Spirit and established a truce in the area so that all could benefit. The Hudspeth Cutoff on the Oregon Trail passed by here, too. Perhaps that's one reason why the trail became so popular with trail-weary pioneers. Whites began to settle in the area in the 1880s, and the present town was platted in 1911. It was incorporated as Lava Hot Springs in 1915.

Lava Recreation Complex

The town's biggest attraction is the state-owned Lava Recreation Complex, which consists of two sites. On the west end of town is the 25-acre swimming facility featuring three 86°F pools, one of which is enormous and offers two Olympic-height diving platforms. Surrounding the pools is a large grassy expanse with volleyball courts and picnic tables. This half of the complex is open daily Memorial Day to Labor Day. Down at the other end of town is the hot springs, where several 110°F hot pools sit amid beautiful landscaping in a hollow between the highway and the Portneuf River. The hot pools are sulfur-free (no odor) and are open daily year-round, except Thanksgiving and Christmas. Hours are April 1–Sept. 30, 8 A.M.–11 P.M.; Oct. 1–March 31, 9 A.M.–10 P.M.

Weekend and holiday admission to the Olympic pool is $5.50 for ages 12 and older, $5 ages 3–11, 2 and under free. Admission is $.50 less Mon.–Thurs. Slide tubes cost an extra $3 every day. For the hot pools alone, an all-day weekend/holiday pass is $7 ages 12–59, $6.50 ages 3–11 and 60 and up; single entry is $1.50 less, and weekday rates are discounted $.50. Combined passes to both the Olympic pool and hot springs are available, as are Mon.–Thurs.

The Lava Hot Springs Olympic pool has lots of room for water fun.

family specials. If you need a swimsuit or towel, you can rent 'em at either place.

For more information about the Lava Recreation Complex, contact the **Lava Hot Springs Foundation,** 430 E. Main St., Lava Hot Springs, ID 83246, 208/776-5221 or 800/423-8597, www.lavahotsprings.com.

Tubing the Portneuf River
In summer, kids love innertubing down the Portneuf River from one end of town to the other. The run is short—less than a mile—and takes about 10–15 minutes, depending on how fast the water's flowing. The put-in point is at Majestic Mart at the east end of town, and the takeout is at the Center Street Bridge just before the swimming pool facility. Some of the many tube-rental companies in town will pick you up at the bottom and shuttle you back to the top. But by the time you wait for the shuttle truck to arrive and load passengers, you'll probably find it nearly as fast just to walk back. Figure on making three or four runs an hour. The crux of the run is the "rapids" right by the Pancake House. The water is shallow there and flows pretty quickly over a rocky riverbed—hang on tight or you might end up singin' the black 'n' blues. You also might want to consider renting one of the deluxe tubes with an added bottom.

Numerous tube companies hawk their wares right on the main drag through town. The going rate for a one-person tube is around $4 an hour; larger multiperson tubes are also rented.

Other Recreation
Thunder Canyon Golf Course, 9898 E. Merrick Rd. (head south on 4th Street), 208/776-5048, offers a nine-hole course playing par 35 over 2,974 yards. A stream winds through the scenic course, which costs about $16–18 a round. The course is closed mid-October to mid-April.

Summertime dinner wagon rides are the specialty of **Baker Ranch,** on Dempsey Creek Road south of town, 208/776-5684. The three-hour rides begin with a 40-minute ride up to a creekside picnic area in the pines. Dinner there is campout-style: corn on the cob, baked potato, hot dogs, beans, and all the trimmings, including lemonade and coffee. After dinner, you'll watch the sunset and ride back as the stars come out. The wagon is pulled by a team of draft horses. Light refreshments are served along the way. To get to Dempsey Creek Road, take Main Street west to 4th Street W. and turn left. Cost is $20 adults, $15 ages 3–13, under age 3 free. Call for reservations and more information.

Historical Museum
The **South Bannock County Historical Center and Museum,** 110 E. Main St., 208/776-5254, offers interesting regional-history exhibits. One set of displays chronicles the history of each of the little communities in the area: Swan Lake, Virginia, Inkom, and McCammon, among others. The museum is open year-round, daily noon–5 P.M. (closed Christmas and Thanksgiving). Admission is free; donations accepted.

Accommodations
$50–100: Lava Ranch Inn Motel, 9611 Hwy. 30, 208/776-9917, is a mile west of town. Each of the standard rooms has a private bath, phone, TV (with a movie channel), microwave ovens, and small refrigerator. One Jacuzzi room is available. Outside you'll find a deck and hot tub, riverfront fishing and picnic facilities, and RV sites. **Lava Spa Motel & Campground,** 359 E. Main St., 208/776-5589, is right across from the state hot springs. In addition to motel rooms, RV sites with full hookups are available at $27.50 a night. No tents permitted.

The elegant **Riverside Inn B&B & Hot Springs,** 255 E. Portneuf Ave., P.O. Box 127, Lava Hot Springs, ID 83246, 208/776-5504 or 800/733-5504, was built in 1914 and restored in 1991. Twelve rooms with private baths and four rooms with shared bath all include continental breakfast and use of the private indoor or common outdoor hot tubs. You'll find a television and phone in the lobby but not in the rooms. Out back is a beautiful patio overlooking the river. Smoking is restricted. **Greystone Manor B&B,** 187 S. 2nd W., P.O. Box 419, Lava Hot Springs, ID 83246, offers three B&B rooms, including a honeymoon suite with its own Jacuzzi. Amenities include a billiard room and an upright piano.

$100–150: Lava Hot Springs Inn, 94 E. Portneuf Ave., 208/776-5830 or 800/527-5830, occupies the old hospital/sanitorium just upriver from the Center Street Bridge. The inn's grounds feature five hot mineral pools, including an 80-by-20-foot pool for swimming. The pools are every bit as nice as anything at the state complex up the street, so if you stay here you can save the admission price you would've paid at the state's pools. A lap pool and 10 private hot mineral-water tubs are out front. Inside the inn, the decor is casually elegant. Several honeymoon suites—complete with in-room Jacuzzis—make for an ultimate romantic getaway. A full breakfast is included in the rates. Some less-expensive rooms with shared bathrooms are available, too, as are larger family suites, massage therapy, and complete spa services.

Camping

The nicest RV campground here unfortunately declined to be listed in this book. Perhaps you'll discover it over on the east side of town. Several others are more than adequate, however. One mile west of town, **Lava Ranch Inn Motel & Campground,** 9611 Hwy. 30, Lava Hot Springs, ID 83246, 208/776-9917, offers sites with full hookups for $35, electric only $30, no hookups/tents $20. Amenities at the campground include showers, restrooms, horseshoe pits, volleyball courts, picnic areas with tables and barbecue grills, and a nice stretch of riverfront for fishing.

River's Edge Resort, 101 Hwy. 30, 208/776-5209, is down on the river near the swimming pool complex. RV sites go for $17–22, tent sites for $13–16. Shower and laundry facilities are available. **Smith's Trout Haven,** 9589 E. Maughan Rd., 208/776-5348, is a mile west of town off Main Street, in a quiet, wide-open spot with great views of the surrounding mountains. The park offers two no-license trout-fishing ponds—one for kids and one for adults. You pay just for the fish you catch; $.25 an inch for the small ones, $2.50 a pound for the big ones. RV sites here cost $10 with no hookups, $13 with electrical hookups. Water is available, and showers are under development.

Food

The restaurant at the old 1917 **Royal Hotel,** 11 E. Main St., 208/776-5216, specializes in pizza and other light Italian fare here. The food is outstanding; everything is made from scratch. Try the wonderful Royal calzone with pepper cheese, which you can accompany with one of the decent imported beers on the menu. A wall full of windows makes for bright and comfortable dining, as well as good people-watching. The hotel has a few bed-and-breakfast rooms, too ($50–100).

The **Pancake House,** 15 N. 3rd St. E. (at the river), 208/776-5559, serves basic breakfasts at great prices. It's open daily from Memorial Day to Labor Day, and on weekends only in the early season, from Easter to Memorial Day. Hours are 7:30 A.M.–noon.

Watering holes in town include **Wagon Wheel Lounge,** 225 E. Main St., 208/776-5015, which has a big sideyard beer garden with horseshoe pits and offers live music every Friday and Saturday night in summer; and **Blue Moon Bar & Grill,** 89 S. 1st St. E., up the hill off the main drag, 208/776-5077, where you can shoot pool with the locals.

Information

For more information about the town, contact the **Lava Hot Springs Chamber of Commerce,** 94 E. Portneuf Ave., Lava Hot Springs, ID 83246, 208/776-5500, www.lavahotsprings.org; or the **Lava Hot Springs Foundation,** 431 E. Main St., P.O. Box 669, Lava Hot Springs, ID 83246, 208/776-5221 or 800/423-8597.

To Bancroft and Chesterfield

On the east side of Lava Hot Springs, a turnoff onto Old Highway 30 takes you north up the Portneuf Valley. You'll soon come to a turnoff for the USFS **Big Springs Campground,** which straddles Pebble Creek, a beautiful trout stream unfortunately plagued by cattle. The campground's 11 fee sites are suitable for either picnicking or overnight camping. A nature trail provides a short leg-stretcher, while other trails lead up into the mountains for higher adventure.

Farther north you'll come to Kelly-Toponce Road, which leads north to Chesterfield, a "town" consisting of 27 buildings in various states of re-furbishment or decay. Most were built around the turn of the 20th century by Mormon set-tlers. Some residents still farm the upper valley here, but there is little of interest for the tourist. You might find the small museum open, but you won't find anything in the way of services—no general store, saloon, or gas station. It's a long way out of the way to get here, and there's no pot of gold at the end of the rainbow. Nearby are **Chesterfield Reservoir** and **24 Mile Creek Reservoir,** both popular local fishing holes. From Chesterfield, you can loop back down the far side of the valley to the town of Bancroft and on to Highway 30 and Soda Springs.

Grace

One more turnoff peels away from Highway 30 before you roll into Soda Springs. Heading south on Highway 34 will take you to the town of Grace, which harbors a few quirky sights.

When the first settlers arrived to claim land under the Carey Act of 1894, they had to irrigate Grace Valley in order to perfect their rights to the land. This meant finding a way to move water west out of the Bear River, not an easy task since the river here weaves its way through narrow canyons of lava rock. In 1895, the settlers tried constructing wooden flumes to carry the water. That worked okay in summer, but heavy snows destroyed the flumes in winter. As the deadline to claim the water rights neared, the settlers formed the aptly named Last Chance Canal Company. More wooden flumes, jury-rigging, and amazing perseverance succeeded in getting water to both sides of the valley in 1902. But it was still just a temporary solution. By then it had become clear that the only permanent so-lution to their water woes would be to dig a tun-nel right through the most problematic lava-rock hill and run an aqueduct in one side and out the other. In 1917, the project became a reality.

The contract for the job—a monumental en-gineering task at the time—fell to none other than Morrison-Knudsen Corporation. Two brothers dug the tunnel for MK, one coming in from either side of the hill. Much of the tunnel was dug by hand, with the rock hauled out by horsedrawn cart. When the two tunnels met in the center, they were almost perfectly aligned, forming a single passage 12 feet wide, nine feet high, and 1,800 feet long. A wooden flume sup-ported by a massive concrete arch was then built on the south side of the tunnel to carry the di-verted water back across the Bear River. Although the flume now crosses the river on a steel bridge built in 1946, the new version was built over the old, leaving the concrete arch intact as evidence of the earlier undertaking. To get to the tunnel, turn east at Last Chance Lane just north of town. You can also continue down the road a short way to Last Chance Dam, to see where the water that ends up irrigating Grace is diverted out of the Bear River.

The waters of the Bear River that aren't di-verted for irrigation make their way down into another unusual area sight, **Black Canyon.** The canyon begins humbly just west of Grace, cutting ever deeper into the broad, flat expanse of Grace Valley. Take 1100 N. Road west to the bridge to see the canyon's upper end, where it starts out as a narrow 100-foot-deep canyon. At the other end, downstream, the canyon becomes a wide, 1,000-foot-deep chasm. Hiding a canyon this big is no small feat, but the valley pulls it off well—you'll never see the canyon driving down Highway 34. To get to the rim, take 1100 N. Road west to Turner Junction, turn south on Hegstrom Road and west on Black Canyon Lane. You can also drive down to the canyon floor: take Highway 34 south of town to Two-Mile Road and turn west, then make a left on River Road and a right down to the power plant. A Sportsmen's Access Area fronts the river here, and a dirt road continues upriver to a string of terraced pools favored by local anglers.

One last sight near Grace will appeal to fans of the cold and dark. When one settler homesteaded property near a prominent lava butte south of town, he was pleased to discover a natural re-frigerator located close by. **Niter Ice Cave** is of the collapsed lava tube variety, created by flows ooz-ing from the shield-volcano butte. This site is well signed and not commercially developed. Just find your way down about three-eighths of a mile in the dark. A large flock of birds also seems to like the cool cave, and they get a little hysterical when you invade their space—you might be wise to bring a hat.

SODA SPRINGS

The Caribou County seat, Soda Springs is named for the numerous naturally carbonated springs that well up in the vicinity. The area was something of a novelty to pioneers, who named one of the water holes Beer Springs for its fizzy-salty taste and dubbed another Steamboat Springs because it sounded like a churning steam engine. Both these springs are now submerged under Alexander Reservoir. Also beneath the reservoir lies the original Soda Springs townsite, which grew around the army fort established in 1863 by Colonel Patrick Connor of Bear River Massacre infamy. The present town didn't take hold, however, until Brigham Young visited and supported the establishment of a new townsite at the current location.

West of town along the highway, you'll note groves of **limber pine,** a species that usually grows at a much higher elevation. It's the weather in this particular spot that suits them; winter wind blows hard through the gap here, making the spot even colder than the surrounding territory.

The Geyser

In November 1937, a drilling crew probing for hot water to supply a proposed municipal swimming pool inadvertently tapped into a pressurized underground chamber of geothermally heated water. They capped off the resulting geyser and now it's on a timer, erupting every hour on the hour. The stream of hot carbonated water shoots 150 feet into the air and runs down over a small mineralized mound at its base. Pathways lead to various viewpoints all around the site, which is on the west side of downtown, at the west end of 1st Street S.

Hooper Spring

Here you'll find one of the naturally effervescent springs that gave the town its name. Oregon Trail pioneers stopped here to partake of the waters, and folks still come from all over to drink the water right out of the spring, claiming it helps

their arthritis or other ailments. How does it taste? "I think it's gross!" said one local. And looking out on the Monsanto slag pour and the nearby Kerr-McGee Chemical Corp. plant, you may lose all trace of thirst. The city built a gazebo over the spring itself, and a park around it. The park holds basketball courts, horseshoe pits, picnic sites, and a playground. To get there, head north on 3rd Street E. and turn left just before the can't-miss-it slag pour.

Monsanto Slag Pour

Amazing as it seems, this is actually a tourist attraction. The 530-acre Monsanto Chemical Co. plant here takes some one million pounds of phosphate ore annually and heats it to 1,400°C, at which point elemental phosphorous is separated from the remainder, called slag. An enormous amount of electricity is consumed in the process—local flyers boast that the plant uses as much power per day as a city the size of Kansas City. The slag is poured into specially designed dump trucks, hauled to a hill at the perimeter of the plant, and dumped over the side. This happens about five times an hour, 24 hours a day, 365 days a year. Locals liken the event to a "manmade lava flow." The plant opened in 1953 and has been in continuous operation ever since. At some point, the slag heaps will be capped with soil, trees, and grass, and no one will ever know that the heaps ever existed. That's the plan, anyway. No tours are offered.

Both the Monsanto plant and the 158-acre Kerr-McGee Chemical Corp. plant right across the street are Superfund sites on the EPA's National Priorities List. Groundwater under the Monsanto plant is contaminated with cadmium, selenium, vanadium, and fluoride. Kerr-McGee's waste ponds have leaked vanadium, arsenic, copper, and silver into the groundwater. Fortunately, testing has found no evidence of contamination of Soda Springs' domestic water supplies.

City Parks

Corrigan Park, downtown at Main Street and 1st Street S., is marked by a couple of old locomotives—the Dinky Engine and the Galloping Goose. The Dinky Engine was used to haul supplies during the construction of Alexander Dam. When the water began to back up into the reservoir, the little engine was trapped and drowned at the bottom of the lake. It remained there until 1976, when the reservoir was drained for repairs. Union Pacific Railroad retrieved and restored the Dinky and donated it to the city. The Galloping Goose carried mine workers and ore between Soda Springs and Conda, from 1922 until 1936. The park also offers tennis and basketball courts and lots of grass.

Oregon Trail Public Park and Marina, west of town on Alexander Reservoir, offers a dock, boat ramp, and picnic shelters; open daily 8 A.M.–10 P.M. On the east edge of town, **Kelly Park** is a large open recreation area with baseball diamonds, tennis courts, a fishing pond, and jogging paths.

Recreation

Oregon Trail Country Club, just west of town at 2525 Hwy. 30, 208/547-2204, offers a special thrill to golfers who also happen to be history buffs. The nine-hole, par-36 course surrounds the old Oregon Trail; wagon ruts can be seen on the course's south side between holes one, eight, and nine. The course managers don't mind if you walk from the clubhouse down between the fairways to take a look. Just be careful you don't get in the way of a drive. Greens fee is around $12 for nine holes, or $18 to go around twice. The course is closed in winter.

Trail Canyon Park N' Ski Area, 12 miles northeast of Soda Springs on Trail Canyon Road, offers 10 miles of trails in five loops, and a warming hut. The trails are groomed periodically and are suitable for all ability levels.

Events

The biggest celebration in town takes place the third full week in August with **Geyser Days.** There's a community potluck, dancing in the park, and some fun contests, but the highlight for most locals is the series of **mud bog races.** Watch the trucks get stuck in the muck. For a full calendar of local events, call the Soda Springs Chamber of Commerce at 208/547-2407 or 888/399-0888.

Guest Ranch

The **Bar H Bar Ranch,** 1501 Eightmile Creek Rd., Soda Springs, ID 83276, 800/743-9505, was once cited in *National Geographic Traveler* as one of the country's top 26 dude ranches. At this working 9,000-acre cattle ranch, you ride right alongside the ranchhands, roping, moving, and doctoring cattle, mending fences, and more. The no-frills ranch books only four to six guests per week for the typical one-week stay, so you'll receive personal attention and quickly become friends with the staff. It's not slave labor—any day you don't want to work, you're more than welcome to just saddle up and head for the hills. Those who find horseback riding to be a pain in the butt, literally or figuratively, can explore the ranch on a four-wheel ATV instead. The summer rate here of $850 for a stay from Monday to Saturday noon includes all meals and activities. In winter, nightly rates are available and you can rent snowmobiles or go cross-country skiing.

Forest Service Rentals

The Soda Springs ranger station handles rentals for three guard stations in the Caribou-Targhee National Forest. Northwest of Grays Lake NWR, 45 miles northeast of Soda Springs, **Caribou Guard Station** lies along McCoy Creek in Caribou Basin. It sleeps up to eight people. **Johnson Guard Station** guards the Webster Range at the upper end of Upper Valley and sleeps six. And just two miles from the Wyoming border, **Stump Creek Guard Station** sleeps four and is reached most easily through Afton, Wyoming. All three rent for $20 a night year-round and are equipped with beds and mattresses, as well as propane lights, heaters, and stoves. For reservations or more information, contact the **Soda Springs Ranger District,** 421 W. 2nd S., Soda Springs, ID 83276, 208/547-4356.

Food

Soda Springs isn't going to win any awards as a culinary capital. But you could do worse than the steak-and-seafood **Cedar View Supper Club,** out at the golf course, 2525 Hwy. 30, 208/547-3301, which has excellent atmosphere. The bar is comfortable, and the tall, A-frame dining room boasts a cathedral-like wall of windows and great views of the hills. Open Mon.–Sat. for lunch ($5–10) and dinner ($12–18).

Information

Contact the **Soda Springs Chamber of Commerce** at 9 W. 2nd S., P.O. Box 697, Soda Springs, ID 83276, 208/547-4964 or 888/399-0888. For more information about recreation opportunities in the Caribou-Targhee National Forest, contact the **Soda Springs Ranger District,** 421 W. 2nd S., 208/547-4356.

HIGHWAY 34 TO WYOMING

Heading north out of Soda Springs, Highway 34 runs past Blackfoot Reservoir to Grays Lake, then makes a 90-degree turn east to Freedom, Wyoming. It's big open country out here. Blackfoot Reservoir has a small fishing-village scene, but Grays Lake can be all but deserted, even in the peak summer travel season.

Grays Lake National Wildlife Refuge

Iroquois trapper Ignace Hatchioraquasha discovered this valley around 1818 while out trapping beavers for the Northwest Company. Fortunately for cartographers, Ignace had an Anglicized name: John Grey. How "Grey" became "Gray" is anyone's guess.

This remote, 20,000-acre refuge—actually a large marsh rather than a lake—holds the world's largest concentration of nesting sandhill cranes, as well as a few rare and endangered whooping cranes. The whooping crane is the tallest bird in North America, nearly five feet from head to toe. Its snow-white body is accented by a red-and-black head and jet-black wing tips, and its wingspan stretches some seven feet. The U.S. Fish and Wildlife Service has tried a number of strategies to bolster the population of whoopers but has met with little success. Only about 230 whooping cranes are left in the world.

The perimeter road encircling the refuge makes for a scenic drive. In addition to the cranes, you'll likely see ducks, geese, white pelicans, herons, egrets, Franklin's gulls, grebes, bit-

terns, and phalaropes. Nonwinged species in the area include moose, elk, mule deer, muskrats, and badgers.

Refuge Headquarters along the southeast side of the refuge holds a visitor center with interpretive exhibits, including a mounted whooping crane. A short road leads from the headquarters up to a nearby hilltop, where you'll find an observation point equipped in summer with a free spotting scope. The visitor center is open daily April 1–Nov. 15. Hiking and cross-country skiing are permitted on the northern half of the refuge Oct. 10–March 31.

For more information, contact the Refuge Manager, Grays Lake National Wildlife Refuge, 74 Grays Lake Rd., Wayan, ID 83285, 208/574-2755.

Camping

Up the Blackfoot River at a point called the Narrows is the USFS **Mill Canyon Campground** (10 sites, fee). It's unremarkable except for its proximity to the river for fishing.

The out-of-the-way USFS **Gravel Creek Campground** (nine sites, fee) is definitely worth going out of your way for. After climbing into the Grays Range you'll enter a lush forest filled with a veritable arboretum of tree species. No doubt much more of the state's forests once looked like this before the coming of the chainsaws. You'll see some little trees, some big trees, some dead trees, some clearings, some incredibly dense groves, and a dozen or more variations on a theme of green. Catch a trail to the top of Henry Peak (elevation 8,319 feet) or just nap alongside Gravel Creek. To get to the campground, take Wayan Loop off Highway 34 and turn south up FR 191.

Pine Bar and Tincup Campgrounds, fronting Highway 34 near the Wyoming border, are more glorified rest stops than anything else. Both have five sites and both are free.

MONTPELIER AND VICINITY

Butch Cassidy Robbed Here

According to local legend—which some locals question—famous desperado Butch Cassidy and his Wild Bunch gang rode into Montpelier on August 13, 1896, and relieved the local bank of some $16,500 in gold, silver, and currency. The deputy sheriff on duty couldn't find his horse, so he grabbed a nearby bicycle and rode off after the gang as they headed up Montpelier Canyon. Needless to say, his pursuit efforts were futile. One of the Hole-in-the-Wall Gang, Bob Meeks, was eventually caught and jailed for his part in the robbery. But Butch and Sundance escaped scot-free for this one. The bank building the gang held up still stands, but it's now a print shop.

National Oregon/ California Trail Center

This interpretive center, 320 N. 4th (corner Hwys. 89 and 30), Montpelier, 208/847-3800, houses interactive exhibits on life along the emigrant trails, among them a computer-controlled covered wagon. The center also offers regular living-history programs. One-hour tours are offered daily May–Sept. from 10 A.M.–5 P.M.; $6 general, $5 seniors 60 and up; $4 kids 5–12.

In the basement of the center is the **Bear Lake Rails and Trails Museum,** offering some great regional-history displays. Among the topics covered are the wild and woolly Bear Lake Rendezvous of 1827; nearby Big Hill, the toughest grade on the Oregon Trail up to this point; and the Native American history of Bear Lake Valley. Artifacts on display include many items brought across the plains on wagon trains by the area's early settlers. The museum is open the same hours as the center, except it's closed on Sunday.

Golf

Montpelier Municipal Golf Course, 210 Boise, 208/847-1981, offers a nine-hole course—3,172 yards, par 36—with a snack bar, pro shop, and driving range. The greens fee runs about $10 for nine holes, $17 for 18. Closed mid-October through mid-April.

Events

The fourth Saturday in July, Montpelier presents the **Oregon Trail Rendezvous Pageant.** Celebrations include a delectable Dutch-oven supper, as well as pioneer-style music, drama, dancing, and more. For more information, call pageant organizers at 208/945-2333.

Accommodations

Under $50: Budget Motel, 240 N. 4th St., 208/847-1273, is adjacent to the busy parking lot of Butch Cassidy's restaurant. **Three Sisters Motel,** 112 S. 6th St. (at Washington), 208/847-2324, has rooms with refrigerators and microwaves. **Park Motel,** 745 Washington St., 208/847-1911, a basic brick road motel, rents 25 rooms. **The Fisher Inn,** 401 Boise, 208/847-8885, another basic road motel, is on the way out of town to the north and boasts a heated pool.

$50–100: Best Western Clover Creek Inn, 243 N. 4th St., 208/847-1782 or 800/528-1234, offers the town's fanciest and most expensive accommodations. Its 65 rooms include both smoking and nonsmoking units. Triple-bed rooms and kitchenettes are available. Amenities include free in-room coffee, free HBO, and a hot tub. Right across the street is **Super 8,** 276 N. 4th St., 208/847-8888 or 800/800-8000, which offers 50 rooms, a hot tub and exercise room, and a free continental breakfast.

Camping and Picnicking

Two campgrounds are near town on Highway 89 north, which here runs more east than north. Closest to town is **Montpelier KOA,** 28501 Hwy. 89 N., 208/847-0863 or 800/562-7576, a particularly clean and pleasant KOA that's quieter and not as much of a circus as some. Rates are $21.50 for full hookups, $19.50 for electricity and water only, $16.50 for no hookups, and $15 for tenters. Kamping Kabins go for $31.50. Amenities include showers, a laundry, seasonal pool, game room, and adjacent fishing on Montpelier Creek. A bit farther east, 3.5 miles east of town, and also on the creek is the relatively primitive USFS **Montpelier Canyon Campground** (13 sites, fee). A trail runs upstream from the campground to secret fishin' holes. If the campground isn't full when you get there, choose the upstream "trailers" loop instead of the downstream "campers" loop—the sites are nicer. Just past the campground is a creekside picnic area.

North of Montpelier, east of Georgetown, is

Caribou-Targhee National Forest's **Summit View Campground** (23 sites, fee). It's a relatively nice one with no evidence of cattle in the vicinity. Equestrians and ORVers are among the most likely users.

Food
Butch Cassidy's Restaurant and Saloon, 260 N. 4th, 208/847-3501, is the town's most reliable restaurant. It's a popular stop on the tour-bus circuit. The diner section in front is casual, the dining room on the side is a little more formal, the bar in back is country and billiards. The restaurant is open daily 6 A.M.–10 P.M.

Information
Contact the **Greater Bear Lake Valley Chamber of Commerce** at P.O. Box 265, Montpelier, ID 83254, 800/448-2327. For Caribou-Targhee National Forest recreation information, contact the **Montpelier Ranger District,** 322 N. 4th St., Montpelier, ID 83254, 208/847-0375.

On to Wyoming
Heading east out of Montpelier on Highway 89 N, you'll soon come to the turnoff to Montpelier Reservoir. Anglers can try their luck either in the reservoir (no motorboats) or just downstream of the dam, where clean and clear Montpelier Creek meanders through verdant meadows, in and out of thickets, over riffles and through cool pools—it looks like trout heaven. The Forest Service's primitive Elbow Campground (unsigned) is just off the highway, right below the dam. Continuing east, you'll crest Geneva Summit (elevation 6,938 feet) and coast down the other side to the state line. From there it's another 30 miles to Afton, Wyoming.

If you instead head south out of town on Highway 30, you'll pass Big Hill. This climb over the Sheep Creek Hills was the toughest grade that Oregon Trail travelers had faced on their journey to this point. It was definitely a shortcut—the Bear River loops many more miles south and back from one side of the hill to the other—but the climb was steep and the descent harrowing. Soon you'll crest Border Summit (elevation 6,358 feet) and drop down into

Wyoming at Border Junction, at the feet of the Sublette Range.

HIGHWAY 89 TO BEAR LAKE
Bear Lake was discovered by whites in 1812, when a party of trappers passed this way on a return trip from Astoria, Oregon. Trappers played leading roles in the area's history, and two of the annual fur-trading rendezvous were held here, in 1826 and 1827.

Half in Idaho, half in Utah, Bear Lake is 20 miles long and seven miles wide. Dissolved limestone particles suspended in the water give the lake a surreal, turquoise-blue color, especially intense at sunrise. Rainbow and cutthroat trout tease anglers here, while another fish, the sardine-like Bonneville cisco, is found nowhere else in the world. Besides fishing, popular summer pastimes on the lake include sailing and powerboating. The nearest boat rentals are at the Bear Lake State Recreation Area marina in Garden City, Utah, about three miles across the state line.

Ovid
On the way down to Bear Lake from Montpelier, you'll pass blink-and-you'll-miss-it Ovid, settled by Mormons in 1864. The town lies at the junction of Highway 36, which heads west to Preston, and Highway 89, which continues south to Bear Lake and the Utah border. Twelve miles northwest of Ovid off Highway 36, the USFS **Emigration Campground** (25 sites, fee) occupies a delightful spot high on the east side of the Bear River Range at an elevation of 7,500 feet. It's surrounded by a beautiful mix of evergreen and deciduous trees, making it an especially nice location in fall. Wildflowers are abundant, and hiking trails lead from here to other parts of the range.

Paris
The little town of Paris, seat of Bear Lake County, was founded on Sept. 26, 1863, by 30 Mormon families led by Charles C. Rich. Here, as happened in Franklin, the settlers thought they were still in Utah at the time.

Presiding majestically over Main Street downtown is the red sandstone **Paris Stake Tabernacle,** a Romanesque Mormon temple designed by one of Brigham Young's sons. It was built between 1884 and 1889. The stone for the temple was quarried 18 miles away and hauled by horsecart to the site, where immigrant Swiss stonemasons carved the stunning edifice. Tours of the tabernacle are offered daily in summer.

Paris Springs Campground (12 sites, fee) is six miles up into the mountains west of town, in a quiet location a short hike from the namesake springs. No mere trickle, these springs gush profusely out of the ground at the head of a steep-walled box canyon. The campground isn't crowded; you may have it to yourself. Ice-cave diehards can take a fork lower down the canyon and continue five or six miles up a gravel road to the small **Paris Ice Cave.**

If you're hungry, try the **Paris Cafe,** 48 S. Main St., 208/945-9900, a friendly eatery serving basic diner fare.

Bloomington

From Bloomington, FR 409 leads west up Bloomington Canyon to some of the most beautiful country in the Caribou-Targhee National Forest. About eight miles up the canyon you'll come to a well-marked turnoff to the **big Engelmann spruce,** a point of interest listed on the Forest Service map. What the map doesn't tell you, however, is that the giant tree—weakened by drought—died in 1992 at the ripe old age of 448. Its hulking carcass still stands and is still impressive and beautiful in its own way. But it may not be the stunning sight you were expecting.

The area right around the big Engelmann spruce is a beautiful place for camping. Several unofficial sites are available along the banks of the South Fork of Bloomington Creek, and wildflowers flower wildly here.

If you hadn't turned left at that last fork on your way to the spruce, but had veered right instead, you'd have eventually ended up at the trailhead for **Bloomington Lake** and the **Highline National Recreation Trail.** It's possible to drive to within about a half mile of the lake, but those with wimpy cars or constitutions will want to park about a mile farther back down the road. The top of the canyon opens out on to a beauti-

ful high meadow resplendent with wildflowers. The trail to the lake is easy and short, and passes a couple of shallow ponds that might be of interest to anglers or splashers. But Bloomington Lake itself is the star attraction here. Its crystal-clear waters lie right at the foot of a towering granite cliff where snow lingers year-round. The high-alpine feeling you get here is rare in southern Idaho.

The Highline Trail runs 55 miles along the crest of the Bear River Range, from Beaver Creek Campground in the south (take FR 411 off Highway 89; five sites, fee) to **Soda Point Trailhead** (five miles northeast of Grace off Highway 34) in the north.

For more information on Bloomington-area recreation, contact the Caribou-Targhee National Forest's **Montpelier Ranger District,** 322 N. 4th St., Montpelier, ID 83254, 208/847-0375.

Bear Lake National Wildlife Refuge

This 18,000-acre reserve, most of it marsh, is one of the largest Canada goose nesting grounds in the western United States and home to the country's largest nesting population of white-faced ibis. Scads of ducks pass through in spring and fall, and deer and moose roam the refuge as well.

Spring is the best time to view the greatest numbers of species. Most migratory species begin arriving in April and begin leaving in August. Access restrictions apply for much of the year; contact the refuge headquarters for complete regulations. The best viewing area is in the refuge's Salt Meadow Unit at the northern end. To get there, take Paris-Dingle Road east out of Paris and turn south just after crossing the canal. The canal road leads to a boat-launching ramp and several parking areas.

For more information, write to Bear Lake National Wildlife Refuge, 370 Webster St., P.O. Box 9, Montpelier, ID 83253-1019, or call the headquarters at 208/847-1757.

Bear Lake State Park

As Idaho's state parks go, this one is pretty humble. You won't find interpretive information, campfire programs, or nature trails here. The key attraction is Bear Lake itself. The park has two units—a day-use beach and boat ramp along the north shore, and a campground on the east shore. The normal state park motor vehicle entry fee of $4 applies. Campsites at the 150-site **East Beach Campground** cost $9 a night plus $4 more for electricity hookups. For more information, contact the park office, 181 S. Main St., P.O. Box 297, Paris, ID 83261, 208/847-1045 or 208/945-2565.

St. Charles and Vicinity

For what it's worth, St. Charles was the birthplace of Gutzon Borglum, the painter and sculptor who carved Mt. Rushmore. He was born here March 25, 1867. Recreation opportunities abound in St. Charles Canyon, which climbs into the Bear River Range west of town. A paved road (FR 412) leads all the way up to **Minnetonka Cave,** 208/945-2407, one of only a few federal show caves in the country. Those who have traveled throughout southern Idaho and have therefore come to expect every "cave" site to be a lava tube are in for a surprise here. This is an honest-to-goodness limestone cave, complete with stalagmites and stalactites. A half-mile guided tour takes you deep inside, up and down some 448 steps, and through nine rooms holding formations such as the Seven Dwarfs and the Devil's Office. Tours are offered daily June through Labor Day, every half hour between 10 A.M. and 5:30 P.M.; admission is $5 general, $4 ages 6–15, free for ages 5 and under. Family rates are available. Bring a sweater; the cave is a constant 40°F.

On the way to the cave you'll pass a string of Forest Service campgrounds. First, lowest, and least interesting is **St. Charles Campground** (six sites, fee), followed by **Davis Canyon Campground,** a free, primitive, and unmarked site down on the creek, at a point where the main road climbs above the creek for a stretch. A spur leads down to the water. If you don't need the fee-campground amenities, this is an excellent place to spend one night or many. Next up is **Porcupine Campground,** right on St. Charles Creek, where a newly added loop among lodgepole pines

and aspens brings the total number of sites to 16 (fee). Continuing ever higher up the canyon, you'll next come to **Cloverleaf Campground,** which offers 20 sites (fee) in three cloverleaf loops. It's not immediately on the creek, but it's convenient to a trail that climbs up to Minnetonka Cave. For more information on the cave or the USFS campgrounds, contact the **Montpelier Ranger District,** 322 N. 4th St., Montpelier, ID 83254, 208/847-0375.

RV sites at **Minnetonka RV Park & Campground,** 220 N. Main, 208/945-2941, rent for $13.50 per night; no-hookup tent sites cost $10.50. Amenities include showers and laundry; volleyball, basketball, and tetherball courts; and horseshoe pits.

Fish Haven

Bear Lake B&B, 500 Loveland Ln., Fish Haven, ID 83287, 208/945-2688, overlooks the lake from up on a hill. The year-round home-style B&B offers six rooms with private or shared bath ($50–100). Rates include a full breakfast, and amenities include an outdoor hot tub and a rec room with TV and VCR. Fish Haven is also home to the **Bear Lake Valley Convention and Visitors Bureau,** 208/945-2072 or 800/448-2327.

Bear Lake West

Just south of Fish Haven you'll find **Bear Lake West Golf Course,** 155 Hwy. 89, P.O. Box 396, Fish Haven, ID 83287, 208/945-2744. The nine-hole, par-33 course challenges the hacker with water and sand traps on several holes. Greens fee is around $12. The course is open April–Oct. Party animals who have been enduring the route south from the last oasis at Pocatello can take heart—a bastion of youthful energy can be found at Bear Lake West's restaurant, 208/945-2222. Students from Utah State in Logan come up here in summer to cut loose at this comfortable resort, where a large back deck offers great lake views. It's easy to miss this place; watch closely for signs just south of Fish Haven. If you hit the "Welcome to Utah" signs, you've gone too far.

Lava Country

North of Pocatello, I-15 hunkers up close to hills on one side and fronts the vast, wide-open Snake River Plain on the other. Highways 26 and 20 head west from Blackfoot and Idaho Falls, respectively, forging bold, straight paths out across the plain's lonely high-desert terrain. Not far from the lifeblood water of the Snake River, the plain doffs its irrigated mask of green to reveal the blacks, browns, grays, and reds of its volcanic origins.

BLACKFOOT AND VICINITY

The Bingham County seat, Blackfoot is a working-class agricultural hub ruled by King Spud; this is the number-one potato-producing county in the nation as well as Idaho's top grain producer. Blackfoot, founded in 1879, is the largest of the county's handful of small towns, most of which have declined in population in the last couple of decades.

World Potato Exposition

It really is worth getting off the highway and seeking out this shrine to Idaho's most famous vegetable. You'll find it in the old Oregon Short Line Railroad Depot at 130 N.W. Main St., 208/785-2517, www.potatoexpo.com. In addition to offering "Free Taters for Out-of-Staters," the museum houses endless potato anecdotes and trivia. Here you'll see the world's largest potato chip, made by Procter & Gamble's Pringles division; a picture of Marilyn Monroe dressed in a burlap potato sack; and a copy of the 1992 letter sent by Idaho governor Cecil Andrus to U.S. vice president Dan Quayle, following Quayle's well-publicized spelling-bee faux pas. The letter, which accompanied a gift box of Idaho bakers, reads: "As far as we're concerned you can spell potato any way you want as long as it's genuine Idaho. P.S. There is no 'e' in Idaho either."

The Potato Expo is open April–Oct., Mon.–Sat. 9:30 A.M.–5 P.M., and Nov.–March, Mon.–Sat. 9:30 A.M.–3 P.M. Admission is $3 adults, $2.50 seniors, $1 children 6–12. Next door to the museum is a gift shop selling boxes of

Got potatoes?

potatoes, potato ice cream cones, potato fudge, potato hand lotion, and other potato products.

Recreation

Jensen Grove Park makes a nice place to get out of the car for a breather. A shady grove of cottonwoods gives the park its name and watches over an inviting picnic area. Water-skiers and summertime splashers make good use of the park's 55-acre lake. To get there, take Exit 93 east off the interstate, then make the first left and follow it to the park. Golfers enjoy the adjacent 18-hole **Blackfoot Municipal Golf Course,** 3115 Teeples Dr., 208/785-9960. Greens fee for the 6,722-yard, par-72 course is about $18. The course is closed Nov. 1–March 1, and it's also closed Monday in season. Club and cart rentals available. Year-round swimming is available at the heated, indoor **Blackfoot Municipal Pool,** 960 S. Fisher Ave., 208/785-8624.

Entertainment and Events

Blackfoot Community Players presents a season of community theater at the historic, art deco **Nuart Theatre,** 195 N. Broadway, 208/785-5344. The troupe typically presents four dramas and a musical each year.

The **Eastern Idaho State Fair** comes to Blackfoot the first week in September. Pigs race, cars crash (on purpose), cowboys hang on for dear life to unappreciative horses and bulls—it's the quintessential Idaho shindig. There's even a "Best Spam Recipe" contest. Also check out **Snake River Days** in May. For a complete events schedule, call the chamber of commerce at 208/785-0510.

Accommodations

$50–100: The **Weston Riverside Inn,** 1229 Parkway Dr., 208/785-5000 or 800/785-9331, is right by Exit 93. Its 80 rooms feature queen beds and cable TV with HBO. Other amenities include a heated outdoor pool (summers only), a restaurant serving three meals a day, and a lounge with big-screen TV. Suites are available. Kids under 12 free with parents in same room. Pets are permitted for an additional $5 a night.

The **Best Western Blackfoot Inn** is close to

I-15 Exit 93 at 750 Jensen Grove Dr., 208/785-4144 or 800/528-1234. All rooms have two queen beds, and amenities include cable TV, an indoor pool, hot tub, and weight room, and a free continental breakfast.

Information

Contact the **Greater Blackfoot Area Chamber of Commerce** at P.O. Box 801, Blackfoot, ID 83221, 208/785-0510, www.blackfootchamber.org. The office is in the Key Bank building in the Riverside Plaza parking lot at the corner of Bergner Boulevard and Parkway Drive.

HELL'S HALF ACRE

Covering some 222 square miles, this brand-spankin'-new lava flow—about 2,000 years old—comprises substantially more than a half acre. It occupies almost the entire eastern half of the triangle formed by I-15 and Highways 20 and 26. You can get a pretty good look at the flow from the rest stop on I-15 just north of Blackfoot. But to really explore the flow, take Highway 20 west of Idaho Falls for 20 miles, then turn south on a quarter mile gravel road to a parking area and trailhead. Here you'll be in the Hell's Half Acre Wilderness Study Area, a 66,000-acre preserve managed by the BLM, Bonneville County, and the Idaho Alpine Club. From here you can head out across the lava on foot in any direction you'd like. A couple of suggested but unimproved trails are marked with colored poles. One of them is a half-hour loop that takes you past several different volcanic features. The other is a 4.5-mile route that leads to the volcanic vent itself, the actual spot from which the molten goo oozed in the B.C. days. From the vent, at an elevation of 5,350 feet, the lava flowed south down to a point near today's interstate at an elevation of 4,600 feet.

The best time to visit is in late spring or early summer, when the wildflowers are blooming brightly and the summer sun has yet to turn the Snake River Plain's oven knob to Broil. For more information on the Hell's Half Acre area, contact the **BLM Idaho Falls District,** 1405 Hollipark Dr. in Idaho Falls, 208/524-7500.

SPUDOLOGY 101

At last, all the studying is over and it's time to see how much you've learned. Your Ph.D. in Spudology rides on this final exam. If you pass, a universe of spudness awaits. The world is your russet! If you fail, it's back to Stove Top stuffing. Pencils ready? Good luck. And . . . begin!

1. The first potato farmer in Idaho was:
   a. Meriwether Lewis
   b. David Thompson
   c. Henry Harmon Spalding
   d. Walter "Big Train-O-Spuds" Johnson

2. What country grows the most potatoes?
   a. The United States
   b. Russia
   c. China
   d. Ireland

3. Which of the following plants is not related to the potato?
   a. chili peppers
   b. petunias
   c. rutabaga
   d. tobacco

4. Which American president first served french fries at the White House?
   a. George Washington
   b. Thomas Jefferson
   c. Abraham Lincoln
   d. Gerald Ford

5. What French celebrity was responsible for introducing the Paris fashion world to potato blossoms as an accessory?
   a. Coco Chanel
   b. Brigitte Bardot
   c. Marie Antoinette
   d. Charles de Gaulle

6. Which of the following government agencies has not conducted potato research?
   a. USDA
   b. INEEL
   c. NASA
   d. CIA

7. Which of the following is not made from potatoes?
   a. blood plasma
   b. biodegradable packing peanuts
   c. artificial crab
   d. heat shields on the space shuttle

8. One 8-ounce baked potato has how many calories?
   a. 100
   b. 250
   c. 500
   d. 750

9. The world's largest potato weighed just over:
   a. 4 pounds
   b. 9 pounds
   c. 18 pounds
   d. 36 pounds

10. The potato chip was invented by:
   a. Lay's Diner in Hoboken, New Jersey
   b. Mrs. Winnifred P. Geuss (grandmother of Martha Geuss-Pringle), St. Louis, Missouri
   c. Sands Resort Hotel and Casino, Las Vegas, Nevada
   d. Moon's Lake Hotel in Saratoga, New York

BIG SOUTHERN BUTTE

You can't miss this landmark rising nearly 2,500 feet above the surrounding plain. It's visible on the horizon from nearly all of southeast Idaho. Like scores of other smaller buttes sprinkled across the Snake River Plain, Big Southern Butte was also created by the forces of volcan-

ism. But unlike the other smaller buttes, the molten rock that spewed from the earth here was not basalt but much more viscous rhyolite. Think of it like an upwelling of Elmer's glue instead of water. The rhyolite cooled and solidified before it had the chance to spread and flatten out across the plain. Unlike the more common black basalt, rhyolite is light-

Answers:

1–c. Henry Harmon Spalding was Idaho's first potato grower. He, wife Eliza, and some curious Nez Perce brought in the first crop at Lapwai Mission in 1836.

2–b. Russia grows the most potatoes in the world. They also drink the most vodka.

3–c. Rutabaga

4–b. Thomas Jefferson introduced french fries to America when he served them at a White House dinner. John Adams scoffed that Jefferson was "putting on airs" by serving "such novelties."

5–c. Marie Antoinette paraded though the French countryside wearing potato blossoms in her hair. They soon became the rage in Parisian court circles.

6–d. The CIA, so far as we know. USDA is always looking to improve the mighty spud. INEEL uses "reverse geometry x-ray" techniques to find hollow heart and other potato diseases. NASA is hoping to grow potatoes in space

stations to sustain the astronauts through extended missions.

7–d. Heat shields. Overcooked potatoes are an abomination—even NASA knows that.

8–a. Just 100. Eat two!

9–c. Thomas Seddal of Chester, England, grew an 18-pound, 4-ounce potato, which he harvested, weighed, and, presumably, ate, on February 17, 1795.

10–d. At Moon's Lake Hotel in Saratoga, a picky customer regularly complained that his fried potatoes were soggy. So one day the chef sent out a batch that he'd literally fried to a crisp. The customer loved them.

Score Ratings:

1–3 wrong: Congratulations, your degree in Spudology is hereby conferred.

4–6 wrong: Uh-oh, better put more starch in those collars.

7 or more wrong: Couch potato! Make another trip back to the World Potato Expo in Blackfoot, Idaho, and take better notes this time.

---

colored, which helps Big Southern Butte stand out in contrast to its surroundings.

You can hike to the top of the 7,560-foot butte, or even drive up in a 4WD. To get to the road to the summit, start from Atomic City on Highway 26. Take Cox's Well-Atomic City Road west. Continue across the railroad tracks, bearing right at the Cedar Butte Road intersection and left at the Cedar-Big Butte Road intersection. From here, the idea is to follow roads clockwise around the south and west sides of the butte, ending up at Frenchman's Cabin (and landing strip) on the butte's northwest corner. From the major intersection at Frenchman's Cabin, the road to the Butte leads off to the southeast. After a mile and a half, you'll come to a gate. If it's locked, hike up

the remaining 3.5 miles from there. If it's open and you have a 4WD vehicle, you have your choice of hoofing it or using the gas-guzzler. In either case, bring plenty of water. You'll pass through Douglas fir forest on the way up, then enjoy spectacular views from the summit. Backpackers can bivvy on top to catch sunrise over the Tetons.

IDAHO NATIONAL ENGINEERING AND ENVIRONMENTAL LABORATORY (INEEL)

The U.S. government established this facility in 1949 to build and test nuclear reactors for both civilian and military purposes. Today, Department of Energy contractor Bechtel

BWXT conducts a broad spectrum of nuclear-related studies here, including research and development of electric vehicles, medical radiation cancer treatments, environmental cleanup technologies, and nuclear waste volume-reduction systems, among others.

You can't see much of INEEL from most roads in southeast Idaho. That's partially by design. The 890-square-mile site was selected for its remote location. The barren desert out on the sparsely populated Snake River Plain seemed the perfect place to toy with the newly uncorked nuclear genie. But even if you never see INEEL, it's hard not to think about it in your travels through the region. "The site," as many call it, holds the nation's highest concentration of nuclear reactors; 52 have been built here over the years, and 13 continue to operate. That's particularly interesting statistic given that the site is located in one of the nation's most geologically active areas, and sits atop an aquifer that supplies drinking and irrigation water to much of southern Idaho. Many people see this as a nightmare in the making.

INEEL is also the federal government's current repository for nuclear waste shipments from all over the country. Spent reactor fuel from the nuclear navy is shipped here by rail from Mare Island, California, and Newport News, Virginia. The U.S. Departments of Defense and Energy have no legal obligation to notify states of these shipments—you wouldn't want terrorists sabotaging or stealing the radioactive cargo. But again, many people look at this process and see potential catastrophe. Storage of the federal waste at INEEL is supposed to be temporary. But since no other plan to safely store nuclear waste is even close to being implemented, what that "temporary" label means is uncertain.

Isolated instances of small nuclear waste spills have been reported over the years, and the site is also on the EPA's Superfund list for chronic contamination that took place over decades of use. Among the toxic substances detected in both monitoring and drinking-water wells on the Snake River Plain Aquifer: hexavalent chromium, acetone, sodium hydroxide, and sulfuric acid. In addition, the EPA reports that "carbon tetrachloride and trichloroethylene (TCE) have migrated from where they were buried to the Snake River Plain aquifer. Soils are contaminated with heavy metals such as lead and mercury, volatile organic compounds, and radionuclides."

You don't hear much protest about any of this in Pocatello or Idaho Falls, where most of INEEL's employees live. The site employs about 8,000 area residents and generates about $612 million in wages and more than $50 million in tax revenues annually.

For more information, call the busy INEEL Public Affairs Office at 800/708-2680.

EBR-1

Experimental Breeder Reactor-1, built in 1951, was the world's first atomic power plant. The reactor was decommissioned in 1964 and designated a National Historic Landmark in 1966. It's open to the public for free tours—either guided or self-guided—from Memorial Day weekend through Labor Day weekend, daily 8 A.M.–4 P.M. The reactor is on Highway 20/26, 18 miles southeast of Arco, 50 miles west of Idaho Falls, 40 miles northwest of Blackfoot. For more information, call the EBR-1 office at 208/526-0050 or the INEEL Public Affairs Office at 800/708-2680.

ARCO

Arco was the first city in the world to be lit up by atomic power. On July 17, 1955, scientists at the National Reactor Testing Station, 18 miles east of town (now INEEL), threw a switch and sent two million watts of electricity from Boiling Water Reactor No. 3 (BORAX-III) into the living rooms of Arco for about two hours.

The Hill with the Numbers

The graffiti-riddled hill behind town is a monument to adolescent fervor. Since 1920, every graduating senior class at the local high school has trudged up the hill to paint its class year on the rocks. The view of town from the cliffs is decidedly romantic. One can only imagine how many fond memories have been conceived up there each moonlit June for the past 80-odd years.

King Mountain

Consistent updrafts make the summit of King Mountain, north of town, a popular launching spot for hang gliders; the Idaho state distance record was set here. And on the south flanks of the peak is one of the most impressive area destinations for hikers—a natural bridge spanning 80 feet. The massive limestone arch frames rugged spruce-covered terrain. A map to the King Mountain area is available at the Arco visitor center.

Events

The **Winter Rose Festival** celebrates the most romantic of flowers on the first weekend in February. If you're gliding through town the third weekend in June, you'll be right on time for the **King Mountain Hang-Gliding Championships** up on King Mountain. If you ask around, you might be able to get a tandem ride on one. The following month, on the closest weekend to the anniversary date of the town's historic electrification (July 17), the whole town lightens up for **Atomic Days.** Featured are parades, a rodeo, quilt show, sidewalk sales, nuclear exhibits, dancing, and other high-voltage festivities. It's the most fun you can have without goin' fission.

The weekend before Halloween, the **Fall Festival** celebrates the arrival of chilly weather with—what else?—a chili cookoff. Don't be surprised to find pirates, vampires, or sugar-plum fairies among the chefs. Come in costume if you'd like, but ghosts should bear in mind that it's hard to get chili stains off a white sheet. The year winds up with the **Festival of Trees,** the first weekend in December, featuring Christmas music and the town's biggest crafts show.

Information

Basic accommmodations and food are available in town. The **Lost River Visitor Center,** 132 W. Grand Ave., 208/527-8977, can give you a map to the natural arch and answer your questions about the area.

CRATERS OF THE MOON NATIONAL MONUMENT AND PRESERVE

Eighteen miles southwest of Arco, Highway 20/26/93 enters an eerie, otherworldly landscape

the alien landscape of Craters of the Moon National Monument

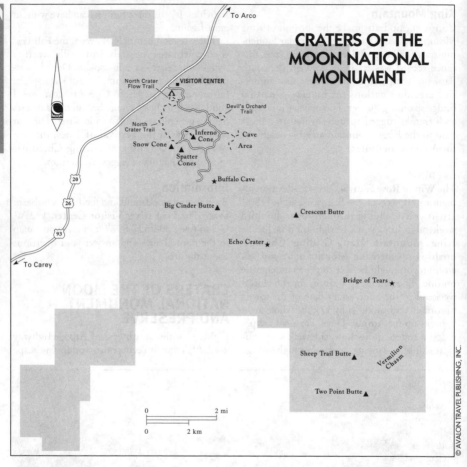

CRATERS OF THE MOON NATIONAL MONUMENT

pocked, cracked, contorted, and charred by lava flows and eruptions occurring at various times between 15,000 and 2,100 years ago. When Oregon-bound pioneers passed by here on Goodale's Cutoff in the 1860s, they considered the area a forbidding wasteland and kept on truckin'. But the area soon caught the eye of local geologists, who began studying it in the early 1900s. In 1921, USGS geologist Harold T. Stearns described the area as resembling the craters of the moon and recommended the creation of a national monument at the site.

That idea, and the name Craters of the Moon,

really took hold after Boise taxidermist-turned-explorer Robert Limbert made several long treks across the lava flows. Limbert brought national attention to the area by describing his adventures in the March 1924 issue of *National Geographic* magazine. In May 1924, President Calvin Coolidge designated the area as Craters of the Moon National Monument. In August 2002, the monument was expanded from about 55,000 acres to more than 250,000 acres now known as Craters of the Moon National Monument and Preserve. It's managed jointly by the National Park Service and the Bureau of Land Management.

Lava fields cover much of southeastern Idaho, but what makes this area unique is the concentration of different volcanic features. Craters of the Moon lies along the Great Rift, a 60-mile-long perforation in the earth's crust along which eruptions have occurred as recently as around 110 B.C., practically yesterday in geologic time. Here the earth's crust is stretching apart, becoming thinner and developing deep cracks and fissures above hot rising magma deeper down. When the magma reaches the crust and finds the cracks, it erupts out onto the earth's surface—sometimes placidly oozing, sometimes spouting forth in geysers of molten rock. Scientists say the area is due for another eruption any day now, sometime in the next thousand years.

From the air, the Great Rift looks like a giant dashed line of enormous cracks, dotted here and there with cinder cones marking the sites of volcanic vents. Craters of the Moon constitutes the denouement of the Great Rift, where an entire textbook's worth of volcanic phenomena can be seen in one place.

A Lavaland Lexicon

Visitors to Craters of the Moon will be faced not only with an alien landscape, but with an alien set of words used to describe the various volcanic features. Many of the words come from the Hawaiian language; the islands were built by similar volcanism, and the process continues today, so it's no surprise that wordsmiths there beat mainlanders to the punch in coming up with names for what they saw. Following are a few of the more common terms you'll need to know:

A'a (pronounced "AH-ah" and meaning "hard on the feet") lava is full of sharp edges that slice open both sneakers and bare skin. You can't walk barefoot on *a'a* and you sure as heck don't want to fall down on it. *Pa'hoe'hoe* (pronounced "pa-HOY-hoy" and meaning "ropy") lava is smoother than *a'a* and won't make mincemeat of your Keds. It's also full of enclosed air pockets, so chunks of *pa'hoe'hoe* are far lighter than equivalently sized *a'a* chunks.

Cinder cones form when an eruption sprays lava into the air. The lava droplets cool on the way down and the resultant cinders accumulate as big ash heaps, generally with shallow-sloped sides that are highest right around the vent. Since the cinders are light, cinder cones are often elongated in the direction of the prevailing wind. **Spatter cones** form where steam vents disgorge denser globs of lava into the air. The heavier globs clot together like a hollow chimney around the vent, generally forming cones that are smaller than cinder cones, with steeper sides. Large globs of lava thrown skyward often solidify in midair and land as **lava bombs.** The bombs come in several different common shapes, including spindle, ribbon, and breadcrust, the latter looking like a fine pumpernickel *batard*.

Kipukas are areas where a lava flow surrounded, but didn't cover, either an older flow or an area as yet untouched by lava. These "islands" of vegetation allow scientists a window on preflow vegetation in an area, and allow them to compare that vegetation to postflow growth. Where lava flows into a tree, it makes a cast of the trunk, then cools around it. The trees themselves are long gone—fried to a crisp—but the impression of their scorched bark remains etched in the lava.

A **lava tube** is formed when the surface of a river of *pa'hoe'hoe* lava cools and hardens into a skin, while the interior of the stream stays molten and pours right on through. After the molten flow drains away, the hardened outer skin forms a hollow tube, often loosely called a cave. Sometimes these "caves" can even have "stalactites," which in this case aren't calcite deposits left by dripping water, but lava that hardened in the act of dripping off the ceiling of the tube.

Flora

Looking at the dry, blackened landscape, you wouldn't expect much life to be found here. Craters of the Moon receives a limited amount of precipitation to begin with, about 15–20 inches per year. Arid conditions are compounded by wind-exacerbated evaporation, and rainfall and snowmelt sink through the porous lava before the plants have much of a chance to make use of it. Nevertheless, many plants have adapted to these harsh conditions.

Of primary importance to all the other plants in this land of abundant rock is the minute

lichen, a schizophrenic character that isn't sure if it's an alga or a fungus. It attaches itself to rocks and over time breaks down the rock into soil in which other plants can get a start. An odd but heroic lifeform, the lichen.

Drought-tolerant desert dwellers such as **sagebrush, antelope bitterbrush,** and **prickly pear cactus** also inhabit the monument, but the author's award for the most striking plant species here goes to the **dwarf buckwheat.** This tiny plant grows only a few inches tall, but its root system spreads out across an underground area up to three feet in diameter. As a result, the dwarf buckwheat plants are spaced out across the lava fields, looking more like a gardener's plantings than Mother Nature's handiwork. In summer, the white-foliaged plants look like snowflakes against the black lava.

The most prevalent tree in the monument is the hardy **limber pine.** Its limber branches bend easily but don't break in the often heavy winds here, and its very large seeds can germinate in cracks in the lava where other trees could never get started. In early summer, it's time for the wildflowers to show off; look for **monkeyflower, desert parsley, Indian paintbrush, bitterroot,** and **scabland penstemon,** among others.

Fauna

Small mammals can make a home in and among the cracks in the lava flows. Don't be surprised to see mice, voles, pikas, squirrels, and chipmunks darting about and keeping a close eye on your food supplies. Of course, those little guys are food themselves for the local raptor population, which includes northern harriers, red-tailed and sharp-shinned hawks, and great horned and long-eared owls. Though you're unlikely to see them, gopher snakes, rubber boas, and rattlesnakes are also found here.

Besides *Homo sapiens,* the **mule deer** is the largest mammal inhabiting the monument. The park's healthy herd of these big-eared Bambis has made remarkable adaptations to life on the lava. In spring, the herd turns up in the wilderness area south of the monument. The deer find high-quality forage there, but since the area provides no pools of open water, the animals get all their

water from dew, condensed fog, and the vegetation they eat. When summer comes and the wilderness area dries out, the herd moves north into the smaller monument proper, congregating in larger-than-normal population densities around the few water sources there. In fall, the rains return and the herd heads back south into the wilderness area. When snow falls, the deer leave the park entirely, off to their wintering grounds. It's a complicated schedule as mule deer migrations go, but it seems to be working well for this ingenious herd.

Visitor Center and Campground

After turning off the highway, you'll find the monument's visitor center on the left. Exhibits and videos explain the geology, flora and fauna, and history of the area, and National Park Service rangers answer questions and sell a variety of related science and history books. The visitor center, 208/527-3257, is open daily year-round, except for winter holidays. Hours are 8 A.M.–6 P.M. in summer, 8 A.M.–4:30 P.M. the rest of the year. Across the road is the monument's single campground. Its 52 sites are densely clustered in a relatively small area, but this is a blessing rather than a curse—it means the rest of the monument is less crowded.

The day-use fee is $5 per vehicle, or $3 per person for those entering by bicycle or motorcycle or on foot, and campsites (first-come, first-served) cost $10 a night. Water and restrooms are available, but showers, hookups, groceries, and other amenities are not. Rangers lead interpretive walks by day and present amphitheater programs in the evening. Check out those stars! Between October and May, day use and camping are free, but there's no running water and the campsites aren't plowed. When the loop road gets covered in snow, rangers turn it into a groomed cross-country ski trail.

Around the Loop Road

From the campground, a seven-mile road loops south into the heart of the monument, past many sight-filled stops. Among the highlights: the **Devil's Orchard,** where a short, wheelchair-friendly interpretive trail loops through some bizarre formations; **Inferno Cone Viewpoint,** where you can hike up to the top of Inferno Cone for sweeping views across the lava flows and the Snake River Plain; the **Tree Molds** area, where a short hike leads to some prime examples of that phenomenon; and the **Cave Area,** where a trail leads to numerous lava tube "caves," most of which require a flashlight to explore.

With multiple stops, a few short hikes, and a picnic lunch thrown in for good measure, plan a leisurely three or four hours to make your way around the loop.

Into the Wilderness
In 1970, Congress designated 43,000 acres south of the monument as Craters of the Moon Wilderness. You'll need a permit from a ranger at the vis-itor center to venture into this area, accessed past the end of the Tree Molds trail. Not surprisingly, the wilderness receives little use. In summer, temperatures are high and water is scarce. In addition, hiking on the lava chews up boots. In winter, it would be tempting to head out into the snow-covered wilderness on cross-country skis, though unstable snow bridges can obscure deep cracks in the lava. A fall into the Great Rift would put an end to your Nordic-ski vacation.

Information
For more information, write Superintendent, Craters of the Moon National Monument, P.O. Box 29, Arco, ID 83213, call the monument at 208/527-3257, or see www.nps.gov/crmo.

Idaho Falls and Vicinity

Idaho Falls, the Bonneville County seat, owes a great deal of its economy to the Idaho National Engineering and Environmental Laboratory; you'll see a regular stream of big yellow buses carrying the site's engineers and physicists to and from work and home. (Man, the yellow paint on those buses is bright! Does it glow or just seem to? New nuclear-waste recycling technologies, perhaps?)

The town (population 51,100) was around long before INEEL, so it exhibits an interesting mix of farmers and nuclear scientists. The two groups seem to coexist well enough. In any case, you'll find just enough culture here—including the state's largest museum—to keep you entertained, as well as plenty of that down-home charm that makes Idaho so great.

SIGHTS
The Falls
The falls at Idaho Falls were just rapids until 1910, when work began on the hydroelectric power plant just south of the Broadway bridge. Then the diversion dam was built, resulting in the cascade you see today. The falls may not be natural, but they're still a pleasant sight (and sound). A greenbelt winds along the riverbank right by the falls, making for scenic jogging, strolling, or picnicking.

Mormon Temple
The big Moroni-topped wedding-cake structure on the city's finest riverfront property is the Idaho Falls Temple of the Church of Jesus Christ of Latter-day Saints, 1000 Memorial Dr., 208/523-4504. The temple offers a place for non-Mormons to learn about the prevalent religion in southeast Idaho. A visitor center has displays and videos about the church; it's open daily 9 A.M.–9 P.M. One-hour tours are offered Mon.–Sat. 9 A.M.–4:30 P.M. Both the tour and visitor center are free.

Museum of Idaho
Once a humble repository of local lore, this newly enlarged and renamed museum, 200 N. Eastern Ave., 208/522-1400 or 800/325-7328, www.museumofidaho.org, has triple the space it did before, which reportedly makes it the state's largest museum. A full-size, fleshed-out replica of a Columbian mammoth is the centerpiece attraction, but you'll also find a neat exhibit showing Eagle Rock (Idaho Falls' original name) as it may have looked on a typical day in 1891. The museum is open Mon. 6–9 P.M. for Family Night

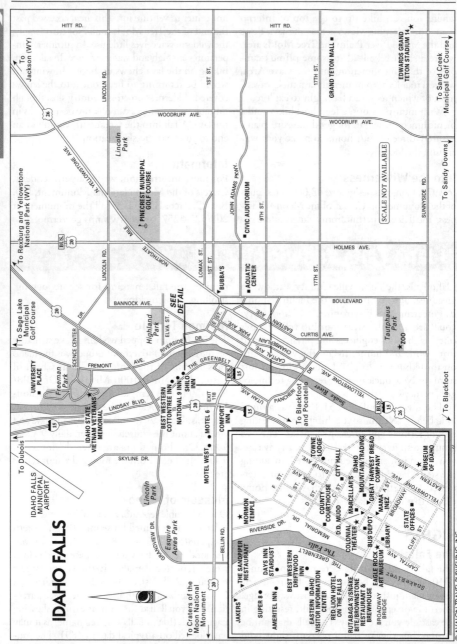

SOUTHEAST IDAHO

IDAHO FALLS

HITT RD.
HITT RD.

To Jackson (WY)

LINCOLN RD.

WOODRUFF AVE.
WOODRUFF AVE.

1ST ST.

17TH ST.

GRAND TETON MALL

EDWARDS GRAND
TETON STADIUM 14

To Sand Creek
Municipal Golf Course

N. YELLOWSTONE AVE.

Lincoln
Park

PINECREST MUNICIPAL
GOLF COURSE

JOHN ADAMS PKWY.

CIVIC AUDITORIUM

9TH ST.

SCALE NOT AVAILABLE

To Sandy Downs

To Rexburg and Yellowstone
National Park (WY)

BUS. 20

20

LINCOLN RD.

NORTHGATE MILE

HOLMES AVE.

17TH ST.

SUNNYSIDE RD.

To Sage Lake
Municipal
Golf Course

20

SCENE CENTER DR.

BANNOCK AVE.

LOMAX ST.

1ST ST.

BUBBA'S

AQUATIC
CENTER

BOULEVARD

Tautphaus
Park

ZOO

To Blackfoot

Highland
Park

ELVA ST.

SEE
DETAIL

E ST.

PARK AVE.

PARK AVE.

EASTERN

CURTIS AVE.

CHAMBERLAIN

RIVERSIDE DR.

CAPITAL AVE.

University
Place

FREEMANT AVE.

THE GREENBELT

SHILO
INN

BUS. 15

15

YELLOWSTONE AVE.

Freeman
Park

IDAHO STATE
VIETNAM VETERANS
MEMORIAL

BEST WESTERN
COTTONTREE INN

NATIONAL 9 INN

LINDSAY BLVD.

MOTEL 6

EXIT 118

20

UTAH AVE.

PANCHERI DR.

COMFORT
INN

15

Snake River

BUS. 15

26

15

To Dubois

SKYLINE DR.

MOTEL WEST

To Blackfoot
and Pocatello

To Blackfoot

IDAHO FALLS
MUNICIPAL
AIRPORT

GRANDVIEW DR.

Lincoln
Park

Esquire
Acres Park

BELLIN RD.

TOWNE
LODGE

SHOUP AVE.

MOUNTAIN TRADING

GREAT HARVEST BREAD
COMPANY

MUSEUM
OF IDAHO

F ST.

PARK AVE.

CITY HALL

D ST.

C ST.

IDAHO

MARCELLAR'S

MEMORIAL DR.

E ST.

COUNTY
COURTHOUSE

D.D. MUDD

BROADWAY

EASTERN
YELLOWSTONE AVE.

MAMA
INEZ

To Craters of the
Moon National
Monument

20

MORMON
TEMPLE

RIVERSIDE DR.

COLONIAL
THEATER

BUS DEPOT

LIBRARY

STATE
OFFICES

CLIFF ST.

CAPITAL AVE.

JAKERS

THE SANDPIPER
RESTAURANT

DAYS INN
STARDUST

BEST WESTERN
DRIFTWOOD
INN

THE GREENBELT

The Falls

EASTERN IDAHO
VISITOR INFORMATION
CENTER

RED LION HOTEL
ON THE FALLS

RUTABAGA'S/SNAKE
BITE/BROWNSTONE
RESTAURANT &
BREWHOUSE

EAGLE ROCK
ART MUSEUM

BROADWAY
BRIDGE

Snake River

SUPER 8

AMERITEL INN

© AVALON TRAVEL PUBLISHING, INC.

and Tues.–Sat. 9 A.M.–5 P.M., with extended hours for special exhibits. Admission costs $5 for adults, $3 for kids 4–18, under 4 free. Families can get in for $18 ($14 on Monday nights).

Eagle Rock Art Museum

When you're out strolling the Greenbelt, be sure to stop in the new **Eagle Rock Art Museum,** 300 S. Capital Ave., 208/524-7777, www.eaglerockartmuseum.org. In addition to traveling exhibits and works by local artists (adults and children), the center hosts such special events as a holiday show the first weekend in December and a spring show in April. Regular hours are Mon. 6–9 P.M., Wed.–Sat. 10 A.M.–4 P.M., Sun. 1–4 P.M. Closed Tues. Admission is free, so spend a few bucks in the gift shop and help this place grow.

Historic Architecture

Many 19th- and early-20th-century buildings still stand in Idaho Falls. An exploratory stroll through downtown yields views of such buildings as the 1917 Hotel Idaho, 482 Constitution Way, which was in use until 1979; the 1918 Underwood Hotel, 347 Constitution Way, built for early Idaho Falls entrepreneur Jennie Underwood; and the 1915 Shane Building, 381 Shoup Ave., a Renaissance Revival retail space with terracotta accents.

Across the railroad tracks, on the east side of Yellowstone Avenue, is the Ridge Avenue Historic District, once the city's prime residential neighborhood. Queen Annes, Craftsmans, and Colonial Revivals—all here and surrounded by expansive lawns and venerable maple trees. Many of the houses are listed on the National Register of Historic Places. Among the most impressive: the 1896 A.D. Morrison house at 258 Walnut St.; the 1916–17 Tudor-Gothic Trinity Methodist Church at 237 N. Water Ave.; and the 1910 Fuller House at 101 N. Placer Ave., which once did double duty as a home and hospital.

The city publishes detailed walking-tour guides to both the downtown and Ridge Avenue districts. Pick up copies at the Eastern Idaho Visitor Information Center, 505 Lindsay Blvd., 208/523-1010 or 800/634-3246.

PARKS AND RECREATION

Snake River Greenbelt

One of the best ways to spend an hour or more in Idaho Falls is a stroll along the city's greenbelt, a 29-acre park lining both sides of the Snake River. The most popular stretch lies between the Broadway bridge and the Highway 20 bridge; it's a 2.3-mile loop enjoyed by joggers, speed-walkers, and bicyclists, as well as squadrons of ducks and Canada geese. In winter, the snow-covered landscape takes on a contemplative air, and the greenbelt becomes a whitebelt suitable for snowshoeing or cross-country skiing.

Tautphaus Park

The crown jewel of the city's 39-unit park system, Tautphaus Park holds acres and acres of grassy expanses, an abundance of trees and flowers, a fountain, baseball fields, tennis courts, a playground, and a tiny amusement park that will keep Junior occupied for at least 10 minutes.

In addition, **Tautphaus Park Zoo,** 208/528-5222, www.idahofallszoo.org, houses more than 250 animals in re-created natural habitats simulating the respective creatures' home turf. Among the rare and endangered species on display here: snow leopards, red ruffed lemurs, Amur tigers, and cotton top tamarins. The zoo is open in April weekends only, 9 A.M.–4 P.M.; May 1 to Memorial Day daily 9 A.M.–4 P.M.; Memorial Day to Labor Day Mon. 9 A.M.–8 P.M., Tue.–Sun. 9 A.M.–5 P.M.; Labor Day to Sept. 30 daily 9 A.M.–4 P.M.; October weekends only, 9 A.M.–4 P.M. (Closing time is when the last admission is sold; gates remain open an hour later.) Admission costs $4 general, $2.50 seniors 62 and over, $2 kids 4–12, free for ages 3 and under. The zoo is closed Nov.–March. Across from the zoo is an ice-skating/hockey rink open in winter, 208/529-0941.

Other Parks and Recreation Facilities

At the west end of Science Center Drive at the river, 75-acre **Freeman Park** offers plenty of open space, along with baseball diamonds, a disc golf course, picnic tables and shelters, a playground, and the **Idaho State Vietnam Veterans Memorial**—a stainless-steel sculpture engraved with the names of Idaho soldiers killed or missing in action in the Vietnam War.

The city's **Recreation Center,** 520 Memorial Dr., 208/529-1480, offers racquetball courts, basketball courts, a weight room, showers, and lockers. It's open Mon.–Fri. 8 A.M.–10 P.M., Sat. 8 A.M.–5 P.M. The **Aquatic Center,** 149 S. 7th St., 208/529-1111 (recorded information), provides an indoor lap pool, hot tubs, and an outside wading pool open in summer. Hours vary by season, so call for details. Admission is $3.35 general, $2.55 ages 4–12 and seniors 62 and over. You'll also find a municipal pool at **Reinhart Park,** 1055 Washburn Ave. (at Grandview Dr.), 208/529-1112.

For more information on the city's municipal parks and recreation facilities, call the **Idaho Falls Parks and Recreation Division** at 208/ 529-1480.

Climbers in need of some good 5.11 can head to **Stonewalls,** 751 S. Capital St., 208/528-8610, an indoor climbing gym with 6,500 square feet of climbing walls. The cost is $7 per day; shoe and harness rentals available. Call for current hours, which change monthly; generally, however, the gym is open afternoons and evenings.

Golf

Area golfers can choose from three city-maintained 18-hole courses to putt around on. In the heart of town, the 6,419-yard, par-70 **Pinecrest Municipal Golf Course,** 701 E. Elva St., 208/529-1485, is probably the toughest of the three, featuring small greens and lots of dastardly trees. On the southeast side of town, par-72 **Sand Creek Municipal Golf Course,** 5200 S. Hackman Rd., 208/529-1115, is the longest of the batch. Its 18 holes stretch across 6,770 yards. On the city's north end you'll find **Sage Lakes Municipal Golf Course,** 100 E 65 N, 208/528-5535, which offers numerous water traps on a 6,566-yard, par-70 course. All three courses are closed in winter, and all three charge $18 on weekends and holidays; $1 less weekdays.

Spectator Sports

The **Idaho Falls Chukars,** 208/522-8363, a Pioneer League team affiliated with the Kansas City Royals, play summer evenings at McDermott Field, in Highland Park at Bannock Ave. and W. Elva St. Tickets cost $8 reserved, $5 adult general admission, $4 for kids and seniors.

Outdoor Outfitter

For backpacking, climbing, skiing, and skating gear, to buy or rent, try **Idaho Mountain Trading,** 474 Shoup (at B St.), 208/523-6679.

ENTERTAINMENT AND EVENTS

Idaho Falls' big arts venue is the renovated **Colonial Theater/Willard Arts Center** complex, 498 A St.; 208/522-0471; www.idahofallsarts.org. There are typically several concerts here each week, including many touring acts. It's also the home of the excellent Idaho Falls Arts Council, which can fill you in (via phone or its website) on all the arts events around town.

Movies are big in Idaho Falls, with the **Edwards Grand Teton Stadium 14,** 2707 S. 25th E., 208/552-0690, leading the pack among the multiplexes. A couple of drive-in movie theaters make anachronistic options. The **Motor Vu Drive In** is at 2095 N. Yellowstone, 208/523-3711; the **Sky Vu Theatre** is at 3000 S. Yellowstone, 208/523-1085.

Mid-April brings the annual **East Idaho Fly Tying and Fly Fishing Expo** to Idaho Falls, with demonstrations by more than 100 top tyers. The sponsoring organization's website is packed with info both on the expo and on the region's great angling opportunities. See www.snakerivercutthroats.com.

The **Mountain Brewers Beer Festival** bubbles forth in early June at McDermott Field, featuring more than 80 breweries in what has to be the Northern Rockies' biggest beer festival. Ironic, given that Idaho Falls is strong Mormon country, but teetotalers will find plenty of handcrafted root beers on tap, too. Call 208/524-0970 for more information.

Mid-June through August, the Idaho Falls Arts Council, 208/522-0471, sponsors free concerts from 7 to 8 P.M. every Tuesday on Memorial Drive between D and E Streets. The arts council also is the sponsor of the annual **Snake River**

Roaring Youth Jam, a kid-oriented arts festival in mid-August. Activities include a battle of the bands, family concerts, hands-on art tents, and the **Great Snake River Duck Race.**

In nearby Shelley, nine miles southwest of Idaho Falls, the **Idaho Spud Day** celebration takes place the third Saturday of September. It's an absolutely taterific event that promises starchy fun for the entire family; for more information, call Shelley City Hall, 208/357-3390.

For more regional events information, call 866/ENJOY-IF (866/365-6943).

ACCOMMODATIONS
Under $50
Out by the interstate at Exit 118 you'll find **Motel 6,** 1448 W. Broadway, 208/522-0112 or 800/466-8356. **Motel West,** 1540 W. Broadway, 208/522-1112 or 800/582-1063, is another good budget choice, with an indoor pool and onsite restaurant.

$50–100
At the low end of this range is the humble **Towne Lodge,** 255 E St., 208/523-2960, worth a mention for its low rates and convenient downtown location.

Most of the city's chain lodgings cozy up to each other on Lindsay Boulevard, along the west side of the Snake River near the falls. From south to north on the riverbank side of Lindsay you'll find: **Red Lion Hotel on the Falls,** 475 River Parkway, 208/523-8000 or 800/RED-LION (800/733-5466); **Best Western Driftwood Inn,** 575 River Parkway, 208/523-2242 or 800/939-2242; **Days Inn Stardust,** 700 Lindsay Blvd., 208/523-8900 or 800/527-0274; **Shilo Inn,** 780 Lindsay Blvd., 208/523-0088 or 800/222-2244, with rates at the top of this range; **National 9 Inn,** 850 Lindsay Blvd., 208/523-6260 or 800/852-7829; and **Best Western CottonTree Inn,** 900 Lindsay Blvd., 208/523-6000 or 800/662-6886, also near the top of this price category.

At all of these lodgings, you can get river view rooms (worth the extra bucks, as the view in the opposite direction is less than exciting), and you'll be able to walk right out the door onto the greenbelt for your evening constitutional. The cylindrical-shaped Red Lion is the tallest and nearest the falls; the Shilo Inn probably has the best location and range of amenities.

Across Lindsay, away from the river, is the spiffy, high-end **AmeriTel Inn,** 645 Lindsay, 208/523-1400 or 800/600-6001, which offers a 24-hour indoor pool. Nearby is **Super 8,** 701 Lindsay Blvd., 208/522-8880 or 800/800-8000, with rooms on the low end of this price category.

By the freeway near Motel 6 (Exit 118) is **Comfort Inn,** 195 S. Colorado Ave., 208/528-2804 or 800/228-5150, also on the easy end of your wallet.

RV Parks
Idaho Falls KOA, 1440 Lindsay Blvd., 208/523-3362 or 800/562-7644, lies north of Highway 20 in an industrial area dominated by a General Mills seed plant. But a long driveway and abundant trees provide a sufficient buffer against the sights and sounds out on the boulevard. Amenities, some seasonal, include a heated pool and Jacuzzi, outdoor movies, miniature golf, a game room, playground, and camp store. In summer, the camp offers pancake breakfasts and evening barbecues. Rates run around $24 for a tent site, $32 for an RV site with full hookups. One-room Kamping Kabins are also available for $35–40.

The city maintains a primitive but free **tourist campground** for visiting RVers. South Tourist Park is on S. Yellowstone Highway, a couple of miles out of town toward Shelley. The park has a bathroom and RV dump. Stays are limited to one night. For more information, call the city's parks department at 208/529-1480.

FOOD
Upscale American
A decidedly off-the-wall alternative in this restaurant category is the **Hawg Smoke Cafe,** 4330 N. Yellowstone Hwy., 208/523-4804, a gourmet biker kitchen. The tiny, eight-table restaurant is the brainchild of Harley owner Dave Musgrave, who knows his way equally well around a shovelhead and a châteaubriand. Musgrave studied

under master chef Paul Bucose of Lyon, France. Look for a varied menu of chef's specials—no telling if you'll be offered squid tacos, tournedos Rockefeller, or Mongolian stir-fry. But you can bet it'll be good. Entrées average $15–19. Open Tues.–Sat. for dinner, with reservations a must.

In the Eagle Rock Station mini-mall near the falls are two excellent locally owned restaurants. **Rutabaga's,** 415 River Pkwy., 208/529-3990, features "semi-tough industrial decor," serves sandwiches, gourmet pizzas, and salads, and offers rotating dinner specials that might include fresh grilled swordfish, teriyaki duck, or herb-crusted rack of lamb. Dinner is served Tue.–Sat.; entrées range $14–25. It's also a favorite for Sunday brunch. Next door is the lighter and less formal **Snake Bite,** 425 River Pkwy., 208/525-2522, which offers pizzazzy burgers, salmon, chicken, steaks, rack of lamb, you name it—all in a Southwestern atmosphere. Bottled microbrews take the sting out of the Bite. Entrées range anywhere from $5–16. It's open Mon.–Sat. for lunch and dinner.

The Sandpiper Restaurant, 750 Lindsay Blvd., 208/524-3344, is part of the small southern Idaho chain that offers consistently good food and atmosphere in a traditional, casually elegant setting. Entrées range $11–30 and include chicken, pasta, and prime rib, as well as a half dozen different cuts of steak to suit your whim. A similar choice with less atmosphere but lower prices is the nearby **Jakers,** 851 Lindsay Blvd., 208/524-5240.

Ethnic Fare

Mexican food is big in Idaho Falls. Good choices include **Melina's,** 187 E. 1st St., 208/524-5430, and **Mama Inez,** 344 Park Ave., 208/525-8968. You can fill up at either one for $5–10. The best Mexican eats in town, however, may be what you get from **La Aguililla,** a.k.a. the Taco Truck—a mobile *taquería* that parks downtown behind Idaho Mountain Trading on certain nights of the week. Ask a local for the where-and-when, and don't miss it for supercheap, superauthentic tacos, tamales, and the like. Or try the reader-recommended **Puerto Vallarta Mexican Restaurant,** 1480 Fremont Ave., 208/523-0437, which is reported to have very good salsa.

The local favorite for Italian food is the chain eatery **Johnny Carrino's,** 2833 S. 25th St., 208/523-4411, where the average entrée runs around $10. It's open daily for lunch and dinner.

It's 20 miles north of town via I-15 in Roberts, but **BJ's Bayou,** 655 N. 2880 E., 208/228-2331, offers downhome Cajun food to die for. Prices range $12–19. It's open Mon.–Sat. 11 A.M.–10 P.M., Sun. 3–9 P.M.

Brew and Barbecue

For barbecue, without a doubt the place to go is **Bubba's,** 118 E. 1st St., 208/523-2822. Menu items range $6–13, and specials are offered. It's open for lunch and dinner daily and even for breakfast Wed.–Sun. Brewpub duties in town are well handled by **Brownstone Restaurant & Brewhouse,** 455 River Pkwy., 208/535-0310. It's a clean, spacious place with good beer and a varied menu ranging from filet mignon to burgers (mostly $8–18). Vegetarian options available. Open for lunch and dinner daily in summer, Mon.–Sat. the rest of the year.

Coffee

D.D. Mudd, 401 Park St., 208/535-9088, sports a bright interior and great people-watching from its downtown corner location. In addition to your favorite bean brew, it also offers a light food menu: bagels during the week, a bigger spread with eggs, waffles, breakfast burritos, and such on Saturday morning. Hours are Mon.–Sat. 6:30 A.M.–10 P.M. There's also an eastside location at 2896 S. 25 E., 208/524-6683.

Bread and Wine

It's worth a stop at **Great Harvest Bread Company,** 360 A St., 208/522-7444, just to breathe. The heady, yeasty, and comforting aroma of freshly baked bread permeates the place, and you can watch the bakers in action. Dozens of different flavors are baked fresh every day but Sunday. The bakery is open Mon.–Sat. 7 A.M.–6 P.M.

An imbiber's oasis in the dry Sahara of southeast Idaho, **MarCellar's Vintage Wines & Brews,** 431 Park Ave., 208/523-0503, stocks a wide selection of premium wines and beers.

SHOPPING

In Idaho Falls, 17th Street is The Road to Mallville. The long strip is encrusted with one fastfood emporium after another, all brightly lit and egging you on toward **Grand Teton Mall**, 2300 E. 17th St., 208/525-8300, the town's largest shopping center. ZCMI, JCPenney, Sears, and Bon-Macy's are the mall's big guns. It's open Mon.–Sat. 10 A.M.–9 P.M., Sun. noon–5 P.M. Across the street, you'll find megabookstore **Barnes and Noble**, 2385 E. 17th St., 208/522-1010, which also sells art notecards and espresso.

INFORMATION AND SERVICES

Information

The all-in-one **Eastern Idaho/Snake River Territory Visitor Center**, 505 Lindsay Blvd., P.O. Box 50498, Idaho Falls, ID 83405-0498, 866/ENJOY-IF (866/365-6943), www.visiteastidaho.com, is staffed by representatives from the Greater Idaho Falls Chamber of Commerce, 208/523-1010, and other agencies. The center offers interpretive displays about the region, sells related books and maps, and stocks free literature on everything from accommodations to recreation opportunities.

The headquarters of the **Caribou-Targhee National Forest** and the **Idaho Falls BLM** field office are both at 1405 Hollipark Dr., 208/524-7500. The forest's **Palisades Ranger District** is at 3659 E. Ririe Hwy. (Hwy. 26 E.), 208/523-1412.

The **Idaho Falls Public Library**, 457 Broadway, 208/529-1460, is one of the state's best. It's open Mon.–Thurs. 9 A.M.–9 P.M., Fri.–Sat. 9 A.M.–5:30 P.M.

Transportation

Idaho Falls Municipal Airport, 2140 N. Skyline Dr., 208/529-1221, is served by **Delta Air Lines**, 800/221-1212, with flights to Salt Lake City and worldwide connections from there; **SkyWest**, 800/453-9417, Delta's commuter affiliate; and **Horizon Air**, 800/547-9308, a commuter affiliated with Alaska Airlines. Car rental agencies at the airport include **Avis**, 208/522-4225 or 800/831-2847; **Budget**, 208/522-8800

or 800/527-0700; **Hertz**, 208/529-3101 or 800/654-3131; and **National**, 208/522-5276 or 800/227-7368.

I-15 NORTH TO MONTANA

Waterfowl Sanctuaries

As I-15 beelines north to the Montana border, it passes three separate preserves that serve as aqueous stepping stones for migratory waterfowl on the Pacific Flyway. In spring and fall, the preserves draw vast numbers of snow geese and Canada geese; mallard, gadwall, and ring-necked ducks; green-winged and cinnamon teal; trumpeter swans; double-crested cormorants; herons, egrets, and sandhill cranes; Franklin's gulls; white-faced ibises; and many other species. Numerous extras with important cameo roles include shorebirds, songbirds, and raptors. All three refuges are open year-round. Camping, fishing, and boating are permitted subject to seasonal restrictions; inquire at the respective headquarters.

Twenty miles north of Idaho Falls is **Market Lake Wildlife Management Area**, a 5,000-acre area surrounding 1,700 acres of spring-fed marsh. A map and birder's checklist are available at WMA headquarters. To reach the headquarters, exit I-15 at Roberts (Exit 135) and head east to Road 2880 E. Turn north on 2880 E. and drive through the town of Roberts. At the fork in the road, bear right to Road 800 N. and follow signs from there to the headquarters. For more information, contact the Regional Wildlife Habitat Biologist, Market Lake WMA, Idaho Department of Fish and Game, 806 N. 2900 E., Roberts, ID 83444, 208/228-3131.

The huge **Camas National Wildlife Refuge** protects more than 10,000 acres of waterfowl-filled wetlands. The two largest lakes on the refuge cover 600 and 700 acres, respectively. In addition, Camas Creek winds through the area. During peak spring and fall migration periods, you might see up to 100,000 ducks here. The birder's checklist for the refuge includes 177 species. Information and a map of the refuge are available from the headquarters, 2150 E. 2350 N., Hamer, ID 83425, 208/662-5423. To get there, take the Hamer exit off I-15 into the town of Hamer, then turn north on the old highway. Go three miles north up the old highway, then two miles west to the headquarters.

West of I-15 (Exit 143) off Highway 33, **Mud Lake Wildlife Management Area** centers around 7,000-acre Mud Lake. The lake is only about five feet deep and is ringed with bulrush, cattail, sedges, and salt grass. This wetlands habitat is a prime staging area for some 50,000 snow geese, who pass through in March and early April. The best place to view this extravaganders is the **Kaster Overlook Tower** along the north shore of the lake in the heart of the 8,853-acre WMA. To reach the tower, turn off Highway 33 at Road 1100 E., 14 miles west of I-15. Take 1100 E. north three miles to 1800 N, and turn right. Follow this road a half mile to the WMA Head-quarters, where you can pick up a map and get more information. From near the WMA head-quarters, near the junction of 1100 E. and 1800 N., a road leads northwest. Follow this road a couple of miles to the first intersection and turn right, then make the very next right in about a quarter mile. The tower is a couple of miles down this road. If you picked up a map at the WMA headquarters, you'll have no trouble navigating around the preserve. For more information, con-tact the Regional Wildlife Habitat Biologist, Mud Lake Wildlife Management Area, Idaho Department of Fish and Game, 1165 E. 1800 N., Terreton, ID 83450, 208/663-4664.

Dubois

Dubois lies in high-desert terrain at an elevation of 5,149 feet. Some 20 miles to the north, the Centennial and Beaverhead Mountains form the Continental Divide. Northwest of Dubois, Med-icine Lodge Road follows Medicine Lodge creek ever higher into the high peaks, eventually crest-ing them at Medicine Lodge Pass (a.k.a. Ban-nack Pass) on the Montana border. Up Medicine Lodge Road, the USFS **Webber Creek Camp-ground** (four sites, free) lies at a lofty altitude of 7,000 feet. The camp is on Webber Creek, but there's no improved water supply. The trail leaving from the trailhead here ascends along-side the creek up into the Beaverheads along the Continental Divide. From here, mountaineers

can make their way over to the scenic Italian Peaks area for a Class 2 ascent of Scott Peak, the highest of the Beaverheads at 11,393 feet. To reach the campground, turn west off Medicine Lodge Road on FR 196 at Edie Creek Ranch and follow the road about five miles to the end.

Dudes who want to do some real ranchin' can contact Dubois-based **Small Cattle Company,** Small, ID 83423, 208/374-5555, a working ranch that lets city slickers play real cowboy for a week, for a price—around $1,000, including meals, not including tax. Only cowpokes 16 and up need apply, and don't be lookin' for no luxury. As the company's website says: "NO tennis courts, NO hot tubs, NO Sealy Posturpedics." The ranch is open for guests Mon.–Fri., May–October.

You'll find the office of Caribou-Targhee Na-tional Forest's **Dubois Ranger District** at 225 W. Main St., P.O. Box 46, Dubois, ID 83423, 208/374-5422.

Spencer

As soon as you get off the interstate at the little outpost of Spencer, you'll be bombarded with signs for a number of different businesses, all imploring you to buy the town's claim-to-fame product: opal. The first opal here was discovered in the area in 1948 by a couple of deer hunters. Precious gem-quality opal is rare because a unique combination of geological circumstances is re-quired for its formation—it only forms at the bottom of still pools of underground water. The mineral's layers of microscopic silica spheres reflect light like millions of miniature prisms, brilliantly flashing the colors of the rainbow.

Spencer Opal Mines, HCR 62 Box 2060, Dubois, ID 83423, 208/374-5476, sells visitors permits to dig for opal at its commercial mine. Permits cost $30 a day for up to five pounds of opal-bearing ore and $5 per pound for anything over five pounds. The mine is only open on select days, usually around summer holidays (Memorial Day, Fourth of July, and Labor Day) plus a few other weekends. You need to bring your own tools, including a rock hammer, sledge hammer, bucket, spray bottle, gloves, boots, and safety glasses. The safety glasses are required. The mine itself is a short drive from the office, which is at the gas station on the north end of Main Street; get directions to the mine at the office. The company also maintains a "mini-mine"—a pile of ore trucked down from the mine—next to the office. You can dig through this heap for $5 per pound per person, minimum one pound. The office is open May–Sept.

A couple of USFS campgrounds are in the area. **Stoddard Creek Campground** (13 sites, fee) lies three miles north of Spencer up the interstate (Exit 184, then turn west), while the remote **Steel Creek Campground** (four sites, free) is in the Centennial Mountains northeast of Spencer, midway between Spencer and Kilgore on FR 006. To get to FR 006, head north from Spencer to the Stoddard Creek Campground exit (Exit 184), then turn east instead of west (right instead of left). You'll climb up Miner's Creek, crest Porcupine Pass, and drop down West Camas Creek about six miles to the campground.

Highway 26 to Wyoming

A DETOUR TO NOWHERE

On the northeast edge of Idaho Falls, Lincoln Road (17th St. N.) turns east off Highway 26. If you follow this road as far as it goes, you'll come to the boat ramp at **Ririe Lake,** a 1,500-acre impoundment popular with local anglers. If, instead, you turn southeast onto Bone Road, you'll be on the lonely way to Blackfoot Reservoir or Grays Lake NWR. Along this route are the towns of **Ozone** and **Bone.** Well, "towns" is probably too strong a word. Windbreaks, perhaps, or timeposts—brief flashes of human habitation that will someday soon disappear off the land, then off the maps, then out of the collective consciousness.

RIRIE AND VICINITY

Cress Creek Nature Trail

If you cross the Snake River headed toward Heise Hot Springs and Kelly Canyon, but turn left instead of right just across the bridge, you'll soon come to a small parking area for the BLM's Cress Creek Nature Trail. The trail climbs steeply up a sage- and juniper-covered hillside and leads to sweeping views across southeast Idaho—from the lazy Snake River in the foreground all the way out to Big Southern Butte on the horizon. Cress Creek is a sparkling clear gem, and its incessant babbling provides the perfect soundtrack for your picnic. A trail-map box at the bottom of the hill was empty when I was there; best pick one up in Idaho Falls at either the

BLM District Office, 1405 Hollipark Dr., 208/524-7500, or the multiagency **Eastern Idaho Visitor Information Center,** 505 Lindsay Blvd., 208/523-1012.

Heise Hot Springs

This venerable mini-resort along the South Fork of the Snake River, 5116 E. Heise Rd., Ririe, ID 83443, was established in 1896. Hot springs flow from the ground here at 105°F—perfect hot-tub temperature. You can soak in a soaking pool at that temperature, or swim in a cooler 92°F pool; both open year-round except November. A large, 82°F filtered-water swimming pool is open May–September. Bathing suits are required. In addition to the pools, the resort offers a 350-foot waterslide, pizza parlor (serving regionally renowned pizza), nine-hole golf course, cottonwood-shaded RV park and campground, and picnic area.

Pool admission costs $6 general, $4.50 for children under 12. An all-day pass to the big pool and hot tubs runs $7/4, respectively. Unlimited rides on the water slide cost an additional $6; $1 for just three rides. A round on the golf course costs $7.50 for nine holes, $14 for 18 holes. RV sites cost $20 a night with hookups, $12 without. A two-bedroom cabin is also available ($80 d, $110 for four people). Ask about the Heise Expeditions guided fishing packages. For more information, call 208/538-7312 (pools), 208/538-7327 (golf course and restaurant), 208/538-7944 (campground), 208/538-7453 or 800/828-3984 (Heise Expeditions).

Alpine Skiing

Kelly Canyon Resort, 5488 E. Kelly Cyn. Rd., 208/538-7700, snow report 208/538-6251, is about 25 miles from Idaho Falls. Take Highway 26 toward Swan Valley and watch for a signed turn to the left, a mile or so past the turnoff to Ririe. After crossing the Snake River and sidling past Heise Hot Springs, the road turns up the canyon and leads to the ski area. A shuttle bus is available from Idaho Falls on Saturdays and holidays; call for current schedule and route.

Call it a big small hill, or a small big hill. Either way, it's a mellow, family ski area with reasonable prices and enough varied terrain to satisfy everyone. Four double chairs serve 27 runs on 740 acres with a maximum vertical drop of a thousand feet. The runs are 35 percent beginner, 45 percent intermediate, and 20 percent advanced; 70 percent of the area is groomed. There's a terrain park for boarders. Day skiing operates Tues.–Sat. 9:30 A.M.–4:30 P.M., and the area draws locals for after-work and after-school night skiing Tues.–Sat. 6–10 P.M. A day lodge holds a cafeteria and plenty of space to thaw out.

Full-day lift tickets cost around $29 for adults, $20 for kids 5–11. Half-day tickets are $21 and $15, respectively, as are night-skiing tickets. Skiing is free for senior citizens age 65 and up, and for junior citizens under age 5. Rentals and lessons are available.

Nordic Skiing and Mountain Biking

Just past Kelly Canyon Ski Area, a network of cross-country ski trails laces the hills on Caribou-Targhee National Forest land. Of the 20-some miles of trails, some are periodically groomed—others are marked but not machine-tracked. Trails of all ability levels are available. Easiest is the one-mile Tyro Loop, beginning and ending at the Y junction just above the ski lodge. Most difficult are the five-mile Hawley Gulch Loop, which leads to a remote area and offers lots of big ups and downs along the way, and the Kelly Mountain Trail, which offers advanced skiers a chance for panoramic views of the Snake River Valley. In summer, these logging roads become prime mountain biking terrain. For more information, contact the **Palisades**

Ranger District, 3659 E. Ririe Hwy. (Hwy. 26 E), 208/523-1412.

SWAN VALLEY

Named for the whistling swans that once frequented the area, idyllic Swan Valley lies between the lofty Snake River Range to the northeast and the lower Caribou Range to the southwest. The south fork of the Snake River—a blue-ribbon cutthroat trout stream—flows gently through the valley, from Palisades Reservoir back toward Idaho Falls. The reservoir and river provide water recreation, while hiking possibilities abound in the mountains to either side.

Fall Creek Falls

Fall Creek makes a beeline down out of the Caribou Range, plunging 60 feet into the Snake River at Fall Creek Falls. The falls are on the southwest side of the Snake River, west of the town of

boat fishing on the South Fork of the Snake River near Swan Valley

Swan Valley. Coming from town, turn left onto Snake River-Palisades Dam Road, just after the highway crosses the Snake River. Follow the road a short distance just across Fall Creek, then park. An overgrown trail leads to a view from the top of the falls. It's a beautiful cascade, but best viewed from a canoe or boat on the river.

Palisades Dam and Reservoir

At the time it was completed in 1959, Palisades Dam on the Snake River was the largest earthen dam ever built by the Bureau of Reclamation. An overlook at the outlet provides good views of the lake, dam, and spillway. The 16,100-acre lake holds both wild and stocked cutthroat trout, as well as smaller populations of brown trout, kokanee, and mackinaw. Ice fishing is popular in winter. Five boat ramps dot the east shore, and two more are found at either end of the west shore.

Fishing

While Henry's Fork gets all the press, fly-fishing for trout on the South Fork of the Snake between Palisades Dam and the Henry's Fork is also outstanding and less crowded. You'll be chasing cutthroats and browns here primarily. Both South Fork Lodge and the Lodge at Palisades Creek specialize in helping anglers hook the big one, offering fishing-only trips and fishing/lodging packages.

Hiking

Trails lace the Caribou-Targhee National Forest units surrounding Swan Valley. The most noteworthy hike in the region is to **Palisades Lakes,** high in the Snake River Range northeast of the reservoir. To get to the trailhead, take the highway north from Palisades dam about four miles, then turn right onto FR 255 and follow it three miles to the parking area. The trail climbs seven miles along Palisade Creek to the two lakes, both of which offer excellent fishing. Upper Palisades Lake, the larger of the two, sits at an elevation of 7,000 feet. It's

the gem of the region—the only lake of appreciable size in the Snake River Range. The Palisades Peaks add a majestic background to the high alpine setting, and the lake is a good base camp for a couple of sidetrips. Another two miles up in **Waterfall Canyon** is a beautiful waterfall (surprise!). And ambitious mountaineers can continue from there up the canyon trail to its T junction with the Little Elk Creek trail, then scramble straight ahead up the Class 3 north ridge of **Mt. Baird,** which, at 10,025 feet, is the range's highest peak.

Float Boating

The South Fork of the Snake River—from below Palisades Dam to its confluence with the Henry's Fork near Menan—is a beautiful, 64-mile-long, trout-filled watercourse perfect for those who eschew white-knuckle whitewater in favor of calm currents and placid pools. It's an easy, eight-hour float in your raft, canoe, or kayak from below the dam to Heise. Along the way you'll pass 39 islands—some suitable for camping—and float through a magnificent canyon with hundred-foot-high walls. Glorious stands of cottonwoods line the banks, holding in their uppermost branches nests of bald and golden eagles. Ducks and geese are plentiful, and you might also spot great blue herons, grouse, deer, moose, otters, beavers, bobcats—maybe even a mountain lion or mountain goat. All have been seen in the area. Side trails leading up Dry Canyon, Black Canyon, and Table Rock Canyon allow you to paddle ashore and explore terra firma if you so desire. The three canyons are linked by another trail that parallels the river's northern bank.

The river is floatable year-round, but some hazardous obstacles—notably canal diversions—do exist; be sure to pick up the *South Fork of the Snake River Boater's Guide* from the Forest Service, BLM, or Fish and Game office in Idaho Falls. The guide also describes

> *The South Fork of the Snake River—from below Palisades Dam to its confluence with the Henry's Fork near Menan—is a beautiful, 64-mile-long, trout-filled watercourse perfect for those who eschew white-knuckle whitewater in favor of calm currents and placid pools.*

the campsites available en route, some of which also bear use restrictions.

Camping

Numerous Forest Service campgrounds are scattered between Fall Creek Falls and the south end of Palisades Reservoir. **Falls Campground** provides 24 fee sites just south of Fall Creek Falls on Snake River-Palisades Dam Road. **Palisades Creek Campground** (seven sites, fee) is at the Palisades Lakes Trailhead at the top of FR 255. It offers restrooms, trailer parking, and good fishing in the creek. **Calamity Campground** is the valley's largest, with 60 fee sites on the northwest shore of the reservoir near the dam. A boat ramp here makes this campground convenient for campers heading out on the water. Continuing around the west shore of the reservoir, you next come to the small and quiet **Bear Creek Campground.** Its eight free sites are on Bear Creek about a mile from an arm of the lake. Past Bear Creek, you can continue to follow the road as it winds west through the mountains and eventually circles back to the southern end of the lake and **McCoy Creek Campground.** This one is more easily reached, however, from the south off Highway 89 in Wyoming. McCoy Creek's 19 fee sites are next to a boat ramp.

Coming back up the east shore, **Alpine Campground** offers 33 fee sites by a lakeshore trail—a nice place to watch the summer sun go down over the lake. The 19 fee sites at **Blowout Ramp Campground** are adjacent to the Blowout boat ramp. **Big Elk Creek Campground** offers 21 fee sites at the mouth of Big Elk Creek. From the trailhead here you can hike up the creek into the heart of the Snake River Range.

All the Forest Service campgrounds open for the season around June 1; Alpine opens a little earlier, Palisades and Blowout Ramp a little later. Bear Creek and Blowout Ramp stay open through the end of October; the others all close for the season between Labor Day weekend and mid-September.

Bed-and-Breakfast

$100–150: The cabins and corrals of **Hansen-Silver Guest Ranch,** 956 Rainey Creek Rd.,

Swan Valley, ID 83449, 208/483-2305, are surrounded by the cottonwoods lining Rainey Creek. Upscale accommodations are available in a variety of buildings, including a renovated century-old barn, a cottage, cabins, and the ranch house proper. All rooms have private baths and queen beds. The ranch is primarily a summer operation, although you're welcome to call and try to arrange something other times of year.

Fishing Lodges

Over $250: Overlooking the Snake River, **South Fork Lodge,** 40 Conant Valley Loop, P.O. Box 22, Swan Valley, ID 83449, 208/483-2112 or 877/347-4735, is one of the West's most plush angling lodges. It offers eight rooms in a new lodge, plus two new log buildings holding five rooms each, a restaurant, and tackle shop. Guided fishing is the specialty here, and packages are available.

Just upstream from Swan Valley is the hamlet of Irwin and **The Lodge at Palisades Creek,** P.O. Box 70, Irwin, ID 83428, 208/483-2222. The Lodge sits right along the highway, but also right along the Snake River at Palisades Creek. The log-cabin-style accommodations are upscale rustic. You'll be exceedingly comfortable here, whether lounging on the porch of your cabin overlooking the Snake, or enjoying a gourmet meal served alfresco on the beautiful lodge deck. A minimum four-night stay is requested. Rates include meals and many activities; fishing guides cost $395 per day for one or two people. The lodge is open June–Oct.

Guest Ranch

A couple of the valley's working ranches let you experience the cowboy or cowgirl life up close and personal. **Granite Creek Guest Ranch,** P.O. Box 340, Ririe, ID 83443, 208/538-7140, lies on a 4,000-acre spread up an idyllic valley on the south side of Highway 26—look for the sign at mile marker 368. The ranch borders on Caribou-Targhee National Forest land. Trail rides, cattle drives, fishing, hiking, canoeing on the ranch's lake, and evenings around the campfire are just some of the Old West activities you can enjoy at Granite Creek.

Accommodations are in rustic cabins, each with

private bath and shower. All-inclusive package stays cost about $960 a week for adults, $720 ages 6–12, $480 ages 2–5. Shorter stays are also possible at about $175/135/95 per person per day including three meals. The cabins can also be rented exclusive of meals and ranch activities, at lower rates. No smoking is permitted inside any of the ranch buildings, and no alcohol is permitted anywhere on the ranch. You can also come up for just a couple hours or a day and enjoy some of the ranch's facilities and activities; call for rates.

Information

For more information about the area and recreation in the Caribou-Targhee National Forest, contact the **Palisades Ranger District,** 3659 E. Ririe Hwy., Idaho Falls, ID 83401, 208/523-1412.

Teton Basin

Teton Basin was once known as Pierre's Hole, after Iroquois trapper "Old Pierre" Tevanitagon. Old Pierre trapped here frequently until he was killed in Montana by Blackfoot Indians in 1827. In 1832, Pierre's Hole was the site of the annual rip-roarin' rendezvous of fur trappers, mountain men, and Native Americans—the original trade show.

The 6,000-foot-high valley is spectacularly situated between the Big Hole Mountains on the west and the Teton Mountains on the east. The Tetons are the youngest range in the Rockies; their steep, granite faces tower over the landscape from just across the border in Wyoming. Beneath their western flanks lies Grand Targhee ski area, one of the West's finest, funnest ski and summer resorts.

Both the Tetons and the Big Holes are laced with hiking/mountain-biking trails. Several of the most popular trails are noted below. For a complete hiking guide to the area, stop by the office of Caribou-Targhee National Forest's **Teton Basin Ranger District,** 515 S. Main St. in Driggs, 208/354-2312.

VICTOR

At the south end of the valley, Victor is an important crossroads, especially for skiers. Coming in on Highway 31 from Swan Valley, you'll turn right to get to Jackson Hole, left to get to Grand Targhee—what a wonderful decision to have to make.

Victor is named for mail carrier George Victor Sherwood, who courageously made his ap-pointed run from here over to Jackson at a time when the local Indians were in a threatening and hostile mood.

Recreation

Among virtually endless hiking opportunities in the area, the **Moose Creek Trail** (#038) follows Moose Creek up to the Teton Crest, past a waterfall and alpine lakes. To get there, take Highway 33 southeast from Victor. Just before Mike Harris Campground, FR 276 leads 1.5 miles east to the trailhead.

Across the valley in the Big Hole Mountains, the **Patterson Creek Trail** (Trail 054) climbs alongside Patterson Creek up to Mahogany Ridge and on to Red Mountain (elevation 8,715 feet) for panoramic views of the Tetons and the valley. To get to Patterson Creek, take Cedron Road west out of Victor. After several miles, the road bends north. Continue north one mile and turn left out to the trailhead.

Entertainment

Old Pierre Tevanitagon would no doubt enjoy knowing that Victor remembers him to this day. **Pierre's Playhouse,** 27 N. Main St., 208/787-2249, is the venue for old-fashioned melodrama, presented mid-June to late August by the Teton Valley Players. Performances are usually scheduled Thurs.–Sat. at 8 P.M., with an additional Saturday evening matinee at 5:30 P.M. A Dutch-oven chicken dinner is served before the show. Rates run around $10 for the show alone or $18 (adults) for the show and dinner.

Accommodations

$50–100: Timberline Inn, 38 W. Center St., 208/787-2772 or 800/711-4667, a nice, basic road motel, offers 22 rooms with one or two queen beds.

Camping

Teton Valley Campground, 128 W. Hwy. 31, Victor, ID 83455, 208/787-2647, is a tidy, pleasant, and friendly RV park just outside town. Amenities include a heated pool, coin laundry, rec room, large grassy sites, restrooms, and showers. Rates run $22–42.

Forest Service campgrounds in the area include **Pine Creek Campground** (11 sites, fee), back down toward Swan Valley on Highway 31, just on the Victor side of Pine Creek Pass, and **Mike Harris Campground** (12 sites, fee), about the same distance southeast of Victor on Highway 33.

Food

The intimate **Old Dewey House Restaurant,** 37 S. Main St., 208/787-2092, serves a wide menu of delicacies (steak, veal, seafood, pasta, and more), plus its own homemade bread and goat cheese, nightly for dinner. Entrées range $12–25. Wines and microbrews are available. Reservations required.

A little more casual is the **Knotty Pine Supper Club,** 58 S. Main St., 208/787-2866. Hickory-smoked baby back ribs are the house specialty; they're slathered with your choice of regular, "el scorcho," or Jamaican jerk barbecue sauce. Steak, chicken, and fish dishes are also available. Entrées range $12–25; burgers and salads are less expensive. Look for a good beer selection, pool table, big-screen TV, and occasional live entertainment. Open daily for dinner.

Don't miss the huckleberry milk shakes in season at **Victor Emporium,** 45 N. Main St., 208/787-2221. The store sells sporting goods and assorted miscellany, and boasts an old-fashioned soda fountain that gets jam-packed with locals and passersby in summer.

DRIGGS

Driggs is the "urban" hub of Teton Basin—the valley's largest town and a service and supply center for skiers, hikers, and horsepackers heading off into the Tetons or the Big Hole Mountains. Its atmosphere carries vague reminders of the valley's wild rendezvous heritage; Driggs still feels like a remote party town, full of independent outdoorspeople.

Recreation

The road to the ski resort forks on the far side of Alta; the left fork takes you to Grand Targhee, the right fork to Teton Canyon. At the end of the road up Teton Canyon is the area's most popular trailhead. From here, you can continue on foot up Trail 027 for 7.7 miles to the top of Teton Canyon and **Alaska Basin,** a scenic alpine valley holding a number of gemlike lakes. You're up in the high and wild here, surrounded by 10,000- to 12,000-foot peaks. The down side is that the area is heavily used. Another shorter trail offering an exceptionally scenic hike is the **South Darby Trail** (Trail 033). This 2.7-mile one-way trail begins at a trailhead at the end of Darby Canyon Road (FR 012), which turns east off Highway 33 three miles south of Driggs. The trail climbs along the South Fork of Darby Creek, past waterfalls and beautiful, wildflower-filled meadows.

If you think the Tetons and Teton Valley are impressive from the ground, wait till you see them from the air. **Teton Aviation,** 208/354-3100 or 800/472-6382, can take you aloft from Teton Peaks Centennial Airport in Driggs for a scenic airplane or glider flight. Flights in the single-passenger gliders cost about $200 for an hour. Airplane flightseeing costs $165 an hour for a plane load of up to three passengers.

Outfitters

Your year-round recreational rental needs are deftly handled by **Yöstmark Mountain Equipment,** 12 E. Little Ave., 208/354-2828. Telemark packages and snowshoes are the hot rental items in winter. In summer, the store rents tents, backpacks, stoves, sleeping bags, duckies, fishing gear, and more. Hours are 8 A.M.–7 P.M. daily. Yöstmark also manufactures the famous "Mountain Noodle" backcountry ski. Another good shop to try—something like a cross between a hardcore mountain shop and a surplus store—is

Mountaineering Outfitters, 62 N. Main St., 208/354-2222 or 800/359-2410.

Entertainment and Events

Driggs enjoys the classic **Spud Drive-In Theatre,** 231 S. Hwy. 33, 208/354-2727. Look for the big potato marquee.

Idaho offers no shortage of hot-air balloon rallies, but the **Teton Hot Air Balloon Race and Great American Outdoor Festival** has to be the tops. On July 4th weekend, some 30–40 balloons chase each other across the crystal-clear blue skies above the Tetons. If you can't drag yourself away when it's all over, stick around for the subsequent events up at Grand Targhee. In August, look for the **Teton County Fair.**

For more information and a complete events calendar, call the Teton Valley Chamber of Commerce, 10 E. Ashley Ave., P.O. Box 250, Driggs, ID 83422, 208/354-2500, www.tetonvalley-chamber.com.

Accommodations

$50–100: Pines Motel Guest Haus, 105 S. Main St., P.O. Box 117, Driggs, ID 83422, 208/354-2774 or 800/354-2778, offers eight rooms, six with private bath, in a refurbished and expanded turn-of-the-20th-century log cabin. Breakfast is available for an extra charge. Amenities include cable TV, in-room phones, a Jacuzzi, a large lawn for summer picnics and barbecues, and an ice-skating rink in winter. Kids and pets okay. Rates are right at the low end of this price category.

Best Western Teton West, 476 N. Main St., P.O. Box 780, Driggs, ID 83422, 208/354-2363 or 800/528-1234, offers a tidy and amenity-filled Best Western package. Luxuries include indoor heated pool and hot tub. Pets allowed at discretion of manager.

Intermountain Lodge, 34 Ski Hill Rd., P.O. Box 468, Driggs, ID 83422, 208/354-8153, is right on the road to the ski area and has a hot tub and motel-like cabins.

Information

Contact the office of the Caribou-Targhee National Forest's **Teton Basin Ranger District,** 525 S. Main St., P.O. Box 777, Driggs, ID 83422, 208/354-2312. The **Teton Valley Chamber of Commerce** is at 81C N. Main St., P.O. Box 250, Driggs, ID 83422, 208/354-2500.

ALTA, WYOMING

Yes, *technically* both the little town of Alta and the Grand Targhee resort are in Wyoming, not Idaho (who drew *that* border, anyway?), but unless you're Joe Mountaineer, the only way to get to either of them is through Idaho. How strange life must be for the residents of Alta—cut off from the rest of their state by the mighty Tetons. But I doubt they complain; this is one beautiful neck of the woods. A handful of lodgings, a restaurant of note, and a golf course are all you'll find in Alta—most area services are in Driggs.

Guided Ski Tours

Rendezvous Ski Tours, 1110 Alta N. Rd., Alta, WY 83414, 307/353-2900 or 877/754-4887, guides guests on day trips and overnighters to three remote yurts near the Tetons. Guided day trips cost $175 for the first person, $205 for a couple, $50 each additional person. Overnight hut tour prices vary; call or see www.skithetetons.com for details.

Golf

Targhee Village Golf Course, Stateline Rd. at Golf Course Rd., 208/354-8577, is a nine-hole, par-35 course stretching just under 3,000 yards. Greens fee is $14 for 9 holes, $22 for 18. Also here are a driving range and great views of the Tetons. The course is open April–Oct.

Accommodations

$50–100: At its inception, **Alta Lodge Bed & Breakfast,** State Line Rd. at Targhee Towne Rd., P.O. Box 135, Alta, WY 83422, 307/353-2582 or 877/437-2582, was intended to be an outdoor school. Mountaineer Paul Petzoldt began the building in 1978 but never finished it. The current owners purchased the property in 1992 and built this luxurious B&B atop the foundation. Views of the Tetons are especially grand from the indoor hot tub. Four guest rooms are available; two have private bath, two share a bath. Rates include a full gourmet breakfast. To get to the B&B from Driggs, take Ski Hill Road 4.5 miles east to State Line Road, and follow State Line Road north six-tenths of a mile.

Over $250: Without a doubt, the award for the hippest lodging in the Teton Valley area goes to **Teton Teepee Lodge,** right on the road to Grand Targhee, Alta, WY 83422, 307/353-8176 or 800/353-8176. The high rates for double occupancy are not because of a superhigh luxury level, but rather because of what the rates include, namely lift tickets, a shuttle to and from the resort each day, and a full family-style breakfast and wine-accompanied dinner daily. The lodge building is loosely shaped like a tepee—highest at center, low around the edge—and much larger inside than it would appear from the outside. A large, high-ceilinged common area—warmed by a big, open-pit fireplace—is ringed by the standard guest rooms, each of which has a private bath. Dorm rooms are down on the lower level. Après-ski amenities include a big hot tub and evening socializing. In fact, the social scene is what really sets this place apart—you'll feel part of a big, fun family.

The lodge operates in winter only. Daily rates for the downstairs dorm bunks are $148 double occupancy ($166 single occupancy) adults, $114 for teens, and $60 a night for kids ages 6-14. For the private rooms it's $166 double occupancy, $198 single occupancy per person. These rates are based on the three-night stay minimum; daily rates go down for longer stays. They'll shuttle you to and from the Jackson Hole or Idaho Falls airports for $30 per person roundtrip; also ask about ski shuttles to Jackson Hole.

Food

A local tradition in the Teton Valley is the unique **Lost Horizon Dinner Club,** six miles from downtown Driggs right on the road up to the ski area, 307/353-8226. The husband-and-wife proprietors prepare and serve a gourmet half-Japanese, half-Chinese, 10-course dinner in their restaurant/residence. Diners will enjoy incredible views of the Tetons and savor every moment of the 3.5- to four-hour experience. Reserva-

tions and appropriate dinner dress are required. Call for details.

GRAND TARGHEE SKI AND SUMMER RESORT

The Tetons are some of the West's most magnificent mountains, and Grand Targhee is certainly one of the West's most magnificent resorts. It's a little gem of a place—uncrowded, well designed, and reasonably priced. It's also just far enough off the tourist track to make you feel as if you've discovered your own personal shangri-la, and that's a feeling the resort's friendly staff will be all too pleased to encourage.

Alpine Skiing

If you listen to ski-area marketing departments, you might wonder how it is that every resort in the nation can have the best powder. Snow-quality superlatives are a dime a dozen in the industry. But *Moon Handbooks Idaho* is not a marketing department. So believe me when I tell you, Grand Targhee gets the real thing—killer powder as light as it comes, and plenty of it. Snowmaking? At Grand Targhee? You've got to be kidding! Targhee's motto is "Snow from heaven, not hoses." Praise the Lord and pass the snorkel, this 3,000-acre, two-mountain ski heaven gets more than 500 inches of snow a year. In one recent year, the total topped 650 inches.

While Grand Targhee is by no means unknown, you have to work a little to get to it. That fact automatically keeps the dilettantes at bay, leaving the slopes wide open for worshippers of Skadi, the Scandinavian ski goddess, or her impetuous little sister Fluffi, the powder goddess. Fred's Mountain—yes, that's really the name—has 2,000 vertical feet and 1,500 acres of skiing, with the runs rated 10 percent beginner, 70 percent intermediate, 20 percent expert. It's served by two quad chairs, one double, and an easy-on, easy-off "Magic Carpet" lift for the beginners' area. The other mountain, Peaked, has 500 acres and 1,277 acres of lift-served terrain, but another 1,000 acres are reserved for powder skiing and riding. Snowboarders will find a new terrain park, as well as board rentals and lessons.

Full-day lift tickets run $51 general, $37 for children 6–14 and seniors 62 and over. Toddlers 5 and under are free. Half-day passes cost $37. Passes for the Shoshone Lift only, which serves the kids' area, are $29. Guided snowcat skiing over on Peaked Mountain is offered daily, weather permitting, and costs about $300 per person per day.

Targhee's ski and boarding school is widely acclaimed and aimed at all ages and levels of skiers. Adult and teen learn-to-ski or ride packages with a Shoshone lift ticket, two-hour group lesson, and rentals cost $59. For kids ages 6–14, the Powder Scouts program includes fun time in a private clubhouse and snow sports instructors who really know and like kids. A full day is $79, $89 with rental. The Kids Club program for ages 2 months–5 years offers fun for the littlest visitors and learn-to-ski and snow play for the preschoolers; full-day cost ranges from $47 for infants to $80 for preschoolers who take two group lessons.

Nordic Skiing

Twenty kilometers of immaculate cross-country tracks—both skating and traditional—leave from the resort's base area and head out into the surrounding glades. The tracks are groomed to perfection—it's the kind of place where you can work on your *uphill* glide. The farthest five-kilometer loop leads to a view of Grand Teton, and chances are good that you'll have the whole trail system to yourself. A warming hut on the far side would be a nice addition, as would trail names and marked junctions. But all in all, this is one of the state's finest tracked Nordic areas. A full-day trail pass costs $10 adults. Lessons and rentals are available.

To find out all about the mountain's Nordic scene, check in at the Nordic Center at the base of Shoshone lift. It's open daily in winter, 9 A.M.–4:30 P.M.

Summer Recreation

Grand Targhee is a great place to be in summer, too, when the Tetons pierce the brilliant blue sky and wildflowers paint the alpine meadows of Targhee National Forest in a rainbow of brilliant colors. The resort offers **chairlift rides** up the mountain in summer, allowing you to ride up

for great views—including the back side of the Tetons—and enjoy a leisurely hike back down. The lift operates in June on Wednesday, Saturday, and Sunday, and daily July–Labor Day. Cost per person is $8 general, $5 kids 6–14.

Mountain bikers will appreciate the resort's trail system. You can even load your bike onto the chairlift ($12 one ride; $16 all day) and ride down from the summit. Bike rentals are available at the resort's activity center; $25 for a half-day, $40 a day, less for kids' bikes. Guided bike tours are available. If **rock climbing** is more your style, check out the climbing wall at the base of Shoshone lift; it costs $6 for one climb, $10 for two. Free activities include hiking and disc golf.

Horseback riding fans can gallop over to Bustle Creek Outfitters' equestrian center at Grand Targhee. Take a lesson in either Western or English riding, or sign up for a trail ride. One- or two-hour trail rides cost $25 and $42, respectively. Half-day (four-hour) trips ($81) and full-day trips ($150) might explore the Jedediah Smith Wilderness. On all the trips, you'll likely get views of the Tetons, the Big Hole Mountains, the Teton Valley, and the Continental Divide.

Summer kids programs include Camp Targhee (ages 3–5) for $30 a day, including swimming lessons and other fun. The resort's **Science Explorers** program, run by the Targhee Instititue, offers a series of four-day classes for ages 6–9 mid-June through mid-August on such themes as rock climbing, nature art, photography, mad scientists' experiments, and animals. Cost is $94 for the session, with a $32 daily drop-in rate available. A few sessions for ages 10–12 are offered each summer, too. With the kids out of the way, parents can indulge themselves at the resort **spa,** where you can enjoy a massage (one hour, $72) or facials ($70–82), as well as the resort's pool, hot tubs, steam bath, sauna, and exercise room. For more information on summer recreation and programs, call the resort's Activity Center.

Activity Center

The folks at the resort's Activity Center in the base-area village can set you up with just about any activity that interests you, on or off the mountain, at any time of year. In many cases, they can handle all the arrangements for you right from the office. In winter, try snowshoeing or even dogsledding. In summer, the Activity Center offers fishing, river rafting, ballooning, or soaring. For more information on these or other activities, call the center at 800/827-4433, ext. 1355.

Events
The second week of August brings the annual **Grand Targhee Bluegrass Festival,** packed with big-name pickers and fiddlers. To find out who's playing and when, call the resort at 800/827-4433.

Accommodations
Three separate lodging options are available right at the resort's base area. **Targhee Lodge** ($100–150) offers standard rooms with two queen beds. The plush rooms of the exquisite **Teewinot Lodge** ($150–250) are furnished and decorated in Southwestern and Native American motifs. Each room holds two queen beds, and amenities include a hot tub and a large lobby with a fireplace and ski racks. The **Sioux Lodge Condominiums** come in various sizes that sleep anywhere from two ($150–250) to eight (over $250) people. The midrise Sioux Lodge building

lacks architectural character, but you get great views from each of the fireplace- and kitchenette-equipped rooms. Rates vary depending on date. Various discount packages are available. No pets allowed.

Food
The resort's top-of-the-line dining room, the **Targhee Steak House,** is itself a work of art; a high, open-beam ceiling caps two-story-high windows and a massive fireplace. Casual elegance is the watchword. Entrées on the distinctive gourmet menu range $14–22. The wine list offers a wide selection of California wines, as well as a few from Idaho and Washington. The restaurant is also open for breakfast and lunch.

Other eateries include the **Trap Bar & Grille,** a favorite après-ski and evening spot, and **Snorkel's,** with espresso, deli sandwiches, and pastries.

Information
For more information on the resort or any of its offerings, call 307/353-2300, 800/827-4433, or 888/766-7466 (toll-free snow report); write P.O. Box SKI, Alta, WY 83422; or see www .grandtarghee.com.

Highway 20 to West Yellowstone

RIGBY TO ST. ANTHONY

Rigby
Rigby's claim to fame is as the "Birthplace of Television." Inventor Philo T. Farnsworth (1906–1971), holder of more than 125 patents, first came up with the idea of the cathode ray tube while living in Rigby. You can find out more about Farnsworth and Rigby at the **Jefferson County Historical Society and Farnsworth TV & Pioneer Museum,** 118 W. 1st S., 208/745-8423. The museum is open Tues.–Sat. 1–5 P.M. Admission is $1 adults, $.50 seniors, $.25 children. For more information about Rigby, contact the **Rigby Area Chamber of Commerce,** 134 W. Main St., P.O. Box 37, Rigby, ID 83442, 208/745-8701.

Rexburg
The squeaky-clean lifestyle of the Latter-day Saints is much in evidence in Rexburg, home of the LDS-owned Brigham Young University-Idaho. Established in 1888, the onetime junior college originally was named for Thomas Ricks, the Mormon leader who came north from Logan, Utah, in 1882 to found the town, but it got the BYU moniker and became a full-fledged university in 2001. Rexburg is also a favorite among "sunbirds," senior citizens who spend winters down south and summers in a cooler clime. Between the strait-laced Mormon collegians and the senior set, you might expect Rexburg to be one of Idaho's more sedate towns—and it is.

There's a pretty good arts and culture scene, though. The main event is the **Idaho Interna-**

The Farnsworth TV & Pioneer Museum in Rigby has exhibitions about Philo T. Farnsworth, the inventor who made television possible.

tional Folk Dance Festival, held from the tail end of July (with a few performances down in Pocatello) through the first week of August. Folk dance groups from all over the world come here to share their fancy footwork and culture. A street dance, parade, rodeo, country-western concert, and lots of food accompany the wide variety of dance styles presented. Tickets for each performances range $5–12.50. For more information contact the **Rexburg Chamber of Commerce,** 420 W. 4th St. S., Rexburg, ID 83440, 208/356-5700, www.rexcc.com.

Teton Dam Site

It seems amazing that a dam whose construction was opposed by the EPA, the Idaho Fish and Game Department, and the Idaho Conservation League ever got built in the first place. Even the dam-crazy Army Corps of Engineers couldn't bring itself to endorse this turkey. The cost-benefit analysis on Teton Dam never made sense, no matter how you looked at it—not from an irrigation perspective, not from a flood-control perspective, not from a hydropower perspective. The dam wasn't needed or wanted by anyone

other than the U.S. Bureau of Reclamation, presumably seeking to justify its own existence, and the Fremont Madison Irrigation District, seeking to save a little money on its water bill. What's even more amazing is that invincible Idaho engineering giant Morrison "No Task Is Impossible" Knudsen—prime contractor for the project—just plain screwed up.

Congress approved the dam in 1964 and construction began in 1972. The dam was completed in spring 1976 and the reservoir behind it began to fill up. On the morning of June 5, 1976, with the reservoir nearly full, crews noticed two leaks in the dam. Workers with bulldozers were dispatched to plug the leaks, but the porous volcanic earth beneath the dam was passing water like a sieve. The design had inadequately addressed the geologic considerations of the site.

Imagine being one of those bulldozer operators and seeing the leaks get exponentially greater despite your best efforts. Imagine thinking about the frail, failed barrier that was keeping 80 billion gallons of water from washing you and that bulldozer to Kingdom Come, or at least to American Falls. When it became clear that the situation was out of control, the 'dozer operators fled for their lives, leaving the heavy equipment behind. At 11:52 A.M. the entire dam burst open, sending a wall of water downstream that destroyed everything in its path. It wiped the village of Wilford off the map—six people drowned and 150 homes were lost. Sugar City was hit at 1 P.M., Rexburg at 2:30 P.M. The flood finally subsided in the Fort Hall bottoms of American Falls Reservoir three days later. When the destruction ended, the cost of the folly was estimated at between $800 million and $1 billion, not to mention the lives lost.

Today, you have to look for the site to find it. Drive out Highway 33 east of Sugar City and look for a sign to the north, three miles east of Newdale. A short spur leads to an overlook of what once was the dam. It's an eerie site. Much of the dam infrastructure—ramps and concrete structures—remains in place, abandoned to time and the elements. Perhaps most fascinating, however, is the lack of any interpretive information at the site, owning up to culpability for the disaster.

Back in Rexburg, however, the **Teton Dam Flood Museum,** 51 N. Center St., 208/359-3063, has extensive displays on the event, as well as Rexburg-area pioneer memorabilia. The museum is open Mon.–Sat. 9 A.M.–4 P.M. in summer and Mon.–Fri. 10 A.M.–3 P.M. the rest of the year.

St. Anthony Sand Dunes

Prevailing wind patterns have created a 35-mile-long, five-mile-wide desert of sand dunes a few miles west of St. Anthony. The 10,000 acres of dunes—some hundreds of feet high—constitute a playground for the off-road-vehicle set. Hiking and camping are possible in the area, but don't expect a wilderness experience; this is an ORV sacrifice area. The two hubs of dune-buggy and ATV activity are the scruffy **Sandhills Resort** on the east side of the dunes, 865 Red Road (N. 1900 E.), 208/624-4127, which offers a bit of grass and RV sites for $18 with hookups, $12 without; and the **Egin Lakes Access Area** on the south side (off 500 N.), a free primitive camping area constantly abuzz with the sounds of internal combustion engines. For more information, contact the **BLM Idaho Falls District,** 1405 Hollipark Dr., Idaho Falls, ID 83401, 208/524-7500.

St. Anthony

All the flies have been tied, the new rod has been purchased, the new waders are ready for that first splash of icy mountain water—now all Idaho's eager anglers can do is wait for the fishing season to open. One signal casting them off on their annual pursuit is St. Anthony's **Fishermen's Breakfast,** held the last Saturday in May 6 A.M.–2 P.M. It's free to one and all, but bring your best fish story to share. The **Fremont County Fair** comes to town for three days in early August; look for livestock shows, a rodeo, and Dutch-oven dinner. To find out more, contact the **Greater St. Anthony Chamber of Commerce,** 114 N. Bridge St., 208/624-4870.

ASHTON AND VICINITY

Ashton was founded in 1906 and named after William Ashton, chief engineer for Oregon Shortline Railroad. As the world's largest seed-potato-producing area, Ashton's life revolves around the familiar tuber. Surrounding the city are some 11,000 acres planted in potatoes, which produce about 10 tons per acre. At harvest time in late September and October, the schools here let out for a two- to 10-week harvest "vacation." It's not much of a vacation for most of the schoolkids—most work their tails off bringing in the crop. But they pick up a nice pocketful of spending money in the process. In addition to potatoes, the local fields grow wheat, barley, canola, hay, and peas.

Highway 47, designated by the state as the Mesa Falls Scenic Byway, is the scenic 25-mile back way between Ashton and Harriman State Park. Most of the sights listed below are on or off Highway 47.

Warm River

At the confluence of Robinson Creek and Warm River lies the tiny town of Warm River, Idaho, population 11. Once the town was squarely on the tourist track, but when Highway 20 was built to replace Highway 47 as the main route to Yellowstone, Warm River was left behind. Today it holds the distinction of being the state's smallest incorporated city. It's also the home of **Three Rivers Ranch,** 1662 Hwy. 47, P.O. Box 856, Ashton, ID 83420, 208/652-3750, a fishing lodge booked years in advance by trout-hungry fly-fishing fanatics. (The third river in the ranch's namesake triumvirate is the Henry's Fork itself, which the combined waters of Robinson Creek and Warm River flow into just below town.) Three Rivers Ranch is open May–Oct. and charges about $3,000 per person (based on double occupancy) for an all-inclusive weeklong package including lodging, all meals, airport transfers, and five days of guided fishing. Guided fishing day trips run about $450 for one to two anglers with a guide. If all that's a little too rich for your blood, try the USFS **Warm River Campground** (12 sites, fee) just north of town.

Mesa Falls

Continuing north up Highway 47 past Warm River, you'll soon come to two impressive waterfalls on the Henry's Fork. At Lower Mesa Falls, the river squeezes through a narrow gorge and drops 65 feet. A turnout at the lower falls offers good but distant views of the cascade. Nearby is the USFS **Grandview Campground** (five sites, free). Farther up the road, 114-foot Upper Mesa Falls offers a well-developed viewing area. Wheelchair-accessible walkways lead down to the top of the falls for close-up views. You'll also find the rustic old Big Falls Inn, which was a roadhouse back in the days before Highway 20 was built. It's now a visitor center. For more information about Mesa Falls, contact the Caribou-Targhee National Forest's **Ashton-Island Park Ranger District,** 30 S. Hwy. 20-191, P.O. Box 858, Ashton, ID 83420, 208/652-7442.

Yellowstone National Park

Although nearly all of Yellowstone National Park—including its major tourist facilities—is found in Wyoming, a thin strip along the western border of the park extends into Idaho. Cave Falls Road leads about 25 miles northeast from Ashton into the southwestern corner of the park. It's a dead-end road, isolated from the rest of the park;

you can't keep driving to Old Faithful without going back to Ashton and taking other highways through Montana or Wyoming. But this corner of the park, the "Cascade Corner," boasts an excellent backcountry trail system leading into the Bechler River drainage and more than half the park's waterfalls. From the end of the road at Cave Falls or from the nearby Bechler Ranger Station, you can hike to Dunanda Falls, Iris Falls, Ouzel Falls, Colonnade Falls, or Union Falls, among others. Pick up a map and a wilderness permit at the ranger station, which is up a spur road a few miles back toward Ashton from Cave Falls. The area didn't get torched in the 1988 firestorm that incinerated 36 percent of the park's forests, so it remains heavily timbered. It's all grizzly country back here, so take appropriate precautions, and check with the rangers for news of recent sightings and for trail-condition updates.

Cave Falls is a low, broad, and beautiful cascade on the Falls River. The nearby USFS **Cave Falls Campground** (16 sites, fee), just outside the Yellowstone park boundary, gets filled up in summer. Come after Labor Day for more breathing room. The campground is open June 30–Sept. 30.

Jedediah Smith and Winegar Hole Wildernesses

Yellowstone National Park is north of Cave Falls Campground, but the beautiful backcountry knows no boundaries. An area south of the park, extending with only one small gap all the way to Teton Pass, Wyoming, has also been protected in the Winegar Hole and Jedediah Smith Wildernesses. Both of these pristine areas are grizzly bear heaven, and both are located entirely within the state of Wyoming. To find out more, pick up Don Pitcher's *Moon Handbooks Wyoming.*

Nordic Skiing

At the **Bear Gulch-Mesa Falls Park N' Ski Area,** about five miles past Warm River on Highway 47 N., you'll find a trailhead for Nordic ski tracks leading to Upper Mesa Falls. The trailhead is at the old Bear Gulch Ski Area. It's 8.8 miles from Bear Gulch to the falls and back; the trail climbs steeply at first, but then becomes more moderate as it traverses the rim of Henry's Fork Canyon.

ck you'll get great views of the
les away. Other, shorter loops are
and groomed. You won't have the
ourself; snowmobile trails parallel the
rails.

River Ridge Park N' Ski Area, 10 miles
east of Ashton on Cave Falls Road (1400 N.),
offers seven miles of beginner-intermediate, periodically groomed trails. Loops of between two
and 6.1 miles are possible, and pieces of the trail
system are shared with snowmobilers. Some of
the trails wind through groves of lodgepole and
aspen, but most of the trails cross open terrain.
Look for tracks of moose, coyote, and snowshoe
hare loping, scampering, or hop-skip-and-jump-
ing, respectively, across the trail.

Golf
Eight miles southeast of Ashton, **Aspen Acres,**
4179 E. 1100 N., 208/652-3524 or 800/845-
2374, sets an 18-hole course around a beautiful
old farm and numerous aspen trees. The 2,992-
yard executive-length course plays par 60. Greens
fee is around $12. An RV park here offers 42
shaded sites with full hookups for $21 a night.
The course is closed in winter.

Forest Service Rentals
Caribou-Targhee National Forest's **Ashton-Island Park Ranger District,** 30 S. Hwy. 20-191,
P.O. Box 858, Ashton, ID 83420, 208/652-
7442, offers three year-round rentals within a
30-mile radius of Ashton.

To the northwest, the one-room **Bishop
Mountain Lookout** overlooks Island Park Reservoir from atop 7,810-foot Bishop Mountain. It
sleeps four in two sets of bunk beds, and has a
woodstove and outhouse but no water or lights.
In winter you'll need a snowmobile for access.
It rents for $20 a night.

The two-bedroom **Warm River Hatchery**
cabin lies 24 miles northeast of Ashton, about five
miles east of Mesa Falls. It sleeps 10 in bunk
beds and is furnished with a wood cookstove
and heater. Water must be taken (and treated)
from the creek. You can cross-country ski to the
cabin in winter. Rental fee is $35 a night.

Finally, 23 miles due east of Ashton out FR

261 you'll find **Squirrel Meadows Guard Station,** a two-room affair with a woodstove and
bunk beds sleeping up to six people. Outside you'll
find an outhouse and a hand pump for water. In
winter, you can ski in. Rental fee is $25 a night.

Camping
In addition to the Warm River, Grandview, and
Cave Falls campgrounds mentioned above, **Pole
Bridge Campground** (20 sites, free) lies in a remote spot between Upper Mesa Falls and Eccles
on FR 150; and **Riverside Campground** (55
sites, fee) is just off Highway 20 north of Ashton
near Harriman State Park. To get to Riverside
Campground, look for Little Butte Road (FR
317) on your left as you drive north up Highway
20, then continue past it a half mile to FR 304 on
your right. The campground fronts the Henry's
Fork at the end of FR 304.

Information
For more information, stop by the **Ashton Visitor's Center,** 108 S. Highway 20, 208/652-7520,
open daily in summer, or contact the City of
Ashton or the Ashton Chamber of Commerce,
both at 714 Main St., 208/652-3355. The City's
mailing address is P.O. Box 689, the Chamber's is
P.O. Box 351, both Ashton, ID 83420. For information about recreation in the local Caribou-
Targhee National Forest, contact the **Ashton
Ranger District,** 30 S. Hwy. 20-191, P.O. Box
858, Ashton, ID 83420, 208/652-7442.

HARRIMAN STATE PARK
Eighteen miles north of Ashton, Harriman State
Park, 3489 Green Canyon Rd., Island Park, ID
83429, 208/558-7368, was formerly a 10,700-
acre cattle ranch and private retreat owned by
several bigwigs of the Oregon Short Line Railroad. Edward H. Harriman, father of Sun Valley
founder Averell Harriman, bought into the ranch
in 1908, and eventually the entire Railroad
Ranch, as it was known, ended up in the Harriman family. The family donated the land to the
state in 1977, stipulating that the property be
used as a wildlife preserve. The park opened to
the public in 1982.

SOUTHEAST IDAHO

TRUMPETER SWANS

Harriman State Park is a prime wintering area for the Rocky Mountain trumpeter swan—a species that was close to extinction at the turn of the 20th century. Hunting and habitat changes brought about by human settlement had wiped out most of the swans. Only a few living in Alaska and the most remote areas of the Rockies survived. Those survivors wintered in this area, where hot springs feeding into the rivers keep the waters open and flowing even in the coldest times. Conservation efforts began in the 1930s. The swans wintering around here were fed grain at Red Rock Lakes National Wildlife Refuge 20 miles northwest of Harriman. The artificial feedings continued for almost 60 years, until 1992. The feedings probably saved the swans from extinction—now the population of the species is about 3,000—but they also created a problem of their own. The swans took to wintering *only* around the artificial-feeding areas, and abandoned their migratory routes to points farther south. As a result, the southerly migratory routes were obliterated from the collective genetic memory and the Red Rock Lakes refuge and the area around the park are now overcrowded with the beautiful swans in winter. The park's aquatic vegetation is insufficient to support their numbers, so once again the species is faced with a threat to its survival. Game wardens now encourage the swans to keep moving south in winter by persistently hazing them so they don't get too comfortable.

The Henry's Fork flows right through the ranch, offering superb fly-fishing for cutthroat trout. Elk, beaver, muskrat, and sandhill cranes also call the park home, and some of the region's trumpeter swans winter on the park's lands.

The park is primarily a day-use-only area. No camping is allowed, although there are several year-round yurts ($40 per night for a maximum of six people, plus a $6 reservation fee) and cabin lodgings are available to larger groups by reservation. Many of the original Railroad Ranch buildings still stand; rangers lead regular free tours in summer.

Hiking, Biking, and Skiing

Twenty-one miles of trails here are open to hikers, mountain bikers, and equestrians in summer, and to cross-country skiers in winter. No motorized vehicles or pets are permitted on the trails. The trails are particularly noteworthy in winter, as the park maintains one of the finest trail layouts in the state's Park N' Ski system. According to one survey of southeast Idaho Nordic skiers, it's also the most popular. About half the trails are groomed; the side closest to the highway is the groomed side and has the easiest trails, most traversing wide-open meadows. Both skating and traditional lanes are set where terrain permits; just traditional tracks are set through the trees. All trails start from the visitor parking area just off the highway.

Trail Rides

In summer, wranglers from Harriman Ranch Outfitters lead guided trail rides through and near the park. Prices start at about $30, and chances of seeing some of the park's abundant wildlife are great. To make reservations or find out more, call 208/558-7077.

ISLAND PARK

In 1939, geologists studying the Island Park area realized that the surrounding landscape was a giant caldera. When this area passed over the Yellowstone hot spot about two million years ago, a huge volcano here erupted, blowing rhyolite tuff over a 6,000-square-mile area and creating a crater some 23 miles in diameter. The crater subsequently collapsed, forming the caldera. Just north of Ashton, Highway 20 crosses Big Bend Ridge, part of the rim of this ancient crater.

In winter, under a glaze of snow, the area is especially beautiful. Unfortunately, it's also very popular with snowmobilers. The Big Springs snowmobiler parking lot is just up the road near Mack's Inn and serves a large trail system on national forest land. As a result, the tranquillity of winter in Island Park is spoiled by the constant two-stroke din and stench of hundreds of snowmachines. If you're here to cross-country ski, go to the snowmobile-free Harriman State Park during the day, and ski the Brimstone and Buffalo River trails in late afternoon or early evening, when you'll have the best chance of getting a little peace and quiet.

Island Park Reservoir

Island Park Dam was built on the Henry's Fork in 1938, creating 7,000-acre Island Park Reservoir. The lake supports a population of landlocked kokanee salmon, as well as whitefish and brook trout, cutthroat and rainbow trout. Ice fishing is popular in winter. In summer, boaters enjoy the reservoir. You can rent personal watercraft at Sawtelle Mountain Resort, but be alert. The lake is known for unpredictable, strong winds, which have resulted in more than one unwary boater drowning in the chilly waters.

Hiking and Mountain Biking

The **Box Canyon Trail** makes an easy six-mile roundtrip day hike. Start at Box Canyon Campground and follow the Henry's Fork south for three miles along the canyon rim. The trail provides access to the river's trout heaven for fly-fishermen and delights the wildflower watcher with bursts of summer color.

Across the highway to the east, the old **Union Pacific Railroad bed** has been converted to a recreation trail running north to south past Island Park. It's a multiuse trail, so you'll be sharing it with motorized vehicles. The closest access road to Island Park is Chick Creek Road (FR 291), which leads east off the highway about three miles south of Island Park. From the highway it's four miles down Chick Creek Road to the trail.

Float Boating

The **Henry's Fork** between Island Park Dam and Last Chance makes a pleasant two-hour float suitable for beginners, and the **Buffalo River** from its headwaters to Highway 20 is equally placid and popular. To reach the Buffalo River headwaters, take FR 291 east off Highway 20 about 2.5 miles south of Pond's Lodge. Follow FR 291 about seven miles to FR 292 and turn north, then in another two miles turn west on FR 1219 to the put-in. The put-in can also be reached out of Mack's Inn; take the Big Springs

Loop to Forest Roads 082, 292, and 1219. Be careful of fences spanning the river.

Brimstone and Buffalo River Park N' Ski Areas

The Brimstone system of multiple loops is extensive enough to give even the accomplished skier a good workout. Avalanche danger is nil, and the trails are basically flat, with a few small dips and rises here and there. Die-hard skinny-skiers can continue past the end of the Antelope Park Loop and ski south all the way to Harriman State Park, a distance of a little over 12 miles one-way. The trail to Harriman is not groomed.

The Buffalo River Park N' Ski trail starts on the other (east) side of the highway, just a little bit farther south at the Forest Service office. It's a single loop, much shorter than the Brimstone system. Part of the loop flanks the Buffalo River, and you'll likely see trumpeter swans, joined now and again by small groups of ducks. The 2.6-mile trail is entirely flat, making it an excellent introduction to the sport for beginners.

Near both trailheads is Pond's Lodge (use it as a landmark to help you locate the Park N' Ski parking area), a great place to warm up and grab a bite before or after your ski.

Golf and Tennis

The nine-hole **Island Park Village Golf Course,** HC 66, P.O. Box 12, Island Park, ID 83433, 208/558-7550, stretches 2,668 yards at par 35. Greens fee is $12 on weekdays, $14 on weekends; $18 and $22, respectively, to play around twice for 18. Tennis costs $4 per hour for singles play, $5 for doubles.

Jacobs' Island Park Guest Ranch

Put on them there fancy spurs, pilgrim, and head on over to Jacobs' Island Park Guest Ranch, 208/662-5743 or 800/230-9530. Trail ridin' ($18 per hour), high-falutin' carriage rides ($10) for you genteel folk, canoes to paddle just like an ol' trapper ($10 per hour)—why, you'll feel just like Buffalo Bill! You'll also work up an appetite, so stick around for a hearty ranch-style supper and Wild West wingding; about $25 per person includin' a carriage ride.

If'n you're lookin' to spend the night, git a cabin ($80 and up), includin' your very own hot tub and gas grill, by golly. And if you're out here when the snow flies, swat 'em! Or go cross-country skiing right here on the ranch. Ya just cain't beat it, pardner. The young 'uns will love it.

Pond's Lodge

Right on the west side of the highway, Pond's Lodge, P.O. Box 258, Island Park, ID 83429, 208/558 7221, may not be the quintessential mountain resort, but it's got a big, down-home café, and its Buffalo River Saloon is a classic bar with a pool table, jukebox, wood stove, old piano, and stuffed heads of various large mammals watching you get loose. The year-round lodge offers 16 cozy cabins of various sizes ($50–100; some less expensive) and RV sites (about $11). All are certified TV- and phone-free, and pets are okay in most cabins for an extra charge.

The venerable Pond's is the bustling hub of Island Park activity, filled in summer with tourists en route to Yellowstone, and filled in winter with boisterous snowmobilers. But the best part is, it's right next to the Brimstone Park N' Ski trailhead. The Brimstone trails are easy and flat, skirting the Buffalo River and the Henry's Fork, where trumpeter swans like to hang out in winter.

Henry's Fork Lodge

The most luxurious lap in town is stunning Henry's Fork Lodge, off by itself on a secluded bend in the river. Between June and October, contact the lodge at 2794 S. Pinehaven Dr., Island Park, ID 83429, 208/558-7953. Between November and May write to 465 California St., Room 800, San Francisco, CA 94104, or call 415/434-1657. Here's modern lodge architecture done right for a change, this time by architect Joseph Esherick. The stone-and-timber lodge and guest cabins are works of art in themselves, yet fit in inconspicuously and harmoniously with the surroundings. The big back porch commands a sweeping 180-degree view of the river, and comes complete with wooden rockers from which to take it all in. You have the river to yourself here; the most ruckus you'll have to contend

with will be the splash of a trout rising on a mayfly, or the splash of swans landing on the crystal-clear waters.

Add to all this a gorgeous dining room serving gourmet fare. Meals are included in the rates of the lodge guests and are also available to the general public by reservation. Dinner entrées such as Idaho trout sautéed with bay shrimp and covered with white wine sauce, or roasted duck leg with sweet and sour plum sauce, run $20–25 for nonguests.

The lodge can arrange nature tours of the region and tours to Yellowstone, and it occasionally offers presentations on area topics by naturalists and historians.

Fishing packages including transportation from Idaho Falls or West Yellowstone, six days of accommodations and meals, and five days of guided fishing run around $2,600 per person, based on double occupancy and two anglers per guide. Without the guide service, the cost drops to $1,620 per person. Shorter stays (three nights minimum) run $300 per person per day, including meals, accommodations, and transportation. Super-deluxe suites are available for $30–50 per person per night additional charge. Fishing-guide service for nonguests costs $395 per day for one or two anglers.

Other Area Accommodations

On Phillips Loop, off the east side of Highway 20 about a mile north of Pond's Lodge, you'll find **Elk Creek Ranch,** P.O. Box 2, Island Park, ID 83429, 208/558-7404, a fishing lodge ($150–250) with a rustic but comfortable lodge and eight cabins. The lodge offers its own, no-license private lake, and Elk Creek flows right past. Rates of $85 per person per day, $25 children 7–14, include lodging, all meals, and fishing on the lake. The dining room is open to the public by reservation. Elk Creek Ranch is closed in winter.

Across the loop road from Elk Creek Ranch, **The Pines at Island Park,** 3907 Phillips Loop Rd., 208/558-0192 or 888/455-9384, offers large fully equipped cabins (with kitchen, hot tub, and barbecue grill) that sleep up to eight adults and cost $299 a night in peak summer and winter seasons. The Lodgepole Grill here serves lunch and dinner, and the lodge building has a cozy lounge with a pool table. It's peaceful out here, set off from the highway hubbub.

Lakeside Lodge, 3857 Lakeside Ln., P.O. Box 470, Island Park, ID 83429, 208/558-7147, sits out on the northeast shore of Island Park Reservoir. Take Kilgore Road (north of Ponds Lodge) west off Highway 20 for 2.3 miles to Buttermilk Loop Road, turn left, and proceed 2.3 miles to Lakeside Lodge's three-quarter-mile spur road out to the lake. Once there, you'll find a small but extraordinarily plush motel with B&B rooms right on the water ($50–100). The beautiful new lodge restaurant also does a mean prime rib dinner, and the bar is comfortable and friendly. Live music is often presented on weekends.

Camping

USFS campgrounds around Island Park Reservoir, accessed by Kilgore Road, include the busy **McCrea Bridge Campground** (25 sites, fee), next to the boat ramp at the lake's inlet; and **Buttermilk Campground** (66 sites, fee) on the northeast shore of the lake, next to a boat ramp. In the Pond's Lodge area are **Buffalo Camp-**ground (127 sites, fee) on the Buffalo River on the east side of the highway, and **Box Canyon Campground** (19 sites, fee), also on the riverbank on the west side of the highway south of Pond's Lodge—take FR 134 then FR 284 off Highway 20. **West End Campground** (19 sites, free) is reached by a long drive west on Green Canyon Road (FR 167), which turns west off Highway 20 just south of Osborne Bridge, near Harriman State Park. The campground offers a boat ramp and receives light use.

For more information on these campgrounds, contact the **Ashton-Island Park Ranger District,** 30 S. Hwy. 20-191, P.O. Box 858, Ashton, ID 83420, 208/652-7442.

Information

Contact the **Island Park Area Chamber of Commerce,** P.O. Box 83, Island Park, ID 83429, 208/558-7755 or 800/634-3246.

MACK'S INN AREA
Big Springs

One of the country's 40 largest springs, Big Springs pours 120 million gallons per day of

Big Springs

© JULIE FANSELOW

super-clear water into the Henry's Fork. The constant-temperature, 52°F water emerges from underground at 186 cubic feet per second and makes ideal spawning habitat for fish. You'll find six different species here, including rainbow, cutthroat, and brook trout; coho and kokanee salmon; and mountain whitefish. You can feed the fish here, but they can't feed you; the area is closed to fishing. Also at the springs, a mile-long interpretive trail heads downstream to the Big Springs boat launch area, and another short trail crosses Big Springs bridge and leads to **Johnny Sack cabin.** The cute little cabin, on the National Register of Historic Places, was built by German immigrant Johnny Sack in the early 1930s and is open July 4 through Labor Day. Sack also constructed a small waterwheel, using the flow of the springs to provide his cabin with electricity and water. The little waterwheel house is as artful as the cabin.

In summer, crowds of rafters, canoeists, and inner-tubers line up at the boat-launch area, three-quarters of a mile downstream from the springs, to put in on the **Big Springs National Recreation Water Trail.** It's a popular, placid, two- to four-hour float trip from here down the Henry's Fork to Mack's Inn. Both Big Springs and the boat launch are on Big Springs Loop Road (FR 059), which leaves the highway right at either Mack's Inn or Island Park Village. At **Mack's Inn Resort,** 208/558-7272, you can rent a canoe for $6 an hour, or get a canoe or raft plus transportation up to the Big Springs put-in for $28–60, depending on the size of vessel you choose.

Hiking

The **Coffee Pot Rapids Trail** offers an easy day hike on the west side of Mack's Inn. It begins from Upper Coffee Pot Campground and follows the Henry's Fork downstream for 2.5 miles, passing both placid pools and turbulent rapids. It's closed to motorized vehicles.

More difficult is the **Sawtell Peak-Rock Creek Basin Trail,** which starts near the top of 9,866-foot Sawtell Peak and crosses the Continental Divide on its way to Rock Creek Basin. It seems odd but it's true—here you'll first cross the Continental Divide heading *west* into Montana,

then cross back to the east side into Idaho again. The trail is six miles roundtrip, some of it steep. Outstanding views are the norm up here. To reach the trailhead, take Sawtell Peak Road (FR 024) west off the highway, about 1.75 miles north of Mack's Inn. Follow the road 11.5 miles to the trailhead, or 13 miles to the summit of Sawtell Peak.

The **Continental Divide National Scenic Trail** passes near Mack's Inn on its meandering high-altitude route between Canada and Mexico. As the Continental Divide surrounds Mack's Inn on three sides, you've got a choice of segments and access points. To access the trail to the east, in the Henry's Fork Mountains, take Black Canyon Road (FR 066) off the Big Springs Loop Road near its easternmost extension and follow it up to Reas Pass Creek. From here you can make your way north on foot to Reas Pass, then north to the east side of Targhee Pass. West of Mack's Inn, the divide runs "sideways," east to west across the Centennial Mountains. Access points here are at the tops of Keg Springs Road (FR 042) and East Dry Creek Road (FR 327), both of which turn north off FR 030 (Kilgore-Yale Road/County Road A2). FR 030 turns west off Highway 20 between Mack's Inn and Island Park. No matter which section of the Continental Divide Trail you choose, take plenty of water and good topo maps—the trail may be sketchy in places. Also note, many parts of the trail are in prime grizzly country.

For more information on any of these trails, contact the USFS **Ashton-Island Park Ranger District,** 30 S. Hwy. 20-191, P.O. Box 858, Ashton, ID 83420, 208/652-7442.

Accommodations

Big, bustling **Mack's Inn Resort,** P.O. Box 10, Mack's Inn, ID 83433, 208/558-7272, holds down the south bank of the Henry's Fork with accommodations and recreation options galore and hundreds of happy campers. Lodging options include cabins and condos, some with kitchens ($50–100 for most), and motel rooms ($50–100). RV spaces cost $18 a night with full hookups; no-hookup tent sites cost $10. A rental shop offers rafts, canoes, and lots more stuff. You won't run out of things to do here, but you might feel like part of the herd.

One mile north of Mack's Inn, **Island Park Village Resort,** 4153 N. Big Springs Loop Rd., HC 66 Box 12, Island Park, ID 83429, 208/558-7502 or 800/272-8824, sprawls across a hillock on the east side of Highway 20. The resort's complex, full of upscale furnished condos (one to four bedrooms, most $150–250) boasts amenities such as tennis courts, an indoor pool, and a nine-hole golf course. All units have kitchens and fireplaces.

On the west side of Highway 20 across from Island Park Village is **Sawtelle Mountain Resort,** Highway 20 at milepost 395, 208/558-9366 or 866/558-9366, offering motel rooms ($50–100; some less-expensive rooms available), a hot tub, and an RV park ($21.50 with full hookups, same price for tenters) with showers and a laundry across the street.

Camping

The Caribou-Targhee National Forest's **Big Springs Campground** (15 sites, fee) enjoys a prime location within walking distance of Big Springs and Johnny Sack cabin. Sites here are reservable. Across the highway to the west are **Flat Rock Campground** (45 sites, fee) and **Upper Coffee Pot Campground** (14 sites, fee).

HENRY'S LAKE AND VICINITY

In a high mountain bowl at an elevation of 6,740 feet, surrounded on three sides by the Continental Divide, Henry's Lake has been a historically important campsite. Major Andrew Henry was the first Euro-American to see the lake—he passed by here in 1810. Jim Bridger camped on the lake's shores with trappers and Flathead Indians in 1835, and the Nez Perce camped here on their flight from Gen. O. O. Howard during the Nez Perce War of 1877.

The lake is popular among anglers, who pursue rainbow-cutthroat hybrids, cutthroat and eastern brook trout, and mountain whitefish in the shallow waters.

Henry's Lake State Park

On the southeast shore of the lake, 586-acre

Henry's Lake State Park, 3917 E. 5100 N., Island Park ID 83429, 208/558-7532, provides anglers with a great base camp for fishing expeditions out on the water. The small park holds a first-come, first-served campground with 45 sites ($12–16), 25 with hookups, as well as showers, restrooms, a boat ramp, boat docks, a nature trail, and a picnic area. There also are two camping cabins that can sleep up to six people for $35 a night.

The park is open from the Thursday before Memorial Day until the end of October (weather permitting). In summer, look for the **Ft. Henry Mountain Man Rendezvous,** featuring a blackpowder shoot, primitive camp, traders' row, and entertainment; dates vary, so call ahead if you're interested.

Backpacking

The 14-mile **Targhee Creek Loop Trail** begins north of Highway 20 near Targhee Pass and leads through dense forests, across wide-open ridgetops with panoramic views, and past five alpine lakes perfect for camping and fishing. The trailhead is at the end of short Targhee Creek Trail Road (FR 057), midway between the Highway 20/87 junction and Targhee Pass. You're in prime grizzly country here, so be careful. Bearproof food boxes are installed at many campsites. Use them if you can; otherwise hang your food well.

Trail Rides

Meadow Vue Ranch lies west of Highway 20 at 3636 Red Rock Pass Rd. (FR 053 on the south side of the lake), P.O. Box 93, Mack's Inn, ID 83433, 208/558-7411. The working ranch offers weeklong camps for youth and some daily activities for the public. Call for information.

Fishing Lodges

On the lake's north shore, **Wild Rose Ranch,** HC 66 Box 140, Island Park, ID 83429, 208/558-7201, specializes in serving the needs of anglers. The ranch has been around since the early 1800s; Zane Grey did some writing here. The resort has a café open early for breakfast and a well-stocked tackle shop. It also boasts boat rentals, boat slips, and boat ramps to get you in and out of the water with ease. Accommodations include cabins ($50–100), condos ($150–250), motel rooms (mostly $50–100), RV spaces with full hook-ups ($25), and tent sites ($14).

Farther west, around the north shore, you'll come to **Staley Springs Lodge,** HC 66 Box 102, Island Park, ID 83429, 208/558-7471. The springs, named after early settler Ed Staley, feed the lake and attract big trout right around the lodge. The lodge rents one- to four-bedroom log cabins with kitchens ($100–150; some more, some less). Inside the main lodge building you'll find a fireplace-equipped restaurant serving breakfast and dinner, along with a rustic bar. Both the bar and restaurant are closed on Tuesday.

A humble county park, a little the northwest shore, offers free pri

Howard Springs

Travelers continuing on to Yellowstone on Highway 20 will find the last best Idaho picnic stop along the east side of the highway at Howard Springs. General Oliver Howard passed these springs in hot pursuit of Chief Joseph and the Nez Perce in 1877. Today it's a day-use area.

Continuing north on Highway 20, you'll cross **Targhee Pass** into Montana. Targhee, a Bannock chief, is remembered for his peacemaking efforts during the turbulent 1860s.

The High Country

For most visitors, the wild heart of Idaho is epitomized by the Wood River Valley—a long, beautiful draw flanked on either side by steep, snow-clad mountains. Oddly enough, this out-of-the-way valley holds the two glitziest towns in Idaho—Ketchum and Sun Valley. Once a pooped-out mining town, Ketchum came back to life in 1936 when railroad scion W. Averell Harriman picked the site for his world-famous Sun Valley Lodge and Ski Resort. It's still this resort

that provides many visitors with their high-country experience—skiing on Baldy or playing 18 holes on the lodge golf course.

Others looking for the high country continue straight through Ketchum to the Sawtooth National Recreation Area a few miles to the north. Here Mother Nature dominates the landscape unfettered. In summer, hikers follow trails up steep-walled canyons to alpine lakes and meadows. In winter, cross-country skiers glide silently

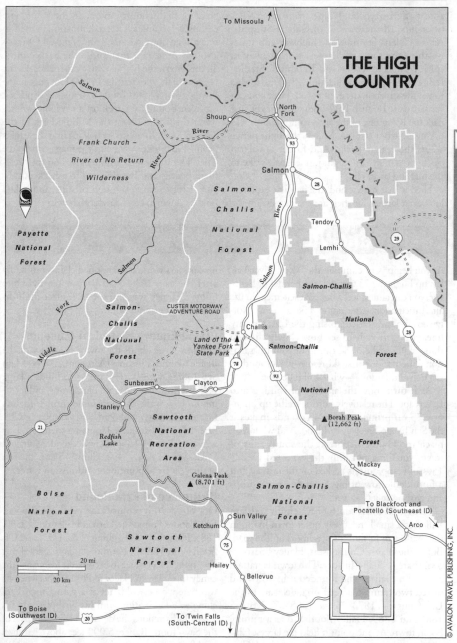

THE HIGH COUNTRY

© AVALON TRAVEL PUBLISHING, INC.

across the frozen landscape from the SNRA boundary all the way up to Galena Summit. Across Galena Summit, the highway continues north to the town of Stanley, worlds away in spirit from Sun Valley and Ketchum. Stanley feels on the edge of civilization. No glitz in this town; the streets aren't even paved. Here you can stay at rustic Redfish Lake Lodge, or maybe just park the RV at one of the area's campgrounds. Go hiking or trout fishing. Watch the light dance across the craggy peaks. And forget the alarm clock; in Stanley you might just as easily wake to the bugling of an elk.

Nice as that may sound, the hardiest explorers look even farther for their adventure, toward the peaks or high-country rivers. To these outdoors enthusiasts, Stanley is not a destination in itself so much as an outpost in the spirit of the Old West—a supply center for forays into the backcountry. To this breed, the high-country experience doesn't begin until they've crested a 10,000-foot ridge in the Sawtooths or White Clouds, or until they've pushed off from Boundary Creek on a weeklong white-water thrill ride down the Middle Fork of the Salmon River. In winter, you won't find these folks paying big bucks to ski with the masses on Baldy. They'll be strapping climbing skins on their telemark boards and heading out to a backcountry yurt, later to carve through pristine, untracked powder down a secret Sawtooth bowl.

Hailey and Vicinity

As you begin your climb up the Wood River Valley, up Highway 75 through the hamlet of Bellevue, you can almost feel a buzz of excitement in the air. Anticipation, expectation. Like a young, Hollywood-bound starlet crossing the L.A. County line, you can't wait to see how closely the real thing matches the florid canvas of your imagination. The nation's first ski resort, playground of the rich and famous—what will it be like?

As it turns out, the analogy of coming into L.A. is apt. The relatively horrific traffic up Highway 75 on prime vacation weekends makes it the San Diego Freeway of Idaho. And when you reach the Hailey airport at the south edge of town, you'll see not only the expected Cessna 150s and crop dusters parked on the tarmac, but a formidable row of big, gleaming turboprops and corporate jets as well.

Hailey, 12 miles south of Ketchum and Sun Valley, is a small, relatively quiet town living in the shadow of its famous neighbors up the road. But as the Blaine County seat, Hailey boasts its own share of Idaho history. The town is named after John Hailey, who founded it in 1881 and served two terms as a Territorial delegate to the U.S. Congress, 1873–75 and 1885–87. Between 1881 and 1889, Hailey flourished as a mining boom town. At one point it held the largest Chinese population in the state; meticulous Chinese miners worked abandoned claims profitably after the easy riches had been taken by white miners. Hailey was also the birthplace of 20th-century poet Ezra Pound.

Blaine County Historical Museum

To learn more about the town's history, visit the Blaine County Historical Museum, 218 N. Main St., 208/788-1801. The museum holds a large political button collection, old mining and farming tools, a walk-through mine tunnel, Idaho's first telephone switchboard, and a display of Chinese dishes and artifacts. Hours are Memorial Day weekend through Labor Day weekend, Mon. and Wed.–Sat. 11 A.M.–5 P.M., Sun. 1–5 P.M.; the rest of the year by appointment. Admission is free.

Birthplace of Ezra Pound

One of the 20th century's most influential poets, Ezra Loomis Pound was born in Hailey on Oct. 30, 1885. His father was Registrar of the U.S. Land Office here in Hailey's boomtown days. Ezra didn't have much of a chance to become an Idahoan—the family moved from Hailey to Philadelphia when he was barely a year old. Yet as a young man Ezra clung to a fascination with his birthplace. In his 1920 "Indiscretions" he described "the vastnesses of the Saw-Tooth Range, 5,000 feet above sea-level (and five million or five thousand miles from ANYwhere, let alone from civilization, New York(ine or other) . . . the scenery, miles of it, miles of real estate, 'most of it up on end.'"

Pound, something of a boy genius, also developed a taste for defying convention, authority, and social norms. He mastered nine languages, got fired as a college professor, and then exiled himself as an expatriate in Europe for 40 years. While there, he befriended William Butler Yeats, fostered the careers of a number of literary greats—among them T. S. Eliot, Robert Frost, Ford Madox Ford, Ernest Hemingway, James Joyce, Amy Lowell, and Marianne Moore—and developed an attraction to the politics of Fascist Italian dictator Benito Mussolini. His irascible anti-Semitic, anti-American radio broadcasts from Italy in the early 1940s got him arrested for treason after that country fell to the Allies in World War II. Pound was adjudged mentally incompetent to stand trial—despite having written the award-winning *Pisan Cantos* while incarcerated—and was committed to a mental hospital in Washington, D.C. He was released after 12 years and moved back to Italy, where he died in 1971.

In later years, Pound's birthplace at 314 2nd Ave. S. (on the corner of Pine Street) was home to Roberta McKercher, a longtime Hailey journalist and community activist. The restored home now serves as the **Hailey Cultural Center,** a community gathering place. Generally, the public is welcome to stop by Thurs.–Sat. afternoon, but would-be visitors are asked to call 208/788-2071 to be sure it'll be open.

Recreation

The onetime Union Pacific Railroad right-of-way between Hailey and Sun Valley is now part of the **Wood River Valley** trails, a system of paved paths available for jogging, strolling, horseback riding, bicycling, rollerblading, or, in winter, cross-country skiing. The highway is in earshot along much of the route, but so is the Big Wood River. Use of the trail is free year-round.

The **Hailey Skate Park,** also free, boasts a 16-foot, full-radius concrete pipe, tall walls, and lots of other challenges for the board set. It's right across from the airport entrance on the south end of town.

When it warms up, head to the **Blaine County Aquatic Center,** 1020 Fox Acres Rd., 208/788-2144. Here you'll find a 25-yard, six-lane heated pool, a wading pool for kids, and a bathhouse with showers and locker rooms. The pool is open daily from Memorial Day to Labor Day. Admission is $4 for ages 17–54, $3 for swimmers under 17 or over 55. Infants under a year old get in free, but are prohibited from using the high dive.

Flightseeing

Sun Valley Aviation, at Friedman Memorial Airport, 208/788-9511, offers hour-long scenic flights over the Wood River Valley and the surrounding montains. Cost is around $100 for 1–3 people.

Company of Fools

This Hailey-based troupe's biggest claim to fame may be that both Bruce Willis and Demi Moore, onetime couple and still part-time locals, serve on its board of directors, and Willis even shows up in its productions from time to time. But even without the celebrity cachet, this is one of the state's most important arts organizations. It presents about three productions per year, both in Hailey at the nifty 1938 **Liberty Theatre,** 110 N. Main St., and in Boise. Tickets run $20 general and $15 for students and seniors; there's also a pay-what-you-can preview before each play's regular run. For more information, call 208/788-6520 or see www.companyoffools.org. For tickets, call 208/578-9122 or buy online at www.ticketweb.com.

Other Entertainment and Events

The town's summer events calendar starts Memorial Day weekend with **Springfest,** an arts-and-crafts fandango in Roberta McKercher Park. On Fourth of July weekend, the **Hailey Days of the Old West** winging features a parade, barbecue, rodeo, and fireworks finale. For more information, call the chamber of commerce at 208/788-2700.

Accommodations

Under $50: Cheapest stay in town, if you can get it, is one of the seven upstairs rooms (shared bath) at the old **Hailey Hotel,** 201 S. Main St.,

208/788-3140, originally a Basque boarding-house built in 1934.

$50–100: The 29-room **Airport Inn,** 820 4th Ave. S., 208/788-2477, is a stone's throw from the airport. Amenities include a hot tub and free coffee in the lobby. Suites and kitchenettes available. The **Wood River Inn,** 601 N. Main St., 208/578-0600 or 877/542-0600, offers all the amenities, including in-room refrigerators and microwave ovens, coffee makers and hair dryers. It also has an indoor pool. Rates include continental breakfast. Suites available.

Povey Pensione, 128 W. Bullion, 208/788-4682, offers a bit of old Hailey history along with its bed-and-breakfast accommodations. English settler and carpenter John Povey built the house around 1890. The restored B&B's three guest rooms all have private baths and come with a full breakfast. No pets or children under 12, and no smoking indoors.

$150–250: Angel Factor Inn, 702 3rd Ave. S., 208/788-6354, is a restful six-room bed-and-breakfast offering onsite massage therapy and intuitive healing sessions. Each room has its own bathroom; guests also have access to a large DVD collection, sun room, and library. No children under 16, pets, or smoking allowed.

Food and Drink

For outstanding Italian fare, try **da Vinci's,** 17 W. Bullion St., 208/788-7699. Dinners range $9–17, and the deck is a great place to dine or sip a beer or glass of wine. Open Wed.–Sun. 5–10 P.M. Fun and friendly **Viva Taqueria,** 411 N. Main St., 208/788-4247, serves up fat, fresh burritos and other Mexican masterpieces ($4–6) and offers a good selection of Mexican beers as well. Locals on a budget come here to get stuffed cheap. More traditional Mexican dining is available at **Chapala,** 502 N. Main St., 208/788-5065. Entrées range $4–12. Open for lunch and dinner daily.

Sun Valley Brewing Company's **Cafe at the Brewery,** 202 N. Main St., 208/788-0805, offers outstanding homebrews and a varied, exciting pub menu as well. Try an appetizer such as clams steamed in the house White Cloud Ale, or one of the specialty pizzas—the delectable Greek version covers a cornmeal focaccia-dough crust with a pesto of kalamata olives, sun-dried tomatoes, feta cheese, garlic, and oregano, and tops it off with mozzarella cheese, red grapes, and red onions. Entrées range $8–17; many are under $12. Tours of the brewery are occasionally offered; call for schedule.

The **Red Elephant Saloon,** 107 S. Main St., 208/788-6047, is a popular locals' hangout known for hearty burgers, hefty prime rib, and strong, cheap drinks. Beware the Jäger on tap. The kitchen's open until midnight. Atmosphere is casual and comfortable.

Shorty's Diner, 126 S. Main St., 208/578-1293, does the '50s retro thing, daddy-o. You can get breakfast all day, as well as burgers and sandwiches for lunch and blue-plate specials (including meatloaf) for dinner. Most lunch and dinner entrées run $6–9. Open 7 A.M.–9 P.M. daily.

At the venerable brick **Hailey Hotel,** 201 S. Main St., 208/788-3140, you can shoot pool in a Victorian West atmosphere, surrounded by a big gorgeous bar and old photos of pioneer Hailey. It's comfortable and decidedly not trendy. Cheap drafts, but no food. Hours are 4 P.M. till closing, Mon.–Sat.

Zou 75, 416 N. Main St., 208/788-3310, one of the newer eateries in town, draws people from Ketchum and Sun Valley for its sushi, seafood, and inventive French-Asian fusion menu. It's open nightly for dinner.

Information

The **Hailey Chamber of Commerce** is at 13 W. Carbonate St., P.O. Box 100, Hailey, ID 83333, 208/788-2700. The **Blaine County Recreation District** is at 308 N. Main St., P.O. Box 297, Hailey, ID 83333, 208/788-2117.

Transportation

When you book a flight to "Sun Valley," this is where you actually end up—Hailey's **Friedman Memorial Airport,** 208/788-4956. It's right along the highway on the south side of town. **Horizon Air,** 800/547-9308, offers daily nonstop flights from Seattle, Los Angeles, and (in winter only) Oakland. Connections are also available through Salt Lake City via **Delta/Skywest,** 800/453-9417.

Avis, 208/788-2382 or 800/831-2847, and **Hertz,** 208/788-4548 or 800/654-3131, have car-rental agencies at the airport.

Ketchum and Sun Valley

As Highway 75 slowly climbs alongside the Big Wood River from Bellevue to Ketchum, property values climb, too, exponentially. Hailey, while by no means undeveloped, is positively rural compared to Ketchum, where you'll find yourself awash in a sea of multimillion-dollar homes. One residential monument to excess visible from Highway 75 has seven chimneys. Clearly, the Ketchum/Sun Valley area is an aberrant element in the state's modest economy.

It's also unlike the rest of the state in its sociopolitical dynamics. Most of the residents here weren't born here. The town is full of people who've made fortunes elsewhere and moved to Sun Valley because they can live anywhere they want, and this is a darned nice place. Their interests lie in keeping the valley beautiful, not making a living from it. The area supports a strong core group of creative, vocal, and oftentimes wealthy environmentalists, who work hard to keep the valley clean and green and to keep what's left of wild Idaho wild. Still, you can't help waxing nostalgic here for the good ol' Idaho

you were just beginning to know and love; Sun Valley may be the one place in the whole state where the word "creek" rhymes with "seek." And in the words of an Idaho native I met down in Boise, "I don't think anyone thinks of Sun Valley as part of Idaho. It's something else that was just dropped down there."

History

Among those impressed by the 1932 winter Olympics at Lake Placid, New York, was W. Averell Harriman, chairman of the board of Union Pacific Railroad. Soon after the conclusion of the games, Harriman, an avid skier, came up with a grand plan mixing business with pleasure. He would build a remote resort that the well-heeled tourist would have to take the train to reach. This strategy had already proven enormously successful for the Canadian Pacific Railway, which started a luxury-lodging empire after its success building the Banff Springs Hotel. Harriman sent young Austrian Count Felix Schaffgotsch scouring the West in search of an ideal site for a destination ski resort,

COURTESY OF THE IDAHO TRAVEL COUNCIL

Ketchum, a mining-era town, became a major destination when Sun Valley Resort was established.

THE HIGH COUNTRY

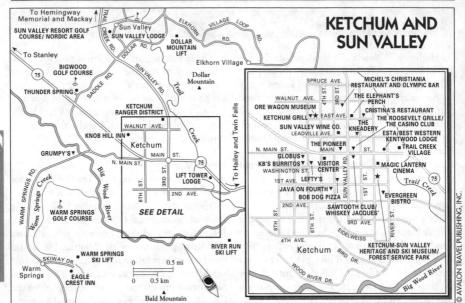

KETCHUM AND SUN VALLEY

one that would draw the tourist throngs via Union Pacific Railroad.

Schaffgotsch toured everywhere, from the Cascades to Colorado, passing up many areas—including Aspen—that would eventually hold first-class ski resorts. Nothing seemed quite right and he was about to give up and waltz home when he heard about a sleepy mining and sheep-ranching town named Ketchum. When he saw it, Schaffgotsch wired Harriman with the news: "Among the many attractive spots I have visited, this combines more delightful features than any place I have seen in the United States, Switzerland, or Austria for a winter sports resort." Harriman was on the scene quick as a wink and writing a check for the 4,300-acre Brass Ranch. Construction of a no-expenses-spared luxury lodge began in May 1936, but now Harriman needed to tell the world of his new baby. He came up with a stroke of genius: draw Hollywood stars and other celebrities here and the lemminglike masses will follow. Shortly after the December 1936 opening of the lodge, Clark Gable and Errol Flynn swashbuckled their way through Ketchum to the delight of the paparazzi

and the public, and the trend began that to this day marks the Wood River Valley as a Tinsel-town playground.

When Harriman's Union Pacific mechanical engineers came up with the world's first chairlift, on Dollar Mountain—developed from the hoist systems used to load bananas into ships' holds—the resort's skiing legacy was firmly established.

Getting Oriented

The Ketchum/Sun Valley mini-opolis consists of three separate areas, each virtually self-contained. **Ketchum,** right on the highway, is the biggest of the trio, and the most like a real city. Here you'll find the services—banks, lawyers, accountants—that keep life flowing smoothly for locals. Ketchum is the closest community to the ski resort's River Run lift.

The **Warm Springs** area lies a short distance northwest of downtown Ketchum, at the base of the north side of Bald Mountain. It has a smaller, quieter feel than Ketchum proper, although you'll still find hotels, condos, restaurants, and nightlife in abundance. The base area here features another plush day lodge and two detachable quads that practically come right down to the street to pick you up and whisk you mountainward.

In the opposite direction from Ketchum to the northeast is famous **Sun Valley,** essentially the Sun Valley Company's company town. Unlike Ketchum, Sun Valley—despite having more name recognition than its neighbors—is a small burg consisting primarily of the original Sun Valley Lodge and its sibling Sun Valley Inn, along with the company's restaurants and activity centers serving guests of those two establishments. The rest of the area is residential; condos and homes galore, but other than a small pedestrian mall with shops in the village you won't find much in the way of basic services. Interestingly enough, Sun Valley is actually farther from Bald Mountain recreation than Ketchum. If staying at Sun Valley Lodge and skiing Bald Mountain is your plan, realize that you won't be skiing out the door of your room or even walking to the lifts, but rather taking a short free bus ride first. Sun Valley is close, however, to the less challenging and less expensive Dollar Mountain ski area, also part of Sun Valley Company's operation.

Note that occasionally you'll find a Sun Valley mailing address listed for an establishment located in Ketchum or elsewhere in the Wood River Valley. In most cases, I suspect those businesses have rented a Sun Valley post office box for the added name recognition and prestige.

SIGHTS
Ketchum–Sun Valley Heritage and Ski Museum
Run by the Ketchum–Sun Valley Historical Society, this museum in Forest Service Park, 180 1st St. E., 208/726-8118, offers exhibits focusing on the town's rich history. Highlights span the days of the fur trappers and Tukudeka tribe all the way to the arrival of Sun Valley Lodge and the Hollywood glitterati. In summer, it's open Mon.–Fri. 11 A.M.–3:30 P.M. and Sat. 1–4 P.M. Call for winter hours. A self-guided walking-tour pamphlet to town is available here. Admission is free.

Ore Wagon Museum
A bit of Ketchum's mining heritage is kept behind glass at East Avenue and 5th Street. Here you can see examples of the giant ore cars that once hauled supplies and mining booty up and down the valley. The heavily laden wagons were often towed in strings, pulled by teams of eight or more mules. This isn't a staffed museum, just a walk-by-and-peek-in point of interest.

Hemingway Memorial
After Averell Harriman completed his Sun Valley Lodge in 1936, he offered complimentary stays to some of the world's most glamorous people. One of the invitees was 40-year-old writer Ernest Hemingway. By the time he first visited Sun Valley in fall 1939, he had written *The Sun Also Rises* and *A Farewell to Arms* and been featured on the cover of *Time*.

Hemingway stayed in Sun Valley Lodge that fall, working on *For Whom the Bell Tolls*. His stay that year agreed with him and he returned in fall 1940 and again in 1941. During these visits, Hemingway found his niche in a rich Sun Valley social scene—duck hunting with Gary Cooper and partying at the Trail Creek cabin with Dorothy Parker and other luminaries.

BOB RACE

Ernest Hemingway

THE HIGH COUNTRY

Although Hemingway enjoyed these trips to Ketchum, after World War II he settled in Cuba with his fourth wife, Mary Welsh. In 1953 he won a Pulitzer Prize for *The Old Man and the Sea,* and the following year he was honored with the Nobel Prize for Literature. In 1958, Fidel Castro overthrew Cuban president Fulgencio Batista, and that, along with Hemingway's deteriorating health, led the couple to leave Cuba and become Ketchum homeowners in 1959.

It was a short-lived residency. Plagued by depression and alcoholism, Hemingway slid into his final chapter. Ernest and Mary dined at Ketchum's Christiana Restaurant on July 1, 1961. Early the next morning, Hemingway turned a shotgun on himself, ending his own life at the age of 61. When Mary Welsh Hemingway died in 1986, she left the couple's Ketchum home to the Nature Conservancy.

Meanwhile, Sun Valley's memorial to the great writer, a short distance up Trail Creek Road from the lodge, is as simple and eloquent as a Hemingway sentence. A bust-topped obelisk stands in a shady nook overlooking Trail Creek. It's inscribed with words written by Hemingway in 1939 as a eulogy for his friend Gene Van Guilder, who was killed in a hunting accident. Ironically enough, the words seem as though Hemingway could have written them for himself:

Best of all he loved the fall. The leaves yellow on the cottonwoods. Leaves floating on the trout streams. And above the hills the high blue windless skies . . . now he will be a part of them forever.

Environmental Resource Center

Equal parts museum, store, classroom, and environmental-action clearinghouse, this center at 411 E. 6th St., 208/726-4333, is a great pace to refill your modern, jaded soul with hope. Here you'll find a lot of great displays and human energy directed toward making the planet a healthier place. Regular video screenings and lectures are held here, and the center's library shelves books, magazines, videos, and CD-ROMs on local and global environmental issues. Hours are Mon.–Fri. 10 A.M.–5 P.M.

WINTER RECREATION
Alpine Skiing and Snowboarding

To the late Gretchen Fraser, America's first Olympic skiing gold medalist (she won the slalom in 1948), Sun Valley's Bald Mountain was "the greatest mountain in the world." Following in her footsteps, local Olympic wunderkind Picabo Street (gold medalist in the Super G slalom in 1998) grew up schussing the chutes off the mountain's lofty summit.

This is one Olympic-size mountain all right, or rather one big mountain and one small mountain; you get a choice of two at **Sun Valley Resort,** Sun Valley, ID 83353, 800/635-4150 or 800/786-8259 (snow report). Bald Mountain—"Baldy" as it's called—is the big one, offering runs up to three miles long down some 3,400 vertical feet from its 9,150-foot summit. What's more, the 2,054 skiable acres are served by a decidedly decadent array of fast lifts and luxurious day lodges.

Seven high-speed detachable quads web the mountain along with four triple chairs and two double chairs. Lift lines? What lift lines? In addition to all the quads, the resort boasts a state-of-the-art computer-controlled snowmaking system to ensure optimum snow conditions throughout the season. And then there are the three lodges, one each at Warm Springs and River Run base areas, and one high on a midmountain ridgetop overlooking the valley. They're all spectacular multimillion-dollar affairs designed in a beautiful mountain-megacabin theme—oversize logs, river rock, and sweeping expanses of glass. Their interiors are positively regal in their furnishings. Marble, chandeliers, and fine wines mix with trophy heads and fireplaces to give each lodge the air of the czar's dacha.

Luxury is the norm here, but if you come more for the skiing than the pampering, you might find a couple of chinks in the royal armor, depending on what you're after. Baldy might be the nation's ultimate mountain for cruisers. You'll find an incredible abundance of moderately steep, consistently pitched, and immaculately groomed intermediate runs, along with some excellent bowls, challenging tree skiing, and a new half-pipe on Lower Warm Springs. But extreme skiers looking for air time would be better off heading to Squaw Valley or Jackson Hole; the Limelight run off the Warm Springs quad is probably Sun Valley's biggest challenge. And while it's true that the lift system covers the entire mountain like a blanket and makes for short lift lines, that can have its own drawbacks. On a busy weekend the summit is like a circus: multiple quads continually dump out skiers in batches, while paragliders jump off the mountaintop, photographers photograph the skiers, and everyone stands around aimlessly admiring the world-class view. You'll also be hard-pressed to find those special, out-of-the-way, non-lift-served areas that reward a bit of a traverse or hike with relatively uncrowded, untracked terrain. Locals probably know a secret spot or two, but you may not be able to ferret them out. Finally, you have to pay for all those fancy quads and lodges. Adult lift tickets here go for a cool $66, which is probably about a full day's pay after taxes for the resort's lift ops and waitstaff. Kids' tickets are $37 a day, and at certain times of the year, kids can ski free when their parents stay at one of the participating lodgings; call for more information.

The resort's other hill, Dollar Mountain, is on the Sun Valley side of Highway 75. It's a relatively uncrowded, wide-open beginner hill (three lifts and a handle tow; 628 vertical feet) great for floundering about on tele-skis, or for kids still "making a pie." Tickets here are about half the price of those on Baldy.

Heli-Skiing

Sun Valley Heli Ski, 260 1st Ave. N. in Ketchum, 208/622-3108 or 800/872-3108, offers a variety of chopper-drop packages. To go diving through the untracked fluff, all you'll need is intermediate or better skiing skills and a small trust fund. The company charges by the vertical foot skied. A full day with five or six runs for a total of around 10,000 vertical feet would cost around $700 per person. A single run goes for around $200 and up. For those who want to spend the night in the woods, the company offers an overnight trip to a sauna-equipped yurt, $325 per person and up, or a lot less for people willing to ski in on their own.

Nordic Skiing

Blaine County's cross-country ski trails rate among the country's best. The **Wood River Trail System** runs 30 kilometers from Hulen Meadows north of Ketchum all the way south to Bellevue along a former Union Pacific Railroad right-of-way. Three miles north of Ketchum, the **Lake Creek Trails** offer a 15.5-kilometer network of loops on the west side of the Big Wood River. The regularly groomed trails are part of the North Valley Trail System, which requires a $9 trail pass. See the Sawtooth National Recreation Area section later in this chapter for more information on the North Valley system, among the best in the West. A free shuttle bus runs to and from the North Valley Trails Wed.–Sat. all winter.

Sun Valley Resort's **Nordic Center,** 208/622-2251, just past the lodge up Trail Creek, sets 40 kilometers of groomed trails on the snow-covered golf course and surrounding hills and canyons. It's popular with the locals for lunch-hour or after-work exercise—you'll see them blasting by impossibly fast in high-powered skating form, a "workout" mindset to be sure. The trails are meticulously groomed, including a set of narrow-spaced tracks provided especially for kids, and the area is beautiful enough. But you couldn't call it a wilderness ski experience; you practically stare into the living-room windows of the extravagant homes built astride the fairways. The best steeps are on the Diamondback Trail across the road—it climbs to a ridgetop for a good view of Ketchum. Alas, the view is dominated by buildings, buildings, buildings, and the sounds of traffic rise up at you from three sides. Your only hope of finding winter tranquility at this Nordic area is to head out past the Trail Creek Cabin to the distant Boundary and Proctor Loops. Somewhere out there, far from town, you'll start to hear the wind, the trees, the creek, and the birds, and begin to appreciate the animal grace of your own body gliding quietly across the winterscape. Trail fee is $12 for adults, $9 for seniors, $6.50 for kids 6–12. Rentals and lessons are available.

Backcountry Skiing

The joys of nearly unlimited skiable terrain in the mountains surrounding the Wood River Valley must be balanced against the backcountry's serious avalanche potential. If you know what you're doing, it could be heaven. If you don't know what you're doing, well, it could be heaven, too, in a different sort of way. Before setting out, visiting backcountry skiers should at the very least call the Ketchum Ranger District's **24-hour avalanche and snow condition report,** 208/622-8027. But there's no substitute for local experience—go with a guide if at all possible.

Sun Valley Trekking Company, P.O. Box 1300, Hailey, ID 83333, 208/788-1966, www.svtrek.com, offers guided tours to one or more of its five cozy and comfortable backcountry huts in the Smoky and Sawtooth Mountains. The huts have woodstoves with plenty of firewood, propane cookstoves, lanterns, toilets, wood-fired hot tubs or saunas, and bunk beds with sleeping pads. You can rent a hut and ski to it on your own, but first-time hut users are required to employ a guide for the first day. The company also offers classes in backcountry ski-touring, telemarking, and avalanche education. Guided tours are $150 per person per day. Hut rental à la carte is $30 per person per night, with a $150 minimum; guide service for first-time users is another $150 per day. The company also offers guided day hikes in the summer, and one of its huts is open for summer use by hikers and mountain bikers.

Sleigh Rides

Dinner sleigh rides out to the historic **Trail Creek Cabin** are offered through Sun Valley Resort, 208/622-2135, www.sunvalley.com. The 1937 log-and-stone cabin was a retreat popular with the Hollywood set—Clark Gable, Gary Cooper, Ava Gardner, and friends—and was Ernest Hemingway's favored New Year's Eve party venue. Sleighs depart from the Sun Valley Inn at 6, 7, 8, and 9 P.M. for dinner. The ride to the cabin along Trail Creek takes about a half hour. Dress warmly; blankets are provided. The ride costs $22 adults, $18 for children under 12 (except during the last week of the year, when prices rise to $24 for adults, $20 for children). These prices include confirmation of a reservation for your meal but do not include the price of the meal itself. The dinner specialty is barbecued ribs, but steaks, chicken, prime rib, and trout are also on the menu; prices range $16–32. A full bar is available, and there's tableside entertainment nightly.

A Winter's Feast, 208/788-7665, offers a horse-drawn sleigh ride to a yurt on the snow-covered Warm Springs Golf Course, where you'll be served a luscious five-course gourmet dinner of beef tenderloin, salmon, rack of lamb, or pork roast, with all the trimmings. The dinner is $60 per person not including wine; the sleigh ride is an extra $15 adults, $12 children.

More traditional sightseeing-style sleigh rides are offered through the **Sun Valley Horsemen's Center,** 208/622-2387 or 208/622-2391, and **Warm Springs Sleighs,** 1801 Warm Springs Rd. (at the golf course, one mile from Ketchum), 208/726-3322 or 208/823-4381. The latter makes a 45-minute circuit around Warm Springs' golf course, occasionally stopping to feed elk if they're in the area; $15 adults, $10 kids under 12.

Forest Service Rentals

In winter, the Forest Service rents two guard stations in the Big Lost River drainage, located over the Pioneer Mountains east of Ketchum in a draw separating the Pioneers and the White Knob Mountains. **Wildhorse** lies just three miles off Trail Creek Road on FR 135/136. It offers both a four-person cabin and a six-person trailer. Way out Copper Basin Road (FR 135) is the **Copper Basin** guard station, a six-person cabin. Copper Basin is a prime fishing spot in summer, but all these rentals are available only Dec. 1–April 30; all are $30 a night. For reservations and information, contact the Salmon-Challis National Forest's **Lost River Ranger District,** 716 W. Custer, P.O. Box 507, Mackay, ID 83251, 208/588-2224.

SUMMER RECREATION

Although Sun Valley started as a ski resort, the Sun Valley Company and local civic leaders about a decade ago pushed to convert the area into a year-round destination resort. They succeeded, and now Sun Valley and Ketchum do even more business in summer than in winter. Summer is an undeniably magnificent time of year here. Hundreds of square miles of the surrounding mountains—accessible in winter only to experienced mountaineers—open up for everyone to enjoy.

Bike Paths

The 10 miles of paved pedestrian/bike paths in the **Sun Valley Trail System** loop around Dollar Mountain from Ketchum to Sun Valley to Elkhorn and out along Elkhorn Road back to the highway. A spur trail follows Trail Creek from Sun Valley Lodge out to Boundary Campground. The Sun Valley system connects with the 20-mile-long **Wood River Trail System,** which traces the old Union Pacific right-of-way from Lake Creek Road, north of Ketchum, down the valley to Bellevue. Ambitious long-term plans call for trails to eventually connect Stanley with Shoshone. For more information, contact the **Blaine County Recreation District,** 308 N. Main, P.O. Box 297, Hailey, ID 83333, 208/788-2117.

Hiking and Mountain Biking

You'll find no shortage of suitable ground for exercise around here; within a five-mile radius from Ketchum lie some 40 miles of unpaved hiking and/or mountain-biking trails. All of these close-in trails are heavily used as workout terrain by area residents. West of downtown Ketchum, the **Bald Mountain Trail** (Trail 201) runs five miles up to the top of Baldy itself. The trailhead for the five-mile hike is at the bottom of the River Run lift. Or be lazy and take your bike up the lift with you—Sun Valley ski area's detachable quads haul mountain bikers and their two-wheeled steeds up in summer.

In the Sun Valley area, several trails leave from Trail Creek Cabin, two miles east of Sun Valley Village up Trail Creek Road. The **Trail Creek Trail** (Trail 305) follows the creek for 1.5 miles one-way and is barrier free. The **Proctor Mountain Trail** (Trail 119) climbs to the summit of that peak for panoramic views of the valley. The easy, 1.75-mile **Aspen Loop Trail** (Trail 119A) and the more difficult, 3.5-mile one-way **Corral Creek Trail** (Trail 119B) wind through aspen and evergreen forest. No bikes allowed on the Aspen Loop or Proctor Mountain trails.

The Adams Gulch Trails are 1.5 miles north of Ketchum; follow Adams Gulch Road three-quarters of a mile off Highway 75 to the trailhead. The network of trails here ranges from the **Shadyside Trail** (Trail 177A)—an easy 1.5-mile stroll—to the demanding **Adams Gulch Trail** (Trail 177, Trail 142), a 14-mile loop. Intermediate-length hikes are also possible. Bikes are permitted on the Adams Gulch trails.

The **Fox Creek/Oregon Gulch Trails** lie a bit farther up the west side of Highway 75 and are accessed by two separate trailheads: the Lake Creek trailhead is right off Highway 75, four miles north of Ketchum; the Oregon Gulch trailhead is three miles farther north, off Highway 75 at FR 143 (just past the North Fork Store). These trails are more difficult than the Adams Gulch trails. Loops ranging 3–10 miles are possible. Bikes okay.

Hikers prepared to spend a long, sweaty day on the dusty trail will want to check out the **Pioneer Cabin Trails.** The Union Pacific Railroad built the cabin in 1937 as a ski hut. It's still in use by hikers and skiers today, and from its lofty 9,400-foot vantage you'll have sweeping views east to the crest of the Pioneer Range. The trailhead to the cabin starts at the end of Corral Creek Road, which branches off Trail Creek Road a mile northeast of Boundary Campground. Take the Pioneer Cabin Trail (Trail 122) on the way up to hut and descend via Long Gulch Trail (Trail 123) for an 8.5-mile loop. No bikes allowed on the Pioneer Cabin Trails.

For more information on these hikes, check out the *Trails Around Town* and *Pioneer Cabin Trails* brochures available at the Ketchum Visitor Center, 4th and Main Sts., and at the Ketchum Ranger Station, 206 Sun Valley Rd.

THE HIGH COUNTRY

Hiking and Biking Guides

Sun Valley Trekking Company, P.O. Box 220, Sun Valley, ID 83353, 208/788-9585, offers half-day and full-day guided hikes anywhere in the Sawtooth NRA and USFS Ketchum Ranger District except the Sawtooth Wilderness. Rates for a group of one to four are $175 a half day, $250 a full day not including lunch (which can be arranged at extra charge).

Venture Outdoors (see Llama Trekking) offers bike tours ranging from three hours to six days. Several different day trips are offered; cost is $85 per person, including lunch.

Llama Trekking

Llamas are a lot cuter than horses, have a lot more personality, and love hiking around in the mountains as much or more than you do. They'll happily carry your gear, leaving you unencumbered to stop and smell the wildflowers along the trail. **Venture Outdoors,** P.O. Box 2251, Hailey, ID 83333, 208/788-5049 or 800/528-5262, is the area's llama-trekking specialist, offering hikes ranging from one to five days in the Sawtooth NRA and Sawtooth National Forest. Day trips cost around $85 per person, including lunch.

Horseback Riding

Sun Valley Resort Horsemen's Center, 208/622-2391, offers one-hour guided trail rides in the area for $29 per person, or 90-minute rides for $40 per person. The rides leave the center on Sun Valley Road (between Ketchum and Sun Valley) starting at 9 A.M. daily in summer. Reservations are required; children must be at least eight years old and 50 inches tall. Spring and fall rides, group hayrides, and stagecoach rides may also be available by appointment.

A bit farther afield, you can escape the Wood River Valley crowds at **Elkhorn Stable at Wild Horse Creek Ranch,** up Trail Creek about halfway to Mackay (21 miles northeast of Ketchum), 208/588-2575. Basic horse-rental rates here are $25 for one hour, $35 for two hours, $65 a half day, $100 a full day. The half-day and full-day rides include lunch; bring a fishing license if you want to try your luck in a beautiful mountain lake at lunchtime.

If you have your own horse, you can head out on one of the numerous trails that lace the Ketchum Ranger District. Stop in at the Ranger Station, 206 Sun Valley Rd., 208/622-5371, for complete information on open trails and usage rules.

Golf

The 6,893-yard, par-72 **Sun Valley Resort Golf Course,** 208/622-2251, was designed by Robert Trent Jones Jr., and it's a beauty. Fairways follow Trail Creek, crossing it seven times on the front nine. Greens fee is $126, including mandatory electric-cart rental. Reservations for tee times are required.

Two nine-hole courses in the area provide less expensive alternatives for linksters. **Warm Springs Ranch Golf Course** offers a 2,647-yard, par-36 course at 1801 Warm Springs Rd., 208/726-3715, greens fee $21. **Bigwood Golf Course,** 125 Clubhouse Dr., on the hill between Highway 75 and Sun Valley, 208/726-4024, is a 3,270-yard par-36 designed by Robert Muir Graves; greens fees run $26 for nine holes, $42 for 18.

The **Elkhorn Golf Club** is closed for renovations. It may open in 2005 or after, but probably as a private club.

Tennis

Sun Valley Resort Tennis Club, 208/622-2156, offers 18 courts, ball machines, lessons, and a pro shop. Rates are $11 per person per day, or $9 per person per day for guests of the resort. The courts are open daily mid-June through mid-October. Courts are also available at **Warm Springs Tennis Club,** 1801 Warm Springs Rd., 208/726-4040, and at **Atkinson Park,** 8th St. and 3rd Ave., 208/726-7820.

Rafting

The local Big Wood River provides great fishing but no boating. However, several raft companies based in Ketchum/Sun Valley offer guided trips on nearby whitewater. **White Otter Outdoor Adventures,** 411 Leadville Ave. in Ketchum, 208/726-4331, www.whiteotter.com, runs the Salmon day stretch out of Sunbeam, as well as the Murtaugh and Hagerman reaches of the

Snake. The Salmon trip costs about $85 for a full day with lunch. Also running the Salmon day stretch are **The River Company,** 208/788-5775 or 800/398-0346, www.therivercompany.com, and Sawtooth Adventures Company, 866/774-4644, www.sawtoothadventures.com.

Several local companies also run trips on the main Salmon River and the famed Middle Fork. See the Frank Church–River of No Return Wilderness Area section in this chapter.

Camping

Six USFS campgrounds south of the SNRA boundary ring Ketchum and Sun Valley. Up Trail Creek Road about two miles past Sun Valley Village is **Boundary Campground,** a free, six-unit campground with a three-day maximum stay. Continuing out Trail Creek Road over Trail Creek Summit in the direction of Mackay are **Park Creek Campground** (16 units, fee), which is 12 miles from Ketchum, and **Phi Kappa Campground** (21 units, fee), 15 miles out.

Up the East Fork Wood River (FR 118 east off Highway 75 between Ketchum and Hailey) you'll find 15-unit **Federal Gulch Campground** and three-unit **Sawmill Campground,** both free. Finally, west of Highway 75 out Deer Creek Road is the free, three-site **Deer Creek Campground,** 20 miles from Ketchum.

For more information, contact the **Ketchum Ranger District,** 206 Sun Valley Rd., Sun Valley, ID 83353, 208/622-5371.

YEAR-ROUND RECREATION

Bowling

You'll find six lanes at Sun Valley Village, 208/622-2191. Rates are $4 a line per person, shoes an extra $2. Also here are video games, a snack bar, and a pool table. Hours are 4–10 P.M. daily.

Fishing

The beautiful Big Wood River flows the length of the valley, offering good trout fishing around every bend. Anglers also enjoy success up Warm Springs Creek (which flows into the Big Wood from the west side of Ketchum), Trail Creek (which flows down from the east), and other tributaries. Through-

out the valley, many sections of riverbank are privately owned. Access points to the public portions are marked by signs and noted in the brochure *Fishing in the Wood River Valley,* published by the Blaine County Recreation District and available at the Ketchum visitor center and ranger station. One favorite place to take the youngsters on a fish hunt is **Penny Lake,** along Warm Springs Road just on the edge of civilization. Also note that fly-fishing heaven, Silver Creek, is not too far away (see North of Shoshone in the North of the Snake River section of the South-Central Idaho chapter).

Trout fishing season runs Memorial Day weekend to Nov. 30, but you can catch mountain whitefish all the way through until the end of March. The Big Wood is catch-and-release only, on artificial flies and lures with single barbless hooks, starting from the bridge south of town at Greenhorn Gulch Road and Highway 75, and continuing upriver to the North Fork confluence.

Local fishing guides include **Bill Mason Outfitters,** in Sun Valley Village, 208/622-9305,

fisherman standing in the Big Wood River

which also offers outings for kids; **Silver Creek Outfitters,** 500 N. Main St. in Ketchum, P.O. Box 418, Ketchum, ID 83340, 208/726-5282 or 800/732-5687, which features an extensive, full-service retail store; **Lost River Outfitters,** 171 N. Main St., P.O. Box 3445, Ketchum, ID 83340, 208/726-1706; and **Sun Valley Outfitters,** in Elkhorn Village, P.O. Box 3400, Sun Valley, ID 83353, 208/622-3400. Expect guide service to run anywhere between $250 and $350 per day for a party of one or two anglers.

Hot Springs

The closest hot springs to Ketchum is **Frenchman's Hot Springs,** 10.5 miles west of town via Warm Springs Road (Forest Road 227). **Warfield Hot Springs** is just a half-mile farther down the road. North of Ketchum you'll find **Easley Hot Springs** and **Russian John Hot Springs** in the Sawtooth National Recreation Area. Far to the west out Warm Springs Road, over Dollarhide Summit, are a number of other hot springs around Fairfield.

Ice Skating

Sun Valley Lodge offers a pair of rinks, one right outside the back door of the lodge, the other indoors in a separate building behind the lodge. Admission is $12 for adults, $11 for kids, including skate rental. Lessons are available. For more information, call 208/622-2194. In winter, you can also skate free on the pond at **Atkinson Park,** 8th St. and 3rd Ave., 208/726-7820.

Paragliding

Join a guide from **Fly Sun Valley,** 260 1st Ave. N. in Ketchum, 208/726-3332, on a tandem flight off the top of Bald Mountain. Anyone young or old, physically fit or physically challenged, can enjoy this thrilling experience, provided they can ante up $145. The company also teaches the activity.

OUTFITTERS AND INFORMATION

Plenty of area shops rent the equipment you need to enjoy a variety of sports. Some of them are listed below.

Ski, Mountain-Bike, and Skate Rentals

Area rental shops include **Sturtevants Ski & Sports,** 314 N. Main St. (at 4th St.), 208/726-4512; **Formula Sports,** 460 N. Main St., 208/726-3194; **Kelly Sports,** in the Colonnade Building, 641 Sun Valley Rd. E., 208/726-8503 (mountain bikes only); and **Pete Lane's,** at River Run Plaza, 208/622-6123, or in Sun Valley Village, 208/622-2279 (no skates).

Best Backcountry Shops

Mountaineering-oriented rental centers include **The Elephant's Perch,** 280 East Ave. N. (at Sun Valley Rd.), 208/726-3497, and **Backwoods Mountain Sports,** at the intersection of Main St. and Warm Springs Rd., 208/726-8818; both are in Ketchum. These two stores carry a full selection of cross-country ski gear, including touring, skating, and telemark skis, boots, and poles. They also carry climbing gear and rent a good selection of camping equipment—packs, tents, sleeping bags, and the like.

Snowboard Specialists

Snowboard-rental headquarters in town is the **Board Bin,** 180 4th St. E. in Ketchum, 208/726-1222. Snowboard packages go for $30 for the first day, $25 each consecutive day, and state-of-the-art tuning is available. In summer, the store's passion turns to skateboards.

Also renting snowboards are **Sturtevants Ski & Sports,** 314 N. Main St. (at 4th St.), 208/726-4512; **Paul Kenny's,** at the base of the Warm Springs lifts, 208/726-7474; **Pete Lane's,** in Warm Springs Village at the base of the lifts, 208/622-6534, in Sun Valley Village, 208/622-2279, and at the River Run base area, 208/622-6123; and **Ski Tek,** 191 Sun Valley Rd. W. in Ketchum, 208/726-7503.

Kayaks

In Ketchum, try **Backwoods Mountain Sports Boats & Bikes,** 760 Warm Springs Rd., 208/726-8826, which also rents rafts and accessories, and **Ski Tek,** 191 Sun Valley Rd. W., 208/726-7503.

Backcountry Information

Before heading out into the mountains around Sun Valley and Ketchum, it's a good idea to check in at the USFS **Ketchum Ranger District,** 206 Sun Valley Rd., P.O. Box 2356, Ketchum, ID 83340, 208/622-5371 or 208/622-8027 (avalanche and weather information). The ranger station stocks numerous flyers and can answer any questions you have about backcountry activities. The two "Best Backcountry Shops" listed above are also excellent sources of information on the up-to-the-minute state of the surrounding wilds.

EVENTS

The area's events calendar is huge. Something's always going on here. Some of the bigger bashes are listed below. For details and a complete list, contact the Sun Valley/Ketchum Chamber & Visitors Bureau, 208/726-3423 or 800/634-3347, www.visitsunvalley.com.

Summer

The world-class **Sun Valley Ice Show** runs Saturday evenings, mid-June through September, presenting Olympic medalists and other world-champion skaters and featuring a lavish pre-show outdoor buffet. It all takes place at the Sun Valley Lodge rink. Tickets run $27–49 adults for just the show, or $77–84 with dinner. For more information, call 208/622-2231.

Music fills the upper Wood River Valley during numerous summertime events. Every Wednesday evening June through August, the **Ketch'em Alive** music series presents bands from throughout the Northwest at Forest Service Park, 6–10 P.M. Throughout July and August, the **Sun Valley Music Festival** brings classical music, jazz, and pop performers from all over the country to town. Past performers have included Lyle Lovett, Willie Nelson, Los Lobos, and Branford Marsalis. For tickets and information, call the Sun Valley Center for the Arts and Humanities at 208/726-9491. In July and August, the **Sun Valley Summer Symphony,** 208/622-5607, performs free outdoor concerts at Sun Valley Lodge. Also in mid-August at the resort is the annual **Sun Valley Arts and Crafts Festival,** 208/726-9491.

Labor Day weekend brings the **Ketchum Wagon Days Celebration,** a festival commemorating the town's mining history. Festivities include the West's largest nonmotorized parade (featuring those glassed-in ore wagons), along with pancake breakfasts, concerts, an antiques fair, and street dances. For more information, call 800/634-3347.

Fall

In mid-October, the saints come marchin' in to Sun Valley for the **Swing 'n' Dixie Jazz Jamboree;** 20-some of the best Dixieland jazz bands from the United States, Canada, and around the world re-create Bourbon Street and the Big Band era for the dancing crowds. The revelry takes place at Sun Valley Resort. If you'd rather see sheep marching than saints marching, look for the **Trailing of the Sheep,** a parade and three-day festival celebrating the Wood River valley's shepherding history. It's also in mid-October.

Winter

Nordic ski races fill the winter calendar. The biggest Nordic event in the valley comes in early February, when the huge **Boulder Mountain Tour** cross-country ski race draws upwards of 700 skiers from all over the world. They race right down the Harriman Trail from Galena Lodge to the Sawtooth NRA Headquarters—the very same 30 kilometer trail you can ski yourself on any other winter's day for around $9. In the world of Nordic skiing, this one's big—at least for an American event.

March brings a less serious race: the **Paw and Pole** fun race for dogs and their human associates. It's held at the Warm Springs Golf Course. The end of Galena Lodge's season brings **Ride, Stride, and Glide,** a bike, snowshoe, and running race, as well as the annual **Gourmet Ski Tour,** on which participants mix skiing and noshing, one course after another.

Spring

As mountain bikers all over the valley are tuning and oiling their mechanical steeds in preparation for summer, a few die-hard Nordic skiers vow to ski right on down to bare earth. You'll find them coated with klister and looking slightly crazed at the **Sun Valley Spring Series** races, held at the Sun Valley Nordic Center the last three weekends of March. For more information, call the center at 208/622-2251. Another major March happening, **Sol Fest,** is a family oriented event with snowboarding exhibitions, live music, and more.

The **Sun Valley Mountain Wellness Festival,** held in late May, features big-name speakers, intimate workshops, and a "Hands-On Hall" where you can try a variety of alternative and holistic health treatments. It's held over Memorial Day Weekend; for more info, see www.svmtnwellness.org.

KETCHUM

Ketchum is the urban hub of the Wood River Valley. And contrary to what you might expect, it's closer to the main ski slopes on Baldy than is Sun Valley Lodge itself. Although not large in total area—the town core occupies perhaps 30 square blocks—every block is packed with restaurants, bars, galleries, outdoor outfitters, and boutiques.

Art Galleries

Ketchum is gallery central. Whatever your taste in art, you'll probably find what you're looking for here. All the galleries are within walking distance of each other, so you might want to make a walking-tour day of it, browsing from one to the next on a visual Movable Feast. The galleries listed below are members of the **Sun Valley Gallery Association,** P.O. Box 1241, Sun Valley, ID 83353, 208/726-8180, a good source of information on the art scene in town. Ask about the guided gallery tours.

The nonprofit **Sun Valley Center for the Arts,** 191 5th St. E., at Washington, 208/726-9491, www.sunvalleycenter.org, has been the hub of the valley's art world for more than 20 years, presenting exhibits, lectures, films, and workshops to community members and visitors alike. Pick up a schedule here of local art happenings—something might be going on tonight.

> *Ketchum is gallery central. Whatever your taste in art, you'll probably find what you're looking for here. All the galleries are within walking distance of each other, so you might want to make a walking-tour day of it.*

Anne Reed Gallery, 391 1st Ave N., 208/726-3036, is the place to go for contemporary paintings, sculpture, and photography, including works by Russell Chatham and Manuel Neri, among others. **Toneri Art Gallery,** 400 Sun Valley Rd., 208/726-5639, features the vivid watercolor landscapes of Lynn Toneri. **African Fine Arts,** Sun Valley Rd. at Leadville Ave., 208/726-3144, offers sculptures from Zimbabwe, handwoven mohair wallhangings and rugs, ceremonial masks, and other African arts. **Broschofsky Galleries,** 6th and Leadville, 208/726-4950, carries an eclectic mix of works from the 19th and 20th centuries, including Native American, Western, and contemporary paintings, jewelry, weavings, and pottery.

On the Baldy side of Main Street, **Gail Severn Gallery,** 400 1st Ave. N., 208/726-5079, features a first-class collection of modern works by a distinguished list of artists including the moody Morris Graves and photographer Edward S. Curtis; **Friesen Gallery,** 320 1st Ave. N. (at Sun Valley Rd.), 208/726-4174, deals in paintings, sculptures, and glass. **Gallery OSCAR,** 291 1st Ave. N., 208/725-5090, features original works of Idaho artists; and **Kneeland Gallery,** 271 1st Ave. N., 208/726-5512, presents and sells works in a wide range of styles and media—mostly landscape paintings—by artists living and working in the western United States.

Accommodations

$50–100: The **Lift Tower Lodge,** 703 S. Main St., 208/726-5163 or 800/462-8646, may not look like much as you drive by, but the rooms are clean, comfortable, and extremely well priced. Out front is the restored 1939 Sun Valley lift tower that gives the lodge its name, but the best rooms are around back, where it's quiet and you'll find a hot tub and views of Baldy. The friendly and welcoming managers set out a complimentary continental breakfast in the lobby each morning. For those on a limited budget who don't need palatial quarters, this place is a steal. No pets. Highly recommended.

The tidy **Christiania Lodge,** 651 Sun Valley Rd., 888/799-1394, sits three blocks from the center of Ketchum on the way toward Sun Valley. It's not as new as some, but offers a heated outdoor pool and year-round hot tub. Rates include a continental breakfast. Nonsmoking rooms available; pets may be permitted at discretion of the manager.

$100–150: Best Western Kentwood Lodge, 180 S. Main St., Ketchum, ID 83340, 208/726-4114 or 800/805-1001, lies along the highway at the south edge of downtown. Log and stone accents mark both the exterior and interior of the modern, nonsmoking motel. Amenities include an indoor heated pool and spa, an on-site espresso bar, and microwaves and small refrigerators in each of the 57 rooms. Full kitchens and spa suites are available.

The Austrian-styled **Best Western Tyrolean Lodge,** 260 Cottonwood, P.O. Box 202, Sun Valley, ID 83353, 208/726-5336 or 800/333-7912, is within easy walking distance of the River Run lift. Amenities include a heated pool, sauna, two indoor spas, and a fireplace in the lobby. All the beds are topped with down comforters, and many different suites are available, some with kitchens or in-room Jacuzzis. Rates include continental breakfast and après-ski cider.

At the corner of Sun Valley Road and Walnut Avenue, **Tamarack Lodge,** 291 Walnut, P.O. Box 2000, Sun Valley, ID 83353, 208/726-3344 or 800/521-5379, features an indoor heated pool and outdoor Jacuzzi, both open year-round. The nondescript **Clarion Inn,** 600 N. Main St., 208/726-5900 or 800/262-4833, sits on the highway at the north end of town. It has a year-round outdoor heated pool and hot tub and offers free continental breakfast. Kids stay free with parents.

$150–250: The **Knob Hill Inn,** 960 N. Main St., P.O. Box 800, Ketchum, ID 83340, 208/726-8010 or 800/526-8010, is a member of the prestigious Relais & Chateaux lodging association. Plush doesn't even begin to describe this place. The foyer library and bar looks out on a lushly landscaped garden with a fountain and a bright palette of flowers in spring and summer. The 24 guest rooms feature marble-appointed bathrooms with tubs and separate shower stalls. Each room has its own private balcony with great mountain views. Amenities include a Jacuzzi, sauna, and year-round lap pool. The on-site restaurant, Felix, garners rave reviews. The only possible drawback here is the busy, if convenient, location. No smoking, no pets. It's easy to hit the high end of this price category (and go well beyond it) here.

Over $250: Thunder Spring, 124 Saddle Rd., P.O. Box 6475, Ketchum, ID 83340, 208/727-9635, is a development of ultra-high-end condominiums that sell for $1.2 million and up each, but they're also available for rent by the night when the owners are away. Very, very expensive, but for a taste of how the way-rich folk live, maybe it's worth it.

Fine Dining

The old guard goes to the small and elegant **Michel's Christiania Restaurant and Olympic Bar,** 303 Walnut Ave. N., 208/726-3388. It's reminiscent of an Old World ski chalet, with a cozy interior tastefully appointed in wood, lace, and linen, and a flower-filled patio centered by a small fountain. On the French/continental menu are upscale delicacies along the lines of escargots bourgignon, lamb shank braised with wine, and various recipes featuring filet mignon, pheasant, salmon, and halibut. Entrées average over $20. The Olympic Bar is the best place in town to enjoy a quiet cognac with a friend. You'll want to look sharp here. Open nightly for dinner.

Felix Restaurant, 380 1st Ave N., 208/726-1166, serves outstanding Mediterranean-influenced continental cuisine. Tapas plates, including a different ravioli each day, run $10–11, while entrées range $22–31. Another high-end restaurant, **Evergreen Bistro,** 171 1st Ave. at Rivers St., 208/726-3888, is known for its romantic atmosphere, superb French-influenced fare, and superior wine list.

Globus, 291 6th St. E. (at Main), 208/726-1301, prepares a pan-Asian menu in casually elegant surroundings. Look for such delectables as homemade Thai sausages with mango chutney, and pan-fried oysters served on baby Asian greens. Entrées range $12–20. In the Trail Creek Village complex at 200 S. Main St., **Chandler's,** 208/726-1776, is a local favorite, especially for its seafood and mouthwatering Yankee pot roast ($16.95). The menu features the chef's fine-dining whims—entrées from elk loin to ahi at prices running $15–$33—while the wine list offers selections from the best of the West. Open for dinner nightly.

The Sawtooth Club, 231 N. Main St., 208/726-5233, broils its steaks and seafood selections over a mesquite grill. Microbrews are available, as are fine wines by the glass. The flower-lined upstairs deck overlooks Main Street. Entrées range $11–23. Open nightly from 5 P.M. for dinner. **Ketchum Grill,** 520 East Ave., 208/726-4660, is another high-class dinner house with a creative nouvelle menu and excellent wine list. Wild game and Northwestern influences are the order here, in dishes such as marinated and fruit wood–grilled elk with huckleberries and wild rice. Prices ($8–19 for entrées) run a little lower and the atmosphere is a bit more casual than the other top-tier places.

Warm Springs Ranch Restaurant, 1801 Warm Springs Rd. (a mile from downtown), 208/726-2609, offers a soothing logs-and-timbers atmosphere with comfortable furnishings and subdued lighting. On the wide-ranging menu are steaks, seafood, lamb, chicken, ribs, and pasta dishes. Entrée prices range from around $10–11 (fried chicken, pasta) up to around $23 for filet mignon and $27 for Alaskan king crab legs. The lounge offers a beautiful creekside deck.

A Bit More Casual

On the classy side of the pub-grub scene is **The Pioneer Saloon,** 308 N. Main St., 208/726-3139, which makes a mean burger and even serves up a locally recommended prime rib. The bar is an old Ketchum landmark where trophy heads and pioneer artifacts line the walls, and locals can tell you stories about the town's glorious past. Entrées range from $9 for a burger to $26.95 for a full cut of prime rib.

The Roosevelt Grille, 280 N. Main St. at Sun Valley Rd., 208/726-0051, is another popular spot offering a casual yet creative menu—Idaho rainbow trout, three-cheese pizza, salads, burgers, and more. The awesome rooftop deck makes this a great place for lunch, which features burgers (about $8), salads (try the raspberry chicken salad, $7.95), and wraps. At dinner, look for entrées priced $10–19, including trout, Idaho pork chops, gumbo, and more. Beer lovers note: There are 10 micros on tap.

Sun Valley Wine Company, 360 N. Leadville Ave., 208/726-2442, is a good place to enjoy a light meal and a glass of fine wine. In winter, you can eat indoors by a crackling fire; in summer, go out on the deck. Something among the offerings—soups, salads, quiches, gourmet mini-pizzas, cheese and fruit plates, pâtés—will complement your favorite wine perfectly. Open for lunch and dinner daily.

A Whole Lot More Casual

A little off the beaten path but worth the effort to find is **KB's Burritos,** 200 6th St. (at Washington), 208/726-2232. The women who run the place are as fantastic as the healthy homemade stuff that stuffs each of their bomber burritos. It's a true Organo-Feminist dining experience. If you keep your ears open, you're sure to find out what the locals are doing tonight. Inexpensive ($6–8), delicious, fun, and highly recommended. It's open Mon.–Sat. 11:30 A.M.–9 P.M., Sun. 4–9 P.M.

For pub grub with an emphasis on the "pub" (i.e., beer), the local institution is **Grumpy's,** 860 Warm Springs Rd., no phone, which serves cheap 32-ounce schooners of domestic beer and offers burgers, dogs, and its famous Tuesday-night ribs to soak it all up. The atmosphere is sloppy casual and unabashedly irreverent; the walls are lined with old beer cans, miscellaneous junk, and various signs including one reading Work Free Drug Place. You can shoot pool at the one table inside or take your schooner out on the deck and watch the sunset.

In the same cheap beer-and-burgers vein is **Lefty's Bar & Grill,** 213 6th St. E. (at Washington), 208/726-2744, with a friendly sports-bar atmosphere. It's open daily 11:30 A.M.–10:30 P.M.

Ethnic Fare

Locals are raving about **Rosina's,** 5th and Leadville in the 511 Building, 208/726-4444, which specializes in hearty home-style Italian cooking in an upscale yet comfortable atmosphere. Pasta dishes run $12–19, and meat dishes cost $17–20. Open for dinner nightly, from 6 P.M. in summer and 5 P.M. in winter.

Panda Chinese Restaurant, 515 East Ave. N., 208/726-3591, serves Mandarin, Hunan, and Sichuan cuisine. Dinners run $8–13, with the General's Chicken ($9) a consistent favorite. Look for lunch specials in the $5.50–$7 range.

There's no gourmet Mexican food in town; Hailey and Bellevue are better bets in this category, since more Latinos and the other service people who make the area tick live down-valley, where rents are slightly—though not much more—affordable. In Ketchum, the best choices are **Desperados,** 4th and Washington Sts., 208/726-3068, which uses no-fat beans and canola oil, and **Mama Inez,** 7th St. and Warm Springs Rd., 208/726-4213, which serves up Southwestern-style Mexican fare.

Pizza
It's a small chain, but **Smoky Mountain Pizza & Pasta,** 200 Sun Valley Rd., 208/622-5625, does a good job. The deck offers a nice view of the snow-clad slopes. It's open Mon.–Sat. 11:30 A.M.–10 P.M., Sun. noon–9 P.M. **Bob Dog Pizza,** at 4th and Washington, 208/726-2358, is known for its great herb crust. Pastas, salads, beer, and wine are also available. The staff here is especially friendly and efficient.

Breakfast
The award for best breakfast place in town goes to **The Kneadery,** 260 Leadville Ave., 208/726-9462. Its funky-Western decor includes stuffed ducks, duck decoys, a carousel horse, and a wooden Indian. On the menu are various omelettes, whole-wheat-cinnamon French toast, and the inimitable Huevos Kneadery. Most items cost $9 or less. No smoking.

Brunch and Lunch
The best Sunday brunch in town is served at **Cristina's Restaurant,** 520 2nd St. E. (at East), 208/726-4499, which also has the best alfresco dining in Ketchum. The restaurant is on the south edge of downtown on a quiet side street. Its

garden back patio feels far removed from the hustle and bustle—the perfect setting to enjoy a mimosa and a romantic tête-à-tête. Cristina's also serves lunch.

Perry's, 131 4th St. W., 208/726-7703, is a longtime local favorite, with lots of seating inside and out, a lively atmosphere, and plenty of good food. Breakfast runs $3–9, while lunch selections cost $4–10. Open Mon.–Fri. 7 A.M.–5 P.M., Sat.–Sun. 7 A.M.–4 P.M.

Esta, 180 S. Main St. in the Kentwood Lodge complex, 208/726-1668, has New York–style fare like challah French toast ($6.25) and corned beef reuben sandwiches ($8.95). Open daily for breakfast and dinner.

Coffeehouse
The original Java in the chain is Ketchum's **Java on Fourth,** 191 4th St. E., 208/726-2882. The floorplan is as funky as the crowd in this small but immensely popular caffeinery. You can't go wrong with either the food or coffee here, and the people-watching is outstanding. When it's too hot for coffee, head next door to **Java Primo,** 208/726-6460, for ice cream and other treats.

Nightlife
Besides the Pioneer, mentioned above, a couple of other bars in town merit a mention for socializing after the sun goes down. **Whiskey Jacques',** 251 N. Main St., 208/726-5297, is a large joint catering predominantly to tourists and over-30 divorced locals; live bands and dancing, good pizza ($13–17), and beer.

The Casino Club, 220 N. Main St., 208/726-9901, has drawn its share of Ketchum characters over the years. It's a dark, unassuming, and somewhat mysterious place, with nooks and crannies suitable for scandalous repartee with the object of your desire. Also pool tables, darts, foosball, and plenty of booze.

If you feel more like a movie, head to **Magic Lantern Cinema,** 100 2nd St. E. (facing Washington Ave.), 208/726-4274 (recorded schedule information) or 208/726-3308, for avant garde and foreign flicks; or to **Ski Time 4 Cinemas,** 100 2nd St. E. (at 1st Ave.), 208/726-1039, for first-run films.

Shopping

Oenophiles heading to an après-ski BYOB will want to check out the **Sun Valley Wine Company,** 360 N. Leadville Ave., 208/726-2442. The store sells the largest selection of wines in the valley, as well as gourmet picnic baskets and gifts for wine fanciers. In addition to retail sales, the store offers light food, coffee and espresso drinks, and wines by the glass, which you can enjoy at one of the comfortable tables.

Iconoclast Used Books, 211 N. Main St., 208/726-1564, specializes in used, rare, and out-of-print books, and also features great art—inside and out—and an excellent video-rental library full of art and foreign films. You'll also find a great selection of films to rent at **Video West,** 560 Washington Ave. N., 208/726-3217.

WARM SPRINGS AREA

On the north side of Baldy, with easy access to the mountain's Warm Springs lifts and day lodge, this area is a little too far from downtown Ketchum for convenient walking. But it does have a pleasant, self-contained village feel, with lodgings (lots of condos), restaurants, and nightlife. Yes, there really are warm springs in the vicinity—occasionally your nose will pick up the alluring aroma of sulfur wafting around on the breeze.

Accommodations

$100–150: The **Eagle Crest Inn,** 100 Picabo St. (yes, named after the skier), 208/726-4776, has a great location, less than a block from the Warm Springs lifts. Each of the 16 rooms has a kitchenette and gas fireplace; common amenities include a hot tub and exercise room. The ministudios are less than $100, even in winter, although most rooms fall in this higher price range.

SUN VALLEY

The incorporated city of Sun Valley starts just outside Ketchum, less than a mile up Sun Valley Road. Besides the ubiquitous ski condos and immodest eight-bedroom, nine-bath vacation homes, everything in Sun Valley proper centers around Sun Valley Company's operations. Here you'll find the famous Sun Valley Lodge, the slightly lower-crust Sun Valley Inn, and Sun Valley Village, with its various shops and restaurants existing primarily to serve guests of the resort. Nightlife is more sedate here, favoring the martini-and-piano-bar crowd over Ketchum's beer-and-rock 'n' rollers.

Sun Valley Resort

Grande dame of the Wood River Valley, **Sun Valley Lodge,** P.O. Box 10, Sun Valley, ID 83353, 800/786-8259, 208/622-2151 (reservations), or 208/622-4111 (switchboard), opened in 1936, the realization of Union Pacific director Averell Harriman's pet project to build a world-class ski resort in the American West. Harriman's intended motif for the resort was "roughing it in luxury," but it's difficult to see where the "roughing it" part comes in, especially after renovations in 1986, 1992, and 2003. Old World elegance is the lodge hallmark, retained in the newly upgraded country-French decor. But new furnishings can't conceal the patina of history gracing these venerable halls. Harriman himself, in the form of a portrait hanging above the fireplace, still presides over the oak-paneled foyer living room, and the ghost of Ernest Hemingway still haunts Room 206, where the author holed up while working on *For Whom the Bell Tolls.*

Amenities at the lodge include a year-round glass-enclosed heated pool; two ice-skating rinks, one indoors, one out; and four restaurants, among them the stellar, continental-cuisine Lodge Dining Room. A great many recreational facilities—in addition to world-class skiing—are available at the lodge or in the immediate area. The bowling alley, golf course, stables, tennis courts, and a trap- and skeet-shooting range are open to resort guests and nonguests alike. The resort's three swimming pools—including an Olympic-size pool adjacent to the tennis courts—and the sand volleyball courts are open to resort guests only. Most rooms in the $150–250 category; higher-priced accommodations available.

In addition to the lodge, the resort offers a number of other accommodations options, including the **Sun Valley Inn** ($100–150 and higher); **con-**

COURTESY OF THE IDAHO TRAVEL COUNCIL

THE HIGH COUNTRY

Sun Valley Lodge

dominium units ($150–250 and higher); and for those who demand the most exclusive lodgings available, a number of **guest cottages** are scattered about the expansive resort grounds. The opulent cottages represent the ultimate in privacy—the View Cottage lies near the shore of Sun Valley Lake and rents for a cool $1,000 a night.

Various specials are offered each year; call for information.

Recreation

The resort's **Sun Valley Sports Center,** in Sun Valley Village, 208/622-2231, can arrange whatever activity you're interested in, either on the resort grounds or anywhere in southern and central Idaho. Examples of off-resort activities the center frequently arranges for guests include whitewater-rafting trips, glider flights, guided fishing excursions, and wilderness pack trips.

Food

The crème de la crème of Sun Valley dining and one of the top-ranked restaurants in the Wood River Valley is the resort's **Lodge Dining Room,** 208/622-2150. The menu features Idaho-influenced continental fare such as red deer chop and breast of pheasant, with most entrées in the $19–30 range, some of the state's most decadent desserts ($6.25), and an outstanding wine list. Sunday brunch here is a major treat, priced at $23 for adults and $13 for children 12 and under.

For a quintessential Sun Valley experience, sign up for a sleigh ride out to dinner at the resort's historic **Trail Creek Cabin.** After a brisk ride through the snow, you'll arrive to a cheery, roaring fire and a menu including steaks, trout, and ribs; entrées range $16–32. The sleigh ride costs another $22 adults, $18 children. You can also make dinner-only reservations at the cabin and get there on your own. It's two miles east of Sun Valley Village up Trail Creek, and you can either cross-country ski or (oh, the horror) drive there. Of course, then you'll be missing out on those sleigh bells jingling, ting-ting tingling, and such. For reservations, call 208/622-2135.

Nightlife

The lodge's elegant **Duchin Bar & Lounge,** 208/622-2145, features live music, often jazz. In Sun Valley Village, the **Opera House,** 208/622-2244, screens first-run movies at around 7 and 9:15 P.M. nightly. It also offers free shows of

Sun Valley Serenade, the 1941 Hollywood classic starring Sonja Henie and John Payne and featuring music by the Glenn Miller Orchestra. The film screens at 5 P.M. daily year-round.

INFORMATION AND SERVICES

Information

The **Sun Valley/Ketchum Chamber & Visitors Bureau,** 411 N. Main St. in Ketchum, P.O. Box 2420, Sun Valley, ID 83353, 208/726-3423 or 800/634-3347, maintains a well-stocked visitor center at the corner of 4th and Main Sts. in Ketchum. The USFS **Ketchum Ranger District,** 206 Sun Valley Rd. in Ketchum, 208/622-5371, offers good advice for both local recreation and backcountry exploration.

Property Management Services

Premier Resorts, 333 S. Main in Ketchum, P.O. Box 659, Sun Valley, ID 83353, 208/727-4000 or 800/635-4444, handles rentals for about 300 condos and 75 private homes in the area. Styles and decors vary widely. Tell them what you're looking for and they'll do their best to match you up. No pets. Other property management companies include **Resort Quest Sun Valley,** 200 W. River St., P.O. Box 21, Ketchum, ID 83340, 888/799-1394, which has some very reasonably priced rentals (from about $80), and **Distinctive Properties,** P.O. Box 1230, Sun Valley, ID 83353, 208/726-7664, which handles higher-end condos and homes.

TRANSPORTATION

Getting There

If you're coming in by air, you'll be flying into Hailey's Friedman Memorial Airport. If you're coming by car, figure on about a two-and-a-half-hour drive from Boise or Idaho Falls, an hour and a half from Twin Falls, and five hours from Salt Lake City. **Sun Valley Express,** 208/622-8267 or 877/622-8267, operates year-round shuttle bus service to and from Boise. Adult fare is $54 one-way.

Getting Around

Trying to walk across, or make a left turn across, one of the valley's main streets during the day can be a challenge. Unlike most of Idaho, here you'll find traffic. Fortunately, you'll also find an excellent **free bus service.** KART (for Ketchum Area Rapid Transit) runs three bus routes connecting the major Ketchum/Sun Valley destinations. Schedules and operating hours on the different routes vary, but in general, you'll probably find a bus heading your way every 20 minutes between 7:30 A.M. and midnight. The buses feature handy exterior ski racks, and they'll probably get you closer to your destination than if you drove there and tried to find a parking space. They're also useful for keeping you out of trouble when you're trying to get back to your room after one too many at the Casino. For schedules and information, call 208/726-7140, or ask any of the bus drivers.

Sawtooth National Recreation Area

Driving north out of Ketchum on Highway 75, you don't need a sign to tell you when you've entered the 765,000-acre Sawtooth NRA. Suddenly, the houses disappear and the grandeur of the mountains and the tranquillity of the wooded river valley return to the forefront of your consciousness.

The dividing line between the two worlds is found at the Sawtooth NRA Headquarters and Visitor Information Center, seven miles north of Sun Valley on the east side of the highway.

From here on up the valley, you'll see no more 4,000-square-foot "cabins," and for every 100 vehicles that plied the highway lower down, now you'll see 10.

The NRA, established in 1972, encompasses parts of four different mountain ranges. From the headquarters in the Wood River Valley, you'll be looking at the Smoky Mountains to the west and the Boulder Mountains to the east. Across Galena Summit to the north, the famous Sawtooth Mountains dominate the western skyline

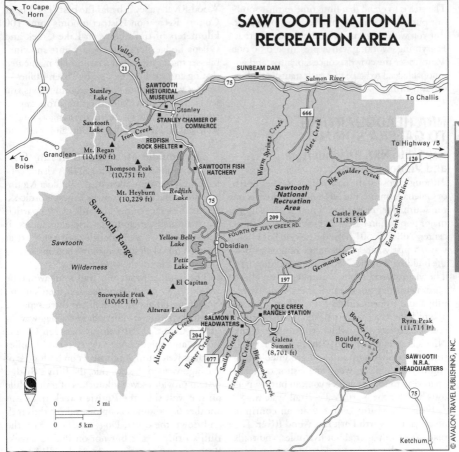

SAWTOOTH NATIONAL
RECREATION AREA

THE HIGH COUNTRY

with a string of jagged summits, while the eastern horizon is shaped by the inscrutable White Cloud Peaks. More than 50 summits in the NRA stand over 10,000 feet.

Among these mountains lie over 300 alpine lakes, all suitable for fishing, some even big enough for boating and sailing (boat ramps are available on Alturas, Pettit, Redfish, and Stanley Lakes). And four major Idaho rivers—the Salmon, South Fork Payette, Boise, and Big Wood—get their starts within the boundaries of the NRA.

Although the entire NRA is spectacular and wild, the centerpiece of the area is the 217,000-acre Sawtooth Wilderness, an alpine realm closed to motor vehicles and even mountain bikes. Hikers and horsepackers here can enjoy some of the country's most magnificent scenery. Unlike most mountain ranges, the Sawtooths seem to rise suddenly out of nowhere. They're not particularly tall as high peaks go—the highest is under 11,000 feet—but their steep relief and abundant granite walls and spires create a mountaineer's paradise. Birders can keep their eyes open for many of the 214 bird species found here either full- or part-time (pick up a checklist at NRA headquarters).

The area is so grand that from time to time some-one pushes to see it recognized as a national park. But you won't hear many locals advocating that. Everything's working well at present and no one wants to see the crowds, concessionaires, and additional federal red tape that such status would inevitably bring.

NRA HEADQUARTERS TO GALENA SUMMIT

Sawtooth NRA Headquarters and Visitor Center

Although most of the Sawtooth NRA lies north of Galena Summit, the NRA headquarters is on the south side, nearer the Wood River Valley's major population base. You can't miss the visitor center, 208/727-5013, on the east side of Highway 75 just where all the fancy houses stop—the building is on the NRA's southern boundary. The visitor center sells a number of excellent natural-history books, and offers copious exhibits and informational flyers. Here you can also pick up a free audio-tape interpretive tour of scenic Highway 75, which you return at the NRA's Stanley office up north. In winter, you'll find an ice-skating pond and groomed cross-country ski trails as well. The visitor center is open year-round; in winter you can buy ski permits here for the North Valley Trail System.

From the visitor center, you can continue north up the **North Fork Big Wood River.** The road poops out after about five miles, and trails head up high into the Boulder Mountains from there. Mountaineers can follow Trail 115 up to West Pass and from there scramble up to the summit of **Ryan Peak** (South Ridge, Class 2); at 11,714 feet, it's the highest peak in the range. From trailhead to summit, the six-mile hike climbs some 5,000 vertical feet.

A less vertiginous day hike in the area is the **Amber Gulch Trail,** (Trails 129-130) which leads about 4.5 miles one-way to Amber Lakes and views of the North Fork and the Pioneer Mountains.

North Valley Nordic Trails

You'll find many superb places to go cross-country skiing in Idaho, but in my book, the upper Wood River Valley is by far the best. The Blaine County Recreation District grooms some 100 kilometers of trails between Lake Creek and Galena Lodge. This is no penny-ante snowmobile-set track system, but a beautifully manicured skating and striding track set by Pisten Bullies—smaller versions of the LMC grooming cats you see at the big downhill ski resorts. You can ski anywhere you like on the trail system, as long as your legs and lungs will hold out, all for around $9 a day.

The **Boulder Mountain Trail** runs from Galena Summit down to the SNRA visitor center. This is the route taken by the Boulder Mountain Tour, one of the country's largest Nordic-ski events. The race draws upwards of 700 participants annually, including world-class racers. If you can arrange a car shuttle, you can start at the top and ski all the way to the bottom, letting gravity do a lot of the work for you.

The Boulder Mountain Trail alone would be worth the $9 per day trail fee. But there's more. Branching off the main trail are three separate side-trail systems on either side of the highway. At Prairie Creek, about halfway between Galena Lodge and the NRA headquarters (11 miles north of Ketchum), loops are set on both sides of the highway: on the east side, the **Billy's Bridge** system provides seven kilometers of trails, while on the west side, the **Prairie Creek** trails run another 6.5 kilometers up one side of the creek and down the other. Dogs are allowed on the Billy's Bridge trails but not on Prairie Creek. Both sides offer scenic views. At the NRA headquarters, the **North Fork Trail System** offers four kilometers of easy trails along the North Fork Big Wood; dogs okay. This trail is recommended for beginners.

In addition to all these trails, Galena Lodge (see below) is the hub of a fantastic 50-kilometer trail system that's also included in the $9 fee.

Day passes are sold at Galena Lodge, the NRA headquarters, and in Ketchum at the visitor center, Backwoods Mountain Sports, the Elephant's Perch. For up-to-the-minute grooming information, call the Rec D **North Valley Trails Hotline** at 208/77

A free shuttle bus travels between S

Ketchum and the North Valley trails Wed.–Sat. through the winter. The bus leaves the Sun Valley Resort at 10 A.M. and travels down Sun Valley Road and Ketchum's Main Street before heading north toward stops at the Sawtooth National Recreation Area headquarters, Baker Creek, and Billy's Bridge, arriving at Galena Lodge at 11 A.M. The return trip begins at 2 P.M. For more information, call the Blaine County Recreation District office at 208/788-2117.

Hot Springs

Commercial or noncommercial—take your pick. **Easley Hot Springs Resort,** 208/726-7522, offers a developed site with a pool and showers, eight miles north of the NRA headquarters; cost is $6 general, $5 for kids. Campers can grab a shower here for $3. It's typically open daily in summer, weekends only the rest of the year. **Russian John Hot Springs** is au naturel, 100 yards west of the highway (near mile marker 146), just south of the turnoff to the 4H camp.

Day Hikes

Recommended by the Forest Service are the **Lakes Trails,** a network of trails accessing a half dozen or so named lakes in the Smoky Mountains on the west side of Highway 75. From a trailhead at the end of Baker Creek Road (FR 162), it's a short, two-mile hike up Trail 138 to the popular (and oft-crowded) fishin' hole **Baker Lake.** A spur partway up Baker Creek Road takes you to a second trail from Trail 135, which leads two miles to **Norton Lakes.** The Forest Service recommends this trail for novice hikers; more athletic visitors might want to continue past Norton Lakes over Norton Saddle and down to **Miner Lake,** where you'll have great views of the Boulder Mountains.

Four miles farther up the highway, a third trailhead at the end of Prairie Creek Road (FR 179) also provides access to the Lakes Trails. From here you can take Trail 136 up to shallow **Mill Lake,** a 2.5-mile one-way jaunt; or pick up Trail 134, which leads to a high-mountain loop that can take you to one or more of Miner, Norton, and **Prairie Lakes.** From this trailhead, it's four miles and a steep climb to Miner Lake, five

moderate miles to Prairie Lakes. For a complete guide to the area, pick up *The Lakes Trails* brochure at the NRA visitor center.

At a hairpin turn on the south side of Galena Summit you'll find the trailhead for a short day hike up to **Titus Lake.** Since you're already at the top of the world here, you won't have too much more "up" to go before you reach the lake—the trail climbs only about 500 feet in the 2.5-mile trek.

Galena Lodge

Almost to Galena Summit, 24 miles upstream from Ketchum, you'll come to the region's Nordic nirvana: the incomparable Galena Lodge, 15187 Hwy. 75, HC 64 Box 8326, Ketchum, ID 83340, 208/726-4010. Here you'll find the crown jewels of the Wood River Valley trails, a 50-kilometer network of loops winding through pristine high-mountain forests and glades, no snowmobiles to disrupt winter's subtle songs, and all included in the standard North Valley Trails user fee of $9 a day.

The lodge itself—just a day lodge, no accommodations—is intimate but not cramped, and the atmosphere is casual and friendly. A small restaurant serves a homemade gourmet lunch, a light après-ski spread, and a Sunday morning special of sticky buns, frittata, and good fresh-brewed coffee. The small bar keeps a variety of wines and a microbrew or two on tap, and a store with a rental and repair shop handles all your equipment needs. Lessons are available as well. After a morning on the trails, it isn't too difficult to spend most of an afternoon out on the sunny lodge deck, serenaded by the quiet rhythm of snowmelt dripping off the roof.

Several programs at the lodge are worth a mention. Once a week beginning in January, the resort offers 90-minute **Ski with a Ranger** outings. A ranger from the Sawtooth NRA will lead you on an easy tour and fill you in on the area's natural and human history, flora and fauna, and varying special topics along the way. It's free with the standard $9 trail pass. The lodge also maintains a popular **backcountry yurt system,** available by reservation beginning Nov. 1 for the

Galena Lodge

following season. The yurts rent for $125 Fri.–Sat. night, $100 a night the rest of the week, for as many people as you can stuff in them. They're popular, and reservations must be booked and paid for at least 30 days in advance.

Another lodge feature not to be missed is the series of **full-moon dinners.** For two nights each month between December and Easter—the night of the full moon and the night before—the lodge restaurant prepares a lavish gourmet dinner accompanied by local live entertainment. You'll need to make reservations well in advance for one of these special nights. If you can swing a full-moon dinner and a yurt reservation on the same night, you'll be in heaven—enjoy a great meal at the lodge then ski out to the yurt under the full moon.

In summer, the trails here are open free to hikers, equestrians, and mountain bikers. The lodge serves lunch Mon.–Sat., dinner usually Thurs.–Sat., and brunch on Sunday. The store is open daily, offering mountain-bike rentals and trail maps of the area. Wildflower walks and a range of other interpretive programs keep the lodge's events calendar full. Summer or winter, Galena Lodge is a fantastic place. Very highly recommended.

Horseback Riding

Across the highway from Galena Lodge you'll find **Galena Stage Stop Corrals,** 208/726-1735. Run by Mystic Saddle Ranch mid-June through Labor Day, the stables offer trail rides in the Galena area ranging from 90 minutes ($35 per person) to all day ($95 per person). Reservations are requested.

Galena Summit

Forgive your car its lack of performance as it struggles up the grade here; Galena Summit, the crest of the hill, tops out at 8,701 feet. The summit marks the separation of two watersheds: the Big Wood to the south, and the Salmon to the north.

Mountain bikers can ride the **Old Toll Road** down into the Sawtooth Valley from the summit. The road was built in the 1880s and was the nightmare of early pioneers attempting to descend it with fully loaded wagons. The trail starts across the highway from the Galena Overlook, a quarter mile north of the summit.

Camping

The 29-site **North Fork Campground** lies across the highway and a bit farther up the road from NRA headquarters. Two miles farther up the valley, **Wood River Campground** offers another 30 sites. At Easley Hot Springs, the reservable, 10-site **Easley Campground** has the advantage of being next to the hot-springs resort. All three of the USFS campgrounds are open June 15–Sept. 15, and all three charge a fee.

SAWTOOTH VALLEY

After cresting Galena Summit, you'll be dropping down to the headwaters of the Salmon River—the famous watercourse that flows undammed for more than 400 miles from here to its confluence with the Snake River in Hells Canyon. **Galena Overlook** is a must-stop turnout just down the north side from the summit. Here you'll usually find a few poor souls trying to revive their cars—the altitude and steep grade put motors to the test—and many more gawkers enjoying a magnificent, sweeping view of the Sawtooths. The road then continues down into Sawtooth Valley, where history buffs will find several sights worth a look.

Historic Sites

Not far from the bottom of Galena grade, FR 194 turns east to the 1909 **Pole Creek Ranger Station,** the first structure built by the Forest Service in the Sawtooth National Forest. It was constructed and occupied by Bill Horton, a district ranger in this area for more than 20 years. Today the site is listed on the National Register. Farther up Pole Creek is a trailhead for hiking and biking into the Boulder Mountains and White Cloud Peaks.

A little farther north up the highway, a couple of tributaries—Smiley Creek and Beaver Creek—flow into the Salmon River from the west. These two streams and their surrounding lands supported a hive of early mining efforts in the Sawtooth Valley. Levi Smiley first found silver ore in this end of the valley in 1878, and other miners found gold on Beaver Creek in 1879. **Sawtooth City,** partway up Beaver Creek, boomed between 1882 and 1886, and held on until the crumbs were exhausted around 1892. **Vienna** was the equivalent boomtown over on Smiley Creek. Its boom lasted a year longer than Saw-

tooth City's. You can drive or mountain-bike to the former sites of both of these towns—Vienna up FR 077, Sawtooth City up FR 204—and picnic with the ghosts among the occasional pieces of mining detritus.

Popular Lakes and Wilderness Trailheads

As Highway 75 continues north from Beaver Creek, it parallels the eastern boundary of the Sawtooth Wilderness, some three miles to the west. Between the highway and the wilderness lie several lakes popular with campers, anglers, hikers, bikers, and, in winter, cross-country skiers.

Alturas Lake (FR 205) is the area's largest. Three fee **campgrounds** along its north shore—Smokey Bear, North Shore, and Alturas Inlet—hold a total of 55 sites. In winter, **cross-country skiing** enthusiasts will find 10 kilometers of periodically groomed trails here; the trails are rated easy to intermediate and wind across open meadows and along a wooded creek.

Continuing north, **Petit Lake** (FR 208) has a small free campground and is the site of the Tin Cup trailhead, a well-used access point into the Sawtooth Wilderness. Backpackers head out from here on the Petit-Toxaway Loop Trail, a two-day trip past several wilderness lakes. Undeveloped **Yellow Belly Lake** (FR 365) is a favorite of anglers; no boat motors allowed.

Off FR 315 you'll find the trailhead to **Hell Roaring Lake.** The moderately difficult 10.4-mile roundtrip trek to the lake makes a great day hike. Surrounded by the granite towers of Finger of Fate and the Arrowhead, Hell Roaring Lake lies in one of the most beautiful parts of the Sawtooth Wilderness.

Mountain Biking

On the south end of Sawtooth Valley, **Valley Road** (FR 194) more or less parallels the highway on the east. It begins at Sawtooth City; to get there, follow the route to Pole Creek Ranger Station, but at the junction of FRs 194 and 197 continue north on 194. Of course, you could always swing up the extra half mile and back and check out the ranger station, too, while you're in the area. The rest of the route north leads through pastures and ranchlands, and rejoins Highway 75 about a half mile south of Fourth of July Creek Road.

If you turn off Highway 75 on FR 315, cross the Salmon River, and turn right, you'll find yourself on **Decker Flat Road** (FR 210), an easy mountain-biking route that parallels the river for some 14 miles north to Redfish Lake Road. The rangers recommend this scenic ride for families.

Just across the highway from FR 315, **Fourth of July Creek Road** (FR 209) leads east up into the White Cloud Peaks. This is the prime west-side access route into the White Clouds, a favored realm of mountain bikers.

Another popular trail begins 1.5 miles farther north up the highway. The 18-mile Fisher Creek-Williams Creek Loop starts at Fisher Creek Road (between mileposts 176 and 177 on Highway 75) and follows that road up to the old Aztec Mine, where it turns into single track. It then descends to the Warm Springs Creek drainage and turns back west, crossing a second saddle before descending Williams Creek to the highway. Hard-core bikers could instead follow Warm Springs Creek north, all the way down to the Salmon River at Robinson Bar east of Sunbeam.

Venture Outdoors, P.O. Box 2251, Hailey, ID 83333, 208/788-5049 or 800/528-5262, leads guided mountain-bike treks in the Sawtooth Valley and surrounding areas. Trips range from easy day rides to technical overnighters; all include bike, helmet, food, and transportation. Rates run about $75–85 for a day trip, around $150–250 per day for a multiday trip.

Day Hikes

On the south end of the valley, **Horton Peak Lookout** provides a high vantage point overlooking the NRA. It's a strenuous eight-mile roundtrip hike that gains 2,700 vertical feet. The trailhead is on FR 459, which turns off Valley Road (FR 194) about midway along its length.

In the Alturas Lake area, the **Cabin Creek Lakes** trail offers an easier trek. The eight-mile roundtrip hike follows Cabin Creek up to a string of small lakes just inside the wilderness boundary. To reach the trailhead, take Cabin Creek Road (FR 207) west off Highway 75, about a mile and

a half north of Alturas Lake Road. Stay on FR 207 at every road junction and find the trailhead about a quarter mile north of Cabin Creek. You can also reach the trailhead from the south, by taking FR 207 north off Alturas Lake Road about a mile.

Farther north, across the highway from the Sawtooth Hatchery, a three-quarter-mile spur road leads to the trailhead to **Casino Lakes.** It's a heart-pounding, five-mile one-way hike up 3,000 vertical feet to the cluster of small lakes at the head of Big Casino Creek.

Guest Ranch

$150–250: Some of the plushest digs on this side of Galena Summit are found at **Idaho Rocky Mountain Ranch,** HC 64 Box 9934, Stanley, ID 83278, 208/774-3544. Look for the signs nine miles south of Stanley on Highway 75, then turn east toward the White Cloud Peaks. The secluded 1,000-acre ranch overlooks Sawtooth Valley from the foot of the mountains. The log lodge and cabins were built in the 1930s and offer a comfortable atmosphere of rustic elegance. Each lodge room and cabin has a private bath, but none of them have telephones or televisions. Fishing, horseback riding, hiking, hot-springs soaks, and swimming are all offered on the premises, and outstanding mountain biking is close at hand in the White Clouds.

The ranch is open to guests mid-June through mid-September. Rates (based on double occupancy) range $92–127 per night per person, depending on length of stay and type of room. (There's technically a three-night minimum, although guests can sometimes be accommodated for shorter stays.) No smoking and no pets, although you can arrange to bring your own horses.

Sawtooth Fish Hatchery

Here, Idaho Department of Fish and Game fisheries biologists are trying to undo the devastating effects of the lower Snake River dams on the Salmon River's anadromous chinook salmon population. It's basically spitting in the wind, but without hatcheries the fish would no doubt disappear entirely. At least it allows the salmon a

THE HIGH COUNTRY

One of the most picturesque lakes in the Sawtooth National Recreation Area is Redfish Lake.

slim chance, until some crazed environmentalist F-16 pilot from Mountain Home Air Force Base makes an unauthorized sortie up the Snake and takes out Ice Harbor, Lower Monumental, Little Goose, and Lower Granite dams with laser-guided missiles.

The small visitor center holds plenty of information about the endangered salmon and explains the hatchery process. Perhaps the most fascinating exhibit is the simple greaseboard at the entrance that lists the number of returning sockeye counted here—usually ranging from zero to a handful (not including the thumb). Several guided tours (45 minutes long) are given each day, and self-guided tours are possible, too. For more information, contact the hatchery at HC 64 Box 9905, Stanley, ID 83278, 208/774-3684.

REDFISH LAKE AREA

The largest lake in the Sawtooths is also the most developed and popular. Here you'll find venerable Redfish Lake Lodge—the region's social hub—as well as several campgrounds, trailheads, and water-sports opportunities. The landscape couldn't be more sublime. Mount Heyburn's

granite walls rise nearly 4,000 feet over the far end of the lake, and views up into the heart of the Sawtooth Wilderness will tempt you to don a backpack and hit the dusty trail.

The lake is named for the sockeye salmon that once spawned in Redfish Lake by the thousands. The fish turn a brilliant orange-red when they spawn, hence the lake's name. Now, thanks to human "progress," these fish are essentially gone here.

Redfish Rock Shelter

Near Highway 75 on the north side of Redfish Lake Road is a rock overhang that archaeologists believe was used by indigenous people for shelter as early as 9,500 years ago. Later, the Tukudeka band of Northern Shoshone—the sheepeaters—also camped here on their bighorn hunting forays into the area. A very short trail begins at a turnout between the north end of Little Redfish Lake and the highway and leads across the creek to the site.

Redfish Lake Visitor Center

The Forest Service's Redfish Lake Visitor Center, 208/774-3376, provides interpretive information about Redfish Lake and the Sawtooth

Wilderness, and hosts guided hikes, campfire programs, slide shows, and children's activities. A short, half-mile interpretive trail here makes a great hike for the little ones. The visitor center is just a short distance from the lakeshore, just east of the lodge.

Day-Use Areas

The Sandy Beach boat ramp and day-use area on the lake's northeast shore attracts crowds of swimmers and sunbathers in summer. The North Shore Picnic Area near the visitor center also features a popular beach. Non-camping visitors are welcome to use the beaches at the Point and Outlet campgrounds. All day-use areas are open 6 A.M.–10 P.M.; no camping.

Horseback Riding

Redfish Lake Corrals, 208/774-3311, about halfway down the road to Redfish Lake, offers trail rides ranging in length from an hour and a half ($35 per person) to a full day ($95 per person, including lunch). The full-day rides head up to one or more of the Sawtooths' beautiful lakes and include lunch along the trail. Anglers are welcome. One special ride includes breakfast at the lodge, a boat ride across the lake, a trail ride to Alpine Lake, box lunch, and dinner back at the lodge that evening ($150 per person).

Day Hikes

Two popular hiking trails begin at the Redfish trailhead parking area, just past the turnoff to the lodge on Redfish Lake Road. The **Fishhook Creek Trail** (Trail 186) leads west several miles upstream along Fishhook Creek; minimal elevation gain. A short distance from the parking area it meets **Redfish Lake Creek Trail** (Trail 101), which heads south to the trailhead at the far end of the lake (5.2 miles) and continues into the Sawtooth Wilderness. Partway along this trail, a turnoff switchbacks up to **Bench Lakes,** four miles from the trailhead, where you'll have a bird's-eye view of Redfish Lake. All these are one-way trails—take them until your stomach growls like a grizzly bear, then eat your picnic lunch and head back the way you came.

You also might consider taking the lodge shuttle across the lake and starting your hike from the trailhead at the other side. The 10.5-mile roundtrip hike from the boat dock up Redfish Lake Creek to **Alpine Lake** (one of at least two lakes in the Sawtooth Wilderness with that unimaginative name) is particularly popular.

Mountain Biking

Trails suitable for mountain biking circle Redfish Lake, but remember, just to the south and west of the lake is the Sawtooth Wilderness, where bicycles are prohibited. Best stay close to water's edge or head north or east in your explorations. Down at the lodge docks, you can rent mountain bikes for $15 a half day, $25 a full day. For more information, call the lodge at 208/774-3536.

Out on the Water

Canoes, kayaks, fishing boats, sailboats, and ski boats—all manner of watercraft ply Redfish Lake. **Boat rentals** of all sorts are available from the lodge; just wander down to the dock and find an attendant. Or sign up for one of the **Lady of the Lake Scenic Tours,** one-hour lake cruises aboard a pontoon boat; $8 adults, $5 kids 6–12. Hikers can get a **boat shuttle** to the trailhead at the far end of the lake. Cost is $5 each way. For more information, call the lodge at 208/774-3536.

Stanley Ranger Station

A couple of miles north of the Redfish Lake turnoff, you'll find the main ranger station serving the Sawtooths and White Clouds. Check in here before you venture into the wilderness. The rangers have up-to-date information on backcountry conditions and can answer any questions about routes or campsites. In winter, a six-kilometer loop **cross-country ski trail** runs through lodgepole pine forest here. For more information, write Stanley Ranger Station—SNRA, Stanley, ID 83278, or call 208/774-3000.

Redfish Lake Lodge

Although its widespread reputation might lead you to expect something along the lines of the

Sun Valley resort, Redfish Lake Lodge, P.O. Box 9, Stanley, ID 83278, 208/774-3536 (for off-season reservations call 208/644-9096), www.redfishlake.com, is instead down-home Idaho all the way. You'll find nothing grand or imposing here. Which isn't to say it isn't nice—it is. But it's more rustic than regal, more folksy than aristocratic. It's like summer camp for the entire family. While Mom's out fishing on the lake, Dad can take the baby on a walk through the woods or a horseback ride along the creek. Meanwhile, the social scene around the lodge and its many neighboring campgrounds will excite even the most jaded and aloof teenager—this place is a natural incubator for adolescent romance.

Rather than one giant, chateau-like lodge, this resort consists of a modest main lodge near the lakeshore and numerous outbuildings. Both private cabins and motel-style rooms are available at wide-ranging rates. A standard motel room is in the $100–150 range, and most cabins are in the $120–175 range, but plainer and fancier digs are available on either end of the spectrum. Two-night stays are required on weekends; three-night stays are the norm for holiday weekends.

Facilities at the lodge include a dining room serving three meals a day, a cozy lounge where locals swap fish stories, a laundromat, stables, general store, gas station, and marina. The resort is open in summer season only, from late May through late September; reservations, taken just after New Year's Day, are highly recommended. Plan on calling January 2 if you want your choice of dates.

Camping

Eight separate USFS campgrounds (fee) with a total of 119 sites dot the Redfish Lake area: **Sockeye, Heyburn, Outlet, Glacier View** and **Point** ring the north end of the big lake; **Mountain View** and **Chinook Bay** are on Little Redfish Lake, closer to the highway; and **Sunny Gulch** is out on the far side of Highway 75. Reservable sites are offered in the Point, Outlet, and Glacier View campgrounds (NRRS, 877/444-6777); Sockeye and Heyburn are first-come, first-served. The Redfish Lake campgrounds start at $11 a night. For more information, call the NRA headquarters at 208/727-5013.

STANLEY AND VICINITY

In 1864, Captain John Stanley led a party of miners into the Valley Creek area. The town that now bears his name started as a supply center for the gold-mining district that eventually dug in here. The little town is the yin to Ketchum's yang. Here you'll find no fancy homes, and no fancy cars; in fact, except for the two highways that intersect here, the streets aren't even paved. Only about 90 people live here year-round, mostly because Stanley's harsh winters are among the coldest you'll encounter anywhere in the state. Recreation fuels the town's economy, which races in summer—when rafters, fisherfolk, campers, and backpackers pass through town on their way into the surrounding wilds—and stays idling in winter with the help of the few snowmobilers and skiers who venture up this way. Besides its decidedly down-home character, Stanley's biggest asset is its incredible view. The Sawtooths rise up like a giant picket fence just south of town; they're so dramatic, it's almost impossible to take your eyes off them.

Stanley Museum

To find out more about the history of Stanley and the Sawtooths, stop by this small museum on the west side of Highway 75, a short distance north of the Highway 21 junction, 208/774-3517. The museum is housed in a 1933 Forest Service ranger's cabin and offers exhibits focusing on pioneer life in the region. It's open Memorial Day to Labor Day daily 11 A.M.–5 P.M. For more information, write the Sawtooth Interpretive and Historical Association, P.O. Box 75, Stanley, ID 83278.

Mountain Biking

Great views of the Sawtooths and White Clouds highlight the 6.5-mile ride down **Nip and Tuck Road.** The old wagon road (FR 633) follows an easy grade west up Nip and Tuck Creek from Lower Stanley, then crests the hill and descends to Stanley Creek, ending at the intersection of Valley Creek Road and Highway 21.

Mountain biking is prohibited in the Sawtooth Wilderness, but east of town the White

Cloud Peaks constitute the Holy Land for area mountain bikers.

Floating the Upper Main Salmon

The stretch of the Salmon just downstream from Stanley is popular for whitewater day trips; between Stanley and Basin Creek it's an easy float suitable even for inner tubes, while between Basin Creek and Torrey's Hole, the river throws two Class III and two Class IV tantrums. The lower segment is usually runnable between April and September. The upper stretch draws most floaters in May and June, as after that it usually gets a tad shallow.

Guide services on the Salmon day stretch include **The River Company,** P.O. Box 2329, Sun Valley, ID 83353, 208/788-5775 or 800/398-0346, www.therivercompany.com, and **White Otter Outdoor Adventures,** P.O. Box 2733, Ketchum, ID 83340, 208/726-4331, www.whiteotter.com. Rates for a full-day guided trip on the river here cost in the $65–90-per-person range, without lunch on the low end, with lunch on the high end.

Floating the Middle Fork and the Lower Main Salmon

Adventurafters looking for something more intense than a day float will want to run the Salmon or its biggest tributary, the Middle Fork, through the Frank Church–River of No Return Wilderness. There you'll have a weeklong thrill ride through big water, big waves, big holes, and big grins, punctuated by prime sunbathing time on sandy beaches and soaks in occasional riverbank hot springs. For more information, see the Frank Church–River of No Return Wilderness Area section, later in this chapter.

Outfitters

Next to the Mountain Village complex you'll find **Riverwear,** Hwy. 21, 208/774-3592, a great outdoor store selling all the supplies you'll need for your raft or pack trip, and renting a variety of gear as well. Sample rentals: bikes, $25 a day; wetsuits, $7–8 a day or around $25 for a Middle Fork trip; kayaks for $20; and rafts from $50 to $95 per day. **River 1 Outdoor Outfitters,** on the east side of Highway 75 just north of the Highway 21 in-

tersection, 208/774-2270, also has a good supply of mountain-related hardware and software.

Sawtooth Rentals, 13 River Rd. in Lower Stanley, 208/774-3409 or 800/284-3185, rents mountain bikes, rafts, kayaks, canoes, innertubes, wetsuits, and other outdoor gear. They also run a motel. **White Otter Outdoor Adventures,** 208/726-4331, rents rafts, kayaks, and related equipment for private trips from its office at the Sunbeam put-in. Figure on paying around $30–40 per day for a kayak, $85–105 for a raft.

Flightseeing and Air Taxi Service

Flying services operating out of Stanley's little airport include **Stanley Air Taxi,** 208/774-2276 or 800/225-2236; and **McCall & Wilderness Air,** 208/774-2221 or 800/992-6559. Either one can take you up to see the sights or fly you into the remote backcountry lodge of your choice. They also fly rafters to Indian Creek on the Middle Fork—the put-in of choice when the water starts to get too low at Boundary Creek.

Events

Stanley's biggest whoop-de-do is the **Sawtooth Mountain Mamas Arts and Crafts Fair** held the third weekend in July. This down-home celebration is enjoyed by locals and visitors alike. You'll find scores of artisans, old-time fiddlers, a barbecue, and a flapjacks breakfast. To find out more about the festival, call the Stanley/Sawtooth Chamber of Commerce at 208/774-3411.

Accommodations

$50–100: Mountain Village Resort, at the junction of Hwys. 21 and 75, P.O. Box 150, Stanley, ID 83278, 208/774-3661 or 800/843-5475, is the most obvious, well-established lodging in town. Rooms are modern rather than rustic, the adjacent dining room is convenient but nothing to write home about, and the lounge often presents live entertainment. The motel's biggest plus is probably the natural hot springs spa on site. Kitchenette suites available.

Heading west on Highway 21 from the big junction, you'll pass a string of motels lining the highway. The motels on the north side front Valley Creek and have a nicer ambience than those on the south side.

Valley Creek Motel, P.O. Box 302, Stanley, ID 83278, 208/774-3606, sits on high ground, resulting in some of the best views in town. All rooms have two queen beds, private baths, color TVs with HBO, and refrigerators. Valley Creek also offers basic RV sites for $23 a day with water, power, and sewer hookups.

Heading down Highway 75 to Lower Stanley, the delightful **Salmon River Lodge,** P.O. Box 272, Stanley, ID 83278, 208/774-3422, sits off by itself on a spacious spread across the river from Highway 75. Turn in and cross the creaky old bridge over the Salmon. The cabins face the Sawtooths, and the river flows right past; anglers could drop a line practically off their cabin porch. The wide-open surroundings provide an expansive feel, in contrast to the sometimes densely packed and claustrophobic cabin complexes in some other parts of town. Kitchenettes available. (Note: This establishment is not to be confused with the backcountry lodge of the same name farther down the main Salmon River near Corn Creek.)

Among the several accommodations in Lower Stanley, **Gunter's Salmon River Cabins,** 208/774-2290 or 888/574-2290, P.O. Box 91, Stanley, ID 83278, and **Redwood Motel,** P.O. Box 55, Stanley, ID 83278, 208/774-3531, offer nice rooms right on the river. Both establishments are closed in winter.

Food

The **Kasino Club,** 21 Ace of Diamonds St., 208/774-3516, is regarded as the finest of dining in Stanley proper. The kitchen specializes in prime rib and also offers a salad bar and a variety of meats, seafood, and pastas. Dinners range $12 and up, and several microbrews are available. You could also take a drive down to **Redfish Lake Lodge,** 208/774-3536, where you'll find a real dining room in the rustic yet plush lodge; dinner entrées run $7–22. Breakfast ($4–8) and lunch ($8–10) are available, too. It's open Memorial Day through the end of September.

Pizza is available downtown at **Papa Brunee's Pizza & Deli and Laundromat,** 208/774-2536, where you can bet they know how to re-

move those pesky pepperoni stains (soak them in beer first).

The **Mountain Village Restaurant and Lounge,** Hwys. 21 and 75, 208/774-3317, may be the easiest to find and the most modern dining establishment in town, but I've eaten there several times and always found the food to be ho-hum at best.

Finally, if you just want a nice peaceful place to caffeinate yourself, head for **River 1 Outdoor Outfitters,** 208/774-2270, on the Salmon River just downstream from the junction of Hwys. 21 and 75. An espresso bar inside will sell you the kind mud, which you can then take out to the store's back deck overlooking the river—the best deck in town.

Nightlife

The best nightlife in town? I'm forever biased on this subject ever since the night I walked into the **Rod & Gun Club Saloon** just in time for a bachelorette party. The gorgeous, already-well-oiled bride-to-be dragged me up on the dance floor and we had a fantastic time . . . until the guy in the gorilla suit cut in and I had to dance with him.

In any case, there's no point in going anywhere else when the sun goes down. The Rod & Gun Club is toward the west end of Ace of Diamonds St., 208/774-9920. Live bands are de rigueur in summer. And, uh, Nicole—if it didn't work out, give me a call.

Information

The **Stanley-Sawtooth Chamber of Commerce,** in the community building on Highway 21, can be reached at P.O. Box 8, Stanley, ID 83278, 800/878-7950 (information packet requests only) or 208/774-3411, www.stanleycc.org. It's generally open around 10 A.M.–6 P.M. mid-May through September.

HIGHWAY 21 UP VALLEY CREEK

Spectacular mountain vistas and vast meadows awash in wildflowers combine to make this stretch of pavement one of the most scenic drives in Idaho. Several angler access roads branch off the highway and lead down to meandering

Valley Creek, while other spur roads lead south off the highway to campgrounds at the foot of the Sawtooths.

Day Hike to Sawtooth Lake

A photographer's favorite, Sawtooth Lake enjoys the sheer granite face of 10,190-foot Mt. Regan as a backdrop. The moderately strenuous five-mile trail to get there takes you up and up past dramatic cliffs, a tall graceful waterfall, and gemlike Alpine Lake. Sawtooth Lake itself is one of the largest lakes in the Sawtooth Wilderness. Snow lingers in these heights until well into summer; don't be surprised to see miniature icebergs drifting across the lake even in July or August. On the hike back down, you'll get glimpses of Stanley on the valley floor below.

To reach the trailhead, take Iron Creek Road off Highway 21, three miles west of Stanley. The trailhead is at the end of the road. Also at the trailhead you'll find **Iron Creek Campground** (12 sites, fee).

Stanley Lake

Boating, fishing, and family camping are the prime pastimes at Stanley Lake, 2.5 miles off the highway on Stanley Lake Road (five miles west of town). Three separate fee campgrounds line the lake's north shore: **Inlet** (14 sites), **Lakeview** (six sites), and **Stanley Lake** (19 sites). It's a beautiful spot offering access into the Sawtooth Wilderness along Stanley Creek. But it's also a dusty, relatively noisy, heavily used area best suited for those who don't like to be too far removed from their fellow human beings. You'll find a boat ramp adjacent to Inlet Campground; water-skiing is permitted on the lake 10 A.M.–6 P.M.

A challenging, 12.5-mile **mountain-biking** trail loops from here north around Elk Mountain to Elk Meadows and back. Stay on Stanley Lake Road past the lake; turn off onto Trail 629, which leads to Elk Meadows and eventually intersects FR 630; return to the lake on FR 630. Elk Meadows is a good spot for wildlife-watching.

Nordic Skiing

In winter, a short, four-kilometer loop is set at **Park Creek** turnout, about three miles northeast of Stanley Lake Road on Highway 21. The trail winds through open meadows and is rated easy to intermediate. It's groomed only periodically.

RV Park

Elk Mountain R.V. Resort and Cafe, P.O. Box 115, Stanley, ID 83278, 208/774-2202, lies four

Sawtooth Lake

miles west of Stanley. Its RV sites rent for $20 a night with full hookups; $15 for tent sites. The small park is in a nice wooded spot away from whatever hustle and bustle you might find in town. Amenities include the usual showers and laundry, and the café is an excellent place for breakfast. The park is open May to mid-October.

To the Middle Fork

To reach the put-in for a raft trip down the Middle Fork of the Salmon, continue out of the NRA and around Cape Horn. Here the Sawtooths at last permit a route around them; the highway makes a lazy 120-degree turn and heads southwest toward Boise. About four miles after rounding the Horn, FR 082 branches off to the west to Boundary Creek and the put-in point, about 18 miles of dirt road away.

Camping and Forest Service Rental

Besides the campgrounds at Stanley Lake, along Highway 21 within the NRA you'll also find reservable USFS campgrounds at **Elk Creek** (two sites, fee), **Sheep Trail** (three sites, fee), and **Trap Creek** (three sites, fee). All are open June 30–Sept. 15.

Just outside the NRA Boundary, Challis National Forest offers its **Cape Horn Guard Station** for rent Dec. 1–April 30. The cabin has electricity but no water, sleeps four, and rents for $25 a night. It's about halfway between the NRA boundary and the Frank Church Wilderness boundary, up FR 203, and offers views of the Sawtooths. For reservations or information, contact the **Yankee Fork Ranger District,** HC 67 Box 650, Hwy. 75, Clayton, ID 83227, 208/838-2201.

HIGHWAY 75 TOWARD SUNBEAM

Heading first north then east out of Stanley, Highway 75 slow-dances with the Salmon River, hugging its every curve as the two glide downstream in unison. It must be a tango they hear, as things get rather steamy—you'll find a string of hot springs along the riverbank in this stretch. From west to east, look for **Elkhorn Hot Springs,** seven-tenths of a mile east of mile marker 192; **Mormon Bend Hot Spring,** 350 yards downstream from Elkhorn (at mile marker 193) on the far side of the river; **Basin Creek Campground Hot Spring,** next to the campground seven miles east of Stanley; and **Kem Hot Springs,** seven-tenths of a mile east of mile marker 197. As all are close to the highway, you won't find bares among the wildlife here.

For panoramic views of Salmon River Canyon and the Sawtooths, make the 12-mile roundtrip **day hike** up to **Lookout Mountain.** You'll climb 2,600 feet to the lookout on the peak, elevation 9,954 feet. Bear left at each of two forks along the way. The trailhead is at the end of Rough Creek Road (FR 626), which turns off Highway 75 10 miles from Stanley.

Between Stanley and Sunbeam on Highway 75, USFS **campgrounds** on the Salmon River include Salmon River (32 sites), Riverside (18 sites), Mormon Bend (17 sites), and Basin Creek (13 sites). All are open June 15–Sept. 15, and all charge a fee.

SAWTOOTH WILDERNESS

Though it's nowhere near the largest wilderness area in Idaho, the 217,000-acre Sawtooth Wilderness is a prime contender for the grandest. Three major Idaho rivers get their start here in snowy tarns beneath granite spires: the South Fork Payette River drains the northwest third of the wilderness; the North and Middle Forks of the Boise River drain the southwest third; and the mighty Salmon is born of the waters flowing off the east side of the wilderness.

Rock climbers have a field day here, on the big-wall granite faces of Warbonnet Peak, Elephant's Perch, and the Finger of Fate, among others. Mountaineers come to bag more than a dozen summits rising over 10,000 feet; the tallest is 10,751-foot Thompson Peak. Hikers and horsepackers are content to keep their feet on the 300 miles of trails lacing the preserve—trails that lead the backcountry adventurer through awesome glacier-carved valleys, past nearly 200 trout-filled alpine lakes and meadows lush with summer wildflowers.

Access Guide

Following is a list of primary access points into the Sawtooth Wilderness, starting at the northern tip of the wilderness and proceeding clockwise:

- **Stanley Lake** trailhead, on Stanley Lake Road (FR 455), six miles west of Stanley on Highway 21; access along western edge of wilderness into Sawtooth Lake and Baron Creek drainage
- **Iron Creek** trailhead, on Iron Creek Road (FR 619), three miles west of Stanley on Highway 21; access across eastern boundary of wilderness into Sawtooth Lake and Baron Creek drainage
- **Redfish Lake** trailheads, at north or south sides of lake, on Redfish Lake Road, five miles south of Stanley on Highway 75; access into heart of wilderness up Redfish Lake Creek, and access to rock climbing on Mt. Heyburn, Grand Mogul, and Elephant's Perch
- **Hell Roaring Creek** trailhead, on FR 315 off Decker Flat Road (FR 210), 17 miles south of Stanley off Highway 75; access to Hell Roaring Lake, Finger of Fate, the Arrowhead, Imogene Lake
- **Petit Lake** trailhead, on Petit Lake Road (FR 208), 20 miles south of Stanley on Highway 75; access to Petit-Toxaway Loop (prime backpacking trail) and on into South Fork Payette River drainage
- **Atlanta** trailhead, at end of Middle Fork Boise River Road (FR 268), about 60 miles northeast of Highway 21 (turn off Highway 21 at Lucky Peak Reservoir); access up Middle Fork Boise River drainage into southern end of wilderness
- **Grandjean** trailhead, on FR 524, about eight miles east of Highway 21 (turn off Highway 21 about 45 miles west of Stanley or 89 miles northeast of Boise); access up either Baron Creek drainage or South Fork Payette River drainage.

Horsepacking and Llama Trekking

Mystic Saddle Ranch, Fisher Creek Road, Stanley, ID 83278, 208/774-3591 or 888/722-5432 (or, mid-October to mid-May: P.O. Box 736, Challis, ID 83226, 208/879-5071 or 888/722-

5432), offers horsepack trips into the wilderness, from day trips to weeklong sojourns. **Sawtooth Wilderness Outfitters,** P.O. Box 81, Garden Valley, ID 83622, 208/259-3408 (summer) or 208/462-3416 (offseason), runs horsepack trips out of Grandjean on the west side of the wilderness. The fishing trips are especially popular, but the company will customize a trip to suit your particular interests.

Llama treks are the specialty of **Venture Outdoors,** P.O. Box 2251, Hailey, ID 83333, 800/528-LAMA (800/528-5262) or 208/788-5049. No, the sure-footed South American beasts won't carry you, but they will carry your gear, leaving you to happily lightfoot it up and down the steep Sawtooth terrain. Figure on paying just under $200 per person per day for a multiday trek.

Mountaineering Guides

The folks at **Sawtooth Mountain Guides,** P.O. Box 18, Stanley, ID 83278, 208/774-3324, know every nook and cranny in the Sawtooths. Rock climbing and mountaineering in summer, hut-to-hut ski touring in winter—whatever your pleasure, they'll show you the way. The company has been in business for almost 25 years and regularly leads ascents of Mounts Heyburn, Thompson, Williams, and Warbonnet, the Finger of Fate, and the Elephant's Perch. Rates for guided summer trekking and climbing run $300 a day for one person, or $325 a day for multiday trips. Larger groups pay less per person. Guided hut skiing is available in winter at similar rates. Experienced backcountry skiers can rent a hut but will need to hire a guide the first time out. The huts rent for $30 per person per night, with an eight-person minimum.

Information

For more information about the Sawtooth Wilderness, contact the **Sawtooth NRA Headquarters,** Star Route, Ketchum, ID 83340, 208/727-5013.

WHITE CLOUD PEAKS

From a distance, you might have to squint pretty hard to distinguish the white limestone peaks here from summer clouds, hence the name. Unlike the

Sawtooths on the other side of Highway 75, the White Clouds aren't within a designated wilderness area, so mountain bikes are permitted here. And while the Sawtooths top out at about 10,700 feet, the White Clouds' tallest peaks tower more than a thousand feet higher. The highest peak in the range, Castle Peak, is a summit highly coveted by mountaineers; its 11,815-foot summit offers no easy route to the top.

Before Congress established the NRA in 1972, mining companies were eyeing the molybdenum deposits in the White Clouds; a large open-pit mine was proposed in the 1960s. Under the rules regulating the NRA, all lands within its boundaries are now closed to new mining claims. Pre-1972 claims can still be worked, however, provided they don't infringe on the area's prime mission as a recreational haven. Thankfully, all old claims are currently dormant, and there's now a proposal to make the Boulder-White Clouds a designated wilderness area.

The White Clouds receive less use than the Sawtooths. Those adventurers taking the time to seek out this pristine high country will find steep granite galore, and water, water everywhere—more than 125 alpine lakes set the range aglimmer in the summer sun. The lakes tend to be smaller than their Sawtooth counterparts, but no less beautiful. Elk, deer, bighorn sheep, and mountain goats inhabit the lofty realm, keeping a sharp eye out for members of the area's small cougar population. Coyotes, foxes, beavers, badgers, and black bears add to the White Clouds' mix of resident wildlife.

Access Guide

Primary access routes are from the west, up Pole Creek/Germania Creek Road (FR 197) and Fourth of July Creek Road (FR 209); from the north, up Slate Creek Road (FR 666), off Highway 75 about six miles west of Clayton Ranger Station; and from the northeast, up the East Fork Salmon River Road (FR 120), off Highway 75 about five miles east of Clayton.

Adventurers taking the time to seek out the pristine White Cloud high country will find steep granite galore, and water, water everywhere— more than 125 alpine lakes set the range aglimmer in the summer sun.

Hiking

The west side's Fourth of July Road will take you from Highway 75 some 10 miles east into the heights before you'll have to park the LeSabre and continue on foot. From there, it's about a mile and a half up Trail 109 to **Fourth of July Lake** and a mile farther to **Washington Lake.** Elevation gain is minimal. Both lakes are only a couple of crowflapping miles to Castle Peak, the monarch of the White Clouds.

On the north side, six miles up Slate Creek Road, you'll come to a four-way intersection. Turn left and go a short distance to the trailhead for the **Crater Lake** trail. The trail follows Livingston Creek four miles and some 2,500 vertical feet up to the lake, from which you'll have views of the striking **Chinese Wall.**

The **Boulder Chain Lakes** attract a healthy share of the backpacking visitors to the range. The trail winds along the shores of eight lakes that lie at elevations averaging around 9,000 feet. Access is via the Little Boulder Creek trailhead, about 22 miles in on the East Fork Salmon Road. From there, Trail 682 ascends Little Boulder Creek about seven miles to the intersection of Trail 047. Turn right there and continue another mile and a half to the first of the lakes.

Mountain Biking

Since all the trails in the area are open to mountain bikes, you can just get yourself a map and take off exploring. The prime access points for mountain bikers are **Fourth of July Creek Road** (FR 209), which leads east up into the White Clouds from Highway 75; **Germania Creek Road** (FR 197), which takes off from Pole Creek/Valley Road (FR 194, off Highway 75 near Sawtooth City); and **East Fork Salmon River Road,** which heads south off Salmon River Road east of Clayton.

A couple of rides in the western foothills are listed under Sawtooth Valley, earlier.

Mountaineering

The White Cloud Peaks aren't known for technical rock climbing; the predominant loose, friable limestone is a climber's nightmare. Still, many peak-baggers can't resist the allure of **Castle Peak,** elevation 11,815 feet, highest summit in the range. All the routes to the summit are Class 3. Access is from Chamberlain Basin, reached via either Little Boulder Creek (Trails 682, 047, and 110) or Germania and Chamberlain Creeks (Trails 111 and 110). The approach to the northside routes is via a cross-country trail from near the junction of the Wickiup Creek and Little Boulder Creek Trails (Trails 684 and 047).

Hot Springs

On the southeast side of the White Clouds, at the end of East Fork Salmon River Road, you'll find a couple of hot springs where you can soak in secluded privacy. **West Pass Hot Spring,** on a hillside above West Pass Creek, offers a pair of tubs with great views. Coming in on the East Fork Road, cross West Pass Creek (29 miles south of Highway 75) and almost immediately bear left on a road that climbs the hillside. Park on the flat and find the short trail past an old mine to the tubs. **Bowery Hot Spring** is in the same area. Continue straight up the East Fork at the West Pass Creek junction to the trailhead. Hike 100 yards up the road toward Bowery guard station, and at the bridge continue a short distance upstream to the spring.

Backcountry Guides

Guides available for summer horse- and backpack trips into the White Clouds include **Mystic Saddle Ranch,** 208/774-3591 or 888/722-5432 (mid-October to mid-May, 208/879-5071 or 888/722-5432); **Pioneer Mountain Outfitters,** 208/774-3737; and **White Cloud Outfitters,** P.O. Box 217, Challis, ID 83226, 208/879-4574. The going rate is around $150–200 a day per person, all-inclusive.

Information

To find out more about the White Clouds, contact the **Sawtooth NRA Headquarters,** Star Route, Ketchum, ID 83340, 208/727-5013 or 208/727-5000. The Idaho Conservation League's website at www.wildidaho.org has updates on efforts to protect the White Clouds with wilderness designation.

FRANK CHURCH–RIVER OF NO RETURN WILDERNESS AREA

Access to this area is relatively easy, which may or may not be a positive attribute, depending on your perspective. When Congress established the wilderness, rather than just drawing a big box for a boundary and letting all the preexisting roads within it grow over, it instead grandfathered out of the wilderness all existing mining and logging roads. As a result, even in the deepest heart of the Frank Church, you're never too far from one of these "cherry-stemmed" roads. Though purists consider this an unwanted intrusion, the roads do permit you to drive to a plethora of trailheads on all sides of the area.

For general information on the Frank Church wilderness, contact the **Salmon-Challis National Forests Supervisor's Office,** 50 Hwy. 93 S., Salmon, ID 83467, 208/756-5100.

Wilderness Trails

Backpackers with a map will be like kids in a candy store here—facing an astounding number of trails to explore. And backpackers entering the heart of the wilderness will be certain to encounter solitude in vast doses; there's an awful lot of land to get lost in out here. Favorite destinations are the Bighorn Crags—a magnificent area of jagged spires and alpine lakes on the east side of the wilderness—and the two big rivers, each of which offers a trail running alongside much of its length. Hot springs abound alongside those rivers and elsewhere in the wilderness, allowing the enterprising backpacker to do a multiday spring-to-spring trip and have a hot soak every night. Horsepackers also enjoy the wilderness. Mountain bikes are not allowed. A compromise that aided passage of the bill creating the Frank Church makes one exception to the no-mechanized-vehicles rule; jetboats are permitted on the main Salmon. Please refer to the accompanying map for common trailheads into the wilderness.

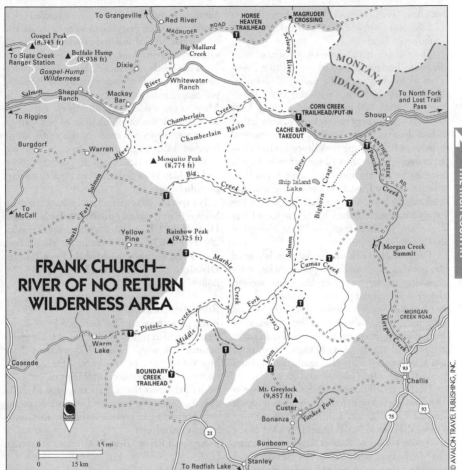

FRANK CHURCH–
RIVER OF NO RETURN
WILDERNESS AREA

© AVALON TRAVEL PUBLISHING, INC.

Whitewater Rafting

When the Lewis and Clark expedition came over Lemhi Pass looking for a route to the sea, they intended to follow the Lemhi River down to the **Salmon River,** then float the Salmon to the Columbia. At camp in the Lemhi Valley, the local Shoshone told Captain Clark that the Salmon River Canyon was impassable, but Clark figured he'd go see for himself. Reaching a point 14 miles downstream from today's town of North Fork, Clark climbed high up the side of the canyon for a better view. From this high vantage point, he saw Pine Creek Rapids (Class III-IV) churning away downstream, and nothing but a deep gorge with steep, rocky walls leading all the way to the horizon. Clark immediately opted for Plan B, and the expedition made a long detour to the north rather than attempt a descent of the Salmon. Later pioneers managed to float some sections of the upper Salmon, but paddling back upstream against the swift current was impossible; hence the river's nickname and the second segment of the wilderness name, the "river of no return." (The first half of the moniker, "Frank Church," comes from the late U.S. Senator from Idaho, a lifelong champion of Idaho's wild lands.)

The Salmon drains some 14,000 square miles and flows undammed for its entire 420 miles—from its headwaters in the southern Sawtooth Valley to its confluence with the Snake River. For more than 180 miles of its length, it flows through a deep gorge rising over a mile on either side of the river. From North Fork to the normal takeout at Riggins, the river drops 1,910 feet—an average of more than 12 feet per mile. Rapids on the river for the most part range Class II to III+, although a few Class IVs—Pine Creek, Big Mallard, Elkhorn, Vinegar—challenge even the experts, and many of the Class IIIs go Class IV in high water. Permits are required June 20–Sept. 7 and are drawn by lottery.

The **Middle Fork of the Salmon** is one of the world's greatest and most popular whitewater trips, drawing rafters and kayakers from around the globe. From the put-in at Boundary Creek, northwest of Stanley, the river flows 100 wet and wild miles through a wilderness little tarnished by man. Bighorn sheep, black bear, mountain goats, salmon and steelhead, bald eagles, and, once again, wolves—the list of magnificent creatures inhabiting this land goes on and on.

The river itself puts up a premier challenge at any flow level. More than 30 significant rapids line the route, almost a third of them running Class IV. From Velvet Falls on Day One to the wild roller coaster of Rubber Rapids on Day Six, the Middle Fork rarely lets up. Another delight of the river is the abundance of hot springs along its banks, making great places for midday breaks or long, stargazing soaks at day's end.

Historical sites along the way include hermit cabins, Native American pictographs, and sites associated with the Sheepeater Campaign of 1879.

Permits are required year-round and are drawn by lottery for trips between June 1 and Sept. 3. The odds of getting a summer permit are about 26-to-1.

Of the two, the Middle Fork is a more technical river, particularly in its narrow upper reaches. The Main Salmon has the big water—the biggest waves, the biggest holes, the most adrenaline-inducing power. The Middle Fork is a wilderness river. Few roads lead to its banks, and only a handful of isolated ranches provide reminders of civilization. The Main also flows past just a few roads and ranches; however, its wilderness quality is sullied somewhat by the permitted presence of jetboats. You'll see more people on the Main, more wildlife on the Middle Fork. The Middle Fork has the lion's share of hot springs, while the Main has most of the wide, sandy beaches. Both rivers offer a lot of history: old mining claims, Indian camps, pioneer cabins, and the like. Trips generally last three to six days on either river.

For specific information on boating the main Salmon River, contact the **North Fork Ranger District**, P.O. Box 180, North Fork, ID 83466, 208/865-2383. For information on Middle Fork float trips, contact the **Middle Fork Ranger District**, P.O. Box 750, Challis, ID 83226, 208/879-4101.

River Guides

If you go with an outfitter (which is by all means recommended unless you've rafted these rivers before), you won't have to worry about those high odds in the permit lottery. Dozens upon dozens of guide services offer trips on either or both of the two rivers. Expect to pay $1,200–1,700 per person for an all-inclusive six-day trip. Following is a quick and by no means exhaustive rundown.

Aggipah River Trips, P.O. Box 425, Salmon, ID 83467, 208/756-4167

ARTA, 24000 Casa Loma Rd., Groveland, CA 95321, 209/962-7873 or 800/323-2782

Echo: The Wilderness Company, 6529 Telegraph Ave., Oakland, CA 94609-1113, 510/652-1600 or 800/652-3246

Far and Away Adventures, P.O. Box 54, Sun Valley, ID 83353, 208/726-8888 or 800/232-8588

Hughes River Expeditions, P.O. Box 217, Cambridge, ID 83610, 208/257-3477 or 800/262-1882

Idaho River Journeys, P.O. Box 1149, Point Reyes, CA 94956, 415/663-8300 or 800/323-4234

Mackay Wilderness River Trips, 4115 W. Wright, Boise, ID 83705, 208/344-1881 or 800/635-5336

Middle Fork River Expeditions, P.O. Box 199, Stanley, ID 83278, 208/774-3659 or 800/801-5146

Middle Fork River Tours, P.O. Box 2222, Hailey, ID 83333, 208/788-6545 or 800/445-9738

Middle Fork Wilderness Outfitters, P.O. Box 575, Ketchum, ID 83340, 208/726-5999 or 800/726-0575

North Fork Guides, P.O. Box 24, North Fork, ID 83466, 208/865-2534 or 800/259-6866

Outdoor Adventures, 306 Broadway, Salmon, ID 83467, 208/756-6102

River Odysseys West (ROW), P.O. Box 579-G, Coeur d'Alene, ID 83816, 208/765-0841 or 800/451-6034

Salmon River Outfitters, P.O. Box 1006, McCall, ID 83638, 208/634-4426

Sevy Guide Service, Inc., P.O. Box 24, Stanley, ID 83278, 208/774-2200

Silver Cloud Outfitters, P.O. Box 1006, Salmon, ID 83467, 877/756-6215

Solitude River Trips, P.O. Box 907, Merlin, OR 97532, 541/476-1875, 800/396-1776, or 208/756-6078 (summer)

Triangle C Ranch, P.O. Box 69, Stanley, ID 83278, 208/774-2266

Warren River Expeditions, P.O. Box 1375, Salmon, ID 83467, 208/756-6387 or 800/765-0421

Wilderness River Outfitters, P.O. Box 72, Lemhi, ID 83465, 208/756-3959 or 800/252-6581

For another extensive list of outfitters, see the Idaho Outfitters & Guides Association website at www.ioga.org. Or for one-stop shopping, check out the **Idaho Whitewater Connection,** 208/733-1921, www.idahorafting.com, a sort of clearinghouse for river trips on both the Main Salmon and Middle Fork, as well as the Snake through Hells Canyon and the Selway.

Rafter Shuttle Service

Independent rafters in need of logistical help can contact **River Shuttles,** P.O. Box 301, Stanley, ID 83278, 800/831-8942. They can drop you off or pick you up—in your vehicle or theirs—at the beginning or end of your paddling adventure. Middle Fork rafters can get their vehicle shuttled from Boundary Creek to Cache Bar for $200; those heading down the main Salmon can get a Corn Creek to Vinegar Creek shuttle for $310. The company, in business since 1963, was formerly known as River Rat Express.

Yankee Fork Country

The Yankee Fork River flows into the Salmon River between the Frank Church–River of No Return Wilderness on the north and Highway 75 on the south. Around the river lies one of Idaho's major historic mining districts, the Land of the Yankee Fork Historic Area. Prospectors first began exploring the area in the 1860s, and mining of one sort or another has been taking place ever since.

SUNBEAM
Sunbeam Hot Springs

These hot springs, emerging from the north bank of the Salmon River, first attracted tourists in

1824. Alexander Ross's fur-trapping party soaked the fall chill out of their bones on Oct. 1 of that year. In 1937, the CCC built a bathhouse on the site. The tubs are long gone, but you can still make your way down the bank to crude pools along the river.

Sunbeam Dam

Another interesting sight nearby provides a useful precedent for those who would save the endangered salmon. In 1910, the Sunbeam Consolidated Gold Mines Company built Sunbeam Dam on the Salmon River to supply hydroelectric power to its mine and mill. The Yankee Fork area had already been logged out by that time, making it too costly for the company to run its existing steam-powered mill.

The dam's power plant operated less than a year before the company went bankrupt; even cheap hydropower couldn't compensate for the poor-quality ore the company was mining. The mill shut down and the dam was left behind, blocking salmon migration up the river. Around 1934, *the dam was intentionally breached with dynamite* to give the salmon their run back.

Granted, the Sunbeam Dam is minuscule in size compared to the monsters on the Columbia. But the idea of purposely breaching a dam to save a fish apparently seemed reasonable in the 1930s and, in fact, was actually carried out. Why do so many people find this solution to the salmon problem so unthinkable today?

Sunbeam Village Services

Up the hill from the river, at the bottom of Yankee Fork Road to Bonanza and Custer, you'll find Sunbeam Village, Yankee Fork Rd., Stanley, ID 83278, 208/838-2211 in summer or 602/979-8332 in winter. The village offers a store, motel, RV park, and café. Cabins are available (most $60–125), while shaded RV sites with water, sewer, and electric hookups go for $18 a night; weekly rates available. Also here is the Sunbeam office of **White Otter Outdoor Adventures,** 208/838-2406, where you can arrange a raft trip down the Salmon.

CUSTER MOTORWAY ADVENTURE ROAD

When gold was discovered on the Yankee Fork, the boomtowns of Bonanza and Custer sprang to life. The miners needed equipment and supplies to work their claims, and the nearest supply center was at Challis. Entrepreneur Alex Toponce saw a moneymaking opportunity. He won a charter from the Territorial Legislature for the construction of a toll road between Challis and Bonanza. It was completed in 1879, and was the sole freight route into the Yankee Fork mines for a decade. In 1933, the road was restored by the CCC and today is known as the Custer Motorway Adventure Road. It's called an Adventure

Road because it would be an unpleasant adventure to attempt the unpaved route with a trailer or large RV. Also note that the road is subject to damage from spring runoff and is sometimes closed between Challis and Custer.

Since the organization of this chapter anticipates that you'll be heading from Stanley to Salmon, the sights along the Motorway are listed below from southwest (Sunbeam) to northeast (Challis). If you're going the other way, turn the book upside down.

Bonanza

Turning north off Highway 75 at Sunbeam—onto Yankee Fork Road (FR 013)—you'll soon come to Bonanza, the first of the Yankee Fork boomtowns. It was founded in 1877 and by 1881 had a population of 600. Fires in 1889 and 1897 gutted most of the town, and most of the townsfolk moved to Custer as a result.

Today the site is a ghost town, less of a developed tourist area than Custer. A CCC-built Forest Service work camp watches over the slowly decaying miners' shacks, their tin roofs banging dirgelike in the wind. A short, dusty spur road (FR 074) leads—appropriately enough—to two separate cemeteries. The first, **Bonanza Cemetery,** is the more typical of the two, holding the graves of a townful of souls who lived and died pursuing their glittering dreams. Among their causes of death: avalanche, black lung, blood poisoning, gunshot wound, heart attack, mining accident, pneumonia, scarlet fever, spinal meningitis, suicide, and typhoid fever.

Farther down the spur is **Boothill Cemetery,** where just three old wooden markers surrounded by a fence record the final resting places of Lizzie King and her two husbands. Husband number one, Richard King, came to Bonanza with Lizzie in 1878. He was subsequently shot and killed in an argument and buried here. Lizzie moved to Butte, Montana, where she met prospector Bob Hawthorne. The two ended up back in Bonanza—running the Yankee Fork Dance Hall and Saloon—and got married in 1880. Hawthorne told everyone in town that he was filthy rich and had a large estate in England. When the truth came out that he was actually dirt poor, he apparently couldn't bear the humiliation brought on by the exposure of his deceit. He shot and killed Lizzie, then turned the gun on himself. Both Lizzie and Bob were buried at Boothill next to Rich King, who no doubt would have killed Bob himself if they both weren't already dead.

Yankee Fork Gold Dredge

Let's see if I've got this straight. A private company finds gold lying deep in the gravel beneath the Yankee Fork—a beautiful mountain stream and a publicly owned natural resource. The company ships in a huge floating dredge that starts at one end of the river and slowly moves toward the other. As it rolls merrily along—24 hours a day, 365 days a year—the monstrous contraption digs out the whole riverbed from beneath the bow, pulls the gold from more than six million cubic yards of gravel, and spews the remainder out its back end to form huge ugly tailings piles. The machine reaps more than a million dollars in gold and silver for its owners—including Idaho billionaire J. R. Simplot and his cronies—and leaves the river lifeless in its wake. When it reaches the end of its journey 13 years later, when there's no more gold and no more river to ruin, the company just ups and leaves its implement of destruction behind, like some kind of space junk on the moon. It also leaves the miles of destroyed river and the miles of tailings piles in place, without so much as a token cleanup effort. Then it "donates" the dredge to the Forest Service, no doubt taking a tax writeoff on it as a "charitable contribution." Restoration of the devastated Yankee Fork is left to future generations and middle-class taxpayers. The dredge, meanwhile, is turned into a "museum" and treated as some holy icon, with gloating volunteers charging admission to tour it. Only in America.

Custer

Established two years after Bonanza, Custer went on to become the more important of the two gold-rush towns. It reached its peak population of 600 in 1896, at which time it held the huge General Custer stamp mill, the Nevada Hotel, the Miner's Union Hall, a cathouse, a brewery, and a sizeable Chinatown. It even had its own newspaper, *The Yankee Fork Herald,* which on April 28, 1880, reported: "There will be no religious services tomorrow; first, because there is no minister, and secondly, there is no church. But there will be several poker games running."

The mines all played out by 1911, and the town disappeared shortly thereafter. Today it's a resurrected boomtown full of Nikons and out-of-state license plates. A museum (summers only) tells the story of the town's heyday, and a self-guided walking tour leads visitors past mining-equipment detritus and other points of interest.

To Challis

Continuing northeast from Custer, the historic sites along the route get fewer and farther between. You'll pass the sites of several waystations where meals, refreshments, and fresh horses were available, and see the remains of the toll station where Toponce & Co. collected the tolls. The rate for a wagon and team was $4. The station operated about a decade, 1879-89. A couple miles later, the road passes the USFS **Mill Creek Campground.** Its eight fee sites have potable water; open June–Sept.

A mile or so farther, FR 080 turns off to the north and leads three miles to **Mosquito Flat Reservoir,** a popular fishing hole—rainbow trout, primarily—with a boat ramp and available drinking water. Just north of the reservoir is the free, nine-site **Mosquito Flat Campground.**

Wilderness Lodge

Deep in the heart of the wilderness, accessible by plane or by car (20 miles past the Yankee Fork Gold Dredge up Loon Creek Road, off Yankee Fork Road) is **Diamond D Ranch,** P.O. Box 1555, Boise, ID 83701 (winter) or P.O. Box 35, Stanley, ID 83278 (summer), 208/336-9772 or 800/222-1269, www.diamonddranch-idaho.com. The ranch offers horseback riding, fishing in a private lake or in the nearby wilderness lakes, boating, a swimming pool, hot tub, two saunas, and more. Both lodge rooms and modern cabins are available at weekly rates of $1,250 adults, $1,050 youth ages 13–18, $850 children ages 12 and under for the cabins, or

THE HIGH COUNTRY

$1,050/895/750, respectively, for the lodge rooms. Rates include three meals a day and all activities. Stays of less than a week may be possible by advance arrangement. The ranch operates early June to mid-October.

CHALLIS

Alvah P. Challis surveyed and platted Challis as a mining and ranching supply town in 1876. Now it's the Custer County seat, but it's still a mining and ranching town. At the Forest Service office on Highway 93, history buffs can pick up a guide to the town's historic structures, including pioneer houses, the old jail, and the old schoolhouse—all constructed between 1877 and 1914. The town claims to harbor the state's largest collection of pre-1900 log homes.

Land of the Yankee Fork Interpretive Center

Travelers heading from Salmon toward Stanley are best poised to take advantage of this modern and informative facility before starting out on the Custer Motorway over to Sunbeam. Travelers coming from Sunbeam on the Motorway will get here last and can at least get answers to any questions they came up with on the way over.

The center commemorates the area's mining history in well-designed educational exhibits. You'll find out about the ghost towns of Custer and Bonanza, the Yankee Fork Gold Dredge, and the other sights along the Custer Motorway. The center, at the junction of Hwys. 75 and 93, P.O. Box 1086, Challis, ID 83226, 208/879-5244, is open April 1–Oct. 1, daily 8 A.M.–6 P.M.; the rest of the year, Mon.–Fri. 9 A.M.–5 P.M.

Challis Hot Springs

This large, developed hot-springs resort has been around since the mining days, although those old sourdoughs missed out on the big swimming pool and the RV sites with water and power hookups. Fishing the nearby Salmon River keeps some guests occupied, while horseshoes and volleyball are on the agenda for others. Campsite rates are $23 for RV sites, $16.50 for tent sites, extra persons (more than two) $6 each. Bed and breakfast rooms are also available ($95 for two people; extra people $15 each). The resort is east of town, 4.5 miles north of Highway 93 at the end of Hot Springs Road. It's open year-round. For more information, contact the resort at HC 63 Box 1779, Challis, ID 83226, 208/879-4442 or 800/479-1295.

Backcountry Roads

A long cherry stem probing 25 miles into the Frank Church–River of No Return Wilderness, Sleeping Deer Road (FR 086) traverses a long, high ridgeline between Twin Peaks and Sleeping Deer Mountain. A spur road at Twin Peaks (not for the new Buick) leads to the West's second-highest manned fire lookout. Farther on, the road is dotted with picnic areas (offering great views of the Frank Church) and several trailheads leading into the wilderness. At the end-of-the-road trailhead, you're within a long day's hike of the Middle Fork. Numerous little lakes also pepper the area.

A bit farther north up Highway 93, **Morgan Creek Road** (FR 055) ascends Morgan Creek, crosses a divide, and descends Panther Creek, joining the Salmon River Road west of Shoup. Along the way you'll pass the BLM's **Morgan Creek Campground** and a turnoff (FR 057) to the USFS Little West Fork Campground. Both are small, with no improved water source and no fee.

Outfitters

Challis is home to several outfitters that can guide you around the local backcountry, including up into the White Cloud Peaks. Try **American Adrenaline Co./Taylor Ranch Outfitters,** P.O. Box 795, Challis, ID 83226, 208/879-4700 or 800/581-0856; **Mile High Outfitters,** P.O. Box 1189, Challis, ID 83226, 208/879-4500; or **White Cloud Outfitters,** P.O. Box 217, Challis, ID 83226, 208/879-4574.

Information

For national forest recreation information, contact the Salmon-Challis National Forests' **Challis Ranger District,** HC 63 Box 1669, Challis, ID 83226, 208/879-4100, or the **Middle Fork Ranger District,** P.O. Box 750, Challis, ID

83226, 208/879-4101. The two ranger districts have different mailing addresses and phone numbers, but they share an office on US 93 at Main Street. The **Challis Area Chamber of Commerce** is at 700 N. Main St., P.O. Box 1130, Challis, ID 83226, 208/879-2771.

Salmon and Vicinity

At the confluence of the Lemhi and Salmon Rivers, the town of Salmon is the Lemhi County seat and another contender for honors as the state's Whitewater Capital. It's the staging center for the start of float trips down the main Salmon River, and the end of trips down the Middle Fork. Although filled in summer with more river rats than you can shake a paddle at, the town has none of the boisterous buzz of Riggins or even Stanley—but it does have some visionary local officials who are helping Salmon make the transition from a resources-based economy better than many other similar Idaho towns. The new Sacajawea Center and an ambitious plan for public spaces and trails are progressive moves. Yet Salmon is too remote to ever risk becoming another upscale resort town, and that's a good thing.

Sacajawea Interpretive Cultural & Educational Center

Or just the Sacajawea Center for short, this brand-new-in-2003 complex, one mile east of Salmon on Highway 28, 208/756-1188, www.sacajawea-center.org, mainly serves to pay homage to the young Shoshone woman, a Lemhi Valley native, who accompanied the Lewis and Clark expedition. Its many facets are still coming together, but right now you'll find a small interpretive facility and walking trail; on weekends (and certainly the third weekend each August, the town's Sacajawea Heritage Days), you might find living history demonstrations and re-enactments, too. The center is open 9 A.M.–5 P.M. daily June–Aug.; Tues.–Sat. May and Sept.–Oct. Admission is $3 general for ages 6 and up or $9 per family.

RECREATION
Rafting and Outfitters

In addition to the many weeklong raft trips that either begin or end in Salmon, the town is a base for several outfitters that offer shorter, half-day to three-day Salmon River adventures. Companies include **Kookaburra,** 706 15th St., Salmon, ID 83467, 208/756-4386 or 888/654-4386, www.raft4fun.com, and **Idaho Adventures,** 6 Adventure Ln., Salmon, ID 83467, 208/756-2986 or 800/789-WAVE (800/789-9283), www.idahoadventures.com. Idaho Adventures also offers gentle, three-hour scenic trips on a traditional Salmon River scow.

History buffs may be especially interested in the Lewis and Clark bicentennial offerings from **Silver Cloud Outfitters,** P.O. Box 1006, Salmon, ID 83467, 877/756-6215, www.silvercloud-exp.com, which plans special trips to mark the captains' decision not to chance survival on the Salmon River in 1805. The August launches, about $1,500 for a six-day trip, will be accompanied by expert historians.

Golf

The **Salmon Valley Golf Course** offers nine holes southeast of town along Highway 28, 208/756-4734. Weekday greens fee is $11.25 for nine holes, $16.25 for 18, $2 higher on the weekend. Cart and club rentals are available.

Salmon Hot Springs

An Idaho classic, this ramshackle old place high in the hills, Rt. 1 Box 223B, Salmon, ID 83467, 208/756-4449, is a relaxing spot with solitude in spades, and the hot springs pool itself is in great shape. It costs $4 for a swim. To get here, follow the signs off Highway 93, just south of town.

Elk Bend Hot Springs

Those who prefer their hot springs undeveloped and au naturel will find a treat in store for them here. Elk Bend (a.k.a. Goldbug Hot Springs) is about 22 miles south of Salmon on Highway

the white waters of the Salmon River

93. Look for a turnoff to the east near mile marker 282. Follow the road a short way down to a well-marked trailhead. The springs—a favorite among Middle Fork raft guides making the weekly commute between Salmon and Stanley—spring forth on a high bench overlooking the valley. It's a magic spot. Matt proposed to Shannon here. What's more, she accepted.

EVENTS

Salmon River Days, leading up to and including Fourth of July weekend, focuses on the twin themes of Old West traditions and river recreation. A free breakfast will give you the energy you'll need to take in the plethora of scheduled events, including a triathlon, kayak and raft races, an auction, rodeo, parade, and a mock bank robbery. **Sacajawea/Heritage Days,** held the third weekend in August, focuses on history, but you can also expect a street dance, arts and crafts fair, and other community-wide partying. The **Lemhi County Fair and Rodeo** arrives the last weekend in August. For a complete events calendar, contact the Salmon Valley Chamber of Commerce, 200 Main St., 208/756-2100.

ACCOMMODATIONS

Under $50

Suncrest Motel, 705 Challis St., 208/756-2294, will save you some money, but it's not on the river and the rooms are on the small side. Pets are OK.

The tranquil **Solaas Bed & Breakfast,** Route 1 Box 59, Salmon, ID 83467, 208/756-3903 or 888/425-5474, nine miles southeast of Salmon down Highway 28, occupies a 1905 building that was first a stagecoach-stop hotel, then a railroad depot. Today the restored structure houses this seven-room B&B. It's surrounded by spacious grounds shaded by 100-year-old poplars, and offers the requisite porch where you can sit and listen to the leaves rustling in the breeze. Rates include a full country breakfast. No credit cards; no alcohol; no smoking indoors.

$50–100

The biggest motel in town is the 100-room **Stagecoach Inn,** 201 Hwy. 93 N., 208/756-2919, right at the Salmon River bridge. Queen beds are standard; some king beds are available. Amenities include a heated pool, free continental breakfast, and a coin laundry. No pets. Get a room facing the river. **Wagons West Motel,** just down the highway at 503 Hwy. 93 N., 208/756-4281 or 800/756-4281, boasts its own island park on the river. Two-bedroom kitchenette suites are available. Kids under 12 stay free.

Syringa Lodge, 2000 Syringa Dr., 208/756-4424 or 877/580-6482, is a large log home on 23 acres. The eight guest rooms, six with private bath, are furnished with antiques; common areas include a great room with fireplace, a dining room, sun porch, and library.

Twelve miles south of Salmon on Highway 93 is **Greyhouse Inn,** HC 61 Box 16, Salmon, ID 83467, 208/756-3968 or 800/348-8097, a beautifully restored 1894 Victorian farmhouse turned into a B&B with four rooms (two with shared bath) plus two cabins and a carriage house. Proprietor Sharon Osgood loves flowers—the grounds are ringed with brightly blooming beds, and the interior is alive with bright floral prints. Rates include full breakfast.

Guest Ranch
Luxurious "rustic" accommodations and a magnificent setting mark the tony **Twin Peaks Ranch,** P.O. Box 774, Salmon, ID 83467, 208/894-2290 or 800/659-4899. The site here at the base of the namesake peaks has been occupied since 1923, but was first developed into a dude ranch by the E. du Pont family in the mid-1950s. Today, the mile-high, 2,850-acre spread offers guest accommodations in Old West–style log cabins providing all the comforts of home (including Jacuzzis) and recreation opportunities including horseback riding, fly-fishing, rafting, hiking, or swimming in the large heated pool. Midsummer rates range $1,636–1,957 per person per week, all gourmet home-cooked meals included. Free transportation is offered to and from the airport at Missoula, Montana, or Idaho Falls. No pets, but kennel service in Salmon can be arranged.

Forest Service Rentals
The Salmon-Challis National Forests offer four cabins for rent. In the Salmon River Mountains, south of Salmon and west of Highway 93, are the **Williams Creek, Peel Tree,** and **Iron Lake** cabins. The first two are open year-round, while Iron

Lake is open Oct. 1–May 1. All three sleep up to six people and cost $15 a night. Across the Salmon River, on the western slopes of the Lemhi Range, is the **North Basin** cabin. It's 19 miles south of Salmon as the crow flies and open year-round (though the trek in isn't recommended in winter). It, too, sleeps six and rents for $15 a night. For directions, reservations, or more information, contact the **Salmon-Challis National Forest,** 50 Hwy. 93 S., Salmon, ID 83467, 208/756-5100. More rental cabins may be on the way, so ask for information on any new developments.

FOOD

The best restaurants in the Salmon area are up past North Fork. But there's some good grub in town, too. **Bertram's Brewery & Restaurant,** 101 S. Andrews St., 208/756-3391, serves up homemade microbrews and sodas in the grand old 1898 Redwine building in downtown Salmon. Open Mon.–Sat. for lunch and dinner; look for burgers and wraps ($6–8) and fine-dining entrées ($12–18). The restaurant is smoke-free, and kids are welcome.

INFORMATION AND SERVICES
Information
The **Salmon Valley Chamber of Commerce** is at 200 Main St., Salmon, ID 83467, 208/756-2100 or 800/727-2540, www.salmonbyway.com. The supervisor's office of the **Salmon-Challis National Forests** is on Highway 93 south of town, 50 Hwy. 93 S., Salmon, ID 83467, 208/756-5100. This is also the office for the Cobalt Ranger District. Next door is the **BLM Challis Field Office,** 208/756-5400. The **Idaho Department of Fish and Game-Salmon Region Office** is at 1214 Hwy. 93 N. (1.5 miles north of town), P.O. Box 1336, Salmon, ID 83467, 208/756-2271.

Transportation
Salmon River Stages, 909 Union Ave., 208/756-4966, runs regular bus shuttles to Idaho Falls. Both **McCall Aviation,** 208/756-4713 or 800/235-4713, and **Salmon Air,**

208/756-6211 or 800/448-3413, fly hunting and fishing charters into the wilderness, make breakfast flights to backcountry guest ranches, and offer scenic air tours. Salmon Air also has scheduled weekday flights between Salmon and both Boise and McCall. The Salmon airport is four miles south of town.

NORTH TO MONTANA

North Fork

Salmon may be the area's largest commercial center, but North Fork—21 miles north of Salmon on Highway 93—is the true gateway to the Salmon River. Here the Main and the North Fork of the Salmon meet. Highway 93 continues up the North Fork to Lost Trail Pass, while Salmon River Road (FR 030) turns west and follows the main Salmon down past Shoup and Cache Bar (the takeout for Middle Fork trips) to Corn Creek (the put-in for main Salmon trips).

North Fork Store & Cafe, P.O. Box 100, North Fork, ID 83466, 208/865-2412, is something of a clearinghouse for river information. In addition to housing a café, store, motel, RV park, post office, laundromat, and liquor store, it also houses **North Fork Guides,** P.O. Box 24, North Fork, ID 83466, 208/865-2534 or 800/259-6866, which offers full-service guided float trips down the main Salmon in dories, duckies, oar rafts, and paddle rafts. There's a small motel at North Fork ($40–55).

It's worth the 24-mile drive from Salmon to eat at **100 Acre Wood Bed & Breakfast Resort,** P.O. Box 202, North Fork ID 83466, 208/865-2165, www.100acrewoodresort.com. Dinner is offered Thurs.–Sat., with reservations a must. Entrées run $13–26, with a lighter menu priced $7–11. The rooms ($55–115) are more of a mixed bag, with some weird configurations. If you're at all fussy, you'll dislike this place, but travelers who don't mind—or even thrive in—a funky, somewhat cluttered environment will enjoy 100 Acre Wood. The inn also offers a wide selection of guided tours, including steelhead fishing, backcountry Jeep tours, hunting, hiking, horseback riding, mountain biking, and more. See the website for options and details.

Lucky 13 Ranch & Guest House, P.O. Box 141, North Fork, ID 83466, 208/865-2065, is a new Hostelling International affiliate in the Salmon area. To get there, drive 4.5 miles north of North Fork via Highway 93, then left on Hull Road, then right on Becker Road The hostel offers eight beds in two shared rooms ($20 each for HI members; $23 for non-members), plus a private room with a queen bed ($45 for one or two people; an extra single bed for a child is available on request). The common room features a full kitchen and a VCR and movies. There's a deck and a grill out back; good recreation (horseshoes, volleyball, river access for swimming and fishing) right out the door; and easy access to lots more hiking, mountain biking, and cross-country skiing. Open all year except about Dec. 23–Jan. 3.

Shoup

Continuing down the Main Salmon, the former gold-mining community of Shoup is the last outpost of civilization on the upper main Salmon. The town also boasts the claim to fame of having had the country's last hand-cranked telephone. **Shoup Store, Cafe & Cabins,** HC 64 Box 1, Shoup, ID 83469, 208/394-2125, is 18 miles west of North Fork. The two small cabins are equipped with kitchenettes, bathrooms, and even electricity, thanks to an antique hydropower waterwheel on nearby Boulder Creek. Another larger cabin, also with kitchen and bath, can sleep up to 10 people (four-person minimum). Rates are $15 per person if you bring your own linens or sleeping bag, or $25 per bed with linen rental.

To Corn Creek

Another 10 miles or so past Shoup, Panther Creek empties into the Salmon. **Panther Creek Road** (FR 055) is a gateway to the eastern edge of the Frank Church–River of No Return Wilderness. The trailheads in this vicinity lead into one of the most spectacular areas of the wilderness—Ship Island Lake and the Bighorn Crags. Besides the wilderness, up Panther Creek you'll find the mining ghost town of Cobalt and the confluence of Panther and Blackbird Creeks. Up Blackbird Creek is the **Blackbird Cobalt Mine,** now a federal Superfund site contaminated with copper, cobalt, arsenic, and nickel. Note that the Clear Creek access to the Bighorn Crags runs through an area of the Frank Church Wilderness that has been set aside for future cobalt mining, should the country's defense operations require more of the mineral. Cobalt is used in jet engine turbine blades. Clear Creek and Blackbird Creek both flow into the Salmon River and are both home to threatened salmon species.

Past Panther Creek Road on Salmon River Road is **Smith House Bed and Breakfast,** 3175 Salmon River Rd., Shoup, ID 83469, 800/238-5915, 208/394-2121 (April–Oct.), or 850/927-3350 (Nov.–March). The B&B sits on three acres with 300 feet of river frontage. Rooms in the main house run $55–65, and a guest house that can sleep up to 12 people rents for $175 a night with discounts for stays of three nights or more. Electricity from a generator is available on request, but its use is not encouraged. Good ol' fashioned lanterns are the preferred light source after the sun goes down. Kids and pets are welcome. The B&B is open mid-April–mid-October.

Way way down at the end of the road, just a quarter mile upstream from the Corn Creek put-in, is **Salmon River Lodge,** P.O. Box 927, Salmon, ID 83467, 208/756-6622 or 800/635-4717. This remote lodge couldn't be more convenient for rafters planning a trip down the main Salmon, or those looking to chill out after their Middle Fork adventure. It's across the river from the Corn Creek launch, accessible only by shuttle across the river in one of the lodge's jetboats. The lodge leads its own guided tours down the Salmon and uses those same jetboats to haul rafters back to the lodge at the end of their float down the Salmon. Other packages available include hunting, fishing, horse-packing, and jetboat trips. Room rates ($50–100) include boat shuttle. Gourmet meals are available for breakfast, lunch, and dinner.

Gibbonsville

A few miles north of North Fork, Gibbonsville is named for one of the worst bad guys of the 1877 Nez Perce War, Colonel John Gibbon, who staged the sneak attack at the Battle of the Big Hole. But don't hold that against it. Gibbonsville is a good base for fall hunting parties or paddlers for whom the North Fork scene is too bustling. The chief attraction here is **Ramey's Broken Arrow,** HC 10 Box 1108, Gibbonsville, ID 83463, 208/865-2241, which serves Mexican food bursting with fresh flavors. It's a local hangout where you may well hear some impromptu live music. Open Mother's Day weekend through the first weekend in November, Thurs.–Sat. 5–9 P.M. and Sun. 2–9 P.M. The resort—on the west side of the road despite its sign across the highway—also has small cabins available nightly during the season above ($45 for two people; extra occupants $5 each) and RV spaces ($15 for a full hookup). The cabins are rustic and share bathroom facilities (except Number 5, which has its own sink and toilet), but some can sleep up to six people.

Lost Trail Pass

Forty-six miles north of Salmon, Highway 93 leaves Idaho and enters Montana at Lost Trail Pass, elevation 7,014 feet. At the top of the pass is **Lost Trail Powder Mountain Ski Area,** P.O. Box 311, Conner, MT 59827, 406/821-3211, www.losttrail.com, a small but popular area that gets some great powder. Four chairlifts and three tows access 1,000 acres and a maximum drop of 1,800 vertical feet. Full-day lift tickets cost $24 general, $14 for kids 6–12. Snowboards are permitted. Lessons and rentals are available. The day lodge holds a cafeteria. Stay-and-ski packages are available with some area lodgings; call the resort for a list. The ski area is open Dec.–April, Thurs.–Sun. and holidays, 9:30 A.M.–4 P.M.

For pinheads, a network of cross-country ski trails laces the national forest lands on either side of the pass. Ask for a trail map at the ski area.

in and Range Country

Southeast of the Challis-Salmon stretch of Highway 93, three parallel mountain ranges separated by road-bearing valleys provide a great example of what geologists call a basin-and-range formation. As the earth's crust stretches apart here at the rate of one-half inch per year, the ground breaks into blocks formed of peaks and valleys. The ranges here—the Lost River, Lemhi, and Beaverhead—and the valleys between them are aligned as neatly as F to B-flat on a piano. The Beaverhead Range forms part of the Continental Divide, while the Lost River Range holds Idaho's highest mountain, 12,662-foot Borah Peak.

HIGHWAY 93: BIG LOST RIVER VALLEY

Up Warm Springs Creek

Turning southeast out of Challis down Highway 93, you'll head up Warm Springs Creek and eventually enter **Grandview Canyon,** a narrow slot perfect for an ambush by desperadoes. Fortunately for you, you're not in an old Glenn Ford western. Geologists will tell you that this odd little canyon was formed by the creek eroding down through a once-buried knob of Devonian dolomite. Past the impressive canyon you'll climb up to **Willow Creek Summit,** elevation 7,160 feet, a favored winter grazing area for elk. When you crest the pass, you'll be heading down the Big Lost River Valley.

Borah Peak

As you head southeast down the Big Lost River Valley, the massive wall of the Lost River Range rises abruptly on your left. From along the highway, this range is nowhere near as exciting a sight as, say, the snowy Sawtooth Range. The terrain here is dry and relatively barren in comparison, and the mountains look not so much like high alpine spires as big hulking blocks of rock. Look for the turnoff marked "Borah Peak Access" and turn your eyes left. This mountain monarch rises abruptly from the valley floor and leads your eye right to the summit, which unlike many high peaks isn't hidden behind lower interlopers.

Those thinking of climbing the peak should plan on 8–12 hours roundtrip, depending on their speed and physical condition. While the route isn't technical, it is very steep and strenuous, gaining almost a vertical mile in less than 3.5 miles. And one short stretch involves third-class climbing (use of hands and feet) across "Chicken-Out Ridge," a knife-edge ridge with serious exposure—if you fall, you'll fall a long, long way. Snow often lingers on a steep saddle near the summit well into midsummer. Use of an ice ax for insurance makes the necessary traverse across that saddle less scary.

While the Forest Service brochure might lead you to think it's an easy walk to the summit, never underestimate the risks associated with

IT'S ALL YOUR FAULT

At 8:06 A.M. on Friday, October 28, 1983, the **Lost River Fault** ripped open with explosive force, releasing 10,000 years of pent-up energy in a devastating, 40-second shift. At the earthquake's epicenter here in the valley, the west side of the fault instantly dropped while the Lost River Range was shoved even higher, creating a 21-mile-long fault scarp up to 14 feet high in places. The quake's energy ran northward up the fault line, scissoring apart the valley floor at a speed of 5,000 miles an hour and sending 400 billion gallons of displaced groundwater gushing forth in springs and geysers. When the quake hit Challis, 20 miles to the north, a masonry wall collapsed, killing two children on their way to school. Within minutes, the temblor rocked Salt Lake City, Portland, Seattle, and western Canada. Measured at 7.3 on the Richter scale, the earthquake caused some $15 million in property damage. It was the worst quake ever in Idaho and one of the worst in the history of the West. A well-marked turnoff from Highway 93 leads a short way to an interpretive site explaining the cause of the quake and providing an excellent look at the scarp.

climbing high peaks. If you're out of shape, or don't have the proper equipment or clothing, don't attempt the hike. If you do attempt it, make sure to check in at the ranger station in Mackay first. Those who are prepared will find the climb exceedingly enjoyable.

A little south of Borah down the highway you'll get a glimpse of another Idaho giant. A roadside sign indicates the Matterhorn-like **Leatherman Peak,** visible through a slot in the nearer ridgeline. Leatherman, elevation 12,230 feet, is the state's second-highest peak and a far more impressive sight than Borah.

Mackay

Copper discoveries in the area led to the founding of Mackay (pronounced "MACK-ee") in 1901. Ranching and recreation have since replaced mining as the mainstay of the local economy. The laid-back little town is the primary supply point for hikers heading up Borah Peak and for anglers trolling for trout in Mackay Reservoir and the Big Lost River. Basic accommodations and food are available.

RVing golfers will appreciate **River Park Golf Course and RV Campground,** 717 Capitol Ave., 208/588-2296. The RV sites lie right between the sixth and eighth tees. The greens fee for the nine-hole course is $8, or $11 for 18 holes. The RV park charges $15 a night, full hookups.

West of town, the White Knob Mountains rise to over 10,000 feet, holding the rugged old mining roads that now make up the course of the annual **White Knob Challenge** mountain-bike race. The race, held on the first Saturday in August, begins on Main Street in Mackay. Hundreds of competitors make the 19-mile loop up toward White Knob Peak and back. The course climbs 2,600 feet in the first nine miles. For more information, call 208/854-1801.

Other big events in Mackay include the **Mackay Rodeo,** held the fourth weekend in June; the **Custer County Fair,** held the first week of August; and the town's legendary **free barbecue** at noon on the third Saturday in September ("Tons of meat—it's Mackay's treat!" reads the sign).

For more information on the town or its events, contact the **City of Mackay,** P.O. Box 509, Mackay, ID 83251, 208/588-2274. For recreation information, contact the USFS **Lost River Ranger District,** 716 W. Custer, P.O. Box 507, Mackay, ID 83251, 208/588-2224.

HIGHWAY 28: LEMHI AND BIRCH CREEK VALLEYS
Lewis and Clark National Backcountry Byway

A turnoff at Tendoy leads to this well-marked loop road that lets you follow in the footsteps of Lewis and Clark. The unpaved but well-graded route first passes an interpretive display that fills you in on the history of the Corps of Discovery in this area. It then climbs up and across a heavily logged plateau before dropping down to historic **Lemhi Pass.** Here an advance party led by Meriwether Lewis first set eyes on the land that would eventually become the state of Idaho. Lewis planted the American flag on the west side of the pass, claiming the land for the United States. When the expedition crossed the Continental Divide here in 1805, they were no longer in territory covered by the Louisiana Purchase, and Britain and the United States would jockey for control of the Pacific Northwest for many years to come.

The pass offers sweeping views into both Idaho and Montana. The small Sacajawea Memorial Camp just down the road on the Montana side has been closed for the Lewis and Clark Bicentennial years (through 2006), but the Agency Creek campground a few miles from Tendoy remains open with primitive sites. The total 39-mile loop takes about half a day to negotiate, including stops for a picnic lunch (bring your own; there are no services along the way) and frequent ooh's and aah's.

Lemhi Pass is usually accessible June–Sept. For more information, contact the **BLM Salmon Field Office,** 50 Hwy. 93 S., Salmon, ID 83467, 208/756-5400.

Lemhi Valley Towns

Mormons founded the town of Lemhi in 1855, naming the settlement after a king in the Book of Mormon. Indians soon drove the settlers out.

The ghost town of **Gilmore** was once a big-money mining town and is named after stagecoach magnate Jack Gilmer (yet another example of the difficulties the Postal Department had with the English language in those days). Contrary to popular belief, the town of **Leadore** was not named for Jack Leadore; it, too, was a mining town.

All three valley towns today are small hamlets (or less) surrounded by arid desert terrain that can make you forget you're still at high altitude. Gilmore Summit on Highway 28 is over 7,000 feet—a fact that can suddenly become apparent if you find yourself trying to cross it without chains in a winter storm.

Birch Creek Valley

Continuing south from Leadore, you'll crest Gilmore Summit and drop down into the Birch Creek Valley. This was a busy mining district in the 1880s, and many remnants of the era still remain. Watch for a turnoff on your right to the Birch Creek **Charcoal Kilns.** The charcoal that fired the blast furnaces of the **Viola Mine** smelter was produced in a series of beehive-shaped rock ovens here. Charcoal is made by "burning" wood in the absence of air. These big clay ovens—each 20 feet tall and 20 feet in diameter—were built in 1886 and operated until the mine ran out of ore in 1888. All together, the 16 kilns here yielded 45,000–50,000 bushels of charcoal per month. Today several still stand, forming an eerily quiet reminder of the boom days gone by. The remote site holds some interpretive signs, but no other facilities.

The turnoff to the Viola Mine itself and the ghost town of **Nicholia** is farther down the valley on your left. Nicholia once was home to 600–700 miners and smelter workers. The busy town boasted two barber shops, two general stores, three hotels, eight saloons, and a jail. During its operating life, the Viola Mine reaped $2.5 million in lead and silver. Now only the bones are left—a couple of log buildings and the rusty remains of an ore-hauling tram.

North-Central Idaho

Lucky north-central Idaho is rich with history. This is the land of the Nez Perce—the proud Native Americans whose ancestors roamed this region for thousands of years and whose age-old and elegant culture echoes off the Camas Prairie and through the Clearwater Canyon in names like Lochsa, Kooskia, and Kamiah. And this was the land of Lewis and Clark, who passed through here in 1805 during their attempt to find an inland water route to the Pacific and again east bound in 1806, camping for nearly a month with the Nez Perce.

This was the land of gold—the region where, in 1860, the first glittering nugget was discovered in Idaho—and the land of big timber, where mighty forests of white pine supplied much of the wood that built the West. Today, mining camps like Orogrande, Florence, Elk City, and Dixie hold faded memories of the bustling saloons and brothels of days gone by. And though the timber barons and the blister rust all but eliminated the white pine, several towering old-growth cedar groves still thrive here—living cathedrals open daily for the masses.

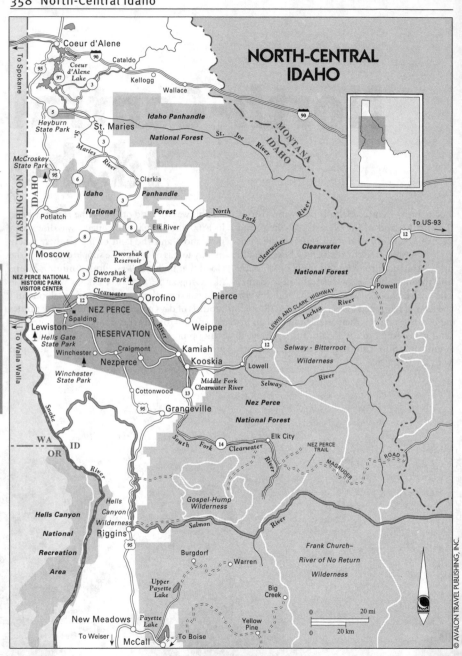

© AVALON TRAVEL PUBLISHING, INC.

North-central Idaho is also rich in its topography. The state's greatest concentration of white-water rivers flows through this region. Here the 1,000-mile-long Snake River enters Hells Canyon, a spectacular gorge even deeper than the Grand Canyon. Joining the Snake in Hells Canyon is the legendary Salmon River—the River of No Return—which draws whitewater rafters from all over the world. To the north is the Clearwater River, a mecca for anglers in pursuit of migrating salmon and steelhead. And far up the Clearwater are two more classics: the Lochsa River, one of the country's most continuously difficult white-water runs, and the Selway River, which flows through a vast and remote wilderness.

Those looking for high-mountain adventure need look no further. The Seven Devils range, part of the Hells Canyon Wilderness, offers an alpine realm filled with granite spires, mountain goats, and awe-inspiring views of Hells Canyon.

Farther east, the Selway-Bitterroot Wilderness and the Gospel Hump Wilderness thrust towering peaks into the clear Idaho skies. Together the three wilderness areas total some 16,000 square miles of pristine backcountry, all of it teeming with fish and wildlife.

For a lower-amplitude landscape, head for the Palouse. Here on the prairie north of the Clearwater, fertile farmland spreads out like a big green picnic blanket across gently rolling hills. Barns highlight the area's distinct architecture, and every town feels like a small town—even Moscow, site of Idaho's oldest university.

Finally, north-central Idaho is rich with good people. Moscow's coffeehouses and classrooms may harbor a cosmopolitan edge, but by and large this part of the state remains a blue-collar, meat-and-potatoes land of just plain folks. Friendly mom-and-pop markets outnumber big chain stores here, and no one stays a stranger very long.

The Hells Canyon Corridor

HELLS CANYON NATIONAL RECREATION AREA

Between Pinehurst and White Bird, Highway 95 parallels the eastern edge of Hells Canyon National Recreation Area, a 652,488-acre preserve straddling the Snake River in Idaho and Oregon. For some 71 Wild and Scenic miles, the Snake carves its way northward through Hells Canyon, the deepest river gorge in North America. This is one mother canyon. A few roads lead down to it in places, but none dare run through it.

Below Hells Canyon Dam, the Snake's raging rapids and placid pools create a recreational haven for rafters and jetboaters. Hikers can follow trails along the water's edge, beneath towering walls of crumbling black basalt, or climb out of the canyon to explore the high country along its rim—most notably the Seven Devils Mountains. This range of high peaks holds some of the state's most magnificent alpine scenery and offers great views of the canyon floor more than a vertical mile below.

The 215,000-acre **Hells Canyon Wilderness** makes up a large portion of the National Recreation Area; motor vehicles and mountain bikes are prohibited here. Though the majority of this wilderness lies across the river in Oregon, Idaho's share includes most of the Seven Devils range, as well as 18 river miles between Hells Canyon Creek and Willow Creek.

History

The canyon has long been popular with humans, thanks to its mild winters, abundant game, and fish-filled river. Some 1,500 Native American archaeological sites have been found in the canyon, including evidence of human habitation going back 7,100 years. At **Upper Pittsburg Landing** you can look at petroglyphs (rock etchings) and pictographs (rock paintings) created by the canyon's aboriginal residents.

Before the advent of whites to the area, Chief Joseph's band of Nez Perce made an annual migration from their summer home in Oregon's Wallowa Mountains to warmer winter quarters here in the canyon. Shoshone, Northern Paiute,

Scale:
0 — 1 mi
0 — 1 km

MooN

White Bird

Snake River

Hells Canyon Wilderness

DEER CREEK RD.

95

UPPER PITTSBURG LANDING

PITTSBURG SADDLE

Slate Creek

HAMMER CREEK RECREATION AREA/ PITTSBURG LANDING

SLATE CREEK

Western Rim Nat'l Rec. Trail

Imnaha River

Imnaha

Hells Canyon

KIRKWOOD RANCH

COW CREEK RD.

Lucile

IRON PHONE JUNCTION

SAWPIT SADDLE

National

LOW SADDLE

Salmon River

BEAN CREEK RD.

Hells Canyon Wilderness

Recreation

Area

Snake River Nat'l Rec. Trail

Riggins

WINDY SADDLE

HEAVEN'S GATE LOOKOUT

Devils Tooth

SEVEN DEVILS

SQUAW CREEK/ PAPOOSE CREEK RD.

Tower of Babel

Seven Devils Mtns.

She Devil Pk.

He Devil Pk.

Seven Devils Loop Trail

SEE DETAIL

Hells Canyon Wilderness

Hells Canyon

HELLS CANYON CREEK VISITOR CENTER

HELLS CANYON DAM

BLACK LAKE

Imnaha River

Snake River

Cuprum

95

OREGON

HELLS CANYON NATIONAL RECREATION AREA

New Meadows

Copperfield

IDAHO

McCall

NORTH-CENTRAL IDAHO

© AVALON TRAVEL PUBLISHING, INC.

and Cayuse people also inhabited the region from time to time. The first whites to the canyon—John Ordway, Peter Weiser, and Robert Frazier, led by several Nez Perce guides—came over from Kamiah in spring 1806, pronouncing the path down to the Snake "the worst hills we ever saw a road made down." Wilson Price Hunt's fur expedition of 1811 explored the upper reaches above today's Hells Canyon Dam, but turned back before seeing the heart of the gorge.

The first population influx occurred in the 1860s, when the West's mining frenzy reached the area. Some placer mining took place along the river, and hard-rock mines soon riddled the southern Seven Devils. Copper was the big find there; today you can drive to what's left of **Cuprum,** an aptly named copper-mining center. Later, homesteading farmers and ranchers made their way into the area. The farmers planted orchards and row crops on the fertile alluvial terraces, supplying both themselves and local miners with high-quality fresh produce. Ranchers grazed cattle and sheep on whatever relatively level areas they could find. A good example of an early sheep ranch is preserved today at **Kirkwood Ranch,** a hike , bike-, or boat-in interpretive site along the river.

After World War II, the Army Corps of Engineers suddenly found itself with nothing to do and latched onto dams as its new raison d'être. The Corps dammed its way inexorably up the Columbia before casting eyes on the Snake. Hells Canyon, with its narrow width and steep gradient, looked like a prime target. In 1964, the Federal Power Commission gave the green light for development of a dam in the canyon. The proposal drew protest from canyon conservationists and eventually ended up before the U.S. Supreme Court. After years of legal wrangling, Congress created the Hells Canyon National Recreation Area on December 31, 1975, ensuring that no more dams would be built here. The Snake is now undammed from Hells Canyon Dam at the south end of the canyon to Lower Granite Dam just beyond Lewiston, a distance of more than 100 miles.

Flora and Fauna

Hells Canyon is a unique biome thanks to the extreme elevation changes that occur within its narrow boundaries. The land rises from 1,500 feet along the river to above 9,000 feet in the Seven Devils, all within about 10 miles as the crow flies. Each altitude zone supports a particular plant and animal community—from cactus and rattlesnakes on the canyon floor to lupines and marmots up high. And since in Hells Canyon those zones are horizontally compressed, you'll find many species there living in abnormally close proximity.

The Snake River is one of the few remaining strongholds of the **white sturgeon,** a huge, primeval-looking monster that can reach lengths of 10 feet or more. If you catch one, the law requires you to put it back. Other fish in the river include steelhead, salmon, rainbow trout, bass, crappie, and catfish—quite a mix. On land, you'll find deer, black bear, elk, mountain goats, and hopefully still some **bighorn sheep.** The sheep have been devasted by recurring plagues that rapidly sweep through the population. Finally, the skies over the NRA are home to more than 100 species of birds, among them hawks, owls, and even bald and golden eagles.

The canyon's unique flora includes rare flowers such as Snake River phlox, rough harebell, the endangered MacFarlane's four-o'clock, and the bartonberry, found only in Hells Canyon. Once-thick stands of ponderosa pine have been logged extensively; logging is permitted in the National Recreation Area outside Hells Canyon Wilderness. Other common trees in the NRA include hackberry, cottonwood, and alder.

Pittsburg Landing

Just south of White Bird on Highway 95, signs mark a turnoff to Hammer Creek Recreation Area/Pittsburg Landing. Cross the Salmon River and make a quick left onto Deer Creek Road (FR 493). Deer Creek Road winds its way up to Pittsburg Saddle and drops steeply down the other side to Pittsburg Landing, a total distance of 17 miles.

This important Native American archaeological site is also the only place south of Hells Canyon Dam where you can drive right down to the river on the Idaho side. Naturally that makes it a popular launch and takeout point for rafters.

At the end of the road you'll find a 28-site NRA campground (fee), a boat-launching ramp, dock, and small ranger information booth. Nearby, a short spur road leads to another boat-launch area at Upper Pittsburg Landing, passing a gallery of Native American rock art on the way. The numerous pictographs and petroglyphs here mark the site as a favored studio for ancient Picassos. Upper Pittsburg Landing also marks the trailhead for the Hells Canyon National Recreation Trail. It can be extremely hot and dry here in summer, and there's little shade. Campers will want to bring big floppy hats, plenty of sunscreen, and ice chests full of cold beverages.

The Seven Devils

Second only to the Sawtooths for spectacular alpine scenery, the Seven Devils Range rises steep and craglike between the Salmon River on the east and the Snake River on the west. From the lofty summit of He Devil Peak—highest point in the NRA at 9,393 feet—it's a dizzying drop of

COURTESY OF THE IDAHO TRAVEL COUNCIL

Snow lingers until midsummer in the Seven Devils.

nearly 8,000 feet in just over five miles down to the Snake at the bottom of Hells Canyon.

You can access the heart of this spectacular mountain range via Squaw Creek/Papoose Creek Road (FR 517), which turns west off Highway 95 on the south side of Riggins at the Hells Canyon NRA headquarters. A 19-mile drive up the gravel road leads you to **Heaven's Gate Lookout,** elevation 8,429 feet, where you'll be treated to possibly the most magnificent view in all Idaho. The 360-degree panorama takes in four states: Idaho, Oregon, Washington, and Montana. To the northeast, the Camas Prairie spreads out all the way to the Clearwater River. To the southwest, Hells Canyon frames the foreground for the snowcapped Wallowa Mountains of Oregon, Chief Joseph's homeland. To the southeast, the Salmon River Mountains roll across the horizon. And practically right in front of you, the Devils' own cathedrals of granite tower over Seven Devils Lake and the USFS **Seven Devils Campground.** A notice posted at the free, seven-site campground warns visitors not to get too close to the mountain goats who occasionally wander into camp.

A number of trails open to hikers and horsepackers start from Windy Saddle trailhead, between the lookout and the campground. The most popular, the Seven Devils Loop Trail, encircles the range's highest peaks while leading past sapphire-blue lakes and verdant, wildflower-painted meadows.

Unlike the low country of Riggins or Hells Canyon, up here it's relatively cool and comfortable even in the scorching days of August. Snowfields linger right through summer in places.

Sawpit Saddle

Another off-pavement route leads to two canyon viewpoints but does not descend to the river. The three-hour loop follows **Bean Creek Road** (FR 241) from its junction with Highway 95 a quarter mile north of Riggins west to Iron Phone Junction. A loop farther west from Iron Phone Junction on rougher roads—FR 2060 and FR 1819—leads to views at Sawpit Saddle, Low Saddle, and Cold Springs. From Sawpit Saddle you can glimpse the Snake River, glimmering in the sun far below. The route returns to Iron Phone Junction, then back the way you came from there.

Boating

In 1865, a riverboat company out of Portland tried to run the first steamboat up through Hells Canyon as a route to the south Idaho goldfields. After four and a half days of slowly chugging up the canyon, the vessel reached the mouth of Oregon's Imnaha River. There the captain discovered an eight-foot-long gash in the bow and decided to beat a hasty retreat. The swift current carried the boat back out of the canyon in less than four hours. Four years later, the steamboat *Shoshone*—built in southern Idaho for a venture that subsequently failed—successfully ran the Snake downstream through Hells Canyon. It was followed in 1891 by another steamboat, the *Norma*. It's unclear how much was left of those boats when they reached Lewiston.

In 1925, Amos Burg became the first bold adventurer—or the first dang fool, depending on your perspective—to canoe down the Snake River through Hells Canyon. He was accompanied by perhaps the first river guide, a man named John Mullins. Before the trip, Mullins told Burg "he knew every rock in the river." After the trip, Burg added, "he ought to, since he hit them all."

The Snake is a big river. Its dam-controlled flow rates range anywhere from 5,000 cubic feet per second in low water to an incredible 80,000 cubic feet per second or more during spring runoff. Both jetboats and rafts are allowed on the river, but certain nonmotorized periods have been reserved for rafters who want to paddle in peace and quiet.

The **Hells Canyon Creek Visitor Center,** on the Oregon side of the river just below Hells Canyon Dam, is the most common put-in point for commercial raft trips. Pushing off from there, you don't have much time to prepare yourself for **Wild Sheep Rapids,** just 5.8 miles downstream. Wild Sheep, the river's longest rapids, is Class IV most of the time, Class V at high flows. Once you make it through that one, you'll barely have time to catch your breath before **Granite Creek Rapids** comes into view. This one's an-

other Class IV–V monster with huge waves and a raft-eating hole at river center. Depending on whether you enjoy or abhor an adrenaline rush, the good (or bad) news is that the hardest part of the river is at the top. More Class II–IV rapids lie ahead, but the trip gets gradually less terrifying as you continue downstream.

Besides rapids, you'll find a few nice beaches (although the silt that would ordinarily keep the beaches alive and replenished is now backed up behind the upstream dams), a few bits of shade, a slew of campsites, and a few historic sites. It's a two- to three-day trip from the put-in at Hells Canyon Creek to the takeout at Pittsburg Landing, a distance of 32 miles. Add another two to three days to continue down to the confluence with the Grand Ronde at Heller Bar, 79 miles from the put-in.

While some jetboat tours also leave from Hells Canyon Creek, more of them leave from Lewiston and head upriver. For more information on jetboat trips, see Lewiston.

Guided trips: Among the commercial guide services offering raft trips down the Snake are **Hells Canyon Adventures,** 4200 Hells Canyon Dam Rd., P.O. Box 159, Oxbow, OR 97840, 541/785-3352 or 800/422-3568; **Holiday River Expeditions of Idaho, Inc.,** P.O. Box 86, Grangeville, ID 83530, 208/983-1518 or 800/628-2565; **Hughes River Expeditions, Inc.,** P.O. Box 217, Cambridge, ID 83610, 208/257-3477 or 800/262-1882; **Idaho Afloat,** P.O. Box 542, Grangeville, ID 83530, 208/983-2414 or 800/700-2414; **Northwest Voyageurs,** HC2 Box 501, Pollock, ID 83547, 800/727-9977; and **River Odysseys West (ROW),** P.O. Box 579, Coeur d'Alene, ID 83816, 208/765-0841 or 800/451-6034. For a complete list, see www.fs.fed.us/hellscanyon.

Permits: Private parties planning a float or powerboat trip through Hells Canyon must obtain a permit from the Forest Service. For information, contact the **Hells Canyon NRA-Snake River Office,** 2535 Riverside Dr. (no mail to this address), P.O. Box 699, Clarkston, WA 99403, 509/758-1957 (float information) or 509/758-0270 (power-boat information).

Flow rates: For daily river flow levels, you

can no longer call God. Instead, you must call **Idaho Power Company,** 800/422-3143, to find out how much water they intend to let out of Hells Canyon Dam during your trip.

Hiking and Horsepacking

The Forest Service maintains some 900 miles of hiker/equestrian trails in the NRA, most on the Oregon side of the river. Some of the lower-altitude trails remain open year-round; in winter, snow closes the mountain trails up on the rim. Water sources at lower elevations are few and far between, and it gets hot down there; carry plenty of water with you. Also be alert for three common pests in the area: rattlesnakes, ticks, and poison ivy.

The **Hells Canyon National Recreation Trail,** a 31-mile footpath along the banks of the river, leads from Pittsburg Landing south to . . . well, south right into the river. Sheer walls of rock block the last two-mile stretch just above Hells Canyon Dam. As a consequence, hikers generally take this trail south to north, paying one of the jetboat operators at the Hells Canyon Creek boat launch to drop them at the beginning of the trail on their way downriver. Note that portions of this trail may be submerged when the river rises above 40,000 cubic feet per second.

Up in the high country, the **Seven Devils Loop Trail** forms a 27-mile circle around the range's highest peaks, passing by or near some 30 alpine lakes along the way. This popular multiday backpack trip offers spectacular vistas looking down into Hells Canyon, and up to the summits of He Devil, She Devil, Devils Tooth, and the Tower of Babel, among others. Main access to the loop is at Windy Saddle, but you can also hike in on Trail 214 from Black Lake to the south (see To Hells Canyon via Kleinschmidt Grade under Hells Canyon Rim Country in the Southwest Idaho chapter). This nine-mile trail follows upper Granite Creek north for a time, eventually meeting the Seven Devils Loop at Horse Heaven Junction, the loop's southernmost point.

For those looking to hike from rim to river, four different trails follow the snowmelt down to the Snake. From south to north, trails descend from the Seven Devils along Devils Farm Creek/ Granite Creek, Little Granite Creek, Bernard

Creek, and Sheep Creek. You can get the appropriate maps at the NRA office in Riggins. Don't forget that down in the canyon it's usually 15–20 degrees warmer than up on the rim.

Access Guide

In addition to the eastern access points listed above, several southern access points are covered in the Southwest Idaho chapter. Following is a summary of all access routes covered in this book. Paved Highway 71 (to Hells Canyon Dam) and gravel Deer Creek Road (to Pittsburg Landing) are usually open year-round. The other routes are unpaved and generally open mid-July–Oct. For current conditions, call the Riggins NRA office at 208/628-3916.

Hells Canyon Dam: The approach from the south is via Highway 71, off Highway 95 at Cambridge (see Highway 71 to Hells Canyon Dam under Hells Canyon Rim Country in the Southwest Idaho chapter). If your vehicle's too wimpy for one of the other routes, don't despair—views of the canyon from along the pavement here are outstanding.

Kleinschmidt Grade: An alternative off-pavement route to Hells Canyon Dam from Council (see To Hells Canyon via Kleinschmidt Grade under Hells Canyon Rim Country in the Southwest Idaho chapter).

Black Lake: An off-pavement route from Council to a southern Seven Devils trailhead (see To Hells Canyon via Kleinschmidt Grade under Hells Canyon Rim Country in the Southwest Idaho chapter).

Windy Saddle: Road from Riggins leads to a viewpoint and trailhead high in the Seven Devils (see The Seven Devils, above).

Bean Creek Road: Rough off-pavement loop to good views of the canyon; begins a quarter mile north of Riggins (see Sawpit Saddle, above).

Kirkwood Ranch: From Lucile, Cow Creek Road (FR 242) climbs toward Kirkwood Bar, but it's a rough road and ends prematurely. You'll need an ATV, horse, or backpack and sturdy boots to make it down to the ranch. You can also hike in to the ranch from Pittsburg Landing.

Pittsburg Landing: Road from just south of White Bird leads to the Snake River, a boat ramp, campground, trailhead, and Native American rock art (see Pittsburg Landing, above).

Accommodations

Beamers Hells Canyon Tours, 1451 Bridge St., Clarkston, WA 99403, 509/758-4800 or 800/522-6966, www.hellscanyontours.com, operates two midcanyon lodges—one at Heller Bar and one at Copper Creek. The Heller Bar lodge is 28 miles south of Clarkston, Washington, at the mouth of the Grande Ronde River. Guests stay in cabins ($120 for up to five people), each with private bathrrom and shower. Rates include continental breakfast but not jetboat transportation, since you can reach this lodge by road from Clarkston. The Copper Creek Lodge is 70 miles upriver from Lewiston, with private cabins overlooking the river. Rates for the cabins include jetboat transportation and all meals; $260 per person for the first night, $125 each additional night. Beamers trips leave from the Port of Clarkston dock, 700 Port Dr. in Clarkston, Washington, behind Quality Inn.

Snake River Adventures, 227 Snake River Ave., Lewiston, ID 83501, 208/746-6276 or 800/262-8874, www.snakeriveradventures.com, also has lodging up the canyon. The Kirby Creek Lodge offers private rooms (with shared bathrooms) in a large guest house 80 miles from Lewiston. You're getting away from it all, but maybe you're not: There's still satellite TV and a DVD player. Overnight rates, including transportation from Lewiston and all meals, are $275 per person for the first night, $110 per person for additional days. At 91.2 miles upriver from Lewiston, considered the end of navigation, the Sheep Creek Ranch was homesteaded in 1913. The rustic quarters can sleep up to eight people for $125 per night, plus $160 per person roundtrip jetboat from Lewiston or Pittsburg Landing. You'll need to bring your own food and sleeping bags.

Information

The three offices of Hells Canyon National Recreation Area are **Hells Canyon NRA-Idaho Office,** P.O. Box 832, Riggins, ID 83549, 208/628-3916, on the south side of town along High-way 95; **Hells Canyon NRA-Snake River Office,** 2535 Riverside Dr. (no mail to this address), P.O. Box 699, Clarkston, WA 99403, 509/758-0616, on the west bank of the river just across the South-way bridge (the "new" bridge) from Lewiston; and **Hells Canyon NRA Headquarters,** 88401 Hwy. 82, Enterprise, OR 97828, 541/426-5546. Online, see www.fs.fed.us/hellscanyon.

RIGGINS

While Salmon and even Banks also compete for the title of "Idaho's whitewater capital," Riggins takes the prize. The Salmon River flows right through town, on the last legs of its run down from Redfish Lake. The Little Salmon River joins it here, and the two flow downstream together another 60 miles, through Lower Salmon Gorge to the Snake River. The Snake's Hells Canyon stretch lies just over the Seven Devils to the west. In short, Riggins is surrounded by a lot of big water. You can feel a buzz of excitement as soon as you enter town. Guide shops and outfitters line both sides of the highway, and packs of river rats—chronically young, tan, and buffed—linger insouciantly outside local delis and coffeehouses, planning the next trip.

Get out on the water as soon as the area's short spring begins to wilt away. Riggins sits at the narrow bottom of Salmon River Gorge, whose walls trap the heat like an oven. It bakes here in summer; shade is at a premium and local ice-cream vendors dish out the sundaes nonstop.

River Trips

Riggins is the center for guide services offering float trips on either or both the main Salmon run above town and the Salmon River Gorge stretch downstream from Riggins. Among the many are **Canyon Cats,** 527 13th St., Clarkston, WA 99403, 509/758-8984 or 888/628-3772, which uses sleek and sporty twin-pontoon catarafts for its trips; **Epley's Whitewater Adventures,** P.O. Box 987, McCall, ID 83638, 208/628-3052 or 800/233-1813; **Exodus Wilderness Adventures,** P.O. Box 1231, Riggins, ID 83545, 800/992-3484, **Salmon River Experience,** 812 Truman, Moscow, ID 83843,

208/882-2385 or 800/892-9223; and **Wapiti River Guides,** 128 N. Main, Riggins, ID 83549, 208/628-3523 or 800/488-9872, which uses gorgeous wooden dories on its trips.

Rates for float trips generally range around $40–55 for a half-day trip, $65–90 for a full day, and about $140–190 per day for longer, two- to six-day floats. Exodus and Wapiti run the priciest, most upscale trips; Wapiti emphasizes natural history, while Exodus makes use of jet-boats on some of its excursions.

If you'd rather float and fish than paddle white-water, call **Natsoh Koos River Outfitters,** P.O. Box 1439, Riggins, ID 83549, 208/628-3131 or 800/539-3963, which leads fishing trips on the Salmon near Riggins. Exodus and Wapiti also offer guided fishing.

Hiking

Riggins is surrounded by great backcountry full of hiking trails. To the west lies Hells Canyon National Recreation Area. About 20 miles east is the Gospel-Hump Wilderness. Access the Gospel-Hump at the Wind River Pack Bridge trailhead, out Salmon River Road (FR 1614) east of town.

Entertainment and Events

The best entertainment in town is the after-dark people-watching at the **Seven Devils Steakhouse and Saloon,** 312 S. Main, 208/628-3351, which hosts live music on a regular basis.

On the Riggins events calendar, the town's annual **Salmon River Jet Boat Races** are held in mid-April; the boats roar up the main Salmon be-tween White Bird and Riggins in an interna-tional competition, the first leg of the U.S. Championships. The first weekend in May, the venerable **Riggins Rodeo** kicks up its heels, bringing Western fun and the obligatory parade. For more information on these and other events, call the Salmon River Chamber of Commerce at 208/628-3778, www.rigginsidaho.com.

Accommodations

Under $50: Around half a dozen mom-and-pop places line either side of the highway through town, most with rates near the top of this category.

The friendly **Riggins Motel,** P.O. Box 1157, Rig-gins, ID 83549, 208/628-3001 or 800/669-6739, has good shade, along with a hot tub, cable TV with HBO, a barbecue, and picnic tables. The motel is in the middle of town on the west side of the highway. On the south side of Riggins is **Salmon River Motel,** 1203 S. Hwy. 95, 208/628-3231 or 888/628-3025, a basic road motel with cable TV and coin laundry. Pets okay.

$50–100: On the town's north end, on the east (river) side of the highway, and on the low end of this price range, sits the two-story **Riverview Motel,** P.O. Box 453, Riggins, ID 83549, 208/628-3041 or 888/256-2322. Each of its 16 rooms has a river view, and a trail be-hind the motel leads to a riverside picnic table. Nonsmoking rooms are available.

The **Best Western Salmon Rapids Lodge,** 1010 S. Main St., 208/628-2743 or 877/957-2743, enjoys prime real estate at the confluence of the Salmon and Little Salmon Rivers. All 55 rooms have refrigerators, hair dryers, and two phones with data ports. More expensive suites available. Amenities include an indoor pool and fitness room, an outdoor patio and hot tub, and a guest laundry.

South of Riggins in the hamlet of Pollock, the Northwest Voyageurs outfitting company, 800/727-9977, runs an **adventure lodge** on the Lit-tle Salmon River. It's a homey place with 11 guest rooms and lots of common space. Rates include breakfast.

Camping

Riverside RV Park straddles Big Salmon Road on the south side of town, offering 15 sites with full hookups but no other facilities; $15 a night. For more information, check in at the Chevron station in town, 208/628-3390. **River Village RV Park,** 1434 N. Hwy. 95, 208/628-3441, is on the Main Salmon and has showers and a laundromat.

Salmon River Road (FR 1614) follows the river 28 miles east from town to Vinegar Creek, a popular boat-launch site. Along the way, you'll pass Ruby Rapids (a good place to look for gar-nets along the shore), **Allison Creek Picnic Area,** the USFS **Spring Bar Campground** (called "heaven on earth" by one reader; 17 sites, fee), and the **Van Creek Picnic Area/Campground** (two sites, free).

Food

The local favorite for a full sit-down meal is **Cattlemens Restaurant,** 601 Main St., 208/628-3195, which offers basic road food three meals a day. Save room for the homemade pie. **Salmon River Inn,** 129 S. Main St., 208/628-3813, looks suspiciously touristy from the outside but offers a spacious and comfortable atmosphere and great grub inside. Homemade pizzas and submarine sandwiches are the specialties, and the dairy case is stocked with first-rate ice cream. Microbrews, wine, and wine coolers are also poured.

Information

Contact the **Salmon River Chamber of Commerce** at P.O. Box 289, Riggins, ID 83549, 208/628-3778, www.rigginsidaho.com. The chamber maintains a visitor information booth in the center of town on the west side of the highway. For recreation information, contact the **Hells Canyon NRA-Idaho Office,** 189 Hwy. 95 (on the south side of town), P.O. Box 832, Riggins, ID 83549, 208/628-3916.

EAST OF RIGGINS

East up the Salmon River from Riggins lie three upscale wilderness lodges. The first you can drive to. Reaching the other two usually entails a jetboat ride up the river. All three charge rates in the over-$250 category once you factor in transportation, but in each case those rates include three meals a day and all activities.

The exclusive **Lodge at Riggins Hot Springs,** P.O. Box 1247, Riggins, ID 83549, 208/628-3785, lies on the shore of the Salmon River, 10 miles east of Riggins up Salmon River Road. Long before today's lodge was built, the Nez Perce frequented the natural hot springs here, which they called Weh-min-kesh, or "Healing Waters." In 1900, Fred and Clara Riggins bought the land, giving the site its current name. Over the years, the property changed ownership and character a number of times, even doing a stint as a haven for moonshiners during the Prohibition

era. Today's lodge was built in 1991. The 10 guest rooms are furnished in Native American–theme decor, and each has a private bath. Some rooms have a private balcony overlooking the river. Inside the lodge you'll find a spa, saunas, satellite TV, and a game room. Outside is the natural mineral hot-springs spa—a beautiful, crystal-clear pool filled with those healing waters. Packages with fishing, hunting, whitewater rafting, or jetboating excursions are available. Reservations are required; no drop-ins.

Shepp Ranch, P.O. Box 5446, Boise, ID 83705, 208/343-7729, lies 45 miles east of Riggins on the north bank of the Salmon, at the mouth of Crooked Creek. The ranch's backyard is the 206,000-acre Gospel-Hump Wilderness, and outdoor recreation in the midst of this wild solitude is the main attraction here. Available activities include jetboating, rafting, trail riding, fishing, hiking, and soaking your cares away in the hot tub. The family-style meals are made with fresh garden vegetables, local berries, and trout from the river. No roads lead into the ranch; you have to come by trail, boat, or plane; call for more information and help with arrangements.

Even farther in than Shepp Ranch is **Mackay Bar Ranch,** P.O. Box 7968, Boise, ID 83707, 800/854-9904, which lies at the confluence of the Main Salmon and the South Fork Salmon. Rates here include roundtrip jetboat transportation from Vinegar Creek, a 26-mile drive east of Riggins. Offerings and amenities include trail rides, jetboat tours, hunting and fishing packages, a hot tub, and more.

NORTH OF RIGGINS

Lucile

In little Lucile you'll find **Prospector's Gold RV Park & Campground,** P.O. Box 313, Lucile, ID 83542, 208/628-3773. Both tenters and RVers are welcome at the riverside park. Besides the river itself, other amenities include horseshoe pits, a volleyball court, and restrooms.

Slate Creek

Ten miles south of White Bird on the highway is the USFS Slate Creek Ranger Station, home of

THE BATTLE OF WHITE BIRD HILL

In 1855, the Nez Perce swallowed their pride and agreed to the white man's treaty creating a 5,000-square-mile reservation for the Indians. Not long thereafter, gold was discovered on that reservation and miners came pouring in. So in 1863, the government drew up a new treaty, reducing the original 5,000 square miles of the reservation to 500. The Nez Perce bands whose lands were not affected by the treaty signed it; the others did not. The government originally took no action against these "nontreaty" Nez Perce. But in January 1877, the government's Indian Agent for the Nez Perce ordered all nontreaty Nez Perce onto the reservation by June 14 of that year.

On June 2, 1877, the nontreaty bands of Chiefs Joseph and White Bird gathered at Tolo Lake, just north of White Bird, preparing to enter the reservation. But then a trio of angry young braves rode out of that camp and killed four whites in the area. The rebel braves were soon joined by 17 others, and went on to kill a dozen more whites over the next couple of days. Word reached army general Oliver O. Howard at Fort Lapwai, who sent two companies of troops under the command of Captain David Perry to put down the uprising. Howard sent off a message to General McDowell in San Francisco, describing the situation and saying, "Think we will make short work of it."

Knowing that troops were on the way, Joseph and White Bird realized there would be trouble. Despite having resigned themselves to entering the reservation and living in peace, it seemed to them now that their only alternative was to fight or flee. They moved their camp to the bottom of White Bird hill and planned their defense for the anticipated attack. As it turned out, their plan was a good one.

Early on the morning of June 17—about a week shy of the one-year anniversary of Custer's annihilation at Little Big Horn—Perry and about 100 cavalrymen rode confidently south from Fort Lapwai, reached the top of this hill, and started down it in search of the Indian camp. For most of the way the soldiers had no view of the camp. The Nez Perce used the topography to their advantage, taking positions hidden from Perry, but ready to spring into action if the need arose.

Some authorities say the Nez Perce sent three warriors riding toward Perry carrying a flag of truce, and that they were fired upon by the soldiers. Other authorities say there was no such effort, and the Nez Perce attack took the army completely by surprise. In any case, suddenly Perry was faced with a barrage of gunfire from the Nez Perce. One of the first Indian gunshots picked off Perry's bugler, which was particularly troublesome for the bluecoats: Perry had spread his men out in three different groups and now had no way to communicate commands. Each of the other two groups had a bugler also, but both had dropped their horns at some point in the panic.

Perry's cavalry found itself in chaos, not knowing how to respond to the well-planned Nez Perce attack. Though the Indians were significantly outnumbered, the battle quickly became a rout. The army troops fled back up White Bird Hill as best they could, with the Nez Perce in hot pursuit.

When the battle was over, the Nez Perce had killed 34 of Perry's men and sustained not a single loss themselves. But they knew General Howard, like the hydra, would come after them with far more troops, hungry for revenge. The Nez Perce packed up their camp and began their now legendary flight, which ended in surrender three and a half months and 1,500 miles later at Bear's Paw, Montana.

the Nez Perce National Forest's **Salmon River Ranger District,** HC 01 Box 70, White Bird, ID 83544, 208/839-2211. Out front, a small 1909 log cabin once used as a firefighter's guard station now serves as a Forest Service museum.

Slate Creek, now a ghost town, formerly supplied the booming mining camp of Florence. Heading east up Slate Creek Road (FR 354) will take you past the BLM's **North Fork Campground** (five sites, free) and on up to the boundary of the Gospel Hump Wilderness, where you'll find the USFS **Rocky Bluff Campground** (four sites, fee). Just south of Slate Creek Road on the river is the BLM's **Slate Creek Campground** (six sites, fee, good wheelchair accessibility).

Hammer Creek

The BLM's **Hammer Creek Recreation Area** is a popular put-in point for rafters heading down the Lower Salmon Gorge. Here you'll also find an eight-site campground (fee) with good wheelchair accessibility. To get to the area, turn off Highway 95 at a well-marked turnoff just before the White Bird exit. The sign is marked Hammer Creek/Pittsburg Landing. Cross the Salmon River, turn right, and follow the road to the campground. For more information, contact the **BLM Cottonwood Resource Area,** Rt. 3 Box 181, Cottonwood, ID 83522, 208/962-3245.

White Bird

Just past the turnoff to the little town of White Bird, Highway 95 climbs White Bird Grade. This hill was long a major stumbling block in the effort to link the north and south halves of the state. Road construction began here in 1915, using convict labor, and wasn't completed for regular traffic until 1921. That old road is east of today's Highway 95, the White Bird Grade portion of which wasn't completed until 1975.

As you drive up the highway today from White Bird onto the Camas Prairie, you'll pass one of the most historic battlefields in the history of the West. **White Bird Battlefield** lies on the expansive hillside to your right (see the sidebar "The Battle of White Bird Hill"). Here on June 17, 1877, the opening battle of the Nez Perce War took place. A turnout along the highway toward the top of the hill describes the fight in detail. But to get the best feel for the history of the event, continue to the top of the hill and take the interpretive drive down the old road. An excellent National Park Service pamphlet, *White Bird Battlefield Auto Tour,* brings the battle to life, moment by moment, as you work your way down the road.

For a copy of the pamphlet or more information about the site, contact **Nez Perce National Historic Park,** Route 1 Box 100, Spalding, ID 83540, 208/843-2261.

Grangeville and Vicinity

After climbing out of White Bird Canyon, you'll top out onto the Camas Prairie, where Native Americans once harvested the roots of the camas plant that grew profusely here. Grangeville began in the mid-1800s as the site of a grange hall and gristmill built by local farmers and ranchers. Later it became a major supply center for miners working the Elk City area. Today, the town of about 3,500 is the seat of enormous Idaho County, an area bigger than the state of New Jersey. The county spans the width of Idaho from Oregon to Montana.

Grangeville is still a hub for Camas Prairie agriculture; the prairie's fertile, volcanic soil produces bumper crops of wheat, barley, peas, clover, hay, and rapeseed. The town also serves as a base camp for recreation trips to Hells Canyon National Recreation Area; the Frank Church–River of No Return and Gospel-Hump Wilderness Areas; and the Clearwater, Lochsa, Salmon, Selway, and Snake Rivers. Basic accommodations, campgrounds, and restaurants are available.

RECREATION
Rafting and Kayaking
Grangeville is a hub for boaters taking to one of the five major rivers within a day's radius of town.

Kayakers often test their skill on the narrow and rocky South Fork of the Clearwater, just east of town along Highways 13 and 14. Rafters like to run the lower 53 miles of the Salmon down to its confluence with the Snake, then continue another 18 miles down the Snake to Pittsburg Landing.

Idaho Afloat, P.O. Box 542, Grangeville, ID 83530, 208/983-2414 or 800/700-2414, runs guided raft trips down both the Snake River through Hells Canyon and the Lower Salmon Gorge. The three- to five-day trips range $850–1250 per person, which includes luxury-level amenities. The company boasts that you "don't have to rough it." Day-end camps with lawnchairs and tablecloth-covered tables are set up by the guides, who prepare and serve three gourmet meals daily. Special trips available include dinner floats and combo float-and-guest ranch trips.

Alpine Skiing

Snowhaven Ski Area, 208/983-3866, is seven miles south of Grangeville on the Grangeville-Salmon Road (FR 221). The road starts on the east end of town opposite the National Forest headquarters; follow it straight up the hill and don't turn left at a junction just outside town.

Snowhaven is a small area: One T-bar and one rope tow serve one 40-acre hill with a 400-foot vertical drop. Lessons are offered for all levels, as well as for telemarkers, snowboarders, and cross-country skiers. A couple of the handful of runs are designated with black diamonds, but at other ski areas, these runs would probably be blue squares. The small day lodge offers light food—burgers, nachos, and the like (no booze)—and the south-facing deck, complete with picnic tables, is sunny and pleasant.

Snowhaven's peak elevation of just 5,600 feet makes for a short season, usually mid-December to mid-March. Hours are Sat.–Sun. (and holidays) 10 A.M.–4 P.M., with some night skiing as crowds and conditions permit. Lift tickets were still a measly $12 for a full day, $8 for a half-day (after 1 P.M.) in 2003, though prices may go up a bit in future seasons. Ski and snowboard rentals and lessons are available and equally inexpensive.

Nordic Skiing

Two miles farther up the road is the **Fish Creek Meadows Park N' Ski Area.** The 10 miles of Nordic trails here are groomed only once a week, and the surrounding area is used heavily by snowmobilers. The area offers a small ski-in cabin with a woodstove, picture windows, and views toward the Gospel-Hump Wilderness. If you've had enough of Fish Creek and want to practice your tele-turns, you can take an ungroomed but marked seven-mile ski trail over to Snowhaven.

For more information, contact the **Grangeville Chamber of Commerce,** Hwy. 95 at Pine St., P.O. Box 212, Grangeville, ID 83530, 208/983-0460, www.grangevilleidaho.com.

Summer and Fall at Fish Creek Meadows

The ski trails here become **mountain biking, horseback riding,** or **hiking** trails after the snow melts. In fall, the area abounds with ripe huckleberries. Near the trailhead you'll find a USFS campground (fee) and a day-use area with a picnic shelter. Much effort has gone into making the area wheelchair-accessible.

Golf

Grangeville Country Club, Rt. 2, Box 845, just south of town along the highway, 208/983-1299, is a private course nevertheless open to the public. The nine-hole, par 35 course has two sets of tees for 18-hole play. It also offers a pro shop, restaurant, and lounge. Greens fee is $12 for nine holes, $18 for 18 holes. The course is usually open from early April until the end of October.

SHOPPING

If you're ridin' into town on your trusty Appaloosa, you might want to head straight to **Ray Holes Saddle Company,** 213 W. Main, 208/983-1460 or 800/527-4526. Founded in 1934, it claims title as the West's oldest saddlery. In addition to saddles, you'll find everything you need for work in the Wild West, including dusters and packer coats, stylish rodeo jackets, and handmade boots.

INFORMATION AND SERVICES

The **Grangeville Chamber of Commerce,** P.O. Box 212, Grangeville, ID 83501, 208/983-0460, maintains a well-stocked visitor center at Highway 95 N. and Pine Street (on the way out of town toward Cottonwood). It's open Mon.–Fri. 10 A.M.–5 P.M.

Recreation information is available from **Nez Perce National Forest Headquarters,** on Highway 13 at the east end of town, Rt. 2 Box 475, Grangeville, ID 83530, 208/983-1950.

HIGHWAY 14 TO ELK CITY, RED RIVER, AND DIXIE

Highway 13 leads east out of Grangeville and soon comes to a junction with Highway 14. Continuing on Highway 13 will take you north from here to Kooskia and Highway 12, while making the hairpin to the right will take you south and east on Highway 14 to Elk City. Either way you'll be traveling through the canyon of the South Fork Clearwater River, a scenic, deep gorge marked in places by massive granite walls rising almost right out of the river. Three small USFS campgrounds line the South Fork on the way to Elk City.

The Elk City area was once part of the booming Buffalo Hump mining district. Today, recreation plays a big role in the local economy, as the area sits in a pocket bordering three wilderness areas. To the northeast is the Selway-Bitterroot Wilderness, to the southeast the Frank Church–River of No Return Wilderness, and to the southwest the Gospel-Hump Wilderness.

McAllister Picnic Area

In addition to being a nice place for a picnic, this is also the trailhead for the **McAllister Trail,** a short day hike that switchbacks up to Earthquake Basin through the old McAllister mining claim and homestead. An interpretive brochure available at the trailhead or Forest Headquarters in Grangeville relates information about the area's fauna, including various birds of prey, spawning steelhead, and wintering elk. The trail is steep in places, and about a mile to the end. It's not a loop

trail, so it'll be that same mile again to get back to the Buick. Bring binoculars, Kool-Aid, and a PBJ. The area is at milepost 11 on Highway 14.

Elk City

Some 50 miles east of the Highway 14/13 junction, you'll come to Elk City, an isolated hamlet lying at the edge of a beautiful broad meadow. The town was founded as a mining camp in 1861, the oldest such settlement in the county. The boom came fast here; within five years of its founding, the town had a population of thousands and more than $3.5 million in gold had been taken from the area. Today the little burg—year-round population approximately 17—is a supply center for campers, hikers, and horsepackers heading out into the surrounding hills. In winter, the area is popular with snowmobilers. Services are limited to a few jack-of-all-trades store/restaurant/motel establishments. One advertises "auto parts and milk shakes." Also here you'll find the office of the USFS **Red River Ranger District,** P.O. Box 416, Elk City, ID 83525, 208/842-2245.

Elk City Wagon Road

Highway 14 is the easy way to get to Elk City. The Elk City Wagon Road is the hard way. Back before asphalt paralleled the South Fork, miners and homesteaders followed an old Nez Perce trail between Stites and Elk City. By 1895, a wagon road was completed along the trail, and soon way stations sprang up. Back then it was a two-day stagecoach trip over the road in summer, or a five-day slog through snowdrifts in winter.

Today, explorers with sturdy vehicles (or snowmobiles in winter) can follow much of the original route between Harpster and Elk City, a 53-mile trip. The west end begins on Wall Creek Road in Harpster. To get there, instead of turning south on Highway 14 at the 14/13 junction, continue a few more miles north on Highway 13 to Harpster. The mostly unpaved road winds east through the mountains, reaching an elevation of more than 6,000 feet near China Point; it's not suitable for monster RVs or trailers. Plan on taking 4–6 hours, and gas up first as you'll find no facilities along the way. A detailed pamphlet describing the route is available from either the

USFS **Clearwater Ranger District,** Rt. 2 Box 475, Grangeville, ID 83530, 208/983-1963, or **Red River Ranger District,** P.O. Box 416, Elk City, ID 83525, 208/842-2245.

Red River Junction

Backtracking from Elk City a few miles down Highway 14, you'll come to the turnoff to Red River and Dixie (County Road 222). The road winds alongside the Red River for a dozen or so miles down to the next major junction at the Red River Ranger District's **Elk City Ranger Station,** P.O. Box 416, Elk City, ID 83525, 208/842-2255. Here you can pick up a travel map to the Nez Perce National Forest and get more local recreation information. Nine USFS campgrounds dot the general area; most are small, free, and have no developed water source. The rangers here can fill you in. If you're so inclined, you can also take a self-guided tour through the nearby **chinook salmon hatchery.**

At the ranger station, you'll have a choice of three routes. Bear left on FR 234 and you'll be headed for Red River Hot Springs. Continue straight and you'll almost immediately be faced with another fork. The turnoff to the left, FR 468, is one of the great Idaho off-pavement adventure roads, known variously as the Southern Nez Perce Trail, the Magruder Road, Parker Road, Elk City–Darby Road, or Montana Road. If you continue straight ahead on FR 222 instead, you'll wind up in the former mining hamlet of Dixie.

Red River Hot Springs and Vicinity

Red River Hot Springs, Red River Rd., Elk City, ID 83525, 208/842-2589, a year-round commercial establishment, offers rustic cabins and modern lodge rooms ($50–100), a hot springs pool, hot tub, and restaurant. Just follow FR 234 from Elk City Ranger Station 11 miles right into the parking lot. Day-use fee is $4 adults, $3 kids 12 and under. Accommodations rates include use of the pool.

Next door, the USFS **Red River Campground** has 40 sites with drinking water and a fee. This place gets crowded in summer due to its proximity to the hot springs. On July 4th weekend, it's like a backcountry city; Winnebagos and Airstreams park cheek by jowl, and scores of campfires blaze on into the wee hours of the morning. It's festive, but lacking in solitude. Other USFS campgrounds along FR 234 include four-site **Ditch Creek** and five-site **Bridge Creek.** Both are free.

Red River Corrals Guest Ranch, HC01 Box 18, Elk City, ID 83525, 208/842-2228, is on the same road but not quite as far as the hot springs. The ranch has been run by Archie and Eileen George for 35 years. It's open mid-May to mid-November and offers three rustic log cabins ($50–100) updated with modern amenities; each has a kitchen and bath, and one is large enough for big groups. You might spot some of the area's abundant wildlife—moose, elk, or ospreys— right from your cabin.

The Magruder Road

From its western terminus near the Red River Ranger Station, FR 468—the historic Magruder Road—winds 95 off-pavement miles up and over the Continental Divide, joining FR 473 18.5 miles southwest of Darby, Montana. It was grandfathered out of the two major wilderness areas here—the Frank Church–River of No Return Wilderness to the south and the Selway-Bitterroot Wilderness to the north— and constitutes a narrow nonwilderness ribbon between them.

The single lane road is often rocky and steep— definitely not suitable for trailers, and not much fun in the old Park Avenue or Riviera. It ranges in elevation from 3,700 feet up to an airy 8,200 feet on the north flank of Salmon Mountain. Along the way you might find the road blocked by blown-down trees, mudholes, snowdrifts, or washouts. Your average speed probably won't exceed 10–12 miles per hour, and absolutely no services are available en route: from gas station to gas station it's 116.5 miles. If this still sounds like fun, fill your tank and double-check your spare before you start out. Carry a shovel, axe, plenty of food and water, warm clothes, a sleeping bag, a good first-aid kit, and your camera.

You can drive from one end to the other in a long 10- to 12-hour day, but after about half

THE MAGRUDER MASSACRE

The Magruder Road has a rich history. Much of the road follows a trail used by the Nez Perce on their buffalo-hunting expeditions into Montana beginning in the mid-18th century. And when gold fever hit the Elk City area in the 1860s, miners and outfitters used the trail to get back and forth between the Idaho and Montana goldfields.

In October 1863, Elk City mining supplier Lloyd Magruder and four companions took the trail on their way back from a profitable sales trip to Virginia City, Montana. Along the way, they were joined by four strangers. Late on the night of Oct. 11, these four men murdered and robbed Magruder and his companions and fled to San Francisco. They might have gotten away with the crime but for the persistent efforts of Magruder's friend, Hill Beachy. Beachy relentlessly tracked down the murderers in California and succeeded in bringing them back to trial in Lewiston. They were found guilty and executed by hanging—the first legal hanging in Idaho Territory. Today you'll find a memorial to the Magruder Massacre along the route, 50.8 miles from the Red River end.

that time you'd be whupped and cranky. Instead, break it into a two-day or longer trip. Six primitive campgrounds are available along the way; only one—**Granite Springs** at mile 17.3—has a developed water source. The **Observation Point** campground is 48.4 miles from the Red River end of the road. At an elevation of 7,620 feet, it offers sweeping views south into the Frank Church Wilderness and Salmon River Mountains. Another, **Magruder Crossing,** at Paradise Road Junction, is 59.7 miles from Red River. Here, rafters take a spur road north to the put-in for the Wild and Scenic Selway River. A third option for overnighters is the USFS **Horse Heaven Cabin,** about 45 miles from Red River Ranger Station. The one-room log cabin lies in a lush, grassy meadow, sleeps four in two sets of bunk beds, and rents for $25 a night, year-round. For reservations and information contact the

USFS **West Fork Ranger District,** 6735 West Fork Rd., Darby, MT 59829, 406/821-3269.

Dixie

From Red River Ranger Station it's 14 miles south to Dixie, population 27. The place began as a mining camp back in 1862, when a couple of Elk City sourdoughs wandered over this way and discovered color in Dixie Gulch. By 1900 Dixie was a boomtown. Today it holds a few loggers, a few miners, and a few hangers-on who like the isolation.

From Dixie you can loop back to Highway 14 via Big Creek Meadows and the Crooked River; take County Road 222 through Dixie about five miles to the old **Dixie Guard Station** and turn north on FR 311 (Orogrande-Dixie Road). A USFS interpretive pamphlet, *The Gold Rush Loop Tour,* describes this route, and interpretive signs are strategically located along the way. The route passes old mines, an old mill, and the **Jerry Walker Cabin.** The cabin is available for rent from the Forest Service year-round. It sleeps four and goes for $20 a night. Inside you'll find a fireplace, wood, and cookstove, but no water. For reservations and more information, contact the USFS Red River Ranger District, P.O. Box 416, Elk City, ID 83525, 208/842-2245.

Near Orogrande, at the confluence of the East and West Forks of Crooked River, FR 233 doubles back to the southwest and heads up the Buffalo Hump Corridor, a snowmobiler's haven excluded from the Gospel-Hump Wilderness. Down this road, the USFS **Orogrande Summit Campground** (free, five sites) and **Wildhorse Campground** (free, six sites) both make great base camps, providing ready access to the wilderness area.

Continuing north down Crooked River, you'll see evidence of how the river and its native fish populations were ravaged by intense dredge and hydraulic mining 1936–58. While restoration efforts have been ongoing here on Crooked River since the 1960s, on rivers elsewhere in the state recreational and commercial hydraulic mining continues, albeit on less visually drastic levels. The free, five-site **Crooked River Campground** is on this stretch of road.

NORTH-CENTRAL IDAHO

Salmon River Access

Two roads lead down to the Salmon River from the Red River/Dixie area. The **Whitewater Road** (FR 421) turns east off the Dixie Road 2.5 miles south of Red River Ranger Station. From there it's another 21 miles to the river. After a long slow descent—during which you'll get a great view of **Mallard Creek Falls** and probably some massive clearcuts as well—the road drops precipitously the last few miles down to the river. At the bottom you'll find a trailhead for the Salmon River trail.

The other road to the river is FR 222, which continues south 29 miles beyond Dixie, around the shoulders of Jersey and Cove Mountains, and on down to **Mackay Bar.** Here you'll find a three-site USFS campground, another trailhead for the Salmon River trail, and Mackay Bar Ranch wilderness lodge, usually accessed by jet boat.

ACROSS THE CAMAS PRAIRIE

Cottonwood

Cottonwood began in 1862, when a Mr. Allen (first name unknown) lopped down a couple of the namesake trees and used them to build a way station here. The outpost eventually included a hotel, saloon, store, and stage station.

Cottonwood Butte Ski Area, 208/962-3624 or 208/746-6397 (snow report), lies seven miles west of town. If you're heading north on Highway 95, turn left two exits past the first turnoff to Cottonwood. The area is pretty humble, just a couple of ramshackle buildings. Driving to the base area involves an adventure in karma—first you pass the cemetery, then the prison.

The ski hill offers an 845-foot vertical drop, served by one T-bar and one rope tow—and excellent views of the Camas Prairie. One local said her snowboarder son prefers this hill to Snowhaven. The season usually runs mid-December through mid-March, depending on conditions. Hours are Fri. 6–10 P.M., Sat.–Sun. and holidays 10 A.M.–4 P.M. Lift tickets cost $8–10, and lessons are available.

Dog Bark Park Inn, U.S. Hwy. 95, 208/962-DOGS (208/962-3647), on the north end of Cottonwood, offers one of the most unusual places to bunk down in Idaho. "Sweet Willy," a 30-foot-high beagle, disguises a studio apartment that can sleep up to four people—two in the main room in the beagle's belly and two in a

beagle for rent—Dog Bark Park Inn in Cottonwood

© JULIE FANSELOW

loft in the mutt's muzzle. It's available April–Nov. for $88 double occupancy ($8 per person for extras), including a refrigerator and pantry stocked with all the makings for a hearty continental breakfast.

For more information about the town, contact the **City of Cottonwood,** 506 King St., Cottonwood, ID 83522, 208/962-3231. Also in town is the office of the **BLM Cottonwood Resource Area,** Rt. 3 Box 181, Cottonwood, ID 83522, 208/962-3245.

You can tune in **NPR** in the area at station KNWO, 90.1 FM.

Keuterville

Keuterville Road separates the tourist from the gypsy. The "big" towns of the Camas Prairie—Grangeville, Cottonwood, Craigmont—aren't big by anything other than rural Idaho standards, but a highway runs through them and you'll find them on your map. Keuterville Road, on the other hand, doesn't go anywhere you need to be. It makes a long lazy loop out around the back of Cottonwood Butte, connecting farms and wooded ranches and eventually entering a maze of lonely gravel roads between the butte and Winchester. Drive slowly: Speeders annoy the white-tailed deer, which outnumber people back here. And make sure your gas tank's full; road signs are minimal, road forks are frequent, and many of the forks dead-end. You may get lost. Which is exactly why you drive out Keuterville Road in the first place.

Near the turnoff from Highway 95 and visible from the highway, **St. Gertrude's Monastery** is impressive enough to pull even pagans in for a gander. The twin-towered Romanesque priory was built of locally quarried stone and has been home to the Benedictine Sisters since 1920. It's now on the National Register. Adjacent to the monastery, the **Historical Museum at St. Gertrude,** 208/962-7123 or 208/962-3224, holds a potpourri of historical artifacts, including pioneer and mining gear, a mineral collection, and utensils handcrafted by legendary Salmon River mountain man Sylvan Hart. It's open May 1–Sept. 30, Tues.–Sat. 9:30 A.M.–4:30 P.M.; Sun. 1:30–4:30 P.M.; Oct. 1–April 30, Tues.–Sat.

9:30 A.M.–4:30 P.M. Admission is $4 adults, $1 students 7–17.

Continuing down the road, you'll enjoy distant views of the Seven Devils mountains; a roadside collection of antique tractors; and finally Keuterville itself. The town, such as it is, was founded around a sawmill in 1883 and named after settler Henry Kuther. Unfortunately for Henry, the Post Office Department needed glasses back then, and what should have been Kutherville came out Keuterville instead. Rafters have been known to float Grave Creek, a tributary of a tributary of the Salmon River, which starts just south of town.

Craigmont and Nezperce

Both these towns are on the Nez Perce Indian Reservation, which the U.S. government opened to white settlers in 1895. Craigmont began as two separate towns engaged in a bitter rivalry. The first town, Ilo, was founded here in 1896. When the railroad came to the area in 1907, it bypassed the town by a mile and started a new town called Vollmer on the north side of the tracks. In the ensuing years, Ilo gradually moved to occupy the south side of the tracks. The two towns each had their own schools, churches, banks, and merchants, and kept themselves segregated from one another. As a result of the intercommunity feud, Nezperce was awarded the county seat in 1911. After World War I, Ilo and Vollmer finally laid down their arms and agreed to consolidate as one town—Craigmont—named after Colonel William Craig, Idaho's first permanent white settler. In 1920, the towns celebrated their reconciliation with a mock "wedding," a tradition that continues as an annual "anniversary" today. It's a good excuse for a party, which Craigmont throws in style—look for a softball tourney, parade, auction, and street dance in June. For more information, contact the **Craigmont City Hall,** 109 E. Main St., Craigmont, ID 83523, 208/924-5432.

From Craigmont, Highway 62 heads east toward Nezperce. Along the way you'll pass a blink-and-you'll-miss-it place called Mohler. Here, those looking for a spectacularly scenic route to the Clearwater Valley can head north on **Mohler Road.** At first, this road continues across the rolling farmland of the Camas Prairie along

Central Ridge, but soon the aptly named Big Canyon comes into sight. It is big all right, and steep, and a very long way down to the waters of Big Canyon Creek at the bottom. Just when you figure the road will dead-end, blocked by this formidable abyss, it makes a dogleg to the canyon rim and drops over the edge. If you can overcome the butterflies enough to continue, you'll probably have to stifle visions of Wile E. Coyote meeting the valley floor in a muffled poof of dust thousands of feet below. The narrow one-lane dirt road with no guardrails clings precariously to the canyon walls as it descends into the depths. If you don't meet oncoming traffic—and there's virtually no traffic of any kind out here—the incredible views are well worth the white knuckles. If you do meet oncoming traffic, keep calm, and remember that the vehicle traveling uphill has the right of way. The road ends at the community of Peck, off Highway 12 about 10 miles west of Orofino.

Back up on the prairie, the town of Nezperce lies in the heart of the Camas Prairie, an area favored by the Nez Perce for its abundant supply of camas roots. The town celebrates Prairie Days the second week of July.

Winchester

Winchester Lake State Park, P.O. Box 186, Winchester, ID 83555, 208/924-7563, occupies a woodsy area at the foot of the Craig Mountains. Its centerpiece is 103-acre Winchester Lake, a **fishing** hole popular with warm-weather anglers in summer and ice-fishers in winter. The lake is stocked with rainbow trout, and also holds largemouth bass and bullhead catfish. A boat ramp is available (electric motors only), and there are some canoe and kayaks available for rent. When enough snow falls here, a small **Nordic skiing** trail system is set. Two beginner-to-intermediate groomed trails skirt the lake and loop around Craig Mountain. Another three-quarter-mile trail is more difficult and ungroomed. The elevation here is only about 4,000 feet, so the snowpack is vulnerable to rain and warm spells. Call for conditions before coming here to ski. The park's campground offers the usual state-park amenities: clean restrooms and showers, campsites with hookups, and picnic tables and grills. There also are three yurts available year-round, each heated and able to sleep up to six people. They cost $45 for up to four people; extra people (up to two) are $4 each.

Winchester Lake is named for the adjacent small town of Winchester, which in turn is named for the rifle that won the West. You can see a giant one suspended above one of the town's main streets.

About a mile past the park (follow signs) is the **Wolf Center,** P.O. Box 217, Winchester, ID 83555, 208/924-6960, www.wolfcenter.org, a joint project of the Nez Perce tribe and the Wolf Education and Research Center. It's the home of the Sawtooth Pack, a wolf pack that was once studied and photographed by Jim Dutcher in a large compound near Ketchum. Inside the visitor center you'll find exhibits on wolves and their place in the ecosystem, as well as information on Nez Perce culture. Interpretive trails and an observation platform surround the visitor center. The center is open daily 9 A.M.–5 P.M. in summer, with self-guiding tours; admission is $5 adults, $3 ages 6–13, under 6 free. Guided tours are available, too; call ahead for cost, dates, and times.

Lewiston and Vicinity

Lewiston (population 30,500) lies at the confluence of the Snake and Clearwater Rivers, a city in the traditional homeland of the Nez Perce, and a pivotal point for Lewis and Clark on their journey west in 1805. At an elevation of just 736 feet above sea level, it's also Idaho's lowest city. The resulting mild winters allow golfers here to enjoy the sport year-round and make for lovely springs that turn the city into a riot of blooming trees.

Amazing as it may seem, this city 470 miles from the Pacific Ocean is a seaport, Idaho's only one. Barge traffic comes up the Columbia and Snake Rivers to serve the Port of Lewiston, which lies at the upper limit of commercial navigation on the Snake.

River, rail, and road connections make Lewiston an important packing and shipping center. The city's largest employer is the big Potlatch mill perched on the south bank of the Clearwater. And the town also likes its jetboats, those nimble aluminum speedsters that hammer up through the rapids on the Snake and Salmon Rivers. Several manufacturers in town make Lewiston the jetboat capital of the West.

© JULIE FANSELOW

the confluence of the Snake and Clearwater Rivers

Like Pocatello in southeast Idaho, Lewiston feels blue-collar to the core. Which isn't to say it lacks in culture—Lewis-Clark State College regularly brings the arts to town, a venerable community-theater troupe draws audiences for live drama, and the historic downtown has made some modest attempts at a facelift. But on a day-to-day basis, when the sun goes down it takes the town with it.

Early Lewiston

When gold was discovered up the Clearwater in 1860, the site of today's Lewiston was transformed from a Nez Perce horse pasture into a port and miners' supply camp. Steamboats cruised up the Columbia and Snake Rivers, dropping off thousands of hopeful prospectors. The community that soon sprouted around the steamboat docks was squatting illegally on the Nez Perce reservation, but the cooperative Nez Perce agreed to give white merchants one square mile where they could sell their goods to the miners. The earliest buildings were simple wood frames covered with canvas, which gave the settlement its early nickname, "Ragtown." Lewiston was formally founded on the site in May 1861.

The miners were just passing through, not looking to acquire land and settle down. But soon farmers showed up to grow crops to supply the mines. The farmers did need land, and lots of it. As the early mining strikes up the Clearwater turned into a full-fledged boom, Lewiston grew exponentially. When Congress created Idaho Territory in 1863, Lewiston was named territorial capital. But there was one small problem: the city was still trespassing on the Nez Perce reservation. In typical fashion, the U.S. government "renegotiated" the original treaty, vastly reducing the reservation's size and moving its boundaries well outside of Lewiston.

The city's capital status lasted just a year and a half. By the end of 1864, the Clearwater mines were in decline. Down south, however, the Boise Basin mines were booming, and Boise sought the coveted capital crown. In April 1865, Territorial

NORTH-CENTRAL IDAHO

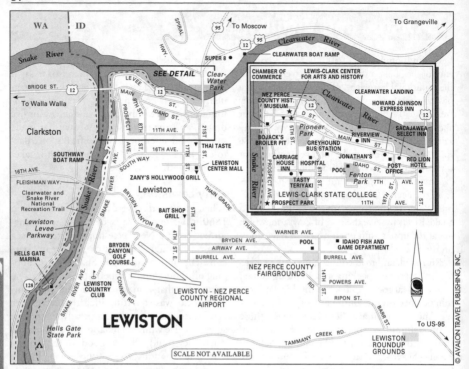

Secretary and Boise supporter C. DeWitt Smith rode into Lewiston with a contingent of federal troops from Fort Lapwai, stealing away the Territorial seal and archives under threat of force. Smith delivered the purloined goods to Boise, and Lewiston's governmental glory days came to an end.

Lewis-Clark State College

Founded in 1893, this four-year state college, 500 8th Ave., 208/799-5272 or 800/933-5272, offers undergraduate degrees in about 20 different fields, as well as two-year associate degrees in a variety of vocational programs. And the school's Warriors men's baseball team is legendary, having won the NAIA world series numerous times. The school's 3,100 students attend classes in one of the most beautiful parts of Lewiston—a hilltop neighborhood full of stately homes and towering trees overlooking the city and rivers below. Even if you're not a student, the small campus—covered with green lawns and tidy brick buildings—makes a nice place for a picnic or an impromptu round of disc golf.

Public Art

While on the LCSC campus, amble across the Centennial Mall, an on-campus pedestrian plaza and sculpture garden commemorating the indigenous Nez Perce people and their first meeting with Lewis and Clark. In fact, Lewiston is packed with public art commemorating the expedition and its Nez Perce hosts. The most impressive are a group of sculptures by David Govedare and Keith Powell, arrayed across the highway medians at the north entrance to town. The Nez Perce ponies look so realistic that the local police have reportedly received calls about loose horses. Other works include a bronze statue of Lewis, Clark, and Sacagawea below the Red Lion Inn; a Sacagawea statue dating to 1911 in Pioneer Park; and an unusual sculpture by Idaho artist Nancy

Dreher at the confluence of the Clearwater and Snake Rivers. Titled *Tsceminicum*—meaning "Meeting of the Waters" in the Nez Perce language—the sculpture depicts a symbolic earth mother sustaining the region's abundant wildlife. The statue is the highlight of an interpretive shelter offering displays about Lewis and Clark's visit. To get there, either park your car in a lot near the west end of D Street and walk across a bridge, or find your way along the Lewiston Levee Parkway bike path from other parts of town.

Prospect Park

This little gem of a park is nothing but a small plot of grass and trees with some picnic tables, but oh what a view. Come up in late afternoon and watch the sunset over the Snake River and Clarkston, Washington. The site was originally a Chinese cemetery. In 1893, the local Chinese community allowed the city to move the graves to Normal Hill Cemetery, on the condition that this site remain, forever, "a pleasant place." And so it is. The park lies along Prospect Avenue, just west of the LCSC campus.

Lewis-Clark Center for Arts and History

Affiliated with Lewis-Clark State College, this downtown museum and gallery, 415 Main St., 208/799-2243, presents rotating shows of local and regional artists, as well as other exhibits of artistic or historical interest. A permanent historical display remembers Lewiston's early Chinese community. The gift shop sells jewelry, crafts, books, and assorted CDs by past performers in the center's concert series. Gallery hours are Tues.–Sat. 11 A.M.–4 P.M.; admission is free.

Nez Perce County Historical Museum

This little museum at 0306 3rd St. at C St., 208/743-2535, once housed the Luna House Hotel, owned by Hill Beachy of Magruder Road fame. In its early days, the hotel was a primitive, timber-and-canvas affair, matching Lewiston's wild and wooly character. Territorial governor Caleb C. Lyon spent the night at the hotel once, reluctantly accepting the sandbags placed around

his bed after he was told they were there to protect him from stray gunshots in the streets.

The museum's exhibits cover all aspects of the area's history, both its Nez Perce and Euro-American heritage. Among the highlights are a fantastic collection of old photographs—a personal favorite being a 1927 ice-cream wagon with a gaggle of goopy gremlins posed alongside—and a huge, stunning triptych of Chief Joseph in three stages of his life. The latter work was painted by Dan Piel, a former member of the fine-arts faculty at Washington State University.

Museum hours are Tues.–Sat. 10 A.M.–4 P.M. Admission is free, but the jar by the door is always hungry.

Spiral Highway

Call it the Lombard Street of Lewiston, this "old road" to Moscow snakes back and forth up some 64 switchbacks to the top of Lewiston Hill, nearly 3,000 feet above the city. Up on the canyon rim you'll get impressive views of Lewiston, Clarkston, and the two rivers. The old road joins the new Highway 95 at the top. From town, turn left at the second exit north of Clearwater Memorial Bridge, then soon make a right onto the old road, following signs.

Champion Trees

When Lewis and Clark came through here in 1805, the only trees they noted were the humble red-stem willow and hackberry. But over the years, Lewiston residents have planted trees of every description all over town, turning the city into something of a giant arboretum. You'll see variegated box elder, blue ash, red maple, umbrella black locust, American chestnut, flowering ash, flowering pink dogwood, and numerous others, many of which are Idaho "champion trees"—the biggest specimens of their respective species in the state. A free map to the champion trees is available at the chamber of commerce.

RECREATION

Hells Gate State Park

Tenters and RVers passing through town will find Hells Gate State Park unbeatable. The 200-acre park, 3620A Snake River Ave., Lewiston, ID 83501, 208/799-5015, just four miles south of downtown, is right on the river; swimming, boating, and fishing are steps from your campsite. It offers fun and informative interpretive programs, plenty of green grass and trees, picnic tables and barbecue grills, and clean restrooms with showers. Here you'll also find boat-launch ramps and trails for hiking, biking, or horseback riding. Thanks to Lewiston's mild, low-elevation winters, the park and marina are both open year-round.

The large visitor center contains a wealth of information on Lewiston's natural and human history, as well as on the exploration and settlement of Hells Canyon. Among other facts, you'll learn that today's park sits on the site of a large and important Nez Perce village—"Hasotino," or "great eel fishery"—that was occupied until the end of the 19th century. Around the back of the visitor center you'll find more interpretive information and panoramic views of the river and Swallows Nest Rock, an impressive basalt cliff on the opposite bank. By late 2004, Hells Gate State Park will have a new interpretive center to help commemorate the Lewis and Clark bicentennial and the expedition's trek across Idaho.

The park charges $4 as its vehicle-entrance fee. Of the park's 93 campsites, 64 have water and power hookups. Eight new camping cabins can each sleep up to five people for $35 a night.

Clearwater and Snake River National Recreation Trail

Urban hikers and bicyclists will appreciate this 25-mile-long trail system, which runs along both the Idaho and Washington riverbanks. On the Idaho side, the trail begins at Lewiston's Clearwater Park. It crosses Memorial Bridge, turns west past Locomotive Park, Clearwater Landing, West Pond, and the Lewis and Clark Interpretive Center, then continues south down the popular **Lewiston Levee Parkway** to Hells Gate State Park. On the Washington side of the Snake, the trail connects Looking Glass Park on the south with Swallows Park and the Clarkston Greenbelt on the north. Southway Bridge (the "new" bridge) provides the connection for the two halves of the trail system. The trail is wheelchair accessible.

Hells Canyon Jetboat Tours

Several companies run jetboat tours up the Snake River through Hells Canyon. Unlike propeller-driven craft, jetboats move forward by shooting a jet of water out the back. Their inboard automobile engines turn powerful turbine pumps. The advantage of this design is its shallow draft; jetboats can navigate shallow rocky rapids that would destroy a standard inboard or outboard motor.

Unlike rafts, jetboats can go both up and down the river. Also unlike rafts, they pound through the rapids with a deafening roar, beating Mother Nature over the head with huge amounts of raw horsepower. In Hells Canyon—much of it surrounded by wilderness—the jetboats seem out of place to many people.

The marina at Hells Gate State Park serves as the departure point for several commercial jetboat operators. Others leave from the Clarkston side of the river—the Clarkston dock is at 700 Port Dr., behind Quality Inn.

Steelhead Fishing

In fall, the Clearwater comes alive when the steelhead season opens. The river draws anglers from all over the country for a chance to hook one of these brawny fighters. Many angling guides lead trips on the Clearwater during fly-fishing season (late Aug.–Nov.) and drift-tackle season (Nov.–April). Plan on spending

BOB RACE

about $375 a day for two people. Guides include FishHawk Guides LLC, 2210 2nd Ave., Clarkston, WA 99403, 509/758-5662 or 888/548-8896, and Tom Loder's Panhandle Outfitters, S. 12601 Thunder Mountain Ln., Valleyford, WA 99036, 509/922-8289 or 888/300-4868.

Outlying Recreation

Under the long-term efforts of the Idaho Department of Fish and Game, the **Craig Mountain Wildlife Management Area,** 10 miles south of Lewiston, has grown to encompass 24,200 acres. The western boundary of the area includes 14 miles of Snake River frontage, which gives anglers hike-in access to the Snake River. Most of the preserve sits up on the tableland above the river, home to several introduced species, including Rocky Mountain bighorn sheep, wild turkeys, chukar partridge, and sharp-tailed grouse. Native to the area are sizable populations of mule deer, white-tailed deer, elk, Hungarian partridge, blue grouse, and ruffed grouse.

No motor vehicles are permitted in the WMA, but three trailheads provide access to hikers, horsemen, and hunters. From Lewiston, take 21st Street south up to the top of the grade and continue southeast after the road becomes Thain Road. Eventually you'll come to a T intersection at Tammany Creek Road, where you'll turn left and continue first east, then south for approximately five miles to the Waha Road turnoff (to the right). Two trailheads are off Waha Road at Redbird Road. A third provides access to the southern end of the preserve. This trailhead is 16.5 miles south of Redbird Road on Waha Road, then 3.9 miles west on a BLM access road from the Madden Corral. Camping is permitted on the preserve. For a map or more information, contact the Idaho Department of Fish & Game, 1540 Warner Ave., Lewiston, ID 83501, 208/799-5010.

The Lewiston Orchards Irrigation District (LOID) manages two small reservoirs in the same general area. Just past the Redbird Road turnoff is **Waha Lake,** a 100-acre fishing pond stocked with kokanee and rainbow trout, and also holding smallmouth bass and crappie. Continuing south from there, you'll come to Soldiers Meadow Road, which leads east about three miles to **Soldiers Meadow Reservoir,** another fishin' hole similar in size and fish supply to Waha Lake. It's pretty remote out here—you're actually closer to Winchester than Lewiston at this point.

A third LOID reservoir is **Mann Lake,** closer to town. Take Powers Avenue east from the south end of Thain Road. This one's a 130-acre impoundment stocked annually with 25,000 rainbow trout. Also swimming toward your hook here might be a channel catfish, or the usual smallmouth bass and crappie. All three

LOID reservoirs have boat ramps; only electric motors are allowed on Mann Lake. For more information contact either the **Idaho Department of Fish and Game,** 1540 Warner Ave., Lewiston, ID 83501, 208/799-5010, or the **Lewiston Orchards Irrigation District,** 1509 Warner Ave., 208/798-1806.

Golf
Bryden Canyon Golf Course, south of the airport at 445 O'Connor Rd., 208/746-0863, offers a public 18-hole course, driving range, pro shop, lessons, putting green, and a restaurant serving breakfast and lunch as well as beer and wine. Greens fee is $18. Across the river in Clarkston, Washington, is the public, year-round 18-hole **Quail Ridge Public Golf Course,** 3600 Swallow's Nest Dr., 509/758-8501. Greens fees run $20–22.

ENTERTAINMENT AND EVENTS
Entertainment
Lewiston Civic Theatre, Inc., 805 6th Ave., 208/746-3401 (box office) or 208/746-1371 (business office), www.lctheatre.org, has presented community theater in Lewiston since 1961. Productions take place at the company's Anne Bollinger Performing Arts Center, 805 6th Ave. The performance season runs concurrently with the academic year, Sept.–June. The **Lewis-Clark State College Artists Series** regularly brings touring opera, ballet, concert music, and drama productions to the city. For more information call the Lewis-Clark Center for Arts and History, 415 Main St., 208/799-2243.

Events
Lewiston's **Dogwood Festival** blooms for 10 days in late April or early May. Garden tours take center stage, while a rodeo, crafts fair, concerts, and winetastings add to the fun.

Hot August Nights are celebrated midmonth with music, merriment, a river cruise, and a classic car show. The **Lewiston Roundup** is the highlight of the year for rodeo fans; you'll find cowboys and cowgirls struttin' their stuff the first full weekend in September at the rodeo grounds, 7000 Tammany Creek Rd. The third week of

September, the **Nez Perce County Fair** comes to town. For a complete annual events calendar contact the Lewiston Chamber of Commerce.

ACCOMMODATIONS

Under $50

The **Riverview Inn,** downtown at 1325 Main St., 208/746-3311 or 800/806-ROOM (800/806-7666), is a good budget option in Lewiston, with a small pool and fitness room and free doughnuts and coffee in the morning. Right at the top of this rate range, the **Super 8,** 3120 North-South Hwy., 208/743-8808 or 800/800-8000, is a good bare-bones bet if you're just passing through town.

$50–100

At the 90-room **Sacajawea Select Inn,** 1824 Main St., 208/746-1393 or 800/333-1393, amenities include a heated pool, spa and fitness room, guest laundry, a fax and copy machine, 24-hour desk service, and an on-site restaurant and lounge. Non-smoking rooms, kitchenettes, and Jacuzzi suites are all available. Just down the street, **Howard Johnson Express Inn,** 1716 Main St., 208/743-9526 or 800/634-7669, offers a small heated pool, spa, guest laundry, and in-room refrigerators.

A nice B&B in this price category is **Carriage House Inn,** 504 6th Ave., 208/746-4506 or 800/501-4506, in an elegant old neighborhood adjoining the campus of Lewis-Clark State College. Rooms in the main building include the Imperial Suite, with a king-size four-poster bed, full bath, and sitting room, and the Windsor Suite, which has a queen-size antique wrought-iron bed, full bath, and sitting room. An adjoining guest house holds the Victoria Room, with a half bath, sun porch, and white wicker furniture, and the Landau Room, which boasts a cathedral ceiling and a full bath with a Roman tub. Rates include your choice of full or continental breakfast; business travelers get a 10 percent discount midweek. Coffee, tea, and cookies are available all day. Smoking outside only; children over age 12 welcome.

$100–150

The nicest place in town, with rooms often available in the next-lower price range, is the **Red Lion Hotel,** 621 21st St., 208/799-1000 or 800/232-6730. The bright and modern inn offers 130 guest rooms, including 43 minisuites. Amenities include two heated pools (one indoor, one outdoor), a Jacuzzi, a full-size health club, and some of Lewiston's most agreeable dining options.

FOOD

American

The traditional special-occasion or hot-date restaurant is **Jonathan's,** 1516 Main St., 208/746-3438. Entrées lean toward steak and seafood and run $15–30. It's open weekdays for lunch ($5–10) and Mon.–Sat. for dinner. In the Morgan's Alley building is local favorite **Bojack's Broiler Pit,** 311 Main St., 208/746-9532. Steak and seafood entrées range $14–15; prime rib is the house specialty. Bojack's is open for dinner Mon.–Sat.

Over at the Red Lion Hotel, 621 21st St., a selection of excellent restaurants awaits. **M. J. Barleyhoppers Brewery & Sports Pub,** 208/746-5300, brews up half a dozen microbrews right on the premises, and also carries a variety of other micros and imports on tap and in bottles—about 60 different beers in all. Don't try them all in one night. The bar offers pub grub, but you can also order anything off the menus of the Red Lion's other two restaurants, which include a casual café and the hotel's formal dining room. The latter, **Meriwether's,** 208/746-9390, offers a full menu of appetizers, gourmet salads, pastas, poultry dishes, steaks, and seafood. Entrées range $12–22. The dining room looks out over the valley through huge picture windows. It's open nightly for dinner and for Sunday brunch. One other not-to-be-missed part of the hotel is the Exchange (see Drinks and Conversation, below).

Zany's Hollywood Grill, 2006 19th Ave. at 21st St. (in the Lewiston Mall complex), 208/746-8131, qualifies as Lewiston's amusement park of restaurants. The decor is part '50s diner, part junk shop. Cool old stuff—movie memorabilia, carousel animals, an old gas pump—covers the walls, hangs from the ceiling, and occupies every available space. The varied menu includes flame-broiled burgers, fish and chips, pastas, ribs, salads, and sandwiches. An old-timey soda fountain on the side scoops out lots of gooey desserts. Burgers go for around $5–7; dinner entrées around $10–14. Beware, this place is a favorite for birthday parties, school groups, and family outings. It gets packed.

Ethnic Fare

When you need your fix of pad Thai, garlic prawns, or eggplant tofu, head to **Thai Taste,** 1410 21st St., 208/746-6192. Dishes can be prepared as spicy as you'd like, from "For Those Who Hesitate" to "Dragon Fire." The restaurant is open daily for lunch and dinner. **Tasty Teriyaki,** 607 7th Ave., across from the Lewis-Clark State College campus, 208/743-7322, offers Japanese food at lunch and dinner ($6–9), plus espresso, doughnuts, and homemade ice cream. Open Mon.–Sat. 8:30 A.M.–8 P.M.

Breakfast and Lunch

For breakfast or lunch, the **Bait Shop Grill,** 3206 5th St., 208/746-1562, is a Lewiston original. A fishing-trip motif (including a gallery of locals' "My Big Catch" photos), friendly service, and just a little whimsy—meals come served with gummi worms—make this a fun spot for a filling, cheap ($4–7) meal. Open Tue.–Fri. 6 A.M.–2 P.M., Sat.–Sun. 7 A.M.–2 P.M.

Coffee

A coffee cart with class, **Yo Espresso** parks downtown right next to Brackenbury Square, a nifty little urban park with benches and a fountain. Grab an espresso, muffin, and the *Lewiston Morning Tribune* and start your day off right in the park. In chilly weather, the coffee purveyors bring blankets for customers to sit under.

Drinks and Conversation

Check out **The Exchange,** at the Red Lion Hotel, 621 21st St., 208/799-1000. The cozy bar is like a tiny den or library. It's furnished with elegant armchairs and tables for two, and surrounded by bookshelves and art—the perfect place for cognac and conversation with a close friend. No smoking.

SHOPPING

The **Lewis-Clark State College Bookstore** in the Student Union Building on campus, 500 8th Ave., 208/799-2242, is open to students and nonstudents alike. In addition to textbooks, the store carries works of many Northwest authors and a great supply of LCSC Warrior T-shirts, sweatshirts, baseball caps and the like. Hours are Mon.–Thurs. 8 A.M.–5 P.M., Fri. 8 A.M.–4 P.M. **Kling's Stationers,** 704 Main St., 208/743-8501, stocks USGS topo maps, Forest Service maps, the DeLorme Atlas & Gazetter series, and many books on regional history.

    Lewiston Center Mall, 1810 19th Ave. (at 21st St.), 208/746-6847, is a part-indoor, part-outdoor shopping center with about 30 shops, including Bon-Macy's, Sears, and JCPenney.

INFORMATION AND SERVICES

Information

The **Lewiston Chamber of Commerce** is at 111 Main St., 208/743-3531 or 800/473-3543, www.lewistonchamber.org. The *Lewiston Morning Tribune,* 505 C St., 208/743-9411 or 800/745-9411, is one of the state's best daily newspapers.

Transportation

Lewiston-Nez Perce County Regional Airport is at 406 Burrell, 208/746-7962. **Horizon Air,** 800/547-9308, provides regularly scheduled flights to the airport. Car-rental companies at the airport include **Budget,** 208/746-0488 or 800/527-0700, and **Hertz,** 208/746-0411 or 800/654-3131.

NORTH-CENTRAL IDAHO

The Lewis and Clark Highway

Highway 12 heads east from Lewiston, winding along the banks of the Clearwater and Lochsa Rivers for 172 miles to the Montana border at Lolo Pass. This most scenic of Idaho highways also traverses lands rich in history. Traditionally this was part of the homeland of the Nez Perce people, who fished for the Clearwater's then-abundant salmon; hunted deer, elk, and other wild game in the Clearwater Mountains; harvested camas bulbs on the Camas Prairie near Grangeville; and regularly crossed Lolo Pass into Montana on buffalo-hunting trips.

In September 1805, the Nez Perce encountered the white man for the first time when members of the Lewis and Clark expedition—cold, weak, and hungry—staggered into Nez Perce Chief Twisted Hair's camp on the Weippe Prairie. The Nez Perce nursed the explorers back to health, sent them off downriver, and tended their horses until the expedition's return trip the following spring.

The Nez Perce and the Lewis and Clark expedition form the historical foundation for the area. Roadside markers along the length of Highway 12—known as the Lewis and Clark Highway—point out one historical site after another. A portion of the route from Lewiston to Kooskia has also been designated by the state as the **Clearwater Canyons Scenic Byway.** As it climbs slowly up the steep-walled gorge, the vegetation gradually changes—from arid grass- and brush-covered hills near Lewiston to lush, green pine forests around Kooskia and points east.

NEZ PERCE RESERVATION AND NATIONAL HISTORIC PARK

Nez Perce Reservation

Thirteen miles east of Lewiston you'll enter the Nez Perce Indian Reservation, home to many of the 3,300 or so enrolled Nez Perce tribe members. The Nez Perce homeland once spanned from eastern Oregon all the way across Idaho into Montana. In 1855, enough white settlers had moved into the area to cause Washington

Territory's governor to clamor for a treaty. The "deal" he negotiated, to which the peaceable Nez Perce reluctantly agreed, established the Nez Perce Reservation across a 5,000-square-mile area. But just five years later, white prospectors discovered gold on the reservation and the deal was off. In 1863 a new treaty reducing the size of the reservation to just 500 square miles was drawn up. Some bands of the Nez Perce signed the treaty; others refused. The nontreaty Indians kept to their traditional lands and the government looked the other way until 1867, when it demanded with threats of force that the nontreaty Nez Perce move onto the pocket-size reservation. Seeing no choice but to comply, most of the nontreaty Nez Perce resigned themselves to this restricted way of life. But on June 13, 1877, three disgruntled Nez Perce braves took revenge on whites in the Salmon River canyon. General Oliver O. Howard was called on to put down the Nez Perce once and for all, and the Nez Perce War began.

After holding off the Army on a 1,500-mile, three-and-a-half-month flight, the Nez Perce finally surrendered at Bear's Paw, Montana, just 42 miles from the Canadian border and freedom. After the war, the nontreaty Nez Perce were exiled to first Kansas, then Oklahoma, and the remaining Nez Perce were subjected to the "allotment" of their lands. In the process, the size of the Nez Perce Reservation was reduced further. Today it encompasses 88,000 acres (137.5 square miles), less than 3 percent of its original size under the 1855 treaty and a microscopic fraction of the land the Nez Perce once roamed. Lapwai, just down Highway 95 from the park visitor center, is the seat of the Nez Perce tribal government.

Spalding Visitor Center

A brief detour from Highway 12 onto Highway 95 leads to Spalding and the headquarters of Nez Perce National Historic Park, 39063 U.S. Hwy. 95, Spalding, ID 83540, 208/843-2261, www.nps.gov/nepe. Call it a "concept" park: it consists of 38 separate historic sites in Idaho,

Washington, Oregon, and Montana. Taken together, the sites tell the story of 11,000 years of Nez Perce culture, from their pre–Lewis and Clark days to the present. To visit them all entails a 400-mile drive.

The park's Spalding Visitor Center is a large facility adjacent to the site of Henry and Eliza Spalding's old Lapwai Mission. Inside you'll find an auditorium screening a film on Nez Perce history, and a bookstore selling books about the Nez Perce and Northwest history. In the exhibit room you'll find a copy of the 1855 Nez Perce

Treaty signed by President James Buchanan, as well as the Spalding-Allen collection of Nez Perce artifacts, recently purchased from the Ohio Historical Society. It seems the good Reverend Spalding—as much as he tried to get the Nez Perce to adopt the white man's ways—also admired and collected Nez Perce handiwork. In 1846, he sent his collection to a friend, Dr. Dudley Allen of Kinsman, Ohio. Allen's son inherited the artifacts and passed them on to Oberlin College, which in turn donated the collection to the Ohio Historical Society in Columbus. The items were

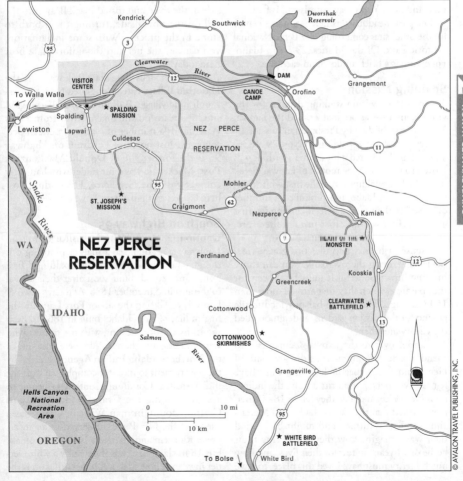

NORTH-CENTRAL IDAHO

"rediscovered" by the National Park Service in 1969 and had been on loan here since the 1970s. In 1994, the Ohio owners said it was time for Idaho to either buy the collection or send it back. After a major fundraising effort, the Nez Perce tribe succeeded in raising the $600,000 acquisition price, and in June 1996, the sale was finalized. The exquisite collection includes gorgeous beaded hide clothing, ornate cradleboards, porcupine quillwork, elk-tooth accessories, and more. The visitor center is open daily Memorial Day to Labor Day 8 A.M.–5:30 P.M., the rest of the year 8 A.M.–4:30 P.M. Closed Thanksgiving, Christmas, and New Year's Day. Admission is free.

The park headquarters here is a nerve center for the other sites composing Nez Perce National Historic Park. Of the 38 sites, 29 are in Idaho. Following is a brief rundown on each site.

Spalding Mission

The mission—within walking distance of the visitor center—was originally called the Lapwai Mission. Established by Presbyterian missionaries Henry and Eliza Spalding on Nov. 29, 1836, and originally located a bit farther south, it was moved to this site at the mouth of Lapwai Creek in 1838. The Spaldings were the first white family to reside in Idaho and produced a number of "firsts" in their tenure here, including the first gristmill, first sawmill, first printed literature, and first white child in the state.

A sense of history pervades this grassy, tree-shaded flat along the riverbank. You can easily imagine how wonderful it must have been for the Spaldings when they first arrived more than 160 years ago. The alluvial bar provided fertile ground for the mission gardens, and salmon filled the Clearwater then.

Wander over to the Lapwai Cemetery and spend a reflective moment at the gravesite of Henry and Eliza. Imagine how they must have felt as a two-person minority among the indigenous Nez Perce, and how they felt in 1847 when they learned that the Cayuse had killed Marcus and Narcissa Whitman and might be headed their way. Imagine how they felt fleeing their home of 11 years, in fear for their lives, and how much Henry must have loved this place, to have

returned later in life to die here among the Nez Perce in 1874.

The site is well aligned along the beaten path but nevertheless an amazingly peaceful spot. Bring a picnic lunch and soak it in.

West of Spalding

West of the visitor center, at mile point 306.7 along Highway 95, is **Coyote's Fishnet.** According to Nez Perce legend, Coyote was happily fishing here one day when Black Bear came along and began to tease him. Coyote lost his temper. He tossed his fishnet onto the hill on the south side of the river, and tossed Black Bear onto the hill on the north side, turning them both to stone in the process. With some imagination, you can see the net and the unfortunate bear here today.

Lewiston's Hells Gate State Park was once the **Hasotino Village Site,** a long-used Native American fishing village. **Buffalo Eddy** archaeological site, upstream on the Snake River from Hells Gate, holds a number of Native American petroglyphs. Just north of Lewiston on Highway 95 is the former site of **Donald Mackenzie's Post.** Mackenzie was a fur trader who had early contact with the Nez Perce. His trading post here lasted less than a year, however.

South on Highway 95

Continuing south from the visitor center on Highway 95, you'll see a marker pointing out the general vicinity where the Spaldings' first home once stood, built soon after their arrival to the area in November 1836. At today's town of Lapwai, you'll find the site of **Fort Lapwai,** the first military fort in Idaho, built in 1862 to keep the Indians from messing with the miners who were flooding into the area. Also here is the site of the **Northern Idaho Indian Agency,** created by the government to monitor compliance with the Indian treaties. Continuing south, you'll come to a sign marking the **Craig Donation Land Claim.** Mountain man William Craig was a friend of the Nez Perce; he served as an interpreter for them and married a Nez Perce woman. His 1846 claim here was the first by a white settler in what is now Idaho. A little farther on is the turnoff to **St. Joseph's Mission.** It was the first Catholic mission among the Nez Perce, built by Father Joseph Cataldo of Old Mission fame and dedicated on Sept. 8, 1874.

Much farther south, outside the reservation, Highway 95 passes five more park sites. Just south of Cottonwood, a sign marks the site of the **Cottonwood Skirmishes,** a couple of early engagements in the Nez Perce War. Small parties of Chief Joseph's band attacked various army detachments and volunteers in this area on July 3 and 5, 1877. The diversionary attacks allowed the main band of Nez Perce to cross the Camas Prairie unnoticed and link up with Chief Looking Glass's band on the Clearwater River. A turnoff here leads seven miles to **Weis Rock Shelter,** a habitation site used by indigenous peoples for more than 8,000 years. West of Grangeville is **Tolo Lake,** where the Nez Perce bands of Chiefs Joseph and White Bird were camped when a few angry braves touched off the Nez Perce War. South of Grangeville on Highway 95 is a site honoring the **Camas Prairie** as a major grocery store for the Nez Perce. Once the prairie was covered with camas lilies, which the Native Americans harvested during late spring and early summer. They mashed the plant's sweet, onionlike root and used it in bread and other staples. As Highway 95 drops down White Bird grade, you'll be looking at a battlefield as historically important as Gettysburg. Here at **White Bird Battlefield,** the first major battle of the Nez Perce War took place (see the sidebar "The Battle of White Bird Hill"). When the dust settled, 34 U.S. Army soldiers had been killed and the Nez Perce had escaped unscathed.

East of Spalding on Highway 12

Ant and Yellowjacket, just east of the Highway 95 turnoff on Highway 12, is another case of Coyote turning something to stone. The two insects were fighting over the right to eat salmon here. Coyote tried to settle the dispute, but they paid no attention to him. To make an example of them, Coyote turned Ant and Yellowjacket to stone. Look up on the hill and you'll see the two creatures—backs arched and jaws locked in combat—now frozen there for all eternity.

Farther east, at the **Lenore Archaeological Site,** evidence indicates that this good fishing hole along the Clearwater was used by the ancestors of the Nez Perce some 10,000 years ago. Continuing east you'll come to **Canoe Camp** near Orofino. On their westward journey in 1805, the Lewis and Clark expedition stayed here 10 days, recuperating from a harrowing crossing of the Bitterroots. Up until this point, they had traveled by horseback; here they left their horses with the Nez Perce and continued downriver by canoe. The dugout canoe you'll see is an example of the sort of vessels the expedition fashioned.

Several sites are found around Kamiah. At mile point 67.6, two signs mark the sites of Lewis and Clark's **Long Camp** and the **Asa Smith Mission.** On their return trip from Astoria to St. Louis in spring 1806, Lewis and Clark camped here for a month while waiting for the snows to melt out of the Bitterroots. By all accounts it was an idyllic time, spent in the good company of the Nez Perce. In 1839, missionary Asa Smith tried to start a mission here among the Nez Perce. But the pioneer life proved too much for him, so in 1841 he moved to a mission in Hawaii. At mile point 75.9, a sign memorializes **Looking Glass's 1877 Campsite,** up nearby Clear Creek. The great Nez Perce war chief Looking Glass tried to remain neutral in the conflict between U.S. Army and the nontreaty Nez Perce. He told the army, "Leave us alone. We are living here peacefully and want no trouble," but the army nevertheless destroyed his village and stole his horses. He then joined Chiefs Joseph and White Bird in the fight and flight for freedom.

According to their legend, the Nez Perce people originated at the **East Kamiah/Heart of the Monster** site. Once again Coyote plays the leading role in the story. Before human beings inhabited the earth, a monster went on a feeding frenzy here, devouring all the creatures in his path. Coyote saw this and came to the rescue. He tricked the monster into devouring him, too. But, little did the monster know, Coyote had a stone knife with him. Once inside, Coyote slashed the monster open, cut it into little pieces, and flung the pieces far and wide. Each piece became a different Native American tribe. Coyote then wrung the blood from the monster's heart, and the Nez Perce people sprang from the drops. What was left of the monster's heart is still visible here today.

Other Sites

South of Kooskia on Highway 13 is the **Clearwater Battlefield,** scene of one of the hardest-fought battles of the Nez Perce War. On July 11, 1877, army general Oliver O. Howard tried a surprise attack on the Nez Perce encampment here. His plan failed. Twenty-four Nez Perce warriors managed to hold off Howard's 600 troops until 100 more warriors could get into position to keep Howard pinned down. Behind the fighting, the rest of the Nez Perce withdrew northward toward Kamiah.

North of Kamiah, up on the **Weippe Prairie,** just west of Weippe on Highway 11, a marker commemorates the first meeting of the Nez Perce with Lewis and Clark. The explorers must have been a scraggly, scrawny bunch at that point. They were near starvation when they stumbled upon the Nez Perce encampment; the Native Americans revived them and sent them on their way. A historical marker at **Musselshell Meadow,** due east of Weippe on the unimproved Lolo Trail, marks the last active camas-gathering grounds of the Nez Perce. Northeast of Weippe on Highway 11 in **Pierce** is a monument marking the beginning of the end of the Nez Perce's glory days. Now Pierce lies outside the reservation, but it was squarely on the reservation in September 1860 when W. F. Bassett, a member of E. D. Pierce's prospecting expedition, found the first gold in Idaho there. Miners came running, and soon a treaty was drafted to take the land away from the Nez Perce.

East of Kamiah up Highway 12, the **Lolo Trail** marker shows the spot where Lewis and Clark crossed the highway—looking both ways—and picked up their old trail on their return trip in 1806. The Nez Perce also came this way in 1877, with General Howard hot on their heels. The sign at **Lolo Pass** also commemorates the Nez Perce trail. It was here in 1805 that Lewis and Clark reentered Idaho after an aborted attempt to negotiate the Salmon River Canyon far to the south.

Finally, in southeastern Idaho, between Spencer and Island Park off County Road A2, is the **Camas Meadows Battle Site,** where the Nez Perce bought time on their pursuers by stealing 200 army pack mules and horses.

Sites Outside Idaho

Other sites included in Nez Perce National Historic Park are **Dug Bar, Joseph Canyon Viewpoint, Old Chief Joseph's Gravesite,** and a **traditional Nez Perce homesite,** all in eastern Oregon; the **Burial Site of Chief Joseph the Younger** and **Nez Perce campsites** in eastern Washington; and the **Big Hole National Battlefield, Canyon Creek battle site,** and **Bear Paw Battlefield,** site of the Nez Perce surrender, all in western Montana.

Reservation Recreation

The Idaho Department of Fish and Game's **Myrtle Beach Campground** offers 16 free sites with no developed water. It's along Highway 12 east of the Juliaetta turnoff. To fish on the waters of the Nez Perce Reservation, you need a permit from the tribe, available, among other places, at Valley Foods in Lapwai, 208/843-2070. Nonresident permits run $10.50 for the first day, $4 for each additional consecutive day.

Picnic areas are available at the Spalding Mission site, the Lenore Archaeological Site, and at **Lawyer Creek Canyon** south of Craigmont.

Nez Perce Businesses

The work of Nez Perce artisans can be found in Orofino at **White Eagle's,** 3405 Highway 12, 208/476-7753, while **Old West Enterprises,** in Lapwai, 208/843-5008, specializes in making traditional tepees.

OROFINO AND VICINITY

The seat of Clearwater County, Orofino's name means "pure gold" or "fine gold" in Spanish, a tribute to the first gold strike in Idaho at nearby Pierce in 1860. The town straddles the banks of the Clearwater River. Logging is the linchpin of

© JULIE FANSELOW

The Nez Perce helped Lewis and Clark build canoes on the banks of the Clearwater River near Orofino.

the economy here; a small park on the north bank of the river holds an infomercial for the industry. Recreation also brings in the dollars. In summer, anglers fish the Clearwater, boaters and campers flock to Dworshak Reservoir, and backcountry explorers head up the North Fork of the Clearwater to the Mallard-Larkins Pioneer Area. In winter, popular area pursuits include snowmobiling and both alpine and Nordic skiing.

Dworshak Dam and Reservoir

The North Fork of the Clearwater River was dammed by the Army Corps of Engineers in 1971. As Cort Conley writes in *Idaho for the Curious:*

> *The North Fork of the Clearwater was an exceptional river with a preeminent run of steelhead trout, and the drainage contained thousands of elk and white-tailed deer. Reports by the Bureau of Sport Fisheries and Wildlife and the Idaho Fish and Game Department indicated the fifty-four mile reservoir would seriously damage these resources. The Army Corps of Engi-*

> *neers proceeded to destroy the river, habitat, and fish; then acquired 5,000 acres for elk habitat and spent $21 million to build the largest steelhead hatchery in the world, maintaining at a cost of $1 million a year what nature had provided for nothing.*

Dworshak Dam is the largest straight-axis dam in North America. That's a fancy way of saying it's a straight line across the dam from one end to the other. At 717 feet high, only two dams in the country are higher.

Before the dam was built, the North Fork was used for log drives out of the forests upriver. The dam put an end to the log drives but allowed water access for loggers into previously inaccessible areas. Logs are still towed across the river and hauled out at several locations. In summer, 90-minute tours of the dam are available at the visitor center on the dam's north end, 208/476-1255.

Dworshak Reservoir is a favorite spot for boaters, anglers, and water-skiers, many of whom whine like the dickens when the reservoir is drawn down to help speed salmon smolts to the sea. Apparently a muddy shoreline is more of a problem than extinction of a species. Anglers probe the lake in search of introduced kokanee salmon, stocked rainbow trout, and obese smallmouth bass; a state-record 117.6-ounce smallmouth was caught here in 1982. Idaho Fish and Game's fishing guide to the lake suggests that nymphs and poppers can add a thrill to your fishing experience. Sounds like fun, eh?

The lake spreads its long skinny tendrils 54 miles back upriver—from the air it looks like a giant neuron. Boat ramps are available at Bruce's Eddy on the dam's east side, at Big Eddy marina and day-use area on the west side, and at several other locations. Big Eddy marina offers the only fuel dock on the lake. Boaters also can take advantage of more than 120 "minicamps" scattered around the lake's 184 miles of shoreline. Each of these primitive campsites has a tent pad, outhouse, picnic table, and grill. The sites are free, and most are accessible only by boat.

The Bureau of Reclamation operates **Dent Recreation Area** on the shore of the lake just over Dent Bridge off the Elk River Road (Wells Bench Road). Here you'll find a boat-launch area, restrooms, and a fish-cleaning station, as well as the large **Dent Acres Campground,** 208/476-3294. The campground features 50 grassy sites on a slope overlooking the lake and offers picnic shelters with tables and grills and a playground. The RV sites cost $16 a night with full hookups. Reservations through NRRS, 877/444-6777.

Fish Hatcheries

The U.S. Fish and Wildlife Service's **Dworshak National Fish Hatchery,** 208/476-4591, and the Idaho Department of Fish and Game's **Clearwater Fish Hatchery,** 4156 Ahsahka Rd., Ahsahka, ID 83520, 208/476-3331, were built just below the dam by the Army Corps of Engineers to compensate for the loss of spawning habitat here, as well as to mitigate the detrimental effects on fish populations caused by the four dams on the lower Snake River. Both hatcheries raise steelhead trout and chinook salmon. Fish migrating upriver are trapped here and milked of their sperm and eggs. The two halves of the genetic stew are mixed together and millions of eggs are hatched. The young fish are raised to smolt size, then either released back into

the Clearwater or barged or trucked down below Bonneville Dam, to begin their return trip to the sea. Despite a big budget, it hasn't stopped salmon and steelhead populations from diminishing. The hatcheries are open daily 7:30 A.M.–4 P.M.; exhibits and self-guided tours are offered.

Dworshak State Park

Although as the osprey flies, this small park lies just four miles from Dworshak Dam, humans have to make a 45-minute drive around the west of the lake to get here. The park is 26 miles northwest of Orofino; head downriver from downtown to Ahsahka and follow the signs: up County Road P1 through Cavendish, then east on Freeman Creek Road to the park, 208/476-5994. Once here, you'll find 105 campsites—each with picnic table and grill, 46 with hookups—surrounded by trees and open meadows. Swimming, water-skiing, boating, and fishing for kokanee and rainbow trout are the most popular pastimes; others enjoy volleyball and horseshoes. Amenities include a showerhouse and restrooms, boat ramp, fish-cleaning station, and a sandy beach. There also are four cabins available for rent; each costs $35 and can sleep up to five people. For reservations, call 208/476-3132 (May 15–Sept.15) or 208/476-5994 (Sept. 16–May 14).

The Bridges of Clearwater County

Two spectacular bridges cross Dworshak Reservoir far out along its eastern reaches. You'll cross **Dent Bridge** to get to Dent Recreation Area or Elk River. The 1,050-foot-long suspension-span bridge is a smaller version of San Francisco's Golden Gate Bridge, though lacking the day-glo orange paint. **Grandad Bridge** is way up the North Fork and connects the town of Headquarters with Elk River. It's a three-span cantilever-deck design; you'll need a Forest Service map to find it.

Golf

Orofino Scenic Golf and Country Club, three miles east of town at 3430 Hwy. 12, 208/476-3117, offers a hilly, nine-hole course as well as a pro shop and snack bar. Greens fee is $12.20 for nine holes, $17.50 to play 18. The course is closed Nov.–March.

Swimming and Floating

Travelers looking to beat the summer heat can head to the **community swimming pool** on H Street, just up the hill from the main drag to Grangemont. On the other hand, who needs a pool when the Clearwater River's right down the street? Tubing and raft floating are popular on the river in late spring and summer.

Events

The highlight of Orofino's annual events calendar is the **Clearwater County Fair and Lumberjack Days** the third weekend in September. Loggers compete; others enjoy a carnival and parade. For more information contact the chamber of commerce.

Accommodations

Under $50: White Pine Motel, 222 Brown Ave., P.O. Box 1849, Orofino, ID 83544, 208/476-7093 or 800/874-2083, offers 18 rooms with queen beds and cable TV. Pets permitted for an extra $10 per night.

$50–100: The fanciest lodging in town is **Helgeson Place Hotel Suites,** right downtown at 125 Johnson Ave., P.O. Box 463, Orofino, ID 83544, 208/476-5729 or 800/404-5729. Its 20 one- or two-bedroom suites—14 of them non-smoking—feature kitchenettes and either king or queen beds. Amenities include tanning booths and a private outdoor Jacuzzi. Some suites are under $50; the rest aren't far over.

Food

For a meal downtown, try the local favorite **Ponderosa Restaurant and Lounge,** 220 Michigan Ave., 208/476-4818. The family restaurant offers prime rib on weekends. Up Grangemont Road (Michigan Avenue) on the outskirts of town is **Konkol's Steakhouse and Lounge,** 208/476-4312, which lies right across the street from the Konkol Lumber Mill. Look for a company-town atmosphere and big, logger-size slabs of meat.

Information and Services

The **Orofino Chamber of Commerce** is at 217 1st St. (at A St.), P.O. Box 231, Orofino, ID 83544, 208/476-4335, www.orofino.com. The USFS **Clearwater National Forest Supervisor's Office,** 12730 Hwy. 12 (west side of town), 208/476-4541, has lots of brochures, maps, and advice for exploring the nearby backcountry.

NORTH FORK CLEARWATER
North Fork–Superior Adventure Road

Here is one of the most beautiful backcountry drives in Idaho—a cruise of some 160 miles up the North Fork Clearwater River and over Hoodoo Pass to Superior, Montana. The CCC built the primitive but well-graded road in 1935, and today it's used by loggers, fly-fishers, campers, and those just looking for a relaxing drive through the great outdoors. Wildlife abounds back here—watch out for moose in the road. Bring your camera and binoculars, and don't forget to fill your gas tank and load up the emergency gear before you go; no services are available along the way.

From Orofino, take Grangemont Road to its intersection with Highway 11 and turn left. Soon the highway becomes a narrow corridor through dense forest, leading to the old Potlatch company town of **Headquarters.** During its logging heyday, some 170 million board feet of cut timber was transported here via the Beaver Creek flume. Logging is still going strong in these parts; watch for trucks.

Past Headquarters, Highway 11 becomes FR 247. The road crests a small saddle, then follows babbling Beaver Creek down to its confluence with the North Fork Clearwater. A few miles east up the North Fork, the pavement ends. From here the dirt road is narrow and occasionally washboard. At **Bungalow Ranger Station,** FR 247 splits off across the river and winds its way up Orogrande Creek, over French Mountain Pass, and down French Creek to Pierce. This allows you to make a nice loop trip from Pierce or Orofino.

Beyond Bungalow, FR 250 continues east to Kelly Forks Ranger Station. You can continue straight up FR 250 through Black Canyon, a scenic but rough stretch through old-growth cedar groves beneath steep canyon walls; or turn right and take the longer loop on FR 255 through the old Moose City mining area. This road, the better choice for RVs, joins up with FR 250 again at Deception Gulch, farther east. East of Deception Gulch, FR 250 climbs to the headwaters of the North Fork on Long Creek and hops the Continental Divide over to Superior, Montana, and I-90.

Recreation

The North Fork and its tributaries are popular with anglers hoping to catch west slope cutthroat trout, rainbow trout, and whitefish. One of the tributaries, **Kelly Creek,** is classified a blue-ribbon trout stream. Kelly Creek and the waters that feed it are restricted to catch-and-release fishing. The North Fork is also a favorite for easy **rafting and kayaking** trips. The water level isn't very high here; the most fun and challenging floating trips usually take place in May and June.

Many hiking trails leave from FR 250 and wind through thick forests up into the mountains. Of particular interest here is the **Mallard-Larkins Pioneer Area,** a 30,500-acre roadless area on the high divide between the North Fork and St. Joe watersheds. Inhabiting the Mallard-Larkins is one of the state's largest mountain goat populations. You also might spy some of the region's resident moose, elk, deer, black bears, or cougars. Access to the Mallard-Larkins is gained via Isabella Creek (FR 700 at the Beaver Creek-Clearwater confluence) or Avalanche Ridge; the trailhead lies on FR 250 three miles east of Canyon Ranger Station.

Camping

A number of USFS campgrounds line the North Fork. From west to east: **Aquarius,** at the Beaver Creek-Clearwater confluence, seven sites, fee; **Washington Creek,** 23 sites, fee; **Weitas,** six sites, free; **Noe Creek,** six sites, fee; **Kelly Forks,** 14 sites, fee; **Hidden Creek,** 13 sites, fee; and **Cedars,** five sites, free. For more information, contact the USFS **North Fork Ranger District,** 12730-B Hwy. 12, Orofino, ID 83544, 208/476-4541.

Lookout and Cabin Rental

Along the North Fork route, turnoffs lead to two Forest Service lookouts available for rent. Between Skull Creek and Quartz Creek, just east of the Canyon Ranger Station, is **Wallow Mountain Lookout.** The 40-foot-high tower rents for $30 a night between June 15 and Sept. 1. It's a three-mile, 1,000-foot climb to the tower, which can accommodate two people. Small children are discouraged because of the tower's height. Farther east, in the vicinity of the Kelly Forks Ranger Station, **Cold Springs Cabin** sleeps two and rents for $25 a night between June 15 and Oct. 1. For more information on either facility, contact the USFS **North Fork Ranger District,** 12730-B Hwy. 12, Orofino, ID 83544, 208/476-4541.

Information

For more information about the North Fork Road or its adjacent backcountry, contact the **Clearwater National Forest Supervisor's Office,** 12730 Hwy. 12, Orofino, ID 83544, 208/476-4541.

PIERCE AND WEIPPE

Pierce

Pierce is named for famous trespasser E. D. Pierce, whose prospecting expedition barged onto the Nez Perce reservation uninvited to find Idaho's first gold here on Sept. 30, 1860. In the subsequent gold rush, thousands of miners flooded in and turned Pierce into a boomtown. By the summer of 1861, some 1,600 mining claims had been filed in the district. In 1862, the **Pierce Courthouse** was built to keep up with registering claims. It still stands today—at Court Street and 1st Avenue—Idaho's oldest standing government building. For more information, contact the **Pierce Chamber of Commerce,** P.O. Box 416, Pierce, ID 83456, 866/665-9736.

Weippe

From high up to the east, Captain William Clark first saw the Weippe Prairie. The Lewis and Clark expedition had been picking its way along the Lolo Trail's steep terrain, and the sight of this relatively level prairie must have given Clark renewed hope. He pulled together an advance party and rode ahead to check it out.

Upon arriving on the prairie, Sept. 20, 1805, he surprised three young Nez Perce boys, who tried to hide in the grass. Clark managed to corral two of the boys and convince them he wasn't a danger. Soon Clark and his men were enjoying salmon steaks and camas roots at the Nez Perce village. The expedition was saved.

The prairie today isn't too terribly different than it was back then. The wide-open vistas remain, and at nearby Musselshell Meadows, the camas bulbs still bloom profusely in spring. In summer, Weippe ("WEE-ipe") makes a good base camp for hiking or horseback riding along the Lolo Trail. In winter, this rolling prairie makes for great cross-country skiing.

THE LOLO MOTORWAY

Although Highway 12 roughly follows the route of the Lewis and Clark expedition—at least closely enough to be labeled the Lewis and Clark Highway—the expedition's actual route followed the Nez Perce's Lolo Trail, up on the highlands north of the river.

The Lolo Trail marked the most difficult conditions the expedition had yet faced on their trip west. Crossing the trail in September 1805, they encountered an early fall snowstorm that not only left them wet and cold but drove the wild game down to lower elevations. The expedition's hunters found little or nothing to kill, and the explorers were forced to eat their own horses to survive.

In the 1930s, the CCC built the 150-mile-long Lolo Motorway (FR 500) on or near the original Lolo Trail. The route runs from Lolo Creek south of Pierce, over Lolo Pass into Montana. It's a primitive road not suitable for trailers and RVs and usually covered by snow from sometime in October until early July. The usual off-road precautions apply: bring warm clothing, extra water, and extra food. Unlike Lewis and Clark, you can't eat your ride.

During the Lewis and Clark Bicentennial years of 2004–2006, the Clearwater National Forest is requiring permits for travel on FR 500 and some adjacent roads between mid-July and Oct. 1. Permits are awarded by lottery, with applications taken in December and January and awarded in February for the next season. For information and an application, call the forest at 208/476-4541 or see its website at www.fs.fed.us/r1/clearwater.

If you're traveling west to east, you'll be retracing the Corps of Discovery's 1806 return trip. Numerous historic sights can be found along the way; pick up a copy of the brochure *Lewis and Clark Across the Lolo Trail,* published by the Clearwater National Forest, 12730 Hwy. 12, Orofino, ID 83544, 208/476-4541.

Access

From Pierce, take Browns Creek Road (FR 100) south from the south edge of town. Stay on FR 100 at every intersection until you reach FR 500 after about 15 miles.

From Weippe, head east where Highway 11 makes a 90-degree turn. After about 10 miles, you'll T into FR 100. Turn right and follow that road about nine miles farther to the junction with FR 500.

From Kamiah, take FR 100 east out of town through Glenwood and follow it another 10 miles to the intersection with FR 500. Heading east to west, the most commonly used access to the trail corridor is Parachute Hill Road (FR 569), which turns north off Highway 12 just east of Powell.

Campground and Lookouts

On or near FR 500 along the way, you'll find one USFS campground and three fire lookouts that can be rented from the Forest Service. None of the locations has developed water. At the junction of Forest Roads 100 and 500 is **Lolo Creek Campsite,** offering five primitive, free sites. Heading east from there, you'll pass the three lookouts. Fourteen miles farther east is **Austin Ridge Lookout,** a 53-foot-high tower that sleeps two and is open between mid-June and mid-September. Farther east, **Weitas Butte Lookout,** also a 53-foot tower-for-two, is open between mid-July 15 and mid-September. Young children are discouraged at both of these high towers. Still farther east is **Castle Butte Lookout,** a cabin sleeping two and open mid-July to late September. The lookouts cost $30 a night. There's a two-night minimum stay; maximum stays may apply, too. For reservations and information on the Austin Ridge and Weitas Butte lookouts, contact the **Lochsa Ranger District-Kamiah**

Office, 103 3rd St. (Hwy. 12), Rt. 2 Box 191, Kamiah, ID 83536, 208/935-2513. For reservations and information on the Castle Butte cabin, contact the **Lochsa Ranger District-Kooskia Office,** 502 Lowry St., Rt. 1 Box 398, Kooskia, ID 83539, 208/926-4274.

KAMIAH

Kamiah ("KAM-ee-eye") was a favorite winter camp of the Nez Perce, who came here to fish for steelhead in the Clearwater. Lewis and Clark hung out here for a month on their way back east in spring 1806, while waiting for Lolo Pass to open up. In modern times, the town became dependent on the timber industry. When that industry suffered a downturn, Kamiah attempted to bolster tourism by refurbishing a three-block strip of downtown in a Victorian Western theme. It doesn't really work, but the great outdoors around here is so beautiful, it hardly matters what the town looks like. The area's abundant elk, ospreys, and bald eagles certainly don't give a hoot (although I suppose the owls might).

Two big events mark summer in Kamiah. The **Clearwater Riverfest,** held the second weekend in July, features arts, crafts, and a bluegrass festival. Mid-August brings **Chief Lookingglass Days,** a pow wow presented by descendants of the famous Nez Perce leader. Look for Native American dancing and traditional Nez Perce ceremonies. On Labor Day weekend, the town fires up the barbies for the long-running **free barbecue,** which also includes assorted fun and games. For a complete calendar of events, call the chamber of commerce.

Just east of Kamiah on Highway 12 is **Lewis-Clark Resort and RV Park,** Rt. 1 Box 17X, Kamiah, ID 83536, 208/935-2556. The large park offers log cabins, each with kitchenette and bath ($50–100); a 21-room motel (under $50); 185 RV sites ($17 with hookups); a restaurant, pool, and spa; license-free trout fishing; and a large clubhouse.

Clearwater 12 Motel, P.O. Box 1168, Kamiah, ID 83536, 208/935-2671 or 800/935-2671, offers 29 rooms (under $50) with cable TV, HBO, and continental breakfast.

For more information about the town, call the **Kamiah Chamber of Commerce,** 208/935-2290, www.kamiahchamber.com.

KOOSKIA

Kooskia ("KOO-skee") got its name from the Nez Perce word *kooskooskia,* which Lewis and Clark translated as "clear water." Historians now believe the explorers didn't get it quite right, that it should have been "where the waters join." Either translation proves appropriate for the town, which lies at the confluence of the Middle and South Forks of the Clearwater River. History buffs will want to check out the renovated 1912 Old Opera House Theatre downtown, a venue for concerts and events.

Forest Information and Lookout Rental

The USFS **Lochsa Ranger District-Kooskia Office,** Rt. 1 Box 398, Kooskia, ID 83539, 208/926-4274, can provide local recreation information. The office also administers two USFS rentals. **Walde Mountain Lookout,** 25 miles northeast of Syringa off FR 101, is available only between Jan. 1 and March 31, making it a favorite of cross-country skiers and snowmobilers. The lookout sleeps four and rents for $30 a night, two-night minimum, $15 each additional night. The **Castle Butte Lookout** is along the Lolo Trail 80 miles east of Kooskia.

Accommodations

$50–100: Between Kooskia and Lowell you'll find three nice B&Bs. **Bear Hollow B&B,** HCR 75 Box 16, Kooskia, ID 83539, 208/926-7146, on Highway 12 at milepost 81, offers three rooms—the Papa Bear ($125), Mama Bear, and Cub Bear—and has a hot tub and a large gift shop.

Reflections Inn on the Clearwater, HCR 75 Box 32, Kooskia, ID 83539-9502, 208/926-0855 or 888/926-0855, sits on 10 acres off Highway 12 between mile markers 84 and 85 (11 miles east of Kooskia). It offers seven rooms, each with queen bed, private bath, and private entrance, and a hot tub out under the starry north-central Idaho skies. There's a common room outfitted with a full kitchen and TV/VCR. Rates include a full breakfast and afternoon refreshments.

Dream's B&B occupies an 18.5-acre spread off the highway at milepost 86, P.O. Box 733, Kooskia, ID 83539, 208/926-7540. Affable proprietors Eugene "Gino" and Helga Tennies designed the place themselves. The two guest rooms—both separated from the main house—have private baths and VCRs, and they face the river. Rates include a full three-course country breakfast and use of the hot tub. Senior citizens get 10 percent off.

LOWELL

At the small town of Lowell, the Lochsa and Selway Rivers meet to form the Middle Fork of the Clearwater. The name Lochsa ("LOCK-saw") is a Native American word meaning "rough water." The Selway, also far from smooth, was likely named after Montana sheepman Thomas Selway, who ran his herds here around the turn of the 20th century and had a cabin along the river. Lowell is supported almost entirely by recreation. In summer, its motels and campgrounds fill up with rafters, kayakers, anglers, bicyclists, and backpackers.

Accommodations and Camping
Three Rivers Resort, HC 75 Box 61, Lowell, ID 83539, 208/926-4430, is the happenin' spot in little Lowell. Enjoying prime real estate right where the Lochsa and Selway come together to form the Clearwater, the resort gets jam-packed with river rats in summer. The resort runs a busy guide service. Rafters aren't the only ones who enjoy this place, though. The resort offers everything for everybody: 40 campsites ($18.50–22.50 a night with hookups, $7.50 a night per person or $5 per child for tent sites); a variety of cabins, some on the river ($50–100) and some with kitchens; a pool, three Jacuzzis, a restaurant, and Lochsa Louie's Bar. In addition, the resort offers two special-occasion cabins up in the woods. Old #1 has a fireplace, a Jacuzzi on the deck, a full bath and kitchen, a VCR, and great views of the rivers, while the Lodge, even farther back in the woods, has its own kitchen and hot tub. Each goes for right about $100.

Just a few miles west of Lowell, back down Highway 12, the USFS **Wild Goose Campground** offers six fee sites right on the north bank of the Clearwater.

UP THE SELWAY

Forest Road 223 crosses the Lochsa at Lowell and follows the Selway River southeast. It dead-ends at a trailhead about 25 miles later, just past the 1912 Selway Falls Guard Station. The road's paved as far as the O'Hara Creek Bridge; after that it can turn washboard.

Amazingly enough, the road up the Selway seems *under*-used. The river can be jammed down at Three Rivers Lodge, but in a few minutes' drive up here you might find a great spot all to yourself. Deer feed in the grasslands along the riverbank, adding to the idyllic landscape.

Fenn Historic Ranger Station and Forest Service Rentals
Four miles down the road you'll find this trim green-and-white building housing the Nez Perce National Forest's **Moose Creek Ranger District,** Fenn Ranger Station, HCR 75 Box 91, Kooskia, ID 83539, 208/926-4258. This office handles reservations for two Forest Service rentals in the area. The **Meadow Creek Cabin** is 15 miles up the Meadow Creek National Recreation Trail and available between mid-May and mid-September. The cabin holds eight people. The **Lookout Butte** rental, a 60-foot-high tower south of the Selway above Goddard Creek, sleeps four and is available between mid-June and late September. Small children are discouraged because of the tower's height. Cost for either rental is $25 a night.

Across the road from Fenn Ranger Station, **Selway Pond** (also called Fenn Pond) is a stocked trout pond with fishing piers, a picnic area, and an encircling wooden plank walkway—all wheelchair friendly.

Selway Falls
Twenty-one miles up the road from Lowell, you'll come upon awesome Selway Falls. It's not a high graceful falls, but a low, wide, awesomely

powerful man-eater. Here the Selway pounds down in a thundering drop between house-size granite blocks. Woe to the unfortunate paddler who misses the warning signs strung across the river upstream from here; this whitewater would undoubtedly be his or her last.

Floating the Selway

The Selway offers two different boating experiences, depending on your experience and interest. The 22-mile stretch from below Selway Falls to Lowell makes a popular day float. During spring runoff, this stretch can be a beginner-to-intermediate whitewater thrill. By July, it's usually a casual float. Upstream from the falls, the Selway offers a difficult, remote, and wild float. Unlike the Lochsa or the Clearwater, no roads follow alongside the river here. Instead, you'll be boating 47 roadless miles through the heart of the 1.3-million-acre Selway-Bitterroot Wilderness. While this makes for an outstanding backcountry experience, it also makes rescue much more difficult. Rapids up to Class IV make this run an expert-only proposition. The river requires a tough-to-get permit; going with a commercial guide is probably best.

Guide services on the Selway include **ARTA**, 24000 Casa Loma Rd., Groveland, CA 95321, 209/962-7873 or 800/323-2782, and **ROW**, P.O. Box 579, Coeur d'Alene, ID 83816, 208/765-0841 or 800/451-6034.

Hiking

The Forest Service has laid out a one-mile **interpretive trail** at O'Hara Creek Campground, explaining the agency's efforts to rehabilitate the salmon-spawning grounds here. Road-building and logging at one time clogged O'Hara Creek with silt, and the fish populations declined. The interpretive sites are situated along the road, so you could even drive to them if you wanted. Along the way you might spot one of the area's resident ospreys, beavers, or belted kingfishers.

Two National Recreation Trails make for longer, more strenuous day jaunts or casual overnighters. The **East Boyd-Glover-Roundtop National Recreation Trail,** a U-shaped 14.5-mile trail, climbs the east side of Boyd Creek up to Roundtop Mountain, then descends the east

side of Glover Creek farther east. You can loop back to the car along the main Selway Road, a scenic little stroll in itself. The **Meadow Creek National Recreation Trail** is part of the Idaho State Centennial Trail. It leaves from Slim's Camp and follows Meadow Creek south. The first four miles are relatively level, winding through lush cedar and fir forest along the creek bottom. The trail then begins to climb and continues south as far as you want to go—be it to Elk City or Murphy Hot Springs, near the Nevada border.

Trailheads in the area at **Big Fog Saddle** (at the end of FR 319), **Race Creek** (at the end of the main Selway Road FR 223), and **Indian Hill** (at the end of FR 290) provide hiker access into the Selway-Bitterroot Wilderness.

Fishing

The Selway is a spawning area for anadromous chinook salmon, steelhead trout, and Pacific lamprey. In addition, the river supports cutthroat trout, rainbow trout, eastern brook trout, mountain whitefish, and bull trout. Bull trout fishing is prohibited along the entire river. Restrictions in effect for all waters of the main Selway require anglers to use artificial flies and lures, single barbless hooks, and no bait. The area between the Selway Falls cable car and Selway Falls remains closed to all fishing. Above Selway Falls Bridge, anglers must confine themselves to catch-and-release fishing on the main river. The tributaries are recommended, but not mandatory, catch-and-release waters, but bear no tackle restrictions. For opening dates and other information, contact **Idaho Department of Fish and Game,** 1540 Warner St., Lewiston, ID 83501, 208/799-5010.

Camping

A string of USFS campgrounds line the Selway up as far as Selway Falls. From northwest (Lowell) to southeast (Selway Falls), these include **Johnson Bar,** seven sites, free; **O'Hara Bar,** 34 sites, fee, good wheelchair access; **Rackliff,** six sites, fee; **Twenty-Mile Bar,** two sites, free; **Boyd Creek,** five sites, fee; **Glover Creek,** seven sites, fee; **Selway Falls,** seven sites, fee; **Race Creek,** three sites, free; and—south up FR 443—**Slim's Camp,** two sites, free.

For more information, contact the USFS **Moose Creek Ranger District,** Fenn Ranger Station, HCR 75 Box 91, Kooskia, ID 83539, 208/926-4258.

UP THE LOCHSA

From Lowell, Highway 12 follows the Lochsa northeast to its headwaters, then continues over Lolo Pass into Montana. Keep in mind it's 64 miles up the highway to the next services at Powell.

The Lochsa Face, a steep 73,000-acre strip of land between the river and the Selway-Bitter-root Wilderness, runs parallel to the Lochsa's south bank. Elk, moose, and mountain lion inhabit this wild paradise of stark cliffs, steaming hot springs, and crystalline trout streams.

Lochsa Historical Ranger Station

Spring 1934 was wet, cool, and green in Central Idaho. But on June 22, a long heat wave began that turned the lush vegetation into a tinderbox. On August 10, a dry lightning storm hit the Clearwater, sparking a number of blazes, including the disastrous "Pete King" fire just downstream from the ranger station. Thanks to abundant ladder fuels, the Pete King blaze turned into a crown fire that rapidly spread. The fire burned out of control for 44 days before a heavy, prolonged rain arrived and extinguished the flames. At one point, fire surrounded the ranger station and threatened to incinerate it, but the 200 firefighters who had gathered here valiantly fought it off. Two were killed by falling trees, but the ranger station and the rest of the firefighters were saved. In the end, the fire charred some 375 square miles.

Today the ranger station serves as tribute to both the Pete King crews and all of Idaho's forest firefighters. A self-guided tour leads from a museum building full of historical photos around the grounds to several outbuildings. The buildings contain old tools of the firefighting trade, as well as the humble 1930s-era furnishings once used by the fire crews. Many of the displays are enlivened with short tape recordings. The site is on Highway 12, 57 miles east of

Kooskia, and open daily 9 A.M.–5 P.M. in summer. Admission is free. For more information, contact the **Lochsa Ranger District,** Rt. 1 Box 398, Kooskia, ID 83539, 208/926-4274.

Colgate Licks and Vicinity

A large turnout on the north side of the highway marks this one-mile loop nature trail to a natural salt lick. It's a nice place to stop and stretch your legs, and wildlife photographers will find this an excellent spot to try to bag a trophy portrait. A bit farther east is Jerry Johnson Campground, and a bit farther east of that the trail to **Jerry Johnson Hot Springs** begins. Look for the pack bridge crossing the river and the cars parked along the road nearby—Jerry Johnson is one of the most well-known hike-in hot springs in Idaho. The trail leads across the bridge and up Warm Springs Creek for about a mile to an area dotted with hot pools. In winter, the hot springs make a great ski or snowshoe excursion. You may never get the place all to yourself, but you can bet the people you share a hot soak with will be cool.

Powell

Lochsa Lodge at milepost 163 on Highway 12 (mail to Lochsa Lodge, Powell Ranger Station, Lolo, MT 59847), 208/942-3405, is a high mountain retreat alongside the upper Lochsa just a short distance from the Selway-Bitterroot Wilderness boundary. Although the business has been here since 1929, it burned to the ground in 2001 and has been entirely rebuilt. The year-round lodge offers both motel-style rooms and private log cabins, most in the $50–100 range. You'll also find a store with gas and a restaurant (open daily 6 A.M.–9 P.M. in summer, 7 A.M.–8 P.M. the rest of the year). Favorite winter activities here include cross-country skiing and soaking in the nearby hot springs.

Just a little farther down the road past the lodge you'll find the USFS **Powell Ranger Station** (mail to Powell Ranger Station, Lolo, MT 59847), 208/942-3113. It's open Mon.–Fri. 8 A.M.–4:30 P.M.

Elk Summit Road (FR 360) leaves Highway 12 just east of Powell and leads south to a trailhead into the Selway-Bitterroot Wilderness. At the trailhead is the USFS **Elk Summit Camp-ground,** offering 15 free but primitive sites. It's not hard to tell where the official wilderness area begins up here: it's the part that's not clearcut.

DeVoto Memorial Cedar Grove

Students of Idaho history remember Bernard De-Voto as one of the elder statesmen of Idaho state scholarship and editor of the annotated *Journals of Lewis & Clark.* A sign here explains: "This majestic cedar grove is dedicated to the memory of Bernard DeVoto (1897–1955), conservationist, author, and historian. He often camped here while studying the journals of Lewis and Clark. At his request his ashes were scattered over this area."

The grove is truly magnificent. Towering cedars on either side of the highway shade the cool forest floor covered with bracken fern, foam flower, maidenhair fern, sword fern, and dogwood. Short loop trails wind through the woods; the one on the south side of the highway offers interpretive signs and leads to picnic tables by the rushing river.

Lolo Pass

Atop the Continental Divide, on the Idaho-Montana state line, is Lolo Pass, elevation 5,233 feet. A spiffy new visitor center here tells the tales of the Nez Perce and of the Lewis and Clark expedition. Outside, a quarter-mile interpretive trail circles a restored wetlands area in warm weather. In winter, snowmobilers and cross-country skiers will find a warming hut.

Running the Lochsa

Whitewater enthusiasts from around the world seek out the Lochsa, considered one of the country's most difficult rivers. Lewis and Clark took one look at it and decided to struggle along the steep canyon walls rather than attempt to float downsteam. The Lochsa tumbles furiously off Lolo Pass in a swirling, whirling, smashing, crashing torrent. Among its more than 60 rapids are nine rated either Class IV+ or V-, including Ten Pin Alley, Bloody Mary, the Grim Reaper, and Lochsa Falls. Although Highway 12 runs right alongside the river, wide-eyed rafters will be far too panicked trying to read the water ahead to care about or even notice the cars going by.

Three Rivers Rafting, HC 75, Box 61, Lowell, ID 83539, 208/926-4430, charges $100 for a one-day whitewater run on the Lochsa. Price includes lunch, wetsuit, paddle jacket, helmet, life jacket, shuttle, and hot tubs and showers after the trip. Also running the Lochsa is **ROW,** P.O. Box 579, Coeur d'Alene, ID 83816, 208/765-0841 or 800/451-6034.

Fishing

As with the Selway, chinook salmon, steelhead trout, and Pacific lamprey come up the Lochsa to spawn. Cutthroat trout, mountain whitefish, and bull trout are also resident. Bull trout fishing is prohibited along the entire river. All waters of the main Lochsa, and Lower Crooked Fork Creek from White Sand Creek to Brushy Fork Creek, are restricted to artificial flies and lures, single barbless hook, no bait. All other tributaries have no bait restrictions. The main Lochsa above Wilderness Gateway Campground is catch-and-release only, as is the section of

chinook

Crooked Fork Creek from White Sand Creek to Brushy Fork Creek. For opening dates and other information, contact **Idaho Department of Fish and Game,** 1540 Warner St., Lewiston, ID 83501, 208/799-5010.

Camping

Numerous Forest Service campgrounds line the Lochsa. From Lowell heading east you'll find **Apgar Creek,** seven sites, fee; **Major Fenn,** five sites, free, also picnic area and nature trail; **Knife Edge,** five sites, free; the humongous **Wilderness Gateway,** 91 sites, fee, good wheelchair access; **Jerry Johnson,** 15 sites, fee, also good wheelchair access; **Wendover,** 27 sights, fee; **Whitehouse,** 13 sites, fee; **Powell,** 39 sites, fee; **White Sand,** six sites, fee; **Lee Creek,** 22 sites, fee; and **Lewis & Clark,** 17 sites, fee.

Moscow and Vicinity

Leaving Lewiston and heading north, Highway 95 climbs steeply out of the Clearwater River Valley and onto a vast tableland of mostly treeless rolling hills called the Palouse. This is rich agricultural land, planted with wheat, barley, peas, and lentils. Each spring when the crops sprout from the furrowed hills, the landscape becomes a sea of green stretching as far as the eye can see.

The Palouse extends north from Lewiston virtually all the way to Coeur d'Alene, spreading west across the border into Washington and east of the highway about 30 miles before giving way to mountains. Plopped down in the middle of the Palouse as if set down by a twister, Moscow (population 21,700) is a cultural oasis in this wide-open, sparsely populated area. It's the home of the University of Idaho and holds coffeehouses, brewpubs, used-book stores, nightlife, and some fine dining—all in a small town with a decidedly friendly, laid-back atmosphere.

Early on, the town was called Hog Heaven thanks to the abundance of hog food (camas roots) covering the prairie. When the town took on a more permanent character, the self-respecting townsfolk sought a name with a bit more panache. They tried Paradise for a while but ended up with Moscow when an early postmaster decided the area reminded him of a northeastern Pennsylvania town by that name.

University of Idaho

As a bone thrown to north Idaho to convince it not to become part of Washington, the Idaho Territorial Legislature established the University of Idaho here in 1889. Idaho's oldest university, the school enrolls about 9,700 students in 10

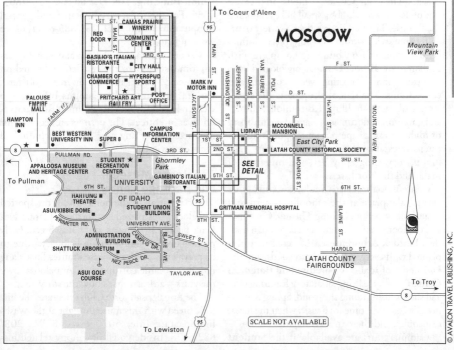

NORTH-CENTRAL IDAHO

COURTESY OF THE UNIVERSITY OF IDAHO

the University of Idaho campus

colleges. The main 320-acre campus, on the west side of downtown, climbs a small hill overlooking the Palouse. The buildings reflect a variety of architectural styles—from the centerpiece Gothic-style administration building complete with carillon to the **Kibbie Dome,** a big bloated bubble hosting indoor sporting events, concerts, and conventions. The school also boasts the state's largest **library**—holding 1.6 million volumes and government documents—and the **University of Idaho Press,** a superb resource publishing an extensive catalog of books on the history, natural history, geography, art, and literature of Idaho and the Northwest.

Concerts, lectures, stage productions, and other events take place at the school's modern and acoustically superior **Hartung Theater.** Gardeners and outdoor lovers will enjoy a walk through both the **Shattuck Arboretum,** a 14-acre forest plot planted with evergreens and hardwoods, and the **University of Idaho Arboretum and Botanical Garden,** a 63-acre living laboratory featuring trees and shrubs from around the world. Spring is an especially beautiful time for a visit, when the lilacs, crabapples, and cherry trees come into bloom.

Campus tours are available at the **Student Union Building,** 709 Deakin Ave., 208/885-4636. For the university operator and general campus information, call 208/885-6111, or see www.uidaho.edu.

Visitors may park on campus at metered spaces any time, subject to the restrictions posted on each meter. Visitors may obtain free, short-term parking permits at the Campus Information Center, located where the Pullman Road curves north at 3rd Street. The permits are required for nonmetered parking year-round, including all vacation periods.

Appaloosa Museum and Heritage Center

The Dalmatian of the horse world, the spotted Appaloosa was prized by northern Idaho's Nez Perce people as a rugged and hardy breed. Early pioneers called this horse "a Palousey," due to its prevalence on the Palouse Prairie. That slang moniker became corrupted to "Appaloosa" over the years—at least, that's how the story goes.

The Appaloosa Horse Club celebrates the historic breed with this museum right at the Washington state line, 5070 Hwy. 8 W., 208/882-5578. Inside you'll find Appy-related historical artifacts, photos, and paintings, as well as the Appaloosa Hall of Fame. In summer, you'll likely find a corral of the critters out back. The museum is open year-round Tues.–Fri. 10 A.M.– 5 P.M., Sat. 10 A.M.–4 P.M. Admission is free; donations appaloociated.

McConnell Mansion

On the east side of downtown Moscow lies the Fort Russell Historic District—a jewel box of gorgeous 19th-century homes presiding over quiet, tree-lined streets. One of these gems, the 1886 McConnell Mansion, 110 S. Adams St., 208/882-1004, was once the home of William "Poker Bill" McConnell, Idaho's third governor. Now the Victorian Gothic house holds a museum offering period-furnished rooms and changing historical exhibits. It's operated by the Latah County Historical Society and open Tues.–Sat. 1–4 P.M. Admission is free; donations encouraged. The historical society also publishes two walking-tour guides, one to other historical residences in the Fort Russell district, the other to historical buildings downtown. You can pick up copies of those guides at the McConnell house or at the chamber of commerce office downtown.

Prichard Art Gallery

The university's downtown art gallery, 414 S. Main St., 208/885-3586, showcases student, faculty, and regional art. The gallery also hosts lectures, readings, and workshops. It's generally open Mon.–Sat., but hours vary, so call ahead.

RECREATION
Parks

Moscow boasts nearly a dozen city parks—some appropriate for a quiet picnic, others for a rousing game of one-on-one. **Ghormley Park,** at 3rd and Home Sts., adjacent to the UI campus, includes a municipal swimming pool, softball fields, tennis courts, barbecues, and horseshoe pits. **East City Park,** 3rd and Hayes Sts., provides a basketball court, sand volleyball court, horseshoe pits, playgrounds, and picnic areas. **Mountain View Park,** a big, open park clear out on the east edge of town (take F Street east to Mountain

View Road), offers plenty of space for you and/or your pooch to get some exercise. In addition to the usual park facilities, here you'll find a bike path along Paradise Creek.

Latah County's **Robinson Park,** 2094 Robinson Park Rd., encompasses almost 55 acres of open space, including picnic areas, two softball diamonds, a sand volleyball court, horseshoe pits, a nature trail, and an ice skating rink.

For a complete list of parks or more information, contact the **Moscow Parks and Recreation Department,** 1515 E. D St., 208/883-7085.

Recreation Center

The U of I's new **Student Recreation Center,** 1000 Paradise Creek St., 208/885-PLAY (208/885-7529), has a 55-foot free-standing climbing pinnacle, the largest of its kind on any college campus in the United States. Other amenities include a running track, free weights, circuit training, and locker rooms with saunas. Non-students can use the center for $5.25 per visit. When classes are in session, it's open Mon.–Thurs. 6 A.M.– 11:30 P.M., Fri. 6 A.M.–9 P.M., Sat. 9 A.M.–9 P.M., Sun. 11 A.M.–11 P.M. Summer hours are Mon., Wed., and Fri. 11 A.M.–8 P.M.; Tues. and Thurs. 6 A.M.–8 P.M., weekends noon–6 P.M. The rec center is on the north side of campus, not far from the campus information center.

The **Outdoor Program Office,** is also in the rec center. Stop by to rent a wide range of equipment, or to learn about upcoming classes and trips, which are usually open to non-students. Hours are Mon.–Fri. 10 A.M.–5 P.M. More information on the Outdoor Program is available by calling 208/885-6810; for rentals info, dial 208/885-6170.

Bill Chipman Trail

This paved 7-mile trail links Moscow with Pullman, Washington. Built on a former railroad bed, it has a nice gentle grade, and it's well used by cyclists, strollers, joggers, and in-line skaters. Catch it on the north edge of the U of I campus or anywhere south of Pullman Road, which it parallels.

Mountain Biking

The city's fat-tire fanatics consider **Moscow Mountain,** five miles north of Moscow, the premier mountain biking destination. To get there, you can take either Highway 95 north to Lewis Road then Lewis east to Foothill Road, or take D Street east to Mountain View Road, Mountain View north to Moscow Mountain Road. Most of the Moscow Mountain trails are on private land, so camping is verboten and you should be on your best behavior.

Other worthwhile biking areas in the region include McCroskey State Park and Palouse Divide Adventure Road.

Whitewater Rafting

Moscow-based **Salmon River Experience,** 812 Truman St., 208/882-2385 or 800/892-9223, runs one- to three-day whitewater or bike-raft trips on the main Salmon River in the Riggins area, three- to five-day trips through Lower Salmon Gorge, and five-day spring trips on southwest Idaho's Owyhee River. Trips include van transportation from Moscow to the river and back. Mountain biking/rafting combo trips and steelhead fishing/chukar-hunting trips are also available. Rates run around $75 for a one-day trip, around $150 a day for a multiday trip.

Outfitters

Hyperspud Sports, 402 S. Main St., 208/883-1150, carries a great selection of mountaineering and climbing equipment, tents, backpacks, and extreme sports gear. Mountain bikers can pick up the *Mountain Bike Guide to Hog Heaven* here. Hours are Tues.–Fri. 10 A.M.–6 P.M., Sat. 9 A.M.–6 P.M.

Golf

The **University of Idaho Golf Course** on the west side of campus, 1215 Nez Perce Dr., 208/885-6171, is open to the public. The 18-hole, par-72 course offers a pro shop, refreshments, driving range, cart rentals, and lessons. Greens fees run $18–23. The hilly, often windy course is closed Dec.–March.

ENTERTAINMENT AND EVENTS

Lionel Hampton Jazz Festival

Los Angeles Times jazz critic Leonard Feather has called this event "the number-one jazz festival in the world." The festival, hosted by the University of Idaho's Lionel Hampton School of

Lou Rawls at the Lionel Hampton Jazz Festival

COURTESY OF THE UNIVERSITY OF IDAHO

Music, draws many of the biggest names in jazz to a four-day blowout of concerts, clinics, and student competitions. It's a rare opportunity to see lots of the masters all in one place—jazz buffs shouldn't miss it.

The event takes place in late February, with the headliner concerts presented in Kibbie Dome on the UI campus. Tickets go on sale in early December and cost $18–28 for the evening concerts; package discounts are available. To order tickets, call 208/885-7212 or 888/884-3246. For more information about the festival, write to Lionel Hampton Jazz Festival, University of Idaho, P.O. Box 444257, Moscow, ID 83844-4257, or call 208/885-6765.

Other Campus Events

The **Idaho Repertory Theater** has presented summer stock productions in Moscow for half a century. Affiliated with the University of Idaho's Department of Theater Arts, the troupe's home stage is E. W. Hartung Theatre on the UI campus. Performances run from early July through early August.

For a complete schedule of entertainment and events on the UI campus, call the University Events Center, 208/885-6662.

Off-Campus Events

The first weekend in March brings Moscow's **Mardi Gras and Beaux Arts Ball.** Never mind that it's not held on a Mardi at all, but on a Samedi and Dimanche—it's still a lot of fun for all but the staunchest Francophone. Cut loose at the parade or boogie to a number of bands.

Spring is in the air when the **Renaissance Fair** comes to town; on the first weekend in May, bold knights, fair maidens, and tankards of grog take thee back to the days before silverware and indoor plumbing. Music fills Moscow's East City Park during **Rendezvous in the Park,** the second and third weekends in July. The festival features all styles of music from blues to bluegrass, and plenty of kids' activities to keep the little dudes

happy. In September, the **Latah County Fair** comes to town beginning the second weekend after Labor Day.

For information on any of these events, call the Moscow Chamber of Commerce at 208/882-1800.

ACCOMMODATIONS

Most of Moscow's motels cluster along one of two strips. The older, established motels are along Main Street (Highway 95), in or close to downtown, while the newer budget chains and a few fancier places are five to 10 blocks from downtown along Pullman Road (Highway 8), which runs west from downtown on its way to Pullman, Washington. The Pullman Road lodgings are convenient to the UI campus, the big shopping mall, and a gauntlet of fast-food establishments. In addition to the motels, a couple of nice B&Bs lie in the country just outside town.

It's a good idea to reserve ahead for a stay in Moscow. There aren't many motels, and everything gets booked up well in advance anytime a major event happens at either the U of I or nearby Washington State University. If you can't find a room through the usual channels, contact **Moscow/Pullman Bedfinders,** www.moscowpullmanbedfinders.com or 208/882-9716, which helps locate overflow bed-and-breakfast accommodations from $75 during big college weekends when the motels are full.

> *The Lionel Hampton Jazz Festival draws many of the biggest names in jazz to a four-day blowout of concerts, clinics, and student competitions. It's a rare opportunity to see lots of the masters all in one place—jazz buffs shouldn't miss it.*

$50–100

At the low end of this category, you'll find the 60-room **Super 8,** 175 Peterson Dr., 208/883-1503 or 800/800-8000. It's four blocks from campus, so rates will be closer to the middle of this range during special events at the university.

Mark IV Motor Inn, 414 N. Main St., 208/882-7557 or 800/833-4240, with amenities including an indoor heated pool and whirlpool tub and an on-site restaurant and lounge. The large **Best Western University Inn,** 1516 W. Pullman Rd., 208/882-0550 or 800/766-2473, offers 173 rooms, an indoor pool, Jacuzzi, sauna, fitness area, restaurant, and lounge.

Behind the Palouse Empire Mall, the new **Hampton Inn,** 185 Warbonnet Dr., 208/882-5365, is a pleasant place to stay, with an indoor pool/hot tub, fitness center, and a big breakfast bar.

$100–150

Five miles north of town, up on the flanks of Moscow Mountain, sits **Peacock Hill,** 1015 Joyce Rd., 208/882-1423, with rates at the low end of this category. The beautiful residence offers a casual, friendly atmosphere and expansive views. One of the two guest rooms features a double-wide sunken Jacuzzi with dual showers; the other has a king-size feather bed and a fireplace. Recreation opportunities begin right off the property; horseback riding, mountain biking, and cross-country skiing trails can lead you all over Moscow Mountain and east all the way to Troy if you want. Those less athletically inclined are welcome to just hang out at the house with Hennessey, the resident St. Bernard. Rates include a full breakfast. To reach Peacock Hill, take Highway 95 north of Moscow 4.5 miles, turn right on Lewis, left on Nearing, left at the fork (Saddle Ridge), left on Joyce, then follow Joyce to the top of the hill.

Like Peacock Hill, upscale **Paradise Ridge B&B,** 2455 Blaine Rd., 208/882-5292, enjoys a hilltop location with great views. Of the three guest rooms, the Palouse Suite is the most luxurious. It offers a king-size bed, a private bath, and a private deck. The other two rooms share a bath, and each has a queen bed; they rent for right about $100 each. Guests can relax in the hot tub outside beneath the trees. Rates include a full gourmet breakfast. No pets, no smoking inside, children over age 10 welcome. To get to Paradise Ridge, head east of Moscow on Highway 8 toward Troy. Continue 1.4 miles past the last stoplight (at Blaine *Street*) and turn right on Lenville Road. Follow Lenville south for 1.5 miles to Blaine Road, then continue on Blaine another 1.6 miles to Paradise Ridge.

FOOD
Breakfast and Lunch

The **Breakfast Club,** 501 S. Main St., 208/882-6481, serves both breakfast and lunch at all open hours, 6 A.M.–2 P.M. weekdays, 7 A.M.–2 P.M. weekends. Its menu is a cut above standard diner fare, and the prices are reasonable (in the $4–6 range for just about everything).

Dinner

Most locals consider the **Red Door,** 215 S. Main St., 208/882-7830, the town's top-tier restaurant. The menu tours the world, from escargot appetizers to such dishes as Thai chicken salad, coconut curry (with tofu or shrimp), sautéed chicken with tequila-ancho sauce, swordfish steak, and Aussie-style tenderloin filet. Entrées range $12–27, though the salads ($8–13) can be meals in themselves. For every main course, the menu lists a recommended wine to go with it. The atmosphere is warm and lively; the staff friendly. If you only have one night in Moscow, eat here.

Basilio's Italian Ristorante, 100 W. 4th St. (in the Moscow Hotel building), 208/892-3848, offers primarily the Italian classics (most under $9), supplemented by salads ($2–6), sandwiches ($5–8), and some seafood and steak entrées ($10–15). It's open for lunch and dinner daily.

Gambino's Italian Restaurant, 306 W. 6th St., 208/882-4545, offers everything from pizza to down-home spaghetti and meatballs to a chicken cacciatora del padrone. The atmosphere alone here is worth the price of admission: red-and-white checkered tablecloths you can really put your elbows on. Just don't let Mama Gambino catch you.

Mexican food fans head to **Casa de Oro,** 415 S. Main St., 208/883-0536, for all the standard menu items plus some bucket-size margaritas. The inside decor might be a bit kitschy for some; go for the tables out on the sidewalk instead.

Winery

Camas Prairie Winery, 110 S. Main St., 208/882-0214 or 800/616-0214, is North Idaho's oldest winery, in business since 1983. It produces and sells a number of varietals, including sparkling wines, as well as unusual items such as mead, herbed wine vinegar, and wine jellies. It's open Tues.–Sat. noon–6:30 P.M.

Groceries

For organic veggies, fresh juices, ginseng ginger ale, whole-grain breads, and the like, head for **Moscow Food Co-op,** 221 E. 3rd St., 208/882-8537. Find the best retail wine selection in town at **Wine Company of Moscow,** 113 E. 3rd St., 208/882-6502. Moscow also has an excellent **farmers market,** 208/883-7036, Saturdays 8 A.M.–noon downtown on Friendship Square.

SHOPPING

Bookpeople of Moscow, 521 S. Main St., 208/882-7957, provides the perfect place to hunt for that old copy of Richard Brautigan's *Rommel Drives On Deep into Egypt.* There's a coffee bar here, too. **Palouse Mall,** 1850 W. Pullman Rd., 208/882-8893, is a big, modern supermall with about 60 stores.

INFORMATION AND SERVICES

Information

The **Moscow Chamber of Commerce** is at 411 S. Main St., Suite 1, Moscow, ID 83843, 208/882-1800 or 800/380-1801, www.moscow-chamber.com. Moscow offers an **NPR** affiliate, station KRFA at 91.7 FM.

Transportation

Pullman-Moscow Airport, just across the border at 3200 Airport Complex N., Pullman, WA 99163, 509/334-4555, is served by **Horizon Air,** 800/547-9308. Rental cars are available at the airport, and most motels offer free shuttle service to guests.

Across the Palouse

Outside Moscow in every direction, two-lane roads wind through pastoral countryside, making lazy curves over and around the scenic, gently rolling hills of the Palouse. It's great for road biking. Dotting the farmland are tidy villages and hamlets, many left over from the logging days. They're commonly tucked away in the draws between the hills, which helps give most of them a pleasant, cozy feel. Time seems to slow down out here, measured not so much by the ticking of the clock as by the turning of the leaves, the first snowfall of winter, foals in the pasture, or laughter at the swimmin' hole.

HIGHWAY 95 TO COEUR D'ALENE

McCroskey State Park

Moscow mountain bikers probably make the most use of this odd little state park. The reserve was the brainchild and labor of love of eastern Washington resident Virgil McCroskey. The son of homesteaders who came west from Tennessee after the Civil War, McCroskey wanted to create a park dedicated to his mother, Mary Minerva McCroskey, and indirectly dedicated to all the Northwest's pioneer women. He bought 4,500 acres here, built the roads, cleared viewpoints, and put in picnic areas and campsites, envisioning an end result similar to the Skyline Drive route through Great Smoky Mountains park in his native Tennessee. When McCroskey was through, he attempted to donate the park to the state, only to have the state refuse it. No money for maintenance, they said.

Eventually a deal was worked out where the state would accept the park if McCroskey would maintain it for 15 years. That was back in 1955. In 1970, his 15-year obligation came to an end and McCroskey promptly died. Since then, the state has taken responsibility for the area, but has kept it minimally developed. You'll never run into crowds here, even in midsummer.

The park lies about 20 miles north of Moscow, along a tall wooded ridgetop with great views of the Palouse. Coming up Highway 95, watch for the turn onto Skyline Drive—the street sign is the only sign you'll see—at the crest of the hill on the west (left) side of the highway. It's a terrible, blind turn across the highway; be careful, though there's not much you can do except make the turn as fast as possible and hope for the best.

Skyline Drive makes a long run down the ridge, past viewpoints, a trailhead, and a nice picnic area, then swings north, giving you a choice of either dropping west into Washington or north and east to DeSmet.

If you're coming from Coeur d'Alene instead of Moscow, turn in at DeSmet, continue for about six miles, and turn left on King Valley Road, just past the cemetery. Follow that road through the valley and up the mountain, eventually reaching signs marking Skyline Drive. For more information, contact the Idaho Parks Department's North Region headquarters, 2750 Kathleen Ave., Coeur d'Alene, ID 83814, 208/769-1511.

DeSmet and Tensed

Heading north on Highway 95, just before you come to DeSmet you enter the Coeur d'Alene Indian Reservation. DeSmet, Tensed, Plummer, and Worley are all Reservation towns. Other than the route to McCroskey State Park, there's nothing in DeSmet to offer the casual tourist, though photographers might appreciate the rolling farmland and open vistas.

The town was named after the early Jesuit missionary, Father Pierre Jean de Smet. The Belgian-born de Smet arrived in North Idaho in 1842 and began a mission near today's town of St. Maries. He became a good friend to the Coeur d'Alene people and succeeded in converting many of them to Christianity. The original mission was built on the St. Joe River floodplain. After being inundated on several occasions, the mission was moved to Cataldo. In 1876, the mission moved again to present-day DeSmet to keep the Indians out of the way of the Silver Valley miners. A new mission was built here and the town that grew around it was named in the missionary's honor. The mission is no longer standing.

Tensed was originally a "suburb" of DeSmet, but when it grew big enough to get its own post office, it needed its own name. The residents applied for the name Temsed, which is DeSmet

spelled backwards. The postal service misprinted it, and the town became Tensed.

Plummer and Worley

Plummer is the commercial center of the Coeur d'Alene Reservation. Although small, it offers sufficient visitor services to make it a good base camp for exploring Heyburn State Park—six miles east on Highway 5—and the northern Palouse country. Farming and logging are two important mainstays of the area's economy, and Plummer supplies those two industries and their workers.

Worley, named for a onetime superintendent of the reservation, is home to one of the tribe's major cash cows, the **Coeur d'Alene Tribal Bingo/Casino**, off Hwy. 95, 800/523-2464. The venture entices passersby with high-stakes bingo and video pull-tab machines. A coffee shop serves the bingo-crazed.

After passing through Worley, the highway bends around Lake Coeur d'Alene (out of sight to the east) through more beautiful rolling farmland interspersed with wooded hillocks. You won't see the lake until just before you drop down across the Spokane River and into the city of Coeur d'Alene.

EAST OF MOSCOW ON HIGHWAY 8

We were south of Troy, in expansive, rolling country patched with yellow wheat and full-leafed autumn groves, and away and away, purple in the purple distance, swam the hills of the Clearwater. And for an instant this was eternity. This was time and place suspended so that a man could have a look and give himself to both.

A. B. Guthrie Jr. (1901–1991)

Troy

Until the Northern Pacific Railroad came to town in 1890, what is today the town of Troy was a place called Huff's Gulch. A Scandinavian settler reputedly later described the gulch thusly: "It wasn't even a road, it wasn't even a town, it wasn't even a horse." Then Idaho millionaire banker John Vollmer stepped in, used his influence to bring the railroad to the gulch, and founded a town there. He wanted to call it Vollmer, and the matter was put to a vote by the locals. Legend has it a Greek settler offered free booze to anyone who would vote for the name Troy. The name was selected by an overwhelming margin. The town became a regional supply center and was the birthplace of today's Key Bank, chartered in 1905 as the First Bank of Troy. Bricks made in Troy were supposedly used on the launch pad at Cape Canaveral.

Just east of town is the turnoff to popular **Spring Valley Reservoir,** a small 35-acre impoundment holding rainbow trout, largemouth bass, crappie, and bluegill. Tranquillity is the name of the game here; gasoline motors are prohibited on the lake. Hiking trails and primitive campsites are found around the shore.

Tatonka Whitepine Bison Ranch
Five miles east of Troy, a little beyond the turnoff to Spring Valley Reservoir, White Pine Flats Road makes a T intersection into Highway 8. Down this road you'll find Tatonka Whitepine Bison Ranch, where Debi and Mike Kerley breed and raise the buffalo that winds up on the menus of Idaho restaurants. The magnificent beasts can be seen on both sides of the road here, and they sure are more handsome than cattle. Imagine when millions of them roamed the Great Plains.

A Short Detour to Juliaetta and Kendrick
At Troy, you can take a bucolic sojourn south down Highway 99 to two small farming towns in the lower Potlatch River Valley. Juliaetta was founded as Schupferville in 1878. But when the first post office was established four years later, the name was changed to honor the postmaster's two daughters, named (you guessed it) Julia and Etta.

Find Juliaetta's **Castle Museum** one block above the post office, 202 State St., 208/276-3081. The unique three-story structure was built in the early 1900s and modeled after a Scottish castle. Displayed inside are 19th-century artifacts such as the town's first switchboard, bank safe, and movie projector, as well as sundry me-

mentos of local history. The museum is open year-round, but hours are irregular; call for an appointment. Admission is free, but donations are gratefully accepted.

Down the road you'll find Kendrick, which got its name from a bit of mutual back-scratching. The town adopted the name of the chief engineer for the Northern Pacific Railroad in order to ensure that the railroad would build a line to town. To find out what's going on in the village, pick up a copy of the **Kendrick Press News,** which under one name or another has been in continuous publication here since 1905. Best time to visit Kendrick is in May, when the locust trees bloom on Main Street and the town celebrates with its **Locust Blossom Festival.** For information, call the City of Kendrick at 208/289-5731.

Deary, Helmer, and Bovill
Back up on Highway 8 and heading east, you'll soon come to tiny Deary, named for big, burly Bill Deary, who worked the area on the payroll of Frederick Weyerhauser. When Potlatch Lumber Co. was formed in 1903, Weyerhauser's son Charles was named company president, and Deary was named general manager. In 1906, Deary platted the company town that bears his name. The town was once the center for some 88 mica mines that dotted the area. The hamlet of Helmer also was founded in 1906 and named for timber cruiser William Helmer.

A little farther down the road is the hamlet of Bovill, amazingly enough *not* named for a timber man but for English settler Hugh Bovill. Born an aristocrat, Bovill was the son of an English Lord Chief Justice of the Common Pleas, and heir to the family tea plantation in Ceylon. But on a postbaccalaureate tour of the United States, he fell in love with the American West and started a Colorado ranch with a fellow cowgentleman named Lord Ogilvie. On a cattle drive to Idaho, he discovered the Moscow area and vowed to return. Hugh, his wife Charlotte, and their two daughters bought a homestead here in 1899 and started ranching, but the area was soon inundated with timber cruisers, homesteaders, and sportsmen—so the Bovills opened a lodge and store instead. The town, incorporated in

1907, appointed Hugh its first postmaster. After the railroad came to town and the logging boom hit, things got a little too bawdy and uncivilized for the Bovills; they left town in 1911.

On the west side of Bovill, Moose Creek Road (FR 381) turns north off Highway 8 and leads a short distance north to small **Moose Creek Reservoir,** which holds rainbow trout, largemouth bass, crappie, bluegill, and bullhead catfish. At Bovill, you can turn north on Highway 3 toward Clarkia and St. Maries or continue east on Highway 8 to Elk River.

ELK RIVER AND VICINITY

Highway 8 ends at Elk River, a town founded in 1909 by the Potlatch Timber company. Potlatch built the world's largest electrically powered mill here, and the Milwaukee Railroad soon arrived to haul out the lumber. Elk River thrived until 1927, when Potlatch built a bigger and better mill in Lewiston. That started Elk River's decline, exacerbated by the onset of the Great Depression. Potlatch abandoned the town in 1936. The town's population, which peaked at around 1,200, today remains under 200.

The little town bills itself as the gateway to Dworshak country—Dworshak Reservoir lies about 10 miles south, or 23 miles east of here, near Orofino. The much smaller but much closer **Elk Creek Reservoir,** a popular fishin' hole, lies just south of town; plumb its depths for rainbow and brook trout, small- and largemouth bass, and bullhead catfish. Elk River is also a great huckleberry-picking area. Fresh huckleberries find their way onto local menus in a number of seasonal recipes.

Elk Creek Falls Recreation Area

Hidden in 960 acres of dense forest three miles south of town, this national forest recreation area is named for its outstanding physical feature. Here Elk Creek cuts through a narrow gorge, plunging 300 feet in three falls on its way to the north fork of the Clearwater River. In winter, access to the falls is theoretically available to cross-country skiers from two **Elk River Park N' Ski** trailheads—one a couple of miles west of town

where the summer road to the falls joins Highway 8, the other on the southeast corner of town. But plowing and grooming at these areas can be hit-and-miss. If you buy a Park N' Ski permit from Huckleberry Lodge, they'll give you a photocopied map of the 24-mile trail system. The east trailhead is within walking distance of the lodge. But it's probably easier (and definitely shorter) to find your way to the falls starting from the access road west of town. From there you follow the snow-covered but well-signed road for 2.5 miles, right to the falls trail. In summer, drive down this road to the falls trailhead.

Winter or summer, the hike to the falls from the falls trailhead is worth the effort. It's a mile and a quarter to the lower falls viewpoint, and about a mile to either of the middle or upper falls viewpoints. The trail to the lower falls descends through a lush enchanted forest of elegant cedars. At the lower falls viewpoint you'll have a great view of a 50-foot cascade dropping over a black basalt cliff. The middle trail, with a drier exposure, leads through fir primarily. The upper falls trail takes you closest to the water, before looping back past two leviathan ponderosa pines. All three trails connect with one another. Wildlife in the vicinity includes black bear, moose, elk, deer, and maybe even a mountain lion or two.

King Cedar

The reigning monarch of Idaho's trees—the state's largest—is a giant Western red cedar north of Elk River on FR 382. Its hulking trunk measures more than 18 feet in diameter, while its crown looms 177 feet above the forest floor. The tree is estimated to be more than 3,000 years old. The area has been developed with a boardwalk providing wheelchair access to the magnificent tree and its beefy old-growth brethren.

Half the fun of checking out the Big Tree is the drive there. The road follows Elk Creek about 10 miles north from town up into Upper Elk Creek Basin, a secluded and quiet area with wildflower-filled meadows and mountain vistas. Informal campsites here make excellent places to kick back and relax for a few days—drop a line in the creek, perhaps, and see if anything fishy happens.

Morris Creek Cedar Grove

High up on the shoulder of Elk Creek basin, along the Morris Creek tributary, you'll find another grove of cedars. The 80-acre grove of 500-year-old trees surrounds a short loop trail. It's a nice place, accessible by a long and winding road. Take FR 1969 off Elk Creek Road (FR 382) and follow it up, up, up to the grove. If you find yourself in the upper basin, you missed the turn.

Oviatt Creek Fossil Beds

Can you dig it? Yes you can, at these fossil beds near Elk River. Some of the most well-preserved fossils in the world are found here, and you're permitted to dig them up and take them home.

Some 15 million years ago, this area looked very different than it does today. Had you been here then, you would have seen a large lake surrounded by dense forests of bald cypress, redwood, magnolia, birch, sycamore, oak, chestnut, and beech. You would've even found avocado trees to harvest for your primordial guacamole. Winds blew leaves from these trees into the lake, where they sank to the bottom. Some catastrophic event caused the lake to rapidly fill with silt, covering the leaves before they had a chance to decay. Over time the lake disappeared completely and the lake-bottom silts turned into sedimentary rock, preserving leaves, stems, seeds, pods, cones, flowers, ferns, moss, and unfortunate insects for modern day archaeologists to uncover.

Scientists appreciate this site as one of few places in the world where they can find "compression" fossils, which actually preserve original organic material. After carefully extracting a 15-million-year-old leaf, they can study its cells under a microscope or even extract its DNA.

To reach the fossil bed, take Highway 8 west from Elk River 5.5 miles to FR 1963. Turn left on that road and follow it another three miles to the site, at the intersection of FR 4704. The best fossils are buried at least six inches deep, in the wedge-shaped plot between Oviatt Creek and the cutbank to its west. No signs mark the spot, and nothing obvious sets it apart. A detailed map and brochure is available from the USFS **Palouse Ranger District,** 1700 Hwy. 6, Potlatch, ID 83855, 208/875-1131.

Events

The town's biggest parties take place on the **Fourth of July**—look for fireworks and festivities—and during the town's annual **Elk River Days** blowout in mid-August.

Accommodations

$50–100: Huckleberry Heaven Lodge and General Store, 105 Main St., P.O. Box 165, Elk River, ID 83827, 208/826-3405, makes a good base camp for area recreation and exploration. Rooms are available in both the lodge and in condos across the street. A hot tub is available. Sites in a 26-unit RV park rent for about $20 per day. The lodge also rents canoes, fishing boats, paddle boats, and a variety of other recreational gear.

Food

For three meals a day of fine family fare, including huckleberry hotcakes, huckleberry milk shakes, and huckleberry pie, try the **Elk River Country Cafe,** 101 S. 1st St., 208/826-3398.

Information

For more information, contact **Elk River City Hall,** P.O. Box H, Elk River, ID 83827, 208/826-3209.

HIGHWAY 6: THE WHITE PINE SCENIC BYWAY

Seventeen miles north of Moscow up Highway 95 you'll come to the turnoff for Highway 6, which leads east 35 miles to its junction with north-south Highway 3. This stretch of Highway 6 is part of the state-designated White Pine Scenic Byway and passes most of the white pines that gave the route its name.

Potlatch

Named for the timber megacompany, this quintessential company town thrived back when the hills around here were covered with enormous stands of white pine. The Potlatch Corp.'s mill here was at the time the world's largest steam-powered mill, and the company owned all the houses, schools, and other real estate in town until 1952.

Now the big timber is gone—cut down by both saws and disease—and so is the mill. Some of the nicer old homes once housing Potlatch bigwigs still stand; they're listed on a walking tour published by the Latah County Historical Society in Moscow.

Princeton and Harvard

These two towns were stops on the Washington, Idaho, and Montana Railway line. Potlatch, the company, built the railway to move logs from throughout the area to the mill in Potlatch, the town. The 47-mile rail line never made it as far as Montana. Eight stops along the line were given university names, reputedly by the student offspring of Midwestern Potlatch execs; the kids worked summer jobs on the railroad here between their academic years back East.

Princeton was founded in 1896, Harvard in 1906. The well marked turnoff to FR 447 and the USFS **Laird Park Campground** lies about four miles east of Harvard. With 31 sites (fee), Laird Park is the largest campground on the Palouse Ranger District. You can use it as a base for exploring the undeveloped North Fork Palouse River area, which offers some decent fishing and some remnant dredge tailings; the area didn't escape the mining onslaught of the 1860s. Hiking, horseback riding, and swimming make for great summertime fun here. The campground is open Memorial Day to Labor Day.

Palouse Divide Park N' Ski Area

From here, the hardcore cross-country skier can tour the entire Palouse Divide Adventure Road, a 31-mile semicircle ending at Laird Park. For less of an epic trek, stay on one of two other marked and periodically groomed loops that keep you closer to the downhill ski area. Grooming here is sporadic. The forest roads are skiable when ungroomed, but the narrow loop trails really aren't. Views of the surrounding mountains are panoramic, taking in clearcuts in every direction. Park in one of two lots: one along Highway 6, the other at North-South Ski Bowl.

Palouse Divide Adventure Road

This off-pavement route leaves Highway 6 at North-South Ski Bowl and follows FR 377 down the Palouse Divide. Along the way you'll get great views of the Palouse, particularly from the Forest Service's **Bald Mountain Lookout Tower** (elevation 5,334 feet). After 17 miles, the road reaches a T intersection with FR 447. There you can turn right (west) and loop back to Highway 6 (14 more miles), or turn east and follow the Emerald Creek drainage about the same distance over to Clarkia and Highway 3. From late spring to late fall, a sturdy car or truck can negotiate the dirt roads; keep an eye out for both ripe huckleberries and rumbling logging trucks. The rest of the year, you'll need a snowmobile or cross-country skis.

Emida

Unless you live in town, the **Western Bar and Cafe,** Hwy. 6, 208/245-1301, *is* Emida. The Western may look like just another backwater roadhouse, but no; this place is something special. As you trudge up to the porch, don't be surprised if the door is opened for you from the inside by one of the waitresses, who might offer a cheery, "Hi, come on in!" This is a genuinely friendly place.

You wouldn't guess there'd be enough happening in Emida to support a three-handed canasta game. But show up here on a summer Saturday night and you'll have a hard time finding a place to hitch up your Buick with all the pickup trucks parked out front. Live music occasionally lights up the night, and everyone living within half a tank of gas in any direction shows up, just so they don't forget what their neighbors look like. If you're anywhere in the area, make a special trip. Highly recommended.

Seven miles past Emida you'll come to the junction with Highway 3, which heads south to Clarkia and north to St. Maries.

HIGHWAY 3: CLARKIA TO ST. MARIES

Clarkia

About 20 million years ago, during the Miocene period, the site of today's town of Clarkia was the bottom of a lake. Plants and insects that floated to the bottom of the lake and were buried in sediments are now fossils waiting to be uncovered. You can dig for these fossils at the Oviatt Creek Fossil Beds near Elk River and at the wacky Fossil Bowl motocross park and fossil dig right here in Clarkia.

About 20 million years later, Clarkia flourishes as a timber town. Passing through today, you'll be amazed by the unbelievably long string of railroad cars, each loaded to the brim with what used to be a forest. The town is a hub for the BLM's Grandmother Mountain recreation area—full of hiking trails—and the Marble Creek recreation area, offering camping and hiking across Hobo Divide in the St. Joe River drainage.

Emerald Creek Garnet Area

The Idaho state gemstone, the star garnet, is found only two places in the world: Idaho and India. Here you can dig the 12-sided crystals from the earth at a Forest Service–managed dig site. The gems are normally found at a depth of 1–10 feet, in alluvial sand and gravel deposits just above bedrock, and range from BB to golf ball–size.

You need a permit to become a garnet miner for a day; the fee is $10 for adults, $5 for kids 14 and under. Permits are available at the site, about a mile hike from the parking area. Each permit is good for five pounds of garnets. If you want more than that, you'll have to buy an additional permit. Digging is permitted in designated areas only.

The Forest Service recommends you budget at least four hours at the site, and bring with you grubby boots, a shovel, bucket, coffee can, and a screen box for washing gravel.

The dig site is open summers only, Fri.–Tues. 9 A.M.–5 P.M. It's in a gorgeous area, surrounded by woods, meadows, creeks, and wildlife, including black bears. Four miles east of the dig site, **Emerald Creek Campground** makes an outstanding place to camp during your rockhounding endeavors. Fee is $6 a night.

For more information on the garnet area or campground, contact the USFS **St. Joe Ranger District** office at P.O. Box 407, St. Maries, ID 83861, 208/245-2531.

Hobo Cedar Grove Botanical Area

If you can visit only one of the several old-growth cedar groves sprinkled through northern Idaho, try to make it this one. The 500-year-old cedars here escaped the saws, axes, and forest fires of the early 20th century. Today they are protected as a National Natural Landmark. The 240-acre grove lies on a gentle slope traversed by a half-mile interpretive nature trail and a longer one-mile loop trail. The easy trails wind through the cool, shady forest, past brooks and lacy beds of lady fern. Sunlight filters through the dense canopy, casting heavenly spotlights now and again on the fairytale landscape. If you stop and wait long enough, perhaps you'll catch sight of one of the gnomes or trolls that must inhabit this mystical realm.

In addition to the western red cedars, botanists will note grand fir, western larch, Pacific yew, and Engelmann spruce. Chances are good you'll have the area all to yourself, particularly on weekdays.

To get to the grove, take FR 321 northeast from Clarkia for 10 miles. Along the way you'll pass Potlatch's Merry Creek clearcut. According to the Potlatch sign here, this 46-acre plot was cut in 1988–89, yielding 730 million board feet (MBF) of lumber. It will be harvested again in 2050 to produce 1.8 MBF. This is sustained yield? And hang on to your hats—thanks to this clearcut, "more than nine jobs were produced." Presumably 10.

Continuing up the road, you'll crest Hobo Pass (elevation 4,525 feet) and almost immediately bear right onto FR 3357. Find trailhead parking about two miles down the road.

For more information, contact the USFS **St. Joe Ranger District**, P.O. Box 407, St. Maries, ID 83861, 208/245-2531.

The St. Maries River

From Santa to St. Maries, the highway follows the St. Maries River, a placid watercourse that was once used as a log-drive highway. Floaters will find it a slow, relaxing paddle. Anglers can drop a line for a cutthroat or rainbow trout; note that the river is stocked between Clarkia and Santa, and that Alder Creek, which joins the St. Maries at the Lotus railroad crossing, is closed to all fishing.

St. Maries

A timber town clinging to life in the wake of the forest-products slowdown and the devastating floods of 1996, St. Maries (pronounced "St. Mary's"), the Benewah County seat, has a gritty blue-collar feel. The city enjoys a beautiful setting. It's surrounded by big mountains, and the lush cottonwoods along the St. Joe River turn a glowing gold in fall. Boating and floating are favorite pastimes, and camping, fishing, and hunting opportunities abound.

The **St. Maries Chamber of Commerce** is at 906 Main Ave., P.O. Box 162, St. Maries, ID 83861, 208/245-3563, www.stmarieschamber.org. A small visitor center and museum occupies the historic log-cabin **Hughes House** at 6th and Main, toward the east end of town, 208/245-1501. The USFS **St. Joe Ranger District** is in the Federal Building at 7th and College, P.O. Box 407, St. Maries, ID 83861, 208/245-2531.

UP THE ST. JOE

The St. Joe River begins on the Continental Divide and flows down through the St. Joe and Clearwater Mountains into Coeur d'Alene Lake, a distance of more than 120 river miles. Timber barges and tourist cruise boats chug upriver as far as St. Maries, leading to the frequently cited statistic that the St. Joe is the highest navigable river in the world.

Floaters and boaters will find a stretch of the river to suit them, no matter what adrenaline level they prefer. The lower river below Avery is a placid float. Above Avery, a 60-mile stretch of the river has been classified as Wild and Scenic. Here rafters and kayakers run whitewater with rapids of up to Class V in difficulty.

Fishing the St. Joe is another productive and popular pastime, though the river isn't the world-class trout fishery it was prior to massive logging operations here early this century. You'll find the biggest angling challenges at road's end, where the rules permit catch-and-release only, and the fish are smarter than most of the fisherfolk.

The Lower St. Joe

Forest Highway 50 begins in St. Maries—on the north side of the river on the northeast edge of town—and treks up the St. Joe, eventually crossing the Continental Divide and continuing on into St. Regis, Montana. It's a beautiful drive. Almost immediately after leaving St. Maries, the road takes on a rural flavor. The lovely **Misty Meadows RV Park,** three miles up FR 50, HCO3 Box 52, St. Maries, ID 83861, 208/245-2639, is right on the river and offers quiet, shady sites with full hookups for $15 a night. Friendly folks run the place, and the park's dock makes a perfect place to tempt a trout or two.

Continuing up the road, the river snakes lazily through a tranquil open valley, belying the furious whitewater found farther upstream. Tall cottonwoods overhang the banks, giving the river its nickname, "the shadowy St. Joe." To the north, a string of draws provides veiled views up into the St. Joe Mountains, where ridge upon distant ridge emerges ever-higher from the morning mists. The adventurous can follow one of these draws, **Phillips Draw** (FR 551), up to the **St. Joe Baldy Lookout.** If the great views there aren't sufficiently thrilling, you might try **hang gliding** off the top—it's a popular spot for that "extreme sports" activity.

About 2.5 miles past Phillips Draw is the 14-site, USFS **Shadowy St. Joe Campground,** which offers public docks and boat ramps, followed closely by the turnoff to **St. Joe City** across the river. At one point, St. Joe City was at the head of navigation on the river. Steamboats stopped here regularly, bringing loggers bound for Big Creek and Marble Creek. When they got time off, those loggers often made their way back here, and a feisty, rip-roaring town it became. But when all the logs were gone, the loggers left, too. St. Maries replaced St. Joe City as the upper terminus for boat traffic from Lake Coeur d'Alene. Today St. Joe City snoozes toward a coma.

Calder and Big Creek

Continuing upriver, you can't miss the turnoff to Calder from FR 50—it's marked by restored railroad signals. The town was founded in the early 1900s as a railroad construction camp, and it's named for one of that camp's crew. In addition to the railroad workers, miners and loggers once kept the hills here buzzing with activity. The area held rich stands of white pine until it all went up in smoke in the great fire of 1910. Many firefighters lost their lives that summer battling the blaze in Big Creek drainage.

Today, those who venture across the St. Joe River to the hamlet of Calder will find a store with gas, but no other tourist facilities. Nearby, however, is **Big Creek Campground,** the trailhead for hiking, mountain biking, and horseback riding on the **Big Creek National Recreation Trail.** The trail system here offers more than a dozen different hikes ranging in difficulty from easy to strenuous, and ranging in length from 2–15 miles. The area holds reminders of its historic boom days, including remnants of logging chutes, steam donkeys, mine shafts, and railroad trestles. Hunters and anglers also make good use of Big Creek drainage.

Marble Creek Historic Area

Marble Creek begins on the west slopes of Lookout Mountain, high in the Clearwater Range, and rushes north to its confluence with the St. Joe. Before white homesteaders showed up at the turn of the century, this area supported the largest stand of mature white pine in the inland Northwest. Had you and I been here then, we might have seen a beautiful old-growth forest. But when the money-hungry settlers and timber barons of the day cast their eyes here, they saw instead 600 million board feet of pure gold.

Under one or more of the government's 1862 Homestead Act, 1878 Timber and Stone Act, or 1906 Forest Homestead Act—all meant to encourage Western settlement and development—settlers could claim up to 160 acres of government land, either free or dirt cheap. When settlers got to Marble Creek, they saw an opportunity to turn this government largesse into personal riches. Here they could claim their spread and then make a fortune by cutting down and selling their 160 acres of prime timber. It was a dream come true; free money, get rich quick. The forest didn't stand a chance.

Most of the homesteaders soon found that cutting down the trees would be easy, but getting them out would not. Most of the tracts were remote, away from the river, and expensive equipment was needed to get the logs to the mill. Homesteaders ended up selling their claims to the timber companies, primarily the Edward Rutledge Timber Co. (a Weyerhauser affiliate later merged into Potlatch Corp.) and a large, independent operation run by Fred Herrick. The companies also took advantage of the Homestead Act, hiring their own shills to file claims, and hiring claim jumpers to intimidate homesteaders off other claims. Between 1918 and 1929 forest fires in the drainage benefitted the timber companies as well; homesteaders who lost their cabins and all their possessions were quick to sell out.

In 1900, the entire 93,000-acre Marble Creek drainage was owned by the federal government. By 1915, over three-fourths of the government-sponsored land in the Marble Creek drainage was controlled by the timber companies. The government policy intended to encourage settlement had failed at that task but had instead enriched the lumber barons and destroyed the forest.

Logging continued in the drainage until the 1930s, when all the virgin pine was gone. At that point, the government decided to reacquire the lands it had given up. Cynics might suspect this was carefully arranged by powerful timber-industry lobbyists. In any case, the government—the American taxpayers—actually bought back the logged-out lands from the timber companies. Go figure.

After moving on to greener pastures, the timber operations left behind some of the tools of their trade. Today you can drive up Marble Creek Road (FR 321) toward Hobo Pass and see the remains of splash dams, flumes and chutes, steam donkeys, logging camps, and railroad trestles. Three small, free Forest Service campgrounds lie en route, and two short historical interpretive trails lead to sites particularly rich with logging debris.

Fishing in the drainage once was outstanding. As one early angler noted, "I have never seen trout fishing, from Canada to California, half as good as the fishing on Marble Creek before the log drives." Post-logging fishing has never recovered to such levels. Still, you might want to drop a line in hopes of attracting a rainbow or a cutthroat.

At the top of the hill at Hobo Pass is the **Hobo Cedar Grove Botanical Area,** a beautiful and tranquil old-growth cedar grove that escaped the handiwork of the goodfellers.

Avery and the North Fork

Like Calder, Avery owes its founding to the Chicago, Milwaukee & St. Paul Railroad, which once employed as many as 150 workers here. The town—named for Avery Rockefeller, grandson of CM&SP director William Rockefeller— was a transfer point, where steam locomotives coming up from St. Maries were replaced with electric ones for the trip up the North Fork and over to Montana. The railroad went bankrupt in the 1970s, and the line from Marble Creek out to St. Maries was purchased by Potlatch Corp. in 1980. The rest of the line was dismantled and today has been restored as the Route of the Hiawatha mountain-biking trail. The old Avery depot now houses a small **community museum.**

In 1909, the Forest Service decided it needed a ranger station here. The following year came the disastrous 1910 fire. A successful backfire set around the town kept the old ranger station and the rest of the town from being incinerated. A new facility has replaced **Avery Historic Ranger Station** for all business purposes, but the original log structure remains, today listed on the National Register of Historic Places.

At Avery, FR 456 turns north up the North Fork of the St. Joe River. When the roads are open, explorers with a map and a hankering for exploration can make their way up the North Fork and over the mountains to either the Silver Valley town of Wallace or to Taft, Montana, across the Continental Divide. Along this route, you'll pass Pearson—western terminus of the Route of the Hiawatha trail—and, farther on, a trailhead for the historic **Arid Peak Lookout,** a Forest Service lookout tower recently restored with the help of volunteers. It's a two-mile hike from the North Fork Road up to the tower, which rents for $25 a night minimum. For more information call the St. Joe Ranger District's Avery office at 208/245-4517.

Above Avery on the St. Joe

Continuing east up the main fork of the St. Joe, you'll pass several USFS **campgrounds** perfect for fishing expeditions. In order from Avery on up, these include **Packsaddle** (two sites), **Turner Flat** (10 sites), **Tin Can Flat** (10 sites), and **Conrad Crossing** (eight sites). Just past Conrad Crossing campground, 29 miles east of Avery, FR 50 makes a 90-degree turn to the northeast and ascends Gold Creek, crossing the Continental Divide and dropping back down to St. Regis, Montana. The road follows the route of the old Montana Trail, a favorite east-west route of early Native Americans. The roads in this area were damaged in the 1996 floods but should be reopened by the time you read this.

Continuing upriver on FR 218, you'll pass two more USFS campgrounds at **Fly Flat** (14 sites) and **Beaver Creek** (three sites) before coming to the old **Red Ives Ranger Station,** a 1935 CCC-built facility now on the National Historic Register. The road continues upriver another couple of miles past Red Ives, before ending at the USFS **Spruce Tree** campground (five sites). From here on up, the St. Joe is designated as Wild and Scenic; no motor vehicles or bicycles are allowed, and only your feet or those of a horse will get you farther upstream. Up here, the water flows clean and clear, and the cutthroat trout are big and hungry. Deep in this angler's paradise is **St. Joe Outfitters & Guides,** HCO 1 Box 109A, St. Maries, ID 83861, 208/245-4002, a remote hideaway geared to the St. Joe sportsperson. After riding in six miles on horseback, you'll find a small, 1940s-era log-cabin lodge and two cabins with four single beds in each. You bring your own sleeping bag, but all the homestyle meals are provided. Electricity is provided by a generator, and hot showers are available. Best of all, you're a stone's throw from the river, where fly-fishing—all catch-and-release only, artificial flies and lures with single, barbless hooks—approaches religion. The cutthroat population up here is all natural; no fish have ever been planted. You can try your luck on your own or arrange a guide for an extra charge. Four- to seven-day packages are offered, ranging $975–1,570 per person. In addition to fishing, the camp offers hunting and horsepacking adventures; call for details. The establishment is an Orvis-endorsed outfitter, and reservations must be made far in advance.

Snow Peak
Wildlife Management Area

Mountain goats love this 32,000-acre back-country area managed jointly by the USFS and the Idaho Department of Fish and Game. The Snow Peak goat herd is large enough to be used as a seed herd for establishing or bolstering herds in other parts of the West. Elk, deer, pine martens, northern goshawks, and pileated woodpeckers also thrive here.

The area lies between FR 50 and the Mallard-Larkins Pioneer Area. To get there, take FR 50 east from Avery about 20 miles to Bluff Creek Road (FR 509). Turn right onto Bluff Creek Road and proceed nine miles to FR 201. Turn left onto FR 201 and proceed four more miles to the wildlife management area. FR 201 is a dead-end road that forms the eastern perimeter of the WMA and passes by seven trailheads leading into the area.

The area is open year-round, but snow usually blocks the roads from November through June. Hunters use the area in fall. Hikers will find creek-bottom stands of old-growth cedar and hemlock, and great views from the top of Snow Peak (elevation 6,760).

Boating

The St. Joe River's 120-plus miles of free-flowing water offer as much of a challenge as you desire, from easy Class I meanders to raging, expert-only Class V whitewater. High in the Bitterroots near the river's headwaters is the first navigable stretch; put in at Heller Creek Campground. Only expert kayakers need apply. At the opposite end of the river, the final 31-mile stretch from St. Joe City to Coeur d'Alene Lake is a placid and pokey stretch that passes by the city of St. Maries—past the tugboats tugging logs to the mill, past majestic cottonwoods lining the banks—and continues down to the "river through the lakes" at Heyburn State Park. This stretch is slow enough for Gramps or Junior. As the Forest Service puts it, "the only serious obstacles are the waves kicked up by passing motor boats." In between you'll find everything from Class II to Class IV water.

One-day guided float trips on the St. Joe are offered by **ROW**, P.O. Box 579, Coeur d'Alene,

ID 83816, 208/765-0841 or 800/451-6034. The season runs June through mid-July, with the more frenetic whitewater on the early end of that range. Cost is around $85–100.

Fishing

Trout fishing on the St. Joe is a venerated and time-honored pastime. In years past the river teemed with fish. Today it's less dramatic. The Forest Service's fishing guide to the St. Joe describes the cause of the decline situation thusly:

"Many of the tributaries of the St. Joe River have received heavy logging. Probably the major direct impact of logging on the St. Joe is in the slack water area, where siltation occurs. Log landings are numerous along both sides of the river. Bank erosion is severe around these areas, as well as in numerous areas where cattle graze on or near the stream's edge."

From St. Maries to around Tin Can Flat Campground east of Avery, the river is open, and no gear or bait restrictions apply to anglers pursuing primarily cutthroat trout (limit one) and rainbow trout—although you'll also find brown and eastern brook trout in the watershed. The limit is six trout total, including your one cutthroat. Rainbows are stocked in Marble Creek and on both forks of the St. Joe above Avery.

In the Wild and Scenic stretch of the St. Joe above Tin Can Flat, the entire drainage—including all tributaries—is open to catch-and-release fishing only, using a single barbless hook and artificial flies and lures, no bait.

Recreation Information

For more information on boating, hiking, biking, or other recreation opportunities in the area, contact the USFS **St. Joe Ranger District** at P.O. Box 407, St. Maries, ID 83861-0407, 208/245-2531, or the **Avery Ranger District** at HC Box 1, St. Maries, ID 83802-9702, 208/245-4517.

HEYBURN STATE PARK

Heyburn is the largest of Idaho's state parks, encompassing more than 5,500 acres of land and 2,300 acres of water, and offering 132 campsites. Boating and fishing are major draws, and hiking and biking trails wind along the forested lakeshore here. The park is home to one of the largest concentrations of nesting ospreys in North America, and deer, elk, bears, and wild turkeys wander through the area. Another odd twist—wild rice is grown and harvested in the shallows of the lake.

The park's several segments are strung one after the other along Highway 5. The biggest segment and the park's "main entrance" is located on Chatcolet Road, six miles east of Plummer or 12 miles west of St. Maries on Highway 5. Here you'll find the large **Hawley's Landing Campground,** as well as the park headquarters (no visitor center) and hiking trails. The **Lakeshore Loop Trail** is an easy, half-mile-plus trail connecting Hawley's Landing Campground and the Plummer Creek Bridge. Along the way, amateur botanists can spot larch, grand fir, and western red cedar trees, as well as bunchberry, oceanspray, and thimbleberry. Look for ospreys, wood ducks, and great blue herons out on the marsh. The **Plummer Creek Trail,** about the same length, is also easy and passes through groves of cedar, grand fir, ponderosa pine, western hemlock, and cottonwood. Here you might spy a rubber boa slithering through the underbrush, or hear songbirds merrily chirping away. The **Indian Cliffs Trail** forms a three-mile loop lined by wildflowers like syringa, heartleaf arnica, and buttercup. The trail takes you up out of the forest to panoramic ridgetop views.

A mile east of the main park entrance along the highway is the park's **Rocky Point** area. Here you'll find a park-managed **marina** with a small store, gas dock, and restrooms, as well as an interpretive center with exhibits on local natural history and Native American arts and artifacts.

Continuing east another mile you'll find a picnic area and public docks at **Cottonwood Point.** And just east of Cottonwood Point on the highway is a turnout offering views of **a river flowing through a lake.** Before Post Falls Dam backed up the Spokane River in 1904, the water level of Coeur d'Alene Lake was significantly lower. The St. Joe River flowed down through the lowlands now under water in Heyburn State Park and was flanked on either side by natural, tree-lined levees. The dam raised the lake's water level enough to flood these southern lowlands, but not enough to crest the levees along the river. As a result, the levees now appear as island strips separating the water of the river from the water of the lake. Eventually, the downsloping topography of the riverbed reaches the surface elevation of the lake, and the phenomenon disappears. Before the dam was built, the four lakes at Heyburn State Park—Chatcolet Lake, Hidden Lake, Round Lake, and Benewah Lake—were four separate bodies of water. Today they're separate in name only; the waters flow together to make up the southern reaches of Coeur d'Alene Lake.

Finally, at the park's eastern end is a turnoff to the **Benewah Use Area,** where you'll find another campground, more docks, and some of the best sunsets in Idaho.

Out on the Water

Fishing at the park is excellent. That tug on the end of your line will most likely turn out to be a bass, kokanee, cutthroat trout, perch, or submerged log. Note that at the east end of the of the lake **Benewah Creek** is closed to all fishing; the bull trout need their privacy while they're doing their spawning thing. Just about any other water-based form of recreation is a sure bet at the park as well; **water-skiing, swimming, kayaking, sailing,** and **canoeing** are all popular pastimes.

Rental Cabins

Two cabins are available for rent in the park. **Chatcolet Cabin** in the Chatcolet Use Area sleeps six to eight persons; **Lakeview Cabin,** right on the shore of Chatcolet Lake, sleeps eight. Both cabins have a full bath, kitchen, dining room, living room, and deck or screened porch. They come with cooking utensils and tableware but no linens. Renters are responsible for daily cleaning. The cabins rent for $85 a night.

Reservations and Information

For campground or cabin reservations, marina rates, or other information, write to Heyburn State Park, Rt. 1 Box 139, Plummer, ID 83851, or call park headquarters at 208/686-1308.

The Panhandle

Up in Idaho's far northern reaches, each bright blue summer day seems to last a lifetime, allowing even staid grownups to feel as immortal and lighthearted as a schoolkid at camp. Boats, fishing poles, and camping gear clutter the garages of homes throughout the region and remain in nearly constant use from May to October. Then it's time to break out the skis and sleds. The Panhandle is one big playground.

On a map, the region looks like a stovepipe hat sitting smartly upon the head of the state. But once you're there, the hat turns into a green velvet crown, covered with dense forests and be-

jeweled with three of the largest and most beautiful lakes in Idaho: Coeur d'Alene, Pend Oreille, and Priest.

The first lake in that trio provides the backdrop and the name for the Panhandle's largest city. Coeur d'Alene, at the intersection of I-90 and Highway 95, is unquestionably the regional hub. It's also a fun resort town, offering visitors a multitude of activities to enjoy—from water-skiing to beach-bumming to world-class golfing. Farther north, Pend Oreille Lake, Idaho's largest lake, is surrounded by the magnificent Coeur d'Alene, Cabinet, and Selkirk Ranges. At the foot of the

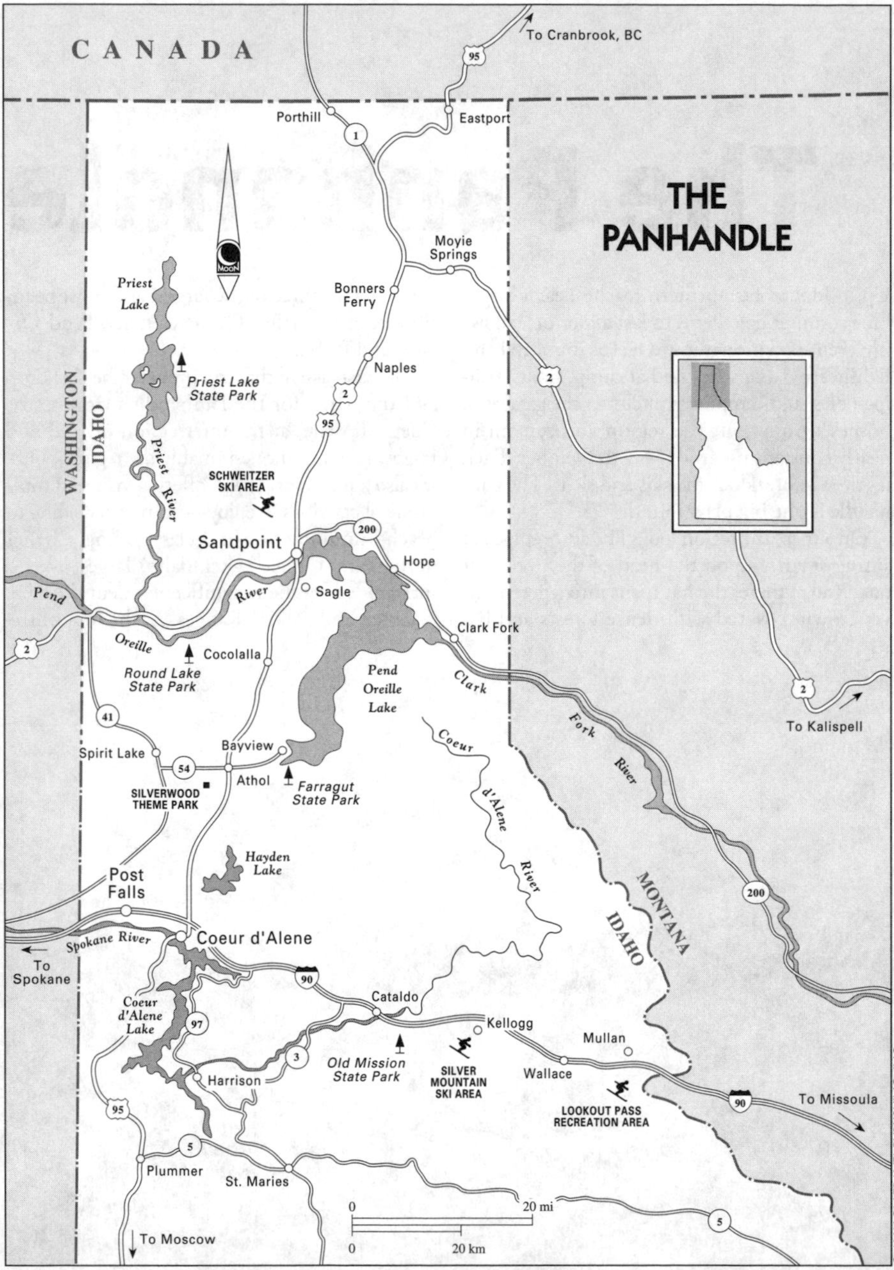

CANADA

To Cranbrook, BC

95

Porthill · Eastport

1

THE
PANHANDLE

Moyie
Springs

Bonners
Ferry

Naples

2

2

Priest
Lake

Priest Lake
State Park

WASHINGTON
IDAHO

Priest River

SCHWEITZER
SKI AREA

95

Sandpoint

200

Hope

Pend River · Sagle

Clark Fork

Oreille

Pend
Oreille
Lake

Clark Fork River

2

Round Lake
State Park

Cocolalla

Coeur

41

Spirit Lake

54

Bayview

Athol

Farragut
State Park

SILVERWOOD
THEME PARK

Hayden
Lake

d'Alene River

MONTANA
IDAHO

To Kalispell

200

Post
Falls

To
Spokane

Spokane River

Coeur d'Alene

90

Cataldo

Kellogg

Mullan

Coeur
d'Alene
Lake

97

3

Old Mission
State Park

SILVER
MOUNTAIN
SKI AREA

Wallace

LOOKOUT PASS
RECREATION AREA

90

To Missoula

Harrison

95

5

Plummer

St. Maries

0   20 mi

0   20 km

To Moscow

5

THE PANHANDLE

© AVALON TRAVEL PUBLISHING, INC.

Selkirks, on the shore of Pend Oreille, lies the small, onetime art colony of Sandpoint, whose splendid setting surpasses even Coeur d'Alene's.

The last major jewel in the crown, Priest Lake, provides the ultimate getaway for those seeking a remote and rustic encounter with the great outdoors. The lake hides in a pocket in the Selkirks, high up in Idaho's northwest cor-

ner. Wildlife is so abundant that if you *don't* see a moose, bear, mountain goat, or other big furry quadruped, you're just not looking. Anglers quietly cruise the lake, sending ripples radiating out across misty morning waters, while campers hunker around shoreline campfires, frying up fresh trout to add to their morning scrambled eggs.

Coeur d'Alene and Vicinity

Shortly after the Mullan Road opened the Panhandle to miners and settlers, U.S. Army general William Tecumseh Sherman came through here scouting locations for a new fort. The army wanted a north Idaho base to protect the burgeoning white populace from Native American attack, and to make sure the Brits didn't push their way south of the 49th parallel. In 1878, construction of Fort Coeur d'Alene began.

The fort, and the town that grew around it, were named for the local Native Americans. Although they called themselves Schee-chu-umsh, meaning "The Ones That Were Found Here," the French trappers called them the Coeur d'Alene—"Heart like an awl." Authorities agree the name arose from the Native Americans' shrewd trading abilities but argue whether the trappers coined the phrase first or adopted it after hearing the Native Americans use it to describe the French. In any case, the name stuck. After Sherman died, the fort's name was changed to honor him, but the town that grew around the fort kept the moniker Coeur d'Alene. In the 1880s, the town became the lake's biggest steamship port; ships carried passengers and supplies to and from the booming Coeur d'Alene Mining District and communities around the lake.

Today, Coeur d'Alene (population 36,300) ranks as the top resort town in the Inland Northwest. In summer, the long lakefront boardwalk bustles with bikini-clad sun worshippers, Frisbee-fetching dogs, ice cream–licking youngsters, and busloads of camera-toting tourists. Out on the lake, jet skis buzz and flit like hopped-up waterborne mosquitoes, while water-skiers race the wakes of the cruise boats, and parasailers

brighten the skies overhead. No question—this city is alive and exciting in summer.

In winter, the crowds disappear and a quiet, intense beauty descends with the first snowfall. Skiers make the morning commute out to one of the region's three downhill resorts, while bald eagles—intent on fattening up on the lake's abundant kokanee salmon—make their annual pilgrimage to Wolf Lodge Bay. It's a great season to relax at one of the town's numerous B&Bs—to sit by a crackling fire, pick up a good book, and drift off to dreams of spring.

SIGHTS
North Idaho College and Old Fort Sherman
The campus of this two-year community college occupies the grounds of old Fort Sherman, one of the major military installations in the Northwest from 1878 to 1901. It was from here that troops were dispatched up the Silver Valley to quell the mining wars of 1892. Today only a few structures from the fort remain, scattered among modern school buildings. The campus is a nice place to just poke around on, thanks to its prime lakefront real estate, expansive lawns, and big evergreens. For more information about the school, write to North Idaho College, 1000 W. Garden Ave., Coeur d'Alene, ID 83814, call 208/769-3300, or see www.nic.edu.

Museum of North Idaho
Kootenai County's history is featured at the Museum of North Idaho, 115 Northwest Blvd. (in front of City Park), 208/664-3448, www.museumni.org. Exhibit topics include the

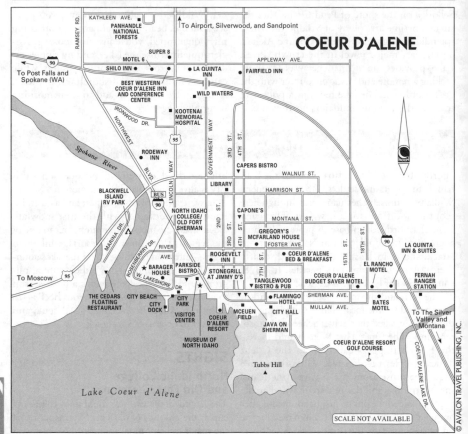

Mullan Road, Fort Sherman, early transportation—including railroads and steamboats—and local industry, especially logging and mining. The museum is open April 1–Oct. 31, Tues.–Sat. 11 A.M.–5 P.M., and also on Sundays 11 A.M.–5 P.M. in July and August.

An annex, the **Fort Sherman Museum,** on the North Idaho College campus, has exhibits including a 1924 smokechaser's cabin, a model of old Fort Sherman, and a lifeboat from the *Miss Spokane*—a passenger boat that plied Coeur d'Alene Lake in the 1920s. The museum provides a walking-tour brochure to the several Fort Sherman structures that have been preserved. The annex is open May 1–Sept. 30, Tues.–Sat. 1–4:45 P.M.

A single admission price of $2 adults, $1 kids 6–16, families $4 is valid for entry to both museums.

RECREATION
Tubbs Hill

One of the city's highlights, this beautiful 120-acre wooded preserve juts out into the lake right next to the Coeur d'Alene Resort. Trails loop around the peninsula through groves of Douglas fir and century-old ponderosa pine. Some paths climb up the hill for panoramic views; others drop down to hidden coves and beaches. It's all a city park, open to foot traffic only and within easy walking distance of anywhere downtown. The best time to enjoy Tubbs Hill is during an after-dinner stroll, when you can walk off your meal and enjoy a gorgeous sunset at the same time. For more information, contact the Coeur d'Alene Parks Department, 710 E. Mullan Ave., 208/769-2252.

Bicycling and Skating

The **North Idaho Centennial Trail,** a 23-mile hiking/biking/skating trail, stretches west from Higgins Point, on Coeur d'Alene Lake's northeast shore, through the cities of Coeur d'Alene and Post Falls to the Washington state line. Ambitious folks can continue west on the abutting Spokane River Centennial Trail; it's another 22 miles to Spokane. For most of its length, the trail is either completely separated from traffic or off on a big, wide shoulder. Animals on leashes are allowed, and interpretive signs mark many points of interest along the way. You can pick up the trail at City Park, downtown, or on Coeur d'Alene Lake Drive. For more information, contact the Coeur d'Alene Parks Department, 710 E. Mullan Ave., 208/769-2252.

Swimming and Sunbathing

When those sunny summer days roll around, **City Beach** is the place to be. The water warms up enough for swimming and splashing, and the beach, boardwalk, and adjacent **City Park** fill with revelers. Skaters, Frisbee-ers, joggers, swimmers, gawkers, and gawkees—the people-watching here can't be beat.

If the tame lakeshore bores you, head to **Wild Waters,** out near the interstate at 2119 N. Government Way, 208/667-6491 (summer) or 208/765-6041 (off-season). This large waterslide theme park also has a grassy area for sunning, hot pools for soaking, a video arcade, and a snack bar. The park is open the last two weekends in May (including Memorial Day Monday), then daily from the first weekend in June through early September. Hours are 11 A.M.–6 P.M., or to 7 P.M. in midsummer. Rates are around $17 for everyone 48 inches or taller, $15 for shorter children, $7 for seniors and disabled sliders, and free for waterbabies 3 and under. Evening sliding, 3 P.M.–closing, is offered at reduced rates. Parents can get a viewing-only pass for about $7, which allows them to keep an eye on Junior without getting wet themselves.

Boating is a way of life in the Panhandle.

Nearby, in Athol, the **Silverwood Amusement Park** offers its new Boulder Beach Water Park.

Sightseeing Cruises

Lake Coeur d'Alene Cruises, P.O. Box 7200, Coeur d'Alene, ID 83816, 208/765-4000 or 800/365-8338, ext. 7143, offers 90-minute tours of the lake daily late April-late Oct.; $14.75 adults, $13.75 seniors, $9.75 children 6–12. Also available are cruises all the way down the lake to the St. Joe River, Sunday brunch cruises, and a Fourth of July fireworks cruise. All public cruises leave from City Dock at Independence Point, next to the Coeur d'Alene Resort.

Another motorized way to tour the bay in summer is offered by **Classic Speedboat Rides,** 208/666-1626 or 208/699-0660, which takes guests out on the lake in *Flashback,* a classic speedboat, of course. Rates for the 30-minute ride run $15 per person. June 15–Sept. 15, the boat leaves every half hour 9 A.M.–8 P.M.

Those who prefer sailing to motoring can call **Coeur d'Alene Sailing Cruises, Inc.,** 208/661-0403, which takes passengers aboard its Elite 37 sloop for cruises tailored to your desires. A four-hour sail runs about $180 for up to six people. Dinner cruises are also available at around $140 per couple.

Flightseeing

Brooks Sea Plane, P.O. Box 1028, Coeur d'Alene, ID 83814, 208/664-2842, 208/772-5649, or 208/772-9059, takes passengers aloft on 20-minute sightseeing flights around the lake. You'll fly aboard either a float-equipped Cessna 206 or a gorgeous seven-passenger De Havilland Beaver, the bush pilot's workhorse. Cost is $40 adults, $20 children under 12. The planes leave from City Dock on Independence Point, next to the Coeur d'Alene Resort. Longer flights are also available. **Big Country Helicopters,** 208/765-0620, offers chopper hops of a half-hour or longer around the area. Prices start at $99.95 for one or two people.

Parasailing

On sunny summer afternoons, the blue skies over Lake Coeur d'Alene are complemented by the brightly colored chutes of **Coeur d'Alene Parasail,** 208/765-5367 (dock) or 208/765-4627 (business office). You'll be towed 400 or more feet in the air behind a speedboat for an eight- to 10-minute ride over the lake. And thanks to the specially designed boat and hydraulic winch system, you won't even get wet. The standard ride costs $40. Boats leave from City Dock at Independence Point, next to the Coeur d'Alene Resort, between 8 a.m. and sunset.

Boat Rentals

Boardwalk Marina, at the Coeur d'Alene Resort, 208/765-4000, ext. 7185, rents 18-foot speedboats or 20-foot pontoon boats for $75 an hour, $225 for four hours, $450 for eight hours. Tax and fuel are additional, and you'll have to leave a credit card for a deposit. You'll also find more humble, people-powered canoes, paddleboats, and such available for rent at City Dock in summer.

Fishing

Coeur d'Alene Lake holds hungry populations of kokanee, chinook salmon, and northern pike. **Fins & Feathers,** 1816 ½ Sherman Ave., 208/667-9304, can help you find the biggest ones and provide the boat and all equipment as well. The going rate for a party of two is around $125 per person for a half-day trip, $175 for a full day. It's a little less per person with a group of three or four anglers.

While the big lake is the obvious centerpiece of the area, don't forget 300-acre **Fernan Lake,** east of I-90 at the Sherman exit. Here you'll fish for wild cutthroat trout and stocked rainbows, as well as warm-water species like largemouth bass, crappie, perch, and catfish. In winter, you can probe beneath the frozen crust, primarily for perch. Boat ramps and docks are found at either end of the lake.

Golf

The star attraction for Coeur d'Alene linksters is **Coeur d'Alene Resort Golf Course,** 900 Floating Green Dr., 208/667-4653 or 800/688-5253. The beautiful lakeside course boasts a great gimmick: the 14th hole features a moveable, floating

lakeside golf in Coeur d'Alene

green. A cute little putt-putt boat ferries you out to it, assuming your ball actually made it to the green and isn't on its way to Davey Jones's locker. Aim carefully.

All the golf magazines rave about the 6,804-yard, par-71 course, designed by Scott Miller and extensively renovated (with 500 new yards to play) in 2003. If you're not staying at the Coeur d'Alene Resort or Inn, a round here will set you back $200 or more. Guests of the resort get a major price break and a free water-taxi ride from the hotel to the course. Rates include a cart and caddie. Clubs and golf shoes can be rented. No plebes please: "Proper attire is required at all times," reads the rule, "Men—slacks or suitable length shorts and shirts with sleeves and collars. Women—dresses, skirts and blouses, slacks, culottes or proper length shorts."

Humbler courses in town include **Coeur d'Alene Golf Club,** 2201 S. Fairway Dr., 208/765-0218, a 6,274-yard, par-72 course where you'll pay about $24 a round, and **Ponderosa Springs Golf Course,** 2814 Galena Dr. (at French Gulch Rd.), 208/664-1101, a nine-hole course with a greens fee of around $15.

Sea Kayak Tours

Three-hour tours of the lake are the specialty of **Kayak Coeur d'Alene,** 208/676-1533, www .kayakcoeurdalene.com, which offers morning, afternoon, and sunset excursions seven days a week May through September. Beginners are welcome, all gear is provided, and the price is right: $32.50 for adults, $25 for children.

Whitewater Rafting

You won't find any whitewater rivers in the Coeur d'Alene area, but you will find headquarters for **ROW,** P.O. Box 579, Coeur d'Alene, ID 83816, 208/765-0841 or 800/451-6034, www.row inc.com, one of Idaho's biggest and best rafting companies. The company runs all the Idaho standards—the Snake through Hells Canyon, the Salmon, the Middle Fork Salmon, the Lochsa and Selway—plus lesser known whitewater like the Moyie, Clark Fork, St. Joe, and Owyhee. ROW is an acronym for both River Odysseys West and Remote Odysseys Worldwide; in addition to domestic rivers, the company runs raft trips in Ecuador, barge trips on French canals, yacht trips along the Turkish coast, trekking trips in Nepal, and more. Call or write for a free catalog.

THE PANHANDLE

The Local Backcountry

The USFS **Fernan Ranger Station** (Coeur d'Alene River Ranger District) is at 2502 E. Sherman Ave., on the east side of I-90, 208/769-3000. Stop by for information on nearby backcountry hiking and biking opportunities. The Forest Service publishes descriptive flyers to several hiking trails, primarily found deep in the Coeur d'Alene Mountains between Hayden Lake, Pend Oreille Lake, and the upper North Fork of the Coeur d'Alene River. A couple of trails to the east begin closer to town, around the Wolf Lodge District. In addition, logging roads lace the nearby mountains; just continue east from the Fernan Ranger Station on Fernan Lake Road, which skirts the north shore of the lake then climbs up toward Huckleberry Mountain. Past that point, dirt roads suitable for hiking or mountain biking spin off in every direction. Inquire at the ranger station to find out which, if any, of these roads are being actively logged.

Mountain Biking

The **Canfield Mountain Trail System** is part of the web of logging roads mentioned above. Its 32 miles of single- and double-track trails are open to hikers, equestrians, motorcycles, and mountain bikes; fat-tire bicyclists currently make best use of the area. Several access points are available along FR 1562, which in a meandering, roundabout fashion links Nettleton Gulch Road with Fernan Lake Road. Nettleton Gulch Road intersects 15th Street 1.1 miles north of I-90 Exit 14, becoming FR 1562 farther east. On the east side, FR 1562 intersects Fernan Lake Road 5.5 miles east of I-90 Exit 15 (Sherman Street). Pick up a map to the trail system at the Fernan Ranger Station, 2502 E. Sherman Ave., 208/769-3000.

Skiing

Although Coeur d'Alene has no downhill ski areas to call its very own, several are close enough for a day trip. North up Highway 95 about 50 miles is **Schweitzer Mountain,** high in the Selkirks overlooking Sandpoint and Pend Oreille Lake. To the east out I-90 are **Silver Mountain**—40 miles from town at Kellogg and home of the world's longest gondola—and **Lookout Pass,** 20 miles beyond that at the Montana border. Popular cross-country areas in the vicinity include **Fourth of July Pass Park N' Ski Area,** 18 miles east of Coeur d'Alene at Fourth of July Pass, and Farragut and Round Lake State Parks to the north.

Outfitters

Vertical Earth, 206 N. 3rd St., 208/667-5503, rents out mountain bikes, snowboards, snowshoes, and cross-country skis, including telemark demo gear. And you're not too far from megaoutfitter **REI,** just over the border at 1125 N. Monroe St. in Spokane, Washington, 509/328-9900.

ENTERTAINMENT AND EVENTS

North Idaho College sponsors the bulk of the area's concerts and dramatic performances. For current listings, call the college's Boswell Auditorium box office at 208/769-7780. The Citizens Council for the Arts, P.O. Box 901, Coeur d'Alene, ID 83816, 208/667-9346, has lots of information on the region's fine and performing arts scene.

Highlights of the town's events calendar include **Fred Murphy Days** the last weekend in May, honoring a locally legendary steamboat captain with good food and drink, contests of strength and skill, street dances, a parade, and a good deal of giddiness; **July 4th,** which brings an Independence Day parade to beat the band; **Art on the Green** at North Idaho College in early August; and the **North Idaho Fair and Rodeo,** which comes to the Kootenai County Fairgrounds later in August. From the weekend following Thanksgiving through after New Year's Day, the Coeur d'Alene Resort area and lakeside boardwalks glow with more than a million **holiday lights.**

HOTELS AND MOTELS

Sherman Avenue runs between Coeur d'Alene Resort and I-90 on the east side of town. A number of mostly inexpensive-to-moderate, older independent motels are along this strip. The area has the advantage of being surrounded by quiet old residential areas and near funky, character-filled shops and restaurants. On the west end, the lodgings are within easy walking distance of downtown. On the east end, you'll be near the interstate.

The other motel district is along Appleway Avenue, which parallels I-90 to the north. This area has the advantages of being close to the interstate and surrounded by modern shopping malls and fast-food emporiums. It has the same disadvantages. Most of the major chain motels are here.

Under $50

The **Coeur d'Alene Budget Saver Motel,** 1519 Sherman, 208/667-9505, doesn't look like much from the outside, but it's well worth the low prices—among the cheapest in town. The rooms are decent, and some have two bedrooms—a nice touch for added privacy. **Bates Motel,** 2018 E. Sherman, 208/667-1411, looks neat and tidy enough to satisfy Mother—I dare you to take a shower there. All of its rooms have just one bed. In the same area, you'll find **El Rancho Motel,** 1915 E. Sherman, 208/664-8794 or 800/359-9791 (reservations only). Over in the Appleway motel area is the ever-faithful **Motel 6,** 416 W. Appleway, 208/664-6600 or 800/466-8356.

$50–100

For budget lodging within walking distance of the lakefront, try the **Flamingo Motel,** 718 Sherman, 208/664-2159 or 800/955-2159, which has a pool and some kitchenettes. Rates start at the low end of this category.

The **Rodeway Inn,** 1422 Northwest Blvd., 208/664-8246 or 800/651-2510, has decent rates, decent rooms (some with balconies overlooking the Spokane River and, at a distance, Lake Coeur d'Alene), complimentary coffee and pastries each morning, and a pool.

Over on Appleway, you'll find **Super 8,** 505 W. Appleway, 208/765-8880 or 800/800-8000, and **Fairfield Inn,** 2303 N. 4th St., at Appleway, 208/664-1649 or 800/228-2800. The La Quinta chain has two motels in town, at 280. W Appleway, 208/765-5500, and at 2209 E. Sherman, 208/667-6777, or either toll-free at 866/

725-1661. The Sherman Avenue motel is the fancier of the two, but rooms at both are mostly in this price range.

$100–150

Among the plushest places in town are the **Shilo Inn,** 702 W. Appleway, 208/664-2300 or 800/222-2244, which offers all minisuites with kitchenettes; and the **Best Western Coeur d'Alene Inn and Conference Center,** 414 W. Appleway, 208/765-3200 or 800/251-7829, a full-service hotel with an indoor pool and spa. Both sometimes have rooms for under $100.

Over $250

By many people's standards, **The Coeur d'Alene, a Resort on the Lake,** 115 S. 2nd St., Coeur d'Alene, ID 83814, 208/765-4000 or 800/688-5253, is *the* hotel in Idaho. It seems to be a pet of travel writers; the resort gets a lot of press and has been included more than once on *Condé Nast Traveler* magazine's "Gold List" of the world's best hotels. It definitely ranks in terms of location, rising high into the sky over the shores of exquisitely beautiful Coeur d'Alene Lake. And it offers a mind-boggling array of extravagant amenities. With all that in mind, is there any room for disagreement with the glowing reviews? Does anyone dare not like this place?

Yes and yes. One wonders what architect R. G. Nelson was thinking, putting a skyscraper on a beautiful lakeshore. Unlike, say, Yosemite's Ahwahnee Hotel, this big tan monster doesn't complement the environment, it competes with it, resembling nothing so much as a giant tower of Legos. In addition, though co-developer Jerry Jaeger was once quoted as saying, "This will be a place to come and play; nobody's going to wear a tie," the self-conscious "informality" here is cloaked in Gucci and Chanel. You'll feel out of place in jeans. Standard rooms usually run $250 or more in summer; pay much less, and you risk getting a depressing "economy" room that'll make you wish you stayed at Motel 6 for half the price. The high-end rooms go for $450 in summer. Lower prices are offered other times of year. Spa, ski, golf, and other packages are available.

BED-AND-BREAKFASTS

Coeur d'Alene is the B&B capital of Idaho; about a dozen are sprinkled throughout town, with a half-dozen or so more in the outlying areas. Unless specified otherwise, the B&Bs below serve a full breakfast, don't permit children under 12 or pets, and don't allow smoking indoors. Note that B&B prices vary widely with the particular room rented. The categories listed below are for each establishment's middle-of-the-road offerings, but less-expensive and more-expensive rooms are often available. Most of the inns below are members of the Bed and Breakfast Association of Coeur d'Alene, with information online at www.bb-cda.com.

$50–100

The **Coeur d'Alene Bed & Breakfast,** 906 Foster Ave., 208/667-7527 or 800/597-1898, occupies a gorgeous 1906 Colonial-style home in a great neighborhood full of big beautiful trees. The five bedrooms all have TVs, and four have a private bath. Outside you'll find a porch with mountain views and a garden with an enclosed, Japanese-style spa and sauna. Rates include a full breakfast and an evening glass of wine.

Cricket on the Hearth, 1521 Lakeside Ave., 208/664-6926, has five rooms. The Molly Brown, Lilac, and Kabuki rooms have private baths; the Garden and Cabin rooms share a bath. The back deck holds a hot tub, the front porch a swing. Pets and small children may be accommodated by advance arrangement.

$100–150

East of town, off the lake's north shore, **Katie's Wild Rose Inn,** E. 5150 Coeur d'Alene Lake Dr., 208/765-9474 or 800/371-4345, sits high on a promontory overlooking Bennett Bay. Wild roses grace the grounds, and a rose motif runs throughout the interior. The inn sits alongside the Centennial Trail bike path. Of the four rooms, two have private bath and two share a bath. One has an in-room jacuzzi.

Baragar House, 316 Military Dr., 208/664-9125 or 800/615-8422, occupies a large Craftsman-style bungalow in the very desirable Fort

ON GUARD FOR HUMAN RIGHTS

Idaho—especially the state's Panhandle region—has long had a reputation as a haven for racists, but events in recent years show that perceptions and reality may both be turning.

From 1973 on, Richard Butler ruled the white-supremacist Aryan Nations organization from a compound in Hayden, Idaho, a few miles north of Coeur d'Alene. The ultra-right-wing racist and his followers were an unending source of embarrassment to the vast majority of North Idahoans. Groups including the Kootenai County Task Force on Human Relations and the Human Rights Education Institute spoke out strongly against the Aryan Nations' presence in their backyard.

Finally, in 2000, Butler was forced into bankruptcy by a $6.3 million civil judgment resulting from a suit filed by the Southern Poverty Law Center on behalf of an Idaho woman and her son who said Butler's group shot at them in 1998. Philanthropist Greg Carr, an Idaho native, purchased Butler's compound and donated it to the North Idaho College Foundation, which now operates the site as a **peace park.** Groups wishing to visit can make an appointment by calling Rayelle Anderson at 208/769-5978. Meanwhile, the Human Rights Education Institute, again aided by a donation from Carr, plans to open a human rights interpretive center in a historic building in downtown Coeur d'Alene's City Park sometime in 2004 or 2005.

Boise, the state's largest city (and its most diverse), has also taken steps to ensure people of all colors and faiths feel at home in Idaho. When a racial slur and swastika were carved into the front door of the Idaho Black History Museum in 2002, city residents swiftly mobilized to repair the damage and hold a rally denouncing the vandalism. Later that year, the city dedicated the new **Idaho Anne Frank Human Rights Memorial,** billed by its creators, the Idaho Human Rights Education Center, as "an educational park inspired by Anne Frank's faith in humanity . . . built to promote respect for human dignity and diversity." More than 3,000 people and businesses, including children from 44 Idaho schools, donated $1.6 million for the project.

Sherman area. Each of the three rooms features an astronomically accurate sky full of stars, professionally painted on the ceiling in irridescent paint. By day you see nothing, but turn out the lights and the Milky Way glows overhead. The upstairs hot tub and sauna are especially nice; the tub looks out on the neighborhood's tall ponderosas through two French doors that can be opened wide. Rates include full breakfast.

The Roosevelt Inn, 105 Wallace Ave., 208/765-5200 or 800/290-3358, occupies the redbrick 1906 Roosevelt School, which was converted to this B&B in 1994. All rooms have private bath and are furnished with antiques; some rooms have a lake view. Common areas include a small exercise center and two parlors—one with a TV/VCR and Internet access, the other a quiet room for reading or writing. Rates include a gourmet full breakfast.

Gregory's McFarland House, 601 Foster Ave., 208/667-1232 or 800/335 1232, offers five rooms in a graceful, turn-of-the-20th-century home furnished with both elegant antiques and modern amenities. A gourmet breakfast and afternoon tea are served daily, and fresh coffee and goodies are always available. Each room has a private bath with a claw-foot tub and a shower. Children over 14 welcome.

Two of the area's most exquisite B&Bs are found off Highway 95 as you head south toward Moscow. **Berry Patch Inn,** 1150 N. Four Winds Rd., 208/765-4994, is just a few minutes from town (take Highway 95 south across the Spokane River and turn right on E. Riverview Drive; about a mile and a half up the hill, turn left on Four Winds Road), yet feels far removed from the hustle and bustle. It's on a quiet wooded hillside overlooking the Rathdrum Prairie, and two-acre grounds feature a big beautiful garden, a peaceful bubbling fountain, and a path leading up to a tepee and the eponymous berry patch.

Inside, the decor is described as "uncluttered country elegant eclectic." The spacious living room boasts an open-beam ceiling and a stone fireplace, and each of the three guest rooms has a private bath stocked with French milled soap, shampoo, and lotion. Rates include a gourmet homemade breakfast—served either in the bright dining room or out on the deck—as well as afternoon tea and biscotti, a dinner-hour glass of wine, and a berry liqueur nightcap. The inn has been extensively praised in many travel publications. Adults only; no smoking anywhere, inside or out.

Someday House, 790 Kidd Island Rd., 208/664-6666, gets the award for the best views of any B&B in Idaho. The house sits on a high hilltop, offering a 180-degree view of Lake Coeur d'Alene and the city lights across the water. Each of the three immaculate rooms is extra large and beautifully furnished in contemporary style. One of them features a Jacuzzi right in the middle of the room, where you and your lovely inamorata can sit buck naked, sipping champagne and gazing like grinnin' fools out the French doors at the exquisite panorama below. On top of all that, innkeeper Sue Fall is an angel. Rates include a full or light breakfast, whichever you'd prefer. To get to the B&B, a 15-minute drive from town, follow Highway 95 for 6.5 miles south of the Spokane River and turn left on Kidd Island Bay Road. Stay on that road for 4.2 miles (stay on the pavement and bear left at every paved fork). At the end of the pavement, turn right up the hill and go to the top. Highly recommended, especially for a romantic Fourth of July getaway when you can watch the Independence Point fireworks from your private aerie across the water.

CAMPING AND RVING

Robin Hood RV Park & Campground, 703 Lincoln Way, 208/664-2306, enjoys a location near the Fort Sherman area, within walking distance of downtown, the lakeshore, and the North Idaho College campus. Rates are about $21 with full hookups, $17 for a tent site. Extra persons $1 plus change. The 80-site campground has the usual shower and laundry facilities.

Blackwell Island RV Park, 800 S. Marina Dr., 208/665-1300 or 888/571-2900, is a large park with boat docks and grassy pull-throughs, just across the Spokane River from town (take Highway 95 south one mile off I-90 and turn left on Marina Drive). Rates run $22–32 with full hookups.

River Walk RV Park, 1214 Mill Ave. (at Northwest Blvd.), 208/765-5943 or 888/567-8700, offers 56 sites with full hookups for $23. Cable TV hookup available at $2 extra per day. The park has showers, restrooms, and a laundry room.

On the north side of town is **Shady Acres RV Park,** 3630 N. Government Way (off Highway 95 N. at Neider Street—turn right at the Kmart), 208/664-3087. The park indeed has shade, as well as hot showers, laundry facilities, and cable TV. Rates are around $16 for full hookups, $14 for tent sites.

The Coeur d'Alene KOA is east of town in the Wolf Lodge District, covered later this section.

FOOD

Standouts

Chic, cozy, and unpretentious **Capers Bistro,** 315 Walnut St., 208/664-9036, offers the finest of fine dining in a Mediterranean-inspired context. Entrées might include such mouthwatering recipes as chevre and portobello fettuccine, or spiced Moroccan lamb served over couscous. Entrées range $15–23 and are complemented by an intriguing list of soups, salads, appetizers, and wines. Open Tues.–Sat. for dinner.

Tanglewood Bistro & Pub, 501 Sherman Ave., 208/667-8612, offers an excellent nouvelle-cuisine menu and comfortable upscale atmosphere in the heart of downtown. Dinner entrées ($12–27) include steak, lamb, pork, chicken, seafood, pasta, and vegetarian dishes—all creatively prepared from a variety of fresh ingredients. Dessert might bring, get this, Frangelico caramelized poached peach and ice cream. Save room. Open Mon.–Sat. for lunch and dinner.

Upscale American

In downtown proper, **StoneGrill at Jimmy D's,** 320 Sherman, 208/664-9774, gets the local nod for its food and atmosphere, including sidewalk dining in season. Meats, seafood, and other dishes are prepared tableside on a heated lava rock. Look for entrées in the $8–11 range at lunch and $15–21 at dinner.

Beverly's, 208/765-4000, ext. 23, is the Coeur d'Alene Resort's premier dining room. It's on the hotel's seventh floor, overlooking the lake. On the menu you'll find entrées that make optimum use of fresh Northwest ingredients. Entrées average $23–43. The restaurant maintains a huge wine cellar; chances are they'll have exactly what you're looking for. Open for lunch and dinner daily. Also in the hotel is **Dockside,** 208/765-4000, ext. 24, a casual family restaurant on the lobby level open for three meals a day.

The Beachouse is at 3204 Coeur d'Alene Lake Dr. (at the north shore's Silver Bay Marina), 208/664-6464. The varied menu ranges from steak and seafood to barbecue to pasta, with prices ranging $12–25. You're paying a lot for atmosphere—this is one of only two places in town right on the water—and for the restaurant's association with the Hagadone corporation. The resort's guests are chauffeured here by boat, which no doubt adds to the overhead. Still, this is a good place for a fancy dinner, preferably out on the deck.

Pubs

Capone's sports pub and grill, 751 N. 4th St., 208/667-4843, entices beer drinkers with some two dozen Northwest microbrews on tap. The decor is vintage sports. Old baseball mitts, skis, golf clubs, and ice skates hang from the ceiling, while historical sports photos line the walls, including one of . . . Jerry Garcia? Seems there's a Deadhead subplot in the bullpen. Whatever game you're looking for, you'll probably find it on one of the five TVs connected to two satellite dishes. The friendly and comfortable place also serves an extensive menu of first-class pub grub, including burgers, subs, and creative, made-from-scratch gourmet pizzas (try the Thai chicken variation). Live entertainment several nights a week draws a fun crowd. Capone's is well worth the short hop up from downtown.

Parkside Bistro, 414 Mullan Rd., 208/765-8220, is in the Fort Sherman area near North Idaho College. Predictably, it gets the college crowd, which can make the tiny place loud at times. But the selection of micros is good and the outdoor bar stools let you enjoy the plein air more or less right in City Park—a nice touch on a summer's eve. Light lunch and dinner fare is available; look for burgers and sandwiches in the $7–8 range.

Seafood

For fresh fish and romantic atmosphere, **The Cedars Floating Restaurant,** 208/664-2922, is the catch of the day. To get there, get on Highway 95 heading south toward Moscow. On the edge of town, turn left onto Marina Drive immediately after crossing the Spokane River. This takes you out onto Blackwell Island, an area of working boat shops and boat storage yards. The restaurant is all the way out at the tip of the island, moored where the Spokane River flows out of Coeur d'Alene Lake.

Fish entrees vary, depending upon availability, but might include mahi mahi, salmon, swordfish, halibut, sea bass, shark, or ahi. All are charbroiled and served with your choice of lemon-butter caper sauce, tropical fruit salsa, or chilled cucumber dill sauce; prices range $15–33. Poultry, pasta, and beef dishes are also available. Dinner nightly from 5 P.M.

Coffeehouses

Downtown, **Java on Sherman,** 324 Sherman Ave., 208/667-0010, is a clean, well-lighted place to enjoy great joe while reading Hemingway or writing the Great American Novel (or Travel Handbook). Big front windows command the best people-watching corner in north Idaho, and many caffeine-laced concoctions are available; go for the trademark Bowl of Soul (coffee and espresso in steamed milk topped with chocolate and cinnamon). The pastries are baked on the premises and thoroughly wonderful. How do they make that Lumpy Muffin so delectably lumpy? Bigger breakfasts are available, too, in the $5–6 range. Both the atmosphere and help are young, hip, and friendly. Highly recommended.

SHOPPING

For an excellent selection of regional art, check out **Art Spirit Gallery,** 415 Sherman Ave., 208/765-6006. This artist-owned gallery offers great stuff from about 30 established and emerging artists from the Idaho Panhandle, Washing-

ton, and Montana. Featured artists include George Carlson, nationally known for his monumental sculptures, and Russell Chatham.

Antiques lovers will have a field day in Coeur d'Alene. The phone book is chock-full of dealers and antiques malls. One of the biggest is **CDA Antique Mall,** 3650 N. Government Way, 208/667-0246. The mall has a second location at 408 Haycraft, 208/664-0579. Between the two locations, more than 150 dealers are represented.

The biggest shopping mall in town is **Silver Lake Mall,** 200 W. Hanley Ave., 208/762-2112, north of I-90 up either Highway 95 or Government Way. The mall's 50 shops are anchored by Sears, JC Penney, and Bon-Macy's. Regular hours are Mon.–Sat. 10 A.M.–9 P.M., Sun. 11 A.M.–6 P.M.

INFORMATION AND SERVICES

The town's visitor center is next to the Museum of North Idaho at 115 Northwest Blvd. (no phone). It's well stocked with maps and brochures on lodging, restaurants, and recreation. For telephone or mail inquiries, contact the **Coeur d'Alene Area Chamber of Commerce,** 1621 N. 3rd St., P.O. Box 850, Coeur d'Alene, ID 83816, 208/664-3194, www.coeurdalene.org.

Recreation information for most of north Idaho is available from the Supervisor's Office of the **Idaho Panhandle National Forests,** 3815 Schreiber Way, Coeur d'Alene, ID 83814-8363, 208/765-7223. The **Idaho Department of Parks and Recreation** maintains its north region headquarters at 2750 Kathleen Ave., 208/769-1511. The **Coeur d'Alene Parks Department** is at 710 E. Mullan Ave., 208/769-2252. The **BLM** Coeur d'Alene Field Office is at 1808 N. 3rd St., 208/769-5030.

NPR listeners can pick up Spokane's **KPBX** at 91.1 FM. Another station, featuring a great jazz repertoire, is **KEWU** at 89.5 FM, the radio station of Eastern Washington University in Cheney.

POST FALLS

Frederick Post planted the seed for the city of Post Falls when he built a sawmill along the Spokane River here in 1800. He needed permission from

THE PANHANDLE

the locals to take advantage of the falls for his mill, so he negotiated a land-use deal with Coeur d'Alene Chief Seltice. Today the riverfront city between Coeur d'Alene and Spokane is one of Idaho's fastest-growing towns, with a population that has more than tripled since 1980 to 17,250.

Parks

Legend has it that Post and Chief Seltice signed their deal on **Treaty Rock,** today preserved as part of a small, four-acre park near the corner of Seltice and Compton Streets (two blocks west of Spokane Street). Short trails wind through the park and lead to the historic granite outcropping. Post's name is indeed carved on the rock, and below it are some Native American pictographs. But as the interpretive information at the site notes, no concrete evidence exists that this rock is actually the "contract" between Post and Seltice.

At **Falls Park,** visitors can walk to overviews of Post's famous falls and the narrow Spokane River gorge. Interpretive signs illuminate early area history; picnic tables, a playground, and a small fish pond make the 22-acre park a pleasant place for a lunch break. To get to the park, head south on Spokane Street from I-90 and watch for a posted right turn at 4th Street.

Q'emiln Riverside Park was once the site of a Coeur d'Alene Indian village. The name (pronounced "ka-MEE-lin") means "Throat of the River" in the Coeur d'Alene language. This 90-acre park on the south side of the Spokane River holds five miles of beautiful hiking trails through steep, rocky gorges. Also here: boat ramps, horseshoe pits, playground areas, and picnic shelters. A parking fee is charged Memorial Day to Labor Day. To get to the park, take the Spokane Street exit off I-90 (Exit 5), follow Spokane Street south across the river, and turn right on Park Way Drive just on the other side.

Corbin Park is named for early Post Falls railroad developer D. C. Corbin. The 24-acre park lies on the riverbank on the west side of town and offers a softball diamond, volleyball court, boat ramp, and picnic areas. To get there, take the Pleasant View Avenue exit (Exit 2) off I-90 and head south to Riverbend Avenue; take River-

bend east (left) to Corbin Park Road and follow that road into the park.

For more information on the city's parks, contact **Post Falls Parks and Recreation,** 408 Spokane St., 208/773-0539.

Centennial Trail

From Post Falls, you can follow the Centennial Trail bike/hike path all the way to Higgins Point on Coeur d'Alene Lake, or west to Spokane and beyond. The 63-mile-long interstate trail system is a favorite of hikers, cyclists, and skaters in summer, and cross-country skiers in winter. Access the trail at Falls Park.

Greyhound Park

Once one of Post Falls' claims to either fame or infamy, depending on your perspective, the Coeur d'Alene Greyhound Park was forced into early retirement by the efforts of an increasingly vocal animal-rights movement. Although live dog races no longer take place here, the park remains open as a bingo parlor and off-track betting center for simulcast horse and dog races elsewhere in the country. The park is at 5100 Riverbend Ave. (I-90 Exit 2 near the Washington state line), 208/773-0545 or 800/828-4880. It's open year-round and admission is free.

Cruises

The *River Queen* sternwheeler cruises up the Spokane River on sightseeing excursions daily in summer. The 90-minute cruises depart Red Lion Templin's Hotel on the River at 1:30 P.M. Cost is $12 general, $11 seniors 55 and up, $7 kids 6–12. Also regularly scheduled are Saturday night cocktail cruises ($15 adults), Sunday and Monday dinner cruises ($27.50 adults), and a July 4th fireworks dinner buffet cruise ($60 adults). Other special cruises are offered from time to time. For reservations or more information, call the resort at 208/763-1611.

Boating

Rent a boat for fishing, paddling, or cruising the Spokane River or Lake Coeur d'Alene at **Red Lion Templin's Hotel on the River,** 414 E. 1st Ave., 208/773-1611, ext. 550 or 571. Rates range from $5 an hour for an inner tube to $10 an hour for a canoe or paddleboat, to $40 an hour plus fuel for a 24-foot pontoon boat.

Golf

The Highlands Golf and Country Club, N. 701 Inverness Dr., 208/773-3673 or 800/797-7339, is an 18-hole, par-72 course stretching 6,369 yards. It's mostly flat and offers nice views of the surrounding mountains. Greens fee is $25 on weekends, $23 on weekdays. For après-golf dining, the club offers Carnegie's Restaurant and Lounge; picture windows make this a great spot to watch the sunset. After dinner, live entertainment is often presented in the lounge.

Rock Climbing

The city's **Q'emiln Riverside Park** offers dozens of single-pitch bolted climbs on reasonably solid river-canyon granite. It's a beautiful spot and seldom gets crowded. If you drive into the park, you'll have to pay a parking fee. Climbers being climbers, most park just outside the gate on Park Way Drive and walk in; from the entrance gate it's just a short hike to the climbing areas.

Accommodations

$50–100: Sleep Inn, 100 Pleasant View Rd., off I-90 at Exit 2, 208/777-9394, 800/851-3178, or 800/627-5337; and **Howard Johnson Express Inn,** 3647 W. 5th Ave., 208/773-4541 or 800/829-3124, are both near the Greyhound Park and the factory-outlet mall. Each offers an indoor pool, hot tub, and free continental breakfast. On the east side of town, **Holiday Inn Express,** 3175 E. Seltice Way, 208/773-8900 or 800/465-4329, offers 47 rooms and a complimentary continental breakfast bar.

$100–150: Red Lion Templin's Hotel on the River, 414 E. 1st Ave., 208/773-1611 or 800/RED-LION (800/733-5466), sits on the banks of the Spokane River and is the state's only hotel listed in *Idaho Wildlife Viewing Guide* as an outstanding critter-watching site. Ospreys and mallard ducks are among the hotel's neighbors. Amenities include an indoor pool, sauna, spa, and fitness center; tennis courts; a marina with boat rentals; guest laundry; and a restaurant overlooking the river. Nonsmoking and wheelchair-accessible rooms are available, as are Jacuzzi suites, family suites, and parlor suites.

River Cove B&B, 212 Parkwood Place, 208/773-9190 or 877/773-9190, bills itself as "a scenic waterfront retreat." From the back deck you can look past the pines to the water's edge below. Each of the guest rooms has a private bath, and rates include a gourmet breakfast. In winter, you can enjoy cross-country skiing right on the premises. Smoking outside only; no small children.

RV Parks

RVers in the area have a couple of good choices. **Coeur d'Alene RV Resort,** 2600 E. Mullan Ave., 208/773-3527, is an upscale park offering 190 spotless sites with full hookups for around $28 a night. Amenities include a beautiful clubhouse with fireplace; a heated pool, spa, and fitness center; a playground; tennis and volleyball courts; horseshoe pits; and a nine-hole putting green.

Suntree RV Park, 401 Idahline, 208/773-9982 or 800/782-3976, offers 111 sites for about $23 a night with full hookups. Amenities include a pool, hot tub, and shower and laundry facilities. It's near the factory-outlet mall and Greyhound Park.

Food

One of the region's best restaurants lies outside Post Falls in sleepy little Hauser Lake, a short and scenic drive away. At **Chef in the Forest,** 7900 E. Hauser Lake Rd., 208/773-3654, owner-chef Richard Hubik and chef de cuisine Jim Jensen prepare a gourmet menu featuring appetizers like warm brie with fresh fruit ($6.95) and entrées ranging from roast duckling with fresh brandied raspberry sauce ($19.95) to a filet mignon Forestière covered with sautéed mushrooms ($21.95). Great food, wine, and atmosphere make this a favorite excursion of area residents. Reservations are highly recommended. From Post Falls, take Seltice west to McGuire Road, McGuire north to Highway 53, Highway 53 west to Hauser Lake Road, and Hauser Lake Road north and east to the restaurant. Open Wed.–Sun. for dinner only.

Shopping

The **Prime Outlets—Post Falls** factory-outlet mall, 4300 Riverbend Ave. (on the west end of town, off I-90 at Exit 2), 208/773-4555 or 888/678-9847, holds more than 40 stores selling name-brand merchandise at deep discounts. Whatever it is you can't live without, you can buy it here at up to 70 percent off. The mall is open daily year-round.

Information

The **Coeur d'Alene/Post Falls Visitors Center** is in the factory-outlet mall on Riverbend Ave., 208/773-4080 or 800/292-2553. Dieters be advised: it's next to a chocolate shop. Summer hours are Mon.–Sat. 10 A.M.–7 P.M., Sun. 11 A.M.–6 P.M. The rest of the year it's open Mon.-Sat. 10 A.M.–4 P.M., Sun. 11 A.M.–4 P.M. The **Post Falls Chamber of Commerce** is at 510 6th Ave., P.O. Box 32, Post Falls, ID 83877, 208/773-5016. Call the **Post Falls Park & Recreation** office at 208/773-0539.

WOLF LODGE DISTRICT

Eagle-Watching

A short distance east of Coeur d'Alene on I-90, you'll come to Exit 22, marked Wolf Lodge District. Wolf Lodge Creek empties into Wolf Lodge Bay here. Wolves are no longer in evidence, but the bay's kokanee salmon population attracts a sizable population of bald eagles each winter. The eagles migrate down from the Canadian northlands to escape the harsh arctic winter. Here they find a relatively mild climate and easy food—the kokanee congregate here to spawn and die at just about the same time the eagles begin arriving in late November. Eagle populations peak here in late December—about 40 birds on average—and by March most of them have moved on. Best viewing time is in early morning, when the eagles do most of their feeding. Best viewing locations are at the Mineral Ridge Boat Ramp, on the south side of the bay, and at the Mineral Ridge trailhead, a little farther down the road on Beauty Bay.

Note: Wolf Lodge Creek is also a prime spawning area for bull trout, yet another Idaho species sliding toward extinction. As a result, all waters in the Wolf Lodge Creek watershed are closed to fishing.

Day Hiking

The **Mineral Ridge National Recreation Trail** leaves from the Mineral Ridge Recreation Area, which you'll come to just after rounding the corner from Wolf Lodge Bay into Beauty Bay on Highway 97. The 3.3-mile nature trail loops past an abandoned mine and cabin. The **Caribou Ridge National Recreation Trail** makes a nice day hike, running 4.6 miles from Beauty Creek Campground up to the Mt. Coeur d'Alene Picnic Area. You'll find huckleberries in season along the way, and you'll get great views of the lake. The trail is moderately difficult, climbing 1,800 feet in four switchbacks up onto the ridge. Beauty Creek Campground is less than a mile down FR 438, which turns off Highway 97 along the east shore of Beauty Bay.

Horseback Riding

Rider Ranch, S. 4199 Wolf Lodge Creek Rd., 208/667-3373, offers guided trail rides, hayrides, and parties for kids on a family-owned and -operated working ranch in Wolf Lodge Creek Valley. Basic 90-minute trail rides run $30 per person, two persons minimum. Chuck-wagon dinner rides are $45 per person, six persons minimum. All activities are scheduled by advance reservation only; no credit cards. Wolf Lodge Creek Road turns off the frontage road on the north side of the interstate, a little less than a mile east of the freeway exit.

Accommodations

$100–150: You'll find the ultimate in solitude at **Wolf Lodge Creek B&B,** 715 N. Wolf Lodge Creek Rd., 208/667-5902 or 800/919-9653. Deer graze alongside the horses in this tranquil valley. You can hear yourself think out here, yet you're less than a half-hour drive from the city. The big and modern wooden B&B sits on 27 acres and holds five guest rooms, all with private bath. A separate cabin is also available. Hiking opportunities are right outside the door—the inn adjoins national forest lands—and a hot tub and sauna provide great evening relaxation. Rates include a full country breakfast.

Camping

Coeur d'Alene KOA is on the south side of the freeway at E. 10700 Wolf Lodge Bay Rd., 208/664-4471 or 800/562-2609. Among the plethora of amenities: lake access with free small-boat moorage for guests; a heated pool and spa; a playground; hiking and bike trails; laundry and shower facilities; and bike, boat, and canoe rentals. Rates are $25–29 with hookups, $20 without, $18.50 for tent sites. Extra persons $2.50 each. The trademark KOA Kamping Kabins are also available for $38–48 a night, and you can stay in a tepee for $25–28 a night.

Along the I-90 frontage road 1.7 miles east of the Wolf Lodge exit (north side of the freeway) is **Wolf Lodge Campground,** 12425 E. I-90, 208/664-2812. The RV park offers 25 grassy sites on a large pleasant flat along Wolf Lodge Creek. Horseshoe pits, shuffleboard and volleyball courts, a putting green, and paddle-boat and canoe rentals are among the recreational amenities offered. Rates for two people range around $20–25 with hookups, $16 for a tent site or no-hookup RV site. Extra persons over age 6 cost $2 each. Cabins ($45) and tepees ($25) are also available.

Also in the area is the USFS **Beauty Creek Campground** (10 sites, fee), just up Road 438 from Beauty Bay.

Food

Folks come from miles around for the steaks at **Wolf Lodge Inn Restaurant,** 12025 E. Frontage Rd., 208/664-6665. Here you can get darn near half a cow served up in front of you; the Rancher cut weighs in at 42 ounces. All steaks are flame-broiled over an open-pit cherrywood and tamarack fire, and served with salad, bread, and buckaroo beans. Also on the menu are shrimp, salmon, trout, lamb chops, scallops, and, yes, Rocky Mountain oysters. The restaurant is open for dinner Tues.–Sun.; reservations required.

LAKE COEUR D'ALENE SCENIC BYWAY

If you continue south from the Wolf Lodge exit around the east shore of the lake, you'll be traveling on the state's designated Lake Coeur d'Alene Scenic Byway. Keep your eyes peeled for ospreys; this area holds the largest concentration of them in the western United States. The beautiful birds love the wetlands around the lake's east shore. You won't have to look so hard to spot the sunsets around here—the showy spectacles light up the sky and lake on a regular basis.

Squaw Bay and Arrow Point

South of Beauty Bay on the way to Harrison, you'll come to a couple of resorts on prime lake-front real estate. Seven miles down the road **Squaw Bay Resort,** Rt. 2 Box 130, Harrison, ID 83833, 208/664-6782, offers cabins ($75–165), a tepee ($25), RV sites ($22–28), tent sites ($18–24), and a marina. This resort has a down-home, family-style feel. Kids will love the slide that shoots them out into an enclosed swimming area. Parents can watch the boisterous fun from the sandy beach. The marina, 208/664-6450, rents a wide variety of watercraft, from canoes ($10 an hour) to 90-horsepower ski boats ($285 a day). The resort's Lakeside Grill and Cafe is open for breakfast, lunch, and dinner on weekends.

Another two miles down the road is **Arrow Point Resort,** 4495 S. Arrow Point Rd., 208/667-0941, which occupies a finger of land jutting into the lake. The secluded, upscale resort offers furnished two- and three-bedroom condo units ($150–250), a marina, beaches, and an indoor pool. For reservations or more information, contact Independent Management Services, 715 N. 4th St., Coeur d'Alene, ID 83814, 208/664-1593.

Bell Bay

At the south end of Powderhorn Bay, Highway 97 turns inland briefly before crossing the Coeur d'Alene River and rolling into Harrison. This inland stretch cuts off the nose of a peninsula jutting out into the lake. Here Road 314 turns off the highway and leads west some three miles across wide open private property to the USFS **Bell Bay Campground** (14 sites, fee) on the lakeshore. You'll feel isolated out here—it's a nice place to kick back.

Harrison

Until 1889, the southeast shore of Coeur d'Alene Lake was part of the Coeur d'Alene Indian Reservation. But then timber companies cruising the area decided that the shore here would be a perfect spot for a sawmill. So they planted a bug in then-president Benjamin Harrison's ear and whoops, now we're going to take this spot, too. Harrison "withdrew" a narrow strip of land from the reservation to accommodate the loggers.

The town was founded in 1891 and named after the president to ensure greasy wheels for the future. By the turn of the century, Harrison was home to 2,000 people, 11 lumber mills, a dozen saloons, and a thriving red-light district. Steamboats plying Coeur d'Alene Lake made Harrison a major port of call, and at one point it was the largest population center on the lake. But fire devastated the town in 1917, and shortly thereafter, the arrival of railroads rendered the steamboats obsolete. Then the local timber industry dwindled and Harrison's glory days were over.

Today the town's 270-some residents rely on tourism to feed the coffers. Fishing and boating were long the primary draws, but increasing numbers of cyclists are using Harrison as a base camp for the Trail of the Coeur d'Alenes (see the sidebar "Bountiful Bike Trails"). Sunsets are stupendous here, too. If you're looking for a refuge from the hectic tourist scene on the north shore of the lake, Harrison offers it.

If you're here to ride, **Pedal Pushers,** 208/689-3436, 101 N. Coeur d'Alene Ave., www.bikenorthidaho.com, is the place to get gear and other information. Owners John Kolbe and Sharon Yablon and their staff rent bikes ($12 for up to two hours, $22 a day) and related equipment including car racks, offer repairs, and run seasonal shuttle service for the Trail of the Coeur d'Alenes.

The first house in town was built in 1891; it's still standing and today houses the **Crane Historical Society Museum** (no phone; call 208/689-3111 for information). Exhibits detail local history. The museum is open in summer Sat.–Sun. noon–4 P.M.; other times by appointment.

Cyclists and other travelers congregate at the **Osprey Inn,** 134 Frederick St., P.O. Box 47, Harrison, ID 83833, 208/689-9502. Built in 1915, the inn was originally a boardinghouse for lumberjacks. Each of the five newly reconstructed rooms has a private bath with shower.

view of Harrison from Coeur d'Alene Lake

BOUNTIFUL BIKE TRAILS

By Julie Fanselow

Over the past few years, North Idaho has become one of the best bicycling destinations anywhere, thanks to the **Route of the Hiawatha** and the **Trail of the Coeur d'Alenes,** two unforgettable biking experiences.

The 13-mile Route of the Hiawatha is a rails-to-trails conversion on the old Milwaukee Road. The main trailhead (accessible via I-90 Exit 5 at Taft, Montana) begins just outside the 8,771-foot St. Paul Pass Tunnel, which means you start and end your ride by cycling through the 1.8-mile tunnel—in the dark, with only a bike light or headlamp to guide you. The packed gravel trail includes eight other tunnels and seven railway trestles, the highest 230 feet off the valley floor. It may sound daunting, but guard rails and a gentle downhill grade make the Route of the Hiawatha an easy and enjoyable ride for nearly everyone. A shuttle ($9 general; $6 kids ages 3–13) runs from the end of the trail back to the first tunnel several times each day late May–early Oct.

Bike rentals (including lights and a rack) and trail passes are available at Lookout Pass ski area (I-90 Exit 0 on the Montana-Idaho border east of Wallace, 208/744-1301, http://wallace-id.com/skilookout/taft.html). Trail passes are also available at the trailhead; cost is $8 general, $4 ages 3–13.

The Trail of the Coeur d'Alenes, now an Idaho state park, spans 72 miles across the Idaho Panhandle from Mullan in the east to Plummer in the west. The fully paved trail sits on the old Union Pacific railbed and marks the railroad's efforts—in conjunction with the state of Idaho and the Coeur d'Alene Tribe, which co-manages the trail—to seal over the mine waste and tailings that contaminated the area in its mining heyday. Signs along the way warn users to stay on the trail and eat at designated waysides, which may make some cyclists feel squeamish about riding the trail at all, but state and tribal officials say casual users need not worry about contamination.

The best, most scenic part of the mostly flat, free-access trail lies between Pinehurst (milepost 48.7), where it leaves the I-90 corridor, and the old Chatcolet Bridge south of Harrison (near milepost 8). Avid cyclists may want to tackle this section in a long day, but most riders will want to savor shorter out-and-back rides along any stretch of it. Be sure to carry your own water and snacks, since services are limited in most areas. Remember, though, you can get a filling meal at the Enaville Resort near milepost 47 and a ridiculously large ice cream cone at The Creamery in Harrison (milepost 15).

Bike rentals and shuttle service are available in Kellogg at **Excelsior Cycle & Sport Shop,** 21 Railroad Ave., 208/786-3751, and in Harrison at **Pedal Pushers,** 101 N. Coeur d'Alene Ave., 208/689-3436. Maps and brochures are available at all trailheads, or contact the trail office at Coeur d'Alene's **Old Mission State Park,** P.O. Box 30, Cataldo, ID 83810, 208/682-3814.

Rates ($50–100) include full breakfast. Harrison also offers RV and tent camping at its waterfront, with a small swimming beach and playground nearby.

Harrison's big annual event is the **Old Time Picnic,** held on the last weekend in July. In addition to potato salad and hot dogs, look for live entertainment and a parade along the lake. For more information, call the **Harrison Chamber of Commerce,** 208/689-3711.

Guest Ranch

At **Hidden Creek Ranch,** 11077 E. Blue Lake Rd., Harrison, ID 83833, 208/689-3209 or 800/446-3833, the staff takes a conservation-oriented approach to the guest-ranch experience. Owners John Muir (a descendant of the famous naturalist) and Iris Behr stress respect for the environment on their spread in the hills east of Coeur d'Alene Lake. Recycling is a given here, and gourmet meals are cooked with organic vegetables straight from the garden. In addition to a wide array of summer and winter recreation opportunities, guests can learn about Native American philosophy, home canning, and environmentally friendly practices.

The 7,000-square-foot log lodge sits in a clearing at the edge of a pine forest. Indoors you'll find a library, a dining room, and a large living room with a fireplace. Outside, a big, sunny deck invites you to bask with a good book or partake of the complimentary beer, wine, and soft drinks served there each evening in summer. Nearby hot tubs, available round the clock, will bubble away your stress.

Accommodations are in luxuriously appointed, modern log cabins ("constructed only from dead standing timber and selectively positioned to save existing trees"), all with private baths and Native American decor. The cabins can hold groups of all sizes, from singles to families. Other facilities include a small store selling fishing tackle, gifts, snacks, and personal items, and a wash house holding free washers and dryers.

Horseback riding on the 250,000 acres surrounding the ranch is the featured summer activity here. Among the ranch's stable of 70 exceptionally well-trained horses is one perfectly suited to you. The staff boasts, "For slow riders, we have slow horses; for fast riders, we have fast horses; and for those that don't like to ride, we have horses that don't like to be ridden!" Trail rides are offered daily and take guests through the forests to spectacular views of the area's lakes. Besides horseback riding, summer activities include fly-fishing, hiking, mountain biking, trapshooting, and archery. In winter, snowshoeing, cross-country skiing, tobogganing, and sleigh rides are on tap.

Six-day packages May–Oct. including accommodations, all meals, beverages, recreation, and evening entertainment cost $2,230 per person double occupancy, $2,570 single occupancy, $1,829 children ages 3–11 June–Aug. (May, Sep-

tember, and October are adults-only months.) Three-day stays are possible, too; cost is $1,339 per person double; $1,549 single occupancy; $857 ages 3–11. Winter rates range from $762 per person for a two-night package to $1,313 for a four-night package (based on double occupancy; singles about 20 percent higher).

A 15 percent service charge covering all gratuities is added to the bill, as are Idaho sales and lodging tax. Off-site kennel services can be arranged, but no pets are allowed at the ranch.

To get to the ranch, head north from Harrison on Highway 97 across the Coeur d'Alene River bridge and turn right (east) on Blue Lake Road (near mile marker 70). Follow signs for five miles right to the ranch.

Chain of Lakes Route

South of Harrison, Highway 97 runs into a T intersection with Highway 3. If you turn right you'll end up in St. Maries. Turn left to stay on the designated scenic byway, which takes you up the South Fork Coeur d'Alene River past 10 major lakes. Most of the wetlands in this Chain of Lakes area are included in the **Coeur d'Alene River Wildlife Management Area,** a favorite stopover for migratory waterfowl.

This beautiful area harbors a dirty little secret. Each spring, tundra swans stop at the Chain of Lakes on their way south; many never make it out. The area lies downstream from the Kellogg Superfund site, and the aquatic plants here hold deadly concentrations of lead. The swans eat the contaminated plants and die of starvation, as the lead and other heavy metals inhibit nutrient absorption. Local environmentalists morbidly dub the annual event "The Rite of Spring." As you drive up this scenic highway, eventually rejoining I-90 near Cataldo, it's hard to imagine environmental problems lurking unseen here. For more information, call the Idaho Department of Fish and Game's Coeur d'Alene office, 208/769-1414.

The Silver Valley

East of Coeur d'Alene, I-90 climbs Fourth of July Pass and drops down the other side into the valley of the South Fork Coeur d'Alene River. In 1859, Jesuit missionary Pierre Jean de Smet described this valley as a verdant paradise: "Imagine thick, untrodden forest, strewn with thousands of trees thrown down by age and storms in every direction, where the path is scarcely visible."

But this almost primeval scene was not to last. In 1885, prospector Noah Kellogg discovered a huge vein of a lead-silver-zinc ore called galena near the present-day town of Wardner. The find brought miners and mining companies flooding into the area, burrowing into the hills like mad, money-hungry moles. Over the next 100 years, more than $5 billion in precious metals would be taken from the earth, making "The Silver Valley" one of the most lucrative mining districts in world history, while at the same time turning it into a lifeless toxic waste dump.

The once verdant forests of the South Fork were cut down for houses, mine timbers, and railroad ties. But that was just the beginning. In 1917, the first lead smelter was built near the Bunker Hill mine so that ore could be processed on site. The EPA's Superfund site description tersely describes the consequences: "During the majority of time the smelters were operating, few environmental protection procedures or controls were used. As a result, there is widespread contamination of soil, water, and air from lead and other heavy metals."

The smelters belched toxic plumes into the air, and the sulfur dioxide fallout killed what vegetation was left on the hillside. Water pollution was an even greater problem. Until 1938, all residues from the Bunker Hill's mine tailings were discharged directly into the Coeur d'Alene River. Thereafter, the wastes were diverted into an unlined settling pond that leaked toxic effluent into the groundwater. In addition, spring floods routinely washed heavy metals from tailings piles into the river and on downstream. Between the 1880s and the 1960s, an estimated 72 million tons of contaminated tailings ended up in the Coeur d'Alene River system; today scientists debate the potential health threat of the heavy-metal sludge coating the bottom of Coeur d'Alene Lake.

Meanwhile, in the mid-1970s, it was discovered that lead had found its way into the blood of the valley's children in alarming concentrations. A class-action suit brought by a number of parents against Gulf Resources and Chemical Corp., then-owner of the Bunker Hill mine, ended in an out-of-court settlement, but the lead problem persists, as evidenced by the Panhandle Health District's publication, *Coeur d'Alene River System and Heavy Metal Exposure, A Public Awareness Message*. Among other precautions, the pamphlet advises local residents to "clean shoes and change soil-stained clothes before going home. Keep soiled clothing in a plastic bag and launder it separate from the rest of your wash. Don't can whole fish caught from the lower Coeur d'Alene River system. Don't eat large amounts of fish, water fowl, or aquatic plants."

The Bunker Hill smelters shut down in 1981, pulling the rug out from under the local economy and leaving behind one of the country's largest Superfund toxic-cleanup sites. A 1992 report by the U.S. Geologic Survey called the Coeur d'Alene River drainage the worst example of heavy-metal pollution in the world. Gulf conveniently declared bankruptcy, sticking taxpayers with the cleanup tab.

The towering smokestacks of the Bunker Hill smelters—built in 1977 in an attempt to disperse toxic clouds away from the local citizenry—were demolished in May 1996, and the blood-lead levels of valley residents today have declined to just above normal. The ongoing Superfund cleanup is making progress on a 21-square-mile area around Kellogg, and the hillsides are recovering their natural blanket of green. But heavy metals continue to leach into the river from upstream mine sites, flowing down to Coeur d'Alene Lake and into Washington.

With its economic one-trick pony gone to the glue factory, the valley looked to tourism to save

THE PANHANDLE

the day. In 1988, Kellogg's citizens voted to tax themselves in order to spruce up the local ski hill and install the world's longest gondola to get people there. Today, Silver Mountain Ski Area is the town's biggest draw in both winter and summer.

For more information on Silver Valley happenings, pick up a copy of the excellent monthly paper, *The Silver Valley Voice,* 208/753-2071. The *Voice* provides a forum for local art, poetry, essays, and the often stormy political dialogue that has accompanied the valley's attempts to re-create itself. It's free and available at shops and restaurants valleywide.

FOURTH OF JULY PASS

East of Wolf Lodge Bay, I-90 ascends and crests Fourth of July Pass, elevation 3,070. The pass gets its name from an Independence Day weekend celebrated here in 1861 by U.S. Army engineer Lt. John Mullan (1830–1909) and his crew of road builders. They were working on what later came to be known as the **Mullan Road,** a historic route connecting Fort Benton, Montana, with Fort Walla Walla, Washington.

Originally intended as a military road and an alternative to south Idaho's Oregon Trail, the route came to be used by railroad builders and miners in the Coeur d'Alene River valley. Today, I-90 overlays much of Mullan's old road.

The freeway exit atop the pass leads to two sites of interest. On the north side of the highway is **Mullan Road Historical Park,** where a half-mile interpretive trail leads to the Mullan Tree, or rather, the place where the Mullan Tree once grew. The tree had been engraved with the words "M.R. July 4, 1861." The "M.R." probably stood for "Military Road," not "Mullan Road." But consensus has it that John Mullan was an intelligent and resourceful man, so what the heck, Mullan Road it is. In any case, the western white pine blew down in 1962, and Mullan's inscription was removed for preservation and is on display at the Museum of North Idaho in Coeur d'Alene. The site is a little anticlimactic as a result, but the path through the woods is delightful. In the parking lot is a monumental bust of Mullan whose face, unfortunately, has fallen off.

On the south side of the highway is **Fourth of July Pass Park N' Ski Area.** A large parking area provides access to two five-mile loop trails and a third, non-looping trail that continues through the woods for just under two miles. Some steep downhills on the loops make those trails best suited to intermediate or better skiers. The other trail is gentle enough for beginners.

CATALDO AND VICINITY

Old Mission State Park

Even from a distance the old Cataldo mission, visible from I-90, is powerful and striking. At once monumental and simple, the Greek Revival–style structure sits atop a grassy hill that slopes down to the placid waters of the South Fork of the Coeur d'Alene River. It fits naturally into its surroundings, a tribute to the man who designed and helped build the mission and served as its first spiritual leader.

That man was Father Antonio Ravalli, born May 16, 1812, in Ferrara, Italy. Ravalli was ordained as a Jesuit priest in 1843 and sent to work with the Coeur d'Alene Indians alongside Father Pierre Jean de Smet. When Ravalli arrived, Father de Smet's mission was located on the St. Joe River near present-day St. Maries. But the regular floods there (a phenomenon that persists today) caused de Smet to look for a higher and drier spot. Ravalli was assigned the task of supervising the relocation.

The park's literature calls Ravalli a Renaissance man; while that might be a cliché, here it fits perfectly. By the time he reached Idaho at the age of 31, Ravalli had studied literature, philosophy, theology, mathematics, science, medicine, art, and architecture.

The Native Americans and missionaries began building the mission in 1847, following Ravalli's plans. The structure was constructed of hand-hewn timbers held together with wooden pegs. The foot-thick walls were made of woven straw and river mud. The result, formally called the Mission of the Sacred Heart, is the oldest building still standing in Idaho.

The exterior is beautiful, but Ravalli's artistic handiwork and creativity really shine in the in-

COURTESY OF THE IDAHO TRAVEL COUNCIL

inside Cataldo mission, the oldest standing building in Idaho

terior. Out on the wild frontier, with no budget to speak of, Ravalli became a master at decorating on the cheap. See that marble altar? It's actually made of wood, carefully painted by Ravalli to simulate marble. And those cast iron chandeliers? They're tin, cut into elegant patterns by the artistic priest. Ravalli also painted the side altars with scenes depicting heaven and hell, and carved the statues of the Virgin Mary and St. John the Evangelist standing on either side of the altar.

The mission opened for worship in 1853 and operated for 23 years. During that time it served as a welcome resting place for Native Americans, pioneers, John Mullan's road-building crew, and military contingents, and it fulfilled its purpose as a center for spiritual guidance. Father Joseph Cataldo, a strong and popular leader of Idaho's Catholics, took the reins in 1865; the nearby town is named in his honor. In 1876, mission activities were relocated to DeSmet in a political move that was heartbreaking for the mission's Native American congregation.

Today, the mission serves as the centerpiece of an outstanding state historic park. A modern interpretive center screens a short film illustrating the mission's history, and offers exhibits about the Coeur d'Alene Indians and the Jesuits. Self-guided interpretive trails lead across the grounds to natural features and points of historical interest.

The park hosts a few events each year. On the second Sunday in July is the **Historic Skills Fair,** where you can watch spinning, quilting, black powder shooting, and other anachronisms, done just the way the old-timers used to do. On Aug. 15 is the annual **Coeur d'Alene Indian Pilgrimage** and its associated "Coming of the Black Robes Pageant." Traditional native foods are featured. That's followed a week later by the Annual Mountainman Rendezvous.

Old Mission State Park is at Exit 439 off I-90, P.O. Box 30, Cataldo, ID 83810-0030, 208/682-3814. It's open year-round, 8 A.M.–6 P.M. in summer, 9 A.M.–5 P.M. the rest of the year. The parking fee is $4 per vehicle.

Snowcat Skiing

Peak Adventures, at Exit 40 off I-90, P.O. Box 50, Cataldo, ID 83810, 208/682-3200, offers snowcat ski trips high into the St. Joe Mountains south of town. Cost for the trips is $175 a day, including guides and lunch. The company

THE PANHANDLE

operates daily from December through April. Reservations are required.

UP THE NORTH FORK OF THE COEUR D'ALENE RIVER

The next town you come to as you head east from Cataldo on I-90 is Kingston, near the confluence of the two major forks of the Coeur d'Alene River. I-90 follows the South Fork here, while Forest Highway 9 leaves the interstate and follows the North Fork up to the old gold-mining towns of Prichard and Murray. Besides its considerable history, the North Fork area is rife with recreation opportunities.

Note: On older Forest Service maps, the North Fork of the Coeur d'Alene is labeled as the main Coeur d'Alene River, while the Little North Fork—the first major tributary of the North Fork—is labeled the North Fork of the Coeur d'Alene. The Forest Service has changed this to reflect standard local usage on its newer maps.

Kingston

Those looking for a bucolic base camp for their Silver Valley explorations might like **Kingston 5 Ranch,** 42297 Silver Valley Rd. in Kingston, P.O. Box 2229, Coeur d'Alene, ID 83816, 208/682-4862 or 800/254-1852. Walt and Pat Gentry have turned their 4,500-square-foot farmhouse into a beautiful B&B. The Rose Room suite upstairs features vaulted ceilings and picture windows; an oak, four-poster queen bed with a down comforter; a private fireplace; a full bath with shower and whirlpool tub; and a veranda with its own hot tub. The ground-floor suite offers sliding glass doors opening onto a big deck with a hot tub. This suite also has a full bath with a whirlpool tub. One- and two-night stays here are pricey, about $200 per night for two people, including breakfast, but discounts apply for stays of three nights or more. Ask about special packages, too.

To get there, take the Kingston exit off I-90 (Exit 43), turn south to Silver Valley Road, and go west on that road to the ranch.

Enaville Resort

Also off the interstate at Exit 43, a mile and a half north on Coeur d'Alene River Road (Forest Highway 9), is Enaville Resort, 208/682-3453. It's not a resort like the Coeur d'Alene Resort—more like a last resort. Enaville was established in 1880 and over the years has held within its log walls a gold rush–era bar, a railroad way station, a boardinghouse, and a whorehouse. Today it's a family restaurant and tavern specializing in such delectables as buffalo burgers and Rocky Mountain oysters. Kitschy Western art and memorabilia—including old swords and a blunderbuss—fills the walls, floors, and ceilings. It's all a bit of living history and definitely worth a stop for breakfast, lunch, or dinner. Open daily.

The Little North Fork

Little North Fork Road leads up to the USFS **Bumblebee Campground** (25 sites, fee) and, after another 20 miles or so, to **Honeysuckle Campground** (eight sites, free). Between the two campgrounds is Laverne Creek, which marks a boundary for anglers. From there on upriver, fishing is catch-and-release only, single barbless hooks, flies and lures only, no bait. The Little North Fork is stocked with rainbows above Bumblebee Campground.

Prichard

Twenty-three miles from Kingston is Prichard, a town named after the first prospector to strike gold in the Coeur d'Alenes. Today there's not a whole lot here. Silver Valley residents come from miles around for the prime rib dinners at **Gloria's Steak House & Lodge,** 21428 Coeur d'Alene River Rd., HC01 Box 245, Prichard, ID 83873, 208/682-3031. It's open daily year-round. Gloria's also rents motel rooms ($50–100; rates include prime rib dinner for two) and has a hot tub.

Continuing Up the North Fork

At Prichard, FR 208 follows the North Fork up toward its headwaters, past three USFS campgrounds: **Kit Price** (21 sites, fee), **Devil's Elbow** (13 sites, fee), and **Big Hank** (29 sites, fee). Fishermen make up a large percentage of the campers here; above Devil's Elbow Campground you're in catch-and-release country.

Also near Devil's Elbow Campground, about 10 miles up from Prichard, is Yellow Dog Creek, where you'll find a turnoff onto FR 1568. Follow the road up three miles to **Fern Falls,** right by the road. A little past Fern Falls is a half-mile trail up to **Shadow Falls.** A path behind the falls allows you to walk right under the cascade without getting wet. Back on the FR 208, a few miles farther up the road toward Big Hank is Flat Creek Road, which leads to **Centennial Falls.**

Past Big Hank, the road makes a lazy curve west, becoming FR 6310 as it enters the Fernan Ranger District, then branches up Tepee Creek. A short distance farther you'll come to the confluence of Tepee and Independence Creeks, also the "confluence" of Forest Roads 925 and 6310. A short distance up FR 925 lies the trailhead to the east end of the **Independence Creek Trail System.** The trails here wind west along and around an old wagon road once used to access mining camps and old homesteads. One of these trails (Trail 22) leads 13.7 miles west to Weber Saddle on the southeast side of Pend Oreille Lake.

If you stay on FR 6310 instead of turning off on FR 925, you'll come to **Magee Historic Ranger Station.** Charley Magee was the first homesteader in this area, arriving in the early 1900s. Sometime after 1905, he built a log cabin here, which in 1908 was taken over by the Forest Service. The cabin, no longer in use, is listed on the National Register of Historic Places. You can poke about in several old buildings here. Just south of the ranger station, on FR 422, is the **Bigfoot Ridge Trail (Trail 700),** a short interpretive loop showing off the area's variety of trees.

From here you can head back the way you came or continue down FR 422 to the Little North Fork and the junction with FR 209. A right turn there will take you past the USFS Honeysuckle Campground (eight sites, free) and eventually into Coeur d'Alene; a left turn takes you down to Bumblebee Campground (25 sites, fee) and Forest Highway 9.

Floating the North Fork

The North Fork offers a scenic and generally relaxed float trip. When the water's high enough, you can put in way up at Senator Creek above Big Hank Campground. From there to Cataldo it's 55 river miles, or 24 hours' worth of floating, a three- or four-day trip. In spring, you'll encounter rapids of up to Class III, most of which dwindle to Class I by midsummer. Numerous access points and campgrounds along the North Fork Road enable you to plan as long or short a trip as you'd like. For more information, contact the USFS **Coeur d'Alene River Ranger District-Silverton Office,** P.O. Box 14, Silverton, ID 83867, 208/752-1221.

To Murray

At Prichard, you can turn off the North Fork and head east up Prichard Creek. At the confluence of Prichard and Eagle Creeks, turning up FR 152, then FR 805, will lead you up the west fork of Eagle Creek to **Settlers Grove of Ancient Cedars.** A trail winds through the grove, which holds many trees six to eight feet in diameter. A trail winds through it.

Continuing east on Prichard Creek Road, you'll soon come to the gold-rush boomtown of Murray. Between Murray and neighboring Eagle City, the area counted as many as 25,000 residents in its heyday. Wyatt Earp ran a saloon in Eagle in the 1880s, and Murray was the Shoshone County seat for 14 years. You'd never guess it looking at the sleepy little town today. You can thank the Coeur d'Alene Mining Company, which dredged Prichard Creek from 1917 to 1924, for the ugly tailings piles along the creekside.

More area history can be gleaned at **The Sprag Pole,** 208/682-3901, which consists of a friendly bar and grill on one side and Walt's Museum, a veritable warehouse full of great old stuff, on the other. A sprag pole was the old-time equivalent of a parking brake—a long pole strategically planted to keep wagons from rolling. The other bar in town is the **Bedroom Goldmine Bar,** 208/682-4394, site of the Bedroom Mine. A former owner sunk a shaft right in his bedroom. It's no longer being used.

From Murray, you can head back to Kingston the way you came, or take FR 456 over King's and Dobson Passes 20 miles to Wallace. The old **Murray Cemetery,** at the bottom of King's Pass grade on the way out of town toward Wallace, holds the graves of such famous locals as Andrew Prichard and Maggie Hall, a kindly madam better known as Molly B'Damn.

KELLOGG AND VICINITY

In attempting to rise anew from the ashes of its mining industry, Kellogg took two major steps: it replaced the narrow winding road up to the local ski hill with the world's longest gondola, which now whisks skiers up some 3,400 vertical feet in 3.1 miles to the snowy slopes; and it gave the town a partial face-lift, turning it into a Bavarian-theme village. The gondola might be called a success—it's certainly a unique attraction and makes it easier for visitors to enjoy the mountain. The Alpine Village, however, is about as appropriate as a Stetson and six-gun on Heidi. Other than snowy peaks, nothing about this gritty mining town or the surrounding area is even vaguely reminiscent of the Alps. Major housing developments are planned here, but that may speak of the hopeful spirit of the locals more than anything else.

Silver Mountain

A ski area has existed on the slopes of Kellogg and Wardner Peaks since the late 1960s. First called Jackass (for Noah Kellogg's famous donkey), then Silverhorn, the resort struggled with one main drawback: the steep, circuitous road skiers needed to negotiate to reach the base area from Kellogg.

When the Bunker Hill and other Kellogg-area mines shut down in the early 1980s, Silver Mountain represented the city's best hope for economic recovery—a chance to fill the void with tourist dollars. The late city councilman Wayne Ross envisioned an aerial tramway that would bypass the road and take visitors directly from town to the mountaintop. He pushed hard for the idea and went out in search of a grubstake. In 1988, a complex deal was successfully negotiated.

Construction of what would be the world's longest single-stage gondola (3.1 miles) began in 1989, and the new, improved Silver Mountain Ski Resort, gondola and all, opened in 1990. The area gets plenty of snow—some 300 inches a year on average. The resort offers 1,500 acres with a 2,200-foot vertical drop and a longest run of 2.5 miles. Intermediate runs are most prevalent, but 40 percent of the runs are either advanced or expert. Besides the gondola, the area is served by one fixed-grip quad, two triple chairs, two double chairs, and a surface lift. The resort is open daily 9 A.M.–4 P.M. in ski season, with lift tickets for $35 adults, $27 for college students and seniors (ages 62 and up), and $25 for juniors (ages 7–17). Night skiing is offered Fri.–Sat. 3–10 P.M. for $10, all ages.

In summer, the resort is open weekends and holidays only and hosts barbecues and entertainment in its mountaintop amphitheater. Other summertime draws include gondola-served hiking and mountain biking on an extensive, newly expanded trail system. A single ride up the gondola in summer costs about $14 adults, $10 juniors; family rates are available. A full-day mountain-bike pass is about $20.

For more information, contact Silver Mountain Ski and Summer Resort, 610 Bunker Ave. (off I-90 at Exit 49), Kellogg, ID 83837, 208/783-1111, 800/204-6428 (information), 800/204-6428 (snow conditions), www.silvermt.com.

Staff House Museum

Otherwise known as the Shoshone County Mining and Smelting Museum, this museum, 820 McKinley Ave., 208/786-4141, occupies the former staff house for resident and visiting bigwigs of the Bunker Hill & Sullivan Mine Co. The house was built in 1906 for a manager of the Bunker Hill mine. Exhibits cover the town's mining history, with an emphasis on Bunker Hill itself. A great collection of old photos includes one of a burro, supposedly Noah Kellogg's famous sidekick. Another display lists the Bunker Hill's staggering statistics: 1,900 tons of ore mined daily; 400 tons of waste rock removed daily; 3,500 gallons of water expelled per minute; 160,000 cubic feet of air circulated each minute. During the mine's 96-year life span, 37 million tons of ore were excavated, yielding more than 165 million ounces of silver, as well as copious amounts of lead and zinc. Don't miss the display in the basement—an ingenious 3D model of the Bunker Hill mine's enormous underground labyrinth. The museum is open late May–Sept., 10 A.M.–5 P.M. daily; admission is free, donations appreciated.

Wardner

To see where it all began, take Kellogg's Division Street up the hill into Milo Gulch to the town of Wardner, population 230. Just 1,000 yards up the gulch from today's Wardner City Hall, Noah Kellogg found the gleaming rock that sparked the Silver Valley's mining boom. In "downtown" Wardner, Mayor Chuck Peterson keeps the memories of the mining days alive at **Wardner Gift Shop and Museum,** 652 Main St., 208/786-2641. The museum holds a fascinating collection of photographs and memorabilia, but the highlight of Wardner is Peterson himself. A native of Milo Gulch, his enthusiastic storytelling brings Wardner's glory days to life. Stop in for a free cup of coffee and an enjoyable earful. You can even catch him and a number of other townsfolk on the web at www.nidlink.com/~signworks/wardner.html.

Noah Kellogg's Grave

On the way up Division Street heading toward Wardner, you'll spot signs directing you east (left) up the flanks of the mountain to the local cemetery. Here you'll find the grave of Noah Kellogg himself, marked by a fence and a tasteless modern monument that steals all dignity from the site. It's a poignant place to ponder the dead miners who couldn't take their wealth with them, and the costs of their obsession on the scarred valley below.

Sunshine Mine Memorial

The Sunshine Mine is recognized as the world's all-time greatest silver producer. But on May 2, 1972, extraction of that bounty exacted a horrific price. Some time after 11 A.M. a fire broke out more than 3,000 feet down in the mine's depths. Warnings spread as soon as the first smoke was noticed. Those among the 173 miners at work that day who got word of the blaze bolted for the hoists that would take them toward the surface. Failure of a mine-wide alarm system prevented others from getting the warning until it

© JULIE FANSELOW

Sunshine Mine Memorial

was too late. Smoke and carbon monoxide soon asphyxiated the hoist operators, trapping the miners left beneath them. Despite the valiant efforts of local, national, and even international rescue workers, 91 miners died in the tragedy.

Just east of Kellogg, off I-90 at Exit 54, is the Sunshine Mine Memorial, a huge sculpture of a miner at work. It's dedicated to those who died in the disaster. The memorial is inscribed with a poem by then state senator, later governor, Phil Batt.

Accommodations

Under $50: On the low-priced end of the spectrum are **Sunshine Inn,** 301 W. Cameron Ave., 208/784-1186, with a small restaurant and a big lounge with pool tables; and **The Trail Motel,** 206 W. Cameron Ave., 208/784-1161. Both are on the north side of I-90.

$50–100: Super 8 Motel, 601 Bunker Ave., 208/783-1234 or 800/785-5443, is especially

THE PANHANDLE

noteworthy for its Superconvenient location adjacent to the Silver Mountain gondola. For a short-term ski stay in Kellogg, you might just as well stay here and eat dinner at Zany's in the gondola terminal. Nothing else in town is all *that* compelling. Amenities at the newish, 61-room motel include an indoor pool and spa, free continental breakfast, cable TV with HBO, a guest laundry, and ski and bike storage. Kids under 12 stay free with parents.

One of the bigger, fancier motels in town is **Silverhorn Motor Inn,** 699 W. Cameron Ave., 208/783-1151 or 800/437-6437. It offers queen beds and an on-site restaurant, guest laundry, and Jacuzzi. Pets okay.

Food

Down at the gondola base, **Zany's Pizza,** 610 Bunker Ave., 208/784-1144, does a good job with pies, pastas, and calzones. The help is hip and the atmosphere casual. You can hear live music here on weekend nights.

The **Silver Spoon Restaurant,** at the Silverhorn Motor Inn, 699 W. Cameron Ave., 208/783-1151, offers homemade baked goods and berry pancakes (in season). Open daily 6 A.M.–9 P.M.

Information

The **Kellogg Chamber of Commerce** operates a visitor center at the Silver Mountain gondola terminal complex, 610 Bunker Ave., Kellogg, ID 83837, 208/784-0821 or 888/333-3737, www.kellogg-id.org.

WALLACE

East of Kellogg, I-90 climbs through Osburn to Wallace. Of all the towns in the Silver Valley, Wallace feels most like the quintessential mining town. It's a compact place—the valley narrows into a tight canyon here, forcing the town to creep off the canyon floor and up the steep wooded slopes. In the small downtown, you'll still find a mining supply store along with many well-preserved 19th-century buildings; the entire town is listed on the National Historic Register. Up on the hill—hidden in the trees up steep, narrow, switchbacking lanes—are old miners' cabins and newer facsimiles. Sometimes after a storm, when mists hang over the hillsides and raindrops drip off the rooftops and pines, the town takes on an almost tangible tranquillity. Walk up the hill then—up the rickety wooden

downtown Wallace

stairs, past the small clapboard houses—and you'll half expect to find a grizzled old prospector sitting on his front porch, plucking the melancholy strains of "My Darling Clementine" on a banjo. It's almost enough to make you want to trade in the station wagon on a pickax and mule.

Museums

A trio of museums commemorate Wallace's three greatest industries. The **Wallace District Mining Museum,** 509 Bank St., 208/556-1592, offers exhibits about mining, miners, and the hard-rock life they led during the valley's boom days. You can ponder historic photos and artifacts and watch two different videos on the valley's mining history. More than one billion ounces of silver were mined in the region over the course of a century. That's 62.5 million pounds, or 31,250 tons. The museum is open daily 9 A.M.–5 P.M. in summer and weekdays 9 A.M.–4 P.M. the rest of the year. Admission is $2 general, $1.50 seniors 55 and over, $.50 children 6–15, under six free, $5 families.

The **Northern Pacific Depot Railroad Museum,** 6th and Pine Sts., 208/752-0111, occupies the beautiful, château-style 1901 Northern Pacific Depot. Bricks used in the building's construction were imported from China and destined for a fancy Tacoma hotel; the hotel never got off the ground, and the bricks ended up here. Until 1980, the Northern Pacific's Yellowstone Park Line stopped at this depot on its run between Chicago and Seattle. In 1986, the depot was carefully moved to its present site after the new interstate threatened to run right over it. Old railroad photos and paraphernalia fill the museum. One of the most interesting exhibits is a huge glass route map that once hung in another Northern Pacific depot. The museum is open daily 9 A.M.–7 P.M. in summer, reduced schedule in spring and fall; closed mid-Oct–March 30. Admission is $2 adults, $1.50 seniors 60 and over, $1 children 6–16, $6 families.

Last and perhaps most interesting of the three museums is the **Oasis Rooms Bordello Museum,** 605 Cedar St., 208/753-0801. Mining towns have historically been populated with a far higher percentage of men than women,

and this imbalance created numerous business opportunities for enterprising ladies of questionable virtue. Wallace was no exception. The Oasis was just one of several brothels that once lined this end of town. Interestingly enough, the Oasis remained in business until 1988—15 years after Idaho's governor officially proclaimed prostitution illegal in the state and some 93 years after the first red light was turned on here. The ladies apparently left in a hurry, and the rooms have been preserved as they were when abandoned.

The 20-minute upstairs tour offers many interesting anecdotes, such as the fact that, in 1982, the Oasis ladies bought the town a new police car with money saved from their earnings. Their relatively recent departure takes this museum out of the realm of a charming Western anachronism and into the somewhat seedier reality of the modern world. Nothing on the tour is particularly graphic or offensive, but it's nevertheless more jeans and g-strings than petticoats and lace. The tour costs $5. Admission is free to the ground-floor store, which sells assorted scents and frillies, and to the basement museum, which offers glimpses of a still and other artifacts from Wallace's rowdy days gone by. The museum is open daily May–Nov.

Sierra Silver Mine Tour

Rarely can someone not drawing a paycheck from a mining company venture down the shafts for a look around. On this tour, run by Sierra Silver Mine Tour, Inc., 420 5th St., 208/752-5151, you'll get to do just that. The mine you'll explore was once a working silver mine. From Wallace, you'll board a trolley for the short ride to the mine, then don hard hats and make your way down into the cool, dark depths. Guides explain the mining process, history, and various techniques. The one-hour 15-minute tours run mid-May through mid-October, leaving the Wallace office every 30 minutes from 9 A.M. to 4 P.M. (extended evening hours in summer). Tickets are $9 adults, $8 seniors over 60, $7.50 kids 4–16, or $33 for a family of two adults with two or more kids. Children under age 4 are not permitted on the tour.

Historic, Not-So-Scenic Drive

For a contrasting perspective on the the beauti-fied-for-tourists version of local mining history, drive up Route 4 heading northeast out of Wallace. Frisco, Yellow Dog, Gem, Mace, Burke—these nearly abandoned, grimy towns provide a far different image of the mining glory days than is gleaned on Wallace's spiffed-up streets. Dickens would feel right at home here, even today. Up in this narrow canyon, buildings had to make way as best they could for the railroad tracks that carried the trains that hauled out the booty that made some men rich and others just tired. The tracks ran right through the lobby of the Tiger Hotel. Other buildings sucked in their bellies and pinned themselves back against the canyon walls. Dirt would've been the dominant decor here. The air would have been thick and heavy with smoke from the mills, with soot from the locomotives, and with the dreams of souls laboring long hours in claustrophobic conditions in hopes of one day earning enough money to escape to somewhere else. One doesn't sense a great deal of remnant joy in this canyon.

Then there's the creek. In its upper reaches, above the mines, Canyon Creek flows clean and clear and carries a background lead level of 63 parts per million. Down in Burke, the creek's lead level has been measured at 76,000 parts per million, some 38 times the EPA's standard for "polluted." The rest of the way down to its confluence with the South Fork Coeur d'Alene River, Canyon Creek is dead. It supports no aquatic life. Restoration efforts are ongoing, with the cleanup process estimated to take at least 100 years.

Recreation

For information on the local backcountry and trail maps for the areas on both the north and south forks of the Coeur d'Alene River, contact the USFS **Coeur d'Alene River Ranger District-Silverton Office,** P.O. Box 14, Silverton, ID 83867, 208/752-1221.

Entertainment

Sixth Street Melodrama, 212 6th St., P.O. Box 1243, Wallace, ID 83873-1243, 208/752-8871 or 877/749-8478, is a long-running local thespian troupe. In summer, the players present old-fashioned melodrama with plenty of audience participation. In winter and spring, the company offers more serious performances, often musicals. Tickets range $8–12. Call for current playbill and schedule.

Events

The second Saturday in May, Wallace celebrates **Depot Days** with a street fair, car show, food, and music. For more information call the Northern Pacific Depot Railroad Museum at 208/752-0111. **Huckleberry/Heritage Days** in mid-August brings a 5K run/walk, pancake breakfast, crafts booths, and more. The chamber of commerce has details; call 208/753-7151.

Accommodations

Under $50: The **Brooks Hotel,** 500 Cedar St., 208/556-1571 or 800/752-0469, is the grande dame of the old Wallace hotels. Off the lobby is a good family restaurant. The **Ryan Hotel,** 608 Cedar St., 208/753-6001, is a historical, old-timey upstairs place, nicely updated. **Stardust Motel,** 410 Pine St., 208/752-1213, is a friendly, 42-room establishment.

$50–100: Best Western Wallace Inn, 100 Front St., 208/752-1252 or 800/528-1234, is the most modern, upscale place in town. Amenities include a heated indoor pool and Jacuzzi, sauna and steam rooms, and a fitness center. The inn offers a free shuttle to Lookout Pass Recreation Area. AAA and AARP discounts apply, and kids under 12 stay free.

The historic **Jameson,** 304 6th St., 208/556-1554, originally opened as a hotel in 1900. Inside its well-restored walls are a dining room, a saloon, and upstairs B&B rooms reflecting Old West elegance.

$100–150: The **Beale House B&B,** 107 Cedar St., 208/752-7151 or 888/752-7151, occupies a 1904 Victorian residence in a quiet residential neighborhood. The house has a long and distinguished history, well documented in a collection of old photographs available for perusal. A crackling fireplace inside and a bubbling hot tub outside combine to take the chill off those après-ski eves. The Beale House has been voted "Best B&B" in a

Silver Valley Voice readers' poll. Four of the five rooms share baths (which often turns out to be exclusive use, depending on how full the place is). Rates include full breakfast. No pets or children under 12.

RV Park

Down by the Depot RV Park, 108 Nine Mile Rd. (just across the interstate from downtown), 208/753-7121, offers 46 sites for $22 a night with hookups, $10 for tents. Amenities include showers, restrooms, a laundry room, game room, and saloon.

Food and Drink

Albi's Steak House, 220 6th St., 208/753-3071, is the local favorite for beef; some say it's the best in the Silver Valley. It's open for dinner nightly, with prime rib offered Fri.–Sun. **Pizza Factory,** 612 Bank St., 208/753-9003, bakes some excellent gourmet pizzas—try the delicious tomato-basil—and pours a couple of microbrews. Open daily for lunch and dinner. **Sweet's Cafe & Lounge,** 310 6th St., 208/556-4661, is a favorite local haunt serving breakfast, lunch, and dinner to a heavy-smoking clientele. The lounge displays a unique collection of model classic cars, each concealing an unopened flask of booze. The restaurant at **Brooks Hotel,** 500 Cedar St., 208/556-1571, offers reliable family fare and a decent salad bar.

The **1313 Club,** 608 Bank St., 208/752-9391, has several sidewalk tables perfect for people-watching. The efficient service and selection of microbrews in bottles and on tap are among the best in town.

Information

The Wallace **Visitor Information Center/ Chamber of Commerce** is right off the interstate at Exit 61, 208/753-7151 or www.historic-wallace.org; look for the caboose. The USFS **Coeur d'Alene River Ranger District-Silverton Office,** P.O. Box 14, Silverton, ID 83867, 208/752-1221, is a couple of miles west of town in Silverton, on Yellowstone Avenue, in the eye-catching brick building that was once a hospital.

LOOKOUT PASS

Lookout Pass Ski and Recreation Area, P.O. Box 108, Wallace, ID 83873, www.skilookout.com, at I-90 Exit 0, right on the state line, may be small in stature, but it's big in heart. The state's second-oldest ski area, Lookout has been faithfully serving Silver Valley since 1938. Over much of its life, the area owed its existence to the volunteer efforts of the Idaho Ski Club and others. It's famous for its family-friendly atmosphere and offers not only skiing, snowmobiling, and other winter activities, but summer fun like mountain biking as well. It's the main outfitting point for the Route of the Hiawatha cycling trail.

Alpine Skiing

Although this is a humble mountain in some ways, the snow quality and quantity—a whopping 387 inches a year average—are excellent, and the sweeping views into two states provide a real "high-mountain" feeling, despite a peak elevation under 6,000 feet. Lookout Pass recently expanded a bit and now has about 18 runs (the longest is 1.2 miles) and 1,150 feet of vertical drop served by a rope tow and two double chairs. The mountain's back side sports a snowboard and ski terrain park.

The lift tickets won't break your budget—weekend rates are $24 for adults, $22 for college students, $16 for juniors and seniors, and midweek rates run $22/20/15. Half-day tickets and various special promotional tickets (such as those for "Ladies' Thursday" and "Boomers' Friday") are even cheaper. And novices can get a rope-tow-only ticket for a mere $6. Ski and snowboard rentals and lessons are available, as is day-care.

The day lodge is cozy and well-kept, offering both food and drink. The bar's lively social scene is especially friendly and intimate, since most of the patrons are locals who know one another. The season here generally runs mid-November through late March or early April. From mid-December through New Year's (except Christmas Day), hours are 9 A.M.–4 P.M. (PST) daily. The rest of the season, it's open Thurs.–Sun. 9 A.M.–4 P.M.

THE PANHANDLE

Nordic Skiing

A 25-kilometer system of cross-country ski trails, ranging in difficulty from beginner to advanced, is accessible from the resort's base area. Some are shared with snowmobiles. Skinny skiers can purchase a one-ride lift ticket for $3 and ski their way back down to the base area on the trails.

Highway 95 to Pend Oreille Lake

HAYDEN LAKE

Heading north on Highway 95 from Coeur d'Alene, you'll soon come to the turnoff to the town of Hayden Lake. a wealthy bedroom community of Coeur d'Alene. The lakeshore is ringed with expensive homes but not much public lakefront, giving the whole area the appearance of an upper-crust country club.

Recreation

In Hayden Lake, babies are born with silver putters in hand. Golf is as natural as breathing here, and you half expect electric golf carts to replace automobiles on the city streets. The chi-chi Hayden Lake Country Club is private, but the semi-chi-chi, semi-private **Avondale Golf & Tennis Club,** 10745 Avondale Loop Rd., 208/772-5963, has been known to accommodate plebeian passers-through. Greens fee for the 6,525-yard, par-72 course is about $38, with $20 specials on Mondays. It's open year-round.

Hikers in summer, and cross-country skiers in winter, enjoy the trails at **English Point,** a bit of national forest preserved along the lake's north shore. To get there, turn east off Highway 95 onto Lancaster Road and drive about 3.5 miles to English Point Road.

Accommodations

$100–150: On the lake's north side, reached by turning east off Highway 95 at Lancaster Road (the first major intersection north of Hayden junction), is **Bridle Path Manor,** 1155 E. Lancaster Rd., Hayden Lake, ID 83835, 208/762-3126, a large Tudor-style house on an expansive horse ranch. Horse fanciers can take trail rides through the woods here; others can stay at home and play billiards or relax by the fireplace. Rates for the five rooms include a full breakfast. Kids are welcome.

$150–250: One of the biggest old mansions on Hayden Lake is now a gloriously refurbished B&B. The **Clark House,** E. 4550 S. Hayden Lake Rd., Hayden Lake, ID 83835, 208/772-3470 or 800/765-4593, was built in 1910 as a summer home for millionaire F. Lewis Clark and his wife, Winifred. At the time of its completion, the 15,000-square-foot manse was the most expensive residence in Idaho. After extensive reconstruction, the mansion once again recalls its glory days, though the sprawling estate it reigned over has shrunk over the years, from 1,400 acres to 12.

Rates at the house include a full gourmet breakfast. All rooms have private baths, and you'll enjoy king or queen featherbeds, fireplaces, Roman tubs built for two, and great views of the lake. No smoking, pets, or children under 12. The B&B's dining room also has a good reputation; it serves a six-course dinner (about $50 per person) to both guests and nonguests, Tues.–Sat., by advance reservation.

Camping

Way around the lake's east side is the USFS **Mokins Bay Campground,** offering 16 sites (fee) on a six-acre lakeshore plot. Take FR 3090, which circles the lake; it's a long dozen or so miles from town to the campground along either the north or south shores—the northern route is probably the best bet. Four miles north of Hayden Junction up Highway 95 is Garwood Road and the **Alpine Country Store & RV Park,** N. 17400 Hwy. 95, 208/772-4305. The tidy, wooded, 25-site park offers restrooms, showers, a laundry, pet area, and barbecue pits. The rate is $22 a night including tax and full hookups. The store is open 24 hours. Three miles east out Garwood Road, the bucolic **Coeur d'Alene Sunrise Campground,** 4850 E. Garwood Rd., Hayden Lake, ID 83835, 208/772-4557, has 64 sites for $16–20 a night.

ATHOL AND VICINITY

Silverwood Theme Park

This 700-acre amusement park is a scream. Literally. Let's see you keep your mouth shut on that upside-down corkscrew roller coaster, or on Tremors—a coaster that plummets into the bowels of the earth—or on the Timber Terror, a 55-mph wooden coaster sure to please even the most obsessed rollermeister. Monster, Roundup, Scrambler, Skydiver, and other "high-intensity" rides will scare the living daylights out of you. Admission is $28 general, $17 for kids over 65 and for almost-grown-ups ages 3–7. Don't miss the magic show nor the ice spectacular. In 2003, Silverwood debuted its new **Boulder Beach** water park, with waterslides, a wave pool, lazy river, and treehouse-themed kids' area. Admission is included in the Silverwood rates.

Those wanting to make a week or weekend of it will find the park's own 127-site RV park right across the street. Rates are $21 per site per night, and amenities include full hookups, shaded sites, showers, picnic tables, volleyball courts, horseshoe pits, barbecue grills, a laundry, and a small store with propane. Tenters are welcome, maximum two tents per site. Guests receive discount tickets to the amusement park.

Silverwood, 26225 N. Hwy. 95, Athol, ID 83801, 208/683-3400, is open from early May into October—daily in peak season, weekends only in early and late season.

Farragut State Park

During World War II, this 4,000-acre spread on the southern shores of Pend Oreille Lake held a large U.S. Naval Training Center. The site was supposedly "discovered" by Eleanor Roosevelt on a flight from Washington, D.C., to Seattle. FDR was looking for an inland body of water to train submariners in safety, away from the eyes and ears of the enemies. Eleanor saw Pend Oreille Lake and described it to her husband, who deemed it perfect for the task. Construction of the base began in 1942. By the fall of that year, the base's population of 55,000 military personnel made it the second-largest naval training facility in the country and the largest "city" in Idaho. At war's end the base was decommissioned, and in 1964 Farragut State Park was established. In keeping with its naval heritage, the park was named after Civil War hero Adm. David Farragut (1801–70), whose important victories on the Gulf Coast and Mississippi River allowed the Union Army to capture and control the region.

Today, the sprawling park with its many long loop roads and open areas still retains a military-base ambience. Four separate campgrounds hold a total of 135 sites plus several camping cabins that can sleep up to five people ($35); the Whitetail campground is closest to the lake, the park's prime recreational attraction. Sunbathing and splashing are favorite activities here, and a concessionaire rents pedal boats, rafts, and beach chairs. A boat-launching area is available for those hauling their own vessels. Those who prefer terra firma fun can explore the park's hiking, biking, and horseback-riding trails (you can rent horses at the Thimbleberry Group Area, off Highway 54 toward the west end of the park). The north-side trails wind through beautiful woods, while the south-side trails skirt the lakeshore. In winter, the park sets and grooms 15 kilometers of mostly flat cross-country ski trails.

Unusual offerings here include a model-airplane flying field and a shooting range often used by black-powder enthusiasts (watch for the occasional cannon shoots).

The park is at 13400 E. Ranger Rd., Athol, ID 83801, 208/683-2425. Take Highway 54 four miles east off Highway 95 at Athol.

The little fishing village of Bayview is an uncrowded hideaway. Docks, boats, and fishing resorts ring the calm waters of Scenic Bay, and the views across the lake are superb.

Bayview

The little fishing village of Bayview is an uncrowded hideaway. Docks, boats, and fishing resorts ring the calm waters of Scenic Bay, and the views across the lake are superb. Front and center on the water is friendly **Boileau's Resort,**

208/683-2213, where you can walk out the dock to the marina bar and grill for a sandwich, a can of beer, and an earful of fish stories.

Though the Naval Training Center has disappeared, the navy still makes good use of Pend Oreille Lake for submarine research and development. On the south edge of Bayview is the **Naval Surface Warfare Center, Acoustic Research Detachment,** where the navy develops "stealth" technology for submarines. Pend Oreille Lake is the ideal spot for such work for a number of reasons, including its deep, still water; flat bottom contour; isothermal temperature profile; low ambient noise; low echo interference; and large, unobstructed operating areas.

Bayview's events calendar is highlighted by **Bayview Days** on the 4th of July weekend. To get to Bayview, continue on Highway 54 from Athol through Farragut State Park. Coming from the north, turn east off Highway 95 at Careywood.

West of Athol

Heading west from Athol on Highway 54 will take you to **Twin Lakes, Spirit Lake,** and **Blanchard.** Anglers like the relaxed pace of the first two resort towns. The White Horse Saloon in Spirit Lake claims to be the oldest continuously operating saloon in the state. Golfers enjoy playing **Twin Lakes Golf and Country Club,** 5500 W. Village Blvd. in Rathdrum, 208/687-1311, a wooded course with eight ponds and lakes (greens fee around $30); and **Stoneridge Golf Course** at Stoneridge Resort, on Blanchard Road in Blanchard, 208/437-4682, a hilly course favored by those staying at the resort (greens fees around $20). Both are 18-hole courses, and both are closed in winter.

Stoneridge Resort rents condos and offers a pool, health club, and tennis and racquetball courts. For more information, contact the resort at P.O. Box 135, Blanchard, ID 83804, 208/437-2451.

COCOLALLA, SAGLE, AND VICINITY

Cocolalla Lake

Stretching between the towns of Cocolalla and Westmond, this 800-acre lake attracts anglers all year. They come to round up the usual suspects: rainbow, cutthroat, brown, and brook trout; channel catfish; largemouth bass; crappie; and perch. In winter, you'll see the diehards out on the lake bundled up in their snowsuits, drilling holes through the ice to sink a line. In summer, you can launch a boat onto the lake from a ramp at the northeast end.

Also at the north end of the lake is **Sandy Beach Resort,** 4405 Loop Rd., 208/263-4328, offering RV and tent sites, a restaurant and cocktail lounge, restrooms, showers, a boat ramp and boat rentals, and a guest laundry, among other amenities.

Round Lake State Park

This small park, 208/263-3489, lies two miles down Dufort Road, which turns west off Highway 95 four miles north of Cocolalla. Here you'll find 53 wooded campsites ringing beautiful, 58-acre Round Lake. The shallow lake warms up in summer, making for pleasant swimming. Fishermen drop a line for brook and rainbow trout, largemouth bass, sunfish, perch, bullhead, and crappie; ice fishing is popular in winter. Hikers and cross-country skiers enjoy seven miles of trails (groomed in winter) that follow the lakeshore or head off into the forest through lush stands of western red cedar, western hemlock, ponderosa pine, Douglas fir, and western larch. Keep your eyes peeled for some of the park's abundant resident wildlife. Winter also brings out ice skaters and sledders here; areas are specifically maintained for both of those slick activities.

Sagle and Garfield Bay

Another goofy postal story explains Sagle's name. Back in 1900, the first resident to apply for a post office here applied for the name Eagle. That name was already taken so he changed it to Sagle. The town marks the turnoff to Garfield Bay, a great out-of-the-way spot with a couple of character-laden bar/restaurants, a couple of campgrounds, and a small golf course.

Just as you come into Garfield Bay from Sagle, a road branches left and climbs up the hill to the north. A short distance down that road, FR 532 branches off to the right and leads to the **Mineral Point Interpretive Trail** (Trail 82), a short and pleasant nature trail winding through groves of Douglas fir, ponderosa pine, Pacific yew, and western red cedar. Along the way you'll find benches where you can sit and enjoy superb views of the lake. This peaceful spot is perfect for a picnic. Chances are good you'll have it all to yourself. The trail connects with another that leads down to the water at the USFS **Green Bay Campground** (three sites, free). Pick up an interpretive brochure or get more information at the office of the USFS **Sandpoint Ranger District,** 1500 Hwy. 2, Sandpoint, ID 83864, 208/263-5111.

Bottle Bay

This major bay opening onto the northern arm of Pend Oreille Lake is a favorite stop-off of cruise boats and anglers. **Bottle Bay Resort & Marina,** 115 Resort Rd., Sagle, ID 83860, 208/263-5916, is best known for its Kokanee Roe Restaurant and cocktail lounge, though the resort also offers some cabins and RV sites.

Bottle Bay can be reached via Bottle Bay Road—accessed from Sagle or from just across the long bridge from Sandpoint—or via a cutoff from Garfield Bay Road. The former leads around the lakeshore, approaching Bottle Bay from the north; the latter winds around Gold Mountain and finds its way up to Bottle Bay from the south.

Sandpoint and Vicinity

Sandpoint and Pend Oreille Lake sneak up on the driver heading north up Highway 95, thanks to dense woods on either side of the highway. When the road rounds the last bend and the view opens up, it's hard to stifle the oohs and aahs. The huge, brilliant blue lake is ringed by high mountains, and you have to drive right across the water on a very long bridge to enter Sandpoint. What a grand entrance.

The town perches on the lake's northwest shore, on a "sandy point" first noted by Canadian fur trapper/geographer David Thompson in 1808. In that same year, the first white settlement was established, and when the railroads and timber companies found their way here, the town took root. It's still a mill town, but a couple of other elements add to the economic and cultural mix.

Back in the 1970s, the town's cheap rents and stunning surroundings were discovered by artists. Then recreation-minded visitors latched on to the area's great skiing, fishing, and other outdoor activities. Today, the logger, artist, and outdoor recreationist all are woven into a pleasantly diverse cultural tapestry.

Sandpoint is full of outstanding restaurants and lively nightclubs, and it offers a full calendar of performing-arts events.

Bonner County Historical Museum

A good place to start your study of Sandpoint is this museum in Lakeview Park, 611 S. Ella Ave., 208/263-2344. Exhibits explain the region's history, beginning with the indigenous Kalispel and Kootenai peoples and continuing through the days of steamboats and railroads. The museum is open April–Oct., Tues.–Sat. 10 A.M.–5 P.M.; Nov.–March, Tues.–Sat. 10 A.M.–4 P.M. Admission is $2 adults, $1 students 6–18, under 6 free, family $5.

PEND OREILLE LAKE RECREATION

Largest of the state's lakes, Pend Oreille is 43 miles long and more than 1,100 feet deep in places. In summer, swimmers splash along the shores, sailors glide silently across the clear waters, water-skiers skim over the surface, and anglers troll the depths searching for some of the 14 species of resident game fish. Following is a rundown on some of the town's water-based recreation.

City Beach

As soon as the hot summer sun arrives, it seems the whole town heads for City Beach. On a July weekend, you'll find blankets covering nearly every square inch of this relatively small

THE PANHANDLE

spit of sand extending out into Pend Oreille Lake. Besides the beach itself, the recreation area here includes a playground; areas for basketball, volleyball, and picnicking; and docks from where the lake cruise ships depart. In winter, City Beach takes on a quieter, more contemplative air, but it's still a great place to watch the whitecaps on the water and let the chill wind cleanse your spirit. The beach is at the foot of Bridge Street, off Highway 95 downtown.

Boat Rentals

Windbag Marina, at City Beach in front of Edgewater Resort, 208/263-7811, rents people-powered boats ($10 per hour) and sailboats ($20–60 per hour; lessons available), while **Sandpoint Recreational Rentals,** 120 E. Lake St. (at the Old Power House), 208/265-4557, is the place to try for power-boat rentals—from personal watercraft ($50 per hour) to 20-foot pontoon boats (also $50 per hour). Sandpoint Recreational also rents pedal boats, canoes, bicycles, and water-ski equipment (all $5 per hour).

Houseboats are available in two sizes from **Pend Oreille Houseboat Rentals,** 533 Olive St., 208/263-2675. The smaller size sleeps six people and rents for around $700 a weekend or $1,300 a week in peak summer season. The larger size sleeps 10 and goes for around $995 a weekend or $1,995 a week in summer. In the shoulder seasons, rates are about 25 percent lower. A fully refundable damage deposit of $300–500 is required. You can also rent houseboats in Hope, east of Sandpoint.

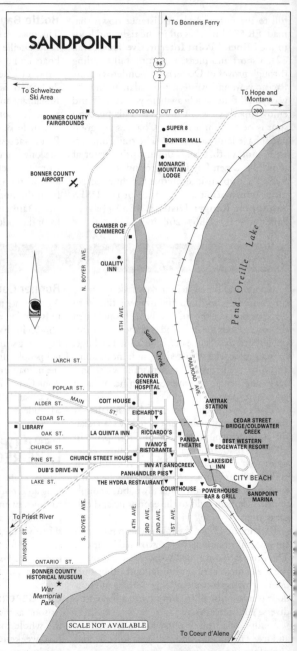

Pend Oreille Lake is the largest lake in Idaho.

Cruises

To get a duck's-eye view of Sandpoint, hook up with **Lake Pend Oreille Cruises,** c/o Tamarack Knoll Enterprises, 303 Pine St., 208/255-5253 or 888/726-3764. From late June through mid-September, 2.5-hour sightseeing cruises aboard the custom-designed *Shawnodese* leave daily at 2:30 P.M. from the Lakeside Inn off Bridge Street; adults $14, seniors $13, children under 12 $10. Also offered are Thursday dinner cruises to Bottle Bay Resort, $29 adults; Friday sunset dessert and eagle-watching cruises, $19 adults; and occasional special cruises such as wine-tasting tours (call for full schedule).

Fishing

Kamloops, kokanee, whitefish, perch, crappie, bluegill, largemouth bass, rainbow, brown, brook trout—whatever your piscatory pleasure, it's waiting for you here. World-record rainbows and bull trout have been pulled from Pend Oreille Lake's depths. You can rent a boat and head out on your own, but it probably makes more sense to avail yourself of local expertise. Fishing guides in the area include **Pend Oreille Charters,** P.O. Box 905, Sandpoint, ID 83864, 208/265-6781; **Seagull Charters,** P.O. Box 208, Kootenai, ID 83840, 208/263-2770; and **Diamond Charters,** P.O. Box 153, Hope, ID 83836, 208/265-2565 or 800/487-6886. Seagull and Diamond are both based east of Sandpoint at the Floater in Hope.

Kayak Tours

Pend Oreille Lake's many bays and islands make for prime exploring by kayak. **Full Spectrum Kayak Tours,** 321 N. 2nd Ave., 208/263-5975, can teach you kayaking or take you on a tour. Special-interest tours combine kayaking with other pursuits such as photography, music, and massage. Rates range from about $70 for a half-day trip with no food to $450 for a three-day, two-night adventure. The season runs June–Sept.

Also offering guided half-day kayak tours around the Lake Pend Oreille region is **Celtic Kayak,** P.O. Box 316, Sagle, ID 83860, 208/265-0780.

Parasailing

Wind Walker Parasails at Sandpoint Marina, 208/263-2136 or 888/727-2724, can get you 300 or 600 feet high above the lake for a real bird's-eye view. The crew uses a hydraulic winch system that allows you to take off and land right off the back of the boat without even getting wet. Flights last 10–15 minutes and start at about $40. Call ahead for reservations.

SCHWEITZER MOUNTAIN RESORT

High in the Selkirk Mountains, a short 11-mile drive north of town, is Schweitzer Mountain Resort, 10000 Schweitzer Mountain Rd., Sandpoint, ID 83864, 208/263-9555 or 800/831-8810, snow report 208/263-9562. One of Idaho's top ski areas, Schweitzer offers a vertical drop of 2,400 feet, two massive bowls, and outstanding base-area lodging and dining. After the snow melts, you can come up the hill for hiking, horseback riding, and even lift-served mountain biking.

Alpine Skiing and Snowboarding

Seemingly underused, Schweitzer's lifts seldom have any appreciable lines. The resort's new high-speed "six-pack" chair (the first in Idaho, nicknamed "Stella") plus a single detachable quad, four double chairs, and two handle tows serve 2,500 acres of terrain and 59 named runs rated at 20 percent beginner, 40 percent intermediate, 35 percent advanced, and 5 percent expert. More than half the runs are groomed, including some of the steep upper slopes, by means of winch cats. The longest run measures a quad-burning 2.7 miles. Racing enthusiasts can try out the NASTAR course, while snowboarders enjoy the resort's terrain park.

Full-day lift tickets cost around $42 adults, $37 seniors, $32 students ages 7–17; kids 6 and under free. After 12:30 P.M., lift rates drop to $35/26/24. Two lifts are lighted for night skiing Fri.–Sat. and holiday evenings until 9 P.M. Lessons and a wide range of rental equipment such as skis, snowboards, tele-gear, and snowshoes are available at the base area. The resort offers discounted beginner packages including rentals, lessons, and lift tickets.

Nordic Skiing

Schweitzer sets and grooms 30 kilometers of Nordic trails just to the north of the base area. The trails are better groomed than any Park N'

Ski area and offer great views and pleasant, rolling terrain. The well-marked trails leave the busy lodge area and climb around the ridge to the north. Both a wide skating lane and traditional tracks are set. An all-day trail pass costs $10; rental gear is available.

Kid Stuff

The resort's day care and learn-to-ski programs are open to kids ages 3 months to 12 years. Day-care rates run around $50 a day for babes in diapers, $40 for kids out of diapers. A combined day-care and ski experience is open to youngsters ages 4–6; they'll get two ski lessons, including explorations of the Enchanted Forest terrain garden (it's pretty neat!) and lunch, all for about $75. And older kids ages 7–12 can get in on the Mogul Mice program—an all-day lesson with lunch for $65.

Mountain Biking

Schweitzer maintains 20 miles of mountain-bike trails on the resort property, and those trails connect with many more miles of logging roads that wind through the Selkirks. You can rent top-notch bikes at Schweitzer for about $30 per half day, $50 per full day. Those who love the downhill but loathe the uphill can load their fat-tire friend onto the resort's quad chairlift and get a ride to the top; $20 for an all-day pass.

Horseback Riding

Mountain Horse Adventures offers guided horse treks around the mountains here in summer. Two-hour rides cost about $45. For reservations, call 208/263-8768 or 800/880-8310.

Hiking

In summer, the hills around Schweitzer are bursting with berries and wildflowers. Add panoramic views of Pend Oreille Lake and you've got ideal hiking country. Ten miles of trails meander through the hills here. Those who want the mountaintop views without the toil can ride the resort's quad chair to the summit for $8, then enjoy a downhill stroll from there. Free trail maps are available at the base area, and guided hikes are offered on Saturday mornings in July and August.

Accommodations

$100–150: Schweitzer Mountain Bed & Breakfast, 110 Crystal Court (head up Crystal Springs Road from the main Schweitzer parking lot), 208/265-8080 or 888/550-8080, is a chalet-style B&B with five guest rooms, each with private bath. Amenities include a hot tub, TV/video room, and ski-in/ski-out access. Rates include breakfast, as well as tea, coffee, and beverages throughout the day. No smoking, children, or pets.

$150–250: The resort has two slopeside lodges—both part of the Red Lion chain—plus condos in the base area. The **Selkirk Lodge,** 208/263-9555 or 800/831-8810, sits right at the base of the lifts, its tall gabled roof giving it the air of a Bavarian château. Some rooms have jetted tubs, and there's an outdoor heated pool and hot tub complex. The newer **White Pines Lodge,** 208/263-0257 or 800/831-8810, has one-, two-, and three-bedroom accommodations, plus outdoor hot tubs and a shopping and dining village. Depending on the season and room size, rates might be lower or higher than this range.

OTHER RECREATION

Golf

The Lower Pack River meanders through the course at **Hidden Lakes Golf Resort,** 151 Clubhouse Way, 208/263-1642 or 888/806-6673, creating water hazards on 17 of the course's 18 holes. Your tee shots might be critiqued by some of the area's abundant wildlife, including elk, deer, bald eagles, and ospreys. The moose play through. Traversing the fairways of the scenic course, you'll play past stands of cedar and birch, the latter glimmering gold in fall. Greens fee is around $55 at the recently lengthened 6,923-yard, par-71 course. Lessons and a snack bar are available. To get to the course, take Highway 200 east from Sandpoint about seven miles (straight through the stoplight at the junction with Highway 95 North) and turn left just past milepost 37. Golf and lodging packages are offered in conjunction with many area motels; call for current list. The course is closed in winter.

For a quick nine holes, head to **Elks Golf**

Course, P.O. Box 338, Hwy. 200 E., 208/263-4321. The par-35 course plays a little under 3,000 yards; greens fee around $15.

Hiking and Biking

One of the best places for a hike, run, or bike ride in town is also one of the easiest to get to. The **Long Bridge** that you drove into town on has a pedestrian/bike path along one side of it. To access the trail from downtown, follow signs from the foot of Lake Street. Bikes are available for rent at **Sandpoint Recreational Rentals,** 120 E. Lake St. (at Sandpoint Marina by the Old Power House), 208/265-4557.

A pamphlet titled *Sandpoint Ranger District Trails* is available from the office of the **Sandpoint Ranger District,** 1500 Hwy. 2, Sandpoint, ID 83864, 208/263-5111. The pamphlet describes a dozen trails on the district, some of which are described elsewhere in this book.

South of town across the lake, the 3.7-mile each way **Gold Hill Trail** (Trail 3) climbs the northern flanks of Gold Hill, providing panoramic views of the city and the lake. The lower trailhead is on Bottle Bay Road, about five miles north from Sagle. To get to the upper trailhead, take Sagle Road six miles to Contest Mountain Road (FR 2642) and follow that road six more miles to the trailhead.

North of town, the easy half-mile one-way **Caribou Lake Trail** (Trail 58) leads to a small lake in the Selkirks north of Schweitzer Mountain Resort. Take Highway 95 north from town 13 miles to Pack River Road. Follow that road five miles to Caribou Creek Road (FR 2684), and continue down that rough road seven miles to the trailhead.

East of town, the long **Round Top-Bee Top Trail** (#120) is especially popular among mountain bikers. The route traverses a long high divide linking Trestle Peak, Round Top, Cougar Peak, and Bee Top. It's about 20 miles long and provides many great views from its 6,000-foot heights. The northwest trailhead is on FR 275, which takes off from Highway 200 at Trestle Creek between Sandpoint and Hope. Look for the trailhead at a hairpin turn in the road about 15 miles in. The southeast trailhead is off Lightning

Creek Road (FR 419), about five miles north from Clark Fork.

Outfitters

For backcountry gear, head to **Outdoor Experience,** 314 N. 1st Ave., 208/263-6028. The full-line adventure-gear store sells packs, mountain bikes, and backcountry duds, and also rents cross-country skis, snowshoes, telemark skis, and kayaks. Bike mechanics are on duty here seven days a week. **Ground Zero,** 317 N. 1st Ave., 208/265-6714, specializes in skateboards, wakeboards, and both sale and rental snowboards. **Sports Plus,** 102 S. Boyer Ave., 208/263-5174, is a local favorite selling water-skis, skateboards, and mountain bikes. Bike mechanics are on duty.

ENTERTAINMENT AND EVENTS

The **Panida Theatre,** 300 N. 1st Ave., 208/263-9191, forms the focus of Sandpoint's flourishing entertainment scene. The Spanish Mission–style theater hosted vaudeville and movies after its construction in 1927. Age took its toll over the years, but in 1985, the city purchased the theater and is in the process of restoring it to its former glory. Today, the beautiful Panida is on the National Register of Historic Places and stages local drama productions, a foreign/art-film series, concerts by touring and local musicians, and many other special events. The theater's name is an amalgamation derived from *Pan*handle of *Ida*ho, but it's nevertheless pronounced "PAN-idda."

Eichardt's, 212 Cedar St., 208/263-4005, is the most reliable place to hear live music.

Events

In late July or early August, the big, 10-day **Festival at Sandpoint** concert series takes place at various venues around town. For more information, contact the festival office, 120 E. Lake St., 208/265-4554 or 888/265-4554. The **Sandpoint Arts and Crafts Fair** brightens the town for three days over the second weekend in August. Late August brings the **Bonner County Fair** to town. The **Idaho Draft Horse International** shows off the best of the brawny breeds in early October at the Bonner County Fair-

grounds. For information call Anne Brower at 208/263-2117 or the Sandpoint Chamber of Commerce at 208/263-0887.

On the cold side of the calendar, Sandpoint's five-day **Winter Carnival** celebrates snow season with snow sculptures, snowshoe softball, and a torchlight parade. It all takes place at the tail end of January.

For a complete calendar of events, contact the **Greater Sandpoint Chamber of Commerce,** 100 Hwy. 95 N., P.O. Box 928, Sandpoint, ID 83864, 208/263-2161.

ACCOMMODATIONS

Summer is peak season in Sandpoint, and summer rates are listed here. Winter rates are significantly lower.

Motels

$50–100: At the **Lakeside Inn,** 106 Bridge St., 208/263-3717 or 800/543-8126, you don't get to look out on the lake, but you do overlook the mouth of Sand Creek, where the inn has its own marina for the exclusive use of its guests. Amenities include a complimentary breakfast bar, a sauna, and both an indoor and a 24-hour outdoor whirlpool tub. A whirlpool tub suite and family suites with kitchenettes are available. The inn specializes in putting together recreation packages—golf, parasailing, lake cruises—for its guests.

Quality Inn, 807 N. 5th Ave., 208/263-2111 or 800/635-2534, is in a hectic location right on Highway 2/95. It's got an indoor pool, a decent restaurant, and 62 rooms. **Super 8 Motel,** 476841 Hwy. 95 N., 208/263-2210 or 800/800-8000, has 61 rooms and a hot tub. Kids 12 and under stay free when accompanied by an adult.

In the Bonner Mall area on the way to Schweitzer, you'll find **Monarch Mountain Lodge,** Hwy. 95 N., Bonner Mall Station, P.O. Box 3171, Sandpoint, ID 83864, 208/263-1222 or 800/543-8193, offering 50 rooms, two spas, a sauna, and a free continental breakfast. Some rooms have fireplaces.

$100–150: La Quinta Inn, 415 Cedar St., 208/263-9581 or 800/282-0660, is right in the heart of downtown. Amenities include a heated pool, whirlpool tub, and an adjacent restaurant open for breakfast, lunch, and dinner daily. Most rooms are at the low end of this price category. Golf packages available.

Best Western Edgewater Resort, 56 Bridge St., P.O. Box 128, Sandpoint, ID 83864, 208/263-3194 or 800/635-2534, enjoys a prime piece of lakefront real estate overlooking City Beach, just a block from downtown. All 55 rooms face the water and offer either a private balcony or a private patio; for a luxurious splurge, try one of the Jacuzzi or fireplace suites. The resort has an indoor pool, and rates include continental breakfast. The inn's Beachhouse Restaurant is a great place for dinner or a sunset cocktail.

Bed-and-Breakfasts

$50–100: The 1907 **Coit House,** 502 N. 4th Ave., 208/265-4035, is a B&B within easy walking distance of downtown. The creaky, character-filled Victorian is full of antiques, and each room has its own bath, cable TV, and phone. Rates include a full breakfast featuring fresh-baked breads. Children under 12 are discouraged, and discounts are offered for longer stays. Smoking outside only. One room is over $100.

Oh, the stories told by the **Church Street House,** 401 Church St., 208/255-7094. Alan Barber and Heather Hellier are the innkeepers of a house that Barber's grandparents lived in back in the 1940s before they moved to Alaska. A splendidly restored Arts-and-Crafts home, the inn offers two rooms: one honoring the family's Texas heritage, another paying tribute to the Barbers' Alaska years. Each has a queen bed and its own bathroom.

$100–150: The **Inn at Sandcreek,** 105 S. 1st Ave., 208/255-2821, offers three guest rooms, two with Victorian decor and one with Western decor. Two of the rooms have a fireplace, and all have a TV/VCR. One room tops the $150 level. Amenities include a hot tub, sun deck, and a picnic/barbecue area. No smoking.

Guest Ranch

Western Pleasure Guest Ranch, 1413 Upper Gold Creek Rd., Sandpoint, ID 83864, 208/263-9066, sits on a 960-acre spread about 16 miles

northeast of town (call for directions). The working cattle ranch has been around since 1940. Summer trail rides—through forest inhabited by deer, elk, bear, moose, and wild turkey—lead to views of Pend Oreille Lake and the Selkirks. Winter sleigh rides are provided courtesy of a beautiful team of Percherons; the horses pull guests through whitewashed woods on a 45-minute ride culminating in hot drinks and popcorn. Cross-country ski trails are also set and groomed here in winter.

Accommodations are in either modern log cabins or a new lodge building. Each of the cabins has a full kitchen and woodstove and can accommodate up to six people. The 10,000-square-foot lodge sports a massive river-rock fireplace and holds six guest rooms. In summer season, late June to mid-September, package stays are offered that include daily rides, evening entertainment, lodging, and all meals for $130 per person per day, $85 for kids 6–10, three nights minimum. Packages without the trail rides and packages with breakfast only are also available. The rest of the year, all the facilities and activities are "à la carte"; nightly rates are available in your choice of cabins ($115, breakfast extra) or lodge rooms ($85, breakfast included).

Camping and RVing

On the south side of the long bridge, Lakeshore Drive leads west around Murphy Bay to the Corps of Engineers' **Springy Point Recreation Area,** 208/265-2676. The campground here (40 sites, fee) is open mid-May through Labor Day. For campground reservations or more information, call NRRS at 877/444-6777.

FOOD

Fine Dining

Relatively new in town is the **Powerhouse Bar & Grill,** 120 E. Lake St. (in the recently restored old powerhouse building on the north side of the Long Bridge), 208/265-2449. The menu features steak and seafood, but you can also choose from pastas, salads, poultry dishes, burgers—even breakfast on weekends. Dinner entrées range $8–16. You can eat inside or out, weather permitting. Full bar available. Open from 11 A.M. daily.

Walk into **The Hydra Restaurant,** 115 Lake St., 208/263-7123, and you'll think you're in a plant-filled grotto. The rambling interior is done up in green with lots of wood, and subdued lighting adds to the aura of cool tranquillity. The menu offers steak, chicken, seafood, and pasta entrées in the $8–18 range, plus a large salad bar. A good wine list offers several selections by the glass, and a half dozen microbrews are on tap in the lounge. Other highlights include a complimentary Friday evening buffet in the lounge. Open for dinner nightly (buffet on Sunday), for lunch Tues.–Fri., and for brunch Sunday.

On the south side of the Long Bridge, **Swan's Landing,** 41 Lakeshore Dr. (at Hwy. 95), 208/265-2000, offers a steak and seafood (and more) menu in an atmosphere reminiscent of a rustic lodge. Dinner entrées range $14–23, or $8–13 for the "lighter fare" menu. Boaters can sail across the lake and tie up here, capping their cruise with a cocktail or microbrew from the full bar. Open daily for lunch (brunch on Sunday) and dinner.

The **Beachhouse** restaurant at the Edgewater resort, 56 Bridge St., 208/255-4947, is also an option for seafood and regional specialties, with dining alfresco in fair weather.

A Bit Less Fancy

It's hard to beat **Eichardt's,** 212 Cedar St., 208/263-4005, a pub and grill suitable for all but the fanciest night out. The restaurant pours a dozen great microbrews, including pale ales, IPAs, ESBs, and thick cream stouts. Nearly everything on the wide-ranging menu—burgers, sandwiches, steaks, and seafood—is priced under $10. The atmosphere is warm and casual, and Eichardt's regularly presents live acoustic entertainment on weekend nights. Open daily from 11:30 A.M. Highly recommended.

Just a few doors away is the **Pend Oreille Brewing Co.,** 220 Cedar St., 208/263-7837. In addition to concocting outstanding house micros right on the premises, the pub serves up a menu of good soups, salads, and sandwiches. Prices range $6–13. The dining room is non-

smoking. Open daily for lunch and dinner. Brewery tours available.

Ethnic Fare

Ivano's Ristorante, 102 S. 1st Ave., 208/263-0211, is an excellent Italian restaurant with an elegant but comfortable atmosphere. The upscale menu offers gourmet appetizers, various pasta dishes, and entrées of chicken, veal, seafood, and steak. Entrées range $9–25. Open for dinner nightly.

Jalapeño's, 314 N. 2nd Ave., 208/263-2995, is the local favorite for Mexican food. It's geared toward the Yanqui palate, perhaps, but offers large portions and reasonable prices; dinner entrées range $7–10. Open for lunch and dinner daily.

Get your Thai fix at **Bangkok Cuisine,** 202 N. 2nd Ave., 208/265-4149, where you can find MSG-free dishes with or without meat, either spicy or mild. Dinner entrées average $8–13. Beer and wine available. Open Mon.–Fri. for lunch, Mon.–Sat. for dinner.

Pizza

Second Avenue Pizza, 215 S. 2nd Ave., 208/263-9321, is one of the two local favorites. Here you can get creative veggie concoctions like the Schweitzer Mountain Ski Flakes Special, which includes "fresh spinach, tomatoes avalanched with feta cheese, garlic, moguls of mushrooms, black olives, and at the peak—knee deep in asiago cheese." Seven microbrews on tap help wash it down in style. Open daily; no smoking. The other locally preferred pie comes from **Riccardo's,** 223 Cedar St., 208/263-6764, open daily from 11 A.M. Wood-fired sourdough pizzas are the house specialty, and the dough is made fresh daily. You can also play pool here.

Breakfast, Burgers, and Basics

Best bet for a full breakfast is **Panhandler Pies,** 120 S. 1st Ave., 208/263-2912. The restaurant offers a full menu for breakfast, lunch, and dinner, and bakes 23 different kinds of pie for dessert. Most everything on the big breakfast menu is under $6. It's open Mon.–Sat.

The bright and cheery **Sandpoint Bagel**

Company, 329 N. 1st Ave. (at Cedar), 208/265-5851, enjoys a location at the busiest people-watching corner in town. Its large selection of bagels and toppings is sure to suit anyone's taste, and espresso drinks are also available. It's open at 7 A.M., seven days a week.

Dub's Drive-In, Hwy. 2 W. at Boyer St., 208/263-4300, is a Sandpoint institution offering traditional artery-clogging burgers in sizes suitable for big and little tykes alike. For dessert or a summer cooler, try a soft ice-cream cone. The little guy can get a baby cone for $.20 and add chocolate or rainbow sprinkles for just an extra dime.

Coffee and Light Bites

The quintessential locals' coffeehouse is the tiny **Java Adagio at the Panida,** 300 N. 1st Ave., 208/263-4607. Since it's right next to the Panida Theatre, it's the perfect place for pre- or post-movie coffee and dessert. It's also a good place to find out what's going on in town. The downside: only a few tables, and a management aloof to tourists.

At the delightful **Annie's Main Street Bakery/Flip Side Cafe & Pizza,** 111 Main St., 208/265-2253, the smell of freshly baked-from-scratch treats of every description permeates the room. You won't find anything this good short of Gramma's own kitchen.

On the edge of downtown, one step removed from the beaten path, is **Monarch Mountain Coffee,** 208 N. 4th Ave., 208/265-9382. It's a spacious, bright and shiny place great for writing that postcard to the folks back home. And yes, since last edition, **Starbucks** has made it to Sandpoint (and probably everywhere else in the known universe for that matter); look for it at 108 N. 1st Ave., 208/263-1330.

Groceries

From May to October, Sandpoint's **farmer's market** fills Farmin Park (3rd Ave. at Main St.) with fresh produce, house plants, flowers, and crafts. The market takes place Sat. 9 A.M.–noon and Wed. 3–5:30 P.M.

For natural foods, bulk foods, vitamins, juices, and organic health products, try **Winter Ridge Natural Foods,** 421 Main St., 208/265-8135, or **Truby's Health Mart,** 113 Main St., 208/263-6513.

Just say "cheese" at **Pend Oreille Cheese Company,** 125 S. 2nd Ave., 208/263-2030. If you're heading out on a pickuhnik, stop in here first and pick up some stinky imported cheese you've never heard of (closed Sunday). Then head right over to **Wine Sellers,** 206 N. 1st Ave., 208/265-8116, for a bottle of wine to go with it. Check out Wine Sellers' gourmet food items too, including highly picnicworthy smoked salmon, locally baked bread, and chocolate truffles. Open daily.

To witness wine production firsthand, tool on over to Sandpoint's own **Pend d'Oreille Winery,** 1067 Baldy Industrial Park Rd., P.O. Box 1821, Sandpoint, ID 83864, 208/265-8545. The winery produces its own chardonnay, merlot, cabernet sauvignon, pinot noir, and cabernet franc, from grapes grown throughout the Northwest. It's open for free tastings in summer, Wed.–Sat. noon–5 P.M.; by appointment the rest of the year. Call for directions.

SHOPPING

Wolf sweatshirts, moose clocks, Native American jewelry, and much, much more—**Coldwater Creek** carries nature-inspired goods of every description. One of Sandpoint's biggest employers, this mail-order company fills the entire Cedar Street Covered Bridge with its showroom and factory outlet. The two-story, 350-foot-long span across Sand Creek is packed with great stuff; shopping here is like walking through the store's catalog. The store is at 1st and Cedar Sts., 208/263-2265, and open Mon.–Sat. 9 A.M.–9 P.M., Sun. 10 A.M.–7 P.M. (Note: As a quirky, scatalogical aside, the far stall of the upstairs men's room, and presumably the women's room, too, offers the best view of any commode in Idaho. It's worth a special trip if you're in the area when nature calls.)

World-beat goods fill the small **Little Bear Trading Co.,** 324 N. 1st Ave., 208/263-1116. Jewelry from around the world, flutes and drums, bead goods, clothing, alabaster pipes, and cool tunes—it's a classic. **From Sea to Sí,** 308 ½ N. 1st Ave., 208/265-1609, sells imports from Ecuador exclusively, owing to the fact that the male half of the husband-and-wife proprietor team is a native of Ecuador. Clouds of incense fill **Zany Zebra,** 109 Main St., 208/263-2178, which sells tie-dye, hemp hacky-sacks, funky art postcards, and more. **Elfin Rhythm,** 107 N. 1st Ave., 208/265-8206, sells a range of crystals, tarot decks, and jewelry.

Named after one of the great Northwest trappers, **Finan McDonald Clothing Company,** 305 N. 1st Ave., 208/263-3622, is an upscale store carrying Northwest-inspired mens- and womenswear. Around the corner is **Cabin Fever,** 113 Cedar St., 208/263-7179, which offers three floors of trendy women's clothing, Northwest-oriented furniture, and gifts. The stuff is great, if pricey. It's worth a peek inside just to see the huge moose. The more down-home **Antique Arcade,** 119 N. 1st Ave., 208/265-5421, has some neat old stuff, especially in the way of various indispensable doodads from times gone by.

Art Stores
Sandpoint enjoys a reputation as an art colony, and some 15 galleries are scattered through the downtown area. A couple of favorites are **Eklektos Gallery,** 214 Cedar St., 208/263-0325, selling a magnificent array of artwork by both local and regional artists, and **Art Works Gallery,** 309 N. 1st Ave., 208/263-2642, a local artists' co-op gallery offering an eclectic collection of paintings, sculpture, pottery, jewelry, wood and glass works, and more.

Many local galleries, restaurants, and shops participate in **Artwalk,** a self-guided art tour of the town. You can pick up a list of the featured artists, their respective media, and the locations of their works at the chamber of commerce or many of the galleries around town. For more information, call the Pend Oreille Arts Council at 208/263-6139.

Bookstores
The **Book Gallery,** 823 Main St., 208/263-0178, stocks more than 44,000 used books. It's open Mon.–Sat. 10 A.M.–5:30 P.M. **Books at Foster's Crossing,** 504 Oak St., 208/263-7620, sells new and used books, and also buys and

trades books. **Vanderford's,** 800/232-0201, has two locations: 201 Cedar St., 208/263-2417, and Bonner Mall, 208/263-0031. The store carries an excellent selection of travel books and also sells office products.

INFORMATION AND SERVICES
Information
The **Greater Sandpoint Chamber of Commerce** is at 100 Hwy. 95 N., P.O. Box 928, Sandpoint, ID 83864, 208/263-0887 or 800/800-2106. Recreation information is available from the USFS **Sandpoint Ranger District,** 1500 Hwy. 2, Sandpoint, ID 83864, 208/263-5111. Sandpoint's gorgeous **public library,** 1407 Cedar St. (at Division St.), 208/263-6930, offers free Internet access.

Transportation
The **Amtrak** station is on Railroad Avenue; turn left off Bridge Street, which is just across Sand Creek on your way toward City Beach. Amtrak's Empire Builder stops here on its run between Chicago and Portland. Eastbound trains arrive at 2:47 A.M., westbound at 11:49 P.M. The closest lodging to the train station—within bleary-eyed, suitcase-lugging stumbling distance—is the Best Western Edgewater Resort. The Amtrak reservations line is 800/872-7245.

HIGHWAY 2 WEST
West of Sandpoint, Highway 2 follows the lazy and scenic Pend Oreille River down to the town of Priest River and on to the Washington state line. In the town of **Laclede,** named after a French engineer on the Great Northern Railway, you'll find the Corps of Engineers–built **Riley Creek Recreation Area,** where you'll find a 67-site campground (fee), 208/263-1502. It's open mid-May through Labor Day. For campground reservations, call the NRRS at 877/444-6777. Laclede is also well known to **rock climbing** enthusiasts for Laclede Rocks, right off the highway two miles west of Laclede. The area has a couple of easy routes, but most are in the 5.8–5.10 range. One 5.12 top-rope problem challenges the superstuds and -studettes.

Come in summer when it's hot and you can end your climb by jumping into the nearby Pend Oreille River.

Like Priest Lake, the town of **Priest River** was named in honor of Jesuit priest and early area missionary Father John Roothaan. Logging has long been its lifeblood; great log drives down the Priest River once fed the big mills here. Today the town is in the process of sprucing itself up for a tourist economy.

West of Priest River is **Albeni Falls Dam,** another Corps of Engineers project built in 1951. As the dam was built right at the falls, the falls themselves are now gone. In summer, tours of the dam are offered daily at the powerhouse, 208/437-3133.

Priest Lake

Surrounded by the dense forests and lofty, snow-capped peaks of the Selkirks, Priest Lake is a secluded, off-the-beaten-path gem. No cities the likes of Coeur d'Alene or Sandpoint will you find along the lakeshore here. The biggest towns on the lake, Coolin and Nordman, are not much more than small supply stations for anglers, campers, and the few hardy souls who live up here.

The area is a haven for wildlife. Black bears are common at the lake, and a few grizzlies roam the high country around the periphery. Deer and moose are plentiful, mountain goats inhabit rocky crags near the east shore, and a small herd of endangered woodland caribou survives tenuously in the wildest reaches of this northern realm. Wildlife photographers will love it here.

The lake is also a favorite of anglers, who fish for lunker mackinaw in forest-shaded coves along the lake's edge. Campers looking for solitude camp on one of several islands in the lake, or boat or hike north to Upper Priest Lake. The upper lake—connected to the much larger lower lake by a two-mile-long, narrow and shallow channel called the Thorofare—is preserved for the wilderness experience. Water-skiing and jet skiing are prohibited on the upper lake, where canoes are the vessels of choice. Trails through cool, dense forest lead between the lower and upper lakes, to campgrounds reached only by boat or on foot.

Around the shore of the lower lake you'll find numerous resorts, lodgings, and campgrounds of varying degrees of luxury, as well as several marinas and a couple of villages offering convivial contact with members of your own species. Many of the restaurants feature huckleberry dishes of every description. Priest Lake is huckleberry heaven—people come from all over the region in mid- to late summer to pick the delectable fruit.

Priest Lake Museum and Visitor Center

A good place to begin your exploration of the area is this informative center just north of Hill's Resort on Luby Bay, 208/443-2676. The museum occupies a log cabin built by the Civilian Conservation Corps in 1935. It was originally a residence and office for the Kaniksu National Forest's first ranger. Inside you'll find exhibits on the threatened grizzly bear and woodland caribou—including sand castings of their tracks—and on rare area plants such as the northern beechfern, deerfern, black snakeroot, and salmonberry.

The most entertaining fact you'll learn here is how the name of the local national forest came to be changed from Priest River National Forest to Kaniksu National Forest. It seems the Forest Service wanted a fresh start after the antics of Priest River National Forest's first supervisor, Benjamin McConnell, gained public attention. McConnell was dismissed for "public drunkenness, habitating with a newly divorced woman, and shooting his pistol in the middle of town." The new name, Kaniksu, was the local Native Americans' term for the Jesuit missionaries in the area. Friendly volunteer docents at the museum are on staff to answer your questions. Admission is free, and hours are Memorial Day to Labor Day, Tues.–Sun. 10 A.M.–4 P.M.

children canoeing on Priest Lake

RECREATION
Hanna Flats Cedar Grove
This small area just south of the Priest Lake Ranger District office in Nordman (look for signs marking the turnoff to the west) offers a short nature trail in summer, cross-country ski trails in winter, and a soggy, mosquito-infested bog in spring. Pick up the interpretive trail brochure at the ranger station; it explains that one reason these cedars survived is because they weren't considered valuable by early loggers. An interesting subplot dates from the settler days. A man named Gumpp built a cabin here once. He moved away for the winter, and when he returned, he found Jim Hanna and family living in his house. They had come upon the cabin, assumed it was abandoned, and moved in. Gumpp didn't raise a stink; he just moved on.

Beaver Creek Recreation Site
This is the main jumping-off point for hiking, mountain biking, and canoeing to Upper Priest Lake Scenic Area. Once the site of the Beaver Creek Ranger Station, the area offers a campground, picnic area, boat launch into the main lake, trailhead parking for the hiker-biker Navigation and Lakeshore Trails, and a 1,600-foot canoe-portage trail directly to the Thorofare. The site is on the lake's northwest shore; turn east on FR 2512 at Nordman and follow it north 12 miles.

Granite Falls/Roosevelt Grove
Actually just over the border in Washington, but reached only via Idaho, the short Granite Falls Trail (Trail 301) leads to views of upper and lower Granite Falls and continues to the Roosevelt Grove of Ancient Cedars. To get to the trailhead, continue north on Highway 57 past Nordman; the road eventually becomes FR 302. Most of the old-growth cedar grove here went up in flames in 1926. About 22 acres are left. The cedars—estimated average age 800 years—are impressive, but it's lower Granite Falls that steals the show. The roaring water rounds a corner at the top of the falls and plummets down a huge granite dihedral. Clever Forest Service engineers have constructed a truly scary viewpoint right out over the cliff edge.

Also at the trailhead is **Stagger Inn Picnic Area.** The area was named by firefighters who used it back in the 1920s as a base camp. At that time, the road up the east shore ended at Nordman, and the firefighters had to hike in from there—a distance of about 14 miles. By the time they got there, they were flat pooped, and many had to "stagger in."

On the way back to Priest Lake, don't miss the wacky **Shoe Tree.** You won't believe your eyes. In a gnomish scene right out of a fairy tale, old pairs of shoes completely cover the trunk of a huge cedar just off the highway. The local tradition started decades ago, but no one seems to remember why. If there's a Priest Lake local out there who knows the whole story, please fill me in. The tree is at the short spur to Trails 261 and 264, south of Granite Falls on the west side of the road.

Vinther-Nelson Cabin

You'll need a boat to get to this historic log cabin on Eightmile Island. The cabin was built in 1897 by the Crenshaw brothers, who tried their hand at mining on the island. After a year with no luck, the Crenshaws gave up and sold the cabin to W. J. Anders and family. Anders cleared the land and planted crops, but couldn't make a go of it. In 1900, he sold out to two cousins—Sam Vinther and Nels Nelson. Vinther and Nelson intended to revive the mine and make a fortune, but they never struck paydirt. Nevertheless, the two men and their families continued to live on the island. In 1967, the U.S. Dept. of Agriculture ordered that all private buildings on Priest Lake's federally owned islands be demolished. The descendants of Vinther and Nelson negotiated an agreement to allow the cabin to remain standing as a historic site open to the public. Inside the cabin you'll find a restored kitchen and a small museum. Outside, trails lead to great views and the old mine site, long since caved in. The cabin is open to visitors Wed.–Sun. 10 A.M.–3 P.M. in summer only; free admission.

Hiking and Biking

A favorite for hikers and mountain bikers alike is **Navigation Trail** (Trail 291). It begins at Beaver Creek Recreation Site and first enters a dense, fern-filled cedar forest. The trail can be mucky in places, but it's always beautiful. You'll pass an abandoned trapper's cabin before arriving at Plowboy Campground on the southwest shore of Upper Priest Lake. It's an easy three-mile hike to this point. You can picnic and head back from there, or continue north another three miles to Navigation Campground at the upper end of the lake. Between the two campgrounds the trail traverses a wooded lakeside slope, offering great views of the water and mountains at many points along the way. This portion of the trail is also easy. Fit hikers will have no problem hoofing it all the way from Beaver Creek to Navigation Campground and back—a roundtrip distance of 12 miles—in half a day.

Beaver Creek is also the trailhead for **Lakeshore Trail** (Trail 294), which heads south along the western edge of the lake for 7.6 miles. It's an easy and popular trail open to both hikers and bikers. Along the way you'll cross five streams, pass numerous campsites, and get great views of the lake.

Probably the most popular and heavily used trail at Priest Lake is the **Beach Trail** (Trail 48), which runs right by Hill's Resort, Luby Bay Campground, and several summer cabins. It's open to hikers only—no mountain bikes. The nine-mile trail runs between Kalispell Bay boat launch on the north and Outlet Bay on the south. Along the way it meanders through woods and along the beach, jumping back to Lakeshore Road for two short stretches.

Mountain bikers can make best use of the east side of the lake, particularly the northeast shore north of Priest Lake State Park's Lionhead Unit. Here, numerous gravel roads have been closed to motor vehicles, making for ideal mountain-biking country. For starters, try Caribou Creek Road, right out of the Lionhead campground.

For a map of the area and a longer list of trails, stop by the Priest Lake Ranger District office in Nordman. You can rent a mountain bike on the west shore at Hill's Resort on Luby Bay, 208/443-2551; cost is $15 per hour, $25 per half day, or $35 per full day.

Rock Climbing

How can you resist the looming block of **Chimney Rock** on the skyline of the Selkirks above the east shore of the lake? To anyone who has ever

THE PANHANDLE

strapped on sticky shoes and a harness, this granite monument cries out to be climbed. The 350-foot-high west face is split by several flake and crack systems, offering routes ranging from 5.3 to 5.11b. Access is via Horton Creek Road, which turns east off the lake's east shore road about 2.5 miles south of Priest Lake State Park's Indian Creek Unit. Follow the road all the way to the end and park. It's a one- to two-hour hike up to the base of the rock from there. And as long as you're up there, you might want to check out neighboring **Mt. Roothan,** which offers several other good routes. For more information, consult Randall Green's excellent book, *Idaho Rock,* now out of print but available via used book sources.

Floating the Priest River

The 44-mile stretch of the Priest River between Priest Lake and the town of Priest River makes a relatively easy float trip, taken either in segments or one long 14-hour day. The toughest rapids, Binarch and Eight Mile, are rated Class III. You'll also encounter three other Class II rapids along the way. In periods of high water—spring and early summer—the Class III rapids are unsuitable for novices. Later in the summer, the river's average depth decreases to three feet or less, and the slow, lazy stretches dominate; after mid-July, plan on dragging the bottom in places. For more information, contact the USFS Priest Lake Ranger District, 32203 Hwy. 57, Priest River, ID 83856-9612, 208/443-2512.

Fishing

Kokanee, cutthroat trout, rainbow trout, mackinaw—Priest Lake is full of scaly dinners-in-waiting. The Idaho Parks and Recreation Department suggests trying the following not-so-secret fishing spots: off East Shore Road about 5–6 miles south of Indian Creek; off the end of Pinto Point; and, for deep trolling, off the Kalispell-Papoose-Bartoe Island group (try a chartreuse crocodile as a trolling lure). If you'd like a local expert to take you out to the *real* secret spots, call **Priest Lake Outdoor Adventures,** at 208/443-5601.

The Priest Lake area is loaded with huckleberries. That's why the menus of so many local restaurants boast huckleberry pies, milk shakes, pancakes, cocktails— you name it.

Boating

The west shore resorts all have marinas with boat rentals. In and around Coolin you'll find **Bishop's Marina,** 208/443-2469, right next to Bishop's Resort on Coolin Bay, and **Blue Diamond Marina,** about five miles from Coolin at 958 Blue Diamond Rd., 208/443-2240, both of which rent boats.

Free **boat-launching ramps** are available at Coolin and at the USFS Luby Bay Campground on the west shore. Fee ramps can be found on the east shore at Cavanaugh Bay Marina and on the west shore at Priest Lake Marina (Kalispell Bay), Elkins Resort (Reeder Bay), and Grandview Resort (Reeder Bay).

Note: The Thorofare is a no-wake zone, and water-skiing and jet skiing are prohibited in Upper Priest Lake.

Golf

On the west shore, **Priest Lake Golf Club,** 152 Fairway Dr., Priest Lake, ID 83856, 208/443-2525, is a nine-hole, par-36 course measuring 3,097 yards from the long tees. It's a beautiful spot, and water comes into play on five holes. Greens fee is about $20. Club and cart rentals, lessons, and a driving range are available. In the winter, you can cross-country ski here.

Huckleberry Picking

The Priest Lake area is loaded with huckleberries. That's why the menus of so many local restaurants boast huckleberry pies, milk shakes, pancakes, cocktails—you name it. Berry-picking season runs mid-July to October. The berries like sun, so the best places to find them will be in open areas along logging roads and trails, mostly west of the lake. You can pick up a berry-picking map from the USFS Priest Lake Ranger Station, on Highway 57 just south of Nordman. Remember, bears love huckleberries, too. If you hear something big thrashing around in the bushes nearby, best yield dibs on the area.

Nordic Skiing

In winter, cross-country skiers and snowmobilers take advantage of the hundreds of miles of groomed and marked trails in the area. About five miles of mostly easy ski trails wind through the Indian Creek Unit of **Priest Lake State Park** on the lake's east shore. Across the lake, **Hanna Flats Cedar Grove** just south of Nordman tracks about four miles of easy loops as well. Heading south toward Priest River, the **Chipmunk Rapids Trail System** offers another 10.5 miles of trails.

CAMPING

Priest Lake State Park

Historical sites, natural-history interpretive information, and abundant recreation opportunities make Priest Lake State Park an outstanding destination. Two of the three units of the park are found along the lake's east shore.

Park headquarters is at the **Indian Creek Unit,** 11 miles north of Coolin on East Shore Road. Once a logging camp for the Diamond Match Company, the site displays a remnant of the logging operation—a section of the old flume that once floated logs into the lake from up to three miles away. It was built in 1946, at a cost of $30,000 per mile.

The campground's broad sandy beach attracts swimmers and sunbathers; others prefer to hike one of the two easy hiking trails meandering through the woods, or play volleyball or basketball on the campground's courts. A boat-launching ramp lets you float your boat. Throughout summer, the interpretive center presents a full slate of events, including educational campfire programs, guided walks and bike rides, and junior ranger activities. In winter, the park offers easy access to more than 300 miles of groomed and marked snowmobile and cross-country ski trails.

The Indian Creek Unit's 93 campsites—some with hookups, some without—range $12–18 per site per night. Two cabins are also available for $35 a night. Other on-site facilities include a camp store, showers and toilets, and an RV dump station. The campgrounds are popular and fill up in summer. Reservations can be made by contacting the park manager, Priest Lake State Park, 314 Indian Creek Park Rd., Coolin, ID 83821, 208/443-6710.

Twelve miles farther north along the east shore, at the mouth of Lion Creek on the lake's northern tip, is the park's **Lionhead Unit.** From 1922 to 1925, Canadian-born silent-film actor and filmmaker **Nell Shipman** operated a movie studio on this site, producing wildlife/outdoor-adventure films and maintaining a veritable menagerie of 70 animal actors used in the films. Although several of the shorts and features filmed here were successful, the studio's high-overhead operation eventually drove it into bankruptcy. The animals were shipped off to the San Diego Zoo, and Shipman returned to Hollywood. She continued to work in the film industry, though no longer as a star, and died in Los Angeles in 1970. Several of her films have been rediscovered, restored, and assembled in a collection at Boise State University.

Also here you'll find the sunken shell of the *Tyee II,* lying in the shallow waters of Mosquito Bay just offshore. The vessel was a steamer tug used to haul large booms of logs from the Diamond Match flume site to the lake's outlet, where the logs were ferried down the Priest River to the sawmill. Towing a full load of logs, the tug managed just a half mile an hour and took some 60 hours to reach the end of the lake. On such a trip, the tug would typically burn 10 cords of wood. The operation lasted until 1959, when the *Tyee* was stripped of its iron and scuttled where you see it today.

The Lionhead Unit is smaller than the Indian Creek Unit and less developed. The 47 sites don't have hookups. Hiking trails wind through the woods, across Lion Creek, and out to the beach (where you just might find moose tracks in the sand). The park is also an excellent launching place for boaters heading to Upper Priest Lake. The Lionhead Unit is open in summer and fall only. Camping fee is $9 a night.

The **Dickensheet Unit** is the most primitive of the state park's three units. It's on Priest River south of the lake, between Coolin and the junction with Highway 57. The campground offers 11 sites with minimal facilities for $7 a night.

It's a great place to kick back with a fishin' pole, away from the crowds up on the lake.

Forest Service Campgrounds

Forest Service campgrounds ring both lower and upper Priest Lake. Many more are found on two islands out in the lake (see Island Camping, below). All campsites charge a fee and are open mid-May to the end of September, weather permitting. Camping is limited to 14 days.

From south to north on the west shore, the campgrounds are: **Outlet,** 31 sites; **Osprey,** 18 sites; **Lower Luby Bay** (lakefront) and **Upper Luby Bay** (across the road in the woods), 54 sites total, RV dump station; **Reeder Bay,** 24 sites; **Beaver Creek,** 41 sites. Fees at the campgrounds range $8–10 per night. Reeder Bay, Beaver Creek, and the two Luby Bay campgrounds accept reservations. To reserve a site, call NRRS at 877/444-6777. For more information, call the Priest Lake Ranger District at 208/443-2512.

Four more campgrounds on Upper Priest Lake are accessible only by boat or by a hike. On the west side of the upper lake are **Plowboy Campground,** with four sites at the south end of the lake, and **Navigation Campground,** offering five sites on the lake's north end. Along the east shore of the upper lake are **Geisinger's Campground,** with two sites, and **Trapper Creek,** with five more. All four upper-lake campgrounds are free.

Island Camping

In addition to the mainland campgrounds listed above, the Forest Service maintains extremely popular boat-in campgrounds on Kalispell Island (12 campgrounds and two day-use areas), Bartoo Island (five campgrounds and two day-use areas), and Fourmile Island (one campsite). All are first-come, first-served and cost $5 a head.

Some of the campgrounds have vault toilets, others don't. Because of the heavy summer use, the Forest Service now requires campers staying at campgrounds without vault toilets to carry and use their own portable toilets while on the island. When they return to the Kalispell boat launch—the most commonly used public boat launch for trips to the islands—a free SCAT (Sanitizing Containers with Alternative Technologies) machine there will clean their portable toilets. The machine works like a giant, coin-operated dishwasher, flushing the waste into the mainland sewage system and sterilizing the container.

Island campers are permitted to stay 14 days maximum. Pick up a map to island campgrounds at the Priest Lake Ranger District office.

One Further Reminder

This is bear country, so keep a clean camp. Dispose of all trash properly and promptly, and don't leave food out on picnic tables.

ACCOMMODATIONS

Resorts

Several resorts dot the lake's west side. The biggest, plushest, and most popular with the tourist set is the venerable **Hill's Resort** at Luby Bay, 4777 W. Lakeshore Rd., Priest Lake, ID 83856, 208/443-2551, www.hillsresort.com. Both *Better Homes and Gardens* and *Family Circle* magazines have named Hill's as one of their favorite family resorts in the country. The Hill family has run the resort since 1946. They offer accommodations in either private cabins or condolike housekeeping units, most with fireplaces. Amenities include a marina; swimming areas; tennis and volleyball courts; hiking, biking, cross-country skiing, and snowmobiling trails; a gourmet restaurant; and a lounge with live entertainment in season. In summer, bookings are taken only for stays of a week or longer. Summer rates (in effect from the last Saturday in June until the Tuesday after Labor Day weekend) range from around $970 to $2,775 per unit per week. The rest of the year, rates are about 15 percent lower, and nightly rates are available. Units vary in size, sleeping anywhere from two to 12 people.

Elkins on Priest Lake, 404 Elkins Rd., Nordman ID, 83848, 208/443-2432, www.elkinsresort.com, is another year-round, full-service resort. Accommodations are in individual log cabins, most with fireplace and all with kitchen, full bath and private bedroom(s); you need to bring your own soap and towels. The lodge restaurant, overlooking the lake and nicely landscaped grounds, serves top-notch Pacific Rim–inspired cuisine daily in summer and between Christmas and New Year's (limited schedule the rest of the year). The Trapper Creek Lounge is one of the west shore's social hubs, often presenting live music that draws in the locals. Other amenities include a marina, beaches, volleyball, and recreation trails. You must book for a week or longer here in the peak summer season, early July to late August. Weekly rates range $990 for a creekside cabin sleeping four to $2,895 for a lakefront cabin sleeping 14. The rest of the year, rates are about 15 percent lower and a two-night minimum (three nights on holiday weekends) is in effect.

Grandview Resort, 3492 Reeder Bay Rd., Priest Lake, ID 83848, 208/443-2433, offers cottages, lodge rooms, and suites with, yes, grand views of Reeder Bay. Amenities include a small swimming pool, a marina with boat rentals, and a bright dining room overlooking the lake. It's open year-round. Peak season rates range from $75 a night, for a lodge room with one queen bed, up to $245 a night for a private lakeview cottage sleeping 10. Weekly rates are available. No pets.

Motels
$50–100: The Inn at Priest Lake, 5310 Dickensheet Rd. (at Cavenaugh Bay Rd.), Coolin, ID 83821, 208/443-4066, is a short distance away from the lake and offers little in the way of views. The big hexagonal structure looks something like a stone fort dropped incongruously into the woods. But the inn's modern amenities are welcome and include a year-round heated pool and spa, restaurant, and lounge. Spa suites and kitchenettes are available. The inn has a nicely landscaped backyard and is within walking distance of Coolin culture. Pets okay for an extra $10. The inn's RV park offers 12 well-kept, pull-through sites with full hookups (including TV) for $25 a night. Restroom and shower facilities available. It's also open year-round.

Bed-and-Breakfasts
$50–100: On the banks of the Priest River at Outlet Bay is **Whispering Waters B&B,** 360 Outlet Bay Rd., Priest Lake, ID 83856, 208/443-

3229. Each of its three immaculate and superbly decorated guest rooms has a private bath, propane fireplace/stove, and outside entrance. You can go swimming right off the private dock, borrow a mountain bike to explore the lakeshore trails, or take a rowboat out for a spin. Morning brings the aroma of fresh-brewed coffee, followed by a full breakfast, as heavy or light as you'd like. No pets, or children under 12; smoking permitted outside only. To get to Whispering Waters, follow Highway 57 to the west shore and turn right on Outlet Bay Road; look for a sign about a half mile down on the right. This is a very nice, very friendly place.

$100–150: In Coolin, **The Old Northern Inn,** 220 Bayview Dr., P.O. Box 177, Coolin, ID 83821, 208/443-2426, occupies the former Northern Hotel, a turn-of-the-20th-century haven for travelers to the secluded shores of Priest Lake. The restored two-story wooden structure holds antique furnishings and first-class modern amenities. The atmosphere is one of rustic elegance. The beautiful, cedar-paneled living room features a stone fireplace and picture windows looking out on the lake. Old photographs and newspaper clippings provide a historical accent. The lake is practically at your doorstep—just a short walk down a wooded slope to the private dock and beach. The four standard rooms (two at $50–100) and two suites all have private baths. Rates include a full breakfast (look for huckleberry pancakes) and afternoon wine and cheese. Children over age 12 are welcome, pets aren't. Smoking is permitted outdoors only. The inn is on your left just before you come to the Leonard Paul Store and Bishop's Marina.

FOOD
The resort restaurants are safe bets for good grub in Priest Lake. On the west shore, **Hill's Resort** in particular has an excellent reputation for fine cuisine. Also on the west shore are **Frizzy O'Leary's Corner,** corner of Hwy. 57 and Luby Bay Rd., 208/443-3043, a quiet, comfortable American-food café and lounge filled with quiet, comfortable old locals; and **Millie's,** a bit farther south, 208/443-2365, serving respectable south-of-the-border fare and offering a more youthful energetic

atmosphere than Frizzy's. As a bonus, Millie's features several microbrews on tap.

On the east side, you'll get a good meal for a reasonable price at **Bishop's Resort,** 352 Bay View Dr., Coolin, 208/443-2191. The place is run by friendly folks and attracts a fair share of local characters. **The Woods** tavern and restaurant, 208/443-2042, is up the hill from Bishop's. It's a local institution serving breakfast, lunch, and dinner daily.

INFORMATION AND SERVICES

The **Priest Lake Chamber of Commerce** can be reached at P.O. Box 174, Coolin, ID 83821, 208/443-3191 or 888/774-3785, www.priest-lake.org. For national forest recreation information, contact the USFS **Priest Lake Ranger District,** 32203 Hwy. 57, Priest River, ID 83856, 208/443-2512. The ranger station is just south of Nordman on the east side of the highway.

Highway 200: Pend Oreille Scenic Byway

HOPE AND VICINITY

East of Sandpoint, Highway 200 skirts the north shore of Pend Oreille Lake, soon coming to Hope, East Hope, and even Beyond Hope. On a warm summer's day, this area of big trees and big water is sublime. Perhaps that's why famed Canadian geographer and explorer David Thompson built the very first fur-trading outpost in Idaho, Kullyspell House, on the Hope peninsula way back in 1809. Today, Thompson is commemorated with the David Thompson Game Preserve here. Also on the peninsula are posh homes hidden away in the woods, a superb national forest campground, and great views of the lake at every turn.

The Floater

Known all over the Panhandle as "the Floater," the **Floating Restaurant and Lounge** at Pend Oreille Shores Resort, Hwy. 200, East Hope, 208/264-5311, is a local landmark. You walk out a creaky-tippy dock to get there, past sailboats and motorboats and rowboats. Once there, you can sit either inside or out on the big, marina-side deck. Seafood seems appropriate here—try the scrumptious Copper River sockeye salmon with orange-ginger sauce. Dinner entrées range $15–22. The food is good, but aah, the atmosphere. Kick back with a good microbrew or glass of wine; watch the sun set over the boats bobbing in the harbor; listen to the cry of the seagulls so far from Pacific shores. Highly recommended.

Houseboat Rentals

You could spend a far worse two-week vacation than lazily cruising Lake Pend Oreille with some friends on a houseboat. **BC & M Houseboat Vacations,** at Hope Marine Services, 1245 Hwy. 200, 877/909-BOAT (877/909-2628), rents houseboats in sizes sleeping eight and 10 people, respectively. In peak summer season, the smaller size costs around $900 for a three-day weekend/$1,350 a week, while the larger rents for around $1,200/1,900. In early and late season you'll pay about 10–15 percent less. A refundable $500 damage deposit is required. All boats have a propane barbecue, a swim ladder and water slide, an AM/FM radio and CD player, a TV/VCR (usable when plugged in at the dock), a VHF radio, charts, a fishfinder, and all safety equipment. The layout includes a full kitchen, bathroom, stateroom, living room, and full-length sundeck up top. You may never want to come home.

Fishing Guides

Hope's marina is a center for charter boats on Pend Oreille Lake. Twenty- to 30-pound rainbow trout are the sought-after prize for many anglers. Others fish for mackinaw, kokanee, or cutthroat trout. **Seagull Charters,** 208/263-2770, docks its funky, comfy 34-foot cruiser right next to the Floater. The boat will accommodate up to eight anglers, or up to 30 non-fishing folks out for just a cruise. Other charter companies based in Hope include **Diamond Charters,** P.O. Box 153, Hope, ID 83836, 208/265-2565 or 800/487-

6886, and **Eagle Charters,** P.O. Box 101, Hope, ID 83836, 208/264-5274.

Accommodations

$100–150: Red Fir Resort, 1147 Red Fir Rd., 208/264-5287, is a little gem tucked away on the secluded northwest side of the Hope Peninsula, facing Ellisport Bay and the Cabinet Mountains beyond. Twelve cabins perch on a quiet and gentle tree-covered slope overlooking the lake. The cabins vary in size, with some sleeping up to eight people; a few are below and above this price range. Each cabin has a private deck, barbecue, full kitchen, and bath. The resort also has its own dock and swimming area. Open April–Nov.

Right next to the Floater is **Pend Oreille Shores Resort,** 47390 Hwy. 200 (between mile markers 47 and 48), 208/264-5828. It's a plush condo development with rental units available in this price range and above. Each unit has a kitchen, washer and dryer, stereo, TV/VCR, and fireplace. An on-site athletic club features an indoor pool, hot tubs, racquetball and tennis courts, sauna, weight room.

Camping and RVing

West of Hope in the Trestle Creek area is the 180-site **Idaho Country Resort,** 141 Idaho Country Rd., Hope, ID 83836, 208/264-5505 or 800/307-3050, one of the nicest RV parks on the lake. This is a great spot, right on the water. The beautifully maintained park is comprised of two separate units, both of which offer dock space as well as RV sites. Rates are around $25–30 a day for up to four people, including electric hookups. Tent sites and summer cottages are also available, as are boat, jet ski, kayak, and bicycle rentals.

Out on the Hope peninsula, you'll find two RV parks and a superbly located National Forest campground. To get to the peninsula, continue east two miles past Hope and watch for the Samowen Road turnoff on the right. Especially appealing here is the area's status as a game refuge. In the early morning and evening hours, large numbers of nearly tame deer feed on the grassy hills, very near to the Winnebagos and awestruck, clucking campers. Keep your camera ready.

Beyond Hope Resort & RV Park, 1267 Peninsula Rd., 208/264-5251, offers 85 sites with full hookups on about 50 acres of neatly manicured grounds right at the edge of the lake. A 600-foot beach makes for easy splashing. Other amenities include a cocktail lounge, rec hall, snack bar, and laundry. Rates are $27 a night with cable TV hookup, $25 without, $2 more for every extra person over age 6.

Island View RV Resort is just down the road at 1767 Peninsula Rd., 208/264-5509. It's more crowded than Beyond Hope, but the general idea is the same—great lakefront property. Facilities include a marina, gas, boat rentals, rec room, small store, laundry, and hot showers. The rate is about $25 a day for two people, including full hookups. The park is open May 1–Oct. 1.

Also on the Hope peninsula, the Forest Service's **Samowen Campground** offers million-dollar lakefront property for $13–14 a night. This is without a doubt the Ritz of the state's USFS campgrounds. Locals love it, so it fills up in summer. But it's a big area and the sites are large. Head straight for the Skipping Stone Loop; units 32, 33, and 35 are among the choicest, just steps from the water. The area also makes a great day-use destination; day-use fee is $5. Reservations are available through NRRS, 877/444-6777 or www.reserveusa.com. For more information call the USFS **Sandpoint Ranger District** at 208/263-5111.

CLARK FORK AND VICINITY

Clark Fork is the last outpost of civilization you'll pass through before crossing into Montana. The town enjoys a scenic location in the shadow of the Cabinet Mountains, at the confluence of the Clark Fork River and picturesque Lightning Creek. "Downtown" holds a couple of stores and taverns but not much else. A couple of RV parks are in the vicinity.

University of Idaho, Clark Fork Field Campus

Lucky forestry students from UI in Moscow get to come out here to study. The "campus," formerly the old Clark Fork ranger station, is tucked away in the forest at the foot of Antelope Mountain, on the banks of Mosquito Creek. An outstanding interpretive trail loops along the creek, offering a cool, leg-stretching break from your road trip. In addition to classes attended by students in UI's College of Forestry, Wildlife, and Range Sciences, the school hosts an Elderhostel course and regular seminars open to the public. Topics have included grizzly bears, Native American history, medicinal plants, and local natural history. To get to the campus, take Main Street in Clark Fork first north, then east, for about 1.5 miles, following signs. For more information, call the campus manager at 208/266-1452, or write to University of Idaho, Field Campus, P.O. Box 87, Clark Fork, ID 83811.

Cabinet Gorge Dam

Virtually at the Idaho-Montana border, this is the last point of interest along Highway 200 before you leave the state behind and venture into Montana. The dam is 208 feet high and 600 feet long, and backs up the 20-mile-long Clark Fork Reservoir, almost entirely in Montana. The spectacle of the water surging through narrow Cabinet Gorge is a powerful one indeed. Imagine what it must have looked like when ancient glacial Lake Missoula broke through here to carve out the gorge in the first place.

Day Hike

A popular and strenuous trail starts outside Clark Fork and leads to the top of **Scotchman Peak,** a 7,000-foot sentry watching over Pend Oreille Lake to the west and the lofty Montana skyline to the east. The views from the summit can't be beat. The trail is only seven miles roundtrip, but climbs some 3,700 feet in less than four miles. To reach the trailhead, follow Clark Fork's Main Street north. It soon turns into FR 276. Continue past the turnoff to the UI Field Campus. When the road forks about a mile farther down the road, bear right, following signs to Trail 65. One mile farther, turn left on FR 2294A, then turn left again a half mile down that road. After a little over two miles, make one last left and proceed one-eighth mile to the trailhead. If all that seems too confusing, ask the rangers at the Sandpoint Ranger District Office in Sandpoint to draw you a map.

Horseback Riding

At **Idaho Outdoor Experience,** Cabinet Gorge Rd., Box 25, Clark Fork, ID 83811, 208/266-1216, you can rent a horse for around $20 an hour ($30 minimum). The outfit also offers all-day lunch rides (around $75) and dinner rides (around $85), summertime wagon rides, and wintertime sleigh rides. Reservations required; call for directions.

North to Canada

NAPLES

From Sandpoint, Highway 95 continues north toward the Canadian border. Ten miles south of Bonners Ferry is the tiny farming and logging community of Naples. Other than an occasional rowdy night of darts at the Northwoods Tavern, the tiny hamlet is usually quiet as can be. Its setting is magnificent. Just west of town, forested ridges climb in ever-higher waves up into the lofty Selkirk Mountains. The rugged peak of Roman Nose—usually snowcapped well into summer—dominates the skyline, sending several creeks rushing down toward Naples from the alpine snowfields. Heading north from town

on the scenic old road, you'll cross one beautiful creek after another. One of these, Ruby Creek, flows past Ruby Ridge just outside town.

Spend some time pulled up to the bar at the Northwoods and you'll quickly get a neatly distilled view of what draws a certain independent breed to northern Idaho. First off, there just aren't many people here. The state's visitors guide dutifully lists population figures for almost every town in Idaho, but not Naples. One suspects the local residents probably like that. Everyone here knows everyone else, and the social code they all live by can be summed up by one word: respect.

First and foremost, they respect each other's privacy. Folks live here because they want to be left alone—by the government, by tourist hordes, by strangers. But that doesn't mean they're antisocial. In appropriate places—down at the Northwoods, for example—locals treat visitors with the same respect they give each other. Call it old-fashioned common courtesy, but it's refreshing in this day and age. Folks here call you "sir" or "ma'am" until you suggest otherwise. They'll be friendly and polite, and answer, without snickering, any dumb tourist questions you might have.

They respect each other's property as well. If you stop in at the Northwoods for a quick beer, then get to Bonners Ferry and realize you left your wallet back on the bar—don't worry, it'll be waiting for you behind the bar with all your money in it. Folks here look out for each other. If your car breaks down in Naples, half the town will probably come to your aid.

The other side of all this neighborliness can be encountered also, should you for some unknown reason go looking for trouble. If you drive into the hills and ignore a No Trespassing sign, don't be surprised if you're promptly turned around, very likely facing a loaded 30.06 as added inducement.

Just about every residence prominently displays a familiar green sign reading "This Family Supported By Timber Dollars." Depending on your point of view, logging might be a topic of conversation to avoid down at the Northwoods Tavern. But there's a lesson to be learned here. Even if you're diametrically opposed to the loggers' environmental stance, you can't make the disagreement personal; the people you meet at the Northwoods—and places like it in little logging towns across the state—are by and large some of the finest, most honest and upfront people you'll ever meet.

Accommodations

Under $50: The **Naples HI Hostel,** Hwy. 2, Naples, ID 83847, 208/267-2947, occupies a former 1940s dancehall adjacent to the Naples General Store. It's open year-round with 23 beds; the dorm bunks cost just $10–12. The friendly managers, who also run the store, will gladly share their knowledge of the area with you. The hostel offers a large, comfortable common area with a woodstove, piano, TV, radio, sofa, and large dining table. Near the door you'll find the hostel log, recording the comments of visitors from all over the globe. One of them wrote that he had the "freight-train blues," a reference, no doubt, to the frequent and somewhat noisy passage of freight trains on the tracks very near the hostel. Off the common area are a kitchen, two bathrooms, the usual hostel-style dormitory rooms, and several private bedrooms offering comfortable beds with fresh linens. Unless the place is nearly full, you can have your choice of any empty room, including one of the private ones, at no extra charge. A separate building out back houses showers and a coin laundry. Office hours are 8–10 A.M. and 3–8 P.M. Reservations (not essential) are accepted; credit cards aren't. Highly recommended.

Camping

A bit farther north on Highway 95 is **Blue Lake RV Park,** HC1 Box 244C, 208/267-2029, a large and very clean, full-facility park surrounding a nice, no-license fishing pond. Sites go for around $18–22 a night with hookups; tent sites $12.

Another option in the area is to spend the night in the lofty perch of the USFS **Black Mountain Lookout,** a fire lookout tower northeast of Naples that is now rented out by the Forest Service. Four people at a time are allowed atop the 53-foot tower, but it has only one twin bed. It's available for $25 a night, usually from mid-June until the end of September. Small children are discouraged. For directions and more information, contact the **Bonners Ferry Ranger District,** 6286 Main St., Bonners Ferry, ID 83805, 208/267-5561.

Food and Drink

Right next door to the Naples General Store is the **Northwoods Tavern,** the town's social hub. Inside you'll find a couple of pool tables, dartboards, a jukebox, good conversation, and plenty of basic American beer.

North a few miles on Highway 2 (old Highway 95, which parallels Highway 95 just to the west), you'll find **Deep Creek Inn Bed and Breakfast,** 208/267-2729. Naples locals consider this the

THE PANHANDLE

area's "fancy" restaurant. The restaurant hugs the idyllic banks of Deep Creek and serves breakfast, lunch, and dinner every day but Monday. The dinner menu offers traditional American fare—steaks, prawns, chicken, prime rib. Entrées average around $15. The dining room is lined with knotty pine and big bay windows, while the creekside deck is the place to be on a sunny summer's day. Cabins ($35–65) and RV sites are also available.

BONNERS FERRY AND VICINITY

In 1834, 24-year-old New Yorker Edwin Bonner came west, intent on using his already considerable experience in the retail trade to establish himself as a successful frontier businessman. After opening a department store in Walla Walla, Washington, he passed through Idaho's northernmost reaches and noted that the well-traveled ford of the Kootenai River—used by miners stampeding north to British Columbia's goldfields—needed a ferry. By 1864, he had built his ferry and begun to operate it successfully. Eventually Bonner left the area and settled in Missoula, Montana, where he became a wealthy and powerful merchant and political leader. Despite his departure, the town that grew up here stuck with its original name.

Boundary County Historical Society Museum

A repository of regional history, this small museum at 7229 Main St., across from City Hall, 208/267-7720, holds a wealth of historical photos and artifacts. Check out the proud portraits of the Bonners Ferry High School class of 1925—all 20 graduating seniors. The museum is open Mon.–Fri. 10 A.M.–4 P.M. in summer season only. Admission is free, donations appreciated.

Kootenai National Wildlife Refuge

Before the building of dikes and Montana's Libby Dam tamed the Kootenai River, annual spring floods washed over the valley floor here, creating prime wetlands for migratory waterfowl. The dikes made for flood-free farming but took away the wildlife habitat. This 2,774-acre refuge west of town was created to mitigate that loss. The refuge is kept flooded with water diverted from the Kootenai River and two local creeks. Today, tens of thousands of waterfowl pass through the refuge every year.

In spring, look for mallards, northern pintails, American wigeon, and tundra swans on their way north. In late summer and early fall, the refuge attracts large numbers of Canada geese. Birdwatchers might also catch sight of bald eagles and ospreys. Among other wildlife occasionally seen: black bears, white-tailed deer, moose, and elk. In all, 230 bird species and 45 mammal species have been observed here.

A 4.5-mile loop road circles the refuge, and several hiking trails (one wheelchair-accessible) lead to good photo vantage points. The refuge is open during daylight hours only. To get there, take Riverside Road five miles west from town. For more information, stop in at the on-site refuge office (open weekdays 8 A.M.–4:30 P.M.) or contact Kootenai National Wildlife Refuge, HCR 60, Box 283, Bonners Ferry, ID 83805, 208/267-3888, http://kootenai.fws.gov.

Day Hikes

Hiking opportunities abound in the mountains surrounding Bonners Ferry. The easiest day hike is to **Snow Creek Falls.** The short (less than a mile), well-maintained footpath leads down a gentle grade to either the lower or upper falls. Cedars, Douglas firs, and birches shade the trail, while lupine, Indian paintbrush, and other wildflowers provide the color commentary. Along the way are a couple of short spurs to tranquil rest spots complete with benches. Though not high, the falls are very powerful. A whole lot of water roars through here when the spring sunshine puts the Selkirks' snowpack on a diet. This hike is suitable even for couch potatoes. Highly recommended.

Other USFS-suggested day hikes in the area include **Black Mountain to Clifty Mountain,** a ridgetop hike offering great views, and the **Burton Peak** trail, which climbs three miles to the remnants of a Forest Service lookout tower and is negotiable for much of the year. Carry water with you on both of these.

As with all backcountry users, day-hikers are advised to check with the local Forest Service office for current conditions and restrictions. The **Bonners Ferry Ranger District** office is at the south end of town, 6286 Main St., Bonners Ferry, ID 83805, 208/267-5561.

Long Canyon

Notable as a roadless, unlogged drainage, Long Canyon climbs from West Side Road up toward the Selkirk Crest. It's seven miles up the trail to the first crossing of Long Canyon Creek—a good distance for a strenuous day hike. The good news is the Forest Service has no plans to open the drainage for logging. The bad news is, as one ranger put it, "it's a ho-hum forest" here. Still, keep your eyes open and you might see a rare goshawk or two. A nest has been spotted on the lower part of the trail.

The Selkirk Crest

The snowy heights of the Selkirk Crest are home to two endangered mammals: the grizzly bear and the woodland caribou. Despite efforts by government wildlife agencies to encourage the growth of the griz and caribou populations, the

Kootenai River near Bonners Ferry

two species cling to a precarious existence in the Selkirks. Roads lead high up toward the crest, and as a consequence, the area is heavily used by backpackers. Give the wild things a break. Idaho is full of high, snowy realms that are *not* home to endangered species. Go somewhere else.

Lookout

Up in the Selkirks about four miles south of the Canadian border is the rentable USFS **Shorty Peak** lookout. It's a 2.5-mile hike to the 15- by 15-foot cabin, perched at an elevation of 6,515 feet. The tower sleeps two and offers panoramic views of Creston Valley and the surrounding peaks. It's open from around July 1 to Sept. 30. This lookout is in the domain of Mr. Griz, so take all appropriate precautions. Rental fee is $20 a night. For reservations, directions, and more information, contact the **Bonners Ferry Ranger District,** 6286 Main St., Bonners Ferry, ID 83805, 208/267-5561.

Rafting

Northeast of Bonners Ferry, the **Moyie River** provides Panhandle rafters with a one-day whitewater stretch during its high-water season, April–June. Lots of rock gardens among the Class II and III rapids can make it an interesting ride. **ROW,** P.O. Box 579, Coeur d'Alene, ID 83816, 208/765-0841 or 800/451-6034, runs guided Moyie trips that begin and end in Moyie Springs. Cost for the day trip is around $85–100.

The lazy **Kootenai River** isn't in a hurry to do much of anything. It eases out of Montana into Idaho, wanders aimlessly back and forth up the Purcell Trench, then crosses the border into British Columbia to feed Kootenay Lake. The Class I float is perfect for leisurely canoeing and wildlife watching, particularly west of town where the river flows past Kootenai National Wildlife Refuge.

Golf

Bonners Ferry's **Mirror Lake Golf Course** is just south of town on Highway 95, 208/267-5314. The popular, nine-hole course offers broad, unimpeded views of the Purcell Trench looking out toward Kootenai National Wildlife Refuge. Greens fee is about $15 for nine holes. Cart and

THE PANHANDLE

club rentals available. Ask about local "Stay and Play" packages.

Nordic Skiing

The northernmost of the state's Park N' Ski areas, **Snow Creek Park N' Ski** lies 14 miles west of Bonners Ferry. Turn west off Highway 95 south of town just before the golf course. The turnoff is marked with a sign for the Park N' Ski area. Follow the road west for a short distance, then watch for Snow Creek Road 402 on the right. Snow Creek Road heads north up the valley a couple of miles before branching west once again and beginning its climb into the Selkirks. You'll probably need chains to make it to the trailhead; the road is steep and very icy in places. Parking at the trailhead may consist of no more than one small plowed slot, depending on the good graces of the plow driver.

The well-marked trail system provides a variety of interesting routes. On the Hemlock trail, you'll see numerous examples of the trail's namesake, the delicate mountain hemlock. It was John Muir's favorite tree, easily recognizable by its graceful drooping crown. Another trail, the Toboggan Run, should be avoided by all but expert skiers—it's a long, steep climb on a narrow trail through many trees. If you have climbing skins with you, use 'em. Otherwise, prepare for herringbone hell. The only thing I can imagine worse than going up Toboggan Run would be going *down* Toboggan Run. Unless you have a death wish, don't try to descend this trail unless plenty of soft, fresh snow is on the ground to cushion your inevitable face-plant.

Although these trails are high in the mountains, they're not high enough to offer any panoramic views. Most of the views you do get, unfortunately, are of ugly clearcuts on the neighboring hillsides. The trail system here is not extensive. The longest loop will take you just over an hour, about the time it takes to drive to the trailhead from Bonners Ferry in all but the best conditions. Grooming is minimal, and on weekends, snowmobilers will be buzzing about the vicinity. Although some of the trails are rated for beginners, I wouldn't recommend the area for novices. And it's a tough call to say whether more experienced skiers will find the area worth their while.

Outfitters

Rent rafts, kayaks, canoes, mountain bikes, cross-country skis, and ice skates at **Far North Outfitters,** 6802 Main St., 208/267-5547.

Accommodations

$50–100: On the south approach to town is **Bear Creek Lodge,** Hwy. 95 S. (at County Rd. 2C), Rt. 4 Box 5010, Bonners Ferry, ID 83805, 208/267-7268, which offers log-style rooms, a hot tub, bistro-style restaurant, and complimentary continental breakfast.

Kootenai Valley Motel, 208/267-7567, is a short distance north of Bear Creek Lodge, also on Highway 95. This one has a large grassy area out front and some nice specialty rooms with kitchenettes or fireplaces. An indoor spa takes the chill off the cold winter nights. A couple of other motels can be found along the highway in this area.

On the north end of town, two miles north of the Kootenai River on the west side of Highway 95, is **Bonners Ferry Log Inn,** HCR 85, Box 6, Bonners Ferry, ID 83805, 208/267-3986. Like Mama's, it's a modern log design. Although it's right along the highway, it's farther away from the hustle and bustle than the motels on the south side of town. The gardenlike, beautifully landscaped grounds; warm, comfortable rooms; and toasty hot tub will combine to drop your blood pressure off the bottom end of the sphygmomanometer. All things considered, this place is a steal.

$100–150: The largest and swankest lodging in town is the **Best Western Kootenai River Inn and Casino,** downtown on the east side of the Kootenai River bridge, Kootenai River Plaza, Bonners Ferry, ID 83805, 208/267-8511 or 800/346-5668. The inn is owned by the local Kootenai tribe, and for better or worse, Indian gaming is here to stay. Slot machines and bingo in north Idaho may seem tacky, but the money the gambling operation sucks in—primarily from white tourists—helps keep the tribe alive. Perhaps it's an appropriate payback for the long-downtrodden Kootenai people, though it's hard to say whether old Chief Michel is laughing or rolling over in his grave. In any case, the inn boasts the best location in town and offers all the finest amenities. Some rooms under $100 are available. The inn's Springs Restaurant overlooks the river and offers upscale fare and outstanding ambience.

Paradise Valley Inn, 300 Eagle Way, P.O. Box 689, Bonners Ferry, ID 83805, 208/267-4180 or 888/447-4180, offers elegant and comfortable B&B accommodations on a secluded 64-acre spread 10 minutes southeast of town. Views from the modern rustic-lodge-style ranch house are impressive, and all five guest rooms (one at $175) have private bath. Rates include gourmet breakfast, served inside or out on the log porch. Lunches and four-course dinners are available at extra charge. To reach the inn, take Paradise Valley Road east off Highway 95 at the stoplight in Bonners Ferry and follow the signs for 3.5 miles. Open year-round.

Food
A rare treat awaits discriminating diners in Bonners Ferry. **Alberto's,** 6536 S. Main St., 208/267-7493, is a superb, gourmet-caliber Mexican restaurant, among the very best in all of Idaho. Alberto hails from Mexico City, bringing with him his favorite recipes from Central Mexico. Everything on the small but artful menu is made from scratch. Try the heavenly Azteca, a baked concoction consisting of layered corn tortillas, shredded chicken, cheese, and an out-of-this-world homemade mole. *Carne asada* and *camarones* (shrimp), separately or together, are other specialties of the house. Entrées average around $9–11 and come with excellent tortilla chips, salsa, and soup. Choose from six Mexican *cervezas,* all served in chilled mugs.

The decor here is as artistic as the food. Before opening his restaurant, Alberto was a professional photographer; his photographs of Old Mexico line the walls, along with an exceptional collection of Mexican folk art. Even the woven-cane baskets for the tortilla chips are simple and elegant. Taped Mexican folk music rounds out the ambience. Alberto himself is the sort of character you'd love to hang out with, exchanging tales of love and life over a pitcher of sangria.

All in all, Alberto's is as close to perfection as it gets. Highly recommended.

At the Kootenai River Inn, **The Springs Restaurant,** 208/267-8511, offers upscale atmosphere, an eclectic menu of steaks, seafood, poultry, and pastas, and great views of the Kootenai River. It's open for three meals daily. Dinner entrées range around $12–18.

When caffeine calls, **The Creamery** answers. In addition to great high-octane espresso, you can also get sandwiches, frozen yogurt, and other goodies here. The smell of fresh-made waffle cones beckons halfway down the block. The little storefront emporium is at 6426 Kootenai St., 208/267-2690; open Mon.–Fri. 8 A.M.–4:30 P.M.

Information and Services
The **Bonners Ferry Chamber of Commerce Visitor Center** is in the parking lot across the highway from the Kootenai River Inn, 208/267-5922, www.bonnersferrychamber.com. It's usually closed in winter (though if you drive by, you might find someone there). Inquiries year-round can be addressed to P.O. Box X, Bonners Ferry, ID 83805, 208/267-2883. The USFS **Bonners Ferry Ranger District** office is on the south edge of town, 6286 Main St., Bonners Ferry, ID 83805, 208/267-5561.

Bonner's Books, 7195 Main St., 208/267-2622, offers a great map section with topographic maps, 3D relief maps, even a globe of the moon. Art postcards tempt you to catch up on your correspondence, and a comfortable sofa gives you just the place to do it. The delightful little store is open Mon.–Fri. 9 A.M.–5 P.M. (until 5:30 Friday), Sat. 10 A.M.–5 P.M.

HIGHWAY 2: MOYIE SPRINGS TO THE MONTANA LINE
Moyie Springs
This small logging community boasts a beautiful, forested setting but holds little to offer the tourist. One highlight for RVers passing through the area is **Twin Rivers Canyon Resort,** HCR 62 Box 25, Moyie Springs, ID 83845, 208/267-5932 or 888/258-5952. The large, 67-site RV park occupies a beautiful tree-filled flat at the

confluence of the Kootenai and Moyie Rivers. Facilities include a store, restrooms, showers, laundry, a swimming pond, ballfield, horseshoe pits, volleyball, and minigolf, a playground, and even a small petting zoo. Rates are $22 a night for full hookups, $20 for water and electricity, $15 for a tent site. Weekly rates available. The resort is usually open mid-April to November.

Up the Moyie River

Out on the highway, **Moyie Bridge** crosses the Moyie River some 450 vertigo-inducing feet above the water. A pullout on the southeast corner of the bridge is intended to provide views of Moyie Falls and Dam, but it doesn't, unless you risk your life by evading the viewpoint boundaries.

About a mile and a half east of the bridge, Deer Creek Road (County Road 72) branches north and leads up the Moyie River drainage into the Purcell Mountains. Armed with a Forest Service map, you can continue up the Moyie, eventually joining Highway 95 at Good Grief. Along the way you'll find the USFS **Meadow Creek Campground** (23 sites, free) in a secluded area at the confluence of Meadow Creek and the Moyie River. For even more seclusion, you can rent the nearby USFS **Deer Ridge Lookout.** From its lofty perch, you'll look down on the Moyie River Valley and enjoy great views of the Selkirks to the west. The tower has just one twin bed, though four people are allowed in it at a time. It's 40 feet off the ground, so young children are discouraged. Rental fee is $25 a night.

Another USFS rental property is a little farther up the Moyie. **Snyder Guard Station** is on the river, about 4.5 miles south of Good Grief. The cabin holds five twin beds and rents for $35 a night or $175 a week. Its relatively cush amenities include a refrigerator, stove, electric heat, hot showers, and a horse corral. Snyder is usually available from early June until the end of September. For reservations or more information on either of these rentals, contact the USFS **Bonners Ferry Ranger District,** 6286 Main St., Bonners Ferry, ID 83805, 208/267-5561.

For information on raft trips down the Moyie River, see River Rafting under Bonners Ferry and Vicinity.

HIGHWAY 95 TO EASTPORT

Highway 95 leaves Bonners Ferry heading north, following the Kootenai River for a time. Then it branches east, winding its way through the Purcell Mountains to the Canadian border crossing at Eastport. For much of the way you drive through a veritable tunnel of trees. Several nice lakes line the route, but they're all sheltered from view.

Camping

At **Smith Lake,** anglers will find a boat ramp and a small lake full of rainbow trout, bass, and catfish. The USFS **Smith Lake Campground** offers seven free sites. To get there, take Smith

BORDER CROSSING REGULATIONS

Citizens of the United States or Canada can cross the border with just a valid ID; usually a driver's license will suffice. Citizens from other countries will need passports and appropriate visas. You may also have to prove to officials that you are carrying enough money to support yourself for the length of your stay. If you're towing a $50,000 fifth-wheel, you're not going to get hassled. But hitchhikers and obviously low-budget road-trippers might even be asked to open their wallets and show cash or credit cards.

Customs regulations for both countries are extensive. Generally, you can transport a limited dollar amount of foreign-bought goods across the border duty-free. Above that limit, you must declare your purchases and pay duty on them.

Some items may require a permit for transport between the two countries. Red flags immediately arise with firearms and other weapons, pets, agricultural products, and drugs—prescription or otherwise. For customs regulations and information, you can wing it at the border or write ahead for advice to: **U.S. Customs & Border Protection,** 1000 2nd Ave., Suite 2200, Seattle, WA 98104-1049, USA, 206/553-6944, fax 206/553-1401, www.customs.ustreas.gov; or **Customs Office,** 220 4th Ave. S.E., Calgary, AB T2G 0L1, Canada, 403/233-5130, fax 403/264-5843, www.ccra-adrc.gc.ca.

Lake Road (FR 36) off Highway 95, seven miles north of Bonners Ferry. Another 12 miles down Highway 95 is Brush Lake Road (FR 1004), which leads to **Brush Lake** and a free, four-site campground.

Nineteen miles from Bonners Ferry you'll come to Robinson Lake Campground Road (FR449), which leads into large **Robinson Lake** and a 10-site campground (fee). A two-mile interpretive trail here points out the intricate interactions within the forest ecosystem. Boaters note: The boat-launching ramp at Robinson Lake is on the lake's north side, accessed a little farther down the highway. No gasoline motors permitted on Robinson Lake.

Copper Falls

Take time to stretch your legs at this exquisite spot just a short distance off the highway. Turn east at the Copper Creek campground sign and head down FR 2517 a couple of miles past the campground (16 sites, fee). Be careful of logging trucks here. A pullout on the right and a sign on the left mark the trailhead. The easy trail climbs briefly, then traverses a beautiful slope of mixed conifers before descending slightly to the falls. An interpretive brochure, hopefully available at the trailhead, explains the biological points of interest along the way. The falls make a beautiful 80-foot cascade, perfectly proportioned to allow you an up-close look without getting soaked. After crossing the creek, the trail loops back to the trailhead a little lower down Copper Creek—a total distance of less than a mile. Benches are well placed at particularly tranquil spots. Bring a picnic lunch and enjoy an alfresco repast in the cool clean air by the rushing waters. Highly recommended.

Eastport

The Eastport border station marks the international boundary between the United States and Canada. It's open 24 hours. Those interested in cultural differences will note that here canary-yellow Union Pacific locomotives rub elbows with their cherry-red Canadian Pacific cousins, while the Yankee-sharp American customs and immigration building contrasts nicely with its older, more civilized Canuck counterpart. The Moyie River knows no border, however. It flows past here unimpeded on the way to its confluence with the Kootenai, some 20 miles to the south as the Canada goose flies.

HIGHWAY 1 TO PORTHILL

From its junction with Highway 95, Highway 1 continues up the Purcell Trench, past fertile farmland and the Kootenai River on the west, and the abruptly steep Purcell Range on the east. The Purcells continue on up into British Columbia, Canada. They don't have to stop at the border—you do. The Porthill border crossing is open 7 A.M.–11 P.M. At Porthill, you might notice the tall trellises of the Elk Mountain Farms hops plantation on the valley floor to the west. The plantation cultivates about 2,000 acres of aromatic hops for use in Anheuser-Busch beers.

Resources

Suggested Reading

Description and Travel

Alt, David D., and Donald W. Hyndman. *Roadside Geology of Idaho*. Missoula, MT: Mountain Press Publishing Company, 1993. A great overview for the layperson, this book describes in easy-to-understand fashion just what you'll be looking at as you drive the roads of Idaho. The introduction provides a crash course in plate tectonics.

Conley, Cort. *Idaho for the Curious*. Cambridge, ID: Backeddy Books, 1982. Although some descriptions are dated, this massive tome is tailor-made for travel down the highways of Idaho. Organized by region and highway number, this monster masterwork provides historical context for virtually every sight of significance you'll come across. Conley pulls no punches in his observations, lustily attacking the greedy magnates and bungling bureaucrats who have done damage to his precious home state. How about a new edition, Cort?

Johnson, Frederic D. *Wild Trees of Idaho*. Moscow, ID: University of Idaho Press, 1995. A comprehensive guide to Idaho's trees and shrubs, with abundant large drawings and a helpful set of color plates. Johnson is Professor Emeritus of Forest Resources at the Universty of Idaho.

Shallat, Todd, ed. *Snake: The Plain and Its People*. Boise: Boise State University, 1994. Expertly written by a group of Idaho professors and other academics, lushly illustrated with both modern and historical photographs, and superbly laid out and edited, this book is a must-read for those who want to learn more about southern Idaho and its central feature: the Snake River. Obviously a labor of love, the book provides an intimate understanding of life on the Snake River Plain.

History and Politics

Arrington, Leonard J. *History of Idaho*. Moscow, ID: University of Idaho Press, 1994. Commissioned for Idaho's 1990 Centennial celebration, this is the definitive Idaho history text. Arrington is an Idaho native and a lifelong student of Idaho history. The two-volume set covers all the bases succinctly and points the way toward further research with copious footnotes. It's highly readable—not too dry—and boasts some great historical photos. Highly recommended.

Boone, Lalia. *Idaho Place Names: A Geographical Dictionary*. Moscow, ID: University of Idaho Press, 1988. How did Foolhen Creek get its name? Or Deadman Gulch or Whiskey Bob Creek? This book provides the answers for those places and thousands of other Idaho towns and physical features. In sum, the entries provide an interesting history of this most interesting of states.

Josephy, Alvin M. *The Nez Perce Indians and the Opening of the Northwest*. Boston: Houghton Mifflin Company, 1965; abridged edition 1997. Josephy tells the whole sad story of the Nez Perce from their welcoming encounter with Lewis and Clark in 1805 to their defeat at the hands of the U.S. Army in 1877. This account is recommended by the Nez Perce.

Lukas, J. Anthony. *Big Trouble: A Murder in a Small Western Town Sets Off a Struggle for the Soul of America*. New York: Simon & Schuster, 1997. At 880 pages, this sprawling account of Idaho labor strife and the 1905 assassination of former governor Frank Steunenberg is no light read. Pulitzer Prize–winning journalist Lukas killed himself after completing *Big Trouble*, feeling he wasn't living up to his reputation, but the book still offers an unmatched look at early Idaho politics and class warfare.

Moulton, Gary. *The Definitive Journals of Lewis & Clark: Volume 5—Through the Rockies to the Cascades* and *Volume 7—From the Pacific to the Rockies*. Lincoln, NE: University of Nebraska Press, 2003. Volume 5 covers the expedition's arduous summer 1805 travels through Idaho; Volume 7 details the explorers' return trek and long camp with the Nez Perce in 1806. Both are packed with high drama—and unbelievably bad spelling.

Stapilus, Randy. *The Idaho Yearbook*. Boise, ID: Ridenbaugh Press, 2002. Although produced somewhat irregularly, this is the bible of Idaho politics, media, business, and a "who's who" of the state. Stapilus also was author and publisher of the 1988 book *Paradox Politics* (Ridenbaugh Press), probably the best-ever assessment of Idaho's political culture.

Recreation

Bingham, Dave. *City of Rocks, Idaho: A Climber's Guide*. Hailey: Dave Bingham, 2004. This is the classic guide to the rock-climbing destination, and the new edition includes information on the recently opened Castle Rocks State Park, just next door.

Bluestein, Sheldon. *Exploring Idaho's High Desert*. Boise: Challenge Expedition Company, 1988. Sure, Idaho's high peaks usually get all the attention, which is exactly why hardcore adventurers love the state's high desert. Although hard to find, this book can take you to lands seen by just a handful of people (or fewer) each year. Deep into the Wapi flow, down along the Bruneau and Jarbidge Rivers—here is a guide to Idaho's loneliest places.

Carrey, Johnny, and Cort Conley. *The Middle Fork: A Guide*. Cambridge, ID: Backeddy Books, 1992. After a thorough introduction to the history of the Middle Fork's early explorations, the authors take you on a mile-by-mile trip down the river, exhaustively detailing the history of every point along the way. Read this one before your float trip to add an additional layer of richness to the experience.

Daly, Katherine, and Ron Watters. *Kath and Ron's Guide to Idaho Paddling: Flatwater and Easy Whitewater Trips*. Pocatello, Idaho: The Great Rift Press, 1999. Here's a wonderful guide for novice and family boaters, featuring practical advice for canoeing and kayaking nearly 100 routes (up to Class II) throughout the state.

Litton, Evie. *Hiking Hot Springs in the Pacific Northwest*. Helena, MT: Falcon Publishing, 2001. This well-researched, recently updated book is geared toward wilderness springs that you need to hike in to. The descriptions provide information about the hikes as well as about the springs you'll find at the end of the trail. Maps and photos accompany the text; about 120 springs are described.

Lopez, Tom. *Exploring Idaho's Mountains: A Guide for Climbers, Scramblers & Hikers*. Seattle: The Mountaineers, 1990. No guide for the neophyte, this one's for people who love "getting high" no matter what it takes. Climb ratings, peak elevations, and approach access routes to more than 700 summits are provided; appendixes list all of Idaho's named peaks over 10,000 feet and supply information on map quadrangles and first ascents. It's an excellent and comprehensive guide to the state's high country for mountaineers.

MacMillan, Daniel. *Golfing in Idaho & Montana*. Carnation, WA: MAC Productions, 2000. An indispensable guide for linksters, this book describes about 100 courses in the state, providing course ratings, course layouts, slopes, hazards, distances, green and cart fees, and particularly challenging holes for each course. It's small and light enough to put in your golf bag.

Maughan, Ralph, and Jackie Johnson Maughan. *The Hiker's Guide to Idaho*. Helena, MT: Falcon Publishing, 2001. From the Selkirks up near the Canadian border to the Bear River Range in Idaho's southeast corner, this book provides select proven hikes across the entire state. The 100 trail descriptions are thick and prosy, and are accompanied by good maps and photos.

Perry, John, and Jane Greverus Perry. *The Sierra Club Guide to the Natural Areas of Idaho, Montana, and Wyoming.* San Francisco: Sierra Club Books, 1988. This book may be getting a little long in the tooth, but it's nevertheless indispensable for its exhaustive coverage. Even the most out-of-the-way destinations are described, with information on flora and fauna, recreation activities, responsible management agencies, and references for further reading provided for each site.

Stone, Lynne. *Adventures in Idaho's Sawtooth Country.* Seattle: The Mountaineers, 1990. This book (now out of print) describes 63 trips for hikers and/or mountain bikers in the Sawtooth, White Cloud, Boulder, Smoky, Pioneer, and Salmon River mountain ranges. Stone is a Sun Valley resident, so these mountains are in her backyard. The book is well laid out and includes a useful appendix that can help you quickly select a trip to suit your time and ability.

Literature

Bass, Rick. *The Ninemile Wolves.* New York: Ballantine Group, 1993. Bass passionately relates the true story of a lineage of wolves that lived and died across the Bitterroot Range in Montana, shortly before the recent reintroduction process was begun. At times joyful, at times heartbreaking, the account fosters respect for the wolves and the people who tried to help them. You'll read this in one sitting and think about it for weeks afterward.

Blew, Mary Clearman, ed. *Written on Water: Essays on Idaho Rivers.* Moscow, ID: University of Idaho Press, 2001. Many of the state's best-known writers offer celebrations of Idaho

rivers including the Snake, Clearwater, Salmon, St. Joe, and more. Read this and you'll understand why, to many Idahoans, rivers are a religion.

Fisher, Vardis. *Children of God.* Boise: Opal Laurel Holmes, 1939; revised edition 1977. Arguably Fisher's most famous work, this historical novel chronicles the development of the Mormon religion from the first vision of Joseph Smith in 1820 until after the death of Brigham Young in 1877. Along the way, Fisher—raised a Mormon—takes an unflinching look at the controversies surrounding the church, most troublesome among them the Mormons' early adoption of polygamy. Fisher's prose is eminently readable, and this book won the Harper Prize for fiction.

McFarland, Ronald E., and William Studebaker, eds. *Idaho's Poetry: A Centennial Anthology.* Moscow, ID: University of Idaho Press, 1989. The editors—themselves well-known Idaho poets—have pulled together a stunning anthology of the best poetry written by Idahoans, from early Native Americans to settler-era poets to contemporaries. Out of print.

Parkinson, Heather. *Across Open Ground.* New York: Bloomsbury, 2002. This impressive first novel by Parkinson, an Idaho native, is set in the Wood River Valley in 1917. If the two principal characters, a young sheepherder and his love interest, seem older than their years, maybe it's because people had to grow up fast on the Idaho frontier—and in World War I.

Robinson, Marilynne. *Housekeeping.* New York: Farrar, Straus and Giroux, 1997 (reprint edition). When Boise had its first citywide book club, this was the book it read. Set in the North Idaho town of Fingerbone (based on Sandpoint, the author's hometown), Robinson's 1981 novel is full of lyrical writing and memorable characters, especially Ruth and her Aunt Sylvie. It won the PEN/Hemingway Award for best first novel.

State Publications

Idaho Highway Historical Marker Guide. Ever notice how all of those many roadside historical markers you pass in your travels through Idaho are numbered? This catalog describes them all, providing the text of that sign you just passed and were too lazy to pull over and read. It's available for $5 (send check or money order) from the Idaho Transportation Department, Public Information Section, P.O. Box 7129, Boise, ID 83707, 208/334-8000.

Idaho Official Travel Guide. The state's tourism folks put out this lush and lovely guide to the state every year. It's got a wealth of information on sights, lodgings, and recreation opportunities, accompanied by stunning color photography. Best of all, it's free. Request a copy from the Idaho Travel Council, Administrative Office, Idaho Department of Commerce, 700 W. State St., P.O. Box 83720, Boise, ID 83720-0093, 208/334-2470.

Maps

National Forest Maps

The USFS publishes detailed maps to each of Idaho's national forests—an invaluable resource for backcountry users. The maps cost $6 each. You can obtain a particular national forest's map from the office for that forest. But if you're interested in several different forests, it's easier to deal with the USFS regional offices. For maps of the forests in the southern half of the state, including the Bitterroot, Boise, Caribou, Payette, Salmon-Challis, Sawtooth, and Caribou-Targhee National Forests, write to USFS Region Four Information, 507 25th St., Ogden, UT 84401, 801/625-5112 or 801/625-5306. Most of the individual national forests are covered by a single map; however, the Caribou-Targhee and Sawtooth National Forests require two maps each ($6 per map).

Idaho Atlas & Gazetteer

De Lorme Mapping, P.O. Box 298, Yarmouth, ME 04096, 800/452-5931, publishes detailed atlases to many Western states, including Idaho. These are not detailed city street maps, à la Thomas Bros., but rather partially topographic maps that show Forest Service roads, campgrounds, and natural features across every inch of the state. Indispensable for off-the-beaten-path travel in Idaho.

Publishers

Backeddy Books, P.O. Box 301, Cambridge, ID 83610, 208/257-3810. Rafter and dedicated Idaho historian Cort Conley's press.

Carole Marsh Idaho Books, Gallopade Publishing Group, 665 Hwy. 74 S., Ste. 600, Peachtree City, GA 30269, 800/536-2438. Children's educational books on various facets of Idaho, including geography, history, dinosaurs, and trivia.

The Caxton Press, 312 Main St., Caldwell, ID 83605-3299, 208/459-7421. Specializes in books about the West, ranging from hiking guides to history books.

Falcon Publishing, c/o The Globe Pequot Press, P.O. Box 480, Guilford, CT 06437, 888/249-7586. Hiking, wildlife, driving, field-identification, and general-recreation guides to most western and many southern and eastern states.

Farcountry Press, P.O. Box 5630, Helena, MT 59604, 800/654-1105 (outside Montana) or 800/821-3874 (within Montana). An eclectic catalog including calendars and photo-illustrated books focusing on scenic areas.

The Mountaineers Books, 1001 S.W. Klickitat Way, Ste. 201, Seattle, WA 98134, 206/226-6303. Hiking and mountaineering guides and literature on worldwide destinations, including Idaho.

University of Idaho Press, P.O. Box 444416, Moscow, ID 83844-4416, 800/847-7377. Full line of Idaho-related books, emphasizing natural and cultural history.

Westcliffe Publishers, P.O. Box 1261, Englewood, CO 80150-1261, 303/935-0900 or 800/523-3692. Calendars and lusciously illustrated coffeetable books to many U.S. states, including Idaho.

Internet Resources

The following websites can help you explore Idaho, both from afar and once you arrive:

State of Idaho
www.accessidaho.org
Idaho's official website has all the usual links to state agencies, plus some truly useful and fun stuff. You can check road conditions, get fishing license information, and even learn all about Larry LaPrise, the Idaho man who wrote *The Hokey Pokey,* for example.

Idaho State Travel Planner
www.visitid.org
A handy itinerary planner, calendar of events, and lodging guide are among the features of the state's official tourism site. Be sure to look at the "Cool Deals" section, where package deals are available in more than a dozen categories including romantic getaways, family fun, Lewis and Clark, mountain biking, fishing, and more.

Idaho Transportation Department
www2.state.id.us/itd
One of the most practical sites for visitors. Check winter road conditions in Idaho and neighboring states, learn about road closures and detours, and get forecasts from the National Weather Service.

Idaho State Parks and Recreation
www.idahoparks.org
Learn about Idaho's state parks on this website, which also features online camping reservations.

National Park Service
www.nps.gov
The National Park Service site has links to such Idaho attractions as Craters of the Moon National Monument and City of Rocks National Reserve, plus Yellowstone National Park (a small part of which is in Idaho).

U.S. Forest Service
www.fs.fed.us
From the Forest Service's home page, you can search for Idaho, then follow the links to all of Idaho's dozen national forests and one national grassland. (The agency administers more than 20 million acres throughout the state.) This is also a good place to get forest fire information.

Bureau of Land Management
www.id.blm.gov
The BLM manages 11,836,481 acres in Idaho—close to a quarter of the state's total land. This site has information on BLM-related recreation sites, as well as a list of field offices throughout the state.

Idaho Outfitters and Guides Association
www.ioga.org
Plan an outdoor Idaho adventure on this site, which showcases the state's licensed outfitters and guides in hunting, fishing, river running, trail rides, mountain biking, and more.

ReserveUSA
www.reserveusa.com
Go here to reserve campsites, cabins, and fire lookout stays in nearly 100 U.S. Forest Service and Corps of Engineers locations across Idaho. As with the state parks' online reservations, the only drawback is a fairly stiff reservation fee—though it's a small price to pay for a guaranteed campsite on busy holidays and weekends.

In Idaho Reservations
www.inidaho.com
This private McCall-based company is a handy place to research and book accommodations and activities throughout the state. It features good package deals, too, including some you won't see on the official state website.

Idaho Conservation League
www.wildidaho.org

Of the many environmental groups working in Idaho, this home-grown organization ranks among the oldest and best. Its website has regularly updated information on every major environmental issue facing the state, from salmon runs to forest health to efforts to preserve such places as the Boulder-White Cloud Mountains, Owyhee Canyonlands, and even the Boise Foothills.

Idaho Fitness
www.idahofitness.com

Billing itself as "Idaho's sports, fitness, and recreation source," this site has sections on all the state's most popular active pursuits. Lots of links, though some are broken.

The Idaho Statesman
www.idahostatesman.com

The online edition of this Boise-based newspaper, Idaho's largest, is a great place to learn what's going on in the state, especially the Boise metro area. There are also links to the paper's superb entertainment section and its archive of restaurant reviews.

Boise Weekly
www.boiseweekly.com

For an irreverent, informative look at life in and around Boise, check out this alternative weekly's site. See the "Eight Days Out" section for upcoming events around town.

Ridenbaugh Press
www.ridenbaugh.com

Randy Stapilus has been covering Idaho politics for a long time, and this site is a must-read compendium of public-affairs reporting from around the Northwest.

Idaho Commission on Hispanic Affairs
www2.state.id.us/icha

Idaho's growing Latino community can look to this site for information on Spanish-language media, upcoming events, job postings, and more.

Lesbian and Gay Idaho
www.gayidaho.com

A site for Idaho's gay and lesbian community, including links to regional and special-interest websites and an online edition of *Diversity*, the state's gay newspaper.

Idaho Tribal News
www.shobannews.com

The online edition of the tribal newspaper for the Fort Hall Reservation near Pocatello offers a glimpse into modern Native American life, as well as links to other Indian news sources.

Digital Atlas of Idaho
http://imnh.isu.edu/digitalatlas

This site is a wonderful compendium of knowledge about all the natural sciences in Idaho. Whether you're trying to identify a bird or learn more about the state's weird geology, you'll find it here.

Lewis and Clark in Idaho
www.lewisandclarkidaho.org

Look here for information on the famous expedition's travels through Idaho, where it crossed the rugged Lolo Trail in fall 1805 and returned to camp among the Nez Perce tribe en route home in 1806.

Idaho State Library
www.lili.org

Idaho residents can use this site to find a local library, search catalogues statewide, access research databases, and even renew checked-out books.

Index

Index

Fishing

Hiking

Index

Rafting

Scenic Drives

Index

Acknowledgments

Way back when, many moons and editions ago, I found myself pulling the trusty steed off the long and winding road into Atlanta . . . Idaho, not Georgia. It's about as far from anywhere as you can get and an unlikely place to make a life-changing acquaintance. But life's funny that way, isn't it?—handing you gifts when you least expect them. So thank you, Idaho, first and foremost, for bringing Becca into my life.

Mush out of the way, the biggest thanks this edition go to Idahoan and veteran travel writer Julie Fanselow, who did all the legwork to make this edition of *Moon Handbooks Idaho* brand-spankin' new. Here's to you, Jules! It's great to know you.

Others who contributed to making Idaho a special home away from home for me include Cindy Trail, Mike and Pat (thanks for letting me sit in!), Brian and Aaron, Dan Ansotegui, Sarah Lunstrum, Jerry Hendershot (where are you?), Sri Galindo, Krista O., Otter and Marianne, Nancy Juell, Mike and Lisa, Kiley K., Angie DeScalfani, John Stinson-Wilge, Big John Thornton, Breezy, Jay, Deana and Bruce, Bill Loftus, and Officer Root of the Boise PD. Thanks for the memories, and much love to you all.

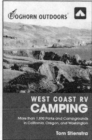

U.S.~Metric Conversion

1 inch = 2.54 centimeters (cm)
1 foot = .304 meters (m)
1 yard = 0.914 meters
1 mile = 1.6093 kilometers (km)
1 km = .6214 miles
1 fathom = 1.8288 m
1 chain = 20.1168 m
1 furlong = 201.168 m
1 acre = .4047 hectares
1 sq km = 100 hectares
1 sq mile = 2.59 square km
1 ounce = 28.35 grams
1 pound = .4536 kilograms
1 short ton = .90718 metric ton
1 short ton = 2000 pounds
1 long ton = 1.016 metric tons
1 long ton = 2240 pounds
1 metric ton = 1000 kilograms
1 quart = .94635 liters
1 US gallon = 3.7854 liters
1 Imperial gallon = 4.5459 liters
1 nautical mile = 1.852 km

To compute Celsius temperatures, subtract 32 from Fahrenheit and divide by 1.8. To go the other way, multiply Celsius by 1.8 and add 32.

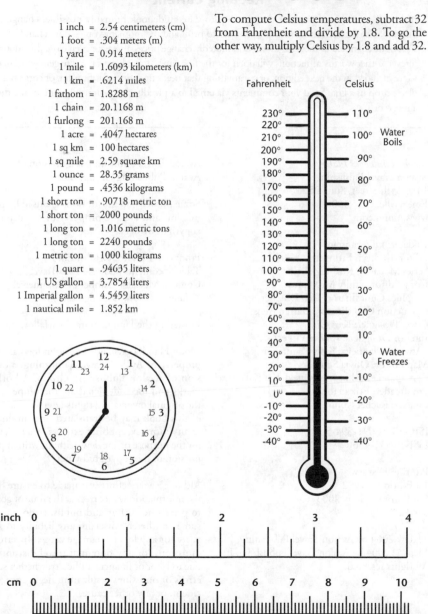

Keeping Current

Although we strive to produce the most up-to-date guidebook humanly possible, change is unavoidable. Between the time this book goes to print and the moment you read it, a handful of the businesses noted in these pages will undoubtedly change prices, move, or even close their doors forever. Other worthy attractions will open for the first time. If you have a favorite gem you'd like to see included in the next edition, or see anything that needs updating, clarification, or correction, please drop us a line. Send your comments via email to atpfeedback@avalonpub.com, or use the address below.

Moon Handbooks Idaho
Avalon Travel Publishing
1400 65th Street, Suite 250
Emeryville, CA 94608, USA
www.moon.com

Updater: Julie Fanselow
Editor: Kathryn Ettinger
Series Manager: Kevin McLain
Copy Editor: Emily McManus
Graphics Coordinator: Deb Dutcher
Production Coordinator: Darren Alessi
Cover Designer: Kari Gim
Interior Designers: Amber Pirker,
  Alvaro Villanueva, Kelly Pendragon
Map Editor: Olivia Solís
Cartographers: Mike Morgenfeld, Kat Kalamaras
Proofreader: Erika Howsare
Indexer: Rachel Kuhn

ISBN: 1-56691-594-5
ISSN: 1531-4960

Printing History
1st Edition—1992
5th Edition—May 2004
5 4 3 2 1

Text © 2004 by Avalon Travel Publishing, Inc.
Maps © 2004 by Avalon Travel Publishing, Inc.
All rights reserved.

Avalon Travel Publishing is a division of
Avalon Publishing Group, Inc.

Some photos and illustrations are used by permission and are the property of the original copyright owners.

Front cover photo: © John Elk III
Table of contents photos: Idaho Travel Council, McCall Chamber of Commerce, © Julie Fanselow, © Craig Hill

Printed in the United States by Malloy, Inc.